COMPREHENSIVE
BUSINESS LAW

REVISED FIRST EDITION

Michael Bootsma, Michael Thieme, Charles Damschen,
Sophia Harvey, Craig Nierman

cognella®
academic publishing

Bassim Hamadeh, CEO and Publisher

Michael Simpson, Vice President of Acquisitions

Jamie Giganti, Senior Managing Editor

Jess Busch, Senior Graphic Designer

Mark Combes, Senior Field Acquisitions Editor

Brian Fahey, Licensing Specialist

Mandy Licata, Interior Designer

www.cognella.com   800-200-3908

CONTENTS

CHAPTER ONE

INTRODUCTION TO LAW, ETHICS, AND LEGAL REASONING

By Michael Bootsma

Figure 1.1 Why would someone deface a piece of art if they knew it was illegal?

Introduction

Raul and Mark are best friends. Raul and Mark have an idea for a new website that will allow college graduates and employers to network. The website will connect college graduates and employers from around the world. Allison and Amy have an idea for a new business as well. Allison and Amy want to provide party planning services for special events such as birthdays and weddings. Allison and Amy are going to provide their services to customers within thirty miles of the city in which they live.

Do Raul and Mark have to have a license to operate a business such as this? What laws will apply to Raul and Mark's Internet-based business? How about Amy and Allison's business? Will they be subject

• Federal law

to a special set of laws if they will also be providing childcare services? Will Amy and Allison need to be concerned with federal law if they are operating in only one state? How about Mark and Raul? Will they be subject to the law of many different states? Will they be subject to federal law or even international law?

The answers to these questions are complicated. Many different types of laws from many different jurisdictions may apply to Raul and Mark as well as Allison and Amy. In this chapter we will discuss the various types and classifications of law that can be found here in the United States. We will also discuss ethical decision-making processes that may be employed by a business owner.

Chapter Objectives

1. Understand and identify the different sources of law
2. Distinguish between different classifications of law
3. Understand the role of common law
4. Distinguish between different types of remedies
5. Identify the difference between ethics and the law
6. Apply different ethical decision-making theories

Sources of Law

Federal Law vs. State Law vs. International Law

In the United States, a person's individual activities or business activities might be governed by various sources of law. The different sources of law can be categorized as international law, federal law, state law and local law. For example, assume Nadia would like to start a bakery where she sells breads and pastries she makes with the help of an employee. Nadia may be subject to federal law governing employee/employer relationships, she might also be subject to state sales tax law, county health laws, and municipal (city) restrictions on her business activities and location.

Federal law refers to laws created by an entity of the federal government or to the US Constitution. The United States Constitution is the highest authority of federal law in the United States. The United States Constitution provides the framework for the federal government by creating the three branches of government. The three branches of government are the Legislative branch, the Judicial branch, and the Executive Branch.

The Legislative branch consists of the House of Representatives and the Senate, which are referred to as "Congress." Both the House of Representatives and the Senate may introduce bills that become statutory law. The House of Representatives and the Senate must both pass a bill by a majority vote, and the President must sign it, before it becomes law.

An example of federal statutory law would be what is called the "Mann Act." 18. USC Section 1421 states "Whoever knowingly transports any individual in interstate or foreign commerce, or in any Territory or Possession of the United States, with intent that such individual engage in prostitution, or in any sexual activity for which any person can be charged with a criminal offense, or attempts to do so, shall be fined under this title or imprisoned not more than 10 years, or both." This statute makes it illegal to transport an individual across state lines if the purpose of such transport is to engage in unlawful sexual conduct.

The Executive Branch is composed of the president, vice president, and several executive agencies such as the Department of Agriculture and the Department of the Treasury (which includes the Internal Revenue Service). The Executive Branch also has indirect control over independent agencies such as the Securities and Exchange Commission and the Environmental Protection Agency.

The Executive Branch's primary role is to enforce legislation passed by Congress. However, the Executive Branch can make law in several ways. The President can issue executive orders. For example, on October 17, 2014, President Barack Obama issued an executive order to improve the security of consumer financial transactions. In addition, federal administrative agencies create regulatory law by issuing regulations. A **regulation** is a law which has the same force as statutory law but is passed by an agency of the federal government whereas a statute is passed by Congress. For example, the Department of the Treasury creates regulations interpreting the Internal Revenue Code. The rules these agencies must abide by is referred to as administrative law. **Administrative law** creates the rules agencies must follow when making regulatory law and when enforcing regulatory law.

The **Judicial Branch** interprets and applies federal law to cases and controversies. The federal court system is made up of District Courts that act primarily as trial courts, Appellate Courts that hear appeals from the District Courts, and the Supreme Court that generally hears appeals from Appellate Courts. The District Courts are considered inferior courts as compared to the Appellate Courts and the Supreme Court is a superior court as compared to the Appellate Courts.

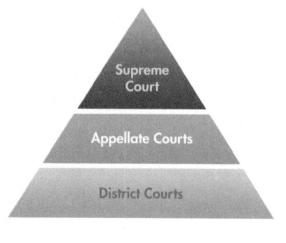

A **judge** is a court-appointed official who governs a court's proceedings. The number of judges who hear a case varies

Figure 1.2 The federal court system

depending upon the court and potentially the type of case. Judges who sit on the Supreme Court are often referred to as **Justices**. In the case of *Marbury v. Madison*, Chief Justice John Marshall of the United States Supreme Court decided the United States Constitution gave the Judicial Branch the power to review the constitutionality of acts undertaken by both the Legislative Branch and Executive Branch.

The Judicial Branch creates law by hearing cases and providing rulings. These rulings are referred to as precedent. **Precedent** is the holding, or legal ruling, provided in a court's opinion. Under the doctrine of **Stare Decisis**, a court should not overturn its previous rulings

- Regulation
- Administrative law
- Judicial Branch
- Judge
- Justices
- Precedent
- Stare Decisis

except in rare situations where Justice requires a departure from precedent. Even though a court may overturn its own precedent, a lower court must always follow the precedent of a superior court in its jurisdiction. For example, all federal courts (both District Courts and Appellate Courts) must follow the precedent of the Supreme Court. A District Court in the jurisdiction of an Appellate Court must follow the precedent of that Appellate Court. The doctrine of Stare Decisis provides legal certainty to both individuals and businesses.

When a court hears a case for the first time, it is referred to as a **case of first impression**. Courts will look to see if similar cases have been decided in different jurisdictions. Courts might also review law review articles written by law professors and law students if the article is related to the subject matter of the case of first impression. When a court comes to a decision, the court renders an opinion. A **majority opinion** means a majority of the judges hearing a case have the same opinion as to the outcome of the case. A **dissenting opinion**, sometimes referred to as a minority opinion, means a minority number of judges hearing a case have the same opinion as to the outcome of a case which is different from the majority opinion. A **concurring opinion** is the opinion of one or more judges who agree with the outcome of the majority opinion but for different legal reasons.

In summary, federal law is composed of the following sources of law (in order of authority):

1. United States Constitution
2. Statutes passed by Congress
3. Regulations passed by federal agencies
4. Federal common law created by judges

State law refers to laws created by an entity of a state government. Most states have a similar structure to the federal government. Each state has its own state constitution. Each state also has three branches of government including an Executive Branch headed by a Governor, a legislative branch, and a judicial branch. State governments do not automatically mirror the setup of the federal government. Some notable differences in the setup of state governments include Nebraska, which has a unicameral legislature meaning it does not have both a house and senate like the federal government does. States might also have a different court system structure. In the state of New York for example, some trial courts are referred to as Supreme Courts and these courts are inferior to the Appellate Court of New York. Finally, states have government agencies that can make regulatory law like the federal agencies but the agencies do not have the same names or even necessarily the same functions as federal agencies. For example, in the state of Iowa, the Department of Natural Resources acts somewhat as a state version of the Environmental Protection Agency which is found at the federal level.

In summary, state law is composed of the following sources of law (in order of authority):

1. State constitutions
2. Statutes passed by state legislatures
3. Regulations passed by state agencies
4. State common law created by judges
5. Municipal law

As a general rule, federal law will trump state law as long as the federal law is found to be valid under the US Constitution.

Counties and cities may also create law. Often the laws made by cities and counties are referred to as ordinances. **Municipal law** is a term used to refer to law made by cities and counties in the United States. **Ordinances** are a form of statutory law that generally applies to a small geographic area such a city or a county. A common example of a city ordinance is one that limits the size of a new building to no more than 25% of the available lot size. A city or county is granted the authority to create law by the state in which the city or county is located. For example, the state of Minnesota grants the city of Minneapolis the right to create ordinances governing citizens within its city limits. Municipal law is a lower level of law as compared to federal and state law. For example, if an ordinance of a city conflicted with state law for the state in which that city was located, the ordinance would be trumped by state law.

Figure 1.3 Supreme Court chamber, April 1910

- Municipal law
- Ordinances

US v. Arizona

132 S. Ct. 2492 (2012)

In 2010, the Arizona state legislature passed statute 1070 named "Support Our Law Enforcement and Safe Neighborhoods," which was designed to curb illegal immigration in the state of Arizona. From the beginning, the law was very controversial. Opponents were worried about the potential effect on the civil liberties of those who might be targeted as illegal aliens. Opponents also believed the law would result in racial profiling of minorities. Proponents cited the number of illegal immigrants in the state of Arizona and believed some of the state's economic problems were related to the illegal immigration. President Obama sought to enjoin the implementation of the Arizona statute.

There were several highly contested provisions of the bill.

Section 3 made the failure to comply with federal alien-registration requirements a state misdemeanor and the Supreme Court struck down this provision because it said federal law preempted state law on this matter.

§5(C) made it a misdemeanor for an unauthorized alien to seek or engage in work in the state and the Supreme Court held this provision to be unconstitutional. It stated the law "would interfere with the careful balance struck by Congress with respect to unauthorized employment of aliens. Although §5(C) attempts to achieve one of the same goals as federal law—the deterrence of unlawful employment—it involves a conflict in the method of enforcement."

- International law
- Sovereign

§6 of the law authorized state and local officers to arrest without a warrant a person whom "the officer has probable cause to believe has committed any public offense that makes the person removable from the United States." The Supreme Court also overturned this provision stating, "Congress has put in place a system in which state officers may not make warrantless arrests of aliens based on possible removability except in specific, limited circumstances. By nonetheless authorizing state and local officers to engage in these enforcement activities as a general matter, §6 creates an obstacle to the full purposes and objectives of Congress."

§2(B) required officers conducting certain stops or arrests to verify with the federal government the person's immigration status. The Court stated "it would disrupt the federal framework to put state officers in the position of holding aliens in custody for possible unlawful presence without federal direction and supervision. The program put in place by Congress does not allow state or local officers to adopt this enforcement mechanism."

However, the Court went on to state, "[e]ven if the law is read as an instruction to complete a check while the person is in custody, moreover, it is not clear at this stage and on this record that the verification process would result in prolonged detention. However the law is interpreted, if §2(B) only requires state officers to conduct a status check during the course of an authorized, lawful detention or after a detainee has been released, the provision likely would survive pre-emption—at least absent some showing that it has other consequences that are adverse to federal law and its objectives. There is no need in this case to address whether reasonable suspicion of illegal entry or another immigration crime would be a legitimate basis for prolonging a detention, or whether this too would be preempted by federal law."

Questions

1. Which sections of the Arizona statute were struck down by the Supreme Court?
2. What does the Court mean when it states federal law "preempts" the Arizona law?
3. Proponents of the Arizona law argued the US government is not enforcing immigration law; why is Arizona then prohibited from enforcing its own immigration law?
4. What do you believe the US government should do about illegal aliens who reside in the US?
5. What political factors will influence governments at both the federal and state levels when confronting illegal immigration?

International law is composed of the laws and judicial customs of all nations or countries. The law of no individual country is controlling since each country is considered to be **sovereign**, which means no one country is superior to another country. In addition, since no one country's laws are superior to the laws of another, international law can be hard to enforce because each nation has an equal amount of authority. The International Court of Justice is located in The Hague, Netherlands, and hears many international court cases. The rulings of the International Court of Justice are often adhered to by individual countries because each country finds it important to maintain relations in order to engage in trade with other countries.

Nuremberg Trials

From 1945 to 1949, a series of thirteen trials were held by the Allied Powers. These trials were a result of the actions of the Nazi regime in Germany. From 1933, when Adolf Hitler and his Nazi party gained power, until 1945, when World War II ended the reign of the Nazi party, more than 6 million Jews were killed either directly at the hands of the Nazi party or indirectly through maltreatment

Figure 1.4 Defendants sitting for the Nuremberg Trials

in Nazi concentration camps. Soviet leader Joseph Stalin is claimed to have wanted to simply execute more than 50,000 German soldiers instead of trying them for their crimes. Winston Churchill discussed the execution of high-ranking Nazi soldiers without a trial. In the end, it was decided to have a series of trials.

The United States, the Soviet Union, and Great Britain issued a proclamation in 1942 that stated those who were part of the mass murder of European Jews would be prosecuted. The Nuremberg trials, as they came to be known by the world, were unprecedented—never before had suspects been tried in an international criminal proceeding similar to this. In the past, suspected war criminals had been tried under the law of one nation. However, this trial would be different.

The Allies started the process by issuing a proclamation stating which crimes the alleged war criminals could be charged with and tried. Three of the most notorious Nazi criminals, Adolf Hitler, Joseph Goebbels, and Heinrich Himmler, committed suicide before they could be tried at Nuremberg. The Major War Criminals' Trial included twenty-four defendants. There were prosecutors who represented the Allied Powers and defense attorneys who represented the defendants. The prosecutors included United States Supreme Court Justice Robert Jackson. There were four Judges, each of whom represented an Allied power.

Only three defendants were found to be not guilty. Ten defendants were hanged. One defendant who was found guilty committed suicide by swallowing a cyanide capsule that was smuggled into his cell. After the initial Major War Criminals' Trial, there were twelve subsequent trials that were governed by the United States military. In the subsequent trials, doctors, lawyers, and even Nazi Judges were condemned for their part in what came to be known as the Holocaust.

Questions

1. Why weren't the defendants just executed as Stalin and Churchill had considered?
2. At the time of the Nuremberg trials, chief Justice Harlan Stone stated the trials were but a "high-grade lynching." Does the fact three defendants were found not guilty in the Major War Criminals' Trial mean the trials were free from bias and were fair in their proceedings?
3. If each nation is considered sovereign, what gave the Allied Powers the authority to hold these trials?
4. What law was applied in the Nuremberg Trials? State, federal, or international?

Classifications of Law

In the United States, the different sources of law can be classified into different categories. For example, civil law versus criminal law or procedural law versus substantive law.

Common Law vs. Statutory Law & Regulatory Law

Common law is a term used to refer to a set of general legal principles and definitions largely derived from the precedent of court cases as opposed to statutes. The United States adopted most of its common law principles from England. This textbook focuses primarily on English and US common law principles and definitions since statutory law varies from state to state in the United States. As an example, "battery" is defined under the common law as an intentional unconsented-to touching of another that results in physical harm or offensive contact. This definition has been used by many state courts and by state legislatures that have written a statute making battery a legal wrong. The easiest place to find the definition of a term or concept under the common law would be a court case summarizing the law regarding that term or concept. For example, a court case involving the civil wrong of battery would provide a definition of battery and possibly the common law defenses against an accusation of battery. Common law is heavily influenced by the opinions of judges in court cases.

Statutory law refers to statutes passed by legislatures such as the United States Congress or a state legislature. For example, the statute 26 USC. Section 61 defines "Gross Income" as income from whatever source derived. The implication of this statute passed by the United States Congress is whatever a taxpayer receives as income is taxable unless another statute passed by Congress excludes the income from taxation. **Regulatory law** refers to regulations passed by an agency such as the Environmental Protection Agency or a state agency such as a state department of human services. Statutory law and Regulatory law have historically been contained in written volumes. However, it is now possible to access Statutory law and Regulatory law through various federal and state government websites.

It is important to remember the common law is still applied by judges when state or federal statutory law and regulatory law is silent on an issue. For example, Frank is continually annoyed and angered by his neighbor Dwight. One day Frank hits Dwight, causing damage to Dwight's body. Dwight can sue Frank for battery, and if their state does not define battery through statutory or regulatory law, a court would apply the common law definition.

Civil Law vs. Criminal Law

Civil law is a body of law that defines private rights and remedies of a citizen. It primarily governs the legal issues arising between citizens and between citizens and their government. Civil law is often enforced by one citizen against another but can be enforced by a government entity in the United States. Both common law principles and statutory law can be labeled as civil law in the United States. For example, Kerry takes Mike's bicycle for a ride without Mike's permission. Mike's state of domicile, Iowa, may have a statute that makes it a civil offense to take another's property without their permission. However, if Iowa does not have statutory law prohibiting Kerry from taking Mike's bicycle, Mike may be able to sue Kerry in court for Trespass to Personal Property as defined by the common law.

Criminal law defines what is a crime. Criminal law can generally be enforced only by a government representative such as the attorney for a city or state. Similar to civil law, both statutory law and common law can constitute Criminal law. If Kerry takes Mike's bike without permission and intends to keep it from him, she may have committed larceny. The police may arrest Kerry, alleging criminal activity on her part, and the city attorney may file criminal charges against her.

- Civil law
- Criminal law
- Substantive law
- Procedural law

Substantive Law vs. Procedural Law

Substantive law refers to rights or obligations of an individual. For example, in the United States, a citizen can move freely from one state to another state without seeking prior approval from a government agency. **Procedural law** defines the process by which an individual's rights can be taken away. For example, before Mike can sue Kerry for taking his bike as part of a civil case, he will have to file a complaint with a court that asks the court to take action against Kerry. The fact Mike has to file a complaint is a requirement of procedural law.

Florida v. Zimmerman

Case# 2012-CF-001083-A

On February 26, 2012, George Zimmerman called 911 to report a suspicious person in his Sanford, Florida, community. George Zimmerman was a neighborhood watch captain. He was told by the dispatcher that he did not need to follow the person which he had reported. The suspicious person was Trayvon Martin, a 17-year-old African American male wearing a sweatshirt with a hood.

Sometime after the call to 911, Trayvon Martin was shot and killed by George Zimmerman. George Zimmerman informed police the shooting was done in self-defense after an altercation ensued. The extent of the altercation will never be known but medical records did show some injury to the back of Zimmerman's head and his face. However, it is not known who or what was the source of these injuries.

Authorities decided not to charge George Zimmerman because they believed they lacked the evidence to refute Zimmerman's story. In the months that followed, unrest grew across the nation in regards to the incident. On March 26, 2012, rallies in support of Trayvon Martin were held in several cities across the nation. Around this time, Florida Governor

Rick Scott appointed a new attorney to represent the state of Florida in this matter. Within weeks of this appointment, George Zimmerman was charged with second-degree murder.

On August 30, 2012, Judge Kenneth Lester was replaced by Judge Debra Nelson after Zimmerman's attorneys raised concerns of bias on the part of Judge Lester due to comments he made in a preliminary hearing. On June 20, 2013, an all-woman jury was selected for the trial. The trial began on June 24, 2013. On July 13, 2013, the jury composed of six women found George Zimmerman not guilty. The jury had the choice of 2nd degree murder, manslaughter, or not guilty.

The not-guilty verdict made international news, with newspapers in European cities even carrying the story on their front page. Rallies were held in protest of the verdict in various locations across the country. The George Zimmerman case also created discussion regarding state "Stand Your Ground" laws. Stand Your Ground laws allow an individual to use deadly force in self-defense and alleviate the requirement of having to retreat or escape if possible.

Questions

1. The prosecution did not prove "beyond a reasonable doubt" that George Zimmerman was guilty of 2nd-degree murder or manslaughter. Does this mean the jury believed what George Zimmerman did was good and acceptable?
2. On May 28, 2013, Judge Debra Nelson ruled that evidence of Trayvon Martin's prior drug use, suspension from school, and familiarity with guns would not be allowed. Why would this information be kept from the jury?
3. Since Zimmerman was found not guilty in a criminal court proceeding, does this mean Trayvon Martin's family cannot bring a civil suit against George Zimmerman?

Types of Damages

Samantha has a profitable clothing business called "Trendy Digs." Stuart starts a competing business and starts to use "Trendy Digs" as his business name. Samantha feels her business is being damaged by Stuart's actions. Customers are becoming confused and buying goods from Stuart instead of Samantha. Samantha sues Stuart. What types of damages should Samantha seek from Stuart?

Remedy at Law vs. Equitable Damages

A **remedy at law** has historically included the plaintiff being awarded money damages or other assets such as land. The **plaintiff** is the party who initiates a lawsuit. The plaintiff is sometimes referred to as a petitioner. The **defendant** is the person against whom a lawsuit is being brought. The defendant is sometimes referred to as the respondent.

Equitable damages are damages not consisting of money damages and include 1) rescission, 2) injunction, or 3) specific performance. **Rescission** means to undo a contract and return both parties to their pre-contract positions. An **injunction** requires a party to quit and refrain from engaging in certain behavior. **Specific performance** requires a party to perform a certain action. The key difference between an injunction and specific performance is an injunction requires a person to refrain from acting while specific performance requires a person to complete a certain action. Samantha may request a court require Stuart to pay her monetary damages to compensate her for lost business. However, she would also be wise to ask a court to issue an injunction requiring Stuart to refrain from using her business name "Trendy Digs."

Ethics

Law vs. Ethics

The **law** defines what is legal and what is illegal. The law provides a minimum threshold for acceptable behavior in society. In the United States, a citizen is not required to come to the aid of another citizen. Samantha could exit her business law class to find her professor lying in a pool of blood, only to walk on past and text her best friend about what she saw. As a general rule, Samantha

Figure 1.5 Socrates, a famous philosopher

has not committed a crime in the United States if she does nothing to help her professor. In addition, the professor could not sue Samantha in a civil lawsuit. However, most individuals would believe Samantha should do something to help her professor and that she is unethical if she does not.

Ethics refers to the principles of wrong and right held by an individual and derived from various sources such as custom, societal norms, and personal beliefs that guide an individual when deciding which behavior is morally acceptable. Samantha may believe it would be unethical if she walked past her professor without providing assistance. **Business Ethics** is a term generally used to refer to the application of ethics in the business context. Some may believe conduct that is not ethical in their individual life may be appropriate in their professional or business life. However, if ethics refers to a person's individual belief of right and wrong behavior, the individual should not be able to act differently just because they are engaging in a business activity. For example, Horace does not believe the practice of lying to be ethical behavior in his personal life. Horace should not then tell lies to his business customers. Horace should not have different standards of wrong and right in business affairs than he has in his personal life. **Integrity** means a person has a strong character for being honest, fair and consistent in the application of their moral beliefs of right and wrong. A person with integrity should not act differently in their personal life than they would in their business affairs. A person with integrity should treat all customers and business associates with honesty and fairness.

At a minimum, one should keep the law if one were to be ethical. Statutory law, as an example, is created by elected officials and represents what the governing body of elected officials believes to be legally acceptable or unacceptable behavior for their society. At times, law may become outdated and one might believe it is ethical to disregard an existing law. However, as a general rule, one should keep the law if one were striving to be ethical even if one disagrees with the law. In addition, an ethical person should do more than that which is required by the law.

Bernard L. Madoff

Figure 1.6 Bernard Madoff

On June 29, 2009, Bernard L. Madoff was sentenced to a 150-year prison term for masterminding what is believed to be the largest Ponzi scheme in history. Madoff was found guilty of numerous infractions, including mail and wire fraud, securities fraud, perjury, and investment advisors fraud. Madoff began his investment career by starting a company in 1960 called Madoff Securities. The firm processed stock trades for customers. After founding the firm, it appears Madoff needed a source of capital in order to grow his firm.

Madoff began to borrow money from investors by issuing promissory notes in exchange. Many of these promissory notes paid returns in excess of fifteen percent! Madoff began to take on more investors in his firm by using sales representatives such as Michael Bienes and Frank Avellino. It is not apparent when the investment firm of Madoff became a Ponzi scheme. A Ponzi scheme is a scheme where existing investors are paid returns using the funds obtained from new investors. However, at some point, Madoff could not generate enough profit from his business to make the required payments to investors, so he paid existing investors with the new investments he was receiving. At this point, Madoff's actions would have been considered a Ponzi scheme because he was paying existing investors a return with the money provided by contributions of new investors.

Eventually, Madoff's fraudulent investment firm became so large that even hedge fund companies were investing in it. The Madoff case was peculiarly interesting for several reasons. First, Madoff claims to be the only living person with knowledge of the fraud. He claims his sons who worked for him had no idea they were part of a Ponzi scheme until he disclosed the truth to them in 2008. Second, Madoff was revered on Wall Street. Madoff was a former chairman of the NASDAQ and even served on panels for discussions led by the Securities and Exchange Commission. Third, Madoff was investigated by the Securities and Exchange Commission on two separate occasions: once in 1992 and once in 2006. In both investigations, the SEC found no evidence of wrongdoing. The Ponzi scheme was revealed only after panic hit the financial markets in the United States as well as global financial markets. Madoff was unable to raise enough new investments to cover the withdrawals made by existing customers. Without the recession he may have been able to operate the Ponzi scheme until his death.

- Duty-Based
- The Golden Rule

On March 10, 2009 a criminal suit was commenced in federal court against Bernard Madoff. Madoff was charged with eleven felonies including crimes such as mail and wire fraud, perjury and money laundering. Madoff pled guilty to all eleven counts and was sentenced to 150 years in prison. In an interview conducted by reporter Barbara Walters, Madoff stated he was happier in prison because he no longer had to keep up the lies he was living. He also tried to claim that his acts were not that reprehensible because he made the rich richer.

Questions

1. What do you believe led Madoff to commit such a large-scale fraud? Was he inherently evil? Did the fraud grow faster than he anticipated?
2. Should white-collar criminals like Madoff receive more severe or less severe prison sentences than someone who commits a violent crime such as assault? Why?
3. Besides Madoff, do you believe the government, accountants, financial investment advisors should share in the blame for this scandal? What about investors?

Ethical Decision-Making Theories

At times, an individual may have to decide what behavior is ethical. There are a myriad of ethical decision-making theories meant to assist individuals in determining what actions are ethical. There are two primary categories of ethical decision-making theories. One is Duty-Based Ethics (Deontological) and the other is Consequential-Based Ethics.

Duty-Based ethical theories determine ethical behavior by focusing on a prescribed set of duties one must follow. Examples of duty-based ethical theories are religious principles, Kant's Categorical Imperative, and Rossian ethics.

Religious-based principles determine which actions are ethical and which are not. The Bible and the Koran are sources of many religious-based principles. **The Golden Rule** states "Do unto others as you would have them do unto you." This rule can be found in the New Testament of the Judeo Christian Bible in Matthew 7:12 and Luke 6:31. The principle is also reflected in other religions such as Buddhism and Hinduism. The Golden Rule is simple and easy to apply. For example, if Tammy would want a seller to disclose a hidden defect, then as a merchandiser and store owner, Tammy should disclose hidden defects to customers. Other duties found in religious texts include the duty to give money to the poor, the duty to care of the elderly and the duty not to lie.

Immanuel Kant's **Categorical Imperative** asks "what if everyone acted this way?" Kant believed human beings had a duty to act in such a way that the individual would find their action to be acceptable as a universal law. For example, Pedro comes out of his office to find his neighbor has parked in his assigned business parking spot. Pedro considers calling the police to have the car ticketed and towed instead of merely asking his neighbor to move the car. What if everyone contacted the police instead of trying to first resolve the situation? Would this be an acceptable world in which one would want to live?

Rossian Ethics focuses on prima facie ethical duties and actual ethical duties. **Prima facie** ethical duties are to be self-evident principles that one must strive to preserve or further. Examples of prima facie duties are fidelity, beneficence, self-improvement, Justice, reparations, gratitude, and non-maleficence. One must consider how proposed actions will further these duties and this inquiry should lead one to their actual duty. An **actual duty** is a duty one must perform in a given scenario. For example, Kayla is a manager at Big Box Electronics. She hears a customer screaming at an employee. Kayla quickly realizes the employee is not at fault but sees the customer holding a damaged item. Kayla must try to create Justice for her employee and engage in reparations if the customer was given inferior goods. Kayla should quickly realize she needs to intervene in the conversation and find a way to compensate the customer.

Outcome-based ethical theories focus on the potential outcomes of a particular situation as opposed to the duties of the actors involved. The most common example of outcome-based ethics is Utilitarianism. **Utilitarianism** requires a cost-benefit analysis to determine the appropriate ethical action. An individual should weigh the positive and negative consequences of each possible course of action available and then choose the action that will result in the most amount of good and the least amount of harm. Utilitarianism is difficult to apply because positive and negative consequences can be hard to quantify. For example, assume Alexa may be injured. What is the value of a person's health? How would you quantify health or even life?

In addition, the consequences themselves might be hard to identify. Who will be harmed? Should we consider the impact on their children? Their employer as well? Finally, society might not like the outcome of the application of utilitarianism, as it may lead to the justification of activities society does not want to condone. For example, assume Henry is a farmer and Chad, his neighbor, is a farmer as well. Henry has lost his entire hay crop because of a hailstorm. However, Chad has a bumper crop. Henry has five children to feed and Chad has no family. Henry might be justified under Utilitarianism to steal part of Henry's hay crop in an attempt to provide for his family. The negative consequences to Chad, a single person, seem to be minimal, while the benefits to Henry and his family may be very large.

The **Stakeholder approach** requires company officials to consider the consequences of their actions on all relevant stakeholders of the firm. Two of the largest stakeholders are the shareholders or owners of the firm as well as the employees. Other stakeholders include the citizens of the jurisdiction where the company is located, suppliers of the company, and customers of the company. Unlike Utilitarianism, the Stakeholder Approach is not a cost/benefit analysis. Similar to Utilitarianism, positive outcomes and negative outcomes should be examined. For example, Bethany is the CEO of Gladd Manufacturing Inc. She is considering whether or not she should shut down an unprofitable manufacturing plant in Minnesota. Bethany should consider the impact of her decision on shareholders, employees, customers, suppliers, creditors, and the local community.

Another outcome-based ethical theory is not necessarily an ethical theory at all but an economic theorem. The **Coase Theorem** holds an efficient outcome will be obtained through bargaining as long as transaction costs are low. The Coase Theorem could then be used as substitute for laws or which determine which person has superior rights. The theorem could be used to eliminate the need for ethical analysis as well. For example, Rod and Marco rent a house next door to Alexis, a college professor. Rod and Marco like to have parties at their home each day of the week. Alexis does not appreciate the noise of their parties. If Alexis values a good night's sleep at $100 and Rod and Marco value having parties in the amount of $75, then Alexis could bargain with Rod and Marco to quit having parties. Alexis would likely pay Rod and Marco between $75 and $100. The Coase Theorem would more than likely not be a good substitute for a legal system, as transaction costs are often high and often parties are not in a position to negotiate. Imagine a country with no stoplights where motorists had to negotiate who would stop using the Coase Theorem!

Optimal vs. Maximum Profits

The basic objective of corporate finance is to maximize shareholder value. This principle often leads students to believe companies must maximize their profits in order to maximize shareholder value. However, if company officials must act unethically to maximize profits, one must consider whether shareholder wealth will really be maximized in the long run. **Maximum profit** is defined as the most profit a company can create even if it means acting unethically. **Optimal profit** is defined as the most profit a company can create without violating its ethical duties. For example, a company might be allowed by law to use non-recyclable inputs in its manufacturing process, but the company might choose to make a smaller amount of profit by using a recyclable input that it believes may be better for the environment.

Walkovszky v. Carlton
18 NY2d 414 (1966)

Walkovszky v. Carlton was a case involving plaintiff (Walkovszky) who was struck and injured by a cab owned by the defendant Seon Cab Corporation. The named defendant is Carlton who owns ten corporations formed under state law. Each corporation owned only two cabs. It was also alleged that the corporations all had the minimum amount of insurance required by state law.

The plaintiff believed the ten corporations were being used to defraud the public by preventing victims such as himself from gaining a proper settlement. The plaintiff believes the

- Coase Theorem
- Maximum profit
- Optimal profit

Figure 1.7 Walkovsky was hit by a taxi cab.

corporations are all the alter ego of Carlton and that the plaintiff is entitled to the assets of all the corporations if he is awarded damages.

The court opined: "[t]he law permits the incorporation of a business for the very purpose of enabling its proprietors to escape personal liability (*see, e.g., Bartle v. Home Owners Co-op.,* 309 N. Y. 103, 106) but, manifestly, the privilege is not without its limits. Broadly speaking, the courts will disregard the corporate form, or, to use accepted terminology, 'pierce the corporate veil, whenever necessary to prevent fraud or to achieve equity'. (*International Aircraft Trading Co. v. Manufacturers Trust Co.,* 297 N. Y. 285, 292.)"

The court went on to state, "The corporate form may not be disregarded merely because the assets of the corporation, together with the mandatory insurance coverage of the vehicle which struck the plaintiff, are insufficient to assure him the recovery sought. If Carlton were to be held individually liable on those facts alone, the decision would apply equally to the thousands of cabs which are owned by their individual drivers who conduct their businesses through corporations ..." The Appellate Court also added: "we agree with the court at Special Term that, if the insurance coverage required by statute "is inadequate for the protection of the public, the remedy lies not with the courts but with the Legislature."

Questions

1. What is the purpose of the corporate business form?
2. Does federal law or state law establish who can form their business as a corporation?
3. Was it ethical for the defendant Carlton to organize his cabs so each corporation owned only two cabs, thereby limiting the amount of assets that could be lost in a lawsuit?
4. Should the defendant Carlton have offered to pay for the plaintiff's injuries even though he was not required to by the court?

Safeguards Against Unethical Behavior

Company officials have a wide variety of tools to incorporate when attempting to safeguard company assets against unethical behavior. Here is a partial list of possible safeguards a company should pursue:

1. **Create a Strong Tone at the Top**. A company should adopt an ethical code of conduct. The code should be communicated to employees and strictly adhered to by all members of the organization. The behavior of management will have a direct influence on the behavior of employees.

2. **Engage in Periodic Employee Reviews**. Companies must have a periodic review of employee performance. Employees benefit from a periodic review by not only getting feedback from superiors but also by getting a chance to express concerns or unmet desires. Ethics should be an integral part of a periodic review.

3. **Establish Separate Employee Responsibility**. Employees should have separate responsibilities in order to alleviate the potential for any one employee to have too much control over assets. Job duties must also be clearly defined. For example, no one employee should be allowed to receive customer payments, deposit customer payments, and update the company's accounting record for those payments. This employee could be tempted to steal a customer's payment and update the accounting records so no one would know.

4. **Institute Physical Controls**. A company should institute physical controls such as padlocks on doors and passwords for computer programs. A company must ensure its employees know who is responsible for these physical controls and checks should be put in place to ensure proper utilization. For example, Big Bank Inc. may require its employees to update their computer login passwords every three months.

5. **Perform a Periodic Review of Safeguards and Risks.** As technology and business operations change, a company must periodically review the risks present in regards to its assets as well as the safeguards in place to protect those assets. For example, most accounting records were once kept on paper and stored in boxes. Now most accounting records are stored in a digital file. Companies must maintain safeguards to prevent loss of the digital files much different from those used to ensure the safeguard of paper files.

Discussion Questions

1. What are the sources of federal law for the United States and which has the most authority?
2. What are the sources of state law for the United States and which has the most authority?
3. Who creates international law?
4. What are the three branches of the federal government and what are the duties of each branch?
5. If a state constitution provision conflicts with the US Constitution, which provision prevails?
6. Where does an agency like the Securities and Exchange Commission get its authority to regulate? Does it make law?
7. What is the common law, where did the common law of the US originate, and what key principles should judges abide by when applying the common law?
8. When do judges apply the common law in the United States?
9. What if common law conflicts with legislation passed by a state? Which prevails?

10. What is the definition of precedent and stare decisis?
11. What are equitable remedies and how are they different from remedies at law?
12. If Jan's car is damaged in an automobile accident, which remedy might she prefer?
13. If Arthur contracted to buy a rare coin collection but the seller refused to deliver it, what remedy might Arthur prefer?
14. How does an injured party know which equitable remedy to pursue?
15. What is substantive law? How is it different from procedural law?
16. How is civil law different from criminal law?
17. What is an example of a substantive right?
18. How do the terms ethics and law differ?
19. How are duty-based ethical theories different from outcome-based ethical theories?
20. What is the Golden Rule? Can you provide an example?
21. What is Utilitarianism? How is it applied?
22. What is the Categorical Imperative?
23. What are the two aspects of Rossian ethics?
24. What is the stakeholder approach and how is it applied?
25. What is the Coase Theorem? What would be an example of its application?
26. How are maximum profits different from optimal profits?
27. What safeguard can a company employ against unethical behavior by employees?

Critical-Thinking Questions

The answers will not necessarily be found in the text to this chapter but an answer should reflect the concepts presented in this chapter.

28. Why are the judgments of an international court hard to enforce against a particular country?
29. Why did the founding fathers of the United States want federal law to preempt state law?
30. What positive consequences and what negative consequences might result if a citizen takes the law into their own hands?
31. Why does a society need a legal system?
32. Would a society need a legal system if everyone followed the same religion?

Short-Answer and Essay Questions

1. Layne is staring a home-repair business. He will provide basic home repairs such as changing door knobs and fixing lights. Layne will also do larger repairs such as building decks or installing windows. Layne will have one employee, Cody. What sources of federal law may apply to Layne? What sources of state law might apply to Layne?
2. Kendra is starting a real estate firm in New York City where she will employ real estate agents to sell only homes that sell for more than $1,000,000. Kendra hopes to employ at

least four real estate agents. Kendra says the only law she needs to worry about is New York statutory law. Is Kendra correct? Could New York City have its own law? Could federal statutory law apply to her business as well? What other sources of law might apply to Kendra?

3. In the following scenarios, which source of law is considered the highest source?
    a. State constitutional provision, federal constitutional provision, or a state statutory provision.
    b. Federal statutory provision, state statutory provision, or a federal administrative agency rule.
    c. State constitutional provision, federal administrative agency rule, or a federal statutory law provision.
    d. State constitutional provision, state common law, or a state statutory law provision.

4. In the following scenarios, which source of law is considered the highest source?
    a. Federal constitutional provision, state common law, or a state statutory law provision.
    b. Federal constitutional provision, state constitutional provision, or a state statutory law provision.
    c. Federal statutory provision, federal common law, or a state statutory law provision.
    d. Federal agency rule provision, state common law, or a state statutory law provision.

5. Mitchel works at Grocery Store Inc. One night Mitchel is working late and leaves his office after dark. Mitchel is attacked in the parking lot by Ryan. Ryan takes Mitchel's wallet. Has Ryan violated civil law? Who would bring a civil lawsuit against Ryan? Has Ryan violated criminal law? Would Mitchel bring a criminal case against Ryan?

6. Samantha buys a new radio online through a website called Dealsforless. Samantha never receives her radio and believes the company has stolen her money with no intent to pay her back. Could this be a violation of civil law, criminal law, or both? If a court requires Samantha to file a formal complaint, is this a procedural law requirement or an example of substantive law?

7. In *Pace v. Alabama* (1883), the US Supreme Court upheld an Alabama law that prohibited blacks and whites from marrying. The Supreme Court held Alabama had a legitimate state interest in protecting the institution of marriage. Can this precedent be overturned? Would the overturning of the precedent violate the rule of stare decisis?

8. In *Plessy v. Ferguson*, the Supreme Court held it was constitutional for states to have separate facilities for the education of white and black children. The doctrine became known as "separate but equal." Can this precedent be overturned? Would the overturning of the precedent violate the rule of stare decisis?

9. Angie recently purchased a greatest hits CD online. Angie paid $50 to the website company that offered the CD for sale. Which remedies should Angie pursue if she does not receive the CD in the mail? Remedy at law? Equitable remedies? Which type of equitable remedy would be most appropriate for Angie to pursue?

10. Craig writes computer software code for his business. Erik works for Craig and copies the code. Erik then quits his employment with Craig and starts selling the software code

to Craig's competitors. Which remedies should Craig pursue? Remedy at law? Equitable remedies? Which type of equitable remedy would be most appropriate for Craig to pursue?

11. Electric Cars Inc. was recently informed by the National Highway Traffic Safety Commission that there might be a government-mandated recall of Electric Cars Inc.'s new model. Electric Cars Inc. is just about to release their quarterly financial data. Conclude as to whether Electric Cars Inc. should tell investors about the possible recall when it releases its quarterly financial data. Apply the Golden Rule, Kant's Categorical Imperative, Rossian Ethics, and Utilitarianism to determine the appropriate ethical action to be taken. Please define each rule before providing an analysis of such rule.

12. Meredith owns and operates a potato farm in Idaho. Meredith currently pays migrant workers minimum wage to harvest her crop. Does Meredith have an ethical duty to provide housing to her workers? Apply the Golden Rule, Kant's Categorical Imperative, Rossian Ethics, and Utilitarianism to determine the appropriate ethical action to be taken. Please define each rule before providing an analysis of such rule.

13. Fast Pharm Inc. creates lifesaving drugs. Fast Pharm has created a drug that will cure ovarian cancer. However, the drug's use will kill at least two out of every one thousand patients immediately after the first dose. The other 998 patients will be saved from ovarian cancer with no side effect. Should Fast Pharm release the drug? Apply Kant's Categorical Imperative, Utilitarianism, and the Stakeholder approach to determine the appropriate ethical action to be taken. Please define each rule before providing an analysis of such rule.

14. Cablecom Inc. provides Internet and cable services to millions of customers nationwide. Cablecom is considering sending out a letter to customers, encouraging customers to sign up for online billing statements. Cablecom is also going to include estimates of how much paper will be saved by this change and the positive effect this will then have on the environment. However, Cablecom is not going to disclose the fact seventy percent of customers will pay less attention to their bill and this lack of attention stands to increase Cablecom's annual profit by five percent. Does Cablecom have an ethical duty to disclose the increase in profit to its customers? Apply Kant's Categorical Imperative, Utilitarianism, and the Stakeholder approach to determine the appropriate ethical action to be taken. Please define each rule before providing an analysis of such rule.

CHAPTER TWO

COURT PROCEDURE

By Craig Nierman

Courts

Holly was recently involved in an auto accident with a delivery truck. The driver of the truck was clearly intoxicated. Holly would like to sue the owner of the delivery truck. Holly is interested in finding out which court would hear her lawsuit.

Nelson was recently harassed by his supervisor at work. Due to the humiliation Nelson suffered at the hands of his coworkers because of the incident, he decided to quit his job. When he informed the human resources director, she told him he would have to submit his claim to an arbitrator. Nelson has never heard of arbitration before and he is wondering what he should do.

Chapter Objectives

1. Understand the role of the judiciary
2. Identify different means for a court to exercise jurisdiction over a defendant
3. Understand the significance of subject matter jurisdiction
4. Distinguish between major aspects of the trial sequence
5. Identify key legal issues associated with alternative dispute resolution

Introduction and Overview

Because business professionals are often involved in decisions related to current or potential litigation, it is important that they have a working understanding of the basic structure of American courts and the judicial process. There is an overlapping and somewhat complicated interplay between the federal and state courts in terms of what cases they have authority over. While their procedure for how cases are processed are significantly similar, their methods for selecting judges and how they ultimately rule

• Judicial review

on issues can vary widely. Because of the expense and delay of litigation, parties and courts have greatly expanded the use of procedures other than trials to resolve cases.

Judicial Review

Federal and state governments have divided their powers into three distinct branches:

1. The legislature, which creates statutory law;
2. The executive, which executes or enforces the law; and
3. The judiciary, which interprets the law.

The extent of the judiciary's power has been controversial since the earliest days of United States. In the foundational case of *Marbury v. Madison* in 1803, the Supreme Court asserted its power of **judicial review**, "to say what the law is" and declare whether a statute passed by Congress violates constitutional principles. By exercising judicial review, the Supreme Court subjected the powers of Congress and the states to its judgment of whether their laws exceed the authority given them by the Constitution. Thus, the power of judicial review is the courts' authority to define and limit the powers of the legislative branch and declare the meaning of laws enacted by the other branches.

Although the holding of *Marbury v. Madison* has not been seriously challenged in over two hundred years, the Supreme Court's approach to interpreting the Constitution remains a flashpoint for political debate. Some see a judge's role as limited to interpreting the text of the Constitution based on the original intent at the time that it was written. This would limit the role of the judiciary and reserve the responsibility of amendment to the democratic process. Others believe that interpretation should occur through the lens of society's evolving definition of Justice and that judges should change the law as they see fit.

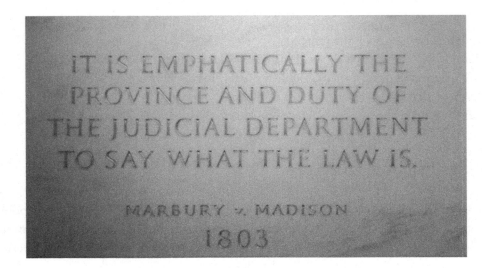

Figure 2.1 Description for the Statute of John Marshall

Marbury v. Madison
5 US 137 (1803)

The following is a summary of the case.

During the last hours of his administration, President John Adams made several judicial appointments. However, their commissions were not delivered before Thomas Jefferson was sworn in as President. Jefferson refused to deliver them. Four of the would-be Judges appointed by Adams, including William Marbury, sued to compel Jefferson's Secretary of State, James Madison, to deliver their commissions. They filed their case directly to the Supreme Court based on the Judiciary Act of 1789, which appeared to give the Supreme Court, rather than a lower court, the power to hear cases affecting persons holding federal government offices.

The Supreme Court ruled that the Judges had been inappropriately deprived of their commissions. However, it determined that the portion of the Judiciary Act of 1789 giving individuals like Marbury the right to bypass lower courts and go directly to the Supreme Court contradicted Article III of the Constitution, which limited the Supreme Court's authority to hear appeals except in very limited circumstances (none of which were relevant to Marbury's case). Accordingly, the Court ruled that provision of the statute to be unconstitutional and affirmed its power "to say what the law is." Supreme Court Chief Justice Marshall wrote that "the very essence of judicial duty" is to determine whether laws are in opposition to the Constitution and, in that instance, to affirm the superiority of the Constitution.

Questions

1. Who was Marbury? Who was Madison?
2. What is the significance of this case?
3. What consequences might exist if Congress were responsible for declaring its own acts constitutional?
4. What consequences might result if the president of the United States were allowed to declare acts of Congress constitutional?

Jurisdiction

Jurisdiction is derived from two Latin words: *iuris* meaning "law" and *dicere* meaning "to speak." **Jurisdiction** is the power of a court to decide a case regarding certain legal matters. Thus, in order to hear case, a court must have the appropriate jurisdiction. There are several aspects of jurisdiction, including the parties, property, and subject matter.

Personal Jurisdiction

Personal jurisdiction refers to the court's authority over a particular person or organization. There are several ways a court can create in personam jurisdiction, meaning jurisdiction over a defendant.

1. Courts have jurisdiction over people who reside in that state
2. Courts have jurisdiction over those found in their state and properly served
3. Courts have jurisdiction over those who consent to jurisdiction in that state
4. Courts may utilize a long-arm statute

For example, an Ohio court clearly has jurisdiction over an Ohio resident who is found in Ohio. On the other hand, that Ohio court does not have any kind of authority over a Nevada resident who has never visited the state of Ohio and who has no connections to Ohio. The Nevada resident could become subject to jurisdiction if the resident visits the state of Ohio and is served with the proper court paperwork while in the state. The Nevada resident could also consent to the jurisdiction of an Ohio court.

Long-arm statutes allow courts to have personal jurisdiction over people who may not be in that state but whose actions relate to the laws there. If a Nevada resident is accused in a lawsuit of causing a car accident in Ohio, the Ohio courts have personal jurisdiction over the Nevada driver, even if the visitor left the state long before he or she was sued in Ohio. That is because state courts have jurisdiction over legal disputes originating in their states regardless of where the parties are located or reside. The mechanism for exercising that authority is often referred to as a **long-arm statute**, which is a law passed by the legislature, giving courts power over people who have sufficient connections with the state. It is said the "long arm" of the law can reach beyond the state's borders.

There are limits on a court's' exercise of its long-arm power. The United States Supreme Court has ruled that a person or organization must have sufficient "minimum contacts" with the jurisdiction to be subject to its laws. Suppose an Idaho business is sued in Alabama even though the business does not have an office there and none of its employees have ever traveled to Alabama. An Alabama court may exercise jurisdiction over the business if its contacts are sufficient that it could reasonably be expected to defend an Alabama lawsuit because of quantity or quality of the business relationships it has there.

Figure 2.2 Burger King Restaurant Franchises Are Located Around the World

Burger King Corp. v. Rudzewicz

471 US 462 (1985)

The following is a summary of the case.

Burger King, which is based in Miami, contracted with Rudzewicz to operate a restaurant franchise in Michigan. The contract provided that Rudzewicz would make certain payments to Burger King for the privileges of using the Burger King name. The contract stated that it was formed in Florida and governed under Florida law. Burger King filed suit in federal court in Florida when Rudzewicz fell behind in making the required payments. The plaintiff alleged diversity of citizenship. Rudzewicz argued that because Rudzewicz was from Michigan and had no Florida connections, the court lacked personal jurisdiction.

The trial court found that the Florida long-arm statute provided the court with authority over the defendant who allegedly signed a contract in Florida that was to be governed under Florida law. The Judge ordered Rudzewicz to stop using the Burger King name, but Rudzewicz refused and appealed. The Court of Appeals reversed, believing that it was unfair to force Rudzewicz to defend the litigation in Florida. Burger King then appealed to the United States Supreme Court.

The Supreme Court held whether or not a defendant is subject to a long-arm statute is determined by the totality of the circumstances. Just because a defendant is not physically in the jurisdiction does not necessarily mean that the defendant is outside the court's power. On the other hand, the defendant must have fair warning of the potential to be sued in that state to be subject to jurisdiction there.

The Court concluded that "Rudzewicz most certainly knew that he was affiliating himself with an enterprise based primarily in Florida. The contract documents themselves emphasize that Burger King's operations are conducted and supervised from the Miami headquarters, that all relevant notices and payments must be sent there, and that the agreements were made in and enforced from Miami." Thus, it was fair to force him to defend the litigation there. The Supreme Court reinstated the trial court's decision.

Questions

1. What were the relevant facts to this case?
2. What form of personal jurisdiction was being exercised by the court?
3. Would the result have been different if Rudzewicz's business had been located in Florida?
4. Would the result have been different if the contract had not said Florida law would apply?

As illustrated by the Burger King case, corporations are subject to jurisdiction in the states where they do business and create minimum contacts. Corporations are also subject to jurisdiction in the states where they are incorporated or where they have their business headquarters. For example, Ballestine Products is incorporated in Delaware and has its business headquarters in Connecticut. Ballestine is subject to jurisdiction in both Delaware and Connecticut. Ballestine is also subject to jurisdiction in a state where it conducted business activities and such business activity gave rise to a lawsuit based upon the theory of a long-arm statute and minimum contacts.

Jurisdiction in Cyberspace

Business activities conducted through the internet could potentially subject a company to jurisdiction under a long-arm statute in any state where the company's webpage or email correspondence is viewed. Courts have developed a sliding scale for determining whether or not a defendant has minimum contacts within a jurisdiction that would satisfy Constitutional requirements. In the case *Zippo Manufacturing Co. v. Zippo Dot Com, Inc.,* 952 F. Supp. 1119 (WD Pa. 1997), a three prong approach was developed for determining whether or not a defendant could be found to have minimum contacts in a cyber-based transaction which would allow a court to exercise jurisdiction over the defendant. The court identified 1) commercial websites, 2) interactive websites, and 3) passive websites. The court found that passive websites were merely viewed by users and the defendant operating the website would not have minimum contacts based upon the passive viewing alone. The court went onto find that commercial websites involve knowing and sometimes repeated contacts and transmissions of information by the plaintiff and defendant. The court reasoned these types of websites should subject the defendant operating the website to jurisdiction in the forum of the user. Finally, the court stated that interactive websites might subject a defendant to jurisdiction in another forum depending upon the type and amount of activity which occurred. Therefore, if a defendant has engaged in a business transaction through cyber-space then the defendant should be considered to have minimum contacts, if the defendant has merely posted information on a website which can be viewed by users, the defendant should be considered to lack minimum contacts, if the website or actions of the defendant is somewhere between commercial and passive (interactive website for example), the court will have to decide whether the facts of the case support finding minimum contacts.

Property Jurisdiction

In rem **jurisdiction** gives a state court authority over a dispute when the property at issue is located within that state, even if its owner is not a resident of that state. The term *in rem* is from the Latin phrase meaning "about the power." The American legal system believes it is appropriate for a court to have jurisdiction (meaning power) to decide who has rights related to land or other property when it is located within that state. However, that does not necessarily mean it has personal jurisdiction over the property owner. Thus, a successful lawsuit based on in rem jurisdiction may allow the plaintiff to make a claim against the defendant's property located within the court's jurisdiction but not for claims that exceed the value of that property.

Subject Matter Jurisdiction

Subject matter jurisdiction refers to whether the court has authority over the specific matter in controversy. In the federal system, some matters may be heard only by courts of the United States government, which are known as federal courts. Other matters can be heard exclusively by state courts. Some legal matters may be heard by either state or federal court.

State Subject Matter

The Tenth Amendment to the Constitution states: "The powers not delegated to the United States by the Constitution, nor prohibited by it to the States, are reserved to the States respectively, or to the people."

In other words, the states have exclusive jurisdiction over all matters that the Constitution does not specifically allocate to the federal government. That means state courts are **courts of general jurisdiction**, which is to say that they have authority over every matter not specifically reserved for other courts. Accordingly, with few exceptions, state courts have exclusive control over matters such as state torts, probate, state criminal law, and domestic and family relations. Therefore, the vast majority of American legal matters are decided in state courts according to state law.

Federal Subject Matter

Article III, Section 2 of the United States Constitution gives the federal courts jurisdiction over cases "arising under this Constitution [and] the laws of the United States." When read in conjunction with the Tenth Amendment, that means that federal courts have the power to hear only cases arising out of the Constitution and laws passed by Congress. Thus, instead of being courts of general jurisdiction, they are **courts of limited jurisdiction**.

For example, the Constitution gives Congress, rather than the states, the exclusive ability to regulate bankruptcies, thus, only federal courts may hear cases where a person or business is seeking bankruptcy protection. Similarly, the Constitution gives the United States government the exclusive ability to hear maritime or admiralty disputes. Likewise, criminal cases arising out of alleged violations of laws passed by Congress are heard only by federal courts.

Legal Matters Heard Only in Federal Court:

1. Patent and copyright law disputes
2. Bankruptcy proceedings
3. Federal tax controversies
4. Maritime disputes
5. Other matters that involve only federal law

Concurrent Subject Matter Jurisdiction

There are a limited number of matters that may be heard in either state or federal courts. These disputes generally fall into one of two categories. The first is based upon diversity of citizenship and the second arises when the lawsuit involves issues of both federal law and state law. **Concurrent jurisdiction** means two or more courts have jurisdiction over the same matter.

Diversity Jurisdiction

The first group of cases that can be heard in either system involves controversies between citizens of different states in matters arising out of state law. The writers of the Constitution were concerned that a resident of one state might not receive equal treatment if they were forced to defend the lawsuit in the court of another state. Accordingly, Article III of the Constitution gives Congress the power to give the federal courts overlapping jurisdiction

- Courts of general jurisdiction
- Courts of limited jurisdiction
- Concurrent jurisdiction

- Diversity jurisdiction
- Removal
- Erie Doctrine

over certain cases between citizens of different states on matters that would otherwise be heard in state court. Currently, the law allows this if the amount in dispute exceeds $75,000. The authority to hear these cases is called **diversity jurisdiction** because it involves people of diverse citizenship. Note that when there is more than one defendant, diversity jurisdiction does not apply if one of the defendants is a citizen of the plaintiff's state. Diversity jurisdiction also applies when one party to the suit is a resident of one country and the other party is a citizen of another country.

As an example of diversity of citizenship, if a Louisiana resident sues a North Dakota citizen in Louisiana state court for $1 million, the defendant, the North Dakota resident, could transfer the case to the federal court in Louisiana. The transfer to another court is called **removal**. Similarly, the Louisiana resident could initially file the action in federal court, either in Louisiana or North Dakota.

In deciding which law to apply to diversity cases, the federal courts apply **Erie Doctrine**, which originates from the 1938 United States Supreme Court decision in *Erie Railroad Co. v. Tompkins*. This case establishes that when federal courts exercise jurisdiction over cases arising out of state law, they must apply state rather than federal law. Thus, theoretically, litigants should expect to get the same result regardless of whether their cases are heard in state or federal courthouses.

Erie Railroad Co. v. Tompkins
304 US 64 (1938)

Figure 2.3 A locomotive of the Cedar Point and Lake Erie Railroad

A summary of the Supreme Court opinion is as follows.

Tompkins was walking along a footpath in Pennsylvania that crossed train tracks owned by New York–based Erie Railroad Co. After being hit by an Erie train, Tompkins, a Pennsylvania citizen, filed a legal action in federal court based upon diversity of citizenship. He filed the case in New York, claiming that the railroad was liable for his injuries.

The trial Judge overruled the railroad's assertion that the case was governed under Pennsylvania law, which provided that railroads had no special duty to pedestrians on railroad property. Tompkins asserted that under federal law the railroad owed him a heightened duty of care. The Court of Appeals affirmed the lower court ruling in favor of Tompkins and the railroad appealed to the Supreme Court.

The Supreme Court ruled that ignoring state law in an area where the Constitution does not specifically allocate power to the federal government is "an unconstitutional assumption of powers" by the federal courts. "Except in matters governed by the Federal Constitution or by Acts of Congress, the law to be applied in any case is the law of the State. And whether the law of the State shall be declared by its Legislature in a statute or by its highest court in a decision is not a matter of federal concern. There is no federal general common law. Congress has no power to declare substantive rules of common law applicable in a State, whether they be local in their nature or 'general,' be they commercial law or a part of the law of torts. And no clause in the Constitution purports to confer such a power upon the federal courts."

Accordingly, the Court held that federal courts must apply state law in diversity cases. As a result, the Supreme Court reversed the Court of Appeals and the case was eventually dismissed.

Questions

1. What were the facts of this case?
2. What was the court's holding?
3. What form of jurisdiction was the court exercising?
4. Why would it be unconstitutional for a federal court to apply state law in a case like this?

The second way that state and federal courts can exercise jurisdiction over the same matter is a controversy where both state and federal law are involved. For example, the federal government and many states have laws that prohibit sexual harassment. So a Colorado resident employed in Colorado who claims to be the victim of sexual harassment can invoke both Colorado state law and federal law in one lawsuit. The plaintiff would have the option of filing the lawsuit either in Colorado state court or in federal court. The court would then decide both the federal and the state issues.

Venue

Venue is the proper court or forum to hear a case. For example, in the state court system, the proper venue for a state court case is generally the county where the defendant resides or where the legal dispute arose. For example, Alex is involved in the state of Iowa in an auto accident with Linda. The accident occurred in Osceola County. The County of Osceola District Court would be a proper venue for Alex to bring a lawsuit against Linda.

In federal court, venue is determined upon what type of case is being heard. If the basis for jurisdiction is diversity of citizenship, as discussed earlier in this chapter, the appropriate venue is the district where all the defendants or the only defendant resides. If there is more than one defendant, and they have different districts of residence, then the district where any one defendant lives is a proper venue. For example, Pol sues Bobby and asserts jurisdiction in federal court based upon diversity of citizenship. Bobby lives in the territory covered by the federal District Court of the Northern District of California; the Northern District is the

• Venue

proper forum. If federal jurisdiction is based upon the fact the case involves a federal question, the proper venue is where the defendant resides or where the alleged wrong occurred.

At times, a defendant may make a motion to have the venue of a case changed. For example, in the high-profile case of Jeffrey Skilling, a former CEO of the defunct company Enron, Mr. Skilling made a motion for a change of venue in federal District Court. He claimed if the trial was held in Houston, Texas, the jurors would be biased against him because of news reports and commentary. The District Court denied his motion for change of venue based upon the fact it believed proper jury selection would eliminate biased jurors.

Court Structure

The court systems in the United States can be separated into many different categories. The main distinction is that of federal courts versus state courts. Regardless of whether a court is a federal court or a state court, it will be required to follow the precedent of higher ranking courts in its jurisdiction. For example, a district federal court in the state of Iowa would have to follow the appellate court decisions for its circuit (the 8th Circuit Court of Appeals) as well as precedents created by the US Supreme Court. A district court in Iowa, however, would not have to follow the precedent of another district court or an appellate court for another jurisdiction such as the 7th Circuit Court of Appeals. A state district court would have to follow the precedent of higher ranking state courts in its jurisdiction as well as the precedent of federal courts.

Federal Judicial System

Although there are minor variations, the federal courts across the nation are largely uniform in terms of procedure.

District Courts

The main federal trial court is known as the **United States District Court** and federal lawsuits typically originate in them. A trial court is a court that acts as a fact finder through the process of listening to testimony and considering other evidence. Each state has at least one District Court and a couple states have as many as four District Courts. **District Court judges**, as well as judges of the Court of Appeals and Supreme Court Justices, are appointed by the president, subject to confirmation by the United States Senate. The judges serve a life term and can be removed from office only for certain egregious misconduct. **Magistrate judges**—who handle cases, or portions of cases, assigned to them by a district judge—are appointed by the chief judge of the District Court. So, a magistrate judge might handle only the initial appearance in a criminal case or a discovery dispute in a civil case while the district judge would normally preside over the trials.

Specialized Courts

The federal system includes several courts that hear cases of a specific nature. For example, there are **bankruptcy courts** that hear only bankruptcy matters. Bankruptcy judges are appointed by the Court of Appeals in their geographic area for a limited term. Other specialized courts include the United States Court of Federal Claims, the United States Court of International Trade, and the United States Court of Appeals for Veterans Claims. Judges of these courts are generally appointed by the president and confirmed by the Senate for a fixed term.

• United States
  Court of Appeals

Court of Appeals

The **United States Court of Appeals**, also known as circuit courts, hear appeals from the District Courts. The Appellate Courts are divided into thirteen divisions called circuits.

Geographic Circuits

With one exception, Circuit Courts are based on the geography of the District Courts they take appeals from. The largest circuit, both in terms of geography and the number of cases, is the Ninth Circuit, which includes nine Western states including Alaska and Hawaii. The District of Columbia Circuit contains only the nation's capital. Most circuits contain three or four states. Below is a representation of the 11 Circuit Courts of Appeals containing multiple states within their jurisdiction. Missing from the picture is the US Court of Appeals for the District of Columbia Circuit , which only hears appeals from the US District Court for the District of Colombia, and the Federal Circuit Court of Appeals, which is discussed later.

Figure 2.4 Pictorial Representation of US Courts of Appeals and District Court Regions

Federal Circuit

The **Federal Circuit**, based in Washington, D.C., is the only division of the Court of Appeals to receive cases based on the subject matter of the case rather than the geography of the lower court. For example, when any case concerning intellectual property is appealed from the District Court, it goes directly to the federal circuit. The federal circuit also receives cases directly from several specific specialized courts such as the United States Court of Federal Claims, the United States Court of International Trade, and the United States Court of Appeals for Veterans Claims. It also hears certain administrative law rulings appealed from government agencies. For example, if a party gets an unfavorable ruling from the Government Accountability Office Personnel Appeals Board, it can appeal directly to the Federal Circuit of the Court of Appeals.

Supreme Court

The **United States Supreme Court** is the final arbiter of federal law and all appeals from the United States Court of Appeals are appealed to the Supreme Court, which decides whether or not to hear the appeal. Litigants generally have one **Appeal of Right**, meaning that they are entitled to appeal to the Court of Appeals. Appeals to the Supreme Court are **Discretionary Appeals**, meaning that the Supreme Court will not necessarily agree to hear a case appealed to it. In fact, the Supreme Court hears only a fraction of the appeals it receives. When the Supreme Court declines a case, the Circuit Court decision stands. The **Rule of Four** requires that at least four of nine Supreme Court Justices must vote to hear a discretionary appeal. If at least four of the nine Supreme Court Justices decide to hear a case, the Supreme Court grants a **Writ of Certiorari**, sometimes referred to simply as a "Writ of Cert," that means the Court is exercising its discretionary power to hear an appeal.

In limited circumstances, United States Supreme Court can hear cases appealed from state courts. This occurs only when the matter in controversy involves interpretation of federal law. As an example, if the Vermont Supreme Court hears a case based on concurrent jurisdiction, meaning the case involves both Vermont and federal law, the litigants may attempt an appeal to the United States Supreme Court to decide the federal issue only. In other words, United States Supreme Court can rule only on the federal law issues. Since the Vermont Supreme Court has the final say on the interpretation of Vermont law, the federal Supreme Court has no authority to reverse the Vermont court's ruling on state law unless such law would violate the federal Constitution.

State Judicial System

Each state has its own unique court system. This section outlines the typical structure only.

Municipal Courts

States generally have one or more lower-level courts that handle minor criminal violations such as traffic tickets as well as civil cases with relatively little money in controversy. A court that hears civil law cases where a small amount of money is in dispute is called a **Small Claims Court**. Generally, states make it relatively easy for people to represent themselves in Small Claims Court and some states prohibit people from having attorneys represent them there.

Depending on the state, the people presiding over municipal courts have different names, such as magistrates, court commissioners, Justices of the peace, and associate judges. Oftentimes the decision of a municipal court may be appealed to the state trial court.

Trial Courts

State trial courts generally hear a broad range of cases such as family law matters, tort claims, state criminal cases, and probate issues. Parties usually have the right to have trial court decisions reviewed by a state **Appellate Court**.

Court of Appeals

About eighty percent of states have an **intermediate Appellate Court** (usually called the Court of Appeals), which is a court that hears appeals from state trial courts and is subject to the authority of a higher court usually called the Supreme Court. Like the federal system, appeals to the intermediate Appellate Court are generally an appeal of right and a second appeal to the highest state court is discretionary. In rare circumstances, appeals from the trial court can bypass the Court of Appeals to the state's highest court.

Supreme Court

Each state has a court of last resort and, in almost all instances, it is called the Supreme Court. A well-known exception is the State of New York, which calls its highest court the New York Court of Appeals. State supreme court decisions interpreting state law are final. However, when a state supreme court renders an interpretation of federal law, then that opinion can be appealed to the United States Supreme Court. In states that have a court of appeals, the supreme court is generally not obligated to review cases reviewed from the intermediate Appellate Court.

Judicial Selection

While some states use the same system to select judges regardless of which court the judge will serve on, others use different systems for trial and appeals court judge selections. There are three main processes by which state court judges are selected.

Gubernatorial Appointment

A number of states have a system very similar to the federal system where the governor appoints a person to be a judge and that person then must be confirmed by the state senate. Of those states, some appoint judges for life, while others require judges to sit for periodic elections to continue serving.

Election

Almost half of the states select judges by public election.

Missouri Plan

The remaining states utilize a system known as the **Missouri Plan**, which utilizes a commission to appoint judges. The commission is generally composed of a judge, attorneys selected by the state's lawyers, and citizens appointed by the governor. The commission narrows the pool of people applying to be a judge to a list of between two and five people. The governor must then select one person from that list. Senate confirmation is not required, but the judge must stand for one or more retention elections.

Judge selection methods have become a source of considerable controversy. Some believe that, like other officials in a democratic society, judges should be elected by a majority of the citizens. Others argue that subjecting judicial candidates to raising money from lawyers or possible litigants taints the impartiality of the courts.

Similarly, the length of a judge's term is also a matter of debate. Some believe that appointing a judge to a specific term promotes accountability, while others assert that life terms are important to insulate judges from being tempted to consider the popularity of his or her decisions. The Missouri Plan is also controversial in that some contend that it removes "politics" from the process, while others say they are even more "political" because the commissions are often heavily dominated by a particular political party.

Civil Procedure

The law can be divided into two broad categories: substantive law and procedural law. **Substantive law** refers to matters of substance and creates legal rights and duties. An example is whether a company is liable for a defective product, the requirements for a valid contract, and what constitutes a criminal act. **Procedural law** is that portion of the law that dictates how rights can be enforced or taken away. An example of procedural law is the amount of a fee for filing a lawsuit. Other common examples of procedural law are what documents a party must share with its opponent, how much time a defendant has to respond to a criminal complaint, or how long a criminal defendant can be incarcerated before a hearing takes place. The procedural law for civil, rather than criminal, cases is called **civil procedure**. While the legislature can mandate certain aspects of civil procedure, the highest court of a jurisdiction generally creates most of the rules of civil procedure.

Standing

Before a person or organization can bring a civil lawsuit, it must have **standing**, which is a sufficient interest in the controversy to bring the case. Courts will generally dismiss a lawsuit if the person bringing it lacks standing.

Imagine that Adams, Beltran, and Chen are neighbors and that Adams accidentally backs Adams' car into Beltran's mailbox. Although Beltran has a right to demand that Adams pay for the damage, Beltran decides to do nothing. Even if Chen feels like Beltran is wrong for not making Adams pay for Adams' negligence, Chen has no right to sue Adams to force Adams to pay Beltran. The reason is that Chen did not incur any damage in the matter. Therefore, even though Chen may be motivated to bring Justice, Chen has no standing to do so.

- Pleadings
- Plaintiff
- Complaint
- Statute of limitations

Litigation Process

Initial Pleadings

Pleadings are documents filed with the court that state the legal position of the parties. It is important to note pleadings do not include discovery documents, which are described in the following sections.

Complaint

Litigation starts with the **Plaintiff** (also known as the Petitioner), who brings the lawsuit (also known as an action). The document that initiates the action is the **Complaint** (also known as a Petition), which is a pleading setting forth the names of the parties, a description of the controversy, and the specific legal theories that justify the plaintiff's request for relief. Courts vary in terms of how specific the complaint must be and whether it must include a specific dollar amount. Sometimes the complaint is amended to make technical corrections or to accommodate new information gained through the litigation process.

The Complaint must be filed before the **statute of limitations**—the maximum amount of time after the alleged incident occurs in which one must file suit—expires. Thus, if Acme Computer Corp. sues

Figure 2.5 First Page of a Complaint

Silicone Express for supplying it with faulty components, but waits until after the statute of limitations has passed, Acme's claims may be dismissed simply because it filed too late.

The length of the statute of limitations varies by jurisdiction as well as by the type of action. Often the statute of limitations for torts is considerably shorter than it is for contracts. For example, a state may decide that the statute of limitations for a breach of contract claim is five years, three years for a property damage claim, and two years for a personal injury claim.

Many jurisdictions apply what is called the **discovery rule**, which, as an exception to the statute of limitations, extends it by the amount of time that a reasonable person would not have had any idea that a claim existed. Suppose in a state where personal injury claims must be brought within three years that a manufacturer was dumping toxic chemicals into a creek starting in 2008, contaminating a nearby family's well. As a result, several family members developed a disease in 2010, did not have symptoms until 2013, did not find out about the chemicals until 2015, and then filed suit against the manufacturer immediately thereafter. The manufacturer may seek to dismiss the complaint because the family waited seven years before taking action against the manufacturer. However, the discovery rule might allow the family to overcome that argument if they filed the suit within three years of having reasonable notice of the chemical dumping.

Summons

The person being sued is the **defendant** (also known as the respondent). A **summons** (also referred to as the original notice) is a document that formally advises the defendant that a complaint has been filed. The law is very specific about the required **process of service**, which is the formal way the summons must be delivered to the defendant. In many cases it must be hand delivered to the defendant or the defendant's spouse. If the defendant is a corporation or similar entity, the summons may be delivered to an officer of the company or the **registered agent**, which is the person officially listed with the government in the state where the company is incorporated or organized. Most states publish an online directory of the registered agents through which a corporation may be served a summons.

Motion To Dismiss

If the defendant wants to assert that the court does not have jurisdiction over the defendant, it must file a Motion to Dismiss (also known as a special appearance) before it files any other documents with the court. The **motion to dismiss** describes the specific grounds for its argument and asks the judge to dismiss the case before any other proceedings are held. A defendant can file a motion to dismiss if the defendant believes that the court does not have jurisdiction over the case, the court does not have jurisdiction over the defendant, the lawsuit fails to state a case that the plaintiff can win even if the plaintiff proves all of the Complaint's allegations, etc. For example, Stan sues his business law teacher for being less-than-average looking. Being less-than-average looking is not against the law and a judge would dismiss this type of complaint.

Answer

The **answer** is the defendant's formal response to the complaint. In a complaint, the defendant states which parts of the plaintiff's claim the defendant disputes. The failure to timely file an answer can lead to a **default judgment**, meaning that the plaintiff obtains a judgment against the defendant because of the defendant's failure to defend the case.

Counterclaim

In many cases when a defendant is sued, the defendant responds with a lawsuit against the plaintiff, which is called a **counterclaim**. The counterclaim is similar to the complaint as it sets for certain allegations that allege wrongdoing. In response to a counterclaim, the plaintiff is required to file a **reply**, just like the defendant is required to file an answer to the complaint.

Judgment On The Pleadings

A **motion for the judgment on the pleadings** is a motion requesting the judge rule based upon the pleadings only. A motion for a judgment on the pleadings would be appropriate when there are no factual discrepancies from the pleadings made by the parties and the judge can provide a ruling by applying the appropriate law. For example, Sue files a lawsuit against Erik. Sue alleges Erik caused an accident in a parking lot by backing into her car, causing $50,000 in damage. Erik does not dispute the act or any facts in Sue's complaint. However, he believes he was not legally at fault under the applicable state law. A judge may render a ruling based upon the pleadings and the appropriate state law.

Discovery

Discovery is the process by which the parties find out what evidence is available to be presented at trial. Discovery involves primarily obtaining documents and other materials from the opposing party. This helps each side to evaluate what the result of the trial will be, thereby reducing surprises and uncertainty.

When parties have a similar estimate of the outcome of a trial, the case will often settle. It is often estimated that over 90% of all civil matters are settled before trial and a large portion of those settle during the discovery phase. Before parties settle, they often take into consideration their ability to win the case at trial, the cost of litigation, the length of the litigation process (including the possibility of an appeal), and the consequences of losing at trial. The settlement process is generally not public information and businesses often include contractual provisions in a settlement that prevent the other party from disclosing related information. The contract between the parties that spells out the terms of the settlement is called a **settlement agreement** or **release** and that portion of the settlement agreement that keeps the terms secret is a **confidentiality clause**.

Judges expect parties to fully disclose all relevant information derived from discovery without unduly hindering the other side. Discovery also helps the parties to narrow down the information relevant to the trial, and, thus, makes the trial more efficient.

Generally, each side must turn over the information the other party requests. For example, the plaintiff might ask for certain documents in the defendant's possession. The failure to provide documents requested by an opposing party can result in sanctions imposed by a judge. These sanctions include monetary fines and/or a restriction on presenting certain evidence at trial.

- Default judgment
- Counterclaim
- Reply
- Motion for the judgment on the pleadings
- Discovery
- Settlement agreement or release
- Confidentiality clause

There are several classes of information that are exempt from discovery. For example, **privileged communication** involves communication between attorneys and their clients. The concept of privileged communication shields client and attorney discussions and other interactions from discovery, which allows clients to privately seek legal counsel without fear that those private communications will be exposed. Communication between a party and that person's spouse, counselor, physician, and religious minister are often, but not always, privileged.

Another aspect of privileged communication is **attorney work product**, which is the attorney's own notes, strategies, and intra-office communication. As a general rule, the work of a CPA or an accountant is not privileged communication.

Interrogatories

Discovery often begins with written requests for information. Among the most common requests are questions, called **interrogatories**, which are written questions that the other side must answer. They include inquiries about whom the other side will call as a witness and the other side's version of the events in controversy. Interrogatory answers often serve as the basic building block for continued discovery.

Request For Production

A **request for production** is a demand for documents that are relevant to the issues being litigated. For example, in a contract dispute, one party might ask the other for all documents related to the formation of the contract, communication between the parties regarding the contract, and letters about the contract.

Depositions

Depositions are an opportunity for each side to interview the other party, or other potential witnesses such as an employee, under oath prior to trial. Depositions serve three main purposes:

1. Finding out what the witness's testimony will be at trial.
2. Identifying other information that may be subject to the discovery process.
3. Evaluating what the settlement value of the case might be.

Depositions are often taken at an attorney's office in front of a court reporter, who develops a **transcript**, which is a written record of everything that is said. The transcript can be used at trial to discredit or impeach the witness if the witness's trial testimony is different.

Request For Admissions

During the discovery process, either side can submit to the other **requests for admissions**, which ask the other side to admit that certain things are true. Admitting a request for admission means that the matter is conclusively established. If the request is denied, but the asking party proves it is true, the denying party can be forced to pay for the costs of proving the truth of the matter.

Suppose that Ricky sued Quality Used Cars, claiming that Quality sold Ricky a lemon and that the salesperson promised to provide a one-year warranty with the car. Ricky might send Request for Admissions like the following:

1. Quality's salesperson promised Ricky that the car would be warrantied for one year.
2. The said statement constituted a valid warrant on the car.
3. The said statement was used to induce Ricky to buy the car.
4. Ricky made a warranty claim four months after buying the car.
5. Quality refused to honor the said claim.

If Quality denies all of the requests, but Ricky proves that one or more of them are true, the judge may force Quality to pay Ricky some of Ricky's expenses in proving that those statements were true. Thus, Quality may admit facts that it knows are true to prevent having to pay Ricky additional court costs.

Thus, requests for admissions can speed up the discovery process by narrowing down the facts and issues in controversy.

Disclosure of Experts

While most witnesses testify merely as to what they actually saw or heard, **expert witnesses** provide opinions about the incident. During discovery, each side is required to disclose not only what experts they may call as witnesses, but also certain information about their experts' credentials and expected testimony.

To qualify as an expert, a person must have specialized knowledge based on training, education, and/or experience. In a legal dispute over whether a board of directors exercised appropriate oversight of a company's officers, one side might call a business professor who has published articles on the subject or an attorney who specializes in that area of the law to opine on the board members' actions, even though they did not actually witness the events as they were happening. Instead, the experts would review the relevant documents, transcripts of depositions, etc., and then formulate their opinions about the appropriateness of what the board did. The expert would then testify in court, but the **factfinder**, who is the judge in a bench trial or the jury in a jury trial, would make the final determination of whether the experts' opinion had merit.

Inspection of Property or Person

Courts try to make sure that both parties have access to the evidence that might be relevant and/or presented at trial. If the case involves tangible property of any kind that is controlled by one side, the other side may ask the court to order an opportunity to inspect it. For example, if a homeowner sues the contractor who built the house over an alleged defect, the judge may order the homeowner to allow the contractor, the contractor's attorney, and/or

- Expert witnesses
- Factfinder

the contractor's expert witness to inspect the house and take pictures. If a person's physical condition is at issue, such as a plaintiff in a personal injury action, the defendant may ask the court to order the plaintiff to be examined by a physician hired by the defendant.

Subpoenas

Some information relevant to the controversy may be controlled by third parties not directly involved in the litigation. In order to obtain the relevant information, the court may issue an order to a third party, called a **subpoena**, requiring them to allow inspection of their property, turn over copies of documents, sit for a deposition, or appear for trial as a witness.

Discovery Disputes

Despite professional standards requiring attorneys to engage in discovery in good faith, disputes often arise as to the extent to which party must disclose data in discovery. If the parties reached an impasse, the party requesting disclosure of information may file a **motion to compel discovery**, which is a pleading asking the court to force the other side to produce the information. The party seeking to limit disclosure may ask the judge to issue a **protective order**, which is a direction from the court to limit discovery or to require the parties to treat certain produced information as confidential. In a patent dispute, for example, one party may ask the court to require the other party keep discoverable information strictly secret to prevent the harm that may result if the information were made public.

Motion For Summary Judgment

A **motion for summary judgment** is often filed around the end of the discovery process to ask the judge to decide some or all matters in controversy before the trial. Summary judgment is granted only when there is so much evidence for one side that a reasonable judge or jury could only decide the issue in one party's favor. Stated another way, summary judgment will not be granted if there is credible evidence favoring each party's position. Because granting summary judgment means a party may lose without trial, courts are generally careful to make sure that it is warranted before granting it. Sometimes a party will ask the judge to decide only one or a few of the matters in a case to narrow the issues left for trial. If, for example, an actor sued a television network, the producer, and the studio in a royalty dispute, but there is no evidence that the studio did anything wrong, then the studio can file for summary judgment asking that it be dismissed from the case.

Other Motions

Sometimes a defendant will file a **confession of judgment**, in which the defendant offers to pay a certain amount of money to settle the case. If the plaintiff rejects the offer and the final judgment is for that amount or less, the plaintiff may be required to pay for the defendant's court costs and/or attorney fees. The existence of the offer and its rejection is not disclosed to the jury.

In jury trials, the parties often file **motions in limine**, which is a Latin term meaning "at the start." The motion in limine is filed just before the trial to prevent juries from hearing about certain irrelevant information learned during discovery. To support a motion in limine, a party has to demonstrate that the disclosure it wants suppressed will distract the jury from focusing on the merits of the case. A common example is when defendants ask the court to keep the existence of their insurance policy that might be used to pay if the plaintiff wins from the jury. The rationale is that knowing that a defendant has insurance money available might tempt the jury to consider the defendant's ability to pay instead of staying focused on the merits of the plaintiff's case and the defenses raised by the defendant.

- Motion in limine
- Bench trial
- Jury trial
- Pretrial conference
- Voir dire

Pretrial Procedure

Bench Trial

A trial without a jury is called a **bench trial** (since it is tried to the judge sitting at the bench). Bench trials are often faster and are sometimes favored by both parties in cases of significant complexity. Generally, small claims cases as well as domestic relations and probate have bench trials only.

Jury Trial

In civil cases, one of the parties must ask for a **jury trial** within a certain amount of time of filing the complaint or answer. The number of jurors varies by jurisdiction ranging from six to twelve. Each jurisdiction has its own rules on whether a jury trial is available depending on the type of case. Family law and probate matters are generally decided only by a judge, while juries are the factfinder in tort and contract disputes if at least one of the parties requests a jury.

Pretrial Conference

A few weeks before trial, especially in jury trials, the judge may summon the parties to the courthouse for a **pretrial conference** to discuss the upcoming trial. At this conference, each party is required to disclose certain documents, such as instructions they would like the jury to receive, a description of the evidence each side plans to submit, and a brief containing legal arguments about the case. The judge may also use this conference as one last attempt to help the parties reach a settlement without a trial.

Voir Dire

In jury trials, immediately before trial, a group of potential jurors go through **voir dire**, which is a Latin phrase meaning "to speak truthfully." During voir dire, the parties have an opportunity to question potential jurors. If a potential juror indicates that he or she is biased against one of the parties or will not be able to conform to the judge's instructions, an attorney may issue a **challenge for cause**, which is a request that the judge remove the juror for a specific reason. If the judge agrees, that potential juror is excused and is replaced by another. This process continues until a group of qualified jurors remains.

Next, each side is allowed to exercise a certain number of **peremptory challenges**, in which potential jurors are excused without the attorneys having to disclose a certain reason. For example, if the state uses eight-person juries for civil matters, voir dire may continue until sixteen unbiased jurors are identified. Then, each attorney exercises four peremptory challenges, leaving eight jurors. Peremptory challenges may be exercised for almost any reason, although courts have started to prohibit challenges based on race and gender.

Edmonson v. Leesville Concrete Co.
500 US 614 (1991)

Thaddeus Edmonson, an African American construction worker, was injured at a Louisiana job site. He sued Leesville Concrete Co. in federal court, claiming that the company caused his injury. During jury selection, Leesville's attorney used two out of its three peremptory challenges to remove African Americans from the jury pool, leaving the twelve-member jury with only one black person. The Judge denied Edmonson's objection to the removal of two African Americans. The trial proceeded and the jury determined that Edmonson was partially responsible for his injury and awarded him less than he was seeking. The Court of Appeals affirmed the trial court by ruling that, while the Supreme Court had held that excluding jurors on account of their race was prohibited in criminal cases, there was no such rule in civil cases.

Figure 2.6 Jury box in a Nebraska County Courthouse

The Supreme Court reversed the lower courts, noting that the constitutional right to a fair jury trial is tainted when jurors are excluded on account of race. Justice Kennedy wrote, "To permit racial exclusion in this official forum compounds the racial insult inherent in judging a citizen by the color of his or her skin." The case was returned to the trial court for a new trial.

Questions

1. What were the facts of this case?
2. What is voir dire?
3. What did the court find to be unacceptable behavior?
4. If race of the defendant makes a juror biased, should this be a reason for dismissal of a juror? Why or why not?

Trial

Opening Arguments

Attorneys use opening arguments to highlight what the factfinder should be looking for during the trial and suggest what conclusions should be drawn from the information presented. The purpose of the opening arguments is to allow each side time to outline what the evidence will be and what it will mean. The factfinder will hear a summary of how the different pieces of evidence fit together before trial begins.

Presentation of Evidence

After opening arguments, each side has an opportunity to present **Evidence**, including witness testimony and certain other information to the jury. The plaintiff presents their evidence first. After the plaintiff has called their witnesses and proffered their evidence to the court, the defense presents their evidence. The plaintiff then has one last chance to rebut the defendant's evidence.

Witness Testimony

Witness testimony involves calling a witness to the witness stand and asking him or her questions. There are three phases to witness testimony:

1. **Direct examination**, where the side that called the witness asks questions.
2. **Cross examination**, in which the other side asks questions, but only on subjects related to the direct examination.
3. **Redirect**, which allows the party that originally called the witness to cover items covered during cross examination.

The latter two phases can be repeated, but the questions must be related to the previously asked questions and answers.

Generally the questions are related either to the subject matter of the case or to the **credibility** of the witness. While credibility often focuses on bias, or past acts of the witness such as lying or cheating, it can also relate to the witness's competence. For example, if a physician is sued for malpractice, one of the other doctors testifying can be challenged as not being credible if he or she is not board certified in the area of medicine at issue.

- Evidence
- Witness testimony
- Direct examination
- Cross examination
- Redirect
- Credibility

Exhibits

Other evidence can include much of the information that was obtained in discovery. When this information is presented in court, the pieces of information are called **exhibits**. For example, in a breach-of-contract case between two companies, exhibits might include the written contract, interrogatory answers, emails exchanged between the parties, photographs, a recording of a voice mail left on an answering system, or transcripts of depositions.

Objections To Evidence

A judge may rule that the factfinder should not see or hear certain information (or should ignore certain evidence already presented) because it is unreliable or irrelevant. For example, an ambulance driver who came to a car accident scene may be able to testify as to where the vehicles were positioned upon arrival or what people said after the collision. However, the driver cannot testify as to who was at fault since the emergency worker did not actually witness the accident.

Judges will sometimes exclude witness credibility evidence if it is too remote or likely to be more prejudicial than helpful. For example, a side that is trying to impeach the credibility of a witness in a jury trial may not be allowed to ask about a conviction for minor drug use fifteen years earlier in light of the fact that it was so long ago and that it might distract the jury from a rational examination of the testimony. Many of these issues are addressed by motions in limine. In the interest of time, judges may also limit parties from presenting evidence that essentially repeats information already presented. Similarly, there are significant restrictions on hearsay evidence.

Hearsay evidence is when a witness states what the witness heard someone else say. The general rule is that hearsay evidence is not allowed because it is not considered reliable; however, there are numerous exceptions. For example, a witness may testify to what one of the parties said; then, of course, that party will have the opportunity to rebut that assertion.

Motion For Directed Verdict

At the end of the plaintiff's case, the defense may make a **motion for directed verdict**, which is a request to dismiss the plaintiff's case because the plaintiff failed to assemble enough evidence to carry the plaintiff's burden of proof. These motions are rarely granted, but are often made for strategic reasons for appeal purposes.

Closing Arguments

After all of the evidence is presented, each side is allowed time to orally summarize the evidence presented and assist the factfinder in how to analyze the evidence through **closing arguments**. The plaintiff goes first, followed by the defendant. After the defendant's closing argument, the plaintiff may briefly offer some rebuttal points in response to the defendant's argument.

Jury Instructions

In a jury trial, the jury decides which side's version of the facts is most credible. However, even in jury trials, the judge is the one who not only makes rulings on evidence, but also instructs the jury on what the law is in the form of **jury instructions**. Each side presents the judge with a list of instructions it would like the jury to hear. Then, right after the evidence has been presented, the judge decides which instructions to give. Generally, if the requested instruction is a correct statement of the law and it is invoked by the evidence, it will be given. For example, in a dispute about whether a will was properly signed, the judge will tell the jury what the requirements are in terms of the number of witnesses or whether the witnesses can be related to the person making the will. An improper jury instruction can be the basis for an appeal.

- Jury instructions
- Verdict
- Judgment

Post-Trial Actions

Deliberation, Verdict, and Judgment

In a jury trial, the jury starts its deliberations after the judge provides the jury instructions. In the jury room, jurors select a foreperson and then review and discuss the evidence to reach their conclusion or **verdict**, which is their rendering of liability, guilt, or the absence of it. Jurisdictions have different rules on to what extent verdicts in civil trials have to be unanimous. To have a unanimous verdict means all jurors are in agreement. In some states a verdict can be reached if the jurors have deliberated for a certain amount of time and all but one of the jurors are in agreement. Therefore, a unanimous verdict will not always be required.

The verdict is then reported to the judge, who incorporates the verdict into a **judgment**, which is a final ruling on the result of the trial. The judgment may differ slightly from the verdict. For example, if the plaintiff prevails on a claim where the plaintiff is entitled to attorney fees, the judge is often the one who rules on to what extent the lawyer fee claim is included in the judgment.

Judgment Notwithstanding the Verdict

In a jury trial, a judge may overrule one or more aspects of the jury's verdict if the judge finds that the verdict is clearly unreasonable or, in other words, that no rational jury could have reached the same conclusion. In such a case, the judge's decision is called a Judgment Notwithstanding the Verdict. Such instances are rare and should not occur simply because the judge would have made a different decision. Rather, it is reserved for times when the jury's decision was not supported by the evidence and/or based on emotion rather than reason.

Attorney Fees

Generally, the winner's attorney fees are not recoverable except in three specific situations:

1. Authorized by Statute. In some types of cases, the legislature has specifically provided for the prevailing party to recover attorney fees. These provisions are sometimes found in laws prohibiting race and gender discrimination or protecting employees when their employers fail to pay their wages.
2. Created by Contract. Some contracts provide for the payment of attorney fees to the non-breaching party. Some states allow contracts to favor one party over the other (e.g., the landlord may recover legal fees but the tenant cannot), while others require that the provisions apply equally to both parties.
3. Court-Ordered Sanctions. Judges have the power to mandate the payment of attorney fees when one side disregards an order or the law. This can happen, for instance, when a party refuses to turn over documents required in the discovery process.

Post-Trial Motions

Either side may ask the judge to adjust the verdict or convene a new trial by arguing that the jury did not follow the right procedure or that the verdict was not supported by the evidence; these are examples of **post-trial motions**.

Appeal

An appeal is not a new trial. Instead, it is merely an examination of whether the trial court judge made correct rulings in a case. For example, a party can appeal if it asserted that the judge gave a jury instruction that was not a correct statement of the law. However, a party cannot appeal merely because the jury believed the credibility of one witness over the other. The party who appeals is called the **appellant**; the other party is the **appellee**.

Notice of Appeal

Either side may file a **notice of appeal**, which is a formal notice requesting an appeals court to review the case. The vast majority of appeals are heard after judgment. However, the parties may seek an **interlocutory appeal**, which is an appeal prior to trial. Interlocutory appeals are discretionary and are often declined until a judgment has been rendered.

Briefs

After the notice of appeal, each party files a **brief**, which is a lengthy written argument with citations to the law and evidence. The appellant files first, explaining why the trial court made an error. The appellee then responds to the appellant's arguments. The appeals court may rule based on the briefs only or it can order oral arguments, where each side has a turn to present their case in person. Generally, at least three appellate judges hear each case, with a simple majority deciding it. However, an appeal from a municipal court such as a traffic court is often decided by only one judge.

Judgment Enforcement

When a plaintiff prevails in an action, the immediate result is that it receives no more than a written judgment stating that the other side owes it money or some other performance. The prevailing party must then actually collect or enforce the judgment. In some cases the defendant, or the defendant's insurance company, pays right away with the condition that the plaintiff files a **Satisfaction**, which is the formal document indicating that the judgment has been paid.

In other cases, the judgment can be satisfied only when the plaintiff finds the defendant's assets and uses the court's power to take them. For example, if a defendant refuses to pay, but the plaintiff knows the bank where the defendant has an account, the plaintiff can ask the court to order the sheriff to levy the defendant's funds held at the bank. **Levy** means to seize assets or funds. A levy can also be on other assets, including what other parties owe the defendant.

Alternative Dispute Resolution

Courts as well as litigants have encouraged the use of **Alternative Dispute Resolution**, which includes ways to resolve legal disputes without a trial. Alternative dispute resolution has gained popularity because it is often less expensive and time consuming than fully litigating a case. It also reduces the burden on the court system. There are three main types of alternative dispute resolution, namely negotiation, mediation, and arbitration.

Negotiation

Negotiation occurs when the parties, with or without an attorney representing them, directly negotiate with each other. Negotiations can take place through written or oral communication. Negotiation is the least expensive form of dispute resolution, as it does not require hiring a third party. It can be attempted during any phase of the litigation process. It is most common for negotiations to take place before suit is filed or after a significant amount of discovery has been completed. However, negotiations have even been successfully attempted during breaks in the midst of trial.

Mediation

Mediation is when the parties rely on a neutral third party called a **mediator** to help them negotiate. The mediator is often an attorney or sometimes a retired judge who does not represent either side. Mediators often have specific training on helping parties to resolve differences. The parties usually split the charge for the mediator's time.

The parties in mediation typically send in advance a written summary of their case to the mediator. At the actual mediation, the parties, their attorneys, and the mediator may meet together briefly to outline their positions before the parties move to separate rooms within the same building. The mediator then shuttles from room to room gradually convincing them to compromise their position. Mediation has gained popularity because of its effectiveness in resolving complex cases as well as disputes where negotiations have failed. While mediation is often voluntary, it can be court ordered. Court-ordered mediation has become increasingly popular in family law cases. Sometimes a judge other than the one who will preside at the trial will serve as a mediator at or around the time of the pretrial conference. Although mediation may involve an attorney representing each side, certain mediation proceedings might prohibit the use of attorneys. For example, in the mediation of divorce cases, attorneys are often not allowed.

Arbitration

Arbitration also uses a third party but differs from negotiation and mediation in that it is more certain to produce a final, legally binding resolution. In a sense, it is like a trial provided by an entity other than the government. Arbitration is used when:

1. The contract between the parties requires disputes between them to be settled by arbitration;
2. The parties agree to arbitrate their case after the dispute has arisen; and/or
3. The law requires the parties to submit their case to arbitration.

As a general rule, if parties have agreed to use the arbitration process to settle a dispute, then a plaintiff is prevented from filing a lawsuit in a court regarding the dispute. For example, Heidi and Eric have a contract for the sale of goods. The contract states that if a dispute arises under the contract then the parties must submit their dispute to arbitration. Heidi believes Eric has breached their contract by providing non-conforming goods. If Heidi does not want to submit her claim to an arbitrator, she cannot try to file a lawsuit in a court instead.

Many employment contracts require employment related disputes be submitted to arbitration. The arbitration process can provide benefits to both employee and employer such as cost savings and time savings. However, in some cases a court might agree to hear an employment related legal dispute even though the employment contract requires arbitration. Courts may intervene in an employment dispute if the contract requiring arbitration is invalid or was improperly formed. For example, a court might intervene if an employee had no ability to seek legal counsel or bargain over the clauses of the contract. Courts might also intervene if the court believes the arbitration is unfair in its process and remedies. For example, if the arbitration clause requires the employee to pay for the entire cost of the arbitration proceeding, the employee is limited in regards to remedies or ability to appeal the arbitrator's decision, the employer is not subject to the same set of rules regarding the arbitration process.

The **award** is the final decision of the arbitrator and is much like a judgment in a trial. The winner can ask a court with jurisdiction to confirm the award as a judgment and then use the power of the court to enforce it. A judge is more likely to reverse an arbitrator's decision if 1) the arbitration proceeding was unfairly one sided, 2) the arbitrator ruled on issues outside the scope of the arbitration agreement, and/or 3) public policy requires the award be overturned.

Taylor v. University of Phoenix
487 F.App'x 942 (2012)

This case was heard in the United States Court of Appeals—Fifth Circuit. Sabrina K. Taylor (Taylor) worked for the University of Phoenix (University) and sustained a workers' compensation injury in 2005 when a co-worked pulled a chair out from under her during game at a company Christmas party. After being on leave for two years, she attempted to return to work in January of 2008, but the University refused to allow her on its premises until her physician released her to work a full eight-hour day. Taylor resigned two months later and filed a discrimination complaint asserting that the University failed to accommodate her disability and retaliated against her for making the discrimination claim. Taylor's claim was eventually transferred to federal court.

The parties agreed to stay the lawsuit while submitting the matter to private arbitration. The arbitrator ruled in favor of the University on all claims. Taylor the returned to federal court and filed motions to revive her claim and vacate the arbitration award. The court denied her requests, granted the University's motion to confirm the arbitration award, and entered a final judgment against Taylor. Taylor appealed and asked the District Court to stay the judgment during the appeal. In response, the Judge imposed $1,000 in sanctions on Taylor to reimburse the University for costs and attorney's fees associated with responding to Taylor's stay request.

The Court of Appeals, quoting other cases, stated that a trial court's review of an arbitration award should be "exceedingly deferential" and that all doubts should be resolved in favor of affirming the award. Under federal law, arbitration awards may only be vacated if:

1.   the award was procured by corruption or fraud;
2.   the arbitrator was clearly impartial or corrupt;
3.   the arbitrator was guilty of misconduct resulting in prejudice; or
4.   the arbitrator exceeded or abused the arbitrator's powers.

Finding none of those factors present, the appeals court affirmed the trial court on all issues.

If the parties have agreed to arbitration to settle their disputes, the losing party is limited in what it can do to challenge the decision. While it is not uncommon for the arbitration loser to sue the winner in an attempt to vacate the award, courts are increasingly resistant to hear lawsuits seeking to overturn arbitration awards. Courts are hesitant to intervene because the arbitration process is often bargained for contractual duty and the process benefits courts by lightening their case load.

Questions

1. What are the facts of this case?
2. Why was the defendant awarded damages by the court?
3. When does a court feel it appropriate to overturn an arbitrator's award?

Discussion Questions

1. What is the power of judicial review and how did the case of *Marbury v. Madison* help to establish it?
2. Would you call the power of a court to decide a legal matter?
3. What is personal jurisdiction and in what ways might a court obtain personal jurisdiction over a defendant?
4. What is a Long-Arm Statute and what are minimum contacts?
5. What is the role of in rem jurisdiction, and how is the plaintiff's right to recovery limited if in rem jurisdiction was exercised by the court?
6. What two types of cases will a federal court have jurisdiction over?
7. What is the difference between exclusive jurisdiction and concurrent jurisdiction?
8. What is the Erie Doctrine and how it is applied in federal courts?
9. What is venue and how is it determined in state court and federal court?
10. How do state judges obtain their position?
11. What is the difference between substantive law and procedural law?
12. What does it mean to have *standing* to bring a lawsuit?
13. What are pleadings?
14. What is the name of the first pleading that is filed in a lawsuit?
15. What is a motion to dismiss and when would it be granted by a judge?
16. What is a counterclaim and what does a party file to respond to a counterclaim?
17. What is discovery and how is it performed?
18. What does a litigant use to obtain information from a party who is not involved in the lawsuit?
19. What are expert witnesses and how are they different from other witnesses?
20. What is the purpose of a Motion for Summary Judgment and during what aspect of the litigation is it generally used?
21. What is the difference between a bench trial and a jury trial?
22. What is voir dire and what is its purpose?
23. What is the difference between a challenge for cause and a peremptory challenge?
24. What are the three situations in which a litigant can collect his or her attorney fees?
25. What is the document that initiates an appeal and what is the document that supports it with legal arguments?
26. How is a judgment enforced?
27. How is negotiation different from mediation and arbitration?

Critical-Thinking Questions

28. Does a court grant in personam jurisdiction in a case based upon the residence of the plaintiff or the defendant and what purpose does this serve?

29. As a general rule, peremptory strikes can be used for any reason to strike a juror unless it is because of the race of the juror; do you believe this rule provides more or less protection to a defendant? Assuming it does not provide less protection, why would a court prohibit race as a reason for striking jurors?

30. Why are a defendant's prior bad acts generally not allowed as part of testimony or evidence in a case if such bad acts might suggest the defendant is guilty?

31. What is the difference between a verdict and a judgment notwithstanding the verdict? Why would a court be reluctant to issue either of these motions?

32. In what instances can a party appeal the award of an arbitrator and why is it important for courts to abstain from interfering with the arbitration process?

Essay Questions

1. Alice was recently involved in the state of Oklahoma in an auto accident with Margie. Alice is a resident of Minnesota and Margie is a resident of Iowa. Margie has never been to Minnesota. Alice would like to sue Margie for damages arising out of the auto accident in the amount of $80,000. What states might have personal jurisdiction in this lawsuit? Assuming Margie never visits the state of Minnesota, is there any way a Minnesota court might gain jurisdiction of Margie?

2. Rex was recently involved in a fistfight while on a spring break vacation in Florida. Rex is a resident of Nebraska. The person Rex would like to sue for battery is named Piper. Piper is a resident of Alabama. Rex would like to sue Piper for $100,000. What courts could claim personal jurisdiction in this matter?

3. Olga, a resident of Maine, was recently injured by a defective product produced by Home Appliance Corporation, which is incorporated in Delaware but has its company headquarters in Virginia. Olga purchased the defective product in Maine. Olga is suing Home Appliance for $60,000. Which courts would have personal jurisdiction in this case? Would a federal court have jurisdiction? Why or why not?

4. Stuart, a resident of California, believes Nole Smith Corporation has been using Stuart's patented invention without his permission. Stuart would like to sue Nole Smith for patent infringement. Nole Smith's principal business location is in Nebraska where it has its headquarters and its factory. Which court would have jurisdiction over this matter? Would California or Nebraska state courts be able to grant jurisdiction in this case? Why or why not?

5. Austin was recently involved in a dispute with his employer. Austin refused to work on Sunday for religious reasons. His employer fired him without making accommodations. His employer has not disputed any of these facts. If needed, the company Human Resources manager is willing to testify that she was ordered to fire Austin immediately

after he failed to show up for work. What motions might Austin make to have a judge render a ruling before a trial begins?

6. Smiley Manufacturing recently dismissed its CEO after four years of dismal results. The CEO has filed complaint against Smiley. Smiley believes that the CEO has no legal grounds to bring a lawsuit. Smiley also believes when the CEO left office the CEO took office furniture that belonged to the corporation. What pleadings and/or motions should Smiley's lawyers make regarding this scenario?

7. Natalie believes her cell phone company has been charging her excessive fees under her cell phone contract. She wishes to sue the cell phone company. However, her contract states she must submit to arbitration any legal claims she has arising out of the contract. The arbitrator is a former employee of the cell phone company. The arbitrator sides with the cell phone company and awards damages to the cell phone company in the amount of $60,000. Can Natalie appeal the decision of the arbitrator?

8. Jeff is considering starting a lawn care business. He is drafting his own contracts using an online legal service. The legal service's software program wants to know if Jeff wants to include provisions regarding negotiation, mediation, and arbitration. What would a lawyer tell Jeff about these forms of alternative dispute resolution and if he chose one, which one should he choose to incorporate and why?

CHAPTER THREE

CONSTITUTIONAL LAW

By Michael Bootsma

Introduction

Mandi and Matt are angry after finding out the United States government has been scanning the phone records of its own citizens in an attempt to identify what it calls "terrorist activity." Mandi organizes a protest near the US Capitol in Washington, DC. Mandi gathers five thousand like-minded individuals and starts a protest. She is arrested and thrown in jail.

After Mandi is arrested, Matt decides to stage his own protest. He starts the website <down-with-the facists.com>. He starts posting articles about government interference with individual rights. Shortly after creating his website, he is contacted by Davis Raindon who is an employee of the US government. Davis has secret government information. Matt posts the secret information on his website. The next day, Matt is arrested and his website is shut down.

Can Matt and Mandi be arrested for exercising their right to free speech? Can Congress pass a law prohibiting websites from posting government information? Does the government need a warrant to search the office where Matt operated his business? The answers to these questions are found in the US Constitution, its Amendments, and the case law interpreting it.

Chapter Objectives

1. Understand the historical context of the US Constitution
2. Identify key constitutional provisions protecting individual rights
3. Identify the differences between the constitutional rights provided individuals and businesses
4. Understand the different levels of scrutiny utilized by the Supreme Court
5. Identify key areas of regulation assigned to the federal government and states' governments under the Constitution

History of the US Constitution

Figure 3.1 Postage Stamp Depicting Signing of the US Constitution

Until the United States Constitution was ratified on September 17, 1787, 13 independent states, referred to as the United States of America, were governed by the *Articles of Confederation*. The drafting of the United States Constitution began with a Constitutional Convention on May 25, 1787. General George Washington was elected the President of the Constitutional Convention. The drafting of the Constitution led to much debate. James Madison believed the United States needed a central government to help regulate commerce and provide order. Patrick Henry, who famously said "give me liberty or give me death," refused to participate in the Constitutional Convention, as he believed it would lead to a strong, central government that would dampen individual rights as well as states' rights. He also feared the President of the United States would have power equal to that of a monarch or king.

The Constitution was to be ratified through state constitutional conventions. The conventions led to great debates as well as many political essays being published in newspapers. Pro-federal government essays authored by Alexander Hamilton were later referred to as the "Federalist Papers." Proponents of the new federal government became known as *Federalists*, while its opponents were known as *anti-Federalists*. In the end, the votes held for ratification in each state were extremely close, but the Constitution was ratified partly because of the addition of a *Bill of Rights*. Some of the Federalists believed the Bill of Rights was unnecessary, as the Constitution has left to the people any powers not expressly granted to the federal government. However, after much negotiation and compromise, the US Constitution was ratified. The first 10 Amendments of the US Constitution, known of the Bill of Rights, were proposed by Congress on September 25, 1789 and eventually ratified by the last state in 1791.

Articles of the US Constitution

- Legislative Branch
- Executive Branch
- Judicial Branch

The US Constitution, which can be found in the appendix to your book, contains 7 articles. The following is a brief summary of the articles comprising the US Constitution.

Article 1: establishes the office of the United States Congress. Article 1 establishes a House of Representatives and a Senate that are to draft and pass legislation. The US Congress is referred to as the **Legislative Branch** because it creates legislation. Section 8 of Article 1 enumerates, or lists, several powers expressly granted Congress, such as the power to collect taxes and the power to regulate commerce.

Article 2: establishes the office of the president and vice president. The president is the executive and enforcer of the laws passed by Congress. The president is also the Commander of the Armed Forces. The vice president is to be the president of the Senate and is allowed to cast a tie-breaking vote if necessary. In the US, the offices of president and vice president are referred to as the **Executive Branch**.

Article 3: establishes a Supreme Court and such inferior courts as Congress may deem necessary. This system of a Supreme Federal Court and inferior, or lower, federal courts is referred to as the **Judicial Branch**.

Article 4: establishes the principle that each state must give Full Faith and Credit to the legal proceedings of other states.

Article 5: establishes the process of proposing Amendments to the US Constitution. The Amendments may be proposed by a 2/3 vote of each the House of Representatives and Senate or by 2/3 of the states. Ratification is required by 3/4 of the states.

Article 6: establishes the US Constitution as the Supreme Law of the Land, meaning it trumps state law or federal law created by the legislative branch.

Article 7: established the process for ratification of the US Constitution and contains the signatures of delegates from 12 states.

Checks and Balances

The US Constitution contains various checks and balances. For example, the president has the power to veto, which means reject, pieces of legislation passed by Congress. The United States Senate must approve of Supreme Court Justice appointments that are made by the president of the United States. In addition, the Supreme Court has the authority to review laws created by Congress to determine whether the laws are constitutional.

Article 2 Section 2 of the US Constitution states: "The President shall have Power to fill up all Vacancies that may happen during the Recess of the Senate, by granting Commissions which shall expire at the End of their next Session."

National Labor Relations Board v. Noel Canning
134 S. Ct. 2550 (2014)

The National Labor Relations Board vs. Noel Canning is a case that was based upon the Article 2 Section 2 of the US Constitution. On January 4, 2012, President Barack Obama appointed three members to the National Labor Relations Board. This board oversees employer and union relations. The Republicans in the Senate held a brief proforma session every three days in order to prevent a recess from taking place during the holiday break. Article 1 Section 5 of the US Constitution states neither house of Congress may adjourn for more than three days without the consent of the other house. Republicans used this clause to prevent the president from making appointments without their consent. President Obama made the three appointments to the National Labor Relations Board regardless of the proforma sessions.

Two of the members appointed by President Obama during the winter recess later found Noel Canning Company guilty of an unfair labor practice. Noel Canning filed a suit claiming these members of the National Labor Relations Board had been unconstitutionally appointed. The DC Circuit Court of Appeals held in January of 2013, the National Labor Relations Board had acted without a quorum because the president can only make appointments during an *intercession* recess and not an *intrasession* recess. In June 2014, a unanimous Supreme Court held the appointments by the president were unconstitutional, as the Senate was technically in session. The Supreme Court did not hold the president was prohibited from making recess appointments if the Senate is on an extended break.

Questions

1. What is the function of the National Labor Relations Board?
2. Why didn't the president appoint members to the National Labor Relations Board while Congress was in session?
3. Why did the Supreme Court rule the president's actions were unconstitutional? What policy was created or preserved through this ruling?

Levels of Scrutiny

The Supreme Court will apply one of three levels of judicial scrutiny when reviewing a case.

Rational Basis Scrutiny

Rational basis scrutiny is the lowest level of scrutiny. It can also be referred to as minimal scrutiny. The Supreme Court will hold an act of government to be constitutional as long as there is a *rational* basis for believing a government action will further a *legitimate* government objective. This level of scrutiny is typically applied when the Court is reviewing a case involving commerce clause analysis and equal protection cases that do not involve a suspect classification such as race, gender, national original, or legitimacy. For example, assume the state of Minnesota passes a law outlawing camera phones in school bathrooms. The state legislature passes the law in hopes of protecting children from being photographed in a state of indecency. A federal court would likely find the state legislature had a legitimate interest in protecting children and a rational basis for believing their law would actually protect children.

Strict Scrutiny

Strict scrutiny is the highest level of scrutiny applied by the US Supreme Court. It requires government action, further a *compelling* government interest and that no *lesser restrictive* means is available. This level of scrutiny is typically applied when the Supreme Court is reviewing a case involving freedom of religion or freedom of expression (including speech), where a restriction was based upon content, and equal protection when race, national origin, and alienage are the bases for different treatment. For example, assume Melinda is mayor of a large city. Rex is running against her in a reelection race. Therefore, Melinda decides to outlaw any communication in the city that is critical of her as mayor. A federal court would strike down this law as not serving a compelling interest if Melinda claimed the law was put in place to make the city a happier place. In addition, the court would hold there are better ways to create a happy city without limiting a person's right of free speech.

Intermediate Scrutiny

Intermediate scrutiny is less restrictive than strict scrutiny but more restrictive than rational basis scrutiny. Intermediate scrutiny review requires government action to be in furtherance of an important government interest and the action taken is substantially related to its objective. This level of scrutiny is typically applied when the Supreme Court is reviewing a case involving freedom of expression (including speech) where a restriction was based upon something other than content, and equal protection when gender or legitimacy is a basis for different treatment under the law. For example, assume North State University requires men and women live on separate floors. The rule is put into place because the university is worried about the safety of female students. A court would have to determine whether this is an important government interest and whether there was a less intrusive way to protect female students.

Commerce Clause

One of the most important powers granted the United States Congress is found in Article I Section 8, which provides the US Congress the right to "regulate commerce with foreign nations, and among the several states, and with the Indian tribes." This clause means Congress has the right to regulate *interstate* commerce but not *intrastate* commerce. Congress can regulate the channels on which interstate commerce takes place, for example, rivers or highways. Congress can also regulate instruments used in interstate commerce such as a semi-truck. Finally, Congress can regulate commercial activities that affect interstate commerce such as hotel lodgings or restaurants.

Figure 3.2 The US saw major movements for civil rights in the 1960's

Katzenbach v. McClung

379 US 294 (1964)

In *Katzenbach v. McClung*, the Supreme Court had to determine whether a motel and a restaurant could refuse service to people of color. Congress passed the Civil Rights Act of 1964 of which Section 201 of Title II prohibited a business from refusing services to customers based upon race, color, religion, or national origin. The owners of the restaurant Ollie's Barbecue and the hotel Heart of Atlanta Motel argued the Civil Rights Act of 1964 did not apply to them because they were involved in intrastate business. The Court found interstate commerce was involved because the restaurant alone purchased at least 46% of its food from out-of-state suppliers. The Supreme Court found the Civil Rights Act of 1964 to be a constitutional use of the Commerce Clause power to regulate interstate commerce.

Questions

1. Doesn't the US Constitution prohibit discrimination? Why did the Supreme Court discuss the Commerce Clause?
2. If the restaurant had grown its own food, would the result of the case have been the same?

Dormant Commerce Clause

If Congress has the power to regulate interstate commerce but chooses not to, does this mean the states can regulate an area of commerce? For example, could the state of Wyoming pass a law prohibiting businesses from using drone devices to deliver fast food across state lines if Congress has passed no legislation regulating drones? The answer is "no":

the states cannot regulate areas of commerce that Congress has chosen not to regulate. The **Dormant Commerce Clause** is a constitutional principle that states only Congress can regulate interstate commerce. It prohibits states from regulating an area of interstate commerce even if Congress has not.

• Dormant
  Commerce
  Clause

Figure 3.3 View of the Hudson River

Gibbons v. Ogden
22 US 1 (1824)

In *Gibbons v. Ogden*, the state of New York gave Aaron Ogden the exclusive right to operate his steamship on the Hudson River between New York and New Jersey. Thomas Gibbons claimed he had the right to operate his steamship on the same waterway pursuant to an act of Congress. The US Supreme Court held Congress had the exclusive right to regulate interstate commerce. Therefore, the state of New York could not regulate interstate commerce by granting such a license. This case is referred to as the birth of the Dormant Commerce Clause because Chief Justice John Marshall wrote Congress had the power to regulate commerce and if it did not, the power lay "dormant."

Questions

1. Why do you suppose the Dormant Commerce Clause is also referred to as the "Negative Commerce Clause"?
2. Would the Dormant Commerce Clause prevent a state from supplementing legislation passed by Congress? For example, if Congress passed legislation prohibiting the sale of automatic rifles, could the State of Ohio pass a law prohibiting the sale of automatic hand-guns as well?

Outer Bounds of the Commerce Clause

Wickard v. Filburn

317 US 111 (1942)

In *Wickard v. Filburn*, Filburn, a farmer, was found guilty of violating the Agricultural Adjustment Act of 1938. The act was designed to help regulate the price of wheat. Filburn had produced more wheat than he was allowed to under the act. He argued the excess was for personal consumption. He argued the Agricultural Adjustment Act was not a constitutional use of the Commerce Clause, as his personal consumption of wheat that he produced was intrastate commerce. The Supreme Court stated, "But even if appellee's activity be local, and though it may not be regarded as commerce, it may still, whatever its nature, be reached by Congress if it exerts a substantial economic effect on interstate commerce, and this irrespective of whether such effect is what might at some earlier time have been defined as 'direct' or 'indirect.'" The Supreme Court stated Filburn had affected the interstate market by consuming wheat rather than purchasing it. Therefore, his personal consumption of the wheat he was raising affected interstate commerce.

Questions

1. Why do you suppose this case is called the Outer Bounds of the Commerce Clause?
2. Would the making of one's own clothes be interstate commerce under the *Wickard* case analysis?

Police Power

The 10th Amendment of the US Constitution provides the "powers not delegated to the United States by the Constitution, nor prohibited by it to the states, are reserved to the states respectively, or to the people." This Amendment is often referred to as the Police Power. The **Police Power** allows a state to regulate the health, safety, and morals of its citizens. For example, a state may pass a law requiring all school children to be immunized before allowing them to attend class. Family law and criminal law are common examples of the implementation of a state's police power.

Often a state's exercise of police power burdens interstate commerce. When this happens, the courts generally balance the objective of the state with the burden being placed on interstate commerce. If the court finds the objective to be important and the imposition of interstate commerce to be small, the court will allow the law to stand. For example, assume the state of Minnesota limits the weight of semi-truck trailers that drive on Minnesota bridges that have only two lanes. The objective is to protect the public from a collapsing bridge and the burden placed on interstate commerce should be minimal.

Privileges and Immunities Clause

• Preemption

The Privileges and Immunities Clause is found in Article IV Section 2 of the US Constitution. It states that "the citizens of each state shall be entitled to all privileges and immunities of citizens in the several states." The Privileges and Immunities Clause prohibits states from discriminating against out-of-state citizens unless its action can meet the test of strict scrutiny, which means the state must have a compelling government interest and no less-restrictive means is available to further such interest. For example, a prohibition against out-of-state booksellers by the state of Ohio would likely be found to be a violation of the Privileges and Immunities Clause. However, a requirement that a married couple live in the state of Ohio for at least one year before applying for divorce in a Ohio court would most likely be allowed. The one-year requirement of residency for divorce would be an appropriate way for Ohio to prevent couples from coming to Ohio for a divorce and creating a burden on Ohio's state court system.

Supremacy Clause

Article IV Section 2 of the US Constitution states "[t]his Constitution, and the laws of the United States which shall be made in pursuance thereof; and all treaties made, or which shall be made, under the authority of the United States, shall be the supreme law of the land; and the Judges in every state shall be bound thereby, anything in the Constitution or laws of any State to the contrary notwithstanding." This clause is known as the Supremacy Clause. The Supremacy Clause has been interpreted as stating federal law will trump state law, even a state Constitution, if the federal law is a constitutional exercise of the federal government's authority. **Preemption** is the process by which federal law overrules or preempts state law. Congress can expressly state its intention to preempt state law. However, Congress can also be found to have implied preemption of state law by leaving no room for state regulation.

Taxing and Spending Powers

One of the most important powers available to the US Congress is the power to levy and collect taxes as well as spend monies. Article I Section 8 states, "The Congress shall have Power to lay and collect Taxes, Duties, Imposts and Excises, to pay the Debts and provide for the common Defence and general Welfare of the United States; but all Duties, Imposts and Excises shall be uniform throughout the United States." Article 1 Section 9 also states, "No capitation, or other direct, tax shall be laid, unless in proportion to the census or enumeration hereinbefore directed to be taken."

The major restriction in Article 1 Section 8 regarding taxes is that direct taxes, such as a tax on real estate, must be based upon population and excise taxes, such as a gasoline tax, must be uniformly applied throughout the United States. In the *Pollock* case, 157 US 429 (1895), the US Supreme Court held an income tax on profits realized from property to be an unconstitutional direct tax because it was not based upon population. Therefore, the 16th Amendment was passed. It states "The Congress shall have power to lay and collect taxes on incomes, from whatever source derived, without apportionment among the several states, and without regard to any census or enumeration." The 16ᵗʰ Amendment allows for an unapportioned tax on income.

The power to tax and spend is a very broad power held by the US Congress. There are a few limitations. First, the purpose of an income tax must be to raise revenue and not to penalize behavior. Second, Congress must spend in order to benefit the "public welfare," which is an easy requirement to meet. However, Congress cannot create restrictions for the receipt of funds unless the conditions are related to the general welfare. For example, in the case *South Dakota v. Dole*, 483, US 203 (1987), the Supreme Court held the US Congress could require a state to have in place a "21 or over" alcohol restriction if the state wanted to receive federal funds for highways if it was related to "General Welfare" and if among other things, the requirement was not ambiguous and furthered a federal interest. In the case *Bailey v. Drexel Furniture Co.* 259 US 20 (1922), the Supreme Court struck down a federal tax on companies using child labor since the tax was primarily a penalty. However, it should be noted this case would probably have a different outcome today, some argue the Supreme Court would likely take the position the 10th Amendment does not necessarily give the states the exclusive right to regulate health, safety, and morals. Therefore, Congress could use its Commerce Clause power to regulate child labor.

Affordable Care Act

National Federation of Independent Businesses v. Sebelius
132 S.Ct 2566 (2012)

Figure 3.4 President Obama signing the Affordable Care Act

In the case *National Federation of Independent Businesses v. Sebelius*, the Supreme Court considered several aspects of the Patient Protection and Affordable Care Act, also known as Obamacare. The most politically contested aspects of the law included 1) an individual mandate, 2) an employer mandate, and 3) a Medicaid expansion program. The Supreme Court considered the individual mandate and the Medicaid expansion program in their opinion.

The individual mandate required individuals to purchase a qualified health insurance policy through an exchange or a health insurance company directly if the individual was not covered by an employer-sponsored health insurance plan, a qualified health insurance plan that the individual already had in place, or a government-sponsored plan such as Medicaid. If an individual does not have a qualified health insurance plan, the individual may face a penalty starting in 2014. The employer mandate required employers of more than 50 full-time equivalent employees to provide health insurance to employees or face a penalty. The final major component of the act was Medicaid expansion at the state level to a larger portion of the population.

The Supreme Court held Congress could require individuals to pay a "penalty" if they did not have a qualified insurance plan. The Supreme Court held the individual mandate to buy insurance was constitutional under Congress's power to levy taxes. The Supreme Court stated the "penalty" for not buying insurance was a tax and not really a penalty because it was reported on the individual's income tax return and it was collected by the IRS. Furthermore, the Supreme Court held the tax/penalty was not a direct tax and so it did not have to be uniformly apportioned. The Supreme Court held the Medicaid expansion program's application was unconstitutional because it withheld federal funding for all Medicaid programs unless the state expanded the program. The Supreme Court held Congress could not take such coercive action. Congress can withhold funding for Medicaid expansion if a state refuses to expand the program, but Congress cannot threaten to withhold all funding.

Questions

1. What are the three main components of the Patient Protection and Affordable Care Act?
2. What parts of the act did the Supreme Court find to be constitutional? Unconstitutional?
3. What clause of the Constitution justified the penalty imposed by the individual mandate?
4. What clause of the Constitution would justify the employer mandate?

Full Faith and Credit Clause

The Full Faith and Credit clause of the US Constitution can be found in Article IV Section 1. It states: "Full faith and credit shall be given in each state to the public acts, records, and judicial proceedings of every other state. And the Congress may by general laws prescribe the manner in which such acts, records, and proceedings shall be proved, and the effect thereof." The Full Faith and Credit Clause requires each state to recognize and give credit to legal documents and proceedings of other states. For example, Hillary dies in the State of New York where she signed her last will and testament. In her will she devises, or gives, land she owns in Arkansas to her daughter Chelsea. The state of Arkansas must generally recognize the gift of land to Chelsea even though the will was signed and later found to be valid in New York. Although the Full Faith and Credit Clause is generally used to validate judgments of out-of-state courts, it has also been extended to cases involving child custody.

The First Amendment

The First Amendment provides several well-known individual rights. "Congress shall make no law respecting an establishment of religion, or prohibiting the free exercise thereof; or abridging the freedom of speech, or of the press; or the right of the people peaceably to assemble, and to petition the government for a redress of grievances."

Freedom of Religion

The First Amendment to US Constitution provides two prohibitions in regards to religion. First, the federal government shall not create a state-sponsored religion. Many of the settlers of the United States had come to the United States in hopes of better economic opportunities as well as the ability to freely exercise their religion. It was important to the states adopting the US Constitution that the federal government be prevented from establishing a state religion that everyone must follow. For example, Congress cannot require everyone to become a Presbyterian Christian.

This prohibition is referred to as the *Establishment Clause* and is often used for the basis of arguments requiring the separation of church and state. The Establishment Clause prohibits religious or sectarian schools from receiving aid, although there are exceptions. In addition, the Establishment Clause prohibits public prayer from being instituted by a school even if the student body votes to have a public prayer recited. However, in the case *Van Orden v. Perry*, 545 US 677 (2005), the Supreme Court has stated it is appropriate for a courthouse to display the 10 Commandments since the 10 Commandments have played a substantial role in the shaping of our country's history.

In the business context, the establishment clause was used by plaintiffs in *McGowan v. Maryland*, 366 US 420 (1961), to attempt to prevent a state from enforcing a statute requiring certain businesses to be closed on Sunday. The plaintiffs claimed the state statute had its roots in the 10 Commandments, which require Christians not to work on the Sabbath and not to cause others to work on the Sabbath. The Supreme Court, however, held the state statute had secular merit since it allowed for a day of rest for all citizens and not just Christians who observed the 10 Commandments.

Second, the federal government must not restrict the right of its citizens to practice their religious beliefs. This is referred to as the *Free Exercise Clause*. Neither Congress nor a state can pass a law prohibiting the ability of an individual to exercise their religion. For example, in *Lovell v. City of Griffin*, 303 US 444 (1938), the city of Griffin's statute requiring approval to distribute pamphlets was found to be unconstitutional, as it violated the right of a member of the Jehovah's Witnesses to pass out information about their religion.

The Free Exercise Clause does allow for states to prohibit certain activity it deems to be a crime. For example, in *Employment Division, Department of Human Resources of Oregon v. Smith*, the Supreme Court held the state of Oregon could refuse unemployment benefits to members of the Native American Church who used peyote as part of their religious practices.

In the business context, Congress passed the Civil Rights Act of 1964, of which Title VII requires employers to provide reasonable accommodations to employees who wish to practice their religious beliefs. The employer is not allowed to determine what an acceptable religious belief is, but the employee must hold a sincere religious belief. The employee must notify the employer of such a religious belief. The employer must provide reasonable accommodations.

Trans World Airlines, Inc. v. Hardison
432 US 63 (1977)

Figure 3.5 Trans World Airlines Jet

The respondent Hardison was an employee of Trans World Airlines. He was also part of a union named the International Association of Machinists & Aerospace Workers. The union contract with Trans World Airlines provided for a seniority system. An issue arose when Hardison requested Saturdays off each week for religious purposes. Trans World Airlines was willing to accommodate Hardison but an agreement could not be reached because the airline needed Hardison to work more than four days a week and the union could not allow Hardison Saturdays off because he did not qualify under the seniority system. Hardison was then fired for refusing to work on Saturdays.

The Supreme Court held seniority systems are permitted under federal law. The Court also held there was no discriminatory intent in the present case involving Hardison.

The Court also stated: "[t]o require TWA to bear more than a de minimis cost in order to give Hardison Saturdays off is an undue hardship. Like abandonment of the seniority system, to require TWA to bear additional costs when no such costs are incurred to give other employees the days off that they want would involve unequal treatment of employees on the basis of their religion."

Questions

1. What were the facts of this case?
2. Why couldn't Hardison have Saturdays off, in accordance with his religious beliefs?
3. Can a seniority system be used to prohibit those with unpopular religious beliefs from being promoted?
4. Hardison had recently adopted his faith. Does it matter if he did not have the religious beliefs in his faith when he started his job?

Freedom of Speech

- Unprotected speech
- Obscene speech
- Commercial speech

One of the most well-known aspects of the First Amendment is the right to freedom of speech. "Congress shall make no law respecting an establishment of religion, or prohibiting the free exercise thereof; *or abridging the freedom of speech, or of the press*" (emphasis added). The federal courts generally provides more protection to individual liberties than they do to businesses, and the area of free speech is no different.

The First Amendment protects more than just the spoken word. The framers of the US Constitution wanted to protect the written word against prior censorship by the government. Freedom of Speech also protects nonverbal expressions such as paintings and even nude dancing. However, a student must remember the First Amendment protects a citizen from government restrictions on free speech. The First Amendment does not directly limit the ability of an employer to limit the free speech of its employees. It also does not necessarily prevent a business from restricting the expressions of its customers.

Individual Free Speech

An individual cannot have his or her speech regulated by the government unless the person in engaging in **unprotected speech**. Examples of unprotected speech include defamation (wrongfully damaging a person's reputation), obscene language, or inflammatory language likely to incite violence (often referred to as "fighting words").

The Supreme Court has established a three-part test, known as the *Miller* test,[1] for determining whether speech is obscene. **Obscene speech** occurs when 1) the work or speech appeals to a prurient interest, 2) the work or speech is patently offensive, and 3) the work or speech lacks serious literary, artistic, political, or scientific merit. To be considered *prurient*, the work must appeal to a deviant subgroup of citizens or portray acts not considered to be acceptable by the general public. An example is bestiality.

To be patently offensive means the work of speech portrays sex in a way that the community finds to be offensive. Finally, to determine whether the work or speech has any value other than being obscene, a reasonable-person test is used to determine whether a reasonable person would find the work to have literary, artistic, political, or scientific merit. Early pornographic movies often contained a scientist being interviewed about human procreation at the beginning of the movie and this led to the factor of the test requiring serious merit. It should be noted the *Miller* test applies to sexual works or speech involving adults and does not prohibit a state from censuring works involving minors.

Commercial Free Speech

Commercial speech includes speech that promotes a product or service, communicates information that benefits the economic interest of the speaker, or intends to create goodwill for the company. Commercial speech receives less protection than individual speech does,

---

1   *Miller v. California*, 413 US 15 (1973).

as a general rule. It should be noted the government has the right to prohibit commercial speech that is misleading or relates to an illegal activity.

Central Hudson Gas v. Public Service Commissioner
447 US 557 (1980)

In the case *Central Hudson Gas v. Public Service Commissioner*, the Supreme Court designed a four-pronged test for determining whether a government's restriction on commercial speech is constitutional.

1. The speech must be protected by the First Amendment (misleading or obscene speech, for example, would not be protected).
2. The restriction on commercial speech must advance a substantial government interest.
3. The restriction directly advances the substantial government interest.
4. The restriction goes no further than necessary.

For example, assume the state of North Carolina has had several accidents arise because a driver was distracted by advertising on the side of a delivery truck. The state of North Carolina's legislature passes a statute that prohibits advertising on or near roadways, including stationary signs. The state has an important government interest. It directly advances that interest by eliminating advertising on or near roadways. However, the legislation probably went further than necessary. The law prohibited the use of moving billboards anywhere near a road and not just on moving vehicles. Therefore, the law would be unconstitutional under the *Hudson* case test.

Lorillard Tobacco Co. v. Reilly
84 F. Supp. 2d 180 (2000)

The Attorney General of Massachusetts created certain regulations that restricted the advertising of tobacco products near a school or playground. The regulations stated "[o]utdoor advertising [of tobacco products], including advertising in enclosed stadiums and advertising from within a retail establishment that is directed toward or visible from the outside of the establishment, in any location that is within a 1,000 foot radius of any public playground, playground area in a public park, elementary school or secondary school." Mass. Regs. § 21.04(5)(a) (2001).

Figure 3.6 Lorillard Tobacco Advertisement

In addition, the regulations placed advertising restrictions on stores located within the thousand-foot zones. The stores had to place the in-store advertising at five feet higher than floor level, in an attempt to keep small children from seeing the displays. This prohibition was referred to as point-of-sale advertising because it applied to stores selling tobacco products. Various tobacco-product manufacturers banded together to bring a lawsuit against the state of Massachusetts, claiming the regulations were an unconstitutional restriction of speech.

After the tobacco companies argued the restrictions at issue should receive a higher standard of review than that provided by *Central Hudson* because the advertising was not deceptive or misleading, Judge Young wrote:

> Cigarette Advertising is Functional Pornography. The metaphor is apt. Both are entirely legal. Both are spawned by and supported by multi-billion-dollar industries generating significant economic activity. While ostensibly clucking in disapproval, millions of adult Americans support each industry with considerable cash outlays yet seek to have the government teach our children to avoid that which so many of us eagerly purchase.
>
> Both cigarette advertising and pornography are protected forms of speech, reaching out to offer messages or products desired by and legal for adults. At the same time we leave it to our government to seek to shield our children from both of these forms of speech, believing them to be either inherently corrupting (pornography) or an inducement (cigarette advertising) to engage in an activity unlawful for minors. This dichotomy in the way we try to administer our visual world—a dichotomy in which adults value certain forms of speech but at the same time wish to eliminate vulnerable children from the audience—lies at the center of this case.

The Judge went on to find the factors of the *Central Hudson* case were met by the state in regards to its probations against outdoor advertising. However, the Judge found the point-of-sale advertising was unconstitutional under *Central Hudson*. The Judge stated:

> It is not the role of the Courts to choose the proper number for the legislature in order to make the Regulations valid. The government must show it has narrowly tailored its regulation to effectuate its purpose. A numerical limitation selected with no particular logical rationale is insufficient to meet this burden, especially when that limit exhibits a real danger of swallowing up everything by being de facto no limit at all.
>
> Here, however, the Attorney General has relied on the conclusions of a federal agency engaged in the very same objective: the protection of children from tobacco products. The Administration selected 1000 feet as the appropriate zone, and described that zone as inclusive of places where children spend a lot of time. This Court will not second-guess the Attorney General's decision to rely on the Administration's conclusions in selecting the numerical limit of a zone of regulation.
>
> That reliance, however, must be seen to relate to substantially the same subject matter. Although the Administration's proposed regulations address all forms of outdoor advertising, they do not address indoor advertising in stores near schools or playgrounds.

Questions

1. What was the Attorney General trying to prohibit?
2. What are the four prongs of the *Central Hudson* case and which was not met here?
3. What could have been done to make the indoor advertising restrictions narrowly tailored?
4. How would you explain to a 13-year-old that pornography and tobacco are acceptable products for adults and not acceptable products for children?

- Probable cause
- Reasonable suspicion

Second Amendment

The Second Amendment states "[a] well regulated militia, being necessary to the security of a free state, the right of the people to keep and bear arms, shall not be infringed." The second Amendment has been subject to much debate over the years. In *Robertson v. Baldwin*, 165 US 275, 281–282 (1897), the Supreme Court stated the Second Amendment applied to federal action and not state action, but the Supreme Court eventually held the Second Amendment applies to states as well. In the *District of Columbia v. Heller*, 554 US 570 (2008) the Supreme Court held a District of Columbia complete ban on the possession of a handgun was a violation of the Second Amendment. The case involved a public official who wanted to register his handgun and apply for a license for the gun so that he could possess it while off duty. The Court stated the right to bear arms was an individual right and the Second Amendment does not require an individual to own a firearm in conjunction with being part of a militia. The Supreme Court also stated the right to bear arms was not an unfettered right and the state can impose restrictions on the possession and purchase of firearms.

Fourth Amendment

The Fourth Amendment provides "The right of the people to be secure in their persons, houses, papers, and effects, against unreasonable searches and seizures, shall not be violated, and no Warrants shall issue, but upon probable cause, supported by Oath or affirmation, and particularly describing the place to be searched, and the persons or things to be seized." As a general rule, the fourth Amendment requires the state to obtain a search warrant before searching an individual, their home, or their business. There are exceptions to this rule, including where the search was necessary to preserve evidence that would have been destroyed, where the evidence was in plain view, and where the defendant consents to the search.

To obtain a search warrant, the state must convince a judge probable cause exists. **Probable cause** is a reasonable belief that a *crime* has been committed. To question a suspicious individual, police need a reasonable suspicion. **Reasonable suspicion** is the belief a person may be engaged in a *criminal activity*. Reasonable suspicion is a lesser standard than

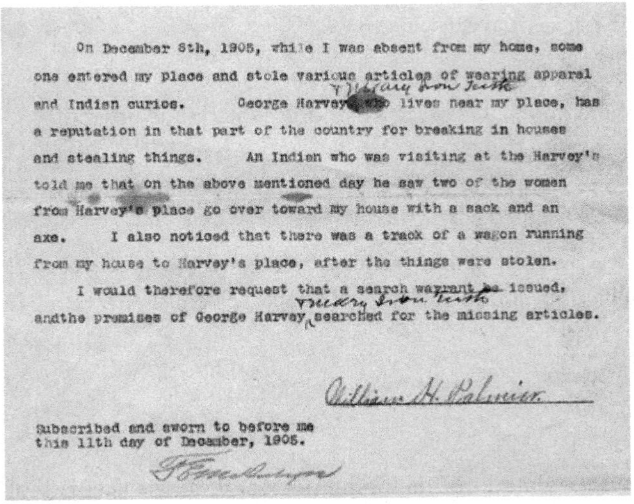

On December 8th, 1905, while I was absent from my home, some one entered my place and stole various articles of wearing apparel and Indian curios. George Harvey who lives near my place, has a reputation in that part of the country for breaking in houses and stealing things. An Indian who was visiting at the Harvey's told me that on the above mentioned day he saw two of the women from Harvey's place go over toward my house with a sack and an axe. I also noticed that there was a track of a wagon running from my house to Harvey's place, after the things were stolen.

I would therefore request that a search warrant be issued, and the premises of George Harvey, searched for the missing articles.

William H. Palmer

Subscribed and sworn to before me this 11th day of December, 1905.

Figure 3.7 Search Warrant

probable cause is. Reasonable suspicion may permit a police officer to stop and frisk an individual.[2]

In the business context, a search warrant is needed for the state to search the location of the business or the records of the business. An employer may consent to a search of the premises even if the state representative, for example an FBI agent, does not have a warrant. The courts are split, however, on whether an employee has an expectation of privacy in regards to electronic files such as computer files. Therefore, an employer could potentially consent to a search of an employee's computer in some jurisdictions.

Fifth Amendment

The Fifth Amendment provides "No person shall be held to answer for a capital, or otherwise infamous crime, unless on a presentment or indictment of a grand jury, except in cases arising in the land or naval forces, or in the militia, when in actual service in time of war or public danger; nor shall any person be subject for the same offense to be twice put in jeopardy of life or limb; nor shall be compelled in any criminal case to be a witness against himself, nor be deprived of life, liberty, or property, without due process of law; nor shall private property be taken for public use, without just compensation."

The Fifth Amendment has several important safeguards for those accused of a crime. First, in certain serious cases, a grand jury must issue an indictment against the defendant. The grand jury is made up of citizens who must vote to allow the state to proceed with a criminal charge against a defendant.

Second, the Fifth Amendment contains the Double Jeopardy clause. **Double Jeopardy** prohibits the state from trying a defendant twice for the same crime. Double Jeopardy even prevents the state from appealing a not-guilty decision in a criminal case to a higher court. For example, Brandy is tried for 1st degree murder. She is found not guilty by a jury. The state that prosecuted Brandy cannot appeal the not-guilty decision as a general rule.

Third, the state cannot call a defendant as a witness if the defendant does not wish to testify. This right applies to both criminal cases and civil cases. The right to refuse to testify against oneself has been expanded to protect spouses from having to testify in a proceeding against their spouse by the Federal Rules of Civil Procedure.

---

2 *Terry v. Ohio*, 391 US 1 (1968).

Fourth, the Fifth Amendment protects property owners from having their property confiscated by the state without just compensation. Just compensation has been held to mean the fair value of the property and does not include lawyer's fees or other costs incurred by the property owner in defending their ownership of the property. The process of a government taking property of a citizen in this manner is referred to **eminent domain**.

Finally, the Fifth Amendment creates what is referred to as due process. **Due process** prevents the federal government from arbitrarily taking a citizen's life, liberty, or property. There are two types of due process. **Substantive due process** means citizens have certain rights that the government cannot take away by legislation; for example, the right to marry, raise children, or work at a job. In cases where legislation seeks to govern a fundamental right, such as the right to privacy, the courts will apply strict scrutiny. **Procedural due process** means the federal government must follow certain procedures when taking away a citizen's life, liberty, or property. Procedural due process rights include the right to an attorney in certain cases, the right to be notified of a legal proceeding, and the right to cross-examine witnesses.

- Due process
- Substantive due process
- Procedural due process
- Equal Protection

Equal Protection Under the 14ᵗʰ Amendment

The 14ᵗʰ Amendment states, "[n]o state shall make or enforce any law which shall abridge the privileges or immunities of citizens of the United States; nor shall any state deprive any person of life, liberty, or property, without due process of law; nor deny to any person within its jurisdiction the equal protection of the laws." The 14ᵗʰ Amendment thus extends the concepts of substantive due process and procedural due process to governmental action by the states. The following information regards the concept of **Equal Protection**, which holds states cannot treat classes of citizens differently under the law unless they have a legitimate, important, or compelling reason for doing so.

Minimal Scrutiny

As mentioned previously in the chapter, when a court applies minimal scrutiny also known as rational basis review, a court will hold an act of a state government to be constitutional as long as there is a *rational* basis for believing a government action will further a *legitimate* government objective. This level of scrutiny is often referred to as deferential review, as a court will look for any conceivable interest a government could have in legislating in a given area. Minimal scrutiny often is applied in cases involving state action affecting economic and social rights of citizens. For example, assume a city has a problem with wild parties being thrown by college students. The city tries to fix the problem by passing an ordinance (law) that states only homeowners may have more than two guests present in their home at once. In this case, homeowners would be treated differently than renters.

Railway Express Agency, Inc. v. New York
336 US 106 (1949)

In New York City, Section 124 of the Traffic Regulations stated:

"No person shall operate, or cause to be operated, in or upon any street an advertising vehicle; provided that nothing herein contained shall prevent the putting of business notices upon business delivery vehicles, so long as such vehicles are engaged in the usual business or regular work of the owner, and not used merely or mainly for advertising."

The Railway Express Agency was a delivery business that was fined under this statute. It had numerous delivery vehicles on which it routinely advertised for other companies. Railway argued the traffic ordinance was a violation of the 14th Amendment. Railway argued there was no greater threat to the general public if it advertised the products or services of another company as opposed to its own product on the side of their trucks.

The Supreme Court stated, "The local authorities may well have concluded that those who advertised their own wares on their trucks do not present the same traffic problem in view of the nature or extent of the advertising which they use. It would take a degree of omniscience which we lack to say that such is not the case. If that judgment is correct, the advertising displays that are exempt have less incidence on traffic than those of appellants."

The Supreme Court went on to hold if "the classification has relation to the purpose for which it is made, and does not contain the kind of discrimination against which the Equal Protection Clause affords protection. It is by such practical considerations based on experience, rather than by theoretical inconsistencies, that the question of equal protection is to be answered."

Questions

1. Which group of citizens was being treated differently under the application of the New York law?
2. What was the holding of the Supreme Court?
3. Do you think advertisements promoting a truck driver's own services are less distracting than those promoting the services of another company? Did the Supreme Court agree with you?
4. What level of scrutiny did the Supreme Court apply in this case?

Strict Scrutiny

In cases involving the Equal Protection clause of the 14th Amendment, a court will apply strict scrutiny to cases involving the suspect classes of race and national origin. Strict scrutiny is the highest level of scrutiny applied by a court. It requires that the government action was furthering a *compelling* government interest and there was no *lesser restrictive* means available to the government. For example, assume a state decides to raise the minimum wage of those of a Latino descent only. Assume the state believes Latino workers have been historically underpaid by businesses. The Supreme Court would likely find this to be a legitimate interest, but not a compelling interest. In addition, the method employed by the state would probably not be narrow enough to withstand strict scrutiny since it would benefit those just entering the workforce and not just those who had been treated unfairly in the past.

Intermediate Scrutiny

Intermediate scrutiny falls somewhere between minimal scrutiny and strict scrutiny. Intermediate scrutiny review requires government action to be in furtherance of an important government interest and the action taken is substantially related to its objective. A court will apply this level of scrutiny where government action treats a class of citizens differently based upon gender or legitimacy. The Supreme Court used intermediate scrutiny in the case of *Mississippi University of Women v. Hogan*, 458 US 718 (1982)and found the university's female-only admissions policy violated the Equal Protection clause of the 14th Amendment.

Discussion Questions

1. Who were the Federalists? Who were the anti-Federalists?
2. What is the significance of the Bill of Rights in regards to the drafting of the US Constitution?
3. What branches of office do the first three articles of the US Constitution create?
4. How does the system of checks and balances work? Give an example of how each branch has the power to check another branch.
5. What are the three levels of scrutiny applied by the Supreme Court in regards to cases interpreting the US Constitution?
6. What does the Commerce Clause allow Congress to regulate?
7. What is the Dormant Commerce Clause and what is its significance?
8. What does the 10th Amendment provide?
9. What will be the outcome of a court case if a state utilizes its police power to pass a law but the law interferes with interstate commerce?
10. What protection does the Privilege and Immunities clause provide to a citizen?
11. When does federal law preempt state law?
12. From where does Congress derive its power to levy an income tax?
13. Can Congress influence state legislation with its power to spend? Can you provide an example?
14. What is the Full Faith and Credit Clause of the US Constitution? Can you provide an example of how it would apply to a verdict in a lawsuit?
15. How is the Establishment Clause different from the Free Exercise Clause?
16. What is the significance of the term "reasonable accommodations" in regards to religious liberties?
17. What forms of speech are unprotected under the First Amendment?
18. Is commercial speech protected under the Constitution? Does it receive more or less protection than individual speech does?
19. What are the factors of the *Central Hudson* test?
20. What are the factors of the *Miller* obscenity test?
21. Can a state outlaw the ownership of handguns under the Second Amendment?
22. How is probable cause different from reasonable suspicion?

23. When wouldn't the police need a search warrant to search a business?
24. What rights does the Fifth Amendment provide to an individual citizen?
25. What does the term "eminent domain" mean?
26. What is the difference between procedural due process and substantive due process?
27. Under the 14th Amendment, discrimination based upon what classes requires strict scrutiny? Intermediate scrutiny? Minimal scrutiny?

Critical-Thinking Questions

28. The US Constitution is referred to as a "living document." What do you think this means?
29. Why did Congress use its commerce power to pass civil rights laws prohibiting discrimination? Doesn't the US Constitution prohibit discrimination?
30. Why is it important to have free speech as a citizen?
31. Andrea believes the Second Amendment was not meant to allow a citizen to have an assault rifle because when the Second Amendment was written, only simple guns like muskets existed. Can you make an argument against Andrea's logic?
32. Why do businesses routinely receive fewer rights than an individual does in constitutional cases? For example, the Fourth Amendment has been interpreted as proving less protection to a business as compared to an individual.

Essay Questions

1. Assume the state of Iowa passes a law that prohibits all advertising on the side of semi-trucks, as the large advertisements often distract other drivers. Assume your client has been found guilty of violating this law by advertising on the side of her truck. What are your best arguments to the court that this law is unconstitutional as applied to your client?
2. Assume the state of Minnesota outlaws advertisements promoting sodas containing sugary drinks at elementary schools or at stores within ten miles of an elementary school because of obesity problems among elementary-age schoolchildren. Your client has been found guilty of advertising soda products within one mile of a school. What are your best arguments to the court that this law is unconstitutional as applied to your client?
3. Assume the state of Minnesota passes a law prohibiting the shipment of milk from out-of-state milk plants. The state has justified this law based upon an incident where a small child became ill after drinking milk that was spoiled. What arguments can the state make in favor of this law being constitutional? What arguments can an out-of-state milk producer use to claim this law is unconstitutional?
4. Assume a state passes a law requiring all sellers of soap and skin products to be registered with the state health inspector office. You represent a client who lives in nearby state and routinely ships soap and skin products into this state. Your client refuses to be registered

and has received a $100,000 fine. What constitutional arguments can you make on your client's behalf as to why this law is unconstitutional?

5. Assume Illinois passes a law requiring doctors to be certified before providing medical services to a citizen of Illinois. You represent a client who is licensed to practice medicine in Indiana. Your client recently administered a drug to a patient in an emergency room of an Illinois hospital located right across the border of Indiana and Illinois. She is fined $50,000 and refuses to pay. What constitutional arguments can you make on your client's behalf as to why this law is unconstitutional as applied to her?

6. Moses is an employee at a local factory. You are the corporate attorney for the factory. A supervisor of Moses comes to you and says Moses refuses to work on Sunday because he has found God. The supervisor does not believe Moses is sincere. What advice would you give the supervisor?

7. Deborah is a nurse supervisor at a local hospital. She recently hired a new nurse named Betty. Betty refuses to touch anyone who has an open sore because it is against her religion. What advice would you give to the hospital? And to Deborah?

8. Your client has been growing plants to make illegal drugs. He has been doing so for at least five years. Last week the police confiscated the plants from his backyard without a warrant. Do the police need a warrant to take plants from his backyard? Will the client have to testify against himself at trial if called by the prosecution to testify?

9. Your client has been dismantling cars that he has been buying from local thieves. The parts from the cars are being sold to out-of-state repair shops. The police entered your client's place of business last week without a warrant. Do the police need a warrant to search a business that is transacting illegal business? What if your client's wife knows all the details of the operation—can she be called by the prosecution as a witness against your client?

10. Assume the state of Montana is concerned about the outbreak of Ebola among those who have traveled to Africa, so the state requires all of its citizens who have traveled to Africa during the last year to undergo testing for Ebola. If a citizen does not comply with this law, they will be fined $10,000. Your client has traveled to Africa in the last four months but refused to get tested. What constitutional concepts will apply to this case? What level of scrutiny will a court apply? Do you think the law will surpass this level of scrutiny?

11. Assume the state of Florida is concerned about the outbreak of a cervical disease among teenage girls, so the state requires all teenage girls who attend public schools to be vaccinated. If a citizen does not comply with this law, they will be fined $15,000. Your client has a 14-year-old daughter but refuses to have her vaccinated because of a fear of government-required vaccinations. What constitutional concepts will apply to this case? What level of scrutiny will a court apply in regards to the 14th Amendment? Do you think the law will surpass this level of scrutiny?

12. Assume the state of Texas is concerned about illegal immigration, so it requires all citizens of Mexico or a South American country to post a bond of $200,000 before entering the state. If a person does not comply with this law, they will be sentenced to ten years in prison. Your client has been arrested for failing to post the required bond. What constitutional concepts will apply to this case? What level of scrutiny will a court apply in regards to the 14*th* Amendment? Do you think the law will surpass this level of scrutiny?

CHAPTER FOUR

INTENTIONAL AND UNINTENTIONAL BUSINESS TORTS

By Craig Nierman

Torts

Jackson is angry because the parking lot of his business is once again flooded. He did not have a problem with flooding until last year when a new Super-Mart was constructed next door. The land on which it was built was raised eight feet higher than the ground on which Jackson's business sits. Jackson is curious as to whether or not he can sue the Super-Mart because the water flooding his business deters customers from visiting his business.

Ramero recently performed work for a client. The client thought he should get certain services for free even though they were not included in the contract that he signed with Ramero. In an act of pure anger, the client went onto the Internet and posted untrue statements about Ramero and his business. Long-time clients are now asking Ramero about these online allegations. Ramero is wondering what actions he can take against this client.

Chapter Objectives

1. Understand what a tort is and the elements of a tort.
2. Identify common intentional torts committed against an individual or business.
3. Identify common intentional torts committed against personal and real property.
4. Identify the elements necessary to prove a case of negligence.
5. Identify defenses against both intentional and unintentional torts.

Introduction

The word **tort** is derived from a French word meaning "wrong" or "injury." In the US legal system, a tort is a civil claim other than a claim for breach of contract. The person who commits a tort is a **tortfeasor**, which finds its roots in a French word meaning "wrong-doer." A tort is committed when the tortfeasor breaches a legal duty to another and that breach causes a legally recognized injury.

Legally, a civil cause of action is considered separate from a criminal cause of action, even though a single act can, and often does, involve both civil and criminal law. For example, if Jake vandalizes Danny's home, Jake may be convicted in a criminal case for vandalism and may be successfully sued by Danny for committing a tort. In that case, one action could spark both criminal and civil legal actions.

There are several reasons a person might be found innocent in a criminal case but liable in a civil action. First, there is a difference in evidentiary requirements for criminal and civil law. Torts generally require that the plaintiff prove his or her case by a preponderance of the evidence. To prove a case by a **preponderance of the evidence** means the trier of fact finds it is more likely than not the defendant is liable for committing the wrongful act. In other words, if 51% of the evidence tends to support the plaintiff's tort case, while 49% of the evidence is in favor of the defendant, the plaintiff should prevail and the defendant would be held liable. However, a criminal prosecutor must prove his or her case **beyond a reasonable doubt**, which is a burden that is much closer to 100%. To prove a defendant is guilty beyond a reasonable doubt means the trier of fact, a judge or a jury, can have no reasonable doubt that the defendant is guilty.

Sometimes a wrongful act results in only a criminal prosecution. An example is attempted arson, where no damage is actually done to a property, but an individual tried to set fire to a structure. The police may arrest the perpetrator for committing a crime but the owner of the property will most likely not pursue a civil action as no damages were incurred. It is also possible that a wrongful act results in only a civil action, such as a car accident in a private parking lot. Assume Jerry backs into Tiffany's car with his automobile. Tiffany might sue Jerry for damages without ever telling the police about the incident.

Purpose of Tort Law

Tort law has two primary purposes: 1) to encourage others to act in a way that does not harm others and 2) to compensate the victims of a wrongful act. Assume John is angry at his former girlfriend Natalie. He is considering posting untrue statements about her online through a social networking website. He knows he might be sued by Natalie for libel, so he does not make the post. This example illustrates the deterrent effect of tort law. When individuals know that they might get sued if they engage in wrongful acts, they may be less likely to engage in wrongful acts. If a person follows through with a wrongful act, the victim may recover damages through tort law. Assume John could not help himself and he made the harmful untrue post anyway. Natalie may be able to recover through tort law for damage to her reputation.

Origins of Tort Law

The origin of US tort law can be traced to the settling of grievances between rival Anglo Saxon clans in what is now known as England. These disputes were resolved through monetary compensation under the common law. The current tort system in the United States has both common law and statutory components. Therefore, the rule of law may be provided by a judge's opinion, resulting in common law or legislation passed by a legislature referred to as statutory law. For example, in a state, what constitutes a nuisance might be defined by a statute or it may be defined through judicial opinions.

Common Law

US tort law originated as almost exclusively judge-made common law. When the country was founded, instead of creating an entirely new civil system, federal and state courts essentially adapted English common law. Much of that system still remains as the backbone of the tort law in the United States. Further, even if applying specific torts created by state and federal legislatures through statutes, courts may still rely heavily on common law principles. For example, the term "reasonable person" is often used in determining whether a defendant has breached his duty of care. A statute might make reference to a "reasonable person," but the definition of what constitutes the actions of a reasonable person often comes from the common law.

One of the benefits of the common law is its ability to change and adapt tort law to meet an evolving society. For example, within the past decade or so, judges have had to consider cyber-bullying lawsuits without clear guidance from earlier court decisions. In essence, the courts have applied longstanding tort principles, such as defamation, to new circumstances involving bullying in cyberspace.

Statutes

Legislatures have codified some common law principles though legislation. Legislatures have also created new torts by enacting statutes that provide for tort remedies for certain activities. For example, tort law addressing racial discrimination and sexual harassment originated from state and federal legislatures.

Legislators have also played a role in limiting the reach of tort law. For example, modern workers' compensation laws resulted from a statutory response to lawsuits against employers as well as the lack of remedies for many workplace injuries. Now workers hurt at work generally receive somewhat predictable compensation for their injuries and are prevented from bringing traditional tort claims against their employers, except in very limited circumstances.

Unintentional Torts

- Unintentional tort
- Negligence

The vast majority of torts are unintentional. An **unintentional tort** involves a situation where the tortfeasor had no intention of creating a wrong, but, because of a lapse in judgment or a failure to be careful, harmed someone else. For example, assume Marissa is thinking about the things she wants to get done that night, instead of the traffic in front of her. She then causes an accident. She has committed an unintentional tort. She did not intend to strike a car with her car.

Figure 4.1 Car Accidents Are Often Caused by Negligence

Negligence

Negligence is the most common type of tort. **Negligence** results when a defendant breaches a duty of care owed to the plaintiff by acting in a way that a reasonable person would not act. It frequently involves property damage and/or personal injury claims. In order to prevail on a negligence claim, the plaintiff must prove all of the following:

1. The defendant owed a duty of care to the plaintiff.
2. The defendant breached that duty of care.
3. The plaintiff suffered a legally recognizable injury.
4. The defendant's breach was the factual and proximate cause of the plaintiff's injury.

The plaintiff must prove all of these elements in a court case against the defendant to prevail in a case of negligence.

Did the Defendant Owe a Duty of Care?

The first question is whether the defendant owed a duty of care to the plaintiff. When a person uses a public sidewalk or a public street, the person owes a duty of care to other members of the public using the same sidewalk or street. As another example, a driver cannot change lanes in traffic if someone is already in that place in the lane.

Although individuals often owe a duty to not act in a certain way, it might not require an individual to act at all. For example, tort law in the United States does not require a private citizen to come to the aid of another individual. The act of coming to the aid of another is sometimes referred to as being a "Good Samaritan." Therefore, Terri could see Andrew lying on the street in pain because of a heart attack. Terri could simply walk past Andrew without offering any assistance. Terri would not be considered negligent unless she owed a special duty of care to Andrew. The special duty may arise because Terri is a physician who took an oath to help those in need of medical attention or Terri is Andrew's legal guardian.

In the earlier development of the common law, a landowner owed no duty of care to trespassers. Therefore, a landowner could keep a vicious dog on his property and he would not be legally responsible if a small child trespassed on his land and was injured by the dog. Modern tort law generally imposes a duty of care to those with an attractive nuisance. An **attractive nuisance** is a potentially dangerous object that might attract others onto a property owner's land. For example, a swimming pool is generally considered an attractive nuisance. The owner of a swimming pool must take reasonable steps, such as putting a fence around her swimming pool, to protect would-be trespassers from injury.

Other landowners, such as business owners, may owe a heightened duty of care as compared to homeowners. In essence, the law holds those who invite people onto their land in order to make a profit to a higher standard than others. Similarly, residential landlords often have an increased duty to keep common areas free from hazards to protect the safety of their tenants and guests. Therefore, storeowners are said to have a higher duty of care towards those visiting their property as compared to those who own property for private use only.

A storeowner is also generally tasked with the duty of patrolling their store in an attempt to uncover newly arisen risks such as a carton of oil which has spilled on the ground making the floor of the store hazardous to invitees. As a general rule, store owners who invite customers into their store to purchase goods owe a duty of care to business invitees that requires the storeowner to warn customers of hidden risks that the store owner knows about. For example, Ashton owns a convenience store. Ashton knew that an ice cream cooler was malfunctioning, but did not check to see if it was leaking in front of it where customers frequently walked. Alex, not seeing the small puddle of water next to the freezer, slipped and was injured. Ashton may be liable for Alex's injuries because Ashton should have known that there was a hazard.

On the other hand, landlords and store owners may not be liable for hazards that are so obvious that the reasonable person should have noticed. So, once Ashton takes reasonable steps to warn of the hazard, like putting a "wet floor" sign next to water, Ashton will likely be shielded from liability.

A few businesses, like common carriers (e.g., taxis and airlines) as well as innkeepers (e.g., hotels and motels), often have a heightened duty to their guests and are more likely to be held liable for their customer's injuries in the context of negligence.

- Attractive nuisance

- Reasonable person
- Legal injury

Did the Defendant Breach His Duty of Care?

Assuming the defendant owed a duty of care, the next question is whether the defendant has breached his or her duty of care. The law imposes a duty to act with a certain level of care when the safety of another person or property is at stake. A person breaches that duty when his or her conduct does not measure up to the standard of what a reasonable person in a similar situation would do. The question "who is the reasonable person?" has perplexed students for decades. The **reasonable person** is the average person in society who exercises an average amount of care when conducting their affairs. For example, it is assumed a reasonable driver would stop for a pedestrian in a crosswalk who has the right of way. A driver then who does not yield to the pedestrian is negligent because that person's conduct was not as prudent as a reasonable person's. An important point is the fact the law asks what *should* the reasonable person do and not what *would* the reasonable person do. The average person might text while driving but the reasonable person when asked would say they should not text while driving. Therefore, it is negligent to text and drive even if the reasonable person would on occasion text and drive.

It should also be noted that a professional such as a doctor, lawyer, or accountant is held to a higher duty of care than the ordinary citizen is when engaging in his or her profession. A professional's conduct is measured against the conduct of a similar professional engaging in a similar activity. A physician's breach would be compared to the level of service provided by doctors practicing in the same area of medicine. In other words, a surgeon would not be able to escape liability by claiming he or she performed a better surgery than the average citizen would have.

Did the Plaintiff Suffer a Recognizable Injury?

The third issue is whether or not the plaintiff sustained a recognizable legal injury. A **legal injury** is an injury that rises above a certain legal threshold. While hurt feelings do not constitute a legal injury, a physical injury or lost money does. For example, Mona owns a retail business located near a busy highway. Lisa drives her car in a negligent manner and smashes into the glass storefront. The damages sustained by Mona are damage to her business property from the accident. She may ask a court to award those damages in a negligence suit.

Was the Defendant's Negligent Action the Cause of the Plaintiff's Injury?

The plaintiff must prove that there is a connection between the breach of duty by the defendant and the legal injury suffered by the plaintiff. Just because there was a breach and an injury arising out of the same incident, it does not necessarily mean that the plaintiff satisfied the requirement. For example, assume that there was a car accident involving Peter and Doug. The plaintiff Peter's car was badly damaged by Doug's car. Even though the plaintiff might be able to prove that the defendant breached the defendant's duty to keep his or her car registration up to date, that breach is not causally (or factually) connected to the plaintiff's damages. In other words, the defendant's tardy registration did not cause the property damage. If, however, the plaintiff can prove that the collision happened because the defendant ran a stop sign or made an illegal U-turn, that would satisfy the causation requirement.

• Cause in fact
• Foreseeability

There are several different types of causation. **Cause in fact** is often referred to as the "but for" cause of the damages. The judge or jury asks "but for" the defendant's breach of duty, would the plaintiff have been injured? In the example above, the car registration was not cause in fact or the "but for" cause of the accident, because the plaintiff's injury would have occurred whether or not the car was properly registered.

Courts have long debated whether **foreseeability** is a requirement of the standard of care. The issue of foreseeability is sometimes referred to as legal causation or proximate causation. Many courts have held that if the connection between the breach of duty and the resulting harm is nearly unimaginable, the negligence claim lacks proximate causation, also known as legal causation. Some courts have held that foreseeability should not prevent a plaintiff from collecting damages just because a defendant was not likely to imagine the resulting harm.

The following case exemplifies the issue of legal causation.

Palsgraf v. Long Island Railroad Co.
248 N.Y. 339 (1928)

The following is a summary of the opinion of the New York Court of Appeals:

Palsgraf was standing on a railway platform waiting for her train. As another train started to depart, a passenger ran toward it while two railroad employees assisted him onto the passenger car. In the process, the man's package containing fireworks fell, detonated, and damaged a scale a number of feet away. The scale then fell onto and injured Palsgraf. Palsgraf sued the railroad for her damages, claiming that the employees were

Figure 4.2 Palsgraf was boarding a railroad car

negligent in the way that they assisted the man onto the train. Both the trial court and the intermediate court of appeals ruled in favor of Palsgraf.

The New York Court of Appeals (the court of last resort in that state) held that although the employees may have been negligent, they could not have possibly foreseen the chain of events leading to Palsgraf's injury. "The conduct of the defendant's guard, if a wrong in its relation to the holder of the package, was not a wrong in its relation to the plaintiff, standing far away. … Nothing in the situation gave notice that the falling package had in it the potency of peril to persons thus removed." Accordingly, Palsgraf did not meet her burden of proof and her case was dismissed.

- Negligence per se
- Res ipsa loquitur
- Contributory negligence
- Comparative negligence

Questions

1. What were the facts of this case?
2. Which of the four prongs of negligence did the defendant fail to prove?
3. Is proximate causation a factual question or legal question for a court to decide?
4. What additional facts might have swayed the court to find for Palsgraf?

Special Negligence Standards

Negligence per se, or "negligence in itself," occurs when a violation of the law establishes a breach of duty on the part of the defendant. Assume a hotel owner, as a result of a fire, pleads guilty to violating a criminal statute for not installing smoke detectors. Assume also that a guest staying at the hotel is injured because of the lack of smoke detectors. The violation of the criminal statute establishes negligence, and if the purpose of the statute was to prevent accidents such as this, negligence per se establishes a breach of duty on the part of the defendant.

Res ipsa loquitur is a Latin phrase for "the thing speaks for itself." It is another special negligence standard that helps prove breach of care by the defendant. Assume a large item at a grocery store falls from a high shelf, hitting a customer. Assume no other customers had touched the item and it is clear that the store had complete control over the object. A court might say "it speaks for itself" regarding the cause of the accident. Under the theory of res ipsa loquitur, the grocery store breached its duty to control the item from falling. In that situation, the plaintiff would not have to spend time proving the breach of duty by the plaintiff because negligence is established by the principle of *res ipsa loquitur*.

Defenses to Negligence

Defendants accused of negligence have several legal principles that they can use to defend themselves.

Under the common law, contributory negligence on the part of the plaintiff was a complete bar against recovery. **Contributory negligence** means negligence on the part of the plaintiff contributed in some fashion to their injury. Imposing a complete bar against recovery by the plaintiff made contributory negligence an easy standard to apply. The judge or jury, whoever was a trier of fact, had to ask only whether or not the plaintiff was negligent. For example, assume Carl is driving five miles per hour over the speed limit. He is hit by Sarah who failed to stop her car at a stop sign. Carl is contributorily negligent by driving too fast if his speeding contributed to the collision in any way. In that event, under the common law, Carl would not be able to collect damages from Sarah.

Because of the harsh consequences of contributory negligence, many states have moved toward a standard based upon comparative negligence. **Comparative negligence** compares the contribution of the defendant toward the plaintiff's injury with the contribution of the plaintiff toward their own injury.

Assume a fire occurs at an office building that did not have a properly functioning warning system. Unfortunately, Bill, who rented space in the building, was hurt in the fire after refusing to leave after the building manager told Bill about the fire. In that situation, the trier of fact could assess 100% of the fault to either the building owner who did not have a properly functioning warning system or Bill for not heeding the manager's warning. The trier of fact could also attribute a portion of the blame to each of them. Bill's damages would be reduced proportionately to his percentage of fault. For instance, if the trier of fact concluded that the owner was 60% at fault and Bill was 40%, Bill could collect only 60% of his damages in a comparative negligence state.

States may impose limitations on the amount of fault a plaintiff can contribute. For example, in a state with a "not greater than" standard, the plaintiff can collect for damages as long as the plaintiff's fault is no more than the defendant's fault. For example, if the plaintiff and the defendant are both 50% at fault, the plaintiff can still collect for the plaintiff's damages, but the plaintiff's award will be reduced by the percentage of the plaintiff's fault. If the plaintiff were 51% at fault, the plaintiff would be barred from recovery.

Other states use what is called a "pure" comparative fault system, where there is no limit on the amount of fault a plaintiff can be responsible for in order for the plaintiff to collect. So, in a pure jurisdiction, a plaintiff who is 80% at fault can still collect 20% of the plaintiff's damages.

Another defense to a negligence action is intervening cause, also known as superseding cause. When a defense is raised based upon an **intervening cause**, the defendant asserts that something beyond the defendant's control intervened to cause the plaintiff's injury. For example, assume that a plaintiff wakes up one morning and finds that the defendant's car crashed into the plaintiff's house during the night. At trial, the defendant might assert that a tornado was an intervening cause, as it lifted the car from its parking spot across the street. If the tornado caused the damage, it is an intervening cause and shields the defendant from liability.

Another defense against the tort of negligence is assumption of risk. **Assumption of risk** results when the plaintiff increased the likelihood of injury by knowingly engaging in a risky activity. For example, assume a skydiver sues an airplane pilot after the skydiver is injured jumping from the pilot's airplane. The pilot might claim assumption of risk by the skydiver because the skydiver engaged in behavior that was inherently risky.

Specific Types of Negligence Actions

The law provides for special applications of negligence. This chapter will discuss malpractice, dram shop actions, and strict liability.

Malpractice is a claim asserted against a professional, such as a physician, dentist, attorney, or accountant, for injuries a plaintiff sustains because the defendant failed to exercise the appropriate standard of care required in their profession. Generally the plaintiff must rely on expert testimony to prove that the defendant breached the defendant's duty to the plaintiff. It is generally not enough for a plaintiff to show that there was a bad result: as an example, the surgery was not successful. Rather that the professional committed a lapse in judgment that was the but-for cause of the negative outcome.

- Intervening cause
- Assumption of risk
- Malpractice

Providing but-for causation in malpractice cases is generally established through **expert testimony**, which is evidence provided through the testimony of professionals with similar credentials to those of the defendant. Experts testify regarding the appropriateness of the defendant's conduct and are generally not involved in the circumstances giving rise to the plaintiff's case. Experts generally form their opinions based on a review of documents, testimony, professional literature, as well as other information related to their experience in the profession.

When malpractice claims are made against professionals like insurance agents or brokers, real estate agents, or other agents who help individual fill out applications or sign purchase contracts, the malpractice claim is often called an **errors and omissions** claim. For example, Rosetta graduates from college and becomes a life insurance agent and sells life insurance policies to consumers. One day while helping a client fill out an application for a $100,000 life insurance policy, she makes a mistake and writes "$10,000" instead of "$100,000." The consumer's beneficiary could make an errors and omissions negligence claim against Rosetta.

A **dram shop** action is brought by a plaintiff against an establishment that served too much alcohol to a patron, who caused the plaintiff's injury. The theory behind allowing an action against a restaurant or bar who over-served a patron is to eliminate the economic incentive to sell more alcohol than is safe. For example, Ted starts drinking at a bar. The bartender tells Ted he should not have any more to drink but Ted becomes angry and so the bartender serves him more alcohol. Ted eventually stumbles off to his car. On his way home, he crosses into oncoming traffic and kills a mother and her young child. The surviving members of the family can sue Ted and can also bring a dram shop action against the bar.

Strict Liability

Strict liability imposes liability on the defendant regardless of whether the defendant acted with reasonable care. Strict liability is applied to situations where a defendant engages in activities that are inherently dangerous like using explosives or possessing vicious animals. Accordingly, when the plaintiff is injured as a result of an activity like these, the defendant is absolutely liable to the plaintiff without any inquiry into whether there was a breach of duty. The defendant may claim they acted with reasonable care but a court may subject the defendant to strict liability because he or she engaged in a dangerous activity.

Take for example Jeremy, who keeps a trained lion in his backyard. He puts a ten-foot fence around the lion and keeps the door to the fence locked with two padlocks. One day an earthquake occurs and the fence Jeremy built falls over. The lion mauls a neighbor who is watering her garden. Jeremy will most likely be held strictly liable by a court for the damages his lion caused. He cannot argue he was more careful than the reasonable person would have been with a lion, nor will asserting intervening cause help because Jeremy engaged in such a dangerous activity.

A plaintiff injured by a defective product can bring a products liability claim, which imposes strict liability. A **products liability claim** is brought against a manufacturer who allegedly produced the defective product that caused an injury to the defendant. To show that the manufacturer breached its duty, the plaintiff must establish that the injury was caused by a defective product and that either the manufacturer failed to warn the consumer about a potential danger or the product was unreasonably unsafe.

- Assault
- Battery

Intentional Torts

While unintentional torts require the plaintiff to prove that the defendant did not act as a reasonable person would believe they should, intentional torts impose a significantly higher burden of proof on the plaintiff. In a case involving an intentional tort, the plaintiff must show that the defendant intended the action causing harm to the plaintiff, while negligence merely requires a showing that the defendant did not conform to the reasonable person standard and subsequently breached their duty of care.

Intentional Personal Torts

Assault and Battery

In order to prevail on an **assault** claim, the plaintiff must prove:

1. The defendant, by word or gesture, intentionally put the plaintiff in fear of imminent physical harm.
2. A reasonable person in the same situation would be fearful of imminent physical harm.
3. The defendant had no permission or privilege to act.

A defendant does not have to touch the plaintiff for an assault to occur. It is enough that the defendant makes some violent gesture. Generally, words alone are not enough to create an assault. The words must be accompanied by some sort of physical movement that puts the plaintiff in fear of immediate harmful contact.

For example, assume Randy threatens to punch Eric. He yells at Eric while pumping his fist in the air. Randy's actions would be considered assault because the words combined with the physical action might be enough to make Eric reasonably afraid that he would be hurt. Now assume Eric yells back that if Randy hits him, Eric will shoot Randy next week with his father's gun. Eric's statement is not assault because the threat is not immediate. Randy has time to alert the authorities or take some other kind of evasive action to avoid being hurt. Therefore, Eric's threat is not immediate and not considered assault.

Battery involves intentional physical contact that is offensive or harmful and was not consented to. The requirements are

1. The defendant touched the plaintiff with an object or the defendant's body.
2. The touching was unwelcome or offensive.
3. A reasonable person in the same situation would find the touching harmful or offensive.
4. The defendant had no permission or privilege to act.

The scope of battery is quite broad and can cover gestures that were innocently intended, but were objectively repulsive. An example is an unwelcome kiss. The question is not whether the defendant had an evil motive but whether the defendant intended the touching to occur and whether it was harmful or offensive.

A defendant can defend against an assault or battery claim by proving that the plaintiff gave the defendant permission to act. For example, if the two parties were acting out a fight scene in a play when one actor was hurt, their willingness to engage in the drama may be considered consent. The law also protects, to a certain degree, certain people when engaging in particular activities, such as police officers when apprehending a criminal suspect.

In regards to athletics, the courts have generally ruled that participants in a sporting event consent to physical contact inherent in the game. For example, assume Tricia is playing basketball. She consents to being pushed when going after a basketball even if pushing is against the rules and results in a foul. However, Tricia may have a valid battery claim against another player who punches her while she is sitting on the bench, waiting to play in the game, since it is so far removed from the hazards expected in the game.

A defendant might also claim they were acting in defense of themselves, another, or their property. To prevail using self-defense, defense of others, or defense of property, the actions taken by the defendant must be reasonable in light of the threat posed.

False Imprisonment

False imprisonment occurs when a defendant confines the plaintiff through the use of physical force or verbal threats without permission or privilege. False imprisonment cannot be brought as a tort claim if a plaintiff had a chance to escape without bodily harm. The plaintiff must have been confined. For example, Monique locks Jim in a refrigerated storage unit without permission or privilege. Jim cannot have a safe means of escape, such as an unlocked back door, if Monique's actions are to be considered false imprisonment.

States differ regarding to what extent a merchant may detain a suspected shoplifter. Some states prohibit any type of detention, while others give the business authority to reasonably confine the suspect if there is a reasonable suspicion of theft.

Defamation

To prove **defamation**, the plaintiff must show that:

1. Defendant made a false statement about the plaintiff.
2. The statement was published to a third party.
3. The plaintiff's reputation was harmed as a result.

There are two types of defamation: libel and slander. **Libel** applies to a defamatory written statement, while **slander** concerns defamatory oral communication.

Under the common law, some defamatory statements are considered so harmful that the plaintiff does not have to prove their reputation was harmed.

These statements include statements indicating that the plaintiff:

a. Is incompetent and/or immoral in the plaintiff's business affairs;
b. Has a loathsome disease such as a venereal disease or leprosy;
c. Is sexually promiscuous; or
d. Has committed a criminal act.

These statements are considered **defamation per se**, meaning that the statements are inherently harmful. The statements can be either written (libel) or verbal (slander).

In order to successfully defend against a defamation action, the defendant can prove defamation did not occur by claiming the statement was true, it did not harm the defendant's reputation, or it was not published to a third party. Defendants are often surprised to find out the truth is not an absolute defense. A defendant who uses the truth in a malicious manner and publishes their

Figure 4.3 Defamation is telling an untruth

statement to a third party causing harm to a defendant's reputation might still be liable for defamation under the theory of **defamation by implication**. For example, Lucille hires Mindy to prepare her taxes. Mindy makes a mistake. Lucille is angry and starts posting statements about Mindy's incompetence online. Lucille then prints off flyers and puts the fliers on windshields of cars at the mall, telling the mall shoppers about Mindy's incompetence. A court could hold Lucille liable for defamation under the theory of defamation by implication.

The defendant can also defend the claim by demonstrating that the defendant had a privilege to make the statement. A **privilege** is a legally recognized justification entitling the defendant to make and communicate the statement. The courts recognize two types of privileges: conditional and absolute.

A **conditional privilege** exists when the defendant's communication was made in good faith with the proper motive. For example, many companies are reluctant to provide references for former employees based upon the fear of the former employee bringing a defamation suit after not successfully getting a job. Some states, such as California, have recognized a conditional privilege on the part of the employer who was acting in good faith with the proper motive when commenting on the performance of an employee.

A conditional privilege also arises in regards to statements made about those who are considered to be a public figure, because they are a celebrity or part of the public sphere. The courts generally only hold a defendant liable for defamation if the defendant made a statement with malicious intent and not just knowledge the statement was untrue. For example, Kristin really hates a certain politician. She published an editorial in a local newspaper stating the individual hates women, children, and pets. Kristin would most likely be protected by a conditional privilege even if she knew the politician actually volunteered at a battered women's shelter and had adopted formerly homeless children and pets.

- Defamation per se
- Defamation by implication
- Privilege
- Conditional privilege

Absolute privilege applies to statements made in legal proceedings such as a trial or debate in the legislature. The privilege is justified by the theory that the government needs to obtain full and complete disclosure and that need trumps any damage caused by the defamatory statement.

Invasion of Privacy

The tort of **invasion of privacy** helps to protect the privacy and identity of ordinary citizens. The tort is committed when a defendant does any of the following:

1. Publishes information that places the plaintiff in a false light.
2. Publicly discloses facts about the plaintiff that a reasonable person would find objectionable or embarrassing.
3. Uses the name or likeness of the plaintiff without permission for a commercial purpose.
4. Invades a person's home or private papers.

However, if a person becomes a public figure like a candidate for office or an entertainer, that person is deemed to have waived any invasion of privacy claims since the public figure is shedding his or her privacy in order to take advantage of a public persona.

Appropriation

Appropriation is the wrongful use of another's name or likeness for the defendant's benefit. It is similar to invasion of privacy, except that public figures are not excluded from making claims.

White v. Samsung

971 F.2d 1395 (1992)

The following is a summary of the opinion of the United States Court of Appeals for the Ninth Circuit.

Samsung developed print advertisements for its video cassette recorders that featured what things would be like in the future. One included a robot standing on a game show set similar to that of *Wheel of Fortune*. The robot's features, including a blonde wig, gown, and jewelry, were intended to resemble Vanna White, who starred on the show. White brought a diversity action in federal court in California based on several arguments. The trial court granted Samsung's Motion for Summary Judgment.

The Court of Appeals affirmed part of the trial court's ruling and reversed another part. The appeals court agreed that White's claim based on California's statute that provided a tort remedy for using the "name, voice, signature, photograph, or likeness" of another for commercial purposes failed because Samsung used none of those in its ad.

However, the Court of Appeals reversed the trial court on White's other two claims. One was based on the California tort prohibiting the use of another's identity for a commercial purpose without consent. The second was based on a federal statute that prohibited using "any false description or representation" of another in a damaging way to sell goods or services. The court concluded that "beneath the surface humor of the series lay an intent to persuade consumers that celebrity Vanna White … was endorsing Samsung products." It reasoned that White could be damaged by the misperception that she endorsed the Samsung VCR.

The court then sent the case back to the trial court for a jury trial. The trial court awarded $403,000 in damages to Vanna White based on her claim for appropriation.

- Intentional inflic-
  tion of emotional
  distress
- Trespass

Questions

1. What were the facts of this case?
2. What torts were involved?
3. What constitutional right of Sony Corporation was infringed upon by the court's ruling?
4. If celebrities are paid large sums of money, why would a court allow them to sue another individual or business for appropriation?

Intentional Infliction of Emotional Distress

When a defendant causes an injury to a plaintiff by engaging in intentionally outrageous behavior, the defendant may be liable for **intentional infliction of emotional distress**. In recent years courts have tried to limit these claims for more egregious violations. In some states, the plaintiff must sustain a physical as well as an emotional injury to claim damages. Some jurisdictions allow damages to a person who sees a close relative endure a personal injury, as in a car accident. Other jurisdictions even extend the ability to sue for this tort to bystanders who witness a particularly gruesome injury, even though they were not physically involved in the incident other than by observing it.

Intentional Business/Property Torts

Wrongful Termination

Most employment relationships are "at will," meaning that the relationship is not governed by a contract for a particular term and either party is free to end the arrangement at any time. However, the tort of Wrongful Termination constitutes an exception by prohibiting the employer for firing a worker for a reason that contravenes public policy. For example, an employer is liable for firing an employee as punishment for making a valid workers' compensation claim. Federal law also protects employees from being fired because of their gender, race, national origin, etc.

Trespass

A **trespass** to real property occurs whenever the defendant enters on the plaintiff's land without permission. Trespass can occur through the defendant's presence on the land or

• Conversion

Figure 4.4 No Trespassing Signs Alert Citizens to Stay-off Property

something that is within the control of the defendant. For example, Michael enjoys hitting golf balls onto his neighbor's land. The golf balls are within Michael's control. Trespass can occur above the plaintiff's land or below it. For example, if Jennifer digs a large swimming pool that causes water to drain from underground and flood Patrick's property below the surface, Jennifer may also be liable for trespass.

The plaintiff does not have to prove actual damages, as it is assumed that any intrusion damages the plaintiff's right to exclusive use of the plaintiff's property. For example, Jennifer walks onto Patrick's property, which has a "No Trespassing" sign. Patrick screams at Jennifer to leave his property. Jennifer does so. Even though Jennifer has caused no damage to his property, Patrick can sue Jennifer for trespass. If Jennifer's dog runs onto Patrick's property, she might also be liable for trespass for her dog's action.

A plaintiff must prove a defendant did not have permission to be on the plaintiff's land. A lack of permission is established by a written or oral statement from the plaintiff that the defendant knew or should have known he was trespassing. For example, Celia is tired of having hunters cross her land to track deer. She posts a sign that reads "No Trespassing." This sign gives notice to the public that they must not enter onto her property. If a hunter does, they have committed trespass.

Defenses against trespass include 1) a license and 2) response to an emergency situation. If a defendant is invited onto someone's property, they have a license to be present on the plaintiff's land until the plaintiff revokes that license. Licenses might be more formal than a mere invitation. Sometimes a license to enter onto someone's property is granted by a purchase contract. For example, Charles sells certain mineral rights to Steadfast Mining Co. He grants Steadfast the right to travel across the northern part of his farmland to reach the place where mining activities will occur.

Public policy sometimes requires a defendant not be found guilty of trespass. One of the most common applications is the response to a dangerous situation. For example, Lisa comes home from work to find her house is on fire. Hunter is standing with a garden hose shooting water at the fire. Hunter's trespass is trumped by the permission the law grants to someone reasonably responding to a dangerous situation.

Conversion and Trespass to Personal Property

Conversion is essentially a civil remedy for theft and is committed when the defendant takes or retains another's personal property. Although it is generally considered an intentional tort, the plaintiff does not have to prove that the property was taken intentionally by the defendant, but only that it was wrongfully taken. For example, a defendant who mistakenly removes jewelry from a home believing that it is her own is liable to the owner for the value of the property under the tort of conversion.

Trespass to personal property occurs when the defendant interferes with the plaintiff's use of plaintiff's personal property. The defendant can be liable even if the property was not actually removed from the defendant's possession. For example, Martina sees Ashley has left her phone on the kitchen table. Martina takes the phone and sends a text to Rudy, who is Ashley's boyfriend, saying the relationship is over. Martina has trespassed in regards to the phone, but has not converted it as her own.

Fraud (or Intentional Misrepresentation)

The tort of **fraud** is designed to provide a remedy to those who are damaged through deceit. The plaintiff must prove:

1. The defendant misrepresented a material fact;
2. The defendant knew of the deception;
3. The defendant intended to influence the plaintiff to act or refrain from acting;
4. The plaintiff justifiably relied on the defendant's misrepresentation; and
5. The plaintiff was damaged as a result.

In many states, fraud is one of the few torts where a plaintiff has an elevated burden of proof. While most tort cases require that the plaintiff prove his or her case by a preponderance of the evidence, a plaintiff pursuing a fraud claim must prove it by clear and convincing evidence, which is higher than a preponderance, but not as high as the criminal beyond-a-reasonable-doubt standard used to decide criminal cases. **Clear and convincing evidence** can be thought of as requiring the plaintiff to prove it is more substantially likely than not that the defendant is liable.

As an example, assume Jeff needs a piece of machinery for mass production of drumsticks. He visits a business that has advertised such a machine for sale. Jeff asks how old the machinery is. The seller responds, "I think it's fifteen years old but I don't know for sure." Jeff then asks if the cylinders have ever been replaced and the seller says "just last year." This statement is false and the seller knows it. If the fact regarding the cylinders is a material fact that influenced Jeff's purchase decision, Jeff may have a case for fraud, also known as misrepresentation.

If the machinery is really twenty-five years old, at best, Jeff may have a claim for negligent misrepresentation, as the seller had said he was not sure of the age. The tort of negligent misrepresentation has the same factors as fraud, but substitutes the test for negligence in place of the requirement of intent.

Interference with Contractual Relationship

A person who induces another to breach a contract with a third party can be held liable for **interference with contractual relationship**. To succeed, the plaintiff must prove that:

1. There is a valid contract;
2. The defendant knew of the contract;

3. The defendant intentionally induced a party to breach the contract; and

4. The plaintiff suffers damages.

This tort commonly occurs when a competitor lures a contracted employee away from the plaintiff's business. For example, assume Kayla is a famous accounting professor. She has a contract with Midwest State University for three years. Sunshine State University approaches Kayla and offers her a new job with better pay. Kayla objects at first but eventually accepts the new job offer after Sunshine State offers her almost twice her current pay. If Sunshine knew of Kayla's contractual obligation to Midwest, it may be liable for interference with a contractual relationship.

Tortious Interference with a Business Advantage

While bona fide competition is not actionable, a business that unreasonably targets a competitor's customers or engages them may be liable for **interference with a prospective business advantage**. While the name of the tort and its elements vary widely from state to state, a defendant can be liable for using tort-like behavior such as defamation to drive a wedge between another business and its customers and possibly its employees. This can happen by spreading false rumors about a competitor's product or employees. Another example is a business that offers free service coupons to customers of a competitor while these customers are sitting in the waiting room of a competing business.

Slander of Title or Property

Slander of property is similar to defamation, but it requires untrue statements that diminish the value of property. For example, assume a famous actor claims red meat contains a cancerous organism that is highly infectious. A specific form of slander of property is **slander of title**, which is committed by knowingly casting doubt on the ownership interest of another in property. A common example is filing an unmeritorious lien on a piece of real estate. Even though the torts are referred to as slander of property and slander of title, they may be committed in the oral form or written form.

Cyber Torts

Cyber torts are torts based on computer-, Internet-, or technology-related activities. The courts generally apply the same traditional tort principles when dealing with cases involving new technology. The fact that allegedly tortious conduct occurred online does not alter the underlying legal principles. For example, the requirements of fraud or conversion remain the same whether the tortious transaction occurred in person or online. However, courts retain their common law power to adapt tort requirements to new developments in society and often modify their previous holdings when they no longer fit new situations.

Damages

Generally speaking, the result of a successful tort action is an award of money damages. Money damages may be based on several different theories of recovery.

Compensatory

As the name implies, **compensatory damages** are an award of money calculated to compensate a person for the harm caused by the tortfeasor. Suppose that Johnson causes a car accident with Lee. In order to compensate Lee, Johnson might have to pay to repair Lee's car, reimburse Lee for a rental car, and give Lee money for anything that was damaged inside the car. Further, if Lee had medical expenses or lost wages because of the accident, Johnson would have to pay for those also. **Special damages** are damages that arise "out of pocket" because of expenses incurred after the tortious act. In this example, Lee's rental car fee and lost property from within the car would be considered special damages.

Nominal damages are awarded for a minimal injury in torts that do not always require the plaintiff to prove specific damages. Examples are trespass to land or defamation per se. In such a case, a plaintiff could be awarded a nominal amount such as $1 or $100. The purpose of awarding a nominal damage is to deter wrongdoing on the part of the defendant.

Another category of compensatory damages is **general damages**, which compensate for losses resulting from the tort that do not have a precise economic value. They compensate the injured person generally, but are not calculated by using a specific mathematical model. In the personal injury context, laypersons often refer to general damages as "pain and suffering" because they are designed to recompense the plaintiff for pain and other losses that are a direct result of the tort. Suppose that Pat wrongfully injures Jerry in an automobile collision. Jerry's medical expenses would be considered special damages, but Jerry's "pain and suffering" are general damages because they do not have a specific economic value, but constitute a legal harm as part of the tort.

Punitive

Punitive damages are money damages awarded primarily to punish the tortfeasor for outrageous behavior. Punitive damages are rarely awarded and only in cases where the tortfeasor's conduct was intentional or reckless. In other words, to obtain punitive damages, the tortfeasor's conduct must be something beyond merely failing to conform to the reasonable person standard. If Cameron ran a red light because Cameron was distracted by thinking about a difficult situation at work, Cameron's conduct would be negligent, and thus, undeserving of punitive damages. If, on the other hand, Cameron decided to intentionally ram into Cosset's car because Cameron was mad at Cosset, the court might award punitive damages to punish Cameron for outrageous conduct.

Punitive damages are often awarded when the tortfeasor's conduct was reckless, which is worse than negligent, but not technically intentional. A tortfeasor acts in a **reckless** manner when a tortfeasor is conscious of a risk but disregards it. Assume that Adrian drove 70 miles per hour through a residential neighborhood before hitting Jonah's boat. While Adrian might not have specifically intended to hit the boat, Adrian's conduct could be considered reckless because he knew or should have known that his outrageous behavior greatly elevated the likelihood of a wrongful act.

Liebeck v. McDonald's Restaurants

CV-93-02419 (1995)

The following is a summary of the trial proceedings in a New Mexico District Court.

In 1992, Stella Liebeck was a passenger in her grandson's car. They went through a McDonald's drive through in Albuquerque, New Mexico, where she got a cup of coffee. Unbeknownst to her, McDonald's had received more than 700 notices of customers receiving coffee burns during the previous ten years and spent $500,000 settling those claims.

Liebeck spilled the coffee and suffered second- and third-degree burns to her groin, buttocks, and legs. She was hospitalized for eight days while undergoing extensive skin grafting. Her medical bills were about $13,000 and her lost income was $5,000. She offered to settle the case for approximately $20,000. McDonald's offered her $800 to settle the case.

At trial, the evidence showed that McDonald's required its franchises to serve coffee at 180–192 degrees—its own employee testified at trial that this was about 50 degrees hotter than what was safe. The jury calculated her compensatory damages to be $200,000, but reduced that by 20% because of Liebeck's comparative negligence for causing the spill. The jury also awarded $2.7 million in punitive damages—equaling two days' worth of coffee revenue—because McDonald's was reckless in selling a product that it knew posed an unreasonable risk of harm. The Judge reduced the punitive damage award to $600,000. Both sides appealed, but the parties reached a confidential settlement prior to an appellate ruling.

Questions

1. What were the relevant facts of this case?
2. What negligence standards from the chapter reading did the court apply?
3. What types of damages were awarded to the plaintiff?
4. Was the $2.7 million in punitive damages excessive? How might the jury have justified awarding this amount of punitive damages?

Attorney's Fees and Court Costs

In some jurisdictions and in specific cases, a successful plaintiff can collect additional damages for attorney's fees. In some situations, a successful defendant can collect legal fees for the expense of defending against a meritless action.

Sometimes statutes provide for additional money awards in specific situations. For example, in some states there are **liquidated damages**, which are damages required by statute.

For example, liquidated damages might be awarded when an employer intentionally refuses to pay an employee's wages. Liquidated damages are a specific amount or multiple of money damages. As an example, three times the amount of the unpaid wages or $50 for each day that the payment was late.

In addition, in some situations, if a defendant made an offer to settle and the amount is more than what is actually awarded by the court, the plaintiff might be forced to pay certain court costs or the interest on the larger settlement amount.

Discussion Questions

1. What is a tort and who is a tortfeasor?
2. How is the evidentiary standard of "by a preponderance of the evidence" different from "beyond a reasonable doubt"?
3. What are the major sources or origins of tort law in the United States?
4. What are the requirements needed to prove a case of negligence?
5. In what situations does a defendant owe a duty of care to those around him?
6. How does a landlord or a business owner owe a heightened duty of care?
7. What is an attractive nuisance?
8. Who is the reasonable person and what is the relevance of the reasonable person in the context of negligence?
9. How is factual causation different from legal causation, which is also known as proximate causation?
10. What is negligence per se and how is it different from res ipsa loquitur?
11. What is contributory negligence and how is it different from comparative negligence?
12. What is an intervening cause and how is it different from assumption of risk?
13. What is a malpractice claim and is it different from an errors and omissions claim?
14. What is a dram shop act?
15. When might a court impose strict liability?
16. What are the factors of battery and how do they differ from the elements needed to prove a case of assault?
17. What are defenses to the torts of battery and false imprisonment?
18. What forms of defamation exist and what privileges exist in regards to potentially defamatory statements?
19. What is the tort of appropriation and how is it different from the tort of invasion of privacy?
20. What is the tort of intentional infliction of emotional distress?
21. What constitutes trespass to real property and what defenses might a defendant raise in regards to a claim of trespass to real property?
22. What is conversion and what is trespass to personal property and how are they different?
23. What are the required factors for proving fraud, also known as intentional misrepresentation?
24. What are the factors necessary to prove a case of interference with a contractual relationship and how is this tort different from tortious interference with a business advantage?

25. What is slander of property and is it different from slander of title?
26. What are compensatory damages and how are they calculated?
27. How are special damages different from general damages?

Critical-Thinking Questions

28. Why is the standard of proof in a criminal case (beyond a reasonable doubt) higher than the standard of proof in a civil case (by a preponderance of the evidence)?
29. Why doesn't the US require one citizen to come to the aid of another citizen?
30. Assume Theodore is upset about a recent court ruling expanding the definition of defamation. Why would Theodore justify his stance based upon the first amendment freedom of speech?
31. Is it correct to say "cyber torts are not new torts"?
32. What are punitive damages and how should a jury determine the proper amount of punitive damages to award in a court case?

Essay Questions

1. Rod owns an auto parts store. Naomi is shopping in the store when she slips on some spilled oil. The oil had been spilled by an employee stocking shelves. What are the four factors Naomi needs to prove a case of negligence? What factors will determine whether or not she is successful?
2. Ruth owns a large gravel and sand pit. Each night she puts a chain across the driveway to the pit. Layne and his friends drive their motorized dirt bikes through the ditch of the sandpit at night. They ride their bikes up and down the sand and gravel piles. One night Layne is hurt after falling in a sinkhole in one of the gravel pits. Could Layne prevail in a case of negligence against Ruth? Discuss any factors that would be relevant to the court's decision.
3. Quinton owns a flower shop. One night he is driving his delivery van when he sees some females walking down the street. Quinton honks his horn and waves at the females in an attempt to get their attention. Unfortunately, he does not see a car parked illegally on the side of the road with a flat tire. Quinton collides with the parked car owned by Susan. Is Quinton liable for negligence? Discuss fully the concepts that may prove his negligence as well as any defenses he might raise against the owner of the car.
4. Nicholas visits a hospital and learns he needs an emergency surgery on his heart. After the surgery, his heart is fine but he has trouble with dizziness. The doctor claims the surgery went as planned. What special negligence theory may help Nicholas prove negligence on the part of the doctor?
5. Rufus is playing soccer with his friends after school. Rufus pushes Samantha while chasing the soccer ball. Samantha falls and sprains her wrist. Rufus also intentionally kicks Bethany while she is lying on the ground after a play. Alex yells at Rufus to get himself under control and Rufus responds by trying to punch Alex with a closed fist.

Who can and who cannot bring a successful lawsuit against Rufus for battery? How about assault?

6. Jonathan works as a bartender. One night a disgruntled patron named Jimmy starts arguing with Jonathan. Jonathan refuses to serve any more alcohol to Jimmy. Jimmy becomes angry and Jonathan tries to physically remove Jimmy from the bar. A struggle ensues and Jonathan ends up pushing Jimmy into a storage closet. He locks the door and calls the police. What torts may Jimmy allege against Jonathan?

7. Phillip was recently let go from his job at Large Corporate Place. He was accused by his former boss of embezzling assets from the company. In particular, his boss was angry about Phillip taking printer paper home to use for personal purposes. Phillip is angry and tells his boss that he thinks he is an ineffective manager. In retaliation against Phillip, his boss sends out a company-wide email telling everyone Phillip is a thief. Could Phillip prevail in a defamation suit against his former employer? Why or why not?

8. Tom just read a news article about a local politician Jodi who proposed legislation requiring all businesses pay their workers a minimum hourly wage of $20. Tom believes this will put him out of business. He writes an editorial about Jodi, claiming Jodi is a shady politician who committed improprieties in business before entering politics. Assuming these allegations are not true, can Jodi recover damages in a lawsuit for libel against Tom? What if Jodi is not a public figure? Discuss fully.

9. Joseph recently parked his delivery truck on the property of a business located right next to his. Joseph has done this in the past many times. However, today the owner of the business next door becomes very angry with Joseph. Is Joseph guilty of trespass? What defenses might he raise? How would the other business owner prove damages?

10. Tim has an idea for a new web program that will affix itself to the computers of users who visit the homepage of a search engine. The web program will then track the users' use of the Internet. Tim plans to sell the data to online advertisers. What torts might have Tim committed if he uses his new software program?

11. Erika is let go from her job. On the way out of the building she takes her boss's cell phone and throws out his eighth-story window. She then proceeds to tell everyone in the office that the company they work for sells stolen goods. Some of the company's best customers are in the building that day to sign contracts. They hear what Erika has to say. What torts may have Erika committed?

12. Ellen has recently been subject to a cyber attack at her business. A file with list of her best customers was stolen by a computer hacker Norman. Tricia, a competitor of Ellen, buys the list online and then uses it to sign new contracts with customers of Ellen. She induces them to break their contract with Ellen by offering them steep discounts. What torts might Ellen allege against Tricia and Norman?

CHAPTER FIVE

CRIMINAL LAW

By Michael Thieme

Mr. Glass, the president and chief executive officer of a small bank, began approving loans to personal friends, including Mr. Riggan. After some time, he began creating fictitious loans for multiple bank customers, again including Mr. Riggan, depositing the proceeds of those loans into his personal account or into his wife's account. In a matter of six months, Mr. Glass increased Mr. Riggan's loan by approximately $130,000 and kept the money for himself. The chief financial officer discovered that the president was transferring funds between client accounts and his personal accounts. Initially the CFO did not report the improper commingling of funds because he was hesitant to accuse the bank president; however, when the vice president of loans and the chief teller also became suspicious, Mr. Glass was confronted and he confessed.

Edward comes home early from class one day to find his wallet missing from his room. He knows his roommate's cousin Ricky was hanging out in the apartment the previous night. Edward becomes suspicious that Ricky has taken his wallet. He starts to wonder whether he can sue Ricky for committing a crime. He also starts to worry about the fact Ricky now might have access to his checking account. Edwards wonders if he should call his bank, the police, or both.

Chapter Objectives

1. Distinguish between criminal proceedings and civil proceedings.
2. Understand the significance of mens rea and actus reus.
3. Identify key elements needed to prove a specific crime has occurred.
4. Identify key defenses raised by defendants in a criminal trial.
5. Understand key evidentiary rules followed by courts.

The Differences Between Civil and Criminal Law

- General deterrence
- Specific deterrence
- Rehabilitation

Sanctions and Goals

Figure 5.1 Prison is a well-known sanction for committing a crime

One key difference between civil and criminal law is the sanctions imposed upon the guilty party. In civil law, the goal largely is to make the injured party "whole," at least to the extent possible. This is done either by providing the injured party with financial restitution or by the court ordering the offending party to act (or to stop acting) in a particular way that is of benefit to the injured party. The plaintiff in a civil case is often a citizen enforcing their rights against another citizen, although the government does have standing to sue in certain civil matters.

In criminal law, however, society is the primary victim of the crime. Therefore, the goals of the sanctions under criminal law are somewhat different from the goals of the sanctions under civil law. Criminal cases are prosecuted by the government on behalf of all of society rather than on behalf of just one or more individual victims. In a criminal trial, when an accused is found guilty, usually the punishment is not financial restitution, but jail time.

Criminal law attempts to deter the criminal act from happening in the first place. By establishing a criminal law and the punishment for breaking the law, society is sending a message to everyone that there are severe consequences for breaking that part of the social contract. When someone commits a crime, society has an interest in punishing the lawbreaker such that the rest of society sees the harsh consequences and is deterred from breaking the law themselves; this is referred to as **general deterrence**. But punishment of a crime can also serve as a specific deterrence for the individual lawbreaker. **Specific deterrence** is a goal of a specific conviction and sentence to dissuade the offender from committing crimes in the future. Once the punishment has been served, the individual is likely to remember the consequences and would be deterred from engaging similar misconduct again.

Unlike civil law, criminal sanctions, such as jail and prison sentences, also serve the important role of removing a dangerous element from society. By locking up those members of society who refuse to comply with the terms of the social contract, incapacitation protects society and gives law-abiding members of the social contract the peace and security they desire.

Fortunately, however, society does not usually lock people up and throw away the key. The US criminal Justice system also has the goal of rehabilitation. **Rehabilitation** is the process of seeking to improve the criminal's character and outlook so he or she can function in society without committing other crimes.

It is society's hope that punishment will help those who commit criminal acts see the value of abiding by the rules and will choose to obey the law in the future, not because they fear another punishment (deterrence) but because they understand the value of the laws in moving society away from lawlessness and toward a state of security and safety.

Burden of Proof

Because the consequences for criminal convictions are potentially far greater than the civil court counterparts are, there are significant additional protections to help prevent an unjust result. Many of these protections are guaranteed by the United States Constitution, some of which will be discussed in greater detail later in this chapter.

One of those protections is the burden of proof required in civil cases. As discussed in previous chapters, civil cases require only a preponderance of the evidence in deciding the case. **Preponderance of the evidence** means the trier of facts, judge or jury, finds it is more likely than not that the defendant is liable.

In criminal cases, the fact finder, either the judge or jury, must find beyond a reasonable doubt that the accused party committed the crime. **Beyond a reasonable doubt** means the trier of fact cannot have any reasonable doubt the defendant is guilty. This is a much higher burden and much more difficult for the government to prove than a preponderance of the evidence.

Civil Liability for Criminal Acts

Just because someone is found guilty of breaking a criminal statute, this does not mean that he cannot also be subject to civil liability for his actions. For example, if Bill kills Bob in a fight, he may very well be prosecuted in a criminal court for some form of homicide. Bob's widow, Mary, might also sue Bill in a civil suit for causing the wrongful death of her husband. Because the burden of proof is different for civil and criminal cases, Mary might be able to show a jury that Bill was responsible for the death by a preponderance of the evidence, and therefore get financial damages awarded in order to make her "whole" (i.e., replace the lost income she will no longer receive from her deceased husband) even if Bill is acquitted in the criminal case because the government did not prove beyond a reasonable doubt that he committed the crime.

In November of 1994 the high-profile murder trial of former NFL football star O.J. "The Juice" Simpson began. Simpson was accused of murdering his ex-wife, Nicole Brown Simpson, and the man she was romantically involved with, Ronald Goldman. After an eight-month trial, Simpson was acquitted of the crime. Despite the acquittal, the families of Nicole Brown and Ronald Goldman sued O. J. Simpson in civil court, where the jury found by a preponderance of the evidence that Simpson was responsible for causing the deaths and awarded civil damages of approximately 40 million dollars.

- Preponderance of the evidence
- Beyond a reasonable doubt

Criminal Liability

- Actus Reus
- Mens Rea

Most of the criminal law in the US is found in criminal statutes passed by state legislatures, although some criminal statutes have been passed by the US Congress. However, most of the principles in state and federal criminal law find their roots in the common law.

In the vast majority of criminal statutes, as well as the common law, there must be both a criminal act and a criminal mindset or intent. The criminal act, often called the **Actus Reus** or guilty act, is the act, or in some cases omission, that society has deemed unlawful. Society does not punish mere thoughts. In order to be convicted of a crime, there must be some sort of action. For example, if Bob is angry at Bill, he might imagine himself walking over and punching Bill in the face. Bob could not be prosecuted for that thought alone. However, if he acted on that thought and walked over and punched Bill, he could be prosecuted for the act of assault and battery.

Most statutes require a certain culpable (blameworthy) mental state in addition to the actus reus. The legal term for a guilty mind is **Mens Rea**. Returning to the previous example, if Bob is angry with Bill and intends to punch him in the face in order to hurt him, then Bob would have the necessary mental state to be convicted of the assault. However, let's suppose that Bob and Bill were walking down an icy sidewalk when Bob slipped. In his attempt to break his fall, Bob reached out and hit Bill in the face. In this example, Bob committed the same act (hitting Bill in the face) but he did not have any blameworthy intent, so he would not be prosecuted for assaulting Bill. Mens rea can be broken down into two categories: specific intent and general intent. If an individual has specific intent, he or she acts with the belief and desire to accomplish that intent. However, sometimes a person may act out of carelessness or neglect and act in such a way as to cause harm to society; this is referred to as general intent. These people can still be held criminally liable for their actions, though typically the punishment will not be as severe.

The Model Penal Code is a model set of criminal statutes that many states have adopted, to varying degrees, into their criminal statute. The Model Penal Code provides several levels of mental intent: **purpose**, **knowledge**, **recklessness**, and **negligence**. *Purpose* requires the defendant act with the purpose of committing the prohibited outcome. For example, Tammie is mad at her ex-boyfriend Javier, so she takes a gun and points it at Javier with the intent to kill him by shooting him. If the crime of first-degree murder in Tammie's state requires a defendant act with purpose, Tammie has acted with purpose and could be found guilty of first-degree murder.

Knowledge requires the defendant know the prohibited outcome may happen but not necessarily commit the act with the purpose that it happen. For example, Tammie shoots Javier in the chest, knowing it will kill him but not acting with the intent of purpose. Knowledge is a lesser culpable or guilty intent than purpose. It could be that Tammie's state requires a showing of knowledge as the mental intent for second-degree murder.

Recklessness requires a defendant knew or should have known the prohibited outcome would occur. For example, assume Tammie shoots into a crowd where Javier is talking to Felicity. Felicity is killed by the bullet. Tammie knew there was a risk that someone would be killed, but disregarded the risk. It could be that Tammie's state requires a showing of recklessness for third-degree murder. Recklessness is an easier burden of proof for a prosecutor to meet than purpose or knowledge. Therefore, crimes involving a state of mind such as recklessness often have a shorter prison sentence than crimes involving purpose or knowledge.

Negligence requires a defendant disregarded a risk the reasonable person would not have disregarded. For example, assume now that Tammie is at a party with Javier. She picks up a gun that she believes to be a toy. She points the gun at Javier and pulls the trigger. Much to her surprise, it is a real gun and Javier is killed. Tammie could be found guilty of a homicide statute but the statute would have to allow for a criminal intent of negligence. For example, negligent homicide is a crime in some states.

Corporate Criminal Liability

The previous discussion focused on what it takes for an individual to commit a crime. The individual must commit a criminal act called actus reus while possessing the criminal mental intent called mens rea. Since a corporation, as a legal entity, does not have a "mind" in the traditional sense, it may seem odd to some that a corporation can possess the requisite mental intent, but it can. Corporations can be held criminally liable for the actions of its officers and employees under certain circumstances. If the employee is acting within the scope of his actual or apparent authority when he committed a criminal act and that the corporation benefited as a result of the criminal act, then criminal liability usually attaches. When criminal liability attaches, the mens rea of the individual is imputed to the corporation as a whole.

An employee acts with actual authority when he or she performs some act with the direct knowledge and

Figure 5.2 Corporations can be charged with crimes too

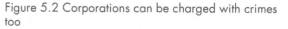

permission of the corporation; however, even if the corporation does not directly endorse the criminal act, the employee may be acting with apparent authority. A person acts with apparent authority if a reasonable person would have believed that the employee was authorized by the company to act in a certain manner because of representations made by the corporation to a third person.

Not only does the employee have to act within the scope of authority, but his or her intent must be to the benefit of the company. It does not matter if the company actually receives the benefit; merely that the employee was acting with the mental intent to benefit the company when he or she broke the law. It also does not matter if benefit the company is the sole or primary reason the employee broke the law.

Imagine Bob worked for a company and engaged in activities that earned both Bob and the company illegal gains. Even though Bob's primary goal was to line his own pockets, he also realized that his actions would and intended for his actions to benefit the company. This would satisfy the mens rea requirement in order to hold the company criminally liable. The act of holding a company or employer liable for an employee's actions is referred to as vicarious liability.

State v. Casey's General Stores, Inc.
587 N.W.2d 599, Iowa (1998)

Jurisdictions may interpret vicarious liability differently. Generally vicarious liability is holding one person or corporation liable, though without personal fault, for the bad or criminal conduct of someone else.

In 1996 a cashier employed at a local general store, in violation of state law, sold an alcoholic beverage to an underage customer without requiring identification. The state prosecuted the corporation for the criminal offense and secured a conviction. On appeal the Supreme Court of Iowa held that vicarious criminal liability extends to a corporation only when the misconduct of the employee violates a specific duty imposed specifically on the corporation by law or when the criminal act was done when the employee was acting within the scope of their authority or was acting for the benefit of the corporation and when the conducted was "authorized, requested, or tolerated" by the corporation's leadership.

The Supreme Court reversed the convictions because there was no evidence that the illegal sales were authorized, requested, or tolerated by the corporation and the criminal statute generally prohibited certain conduct and did not impose a specific duty to corporations.

Questions

1. What was the crime committed in this case?
2. What is vicariously liability?
3. Why was only the employee was found liable for the crime in question?
4. What change in facts might have made the employer liable?

Liability of Corporate Officers and Directors

While the corporation itself may be held criminally responsible, individual corporate leaders may also be subject to criminal prosecution for the crimes committed by employees. If an officer or director of a company knows about a crime being committed by an employee of the company for the benefit of the company, and either approves of the action or turns a blind eye and does nothing to stop it, that official can be held criminally liable.

Furthermore, under the "responsible corporate officer" doctrine, an officer or director can be held criminally responsible even for crimes he or she didn't know about, or approve of, if they failed to meet their responsibility as corporate leaders to ensure compliance with the law.

United States v. Park
421 US 658 (1975)

• Merger doctrine

In 1974, John Park, the president of a national food store chain, was charged and convicted of violating the Federal Food, Drug and Cosmetic Act of 1938 for allowing food stored in warehouses that had become contaminated by rodents to be shipped in interstate commerce.

Mr. Park stated that he had delegated the responsibility for sanitation to "dependable subordinates" and that he had no personal involvement in violating the criminal statute. The trial court instructed the jury that they could find Mr. Park criminally liable if they found that he held a position of authority in the company who had a "responsible relation to the situation, even though he may not have participated personally."

The Court of Appeals reversed the conviction and the case was ultimately appealed to the Supreme Court to decide whether a manager of a corporation, as well as the corporation itself, could be prosecuted.

The Supreme Court noted that the "public interest in the purity of its food is so great as to warrant the imposition of the highest standard of care on distributors." The court held that Mr. Park, by virtue of his position of authority, had a responsibility to ensure the sanitary condition of the food he stored and shipped. The Court upheld the conviction.

Questions

1. Which crime was Mr. Park alleged to have committed?
2. What did he do to contaminate the grocery food his store sold?
3. Whom did Mr. Park blame for the contaminated food?
4. Whom did the Supreme Court blame for the contaminated food?

Lesser Included Offenses

Criminal statutes often distinguish between different degrees of seriousness of a crime. For example, first-degree murder may be the most severe type of homicide under a state's law. The elements of that offense might require proof that the accused planned the murder in advance. It might also require the unjustified killing of another, which is also a required element of second-degree murder. If the government was unable to prove that the accused planned the murder (premeditated) as required for a showing of first-degree murder, but was able to establish that the accused killed another person without justification, the accused may be found guilty of second-degree murder. Second-degree murder is a lesser included offense of first-degree murder because in this example, first-degree murder had the same elements of second-degree murder. The **merger doctrine** holds a criminal defendant cannot be convicted of lesser included offenses and the greater offense. For example, the criminal defendant who is guilty of second-degree murder cannot also be convicted for battery, as battery would be a lesser included offense of second-degree murder.

Types of Crime

There are many different types of crime. Typically the ones depicted on TV crime shows are violent crimes. Homicides (another word for murder) and assaults are examples of this type of crime.

There are also **property crimes**, which include burglary, larceny, arson, or forgery, and include a crime being committed against the property of another.

Public-order crimes, such as being intoxicated in public or prostitution, are generally focused on prohibiting behavior that reflects negatively on society even though there may not be a traditional "victim" of the crime.

Cybercrimes involve the use of a computer or computer-related technology. Examples are cyber hacking and phishing.

Crimes can also be categorized depending upon the punishment the crime carries. When categorizing crimes by punishment, crimes are classified into two main categories: felonies and misdemeanors. Felonies are the more serious of the two and usually carry much more severe punishments. Although definitions vary from jurisdiction to jurisdiction, generally **misdemeanor** crimes are those crimes where the maximum punishment is a year in jail or less. A **felony** is then a serious crime, punishable by imprisonment for more than one year or by death.

Embezzlement

Embezzlement is really a type of theft. However, unlike most thefts, the embezzler does not steal the property nor does he gain it through deception or trickery. Rather, **embezzlement** occurs when a fiduciary is lawfully entrusted with personal property of another and then fraudulently takes or uses that property for his own gain.

Ponzi Schemes

A **Ponzi scheme** is an investment fraud that involves the payment of purported returns to existing investors from funds contributed by new investors. Ponzi scheme organizers often solicit new investors by promising to invest funds in opportunities claimed to have generally high returns and little or no risk. For the scheme to work, the organizer must continue to attract new investors in order to have the money to make existing customers believe they are profiting from a legitimate business. Generally, scheme organizers are personally benefiting from the money invested rather than actually investing that money on behalf of their clients.

If there is not enough new investor money to pay the existing investors the promised return on their investment, then the whole house of cards will collapse. Unfortunately, those who have invested in the scheme could lose their entire investment.

The scheme earned its name after Charles Ponzi scammed thousands of New England investors in the 1920s. Charles Ponzi promised investors a 50% return on investment in just three months. Perhaps the most well-known Ponzi scheme in recent times is that of Bernie Madoff. In the early 1960s Bernie Madoff started his own investment firm, after dropping out of law school, using an initial investment of $5,000 earned during a summer lifeguarding

• Theft of trade
secrets

job. Through family contacts and word of mouth, the investment firm gathered an impressive list of famous investors and the firm garnered a reputation of consistently producing above-average returns on investments. In fact, routine returns of 10% or higher attracted many investors so that by the 1980s, the firm's trading activities constituted up to 5% of the trades made on the New York Stock Exchange.

In 2008, after confessing his actions to his sons, Madoff admitted to the Securities Exchange Commission (SEC) that the firm was actually an elaborate Ponzi scheme that had lost an estimated $50 billion of investors' money. At age 71, Bernie Madoff was sentenced to 150 years in prison. He initially claimed he was the only one who knew of his scheme.

Figure 5.3 Mug shot of Charles Ponzi

Questions

1. What is a Ponzi scheme and how does it benefit those who invest early?
2. Who was Bernie Madoff and how did his Ponzi scheme get started?
3. Do you think Bernie Madoff could have engaged in this fraud by himself?

Theft of Trade Secrets

The **theft of trade secrets** involves the intentional taking, copying, or using another's trade secrets with the knowledge the owner of the trade secret will be injured by such action. Businesses are always looking for ways to gain a competitive advantage over their competition, but there are limits to what they can do legally. In 2006 three employees of Coca-Cola stole confidential documents and samples of products and sent a letter to Pepsi, offering the stolen information for a price. If Pepsi had agreed to pay for this information that it knew had been illegally obtained, it would likely have been held criminally liable. To its credit, Pepsi instead notified Coca-Cola and law enforcement agencies of the scheme and the three employees found themselves facing federal criminal charges.

Fraud

Generally, a society will not make telling a lie a crime. However, there are some instances where giving false information may be criminal. For example, telling a lie to the judge while testifying in court is called perjury and it is a crime. **Perjury** is the intentional telling of an untruth while under oath to tell the truth. Likewise, in many financial transactions, the law imposes a duty to tell the truth and if someone fails to do so, they may be guilty of fraud.

Fraud under the common law was the knowing misrepresentation of the truth or concealment of a material fact to induce another to act to his or her detriment. There are many different types of fraud. For example, mail fraud occurs when someone uses the US Postal Service to make a false representation to obtain an economic advantage. Similarly, wire fraud occurs when the misrepresentation occurs by phone or other means of electronic communication.

In 2013 the Department of Justice indicted Teresa Giudice and Giuseppe Giudice, stars of the reality TV show *The Real Housewives of New Jersey*, with conspiracy to commit mail and wire fraud, among other crimes. The indictment alleged that the couple lied to lenders about their income and hid assets during a bankruptcy. To the reality stars the prosecuting attorney said, "Everyone has an obligation to tell the truth when dealing with the courts, paying their taxes, and applying for loans or mortgages. That's reality."

Bankruptcy Fraud

There is a subset of fraud dealing with bankruptcy cases. **Bankruptcy fraud** occurs when a person knowingly and fraudulently conceals assets or destroys, falsifies, or withholds documents in violation of the law governing a bankruptcy proceeding. In 2010, Grammy Award winner Toni Braxton filed for bankruptcy with an estimated $50 million in debt. Allegations were levied against the pop singer when she transferred over $53,000 to her estranged husband, allegedly in order to avoid paying the money to her creditors.

Bribery

In addition the theft and deceit, individuals and businesses can also engage in criminal bribery. **Bribery** is offering, giving, receiving, or requesting something of value with the intent to unlawfully influence a person or entity in a position of trust. **Bribery of a public official** is a federal crime designed to ensure that government officials act with the interest of the constituents in mind instead of their own financial interests.

In 2009, JPMorgan, the well-known securities company, forfeited hundreds of millions of dollars as part of a settlement agreement with the SEC because it had made payments to an Alabama county commissioner, Larry Langford and his friends in exchange for being awarded lucrative contracts. Langford had become the mayor of Birmingham, Alabama when he was indicted and subsequently convicted of receiving more than $235,000 in bribes.

Securities Fraud and Insider Trading

The Securities Exchange Commission takes fraud very seriously. Its role is to protect investors and maintain fair, orderly, and efficient securities markets. **Rule 10b-5** of the Securities Exchange Act of 1934 makes it illegal to engage in any act, practice, or course of business that would operate as a fraud or deceit upon a person when purchasing or selling securities.

Insider trading falls under this prohibition. Insider trading is sometimes legal, for example, when corporate directors buy and sell stock in their own company, though such actions must be reported to the SEC and placed during certain times of the year specified by the SEC. **Insider trading** becomes illegal, however, when someone buys or sells while possessing nonpublic information. For example, your receiving a nonpublic "tip" from someone inside a corporation that one of its products is going to be recalled and will affect the company's earnings report and then selling your stock before the news is made public is unlawful insider trading.

- Insider trading
- Organized crime

In order to be guilty of insider trading, a person must first have a material fact. That is some fact that would have an impact on the reasonable investor's decision. That material fact must also be nonpublic. Not only is it something the general public does not know, but it must also be something that the public would be unable to learn if they tried. The nonpublic material information must then be used by an insider in an improper way. An insider is anyone who has access to the nonpublic material information and has a duty not to disclose that information before it becomes public. In insider trading cases both the insider and the person who receives the information from the insider can be prosecuted if they use the information to purchase or sell securities.

In 2003 the SEC filed charges against Martha Stewart and her stockbroker, Peter Bacanovic, for insider trading. According to the SEC, Bacanovic gave Stewart a tip that her stock in a pharmaceutical company was in jeopardy because the FDA was about to reject the company's application to produce a new drug. Stewart sold her stock before the news was made public and the stock value crashed. Although Stewart denied the allegations and was never convicted of insider trading, she was convicted of obstructing Justice and lying to the government about the circumstances surrounding the sale of the stock.

Foreign Corrupt Practices Act (FCPA)

The FCPA was passed in 1977 and made it illegal to make payments to foreign government officials in order to gain or retain business opportunities. In 1998 the act was amended to make it a crime for foreign firms to bribe any official within the United States. In 2011, seven Siemens executives were charged with bribing Argentine officials in order to keep a government contract producing national ID cards worth over $1 billion. Since some of the bribe money was paid through accounts at US banks, Siemens' actions fell under the FCPA.

In April 2013, the Parker Drilling Company entered into a three-year deferred prosecution agreement with the Department of Justice after top executives authorized the company to pay $1.25 million to a third-party intermediary, knowing that the funds would be used to bribe Nigerian officials to favorably resolve a customs dispute. In addition to the criminal settlement, the company also had to pay a civil fine to the SEC of almost $12 million and to return more than $3 million of the benefits it received as a result of the bribes.

Another category of crime is called organized crime, which covers a wide range of criminal activities that are coordinated by a central power structure, such as a powerful Mafia crime family. **Organized crime** is defined as widespread criminal activities that are coordinated and controlled through a central syndicate. Businesses can be part of the organized crime, either by being a front for clandestine illegal activity or by laundering illegally obtained money and making it appear that it was earned honestly.

Money laundering is the act of transferring illegally obtained money through legitimate people or accounts so that its original source cannot be traced. With new technology comes new ways to engage in criminal enterprises. In 2013, the United States shut down an online global currency exchange, Liberty Reserve, alleged to have laundered more than $6 billion in ill-gotten gains from a wide variety of criminal enterprises, ranging from child pornography to stolen identities. Founder Arthur Budovsky, who renounced his US citizenship in 2011, was arrested in Spain and is facing multiple counts of money laundering, each carrying a maximum twenty-year prison sentence.

Racketeer Influenced and Corrupt Organizations Act (RICO)

The RICO act was passed in 1970 with a specific goal of targeting the Mafia by enabling prosecutors to charge the "bosses" of a criminal organization with the crimes of their underlings under the theory that all the criminal acts were part of a large "criminal enterprise."

Originally, the RICO act was used to target "illegitimate" enterprises; however, in 1981, the Supreme Court ruled (*US v. Turkette*) that RICO applies to both legitimate and illegitimate enterprises, which means that RICO may now be used against corporations, labor unions, and protesting organizations.

In order to violate the RICO act a person must engage in a "pattern of racketeering activity." The list of racketeering activities is a long one. It includes such crimes as conspiracy, kidnapping, murder, and arson as well as other types of fraud and bribery.

Property Crimes

Figure 5.4 Property Crimes Often Include Forced Entry

Theft crimes include larceny, burglary, and robbery. State law differs in regards to its definition of theft and the degrees of theft the state recognizes. Therefore, the common law definitions for property crimes will be discussed here.

Larceny is the taking and carrying away of another's tangible property with the intent to deprive them of such property. Andrea takes Becca's bag, thinking it is actually hers. Andrea has not committed theft. She did not take the property of another knowingly with the intent to deprive the person of their property. Now consider Rex who takes a six-pack of beer from a gas station when the gas station clerk is not looking. Rex intends to keep the beer and consume it. He has committed larceny.

Under the common law, **burglary** was the breaking and entering into the dwelling house of another at nighttime with the intent to commit a felony. Assume Chris breaks into Loren's house with the intent to steal her purse, which is a felony. If Chris does this at night, he has committed burglary under the common law definition. Chris does not have to be successful in stealing the purse as long as he intends to commit the felony. Some states have removed the requirement the crime be committed at night and have expanded the crime to include buildings other than a dwelling.

Robbery under the common law was the taking by force, intimidation, or threat of violence of a person's tangible personal property with the intent to deprive them of that tangible personal property. The taking must have been from the person or in the person's presence to be considered robbery. An example is Jean who uses a gun to stop Alex while he is driving his car. Jean then approaches the window of the car and tells Alex he has to get out of the car and leave the keys in it or he will be shot. Alex does so and Jean drives off in the car.

Common law **arson** required the malicious burning of the dwelling of another person. If Nathan sets fire to Gregory's barn, Nathan has not committed arson because it was not the dwelling of another. If Nathan sets fire to Gregory's house, Nathan has committed arson. Some states have expanded the definition of arson to include structures other than a dwelling.

Obtaining goods by false pretenses was the act of intentionally misrepresenting a material fact to a person in order to persuade the person to transfer property to the person making the misrepresenta-

Figure 5.5 Arson includes more than just burning a home in most states

tion. For example, Connie dresses up as a doctor and tells Mark who is waiting in a hospital waiting room that Connie is a doctor and needs Mark's social security number and driver's license to check on his medical records. Connie is obtaining goods by false pretenses.

Forgery was the making or altering of a writing with the intent to defraud another. The most common example is signing someone's signature without their permission.

Extortion was the fraudulent use of one's public office to obtain assets from a victim. Today most states have a criminal statute outlawing blackmail, which is the obtaining of assets by threatening harm to a victim or their property. For example, Julie knows Simon has cheated on his wife with a woman named Jezebel. Julie threatens to tell Simon's family what he has done unless Simon gives Julie $12,000.

Receiving stolen goods is the act of receiving property that the defendant knew or should have known was stolen with the intent to deprive the true owner of such property. As an example, Paul is outside his place of employment during break time. A white van pulls into the parking lot. Two men get out and ask Paul if he wants to buy a car stereo for $20. The price is too good to be true. Paul asks where the stereos were gotten. The two men say, "We stole them in another state." Paul buys two stereos. He has committed the crime of receiving stolen goods.

Modern property crimes include credit card fraud, identity theft, and cybercrime.

Credit card fraud is committed when, without authorization, a criminal uses a credit card holder's information to obtain a benefit with such information. For example, Loretta overhears Dan giving his credit card information over the phone to make a purchase. Loretta writes down the information and then uses it to make purchases online.

Identity theft occurs under federal law when a person has been found to "knowingly transfer or use, without lawful authority, a means of identification of another person with the intent to commit, or to aid or abet, any unlawful activity that constitutes a violation of Federal law, or that constitutes a felony under any applicable State or local law" 18 USC. § 1028. For example, Norton is in the US illegally. He steals a driver's license from his neighbor Mark. He uses the driver's license to set up a bank account.

Cybercrime is a category of crimes that include the use of a computer or a computer-related technology. **Cyber hacking** is the unauthorized access of another's computer with the intent to change the settings of the computer or to access information on the other's computer. **Phishing** is the act of accessing another's computer with the intent to use information from that computer to commit a fraud. Under the Computer Fraud and Abuse Act it is also a crime to distribute a virus to another's computer. Because cybercrimes may affect computers in international locations, a criminal may face punishment under the laws of another country as well.

Defenses to Criminal Liability

As previously discussed, a crime requires the actus reus and mens rea. Sometimes the defense will negate one or more of the elements of that offense. If that is the case, then under criminal law, if not every element of an offense is proven, the verdict should be not guilty. Sometimes the element negated may mean the person is still guilty of a crime but perhaps guilty of a less severe crime. For example, getting drunk is not a defense to most crimes; however, a person may be so drunk that they are unable to form the specific mental intent to commit the crime, therefore, the element that someone has a specific intent may be negated and the person may be guilty of a less severe general-intent crime instead. For example Chris is extremely intoxicated at a party he hosted. He shoots Rita with a gun Chris had in his home. Chris might not have had the requisite mental intent for 1st degree murder but he may be guilty of a lesser offense such as negligent homicide.

Even if a person performed the prohibited act, and had the necessary culpable mental state, under some circumstances, society might still not punish them for the crime. Typically this occurs when the individual accused of the crime has a valid justification or a legal excuse. While legal excuses are similar to justifications, they are slightly different. With both types of defense the defendant technically commits a crime (both commits the act and has the necessary intent) but with a justification society generally condones or approves of, whereas with a legal excuse, the conduct is not condoned by society but society determines punishment is less appropriate because of other mitigating circumstances.

Self-defense is a common example of a justification type of defense. Assume that Bob is mad at Bill and wants to punch Bill in the face. Bob approaches Bill and takes a swing at Bill. Unfortunately for Bob, Bill has excellent reflexes and ducks Bob's punch and counters with a punch of his own that lands squarely on Bob's jaw.

Bill engaged in an act that society normally prohibits, in this case punching another person in the face. Moreover, Bill had the specific intent to punch Bob in the face; it wasn't an accident. It appears that Bill has satisfied the elements necessary to commit the crime of assault and battery, yet society would not hold Bob criminally liable under these facts since Bob was acting in self-defense and was therefore justified in striking Bob.

Justifiable Use of Force

A person may be justified in using force against another person; however, there are limits to this rule. While a person can use force to protect himself or others from a real or threatened attack, the force used must be reasonable and not excessive under the circumstances. For example, a person threatened with having their wallet stolen cannot use a gun to kill the would-be thief, unless they reasonably believed that their life was in danger.

At one time, lethal self-defense could be used as a defense only if the victim of an attack had no option to escape the attack. This was referred to as a duty to retreat if possible rather than using force. Today most states allow a victim to use lethal self-defense without retreating if they are attacked in their own home, often referred to as the castle doctrine. Some states have changed the retreat requirement by passing "stand your ground" laws, which allow people to use lethal force to defend themselves, without requiring them to retreat when possible. Of course, as mentioned before, the amount of force used must still be reasonable in response to the threat against them.

Figure 5.6 Self-defense cannot involve unreasonable force

Mistake

An example of a legal excuse type defense is "mistake of fact." There is a well-known legal maxim that says "ignorance of the law is no excuse" and generally that is true. A defendant can usually be held criminally liable even if the defendant was not personally aware that there was a criminal statute prohibiting the act. However, a mistake about the facts may be a defense for some crimes.

For specific-intent crimes an honest mistake may negate one of the elements of the offense. For example if Harrison cuts down a tree on Ford's adjacent property and hauled it off

• Self-defense

for firewood, he may be guilty of the offense of larceny. However, if Harrison was mistaken about the property line and truly believed the tree was on his property, then he may not have the specific intent to steal necessary for the crime of larceny (although he may still owe Ford civil damages for the value of the tree). In most cases, the mistake must be reasonable in order for the mistake to constitute a defense.

Necessity or Duress

Necessity or duress provides another good example to contrast justification and excuse defenses. Sometimes circumstances are such that a person must choose the lesser of two evils. A necessity defense may be available to a person who breaks the law but did so to avoid an even greater harm to society. Typically this type of justification defense arises when a person is acting in response to an emergency (not of his or her own making) and breaks one law in order to save the life or health of another. For example, Herman may break the posted speed limit in order to get his wife to the hospital in time to save her life. Society would approve of Herman's action under these circumstances and determine that Herman was justified in breaking the speed limit and that he should not be guilty of the related crime of speeding.

Duress is a little different from necessity. Unlike necessity, where under the circumstances society approved of the act normally considered unlawful, in a duress situation, society still condemns the act but understands that under the circumstances punishment would be inappropriate or unfair and therefore excuses, rather than justifies, the action. For example, if Horacio was forced to steal something for Matthew, because Matthew is holding Horacio's wife and threatening to harm her if Horacio refuses. Society does not condone the theft, but Horacio may have a duress defense because society understands that the reasonable person would probably act the same way if faced with the same circumstances. In most jurisdictions, to assert a duress defense, the crime committed must be less egregious than the crime threatened.

Insanity

The insanity defense, despite its popularity on TV shows and in movies, is a relatively uncommon and a very difficult defense to establish. This defense is different in another way as well. Instead of negating an element of the offense or providing a justification or excuse, an insanity defense instead results in a special verdict. Instead of being acquitted and going free, an insanity defense, if successful, results in a verdict of "not guilty by reason of insanity" and the accused is then committed to a mental institute. Jurisdictions have differing tests to determine legal insanity. In 1972 the Model Penal Code developed a new rule, stating that a person could use the defense of insanity if the person lacked "substantial capacity either to appreciate the criminality of his conduct or to conform his conduct to the requirements of the law" as a result of a mental disease or defect. Some states follow what is called the *M'Naghten* test. The *M'Naghten* test requires a defendant not know the nature and quality of his act by reason of mental defect. If the defendant did know the nature and quality, he can still claim the defense but he must prove he did not know the act was wrong. Some states have also accepted, either as a separate rule, or as an addition to the *M'Naghten* test what is called the irresistible impulse test (also known as the *Durham rule*). The irresistible impulse test allows insanity as a defense if a party could not resist an irresistible impulse, caused by a mental defect, to commit a crime.

Entrapment

If a law-abiding citizen is somehow persuaded by law enforcement agents to commit a crime that he or she would not have otherwise committed, that citizen might be able to assert a defense of entrapment. However, the entrapment defense is very narrow. The police may engage in conduct that creates opportunities for crimes to be committed. For example, the police often conduct "sting" operations where they provide people the chance to purchase illegal drugs, or engage in other criminal behavior. This is not entrapment because they are not forcing anyone to commit a crime; rather they are providing someone who was already predisposed to commit the crime an opportunity to engage in the crime and then catch them in the act. In practice, the defense of entrapment, like insanity, is very difficult to establish.

Intoxication

A defendant might be able to raise intoxication as a defense. **Involuntary intoxication** is defense against any crime as long as the intoxication rendered the defendant incapacitated. Involuntary intoxication means the defendant did not know they were consuming a substance which would cause them to become intoxicated or the defendant was forced to digest the intoxicating substance.

A defendant who becomes voluntarily intoxicated might be able to use such intoxication to negate the required element of a crime. Stated another way, a defendant who is intoxicated might not be able to form the requisite mental intent required for a crime. **Voluntary intoxication** means the defendant voluntarily consumed an intoxicating substance knowing it would cause impairment. For example, Amy becomes involuntarily intoxicated on her 21st birthday. She then steals a car. There is no doubt Amy has committed a crime, or maybe several crimes. However, Amy might be able to argue her intoxication prevented her from forming the intent to permanently deprive the owner of their car which is a requirement for larceny.

Constitutional Safeguards

The Founding Fathers of our country were concerned about government having too much power, especially as it related to the government's power to prosecute criminal offenses. They had good reason to be concerned, too. Before leaving England and even in the early days of America, the colonists did not enjoy the protections citizens of the US have under the Constitution today. For example, for many years in England the monarch utilized a court called the Star Chamber that provided little, if any, due process protections. Oftentimes the court was held in secret and the accused had little ability to defend against the charges. Additionally, those accused of crimes and brought before this court were required to take

• Exclusionary rule

an oath to answer all questions truthfully. There was no right against self-incrimination. Unfortunately, the court was corrupt and many found themselves in a cruel trilemma with no good options: 1) If they refused to take the required oath, they were imprisoned for contempt; 2) If they took the oath and confessed their crime, they were severely punished; or 3) If they took the oath and plead innocent to the crime, they found themselves locked up for perjury because the court did not believe them.

The drafters of the Bill of Rights ensured that no such court could exist in America. The fifth amendment ensures that the government cannot take any criminal action that would deprive a person of life, liberty, or property without, at a minimum, notice of the charge and a hearing in which to present a defense.

That same amendment also gives every person the right to remain silent and prohibits the government from compelling a person to be a witness against him- or herself.

The sixth amendment also provides important protections to those facing criminal prosecutions. The sixth amendment gives everyone the right to an attorney to represent them at trial, (a right that the Supreme Court has expanded to include the right to an attorney at preliminary proceedings even before trial), the right to have favorable witnesses testify on your behalf, and the right to confront all the witnesses the government brings against you.

If evidence is obtained in violation of the fourth, fifth, or sixth amendments, the courts may apply the exclusionary rule. The **exclusionary rule** excludes any evidence which was obtained in violation of a defendant's fourth, fifth, or sixth amendment rights. The rule also extends to evidence obtained at a later time if it is "fruit of the poisonous tree." This means if the police were to find evidence by searching a defendant's home in violation of the fourth amendment and that evidence led the police to find a murder weapon, the murder weapon would be excluded as fruit of the poisonous tree.

The eighth amendment limits the government's ability to punish you once you have been convicted. Punishments may not be cruel or unusual and fines may not be excessive.

All of these protections were enshrined in our Constitution to prevent government overreaching and to ensure that we never lose too much freedom in exchange for the security we seek.

Amendment	Protection/Right
Fourth	Protection against unreasonable search and seizure Requires probable cause warrants
Fifth	Protection from double jeopardy Right against self-incrimination Right of due process
Sixth	Right to a speedy/public trial Right to an impartial jury Right to be informed of the charges against you Right to confront all witnesses Right to have production of favorable witnesses Right to an attorney
Eighth	Protection against excessive bail Protection against excessive fines Protection against cruel and unusual punishments
Fourteenth	Extended due process and most other constitutional protections/rights to the state level

Search and Seizure

The fourth amendment to the Constitution also provides an important check on government power. It prohibits unreasonable searches and seizures and requires the government to get a warrant based on probable cause before engaging in a search. However, over the years the courts have created numerous exceptions to the warrant requirement whenever the courts have determined that the benefit of letting a warrantless search occur outweighs the danger that the government may abuse its power. These exceptions allow police to search without a warrant. For example, police can frisk a person without a warrant in order to feel for a weapon if they have a reasonable belief that a person is armed and dangerous. The courts have determined that the safety of the police officer is important enough to allow a limited search without a warrant in these cases. Courts created other exceptions to allow for searches when there was a concern that evidence would be lost in the time it took for police to get a warrant. For example, if a police knocked on a door and heard someone inside yell, "The cops are here! Flush the drugs!" the police would be able to enter the home and seize the drugs without a warrant under the "exigent circumstance" exception. Other exceptions include seizing items in plain view from a lawful vantage point and searching automobiles when the police have probable cause that evidence of a crime will be found.

Generally, fourth amendment protections apply to businesses as well as individuals, but a business' expectation of privacy is generally considered less than the privacy interest of an individual. Especially in highly regulated industries, the government does not need a warrant to conduct regular administrative searches. The rationale is that the public interest in regulating the business conduct outweighs the privacy interest. For example, the public interest in a safe food supply allows government agencies to inspect restaurants and other food storage or distribution companies. Likewise, the public interest in safety allows the government to conduct searches at airport screening lines without need for a warrant.

Criminal Procedure

Unlike civil lawsuits, the government is a party to every criminal trial. Often the process starts with an investigation by law enforcement agencies. Once law enforcement believes they have enough evidence that a crime has been committed, the subject of the investigation may be arrested. In order to arrest a person, however, there generally must be an arrest warrant supported by probable cause and issued by a judge.

Once in custody, the Supreme Court has ruled that a person may not be questioned unless he or she is first advised of certain rights. You may be familiar with these rights, called Miranda Rights, from the frequent depiction of them on TV crime shows.

Miranda v. Arizona

384 US 436 (1966)

The Supreme Court examined the facts resulting from a case in which police questioned Ernesto Miranda on suspicion of kidnapping and rape. After two hours of interrogation, Miranda provided police with a written and oral confession. Miranda did not speak English well and was not well educated. His confession was used against him in court and he was convicted.

On appeal, he objected to the use of his confession on the grounds that he would not have spoken to the police if he'd known he had the right to remain silent. The Supreme Court held that the danger of police coercing a confession required additional procedural safeguards. The Court held that suspects in custody must be advised of their constitutional right to remain silent and of the consequences of making a statement.

The court also extended the sixth amendment right to counsel to apply in custodial interrogations, thereby requiring a suspect be advised that he has a right to an attorney and furthermore that one will be provided at no charge if the person is unable to pay for an attorney. Miranda's conviction was overturned.

In an ironic twist of fate, Ernesto Miranda was later stabbed to death outside a bar. The suspected assailant was read his Miranda rights and declined to make a statement.

Questions

1. Who was Ernesto Miranda?
2. What right did the Supreme Court believe he should have been informed of before questioning?
3. If Ernesto Miranda did not speak English, should his rights have been read to him in his native language?

"You have the right to remain silent. Anything you say can and will be used against you in a court of law. You have the right to an attorney. If you cannot afford an attorney, one will be provided for you. Do you understand the rights I have just read to you? With these rights in mind, do you wish to speak to me?"

Criminal Proceedings

After a person has been arrested, they are processed at the law enforcement agency, in a process known as "booking." Fingerprints are taken and other administrative information is completed. The police work with the prosecuting office to draft the charge and then the suspect makes a first appearance before a judge (usually a magistrate judge) where he is advised of the preliminary charge(s) against him. The judge will also appoint a lawyer to represent the suspect in future proceedings and will set bail if appropriate. For certain minor offenses, such as a traffic violation, the suspect may be able to plead guilty to the magistrate and receive his punishment right away.

For more serious offenses, the prosecutor reviews the case and makes a decision about whether to charge the defendant with a crime. Some factors the prosecutor considers are the severity of the crime, the likelihood that is will be repeated if no action is taken, the amount of evidence available to prove the case beyond a reasonable doubt, and the amount of resources available to prosecute the case. Often prosecutors must prioritize cases based on importance because they lack the resources to take every case to court.

For misdemeanor cases, the prosecutor can take a formal charge, called an information, to the magistrate judge who determines if there is enough probable cause to proceed. An **information** is a formal criminal charge made by a prosecutor without a grand-jury indictment.

In federal courts, if the crime is a felony, the accused has a constitutional right to a **grand jury**. This means the prosecutor must present evidence to a panel of citizens and they decide if there is enough evidence to proceed. If the grand jury believes there is enough evidence that a crime was committed by the accused, then they issue an indictment, which is the formal document charging the accused with a crime. An indictment is a formal written accusation of a crime, made by a grand jury, and presented to a court for prosecution against the accused person.

- Information
- Grand jury
- Arraignment
- Immunity
- Bench trial

Arraignment

With an indictment or information in hand, the next step in the process is to arraign the accused. An **arraignment** is the initial step in a criminal prosecution, whereby the defendant is brought to court to hear the formal charges and enter a plea.

Pleas

The accused can enter a plea of not guilty, guilty or, in some cases, nolo contendere. If the accused enters a not-guilty plea, then the case is docketed for trial. If the plea is "guilty" or "nolo contendere," then the judge will schedule the case for sentencing. A plea of nolo contendere is a plea in which the defendant does not admit guilt but does not contest the charges; Latin for "I do not wish to contend."

Often the government and the accused will enter into negotiations called "plea bargaining." As part of a plea bargain, the accused will agree to plead guilty in exchange for some benefit or limitation on the sentence. This is a benefit to the government because it ensures a conviction while freeing up limited resources for other cases and a benefit to the accused because it limits the risk of a severe punishment.

As part of a plea agreement, the accused may also ask for **immunity**, or a promise from the government not to prosecute some or all of the crimes charged, in exchange for the accused's willingness and cooperation in catching and testifying against others engaged in even more serious crimes.

Trial Process

If the crime is a felony or a misdemeanor with a potential punishment of more than six months in jail, the accused has the right to a jury trial, though the accused can waive this right and have the case decided by a judge. If the accused wants to have the judge decide the case, it is called a **bench trial**.

Regardless of whether the case is decided by a judge or jury, the burden to prove every element of the charged offense is on the government. The accused does not have to present any defense, though he may choose to do so if there is a defense available to him.

If it is a jury trial, the panel can be questioned to ensure that they are impartial and can give the accused a fair hearing. The accused also gets to see all of the evidence against him through a process called discovery, as well as the opportunity to question all the government witnesses.

At the conclusion of the trial, the jury (or judge in a bench trial) will consider all of the evidence and render a verdict. If the verdict is not guilty, then the accused is free to leave. The Constitution also prevents that person from ever being prosecuted for that same offense, even if the government later uncovers additional evidence that might convince a jury beyond a reasonable doubt. If, however, the verdict is guilty, then the judge will schedule a sentencing hearing where the punishment will be given. Even after the punishment has been given, the accused has a right to appeal either the finding of guilt or the severity of the punishment to a higher court.

Discussion Questions

1. What are some key differences between civil law and criminal law?
2. What is general deterrence and how is it different from specific deterrence?
3. What does "by a preponderance of the evidence" mean and how is it different from "beyond a reasonable doubt"?
4. What are the two key components needed to prove a defendant is guilty of a crime?
5. What are the levels of intent used to prove mens rea under the Model Penal Code?
6. Can a corporation be liable for criminal activity?
7. How might a corporate officer be liable for a crime committed by those who report to her?
8. What does the term "lesser included offense" mean and how is it related to the merger doctrine?
9. How is a misdemeanor different from a felony?
10. What elements need to be proven to find a defendant guilty of embezzlement?
11. Besides insider trading, what types of fraud are discussed in the chapter and what elements are needed to prove each type of fraud?
12. What is needed for the government to prove a case of illegal insider trading?
13. What is the definition of bribery and is it illegal under the Foreign Corrupt Practices Act?
14. What is the purpose of the RICO statute?
15. How are the elements needed to prove larceny, burglary, and robbery different?
16. What is the definition of arson?
17. How are the crimes of obtaining goods by false pretenses different from forgery and receiving stolen goods?
18. What are examples of modern property crimes, as well as the elements needed to prove the crimes occurred?

19. When is a person allowed to claim self-defense as a justification for or defense to a criminal activity?
20. When can a mistake act as a defense against criminal liability?
21. When might necessity or duress act as a defense against criminal liability?
22. What is the Model Penal Code's test for raising insanity as a defense?
23. What constitutional safeguards are provided by the fourth and fifth amendments?
24. What constitutional safeguards are provided by the sixth, eighth, and fourteenth amendments?
25. What does it mean to be arraigned?
26. What does it mean to make a plea in a criminal case?
27. When does the accused have a right to a jury in a criminal case?

Critical-Thinking Questions

28. Do you think violent crimes should carry a heavier punishment than white-collar crimes carry and why?
29. Why might it be hard for the SEC to uncover cases of insider trading?
30. How might proving a cybercrime has been committed be a more difficult task than proving a property crime has been committed by a defendant?
31. Why do you suppose state legal systems make it difficult for a defendant to prove entrapment as a defense against a crime?
32. What are the Miranda rights and are they necessary this many years later?

Essay Questions

1. Monica is the owner of Fast Dri Cleaning. Two of her employees have been overcharging customers by adding tips to their receipts. The employees split the fraudulent tips at the end of each week. What crimes may have been committed by the employees? What if Monica knew of this scheme but did nothing to stop it; can she be held criminally liable?
2. Low Rent Properties, Incorporated is owned by Don. Don also has an illegal gambling business. Don takes the money received from the gambling business and deposits it into his corporate checking account. Don reports the income from his gambling business on his tax return. During the current year, Don had to file bankruptcy because of declining property values. Before filing bankruptcy Don took $120,000 in cash from the corporate checking account and gave it to his girlfriend. What crimes has Don committed?
3. Mark has a business located in a building with four other businesses. Mark knows the back door to the flower store next door is never locked. One afternoon he enters that door with the intent to steal flowers for his wife. Stealing anything of value in Mark's state is a felony. Mark takes two dozen roses. What crimes may have committed under the common law? Has he committed burglary?
4. Tina is behind on her mortgage payments. She wishes she could sell her home but the home's sales value would not cover her liabilities. Tina decides to burn down her

house during the night when no one can see what she is doing. She then files an insurance claim and collects a large payment from the insurance company. What crimes may have Tina committed?

5. Larissa steals her roommate's credit card. She takes the credit card to a local retail store where she buys a six-pack of beer. Later that night she takes the credit card and buys dinner and drinks for herself and her boyfriend at a local restaurant. She signs the credit card receipt after dinner and gives the waitress a large tip. What crimes has Larissa committed?

6. Nelson owns an unprofitable coffee shop. Nelson has designed a computer program that attaches itself to personal laptops used in his coffee shop through the wireless Internet system. Nelson's virus activates a software program that downloads a customer's bank account information when they visit their bank's website. The virus then destroys the operating system of the laptop computer so his activities cannot be tracked. What crimes may have Nelson committed?

7. Nick is at a football game. He leaves the game to go to a friend's home. When Nick arrives at the house, a person he is not familiar with hands him an illegal substance in a pipe. Nick smokes the illegal substance. He then tells the person about how he vandalized a car owned by an opposing fan after he left the game and before he came to the house. Nick is then arrested by the individual, who is an undercover cop. Can Nick claim entrapment as a defense? Does it matter that Nick was not read his Miranda rights? Can the cop use his statement about vandalizing the car against him?

8. Allison is a waitress at a local restaurant. One night she thinks a customer has told her to write down a tip on the receipt. It was very noisy in the restaurant. In fact, the customer asked her if he had signed the receipt. The customer informs the police of the incident. The police charge Allison with larceny. Has Allison committed larceny? Why or why not?

9. Marty has a business where he buys stolen cars and then disassembles the cars and sells the parts to various auto repair shops. He also does repair work for insurance companies. This repair work is a legal business. Marty puts all the money he receives in one checking account. One day a police officer comes to have his car fixed. He walks into Marty's shop to give him the keys when he sees a car that he believes matches the description of a stolen car. The police officer snaps a picture of the car and shows it to the person reporting the car stolen. What crimes has Marty committed? If the police officer never obtained a search warrant, can the picture of the stolen car be used at trial?

10. One day Alex is working at a local grocery store when his boss comes in and tells Alex he needs Alex to come with him. Alex and his boss walk to the back of the store where all the extra food is stored. Alex helps his boss load eight cases of liquor into the back of a white van. Alex thinks it is out of the ordinary but does what he is told. The next day Alex is charged with larceny. The prosecuting attorney in his case tells Alex's mom that if she pays him $10,000 in cash, he will make sure the charges get dismissed. However, Alex and his mom must never say anything to anyone about the cash payment. Did Alex commit larceny? What other parties committed a crime and what crime did they commit?

CHAPTER SIX

INTELLECTUAL PROPERTY LAW

By Charles Damschen

James has a great idea for a new snow blower that not only removes snow, but simultaneously allows the user to apply rock salt to the cleared surface. James has detailed drawings of how the snow blower would work. He has a great name for his new product, the "Melterator," but wants to make sure that he protects his name and snow blower design before he starts building and selling it. What can James do to protect his snow blower design? The term "Melterator"? Should James be concerned that he could be infringing someone else's rights? How would he find out?

Gabrielle loves to bake, especially whole wheat bread. Her grandmother gave her a recipe that has been in the family for years. Gabrielle tried it, but wasn't satisfied with the consistency of the dough. She made some adjustments to the ingredient proportions and added some new ingredients. The result was amazing, and everyone who tried Gabrielle's bread loves it. Gabrielle would like to start selling her bread at a local food co-op but wants to make sure that no one can just steal her recipe and make the same bread. She also wants to have a unique brand name, so she asked her friend, Claire, for suggestions. Claire came up with a great name and a unique logo. How would Gabrielle protect her recipe? The name and logo? Does Gabrielle need Claire's permission to use the name and logo Claire created? Who owns the name and logo?

Chapter Objectives

1. Identify four distinct types of intellectual property and distinguish the subject matter protected by each.
2. Understand the protection provided by state, federal and international law to intellectual property.
3. Identify ways in which intellectual property law has been affected by advancements in technology.
4. Understand the process and benefits associated with registering intellectual property.
5. Identify key elements in determining how to protect an idea, work of art or business symbol.

Introduction

Intellectual property is the broad term that generally refers to products of the human creative spirit such as inventions, creative works (e.g., songs, plays, visual media), trade and service marks, trade secrets, and other know-how. Intellectual property generally derives its value from a characteristic other than its physical properties. This chapter will focus on a discussion of patents, trademarks, copyrights, and trade secrets.

Intellectual property is generally referred to as intangible property—as opposed to personal and real property, which a person can see and touch. Outside of being intangible, some types of intellectual property have very little in common with other forms of intangible property. The differences among various types of intellectual property present challenges for a clear and concise study, as concepts from one type may not translate to concepts from another type. Therefore, this chapter will focus on patents, trademarks, copyrights and trade secrets.

Even though ideas and their application have always been key drivers in economic advancement, their importance has increased as computers have become more prominent in the industrialized world. Intellectual property generally accounts for a larger portion of a company's value than ever before. In a 2010 study, the US Department of Commerce determined that IP-intensive industries accounted for approximately $5.06 trillion of the GDP of the United States, which equates to 35% of total GDP.

The abstract nature of much intellectual property leads to difficulty in areas outside of academic endeavors. Investors, venture capitalists specifically, have historically struggled when valuing intellectual property. The valuation of intellectual property is especially difficult at early stages before sales, profit margins, and other empirical financial data are available. Furthermore, the process for valuing intellectual property is not a standard process.

International Law

The Agreement on Trade Related Aspects of Intellectual Property Rights (TRIPS Agreement) highlights the fact that intellectual property (and the respect for the intellectual property rights of others) is not only of great importance to fully developed economies but also to economies in the developing world. The TRIPS Agreement is administered by the World Trade Organization, so any member thereof is bound by the TRIPS Agreement. TRIPS applies to patents, copyrights, trademarks, and certain trade secrets. The TRIPS Agreement requires that member countries not treat domestic owners of intellectual property more favorably than nondomestic owners, and that nondomestic owners have the same access to legal procedures and tribunals as domestic owners enjoy when seeking to exercise their rights.

US Law

US law provides certain protections for each type of intellectual property, and the legal basis varies depending on the type of intellectual property. Patents and copyrights find the root of their legal protections in the Constitution (Art. I, sec. 8, cl. 8, commonly referred to as the "Copyright Clause") and acts of Congress, while trademarks are generally governed by both federal and state statutory law as well as common law. Protection of trade secrets is almost entirely dependent on contract law and the owner's ability to maintain secrecy, and is therefore primarily protected by state law.

Most legal protection for intellectual property equates to a **negative right**; that is, the right to exclude others from performing certain acts (infringing the owner's rights) using either a state or federal court system.

• Negative right

Patents

Patents generally provide legal protection for inventions. An invention may be a process, machine, manufacture, composition of matter, or any new and useful improvement thereof.[1] Whether a patent covers a process, machine, or other subject matter is dependent on the claims of the patent, which define the scope of the invention and, therefore, the scope of the patent owner's right to exclude others from using their invention. A claim for a machine will recite a list of specific parts or pieces and how they physically connect or relate to one another. A claim for a process or method will recite a list of specific steps in a specific order.

Perhaps the most famous method patent is US Pat. No. 5,960,411 owned by Amazon®, which includes claims directed to a method of placing a purchase order via a communications network—or more commonly known

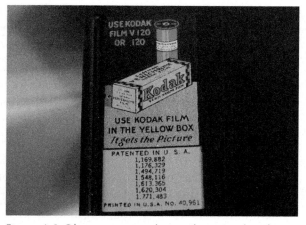

Figure 6.1 Olympus camera box with patents listed

as Amazon's one-click patent. Some products are covered by multiple patents covering both the parts of the product (machine claims) and how the product works (method claims). For example, an iPhone 5 is covered by as many as 1,200 patents owned by Apple, covering various features such as the camera, user interface, calendar, antenna, and voice control.[2] However, this number does not include the thousands of patents that Apple must license from other companies (such as Qualcomm) to make the iPhone work on a 4G network, let alone the tens of thousands of patents Apple must license for 3G, voice, and other aspects required for the telecommunications connectivity consumers expect. By 2008, before most consumers had even heard the term "4G," there were 18,300 patents and over 16,000 pending

---

1   35 USC. § 101.

2   *Inside the iPhone Patent Portfolio*, Thompson Reuters, September, 2012. Available at <http://ip-science. thomsonreuters.com/m/pdfs/iphone-report.pdf>.

patent applications covering various aspects related to the development and implementation of a 4G network.

A patent does not grant the patentee an affirmative right other than to sue infringers. **Infringement** is the unlawful use of another's right without their permission. That is, a patent allows the patentee to prevent others from making, using, selling, offering for sale, or importing to the United States the invention by granting the right to the owner to sue for infringement. A patent grants the patent owner a *right to enforce* a monopoly on the invention. The enjoyment of this monopoly, and monetary benefits associated with it, is designed to reward innovation. As with most other types of intellectual property, the patent owner must police infringement and hold infringers accountable in order to maximize the value of the patent.

USPTO

The United States Patent and Trademark Office (USPTO), which is under the Department of Commerce, has the authority to grant patents in the US. The process for obtaining a patent starts with preparing and filing a patent application. Inventors may draft and file a patent application themselves, or an inventor may hire a patent attorney to do this on the inventor's behalf. The patent application must describe the invention with such specificity that a person familiar with the area of technology could make and use the invention so that when the patent expires and the invention passes into the public domain, competitors of the patent owner can make and use the invention without undue experimentation or research and development costs. This illustrates the quid pro quo ("this for that") of the patent monopoly—in exchange for a time-limited monopoly, the inventor must teach the public how to make and use the invention. However, it is important to remember the USPTO does not police against infringement, the USPTO only grants patents and trademarks. The owner of a patent or trademark must police against infringement.

After an inventor or their patent attorney files a patent application, the USPTO will then examine the application to determine if the claims define an invention that falls within one of the statutory categories for patentable subject matter and that it is useful, new, and not obvious to a person familiar with the technology. During examination the USPTO attempts to discover all relevant teachings and information that pre-date the filing of the patent application, which is referred to as *prior art*. **Prior art** means existing information and concepts that prove the components of a patent are not new or novel. If the invention claimed in the patent application is not sufficiently novel or nonobvious in light of the prior art, the USPTO will reject the application. After a rejection from the USPTO, the inventor may amend the patent application by adding limitations to the claims in order to overcome the rejection. Alternatively, the inventor may present arguments as to why the invention is novel and nonobvious in light of the prior art.

For example, if screwdrivers with a Phillips head do not exist and Jonah has invented one, he might file a patent application with a claim that reads, "An apparatus for applying rotational energy to a fastener, the apparatus composed of a first end formed as a handle and a second end formed as a fastener engager." The USPTO should reject this claim based on the existence of flathead screwdrivers, which are known prior art because the same description would apply to a flathead screwdriver.

Jonah could then amend the claim to add limitations to distinguish the flat head screwdriver that is prior art. Jonah could state, "wherein the fastener engager includes two distinct surfaces intersecting one another along perpendicular lines." This restriction would not be found in a flathead screwdriver, so the USPTO would have to perform another search to find prior art with a fastener engager with two distinct surfaces intersecting one another along perpendicular lines. If the USPTO did not find any prior art teaching this structure, it would grant a patent to Jonah.

- Continuation application
- Continuation-in-part application
- Utility patents
- Design patents
- Plant patents

Practice Tip

Many times multiple patents cover one inventive concept. A patent attorney might include multiple claims in a single patent application with some claims having few restrictions (i.e., broad claims) and some claims having more restrictions (i.e., narrow claims). Because the USPTO judges patentability on a claim-by-claim basis, it may grant a patent on the narrow claims but reject the broad claims. The inventor may allow a patent to issue with the narrow claims and then file another patent application called a **continuation application** that is related to the first application. The continuation application is virtually identical to the first application except for the claims. This allows the inventor to pursue the broad claims in the continuation while simultaneously enjoying an issued patent on the narrower claims. The continuation application and first application are treated as if they were filed on the same date, and therefore, expire on the same date.

Importantly, no new subject matter may be added to a continuation application. If Jonah has improved his screwdriver so that it now has interchangeable bits, he cannot file a continuation application claiming that invention. Instead, he must file a **continuation-in-part application**, which is similar to a continuation application. However, claims to the new subject matter in the continuation-in-part application are treated as filed on the date the continuation-in-part application was filed as opposed to the date on which the first patent application was filed, and new subject matter (new drawings, description, etc.) may be added to the continuation-in-part application.

The USPTO retains a searchable database of issued patents and published patent applications on its website that is accessible to the public. Additionally, Google maintains a patent database that includes US patents and various patents from some foreign countries. Foreign patents are relevant to patent rights in the US because the invention must be useful, new, and not obvious not only in light of the prior art in the US (e.g., US patents and published patent applications predating the patent application) but also in light of prior art around the world.

Generally, there are three types of patents: (1) **utility patents**, which cover the way something functions or the specific arrangement of parts; (2) **design patents**, which cover the nonfunctional ornamental aspects of the invention; and (3) **plant patents**, which cover newly invented strains of asexually reproducing plants.

Utility and plant patents last for twenty years from the date of filing, and design patents last for fourteen years from the date of issue. Because an inventor may also protect new strains of asexually reproducing plants, plant patents are rare and will not be covered further.

Justin has a new idea for a mousetrap that lures the mouse with an audio signal imperceptible to humans, and then traps the mouse without harming it. Justin should file a utility patent application to protect the way his mousetrap works. Jessica has designed a new sweatshirt with a can Koozie® integrated into the front pocket. The design does not include any new structure, but the outline of the can Koozie® is unique in an ornamental way, so she should consider filing a design patent application.

Utility patents may begin as either a provisional patent application or non-provisional patent application. Broadly speaking, a **provisional patent application** allows an inventor to make the invention "patent pending" and preserve his or her patent rights around the world for less expense than that incurred with filing a non-provisional patent application. However, a provisional patent application expires one year after it is filed (along with the "patent pending" status of the invention) and will never mature into an issued patent unless the inventor files a non-provisional patent application related to the provisional before the provisional patent expires.

The examination process for design patent applications is usually much less rigorous than it is for utility patent applications. Utility patent applications may be over 100 pages in length and include many pages of written description of the invention as well as detailed drawings of the invention and how it works.

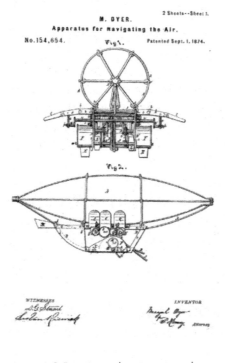

Figure 6.2 Patent applications must have a depiction of the invention

Design patent applications consist primarily of drawings of the exterior features of the invention. If the invention as shown in the pictures in a design patent application looks sufficiently different than the prior art, then the USPTO will grant the design patent. For design patents, the function of the invention is not important—only how it looks. Accordingly, even if existing products function identically to the invention in a design patent, if the invention looks sufficiently different from existing products, the USPTO will grant the design patent.

Design patents have more recently stepped into the spotlight, especially in the business community, because of various high-profile lawsuits Apple has filed against Samsung alleging that Samsung "copied" the look and feel of several of Apple's products, including iPhones and iPads. After a jury trial, the jury in the first *Apple v. Samsung* case awarded Apple an unprecedented $1.05 billion infringement award, although that amount was later reduced on appeal.[3] Additionally, various

3   *Apple, Inc. v. Samsung Electronics Co., Ltd.*, 678 F. 3d 1314 (Fed. Cir. 2012).

technology companies have received design patents for graphic user interfaces for software and web applications. (See D599,372 covering Google Search's homepage.)

International Protection of Patents

Each country has its own patent system, and there is no worldwide patent. Accordingly, if an inventor wants a patent in Germany, the inventor must file a patent application in Germany. However, there is a type of international patent application that is valid in nearly 190 countries. This international patent application is a result of the **Patent Cooperation Treaty** and is called a "PCT application." The **World Intellectual Property Organization** (WIPO), which is governed by the United Nations, oversees PCT applications. As of 2013, 148 countries have joined the PCT, with some of the most notable exceptions being Taiwan and Argentina.

A US inventor can either file a PCT application within twelve months of filing a US patent application (either provisional or non-provisional), or the PCT application can be a US inventor's first application. If the PCT application is the inventor's first patent application, the inventor has thirty months from the filing date to decide in what countries the inventor wants to undergo examination (referred to as entering the national phase) and pursue patent protection.

If the inventor files a PCT application within twelve months of the inventor's first US patent application (either provisional or non-provisional), the inventor has eighteen months from the filing date of the PCT application to decide in what countries to pursue patent protection. Generally, a PCT application is similar to a provisional patent application in the US, because without more than the initial application, the PCT application will never mature into an issued patent.

The inventor must enter the national phase in at least one country for the PCT application to ever mature into an issued patent. Generally speaking, the process associated with procuring patents in multiple countries is expensive, and oftentimes companies or inventors pursue patents only in countries that have the largest existing market for the invention or the largest growth potential.

American Invents Act

Historically, the patent system in the US was based on who invented first as opposed to who filed a patent application first. In a first-to-invent system, an earlier inventor who never filed a patent application could have superior legal rights to that invention as against a later inventor who did file a patent application. By contrast, in a first-to-file system, superior legal rights vest in the inventor who filed a patent application first, regardless of date of invention.

On March 16, 2013, America Invents Act ("AIA") changed the patent system in the US from a first-to-invent system to a first-inventor-to-file system. In the US, to have enforceable legal rights, the first person to file a patent application must be a true inventor. That is, the person must not have stolen or received the idea from another party. This change brought the US patent system into harmony with many other countries in the world, and that harmonization was a key driver in Congress passing the AIA.

- Patent Cooperation Treaty
- World Intellectual Property Organization

Other provisions of the AIA restrict how an inventor may commercialize an invention before seeking a patent. Prior to the AIA, inventors could sell, offer for sale, or publicly disclose the invention for as long as twelve months before seeking a patent. If the inventor did not seek a patent within twelve months, then the inventor was barred from seeking a patent on that invention.

This grace period was often very helpful to small businesses testing a new product. For twelve months the business could market and make sales of the invention to gain insight as to whether the expense of seeking a patent would be worthwhile based on the invention's performance in the marketplace. However, under the AIA, any sale or offer for sale of the invention prior to seeking patent protection forecloses the opportunity to receive a patent. For this reason, some believe that the AIA may have adverse effects on small inventors. Because most foreign countries have historically barred patent protection if the inventor disclosed or sold the invention prior to filing a patent application, the procedures of many multinational companies will probably be unaffected. Congressional records indicate that harmonization with patent laws in other countries was a major factor in restricting the grace period in the AIA.

Patent-Eligible Subject Matter

Figure 6.3 Patent Application for Forecasting Earthquakes

The categories of patent-eligible subject matter in 35 USC. § 101 may seem straightforward, but companies and individuals have spent countless dollars in court arguing over what these categories do and do not include; that is, what patent-eligible subject matter is. Chief among the often-argued classes of inventions are computer-implemented processes (more commonly referred to as software), genetically engineered organisms, and isolated genetic sequences. Historically, Congress desired the categories of patentable subject matter to be very broad and include "anything under the sun made by man."

The Supreme Court first considered the patentability of computer-implemented methods in the case *Gottschalk v. Benson* in 1972.[4] This decision was the genesis for judicially created exclusions to patentable subject matter, which include natural phenomena, laws of nature, and abstract ideas. These exceptions carve out certain types of subject matter that the Supreme

---

4   *Gottschalk v. Benson*, 409 US 63 (1972).

Court has determined Congress did not intend to protect with patents. The most prominent argument for these exceptions is that a monopoly on that type of subject matter would not promote the progress of science and the useful arts, which is the constitutional justification for the monopoly a patent affords, but would instead place undue restrictions on broad areas of research.

For example, most software is composed of one or more algorithms and/or mathematical formulas. The Supreme Court held in *Gottschalk v. Benson* that a patent for a process that would "wholly pre-empt the mathematical formula and in practical effect would be a patent on the algorithm itself" was not patent-eligible subject matter.[5] However, practical applications of abstract ideas may be patent eligible. In other words, a patent claim reciting only a specific algorithm is not patent-eligible subject matter, but a claim reciting a method of using that specific algorithm to determine the cure time required for a given polymer composition may be patent-eligible subject matter.

Even if an invention or idea does not fall within the category of non-patentable inventions based upon the Supreme Court's analysis, a patentable claim must also recite something that is new, useful, and not obvious, in addition to being directed toward patent-eligible subject matter. That is, just because a claim is directed toward patent-eligible subject matter does not mean the claim is necessarily patentable; it must also recite an invention that is new, useful, and not obvious.

Association for Molecular Pathology et al. v. Myriad Genetics, Inc.
569 US 12-398 (2013)

Myriad Genetics, based in Utah, is a genetic research and diagnostic company that employs proprietary technology to identify the genetic basis for certain diseases. This information may allow doctors to determine the likelihood of an individual developing a specific disease and to more effectively treat the disease after diagnosis. Myriad Genetics discovered the precise location and sequence of the BRCA1 and BRCA2 genes and received patents claiming DNA sequences and complementary DNA sequences (cDNA) corresponding to the BRCA1 and BRCA2 genes.[6] Although DNA includes all nucleotide sequences in a naturally occurring human gene, cDNA contains only the portion of the naturally occurring DNA sequence that specifies production of amino acids, and may be synthetically created. Myriad began offering BRCA testing after it had made these discoveries. Other entities also offered BRCA testing, and Myriad filed infringement suits against many of them. A group of medical patients, advocacy groups, and doctors filed suit against Myriad to have the BRCA1/2 patents declared invalid under 35 USC. § 101 as not directed toward patent-eligible subject matter. The District Court held that most claims in Myriad's patents were invalid for claiming products of nature. However, the Court of Appeals for the Federal Circuit (the specialized appeals court for patent law) reversed the District Court, holding that the amount of human work required to isolate the chemical compounds no longer qualified the genes as a

---

5   *Id.*
6   US Pat. Nos. 5,709,999; 5,747,282; 5,753,441; 5,837,492; 6,033,857; 5,654,155; 5,750,400; 6,051,379; 6,951,721; and 7,250,497.

natural phenomenon or product of nature. The court had to decide whether either naturally occurring, isolated DNA or synthetically created cDNA was patent-eligible subject matter.

The court held a naturally occurring DNA segment is a product of nature and not patent-eligible subject matter, but cDNA is patent-eligible subject matter because it is not naturally occurring. The Court focused on the essence of DNA and the fact that it was essentially information. Naturally occurring DNA contained the same information as isolated DNA despite minor chemical differences between the two. Accordingly, the differences between naturally occurring and isolated DNA were not significant enough to push isolated DNA into the patent-eligible category. Myriad argued that isolating DNA requires breaking chemical bonds, and that creates a molecule that is not naturally occurring. The Court rejected this argument because the information in isolated DNA is exactly the same as the information in naturally occurring DNA. Because cDNA included only the portions of the gene that were expressed, the Court reasoned that the information cDNA carried was different from the information naturally occurring DNA carried and, therefore, patent-eligible subject matter.

Questions

1. If cDNA were also naturally occurring, would the result have been different?
2. When drafting patent claims to isolated compounds or their derivatives, what aspects of the invention should be highlighted to ensure the invention is patent-eligible subject matter?
3. How might a monopoly on genes or DNA sequences restrict rather than incentivize innovation?

The debate over what specifically constitutes patent-eligible subject matter and what falls into a judicial exception has continued for over forty years. It is more relevant now than ever due to the enormous amounts of exchanges via e-commerce and wealth attributed to machine-implemented processes. It is likely that this debate will not be completely settled for some time, and that innovation will continue to stretch the application of the Copyright Clause to technology unforeseen by the framers of the Constitution. Let's say Adrianna has developed a new smartphone app that causes her phone to bark every time she comes within three blocks of a pet store. The framers of the Constitution did not foresee this type of innovation and the adaptation of patent law has been difficult at best.

In a 2014 Supreme Court decision regarding patent-eligible subject matter, *Alice v. CLS Bank*, the Supreme Court held that a method for reducing settlement risk for trades of financial instruments was too abstract to be patent eligible. The Court determined that claims at issue in this case were an abstract idea, and implementation of the abstract idea by a computer did not transform the abstract idea into a patentable invention. To be patentable, a claim with an abstract idea must include an element or combination of elements that ensure infringement of the patent requires significantly more than practicing the abstract idea itself. Many commentators have criticized this framework as offering little guidance as to what does and does not constitute patent-eligible subject matter, and inventors and patent attorneys are left to glean as much guidance as possible from patent infringement lawsuits and USPTO patent application examination.

Infringement and Remedies

A patent allows the patent owner to exclude another from infringement. **Infringement** is the making, using, selling, offering for sale, or importing into the United States the invention as defined by the claims of the patent. When a party performs one of these acts without the permission of the patent owner or a license from the patent owner, that party is considered to infringe the patent.[7] This is referred to as direct infringement, and does not require the party's knowledge that a patent exists. For example, RightWay Products starts making a new bicycle mirror, which they sell at a large retail store. Juan Paulo has a patent for the same type of mirror. RightWay did not know about the patent and did not seek a patent of its own. However, they are still liable for direct infringement.

A party's product must meet each and every element of at least one claim in an issued patent before that party is liable for patent infringement. If the party adds additional elements, the party will still infringe the patent if its product includes each and every element of at least one claim in the patent. For example, say John owns a patent with a claim to a stool having a seat, a cushion on the top of the seat, and three legs attached to the bottom of the seat. If Miriam sells a stool having a seat, a cushion on top of the seat, and four legs attached to the bottom of the seat, Miriam will be infringing John's patent even though her stool has one more leg.

Defenses Against Infringement

The most common defense for a patent infringement claim is an attack on the validity of the patent alone or in combination with an assertion that the defendant's product does not include each and every element of at least one claim of the patent. A court may find an issued patent to be invalid for a number of reasons, including:

1. the patent claims recite an invention that would have been obvious to one of ordinary skill in the art to which the patent pertains (i.e., the USPTO should not have issued the patent);
2. there was a sale or public disclosure (either by the patent owner or another party) outside of the grace period or before the earliest application's filing date;
3. the patent owner or some party involved with the patent application withheld information from the USPTO during examination that would have prevented the USPTO from granting the patent.

The defense of laches also applies to the assertion of patent rights. When a defendant raises the **defense of laches,** they are asserting that the patent owner waited too long to bring the infringement claim. Another type of defense arises from the exhaustion of patent rights by an authorized sale of the patented article. The **first-sale doctrine** requires the patent owner to relinquish all rights in an individual article after an authorized sale so that the purchaser is free to use or resell that article without any restrictions. For example, if Jason buys a

- Infringement
- Defense of laches
- First-sale doctrine

---

7   35 USC. § 271(a).

bicycle that is covered by a patent and he decides to sell it to Shauna the next year, he is free to do so. This is because the first-sale doctrine allows Jason to resell the bicycle that he purchased without infringing the patent covering the bicycle.

Indirect infringement requires that the infringer has knowledge of the patent and that the accused infringer intended that its product infringe the patent. A party may indirectly infringe a patent in at least two ways. First, by actively inducing another's direct infringement of a patent by encouraging, aiding, or otherwise causing another to infringe the patent.[8] As an example, let's consider John's patent for a stool with a seat and three legs attached to it. If Miriam sold a kit with a seat, a cushion, three legs, and instructions on how to assemble those pieces so that the cushion was on top of the seat and the legs were attached to the bottom of the seat, Miriam would be indirectly infringing John's patent by actively inducing another (whoever purchased the kit and assembled the stool) to infringe John's patent. Furthermore, whoever bought Miriam's kit and assembled the stool would be liable to John for direct infringement.

A second type of indirect infringement occurs when a party provides a component that has a specific use as part of another article that is covered by a patent, even though that component standing alone does not infringe any patents. This type of indirect infringement is called **contributory infringement**. However, if there are other valid uses for the component, or if the component is a "staple article or commodity of commerce suitable for substantial non-infringing use," the seller of the component will not be liable for indirect infringement.[9] For example, assume Miriam starts selling a seat that can be used for multiple purposes. Her seat would not indirectly infringe on John's patent if Miriam's seat could be used on different products such as chairs and riding lawn mowers.

Historically, either type of indirect infringement required some underlying direct infringement. That is, ultimately one party was required to provide each and every element in at least one claim of the patent (e.g., the party who purchased Miriam's kit and assembled the stool). This requirement may be difficult for a patent owner to prove if the claims of the patent are method or process claims. For example, many patents exist covering various aspects of distribution of digital media over the Internet (e.g., Netflix, Hulu). However, if some of the method claims in one of these patents include a step of displaying the digital media to an end user, the patent owner cannot be sure that this step is performed unless the patent owner observes the end user. This may require entering the end user's home. Accordingly, there is a trend among patent owners to pursue infringement lawsuits when there is no direct infringement, but two or more parties join together to perform all the steps required in a process claim.

Damages for Infringement

Most often a patent owner will pursue an infringing party in a court of law and seek legal remedies from that court. Because all patent laws are federal law, federal courts are the proper forum for patent disputes. All appeals involving patent issues, regardless of what US

---

8   35 USC. § 271(b).
9   35 USC. § 271(c).

District Court conducted the patent infringement trial, are heard by the Court of Appeals for the Federal Circuit so that patent law is uniform across the entire country. The most sought-after remedy for patent infringement is a combination of an injunction (essentially a court order telling the infringer to stop all infringing activities) and monetary damages.

Until the Supreme Court's 2006 decision in *eBay, Inc. v. MercExchange, LLC,*[10] an injunction was nearly an automatic remedy for patent infringement. After that case, the Supreme Court held that an injunction against a patent infringer would be appropriate only if the patent owner could satisfy the standard test for injunctions. This test requires the plaintiff to demonstrate that: (1) it has suffered an irreparable injury; (2) remedies available at law are inadequate to compensate for that injury; (3) considering the balance of hardships between the plaintiff and defendant, a remedy in equity is warranted; and (4) the public interest would not be disserved by a permanent injunction.

To receive money damages for patent infringement, a patent owner must show that it suffered financially because of the infringement. That is, the patent owner would have made more money if the infringement had not occurred. If the patent owner can prove this then it is entitled to either lost profits, which are the profits the patent owner lost due to the infringing sales, or a reasonable royalty from the infringer. The calculation of either lost profits or the royalty for the patent owner may constitute a trial in itself and is often anything but straightforward because so many products in a modern economy are covered by more than one patent. One single feature rarely drives the purchasing choice of consumers so it is hard to quantify the damages caused by the infringement. Finally, if a jury finds that a party willfully infringed the patent, the infringer may be liable for **treble** damages, which is three times the actual monetary damages. Willful infringement requires that the patent owner prove the infringer acted despite "an objectively high likelihood that its actions constituted infringement of a valid patent" *and* then show that the risk was "either known or so obvious that it should have been known" to the infringer.[11]

Recently, non-practicing entities (NPEs) or patent assertion entities (PAEs), often referred to as "patent trolls," have come under the scrutiny of lawmakers and economists. NPEs and PAEs are generally business entities that do not make or sell products covered by the patents they own or license, but instead derive the majority of their revenue through license fees or settlements from infringement lawsuits. Even though NPEs and PAEs are a relatively new development in patent law, patent and economic scholars have provided much commentary and empirical analysis of their effects both on the court system and whether they accelerate or encumber economic advancement. One example that has been in the news is NPEs and PAEs are claiming accountants are using tax strategies for which they hold a patent. The NPE or PAE that is involved sends a letter to an accountant accusing them of patent infringement and offering to settle for a predetermined amount of money.

• Treble

---

10   *eBay, Inc. v. MercExchange, LLC,* 547 US 388 (2006).
11   *In re Seagate Tech., LLC,* 497 F.3d 1360, 1371 (Fed. Cir. 2007) (en banc).

Copyright

Like patent law, the underlying policy of copyright law and the time-limited monopoly it grants to the author is intended to promote creativity. Although some states have provisions for copyright law, federal copyright law is generally far more prominent. Accordingly, the remainder of this section will be devoted to federal copyright law. A **copyright** is an intel-

Figure 6.4
Copyright symbol

lectual property right designed to protect artistic works, and broadly extends to "original works of authorship fixed in any tangible medium of expression."[12] The subject matter of copyright law includes literary, musical, dramatic, pictorial, graphic, and sculptural works, as well as pantomimes, choreographic works, sound recordings, movies and other videos, software, and architectural works.[13]

Originality is key in determining whether a work is copyrightable, and even if the originality requirement is minimal, a copyrightable work generally requires a modicum of creativity. Fixing an original work in a tangible medium of expression may take many forms, from scribbling a sketch on a napkin to posting a poem on Facebook to writing thousands of lines of computer code to a hard disk. Once the author records the work in some manner in which another person or machine may perceive the work, federal copyright protection applies to the work and the copyright owner may use the c-in-a-circle symbol ©. For a copyright in a choreographic work, the author may use dance notation to describe the choreography or otherwise record the work through a video camera or audible description of the choreography.

For additional rights, the copyright owner may register the work with the US Copyright Office. Additionally, the **Berne Convention**, which is an international treaty for copyright, provides international protection for copyrights of citizens of any member country. That is, if a US author owns a copyright, every country that is a signatory to the Berne Convention must recognize that copyright in each member country. As of 2013, 167 countries were members of the Berne Convention.

Length of Protection

For works with one author created in or after 1978, the copyright term generally extends for the life of the author plus seventy years, and works having more than one author generally extend seventy years after the death of the last surviving author. However, certain works are considered a "work for hire," and their copyright term extends for the shorter of 120 years after creation or ninety-five years after publication. A work will be a **work for hire** under copyright law if the author was an employee and prepared the work within the scope of the author's employment, or if the author and a party with whom the author is contracted expressly agree in writing that the parties intend for the work to be a work for hire. If the work is not a work for hire, copyright vests in the author, whereas copyright in a work for hire is owned by the author's employer or the party to whom the author is contractually obligated.

---

12   17 USC. § 102(a).
13   *Id.* at 101.

For example, Balistic Corporation hires Charlie to write a song that the corporation can use in its advertisements. This is an example of a work for hire.

Federal copyright law gives the copyright owner the exclusive right to make and sell copies of the work, create derivative works, and publicly perform or display the work.[14] The legal rights in a copyright are generally analogized to a bundle of sticks, wherein the copyright is the bundle and each individual right is an individual stick. Each right ("stick") in the bundle may be exploited separately. That is, the copyright owner may license the right to create derivative works to a first party and license the right to publicly display the work to a second party. For example, Kate has written a new song with music and lyrics. She may license Faith Hill to use the music, and allow Faith to write her own lyrics for use with that music. Simultaneously, she may license Eminem to use the lyrics, but require him to use his own music and/or beat for those lyrics.

Limitations on Copyright

Copyright protection generally does not extend to the subject matter of patents, nor to an idea, concept, or principle.[15] Although copyright protection is available to a particular expression of an idea, it does not extend to the idea itself. If the idea and its expression are inseparable, copyright protection is not available for the work. The concept that states an idea is not separable from its expression is generally called the **idea–expression dichotomy**. Similarly, copyright protection is not available for the utilitarian aspects of a work, largely because patent protection is available for such works. This situation often occurs in the instance of a software program. Copyright law generally would not protect how the software program functioned but rather the graphical user interface and other aesthetic aspects.

- Idea–expression dichotomy

Mazer v. Stein
347 US 201 (1954)

Stein designed several statuettes of dancing figures and registered the copyright on the various statuettes as "works of art." Stein then partnered with a manufacturer to mass produce some of the statuettes and outfit them with electrical components to be used as lamp bases. Mazer started making lamps identical to those of Stein, and Stein sued Mazer for copyright infringement. The District Court held that Mazer had not infringed a valid copyright owned by Stein. Stein appealed that decision and the Appellate Court reversed. Mazer appealed to the Supreme Court.

Figure 6.5 A dancing figure was at issue in the *Mazer v. Stein* case

---

14   17 USC. § 106.
15   17 USC. § 102(b).

The court had to decide whether copyright protection extends to articles of manufacture, such as lamps and furniture. The court held the artistic/aesthetic aspects of even a utilitarian object may be protected by copyright. The Court looked to legislative history to determine the meaning of the term "work of art." Based on this, the Court determined that the term extended beyond fine works of art to any work that is the result of the original ideas of the author expressed in a tangible manner. Because beauty is a subjective determination, beauty cannot be a criterion for determining whether something qualifies as a "work of art" under copyright law.

Questions

1. Are there instances in which the utilitarian and artistic aspects of an article are so intertwined that copyright protection is not available?
2. Should car designs be available for copyright protection? Shoe designs? Jewelry designs?
3. What should a carpenter who would like to sell a design to Pottery Barn do before showing the design?

Copyright subject matter from 17 USC. § 101 now includes "works of artistic craftsmanship insofar as their form but not their mechanical or utilitarian aspects are concerned." Later cases clarified that the utilitarian and artistic aspects of an article of manufacture must be separable for the article to be protectable by copyright.

Copyright protection does not extend to facts, although specific arrangements or compilations of factual data are copyrightable. In *Feist Publications, Inc. v. Rural Telephone Service Co.*, the Supreme Court held that facts are not original because they don't owe their origin to the author, and are therefore not protectable by copyright.[16] This limitation affects publishers of any sort of directory, as well as publishers of recipe books, since recipes are facts. A copyright on a work consisting of a compilation of facts is sometimes called a "thin copyright," as there may be originality in the author's decision in which facts to include.[17] For example, in a copyrighted news story, the author or publisher does not have the exclusive right to the facts of the story, only to the arrangement, expression, and other creative aspects of the news story.

Copyright Registration, Infringement, and Remedies

Copyright registration is a relatively simple procedure compared to obtaining a patent or even a federal trademark registration. Although many copyright owners engage an attorney for the registration process, a copyright owner might be able to perform the steps themselves. When one performs legal work without the help of an attorney, he or she is said to perform the work *pro se*. Because the filing fee payable to the Copyright Office for registration is

---

16   *Feist Publications, Inc. v. Rural Telephone Service Co.*, 499 US 340 (1991).
17   *Key Publ'ns., Inc. v. Chinatown Today Publ'g Enters., Inc.*, 945 F.2d 509 (2d Cir. 1991).

only $35, the return on this investment may be quite substantial. The registration procedure involves filling out the appropriate form, preparing a copy of the work for submission, and depositing the copy of the work and the completed form with the Copyright Office. A copyright owner may register the copyright at any time during the term of the copyright.

Even though federal copyright law affords an author certain rights upon creation of an original work without registration, registration of the copyright with the US Copyright Office is often advantageous for most copyright owners. Generally, a copyright owner must register his or her copyright before suing another party for copyright infringement. Registration also entitles the copyright owner to certain protections from US Customs and provides evidence of ownership. If a copyright owner registers the copyright prior to infringement or within three months of the work's publication, the copyright owner may be entitled to statutory damages after a successful infringement suit. Statutory damages are between $750 and $30,000 per work, and if a copyright owner is able to prove willful infringement, the copyright owner might be entitled to damages of up to $150,000 per work.

A copyright owner must prove two basic elements to show copyright infringement: (1) ownership of the copyright and (2) unauthorized copying.[18] To prove willful infringement a copyright owner must show either that the defendant intentionally disregarded a known legal duty or acted with knowledge that his or her acts were infringing or reckless disregard as to whether his or her acts were infringing.[19]

Like patent law, copyright law distinguishes direct infringement from indirect infringement. Also like patent law, some underlying direct infringement must be present for any indirect infringement to occur. Indirect copyright infringement may take the form of vicarious or contributory infringement. A party commits **contributory infringement** when that party has actual knowledge of the activity that constitutes direct infringement and induces, causes, or materially contributes to the infringing conduct.[20] A defendant is liable for **vicarious infringement** when the defendant has the right and ability to control the infringer's conduct and receives a direct financial benefit from the infringement.[21] For example, if someone owns a website providing file server space for users to upload digital copies of copyrighted movies and encourages other users to download those digital copies, the website owner may be liable for contributory copyright infringement. An example of vicarious copyright infringement is if a flea market owner allowed counterfeit goods to be sold at the flea market.[22] The line between contributory and vicarious copyright infringement is often blurred, and oftentimes copyright owners assert both types of infringement in lawsuits for copyright infringement.

Some of the remedies available to a successful copyright plaintiff are similar to those for a successful patent owner. For example, injunctive relief and monetary damages are often available to a successful copyright infringement plaintiff. If statutory damages are not available because the copyright owner either did not register the copyright prior to

- Contributory infringement
- Vicarious infringement

---

18 17 USC. § 501.

19 *Island Software & Computer Serv., Inc. v. Microsoft Corp.*, 413 F.3d 257 (2nd Cir. 2005).

20 *Fonovisa, Inc. v. Cherry Auction, Inc.*, 76 F.3d 259, 264 (9th Cir. 1996) (citing *Gershwin Publishing Corp. v. Columbia Artists Mgmt., Inc.*, 443 F.2d 1159, 1162 (2d Cir. 1971)).

21 *Fonovisa, Inc. v. Cherry Auction, Inc.*, 76 F.3d 259, 262 (9th Cir. 1996)

22 *Coach v. Sapatis*, (D.N.H. Han. 31, 2014).

• Innocent
infringement

the infringement or within three months of publication of the work, the copyright owner must prove actual damages. Actual damages are when the infringement resulted in some economic loss to the copyright owner. In addition, a successful copyright plaintiff may be entitled to seizure and destruction of infringing copies (and the articles used to make them) and full costs and reasonable attorney's fees. Criminal prosecution, which the federal government may pursue alone or in addition to the copyright owner's claims in a civil lawsuit for copyright infringement, may result in fines and/or imprisonment.

Defenses Against Infringement

Various defenses are available to a defendant in a copyright infringement suit. The most common defense is that of fair use, which is more accurately described as an exception to infringement rather than a defense to infringement. That is, unauthorized use of a copyright work is not infringement if that use qualifies as fair use. The fair use exception is statutory and requires a court to consider four factors in analyzing the defendant's use:

1. the nature of use (commercial use for profit, educational use, parody);
2. the nature of the copyrighted work (how much creativity the author put into the work);
3. the amount and character of the portion used in relation to the entire work;
4. the effect of the use on the economic value of the work.[23]

This type of multifactor analysis requires courts to determine on a case-by-case basis whether a defendant's use of the copyrighted work constitutes fair use. However, the examples given in the Copyright Act for the types of uses that may constitute fair use are generally directed to noncommercial activities (e.g., news reporting, teaching, scholarship, research). Public policy favors the free dissemination of facts, so a court's determination of fair use will often rise or fall on the nature of the defendant's use and the nature of the copyrighted work, even though none of the factors are decisive.

Innocent infringement occurs when a defendant did not have notice of a copyright. It is allowed by courts as a defense to a claim of copyright infringement. This defense most often arises in situations where the defendant knowingly and intentionally used the copyrighted work but believed in good faith that his or her conduct is not infringing. Generally this defense is not available to a defendant who used a work with a copyright notice affixed to the work. A typical scenario involving an innocent infringement defense arises when someone uses a digital image found via an internet search, thinking that the image was in the public domain.

There are other less common defenses to copyright infringement, including abandonment of the copyrighted work by the copyright owner, laches, or that the portion of the work the defendant used constitutes non-copyrightable material.

---

23   17 USC. § 107.

Copyright in Software

The fact that copyright protection is available for software and certain software may be protected by patents result in two potential and distinct layers of protection for software. Because copyright law and patent law provide different types of protection for software, a dual-protection scheme can be extremely valuable. A patent for software generally protects the way the claimed software program functions, whereas copyright law generally protects the code (both the source code and object code).[24]

Under copyright law, if another party independently writes code (does not copy other code) that results in software that functions identically to that of copyrighted software, it is unlikely that party has committed copyright infringement since that party has not copied anything without authorization. However, if that copyrighted software is covered by a patent, then it is very likely that a software program with the same functionality would infringe the patent. Copyright protection can also extend to the menu structure and even certain aspects of the look and feel of the software, which creates a potential overlap with trademark law, as some companies assert trade dress rights in the look and feel of their software programs.[25]

Copyright law contains a first-sale doctrine similar to patent law. An authorized sale of an individual article of a copyrighted work exhausts the copyright owner's exclusive rights to control that individual article. However, the first-sale doctrine does not allow the purchaser to make copies of the work, which is analogous to the first-sale doctrine in patent law. That is, just as the first-sale doctrine in patent law does not allow a purchaser of a patented machine to make copies of that machine, so too does the first-sale doctrine in copyright law prevent a purchaser of a copyrighted music recording from making additional copies of that recording. For example, Hillary buys a book written by Bill. Bill has copyrighted the book. Hillary may sell the used to book to Monica under the first sale doctrine.

Many software companies circumvent the first-sale doctrine by including click-wrap or shrink-wrap agreements for software that claim the purchaser has received a license only to that individual copy of software rather than a transfer of ownership of that individual copy. This allows software companies to restrict downstream transactions or resale of their software. For example, during his freshman year, Alex purchased a copy of a word processing program to use on his laptop. After he graduated, he got a job that provided him with the latest version of that software. He wanted to sell his old copy, but unfortunately there was a clause in the click-wrap agreement when he installed the software on his laptop that made clear the software purchase constituted a nontransferable license, and he could not resell that copy.

---

24 *Stern Electronics v. Kaufman*, 669 F.2d 852 (2nd Cir. 1982); *Apple Computer, Inc. v. Franklin Computer Corp.*, 714 F.2d 1240 (3d Cir. 1983).

25 *Lotus Dev. Corp. v. Borland Int'l, Inc.*, 516 US 233 (1996); *Whelan Associates, Inc. v. Jaslow Dental Laboratory, Inc.*, 797 F.2d 1222 (3d Cir. 1986).

Copyright in the Digital Age

Of all types of intellectual property, the principles of copyright law are likely the most difficult to apply to digital technology. For example, viewing a webpage, copying the contents of a CD to one's personal computer drive, or copying the contents of one's computer drive to a smartphone or personal music player may all technically qualify as unauthorized copying of a copyrighted work, and thus constitute copyright infringement. Lawmakers attempted to adapt copyright law to software before computers were in common use in households. In 1980 Congress amended the Copyright Act of 1976 to include the Computer Software Copyright Act. Despite this attempt, lawsuits regarding copyrights as applied to digital technology over the last thirty years highlight the difficulty in adapting principles from a paper-and-pen age to the computer age. The mere act of accessing a website requires that the web page (and its attendant copyright material including text and images) be copied, albeit digitally, to some part of the computer. With new technologies in file compression and an increase in computing speed, for many copyright owners, the primary threat of infringement is through digital means.

Digital Millennium Copyright Act

The Digital Millennium Copyright Act, or **DMCA**, went into effect in 1998. The DMCA implements two treaties of the World Intellectual Property Organization (WIPO) and Congress's attempt to update copyright law for the digital age. Notable provisions of the DMCA include the criminalization of the manufacture and distribution of devices designed to circumvent or "hack" software encryption or other software features designed to prevent copying.

The most significant provision of the DMCA is that it provides a safe harbor for online service providers from suits for copyright infringement when a user of the service provider commits the infringement. That is, the DMCA exempts online service providers from direct and indirect liability for copyright infringement committed by users, provided the service provider complies with the notice-and-takedown system of the DMCA. Once a copyright owner becomes aware of infringement, he or she may demand removal of the offending content by sending a takedown notice to the online service provider or the service provider's DMCA agent.

Among other things, the takedown notice must identify the infringed copyrighted work and the material that the copyright owner believes is infringing. Upon receipt of a complete takedown notice, the service provider must either remove the infringing work or disable access to it. The customer to whom the takedown notice is directed may rebut the contents of the takedown notice via a counter notice if either the customer's work was not infringing or the takedown notice was in error or malicious. Although this safe harbor provision of the DMCA is controversial, it is instrumental in facilitating some of the most commonly used websites today, such as Facebook.com and Youtube.com. Without this protection, Facebook would be liable for any post that contained copyrighted material.

The safe harbor provision of the DMCA is especially applicable to file-sharing technology, such as peer-to-peer (P2P) networking. P2P networking generally refers to a network of personal computers in which personal computers may act as both servers and clients, such that any computer in the network can exchange digital information with any another computer in the network directly. In a landmark copyright case, a consortium of record companies sued Napster, Inc. for copyright infringement.[26] Napster provided software through which users could download digital music files from other users' computers through the Internet. The software also allowed users to search an indexed central database Napster maintained of all connected users and their files available. The court held that Napster users were directly infringing copyrighted works, and that Napster committed both contributory and vicarious infringement.

Regarding contributory infringement, internal documents showing that Napster turned a blind eye to infringement was sufficient for the court to determine Napster had knowledge of direct infringement, and the court held that Napster materially contributed to the infringing activity through its search and "hot lists" functions, and because Napster could terminate users' accounts. Regarding vicarious liability, the court found that Napster stood to gain financial benefit from the direct infringement because Napster's ad revenue increased with the number of users, and Napster retained the ability to control some of the infringing activities because it could terminate user accounts.

Shortly after the Napster case, enterprising individuals started companies with software designed to circumvent the material contribution requirement of contributory infringement. The software also was designed to protect against the possibility of vicarious liability by making sure the service provider did not have the ability to control some of the infringing activities. Companies offering this software did not maintain a centralized, searchable database as Napster did, but instead provided a file annotation system so that when a user searched for a specific song, the software searched for it directly on other users' computers. This design resulted in a system that removed a great deal of control from the companies so that neither theory of indirect infringement was applicable. Accordingly, many copyright owners now pursue infringement action against the end user under a direct infringement theory.

File sharing stepped into the spotlight again in 2005 with the Supreme Court decided *MGM Studios, Inc. v. Grokster, Ltd.*[27] This case was similar to the Napster case in that the plaintiffs argued Grokster was liable under both contributory and vicarious theories. Grokster distributed P2P file sharing software (like Napster), but did not maintain a centralized database. In this case, the Court borrowed a liability theory from patent law, which is called active inducement. Under the theory of **active inducement**, one who distributes a device (software in this case) with the intent to induce infringement is liable. This type of infringement is akin (or similar) to an intentional tort, whereas contributory liability and vicarious liability are more similar to negligence or recklessness. To be liable under an active-inducement theory, the plaintiff must show purposeful, culpable expression and conduct attributable to the defendant. Mere knowledge of infringing potential or even actual infringement is insufficient.[28] The Court found Grokster liable for inducing copyright infringement, and as a result Grokster had to cease operations.

- Active inducement

---

26   *A&M Records, Inc. v. Napster, Inc.*, 239 F.3d 1004 (9th Cir. 2001).
27   *MGM Studios, Inc. v. Grokster, Ltd.*, 545 US 913 (2005).
28   *In re Aimster Copyright Litigation*, 334 F.3d 643 (7th Cir. 2003).

- Trademark
- Service mark
- Collective marks

The most recent development in copyright law related to P2P file sharing involved BitTorrent. BitTorrent is a protocol that allows users to rapidly download large files with minimum Internet bandwidth. Instead of requiring a user to download a file from a single source, BitTorrent allows users to simultaneously download and upload from multiple computers joined together as a "swarm." A BitTorrent client generally refers to any program that implements the BitTorrent protocol, and is capable of preparing, requesting, and transmitting files using the protocol. As one would expect, most copyright owners loathe BitTorrent technology, although some organizational copyright owners use BitTorrent to distribute copyrighted material.

Because the file size required for digital movies is generally much larger than that required for a song—an average two-hour movie is 1.5 gigabytes and an average song is 4 megabytes, or 0.003906 gigabytes—BitTorrent has led to a surge in P2P file sharing of copyrighted movies. The legalities of various BitTorrent networks and uses are not completely settled, but copyright owners have made various attempts at curbing file sharing using BitTorrent. Most of these attempts are either sending cease-and-desist letters to the Internet service providers (ISPs) of BitTorrent users or suing BitTorrent users based on the user's IP address (having obtained the user's identity through a subpoena of the ISP). Often lawsuits against users include many defendants in one suit, the legality of which courts have yet to decisively determine.[29]

Trademarks and Other Source Identifiers

Unlike patent and copyright law, which both have an underlying policy of enticing people to innovate and create via the promise of a limited monopoly, a major policy underlying trademark law is to protect consumers from confusion. If one company uses a trademark that is confusingly similar to the trademark of another company on a similar product, purchasers could be confused as to which company produced the product. As the consumer public has become more brand conscious, trademarks have become increasingly valuable. A trademark, if properly maintained, may last indefinitely, and thus may be a very important asset for the trademark owner.

Figure 6.6 Trademark symbols along with a warning

A **trademark** generally refers to a name, logo, tagline, symbol or other distinguishing characteristic of a product or associated with the product, and a **service mark** refers to the same subject matter when associated with a service provided. An example of a trademark is the name "Sony" and the example of a service mark is the name "Expedia." **Collective marks** are marks used by a group of individuals such as a union or an association. Service marks are marks that are used to certify a quality or characteristic of a product or service and is used by someone other than the owner

---

29   *Pacific Century International LTD v. Does 1-101*, No. C-11-02533-(DMR) (Dist. Court, ND California July 28, 2011).

but with the owner's permission. The mark used to identify a teamster's union would be a collective mark. The "FTD" used by a florist means they belong to a group which uses a national floral distribution system and is an example of a collective mark.

Trade dress refers to the aesthetic of a product or its packaging. For example, the décor and general look of a restaurant. A **certification mark** is a mark used to certify a good or service. A common example of a certification mark is the Good Housekeeping Seal of Approval. A **trade name** is the name a business uses when engaging in commerce but is not by itself a type of trademark. However, a trade name might become part of a trademark. For example Coca-Cola is a trade name that has been trademarked.

For legal purposes, trademarks and service marks may be treated uniformly and referred to simply as "marks," and trademark law is a broad term that encompasses trademarks, service marks, trade dress, and some cybermarks. Most people associate a mark with a brand name, but more broadly a mark is an indicator of source or origin. A mark may be a word mark (e.g., Xerox), a logo (e.g., the Nike swoosh), or even a specific color (e.g., John Deere green) or sound (e.g., the NBC three-chime melody).

A party may accrue legal rights in a mark simply by using that mark in commerce. The right to protect one's trademarks arises under the common law. This common law right allows the owner to sue infringers for using a mark that is confusingly similar to the owner's mark. The use of another's mark or a mark similar enough to cause confusion as to the true source of a good or service is called **infringement**.

For example, Dustin has been selling hotdogs at football games under the name "Dusty's Dogs" for fourteen years. Last Saturday another vendor was selling hotdogs at the same football stadium under the name "Dustie's Dogs." Dustin would have legal rights under the common law against this unauthorized use of his trademark. This type of trademark infringement may be referred to as "unfair competition," and is governed mainly by state law. Although 15 USC. 1125(a), commonly known as section 43(a) of the Lanham Act, which is the federal law governing trademarks, provides a cause of action in federal court for unfair competition.

A mark owner may also prevent others from diluting the owner's mark if the mark is sufficiently famous. An unauthorized use might dilute the value of the owner's trademark. Whereas infringement requires another party using the same or a confusingly similar mark on competing or related products, **trademark dilution** allows the owner of the mark to prevent third parties from using the mark on completely unrelated products where there is no likelihood of confusion. Mark owners most commonly bring dilution lawsuits under the Lanham Act, but many states have also codified trademark dilution as a cause of action for owners of famous marks. The policy underlying trademark dilution is necessarily at odds with freedom of speech under the First Amendment. However, the policy underlying trademark dilution is to protect the owners of famous marks from unauthorized use.

Registration

A mark owner may gain additional rights in a mark by seeking state or federal registration of the mark. State registration of marks is generally considered inferior to federal registration and varies from one state to the next. For these reasons, federal registration will be the

- Trade dress
- Certification mark
- Trade name
- Infringement
- Trademark dilution

focus of this discussion. Federal registration of a mark requires filing an application with the USPTO. The application must clearly identify the mark. A clear drawing is also required if the mark is a symbol or logo. The applications must provide a description of the goods and/or services that are associated with the mark. The owner of a trademark must file an application for renewal between 5 and 6 years after the initial application for trademark registration. The first renewal along with subsequent renewals are for a period of 10 years.

Federal registrations for identical marks may coexist if the goods and/or services associated with the marks are different enough that no consumers will be confused. For example, because bathroom fixtures and commercial airline services are very different goods and services, the mark "Delta" may be registered by two different companies.

An application for federal registration may be based on a mark that is already in use in commerce or on a mark that the applicant intends to use in the near future. The USPTO will perform a search to determine if the applied-for mark is confusingly similar to any registered marks, keeping in mind any overlap in the description of the goods and/or services. If the USPTO determines confusion is unlikely, it will publish the mark for opposition in the Federal Register. The Federal Register is publicly available and the opposition period lasts for 30 days. This gives existing mark owners an opportunity to intervene if they feel registration of the applied-for mark would adversely affect their existing mark. If no party opposes the registration of the applied-for mark, or if the applicant successfully defeats any challenges, the USPTO will issue a federal certificate of registration. Unlike patents and copyrights, federal registrations of marks may be renewed indefinitely. Therefore, the owner of a mark must be careful not to allow anyone else to register a mark without providing opposition to such registration, and a company must be careful to renew its mark so it does not lapse.

Advantages of Registration

The owner of a mark with a federal registration enjoys several advantages compared to mark owners relying solely on common law rights and this section will highlight some of the more valuable advantages with federal registration. Most noticeably to the public, federal registration allows the mark owner to use the encircled R symbol "(R)" as opposed to a superscript "TM." A federal registration also affords the mark owner nationwide priority. By contrast, common law rights extend only to the geographic area in which the mark owner is using the mark in commerce. For example, if Sandra owns a landscaping business with common law rights to the mark for the name of her business "Famous Yardscapes," she has rights to that mark only in the geographic area in which she has done business (for example, maybe a 100-mile radius from the physical location of the business). However, if she obtains a federal registration on that mark, she has rights in the entire country. Nationwide expansion for most businesses

Figure 6.7 Lapsed trademark regarding the Year of the Ocean

requires considerable time and resources, so ensuring exclusive ownership of the business' mark prospectively builds value in the company.

The owner of a mark with a federal registration may sue infringers in federal court without proving federal jurisdiction. A federal trademark registration also serves as a powerful tool to deter would-be owners of a domain name. It also allows the mark owner to attack the current owner of an Internet domain name that is confusingly similar to the registered mark.

- Madrid Protocol
- Fanciful marks
- Arbitrary marks
- Suggestive marks

International Law Protecting Trademarks

The **Madrid Protocol** provides mark owners with an international system for registering their marks in multiple countries. The Madrid Protocol finds legal basis in two multilateral treaties: the *Madrid Agreement Concerning the International Registration of Marks*, which chartering members first ratified in 1892, and the *Protocol Relating to the Madrid Agreement*, which went into force in 1996. Like the PCT process for patents, WIPO administers the Madrid System. As of February, 2013, eighty-eight countries have joined the Madrid Protocol, with the US joining in 2003. The Madrid Protocol allows mark owners in member countries to apply for an international registration from WIPO and then procure registrations of the mark in other member countries. In effect the Madrid Protocol allows a mark owner to obtain a registration in any member country by filing a single application for registration.

Strength of a Mark

Legal protection under trademark law is only available to the name, logo, or other characteristic associated with goods or services if that name, logo, or other characteristic such as color is distinctive. The important factor being that a mark must distinguish the goods or services of one company from the goods or services of another company. The distinctiveness of a mark depends on its relation to the goods or services with which it is associated.

Marks almost always fall in one of the five categories, listed here from most distinctive to least distinctive, of (1) fanciful (or coined), (2) arbitrary, (3) suggestive, (4) descriptive, or (5) generic. The strength of a mark is determined largely by the category into which the mark falls, and trademark law provides more protection for stronger marks.

Fanciful marks are those that did not exist in the language prior to their use as a mark, such as "Exxon" or "Kodak." **Arbitrary marks** are those that have no relation to the goods or services associated with the mark other than identifying the source. An example is "Apple" for electronic products. **Suggestive marks** provide some suggestion as to a quality or characteristic of the goods or services associated with the mark, but require some mental exercise to connect the mark with the product, such as "Coppertone" for suntan lotion. Under trademark law, fanciful, arbitrary, and suggestive marks are considered inherently distinctive, meaning the mark owner need not use the mark in commerce prior to accruing legal rights in the mark.

Descriptive marks describe the goods or services, or a quality of the goods or services associated with the mark. For example, the term "Lite" describes a type of beer. There is overlap between suggestive and descriptive marks, and the line between these two categories

• Generic term

is often unclear since it is nearly impossible to suggest something about goods or services without describing some feature of those goods and services. Descriptive marks are not inherently distinctive but may become distinctive through secondary meaning.

A mark owner may gain secondary meaning for a mark through exclusive use of the mark and heavy advertising. Secondary meaning is achieved when consumers recognize the mark as a source indicator for the goods or services associated with the mark. Descriptive marks are inherently weak as a source indicator/identifier but simultaneously provide some information about the goods or services associated with the mark. For example "Holiday Inn" is a name that is not inherently distinctive. The name is descriptive but has been considered to have achieved secondary meaning.

Trademark attorneys and the marketing departments for mark owners may be at odds when choosing a mark. Trademark attorneys often champion a mark that is fanciful or arbitrary even though it conveys no information about the goods or services until the mark has achieved at least some level of recognition by the public. Those in the marketing field often prefer marks that convey some aspect of the good or services so that customers or potential customers have an idea of some characteristic or feature of the goods or services when they see the mark in use.

A generic term is incapable of functioning as a mark. Generic marks do not receive protection under trademark law. A **generic term** is a mark that only names the product associated with the term. An example is "burgers" for ground beef sandwiches or the term "computer" if used to sell a personal computer.

Prohibiting Infringement

It is the owner's duty to police infringement and misuse of a mark. If consumers begin using a mark as the generic term for a product, the mark is in danger of becoming generic. For example, the mark "Kleenex" has been so widely used as a generic term for facial tissues that the mark may not be as strong as it was previously. Also, a mark may be weakened if the public uses a mark as a verb. An example is "Googling." Some of the most common terms that were once trademarks include linoleum, kerosene, escalator, lollipop, and aspirin. If a mark is in danger of becoming generic, the owner often takes great pains to accentuate the source-indicating nature of the mark by using the mark as an adjective whenever possible. An example is "Kleenex brand facial tissues."

Qualitex Co. v. Jacobson Products Co., Inc.
514 US 159 (1995)

Qualitex sells products to dry cleaning firms, and the products have a unique color. Jacobson began using a very similar color for competing products. Qualitex registered the color as a trademark for the products and then sued Jacobson for trademark infringement. The District Court determined that Jacobson had infringed Qualitex's trademark, but the Appellate Court reversed on appeal, holding that color alone cannot constitute a trademark.

The court had to decide whether a color could function as a trademark. The court held colors may function as trademarks. Based on the underlying principles of trademark law, the Court determined that color may function as a trademark, since the legislative intent was for a broad definition of what constituted a trademark. A color may serve to identify and/or distinguish one brand of goods from another, and customers might make color-goods associations when purchasing goods. However, the Court held that a color cannot be inherently distinctive, and can be registered as a trademark only upon a showing of secondary meaning. The Court also allowed for trademark protection for color under the functionality doctrine, which typically bars trademark protection for functional aspects of a product. Specifically, the Court held that to be functional, a product feature must provide some advantage other than the feature's association with the brand (i.e., a non-reputation-related advantage, such as less costly manufacturing and ease of use). If color does not play an essential role in the product's use, does not affect cost or quality of the goods, and other colors are available for competitors, there is no reason to bar the use of color as a trademark under the functionality doctrine.

Questions

1. Should a start-up business rely on the color of its products to serve as a trademark?
2. What should an established brand do to further protect itself from confusingly similar goods or services?
3. For what types of products is color a functional way of identifying the source of its production?

Trade Dress

Trade dress generally refers to the aesthetic of a product or its packaging and may be legally protected if it serves as a source identifier. Certain types of trade dress may be inherently distinctive and other types may acquire secondary meaning as previously discussed for trademarks and service marks. One method to achieve secondary meaning is for a company to protect the trade dress through a design patent. The design patent would thereby ensure exclusivity in the trade dress for fourteen years. As with trademarks and service marks, the owner of trade dress may develop both state and federal common law rights through use of the trade dress. The owner may also register the trade dress with the

Figure 6.8 Restaurants often have a unique décor which constitutes trade dress

• Trademark
  infringement

USPTO to receive additional protection under federal law, which the mark owner ideally would seek prior to expiration of a design patent covering the trade dress.

Trademark law does not offer protection to functional aspects of a product or product packaging. If a competitor must use a feature of the product or product packaging to compete effectively, trademark law will not extend legal protection to that feature of the product or packaging. If a product design or packaging design provides some utilitarian advantage (e.g., it is less expensive to produce) to the owner, then it is likely functional and not protectable trade dress.

Remedies

Encroaching on the rights of a mark owner may take the form of infringement or dilution. **Trademark infringement** exists when a party uses a mark associated with goods or services and that party's use of the mark is likely to cause customer confusion as to the source of those goods or services. Courts will look to various factors to determine if customers are likely to be confused, the most important of which are (1) similarity of the two marks, (2) similarity of the goods or services, (3) strength of the mark, (4) channels of trade of the goods or services, and (5) the sophistication of the ordinary purchases of the goods or services. The remedies for trademark infringement include injunctive relief and/or monetary damages.

Trademark dilution is available for owners of famous marks who have invested heavily in their mark. Trademark dilution allows the owner of a famous mark to forbid others from using the mark even when the public will not be confused by the other's use. Trademark dilution is often divided into blurring and tarnishment. An example of blurring is using the mark "McDonald's" for shoes—the famous mark is blurred from its association with food and restaurant services. An example of tarnishment is using the mark "Samsung" for an adult bookstore—the famous mark is weakened through an unflattering or undesirable association. To prove a mark is famous for purposes of dilution, the owner must show that the public's perception of the term has shifted such that the term "is now primarily associated with the owner of the mark even when it is considered outside the context of the owner's goods or services."[30] This is generally a high hurdle for a mark owner to clear. To determine if a mark is famous under federal law, a court will consider, among other factors (1) the distinctiveness of the mark, (2) the owner's use of the mark, and (3) the amount of advertising and publicity the mark has received. Once the owner proves the mark is famous, the owner may file suit against any party who uses the famous mark in a way that dilutes the distinctive quality of the mark.

---

30   *Toro Co. v. ToroHead Inc.*, 61 USPQ2d at 1180-1181.

Trademarks and the Internet

In general, both traditional trademark and copyright laws were ill suited to adaptation to the Internet and digital technologies. Lawmakers have made several attempts at adapting trademark law to the Internet age, but mark owners and competitors still face a higher degree of uncertainty related to the extent of their rights in the digital world than do business entities based in brick-and-mortar locations.

One of the first areas of law at the intersection of trademarks and the Internet that lawmakers attempted to settle relates to disputes over ownership and use of domain names. A domain name is part of the Internet address for a particular website. Most users think of a domain name as the combination of letters, words, or numbers that the user types into the address bar of his or her web browser to navigate to a particular web page. Every domain name ends with a top-level domain (TLD), such as *.com, .edu, .net*. The portion of the domain name to the left of the TLD is referred to as the second-level domain (SLD). It is this portion of a domain name that, until recently, was the main concern of mark owners.

The Internet Corporation for Assigned Names and Numbers (ICANN), which is a nonprofit corporation headquartered in California and under contract with the US Department of Commerce, is responsible for distribution and regulation of domain names. As the Internet becomes increasingly diversified and widespread through the world, the US-based governance and English-based nature of the Internet are migrating toward a more international scheme. Eventually the United Nations or another international body will likely oversee the distribution and regulation of domain names. ICANN also oversees the Uniform Domain-Name Dispute Resolution Policy (UDRP), which ICANN adopted in 2000. It provides a standardized process for resolving disputes related to domain names. All ICANN-accredited domain-name registrars must abide by the UDRP.

Perhaps the earliest problem mark owners faced regarding the proliferation of the Internet was cybersquatting. **Cybersquatting** refers to a party registering a domain name that was identical or very similar to a well-known mark and attempting to resell that domain name to the mark owner for a profit. Prior to the UDRP, even if the mark owner had a very strong legal case for infringement against the cybersquatter, the cybersquatter may be out of the jurisdiction ("reach") of US courts. For example, a party residing in Russia who was cybersquatting could not be hauled into court in the US, so the mark owner would have no recourse against the cybersquatter directly. Such difficulties led ICANN to commission WIPO in 1999 for a report on trademark disputes as related to domain names. The report was the basis for the UDRP. Also in 1999, Congress amended the Lanham Act to add the Anticybersquatting Consumer Protection Act (ACPA). This act prevents the registration, use, or sale of domain names that are identical or confusingly similar to a mark owned by another if that registration, use, or sale is in bad faith.

A mark owner may pursue a cybersquatter using either the UDRP or the ACPA, whereas the ACPA allows the mark owner to pursue a cybersquatter via a lawsuit in federal court. An issue may still exist in regards to jurisdiction. The UDRP is a policy between the registrar and the registrar's customers. When a registrant purchases a domain name, the registrant must agree to be bound by the UDRP should a dispute arise related to that domain name. Accordingly, the UDRP does away with any jurisdictional problems.

A mark owner may file a UDRP complaint with an ICANN-approved provider, such as WIPO. The mark owner must send a copy of the complaint to the alleged cybersquatter. If the provider determines the complaint complies with UDRP rules, within three days the provider must send a copy to the registrar of the subject domain name. The defendant has twenty calendar days from receipt of the complaint in which to respond to it, and a provider-appointed panel will render a decision within nineteen calendar days of receiving the defendant's response.

To win a dispute under the UDRP, the mark owner must show that the defendant registered the domain name and is using it in bad faith. Evidence of bad faith may include: (1) the defendant's purpose in registering the domain name was primarily to sell it back to the mark owner for a profit; (2) the defendant registered the domain name to prevent the mark owner from using it or to disrupt the mark owner's business; or, (3) the defendant is attempting to attract users for commercial gain by creating a likelihood of confusion with the mark owner's goods or services.

UDRP proceedings are inexpensive, fast, and efficient compared to federal lawsuits. However, the UDRP is not well suited to handle complex legal disputes involving nuances of US trademark law. Furthermore, unlike the federal court system, the UDRP does not have a standard system for appealing arguably incorrect decisions. Even with these and other limitations, the UDRP remains the most widely used process for mark owners to vindicate their rights against cybersquatters and it remains extremely effective against bad-faith registrations.

More recent developments at the intersection of trademark law and the Internet involve meta tags, hidden code, and cyber-stuffing. Each of these terms refers to using the mark of another on a website in a way that is imperceptible to most users. The use affects how search engines rank or evaluate the website. These practices may artificially place a website associated with a competitor of the search term higher in the search results than the website of the true mark owner. Trademark infringement may arise when a party attempts to fool a search engine into listing and/or consumers into visiting websites that are not specifically associated with the search term. Generally, when a party uses meta tags, hidden code, and cyber-stuffing with bad faith or an intent to deceive, that party commits trademark infringement.

Similarly, the sheer amount of content and number of content outlets associated with the Internet raise issues with trademark dilution. For example, if Roger maintains a blog and writes product reviews for small appliances, a mark owner might take exception to a blog post with an unfavorable review of one of the mark owner's products. This example highlights the tension between trademark dilution and First Amendment rights of free speech. To partially resolve this tension, some courts have held that when the mark must be used to identify the goods or services, dilution law does not apply.[31] Therefore, Roger would be able to use the mark associated with a product he is reviewing.

---

31   *Playboy Enterprises, Inc. v. Welles*, 47 USP.Q.2d 1186 (S.D. Cal. 1998), aff'd without op., 162 F.3d 1169 (9th Cir. 1998).

Trade Secrets

A trade secret is knowledge not known to the public or reasonably ascertainable that provides some economic advantage to the owner, and which the owner treats as a secret. Examples are formulas, processes, and designs. Treating the knowledge as a secret requires that the owner control access to the secret. The owner must also contractually bind individuals who may gain knowledge of the secret or aspects thereof via nondisclosure or confidentiality agreements. Accordingly, legal action for trade secret misappropriation is generally subject to contract law and varies from state to state. For example, a high-ranking executive at a company such as Pepsi would have a clause in their employment contract protecting the trade secrets of Pepsi.

Often the subject matter of a trade secret and what could be patented overlap. Inventors may elect to protect their inventions through trade secret law rather than patent law in some cases. As previously explained, a patent has a finite life. However, a trade secret lasts indefinitely if the owner properly maintains its secrecy and no other party is able to reverse-engineer the trade secret. The owners of some extremely valuable pieces of intellectual property protect their intellectual property as a trade secret. For example, the owners of the Coca-Cola formula have successfully kept it as a trade secret for over 100 years.

When an inventor is deciding whether to protect an invention through trade secret law or patent law, the inventor must consider several factors. First, if the invention may be easily reverse-engineered by a competitor, the invention is likely not a good candidate for trade secret protection because independent development is a complete defense to trade secret misappropriation. If a competing cola manufacturer were able to reverse-engineer the Coca-Cola formula, it would not be such a valuable asset. Generally, mechanical products that a company inserts into the stream of commerce are not well suited to trade secret protection because a skilled engineer could purchase the product and reverse-engineer it. Therefore, patent protection is the better avenue.

Another consideration for an inventor is the ease and cost of detecting and enforcing patent rights. Patent litigation is expensive, and some types of infringement are hard to detect, such as process claims that a competitor would likely perform in a closed factory located overseas. Patent protection also requires that the inventor fully disclose to the public how to make and use the invention, and the patent will eventually expire. If the inventor of the Coca-Cola formula had elected to use patents to protect the formula, any patent would have expired long ago and the formula would be in the public domain, free for any competitor's use. In short, the decision whether to use patents or trade secrets to protect an invention is a complex one with many variables and is a decision that an inventor should carefully consider.

For example, Julie has developed a new method for growing herbs that results in much better taste and a longer shelf life. Her method requires various light cycles at specific time intervals and a certain type of growing tray. It might be wise for Julie to keep her specific light cycles and time intervals as a trade secret (because it cannot be easily reverse-engineered based on the herbs grown using that method), but seek a utility patent on the new growing tray if she has publicly disclosed it at a farmer's market, for instance.

Discussion Questions

1. What are intellectual property and the public policy protecting it?
2. What sources of US law and international law protect intellectual property?
3. What types of innovations is the patent system designed to protect?
4. What is patent infringement?
5. What is the USO and what does it do?
6. What is prior art and what is its significance?
7. What is a utility patent, design patent, plant patent?
8. Does international law protect patents and how so?
9. What subject matter is eligible for patent protection and what is not?
10. How is direct infringement different from indirect infringement?
11. What damages are available to a patent owner in an infringement suit?
12. What are some common defenses in a patent infringement suit?
13. What is required to have a protectable copyright?
14. What is the Berne Convention?
15. What is a work for hire?
16. What cannot be copyrighted?
17. What are some benefits of registering a copyright with the Copyright Office?
18. What are some of the sticks in the "bundle of rights" in copyright?
19. What is contributory copyright infringement and how is it different from vicarious copyright infringement and innocent infringement?
20. What is the DMCA and what does it provide?
21. What is a trademark and how is it different from a service mark?
22. What is trademark dilution and how is it different from infringement?
23. What is the definition of a strong mark, arbitrary mark, and a suggestive mark, and how are they different?
24. What is trade dress and what does it protect?
25. What is trademark infringement?
26. What is cybersquatting?
27. What is a trade secret and how is it protected by its owner?

Critical-Thinking Questions

28. How is a first-to-file system different from a first-to-invent system?
29. Why is a natural phenomenon not patentable?
30. What is the fair-use doctrine and why is it important?
31. What action can a trademark owner take if another party registers a domain name that is confusingly similar to the trademark?
32. What is the idea–expression dichotomy?

Essay Questions

1. Rebecca has an idea for a new invention to help remove tree roots from plumbing pipes. Rebecca has drawn up plans for the invention and has started to build the invention in her garage. What must Rebecca do to protect her invention? Assuming she receives a patent, what would she have to do to protect her invention if Stanley, a neighbor, found out about her invention and started making the same invention?

2. Charlie has created a process for melting metal using a bolt of lightning. Mike has created a software program that helps college students schedule classes and part-time jobs to maximize their efficiency. There currently exists a software application that helps students schedule classes only. Discuss whether or not Charlie and Mike should receive patent protection for their inventions.

3. Nigel volunteers at his son's elementary school. As a fundraiser, he thought it would be a good idea to gather recipes to put in a cookbook that the school could sell to raise money. He would like to make sure the cookbook is protected so that others can't copy it without supporting the school. Discuss how Nigel would protect the cookbook and what the legal limitations might be for the protection of the cookbook.

4. Allison owns a business that provides custom embroidery for clothing. She treats the thread she uses with a lavender scent before she performs the embroidery. She would like to register the scented thread as a form of trademark for the services she provides. Discuss whether she could obtain a federal trademark registration on scented thread used in this manner.

5. Jill recently invented a new computer chip that employs different circuitry to consume far less energy than previous chips, and it requires special firmware that Jill coded herself. She has not sold the chip or publicly disclosed how she made it. She would like to start a business to commercialize the chip. She has already coined a term to use for a brand name, designed marketing materials, and secured a domain name. What should Jill do to protect these various items of intellectual property?

6. Sarah is a journalist and interviewed the former governor of Iowa, Sharon, who was recently defeated in an election. Sharon was a good friend of Jessie, who was convicted of securities fraud. The governor pardoned Jessie during her term, and many political analysts believe that pardon was a major factor in why Sharon was not re-elected. Sharon is planning on releasing a book in the next three weeks detailing her thought process regarding granting Jessie her pardon. The former governor shared portions of her upcoming book with Sarah during the interview, and Sarah agreed she would not publish those portions of the book. When Sarah published her interview on a blog, she didn't publish the portions of the book directly, but she reworded those portions and published the main points. Sarah receives advertising revenue from her blog, but it is less than $1,000 per year. Discuss whether Sarah's use of the portion of the former governor's book constitutes fair use.

7. Bill is interested in starting a new restaurant. His last name is McDonald. He is considering calling his business "McDonald's Burgers." He is worried McDonald's Corporation, which is famous for its Big Mac and golden arches, might take issue with his business name. Mariah and her siblings are starting a coffee bean business. Their family name is

McDonald and they would like to call their business "McDonald's Beans." Do Bill and Mariah have to worry about trademark infringement, and what type of infringement might it be?

8. Lisa has developed a new invention for measuring humidity in the air. She is considering the following names for her invention: "humidity detector," "Lisa's rain detector," "Bananas," and "PrecipDeFinder." Discuss the strengths and weaknesses of each name for trademark-protection purposes.

9. Adam operates a catering business that specializes in barbecued ribs. He has six employees who help him cook and serve food at various events. Recently one of his employees, Jack, became disgruntled and quit. Jack started his own barbecue restaurant and uses Adam's recipe. Jack didn't sign an employment agreement with Adam, but Adam did tell Jack that he considered the barbecue recipe to be a trade secret and to not tell anyone what the recipe was. Did Adam have a trade secret in the recipe? What should someone in Adam's position do to ensure his intellectual property is adequately protected?

10. Patents and copyrights are designed to incentivize creation and innovation through the promise of a limited monopoly. This is designed to further progress. However, some argue that these monopolies stifle innovation rather than drive it forward because the monopoly prevents others from exploring derivative technology, and that competitors expend undue resources trying to design around the monopoly. Discuss whether patents and copyrights spur or stifle progress.

CHAPTER SEVEN

CONTRACTS, PART I: INTRODUCTION AND AGREEMENT

By Michael Bootsma

Alice is looking to hire her first employee, a delivery driver. Brady applies for the job. He asks what the pay is and Alice says he will be paid $500 per week. Alice says the job is his as long as he shows up to work on Monday and works through the week. Brady shows up on Monday and makes deliveries to Alice's satisfaction each day that week. Do Alice and Brady have a contract? Is it an informal contract? Is it an express contract? Is it a unilateral contract? When was the contract formed?

Molly sees a motor bike she would like to buy. She asks the owner Ronaldo if it is for sale. He says, "For the right price." She says, "Will you take $2,000?" He says, "Yes." She says, "I promise to bring you $2,000 in cash on June 20." He says, "I accept and I promise to deliver the title of the bike to you on June 20." Do Alice and Ronaldo have a contract? Is it an informal contract? Is it an express contract? Is it a bilateral contract? When was the contract formed?

Chapter Objectives

1. Identify the basic requirements of a contract.
2. Distinguish between bilateral and unilateral contracts.
3. Understand basic terminology for contracts.
4. Understand what constitutes an offer.
5. Understand what constitutes an acceptance.
6. Understand the legal significance of when a contract is formed.

Introduction

The ability to contract is a key component to creating business transactions. The founding fathers provided for the *Freedom to Contract* in the United States Constitution. The ability to have a contract recognized and enforced by a court gives businesses the reassurance their interests will be protected.

- Merchant
- Contract
- Agreement
- Offeror
- Offeree

For example, Monica borrows $10,000 from First American Bank. She signs a promissory note and a debt contract that requires she make $1,000 payments to First American Bank each month plus accrued interest. Monica has entered into a contract with First American Bank. If Monica could simply avoid repaying the debt with no legal consequences, First American Bank would be reluctant to make these types of loans in the future. The Freedom to Contract comes with responsibilities. Monica must repay the debt and the bank must give her the amount of time promised to repay the loan.

Counterbalancing the Freedom to Contract is the Freedom from Contract. As a society we want citizens to be free from unfair or egregious contracts. For example, Katie has too many alcoholic drinks one Friday night. Joel finds Katie in an intoxicated state. He asks her if she will sell him her car for $500 when Joel knows the car is really worth $10,000. Katie agrees to the sale because she is intoxicated and does not understand the consequences of her actions. Since Katie is intoxicated to the point of not understanding her actions, a court would let her decide whether she wants to enforce the contract or not. The Freedom from Contract protects citizens from unfair contracts but does provide less certainty in regards to enforceability and this lessens the Freedom to Contraact. Therefore, courts perform an important balancing act when it comes to Freedom to Contract and Freedom from Contract.

Law Governing Contracts

All fifty states have adopted, in one form or another, what is known as the Uniform Commercial Code. The "UCC" as it is called in this text, primarily governs sales contracts for goods as well as leases. It must be noted, Louisiana did not enact Article 2 of the UCC, which is a major provision regarding contract law. The UCC was designed to provide uniformity to businesses that were transacting across state lines.

In this chapter, the text will often make reference to the fact UCC rules are different when referring to a merchant. As defined in UCC §2-104, a **merchant** is someone who deals in the kind of goods contracted for or who otherwise holds himself or herself out as having special knowledge or skill related to the goods involved. In addition to the UCC, most states recognize the common law of contracts when the UCC is silent on an issue or neither the UCC nor state law governs a contract. Therefore, a student must be familiar with the UCC, state law, and common law.

Elements of a Contract

One rule that is important to remember is a gift is not a contract. If Jonah promises Dwight $500 on Dwight's birthday, this is a promise to give a gift and Dwight cannot legally enforce this promise if Jonah does not deliver the gift. A **contract** is a legally enforceable promise. The elements of a legally enforceable contract are 1) an agreement, 2) consideration, 3) capacity, and 4) legal subject matter.

An **agreement** is generally evinced by an offer and an acceptance. The **offeror** makes an offer to the **offeree** who is the person to whom the offer was made. The offeree can either accept or reject the offeror's offer. If the offeree accepts the offer, then an agreement is formed. Example: Chad offers Henry $50 if Henry will mow Chad's lawn. Henry says,

Figure 7.1 A contract generally forms after an agreement is reached

"I accept and I will mow your lawn this afternoon."

An agreement must be supported by consideration if the agreement is to be considered a legally enforceable contract. **Consideration** is the legal value provided in a bargained-for exchange of a promise. Consideration may consist of a promise or an action. It may consist of a promise to do something or a promise not to do something that one has a legal right to do. For example, Mitch gets into an accident at a convenience store. Mitch believes the accident to be his fault. He says to the other driver, Michelle, "I will give you $250 in cash if you promise not to call the police or your insurance company about this accident." Michelle says, "I promise not to report the accident." The $250 is Mitch's consideration for Michelle's promise not to report the accident. As long as both parties have capacity and this type of contract is legal in their state, Mitch and Michelle have an agreement supported by consideration, which is a contract. Therefore, the fact that a promise cannot constitute a contract without consideration, is another important rule to remember.

Contractual capacity is the capacity required by law to enter into contracts. For example, all fifty states have laws determining the effect of a minor entering into a contract. A minor is someone whom the state decides is too young to understand the consequences of his or her actions and should be treated differently than someone of the age of majority. A minor is considered to have limited contractual capacity and has certain rights, such as the ability to get out of the contract if the minor so desires. Other examples of those with limited, or no capacity at all, are those who are sufficiently intoxicated such that they don't understand their actions and those who do not understand their actions because of a mental illness.

Legal subject matter is a requirement that a contract not accomplish an illegal goal or act. For example, assume Kristen convinces Maggie that Kristen is a doctor. Kristen offers to perform a surgery on Maggie's arm for $500. On the day before the surgery is to take place, Maggie learns Kristen is not a doctor. Maggie does not have to go through with the surgery or pay Kristen if state law allows only doctors to provide this type of surgery. The subject matter of the contract, performing an operation, was not legal because Kristen was not a doctor.

Types of Contracts

Express contracts are contracts that are generally either verbal or written. Amos asks Moses to build him a swimming pool. Moses agrees and demands payment of $30 per hour. Moses and Amos have an express contract. An **implied contract** is often called an implied-in-fact

- Consideration
- Contractual capacity
- Legal subject matter
- Express
- Implied contract

contract and is different from an express contract because it is inferred from the actions of the parties and is not evinced by an oral or written agreement. An implied contract exists when 1) Party A provides Party B a good or service, 2) that Party B had the opportunity to reject, and 3) Party B knew, or should have known A wanted to contract.

Assume Geraldo mows his neighbor Diane's lawn without her knowledge or consent to do so, and Geraldo then asks for payment. This would not be an implied contract because Diane did not have an opportunity to object to the service. If instead Geraldo had been mowing Diane's lawn each week in June and Diane had been paying him, then if Geraldo mows her lawn during the first week of July and Diane had an opportunity to tell him not to mow the lawn anymore, the two parties may have created an implied contract. The implied contract infers the agreement of the parties from the circumstances of the situation.

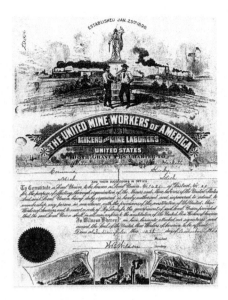

Figure 7.2 This union labor contract is an express contract

Executory contracts are contracts for which one party still owes performance. **Executed** contracts are contracts under which both parties have performed and no performance is still due. For example, assume Lance hires Nathan to put a new seat on his racing bicycle. If Lance promises Nathan $50 for the job, then until both parties have performed, the contract is executory. Once both parties have fully performed, the contract is labeled executed.

Voidable contracts are contracts for which one party has the option of nullifying the contract or enforcing it. Contracts entered into by minors are a prime example of a voidable contract. The minor can decide to enforce the contract or decide not to perform their duties under the contract by disaffirming the contract. A **void** contract is no contract at all and cannot be enforced by a court. An example of a void contract is the contract to achieve an illegal purpose. Assume Kendal hires Kyle to steal a rare car from a local museum. The contract would be void. Neither Kyle nor Kendal could ask a court to enforce the contract and require the other party to perform.

Formal contracts are contracts that, to be enforceable, are required to conform to additional requirements imposed by the law such as the need for a writing signed by the defendant. **Informal** contracts are contracts that are not subject to formal requirements under the law. Assume a state requires all employment contracts for a period of greater than one year to be in writing. An employment contract for a period of greater than one year in that state would then be a formal contract because it must be in writing and cannot merely be a verbal agreement.

Unenforceable contracts contain all the elements of a valid contract (agreement, consideration, capacity, and legality) but are unenforceable by a court. Under the common law Statute of Frauds, a contract for the sale of land must be in writing. Assume Jack and Diane enter into a verbal contract for the sale of land. The verbal contract is a contract; however, if it was not reduced to writing, then it is unenforceable by a court.

A **unilateral** contract contains an offer that can be accepted by providing complete performance only. For example, Xavier offers Kathleen $20 to cut his hair. Kathleen says, "Sit down." She then cuts Xavier's hair. He now owes her $20 because she accepted his offer by performance and the two have formed a unilateral contract. An offer in a **bilateral** contract is accepted by a return promise. Derek offers Hugh $5,000 if Hugh will promise to plow Derek's field. If Hugh accepts by return promise to do so, then the two parties have a bilateral contract. The distinction between a unilateral and bilateral contract can be important for several reasons.

First, in a unilateral contract situation, the offeror cannot revoke their offer once the offeree has begun to perform or has started preparing to perform. If Kenny offers Reba $5,000 to swim across a four-mile-wide river, Kenny cannot revoke his offer once Reba has begun to swim across the river. In addition, Reba has not completed her acceptance until she has provided complete performance, which would mean swimming all the way across the river. Second, a bilateral contract creates legal liability for performance once a return promise has been made, whereas an offer in a unilateral contract will not create liability until performance has been completed.

Carlill vs. Carbolic Smoke Ball Co.
[1893] Q.B. 256 (C.A.)

The Carbolic Smoke Ball Company advertised a smoke ball that it stated would prevent influenza. The company advertised "£100 reward will be paid by the Carbolic Smoke Ball Company to any person who contracts the influenza after having used the ball three times daily for two weeks according to the printed directions supplied with each ball." The defendants, Carbolic Smoke Ball Company, claimed to have placed £1000 in a bank account to pay any claimants. Plaintiff Louisa Elizabeth Carlill used the smoke ball three times a day as required. However, she contracted influenza. Carlill made a claim against the company for her reward. The company refused to pay.

Figure 7.3 advertisement for the carbolic smoke ball

The company claimed the advertisement was too vague to constitute an offer. In addition, Carlill did not give them notice of her acceptance of their offer, if there was indeed an offer. Finally, Carlill did not provide any consideration. A British appeals court found there was a contract. The court stated the advertisement was an offer, and not just an invitation, because it limited who could accept. The court stated the offer was not too vague and it was not just a "puff" or disingenuous sales tactic. The court also stated consideration was provided by the plaintiff because she purchased the ball and attempted to use it, which is what the company wanted.

In regards to notice of acceptance, Justice Bowen stated: "If I advertise to the world that my dog is lost, and that anybody who brings the dog to a particular place will be paid

- Offeror
- Offeree

some money, are all the police or other persons whose business it is to find lost dogs to be expected to sit down and write me a note saying that they have accepted my proposal? Why, of course, they at once look after the dog, and as soon as they find the dog they have performed the condition. The essence of the transaction is that the dog should be found, and it is not necessary under such circumstances, as it seems to me, that in order to make the contract binding there should be any notification of acceptance. It follows from the nature of the thing that the performance of the condition is sufficient acceptance without the notification of it, and a person who makes an offer in an advertisement of that kind makes an offer which must be read by the light of that common sense reflection."

Questions

1. What type of contract was involved in this case? Express or implied? Bilateral or unilateral?
2. Not all advertisements are offers. Why is this an important rule for businesses?
3. Under Justice Bowen's rationale does one ever have to give notice of acceptance?

Agreement

An agreement is generally evinced by an offer and an acceptance. A legally binding offer requires an **offeror**, the person making an offer, to manifest the objective intent to be legally bound by their statement to the **offeree**, who is the person receiving the offer. Courts generally have three requirements for a legally binding offer:

1. The offer must be communicated to the offeree.
2. The offeror must have serious objective intent to be bound.
3. The offer must contain definite-enough terms to bind the offeror.

The first requirement is the offer must generally be communicated to the offeree. This protects the offeror by limiting who can accept. For example, assume Rick offers Karen a job as a salesperson. Elizabeth hears the offer and says "I accept." The offer was not made to Elizabeth so she cannot accept and bind Rick in contract. Rick may have chosen Karen because of her personality and communication abilities.

As another example, assume Kerry loses her dog Dallas. She offers a $10,000 reward to anyone who delivers Dallas to her. Corwin finds Dallas and then returns him to the address on his dog tag. Corwin rings Kerry's door bell. Kerry opens the door and screams with delight because her dog was returned. She then says, "Did you know about the reward?" If Corwin says "no" then Kerry does not have to pay him the $10,000 since he did not know about the offer. It was not communicated to him. He provided the service of returning the dog without knowledge of the offer. His act cannot constitute consideration for Kerry's promise of a reward because her offer had not been communicated to him. It should be noted, some states have created an exception in the context of rewards, and for example, if the reward was offered by a public agency, the offeree does not need prior knowledge of the offer.

Next, an offeror must have serious objective intent to be bound by an offer. An offer made in jest will not constitute a legally binding offer. For example, assume Mike is frustrated with his mower and yells, "I hate this mower—I will sell it to anyone for a dollar!!!" His neighbor Dan walks up and hands Mike a dollar. Mike was not serious and was acting in anger. Therefore, he did not intend to be bound by his statement. The standard imposed by courts is an objective standard and not a subjective standard. A subjective standard would ask what the offeror Mike really meant. The objective standard instead asks what the reasonable person would interpret Mike as having meant by his statement. Therefore, Mike has better be careful when making offers he believes to be made in jest as a court might find a reasonable person would have interpreted the offer to be a serious statement which is legally binding.

Finally, an offer must contain enough definite terms to bind the offeror. The offer must create the power of acceptance in the offeree. Assume Jillian says she will sell Tom her car sometime in the near future at a price she will later determine to be fair. Jillian has not created the power of acceptance in Tom. Tom does not know what the price is or when he will actually be able to obtain the car. In regards to definite terms needed to make an offer legally enforceable, courts generally look for 1) the parties to be named, 2) the price of the service or product to be specified, 3) the time for performance to be stated, and 4) a sufficient description of what the subject matter of the contract is. It should be noted the lack of one of these terms in not always fatal to forming a legally binding offer. For example, parties may refer to "market price" instead of naming an exact price for a good.

In the event an agreement does not contain definite terms, UCC § 2-204(3) states parties may still have a contract if it is clear they meant to be bound and there is a reasonable basis for determining what a reasonable remedy would be. Courts often use "gap fillers" to fill missing terms if they can do so from the conduct of the parties or trade usage.

Lucy v. Zehmer
84 S.E. 2d. 516 (1954)

The following are excerpts from the Supreme Court of Virginia's opinion as written by Justice Buchanan.

This suit was instituted by W.O. Lucy and J.C. Lucy, complainants, against A.H. Zehmer and Ida S. Zehmer, his wife, defendants, to have specific performance of a contract by which it was alleged the Zehmers had sold to W.O. Lucy a tract of land owned by A.H. Zehmer in Dinwiddie county containing 471.6 acres, more or less, known as the Ferguson farm, for $50,000. J.C. Lucy, the other complainant, is a brother of W.O. Lucy, to whom W.O. Lucy transferred a half interest in his alleged purchase.

The instrument sought to be enforced was written by A.H. Zehmer on [Saturday,] December 20, 1952, in these words: "We hereby agree to sell to W.O. Lucy the Ferguson Farm, complete for $50,000, title satisfactory to buyer," and signed by the defendants, A.H. Zehmer and Ida S. Zehmer.

The answer of A.H. Zehmer admitted that at the time mentioned W.O. Lucy offered him $50,000 cash for the farm, but that, he, Zehmer, considered that the offer was made in jest; that so thinking, and both he and Lucy having had several drinks, he wrote out "the memorandum" quoted above and induced his wife to sign it; that he did not deliver

Figure 7.4 A party who makes an offer in jest might still be bound in contract

the memorandum to Lucy, but that Lucy picked it up, read it, put it in his pocket, attempted to offer Zehmer $5 to bind the bargain, which Zehmer refused to accept, and realizing for the first time that Lucy was serious, Zehmer assured him that he had no intention of selling the farm and that the whole matter was a joke. Lucy left the premises insisting that he had purchased the farm.***

In his testimony Zehmer claimed that he "was high as a Georgia pine," and that the transaction "was just a bunch of two doggoned drunks bluffing to see who could talk the biggest and say the most." That claim is inconsistent with his attempt to testify in great detail as to what was said and what was done. It is contradicted by other evidence as to the condition of both parties, and rendered of no weight by the testimony of his wife that when Lucy left the restaurant she suggested that Zehmer drive him home. The record is convincing that Zehmer was not intoxicated to the extent of being unable to comprehend the nature and consequences of the instrument he executed, and hence that instrument is not to be invalidated on that ground.***

If it be assumed, contrary to what we think the evidence shows, that Zehmer was jesting about selling his farm to Lucy and that the transaction was intended by him to be a joke, nevertheless the evidence shows that Lucy did not so understand it but considered it to be a serious business transaction and the contract to be binding on the Zehmers as well as on himself. The very next day he arranged with his brother to put up half the money and take a half interest in the land. The day after that he employed an attorney to examine the title. The next night, Tuesday, he was back at Zehmer's place and there Zehmer told him for the first time, Lucy said, that he wasn't going to sell and he told Zehmer, "You know you sold that place fair and square." After receiving the report from his attorney that the title was good he wrote to Zehmer that he was ready to close the deal.

Not only did Lucy actually believe, but the evidence shows he was warranted in believing, that the contract represented a serious business transaction and a good faith sale and purchase of the farm.

In the field of contracts, as generally elsewhere, "We must look to the outward expression of a person as manifesting his intention rather than to his secret and unexpressed intention.***

So a person cannot set up that he was merely jesting when his conduct and words would warrant a reasonable person in believing that he intended a real agreement.***

Whether the writing signed by the defendants and now sought to be enforced by the complainants was the result of a serious offer by Lucy and a serious acceptance by the defendants, or was a serious offer by Lucy and an acceptance in secret jest by the defendants, in either event it constituted a binding contract of sale between the parties.***

The complainants are entitled to have specific performance of the contract sued on.

Questions

1. Who was the offeror and who was the offeree?
2. Was Mr. Zehmer drunk? Why was it important that he was not extremely intoxicated?
3. Did it matter to the court that Mr. Zehmer says he was joking? Why or why not?
4. What facts led the court to believe Mr. Lucy was justified in objectively believing a legally binding offer existed?

Non-Offers

- Expression of opinion
- Statement of future intention
- Solicitation of bids

Courts generally find certain common scenarios to lack a legally binding offer. For example, an offer made as a joke or "in jest" is not a legally binding offer. Somewhat related is the concept of offers in social situations. Courts often find promises made in the context of social situation to be an offer for which the offeror did not intend to be legally bound. Assume Jack offers to cook Ann dinner if Ann will watch a movie with Jack on Friday night. Ann shows up to Jack's house and watches a movie but Jack refuses to cook dinner. Ann cannot sue Jack for breach of contract because their agreement arose in a social context for which one would not normally expect to be legally bound.

An **expression of opinion** is generally not an offer. An example is Matthew saying, "I would like to sell my business for $120,000." This is an expression of opinion and cannot be accepted by someone hearing this statement. A **statement of future intention** is also not considered a legally binding offer. "I will sell my business in ten years for $500,000" is a statement of intention that cannot be accepted as a legally binding offer. A common example of a statement of future intention is a **solicitation of bids**. For example, assume Gail wants to build a new house. She contacts several construction companies for a bid to build the house. A bid is merely an estimate of costs to complete a project. A solicitation of bids by Gail does not create legally binding offers to the construction companies unless she expressly states the intent to be bound by her solicitation of bids.

Special Offers

- Advertisement
- Auction
- With reserve
- Without reserve

Advertisements

An **advertisement** is generally not a legally binding offer unless it contains words of limitations such as limiting the quantity of the item being sold or the number of people who can accept. Assume a grocery store offers to sell bottles of a certain type of juice for $1 per bottle. As a general rule this is considered an invitation to come to the store and purchase products and not a legally binding offer for juice at the price of $1 per bottle. However, if a grocery store offered "apples at $1 per pound until the first twenty pounds of apples are gone," then a court would generally find the advertisement to be a legally binding offer because the quantity has been limited.

Figure 7.5 an advertisement is generally considered an invitation to bid and not an offer

Auctions

At an **auction**, the auctioneer places an item for sale and solicits bids from those in attendance. The bidders make an offer to purchase and the auctioneer decides which bid to accept. Under the UCC, an auction is **with reserve** unless noted otherwise. At an auction with reserve, the seller or auctioneer may withdraw the item any time before the auctioneer accepts the highest bid and declares the item to be sold. In an auction **without reserve**, neither the auctioneer nor the seller can withdraw an item once bidding has started. Under the UCC, the bidders in the crowd can withdraw their offers any time prior to the finalization of the sale.

Multiple Offers

Courts often must determine whether there was one offer for one comprehensive contract or whether the offeror was making a series of offers that required acceptance by the offeree at different times during the business relationship. For example, assume Smith Manufacturing agrees to sell 10,000 wheels to Gordon Enterprises and promises to make delivery in lots of 1,000 wheels. Is this one offer to contract for the sale of 10,000 wheels or is it ten individual offers? Courts often revert to the rule of what the reasonable person in the place of the offeree would believe the offeror to have meant.

Options Contracts

An **options contract** is a contract under which the offeror promises to keep her offer open to the offeree until a specified date. For example, on September 1, Michelle offers to sell Mark her prized sailboat for $52,000. Mark pays Michelle $250 in return for Michelle's promise to keep the offer open until December 1. Mark and Michelle have a contract under which Michelle must keep her offer open until December 1. She cannot revoke her offer to sell the boat to Mark for $52,000. Mark can accept any time before December 1. A lawyer would say the offer is "irrevocable" during this period.

A firm offer is a similar concept to an options contract. Under UCC § 2-205, an offer can become a **firm offer** if 1) the offer was made by a merchant, 2) there is a signed writing, and 3) the writing clearly states the offer is to remain open. If a period of time has not been stated, the offer is to remain open to the offeree for a reasonable period of time not to exceed three months.

When Offers Terminate

The power of acceptance terminates when an offer can no longer be accepted. Offers terminate, or can no longer be accepted, for a variety of reasons.

Reasonable Amount of Time or Stated Time and Date

First, offers terminate **after a reasonable amount of time**. For example, David offers Michelangelo his business law textbook for $20 on June 1. Ten months later, Michelangelo accepts David's offer by sending him a letter stating his desire to tender the $20 in exchange for the book. David's offer has more than likely terminated because a reasonable amount of time has lapsed. Determining what a reasonable amount of time is depends on the facts and circumstances of each case. Therefore, parties will often make acceptance of an offer subject to the condition that the offeree accepts by a stated time on a stated date.

An offeror is the master of their offer. An offeror can, therefore, determine when the offer will lapse or terminate. Example: John tells Mary, "I will sell you my car for $5,000 but you have to decide by tomorrow." If Mary does not accept by tomorrow, then the offer lapses. It is important to remember if an offeror does not specify when an offer will terminate, the offer terminates after a reasonable amount of time and what constitutes a reasonable amount of time is a factual question for a court to decide.

Rejection

Offers also terminate by **rejection**, which is the offeree's statement or other conduct that states the offeree's desire to reject an offer and refuse acceptance. An offeree may reject an offer by simply stating "no" or by making a counteroffer. A **counteroffer** rejects the original offer and makes a new offer. For example, Mark offers to sell James a used pickup truck for $12,000. James says, "Never, your truck is only worth $10,000. Will you take $10,000?" James has rejected Mark's offer and made a counteroffer. Mark can now accept or reject the offer of James for $10,000. An **inquiry** is not a counteroffer. For example, assume Kristen offers to sell Katie her house for $150,000. Katie says, "That seems like a lot of money, will

• Mirror-image rule

you take $145,000?" Most courts would view Katie's statement as an inquiry that does not terminate the original offer for $150,000.

Under the common law, the acceptance had to be the mirror image of the offer. The **mirror-image rule** prohibits the offeree from accepting an offer while adding additional terms. For example, assume Dennis offered to sell his bicycle to Rose for $50. Rose says, "I accept but you have to install a speedometer on the bike." The common law would label Rose's acceptance as a counteroffer because it was not the mirror image of Dennis's offer.

UCC §2-207

The UCC addresses additional terms in UCC Section 2-207 by abolishing the mirror image rule. Section 2-207 provides that an offeree can accept and make their acceptance conditional upon consent to additional terms expressly provided in the terms of the acceptance. Section 2-207 also allows an offeree to incorporate additional terms in their acceptance. If an additional term is added in the acceptance and one of the parties is not a merchant, the offeror has to agree to the additional term. As defined in UCC §2-104, a merchant is someone who deals in the goods of the kind being contracted for or who otherwise holds himself or herself out as having special knowledge or skill related to the goods involved. In the case where one of the parties is not a merchant, the additional term does not make the acceptance a counteroffer but instead makes the additional term a proposal.

For example, Paul, a non-merchant, offers to sell some of the produce he grew in his backyard to a local grocery store that is considered a merchant. Paul offers the produce at $.50 per pound but states the buyer must transport the produce from Paul's farm. The grocery store accepts his offer but says Paul must help load the truck and must have the produce in plastic cartons that the grocery store will not return. The grocery store has added additional terms that are considered proposals and Paul can now accept or decline these proposals.

If both parties are merchants, the additional term may become part of the agreement under the UCC unless an exception applies. First, the offeror has the ability to reject additional terms. The offeror must notify the offeree of their rejection of the additional terms. The offeror can also state in their original offer that no additional terms may be added by the seller in their acceptance. Second, the other major exception to the rule that additional terms become part of the contract is where the additional terms are considered to "materially alter" the contract.

The issue of whether the additional term materially alters the contact is a question of fact to be considered by a court. For example, assume Merchant A offers to sell 10,000 gallons of fertilizer to Merchant B for the price of $2 per gallon, which Merchant A will deliver on Tuesday March 14. Merchant B accepts but states Merchant A is to provide delivery on two different days: March 14 and March 18. Whether or not the separate delivery dates are an additional term is a factual question. If it is an additional term that materially alters the contract, it will not become part of the contract. If it does not materially alter the contract, it will become a part of the contract unless A expressly objects. There is a third exception and it applies when the original offer prohibited additional terms. Issues arise when the prohibition is part of what is considered to be boilerplate language. The discussion of this third exception is beyond the scope of this text.

Roto-Lith Ltd. v. F.P. Bartlett & Co.
297 F.2d 497 (1st Cir. 1962)

The following are excerpts from the opinion of the First Circuit Court of Appeal.

On October 23, 1959, plaintiff, in New York, mailed a written order to defendant in Massachusetts for a drum of "N-132-C" emulsion, stating "End use: wet pack spinach bags." Defendant on October 26 prepared simultaneously an acknowledgment and an invoice. The printed forms were exactly the same, except that one was headed "Acknowledgment" and the other "Invoice," and the former contemplated insertion of the proposed, and the latter of the actual, shipment date. Defendant testified that in accordance with its regular practice the acknowledgment was prepared and mailed the same day. The plaintiff's principal liability witness testified that he did not know whether this acknowledgment "was received, or what happened to it." The goods were shipped to New York on October 27. On the evidence it must be found that the acknowledgment was received at least no later than the goods. The invoice was received presumably a day or two after the goods.

The acknowledgment and the invoice bore in conspicuous type on their face the following legend, "All goods sold without warranties, express or implied, and subject to the terms on reverse side." In somewhat smaller, but still conspicuous, type there were printed on the back certain terms of sale, of which the following are relevant:

1. "Due to the variable conditions under which these goods may be transported, stored, handled, or used, Seller hereby expressly excludes any and all warranties, guaranties, or representations whatsoever. Buyer assumes risk for results obtained from use of these goods, whether used alone or in combination with other products. Seller's liability hereunder shall be limited to the replacement of any goods that materially differ from the Seller's sample order on the basis of which the order for such goods was made."
2. This acknowledgment contains all of the terms of this purchase and sale. No one except a duly authorized officer of Seller may execute or modify contracts. Payment may be made only at the offices of the Seller. *If these terms are not acceptable, Buyer must so notify Seller at once.*" (Ital. suppl.)

It is conceded that plaintiff did not protest defendant's attempt so to limit its liability, and in due course paid for the emulsion and used it. It is also conceded that adequate notice was given of breach of warranty, if there were warranties. The only issue which we will consider is whether all warranties were excluded by defendant's acknowledgment.***

Now, within stated limits, a response that does not in all respects correspond with the offer constitutes an acceptance of the offer, and a counteroffer only as to the differences. If plaintiff's contention is correct that a reply to an offer stating additional conditions unilaterally burdensome upon the offeror is a binding acceptance of the original offer plus simply a proposal for the additional conditions, the statute would lead to an absurdity. Obviously no offeror will subsequently assent to such conditions.

The statute is not too happily drafted. Perhaps it would be wiser in all cases for an offeree to say in so many words, "I will not accept your offer until you assent to the following:***" But businessmen cannot be expected to act by rubric. It would be unrealistic to suppose that when an offeree replies setting out conditions that would be burdensome only to the offeror he intended to make an unconditional acceptance of the original offer, leaving it simply to the offeror's good nature whether he would assume the additional restrictions. To give the statute a practical construction we must hold that a response which states a condition materially altering the obligation solely to the disadvantage of the offeror is an "acceptance*** expressly*** conditional on assent to the additional*** terms."

Plaintiff accepted the goods with knowledge of the conditions specified in the acknowledgment. It became bound.

Questions

1. What is the significance of the last sentence that states "[i]t became bound."
2. Did the additional terms become part of the contract?
3. Why would it be wise for an offeree to say, "I will not accept your offer until you assent to the following"?

Revocation

An offeror may revoke an offer and the act of revocation eliminates the ability of an offeree to accept. For example, Roger offers Anneshia a notebook computer for $400. Before Anneshia responds, Roger states he has changed his mind and is no longer willing to sell the computer. Roger has revoked his offer to Anneshia. Under the common law, a revocation was effective once it was received by the offeree. However, some states, such as California, have modified the common law rule so a revocation is effective once it is sent. For example, in California, Roger could revoke his offer to sell Anneshia his computer by sending her a letter stating the offer has been revoked. The moment he places the letter in a mailbox, it is considered to be dispatched and the revocation is deemed effective. Anneshia can no longer accept Roger's offer.

UCC § 1-202(e) states a person may receive notice by 1) actually receiving notice of a particular matter or 2) by notice being delivered to the person or a representative of the person; 3) a person may receive notice indirectly from certain facts and circumstances. For example, Sarah offers Jerry a job as an accountant. Jerry does not know if he wants the job but he does not reject Sarah's offer. Sarah may revoke her offer by calling Jerry and telling him the offer has been revoked. If Jerry does not answer his phone, Sarah may leave him a message in his voicemail and this will be deemed to be notice to Jerry that the offer has been revoked even if he does not actually listen to the voicemail. Sarah could also send a letter to Jerry's house. Under the common law and the UCC, once the letter is delivered, Jerry is deemed to have received notice of the revocation. Finally, Jerry may learn of the revocation by facts and circumstances. As an example, assume Jerry speaks with his best friend Kayla and learns she has taken the job. Jerry has received notice through Kayla that the offer to him was revoked. It should be noted that Kayla must have accepted the job. If

Kayla merely mentions she has been offered the job, such a statement would not constitute notice to Jerry. Kayla must actually accept the job so that Jerry knows the offer is no longer available to him.

Another important rule is the rule that if an offer is made to offerees by means of a newspaper advertisement or public flier, it must be revoked by the same means the offer was made. For example, Kelly offers to sell her antique jewelry by placing an advertisement in the local newspaper. As a general rule, advertisements are not offers but Kelly limits who can accept and the quantity that can be accepted by stating, "The first person to tender $5,000,000 to my representative at Ames County Bank shall be deemed to have accepted my offer." Kelly has now created an offer by means of an advertisement. If no one has accepted the offer and after a few weeks Kelly would like to revoke her offer, she must do so using a similar advertisement in a newspaper.

Death or Incapacity

The death or incapacity of either the offeror or offeree terminates the power of acceptance unless the offer was considered to be part of an options contract. For example, assume Raymond offers to sell Qing a calculator for $10. If Raymond dies, Qing cannot accept the offer to buy the calculator unless it was part of an options contract. The result would be different if the offer had been made as part of an options contract. In such case, the offeree Qing could accept and demand the estate of Raymond fulfill the contract.

Acceptance

Acceptance of an offer creates an agreement. Remember, to have a contract, parties must have 1) an agreement, 2) consideration, 3) capacity, and 4) legal subject matter. The agreement is sometimes referred to as **mutual assent** in the legal world. Acceptance of an offer in a unilateral contract situtaion occurs when a party provides complete performance. For example, Suzie offers Addison $100 if Addison will wash Suzie's windows. Suzie says the offer may be accepted only by performance. Addison may accept this offer by washing the windows. However, acceptance is not effective until performance of washing the windows is complete. Fortunately, the modern view is the offer made by the offeror cannot be revoked once performance has begun or the offeree has taken significant steps towards performing. This last rule protects Addison from finishing ½ of the job only to be told by Suzie that the offer has been revoked. In a bilateral contract, an offer is accepted by a return promise. For example, Suzie offers Jon $85 if Jon will promise to wash Suzie's car. Jon's return promise stating, "I will wash your car this Thursday by 4 PM" is his acceptance and legally obligates him to wash the car.

Communication of Acceptance

- Click-on agreement
- Shrink-wrap agreement

Mailbox Rule

The mailbox rule is a common law rule that states acceptance is deemed effective upon dispatch. For example, Ada offers to sell Rachel a motorized bike for $225. Rachel says she needs to think about it. Upon returning to her apartment, Rachel decides she wants the motorized bike and so she mails a letter to Rachel saying she accepts. When Rachel places the letter in the mail, acceptance has been made. The mailbox rule also applies to other forms of communication such as facsimile or email. Finally, it should be noted an offeror can suspend the application of the mailbox rule by stating it does not apply in their offer. For example, Emily offers to sells Scott a truck for $14,000 and says Scott must accept verbally and in person by the end of the following day. Emily has suspended the mailbox rule.

Figure 7.6 The mailbox rule states an offer is accepted upon dispatch of the letter of acceptance

Cyber-Based Acceptances

Cyber-based transactions have presented their own unique challenges in regards to contracting. For example, many online purchases of software or products require the user to agree to the terms of the online offer by clicking a box that certifies the user has read the terms and conditions of the seller's contractual offer. The term **click-on agreement** has been used to describe these transactions because the user must click on the box to certify their assent. Courts have been willing to enforce the terms of these click-on agreements even if the user did not read the terms and conditions. In addition, courts have also been willing to enforce the terms of shrink-wrap agreements if the buyer knew of the existence of the terms and conditions inside the package before making the purchase. A **shrink-wrap agreement** exists when the terms and conditions of the contract are contained in a product's packaging but the terms cannot be accessed until the plastic wrap is removed from the box. Once the plastic wrap is removed, however, the purchaser cannot return the product.

In regards to the mailbox rule as applied to cyber transactions, most courts have held an acceptance is deemed made once an email or fax has been sent, just like the letter being deposited into the mail. However, it is deemed received in most cases when it enters the technological system of the recipient. For example, a revocation made by email would be deemed received by an employee of a corporation once the email enters the company email system, regardless of whether the recipient opens or reads the email.

Nonverbal or Non-Written Acceptance

Acceptance generally requires an affirmative action such as stating "I accept" by verbal or written communication. Acceptance may also be made by action such as shipment of goods after receiving an offer for purchase of goods. However, silence is generally not considered acceptance under the common law.

In certain situations, silence can be considered acceptance. For example, silence constitutes acceptance in the context of an implied-in-fact contract where the defendant knew or should have known the plaintiff wanted to contract and the defendant had a chance to say "no" to the plaintiff's service or goods. Prior dealings might give rise to a situation where silence is considered acceptance. For example, assume Bernie routinely delivers to fresh apples to a local grocery store. The store pays Bernie the current market price. One week, Bernie delivers the apples and the grocery store receives the delivery. A week later, it refuses to pay. The grocery store states it never accepted his offer for sale of the apples. A court would likely say an implied-in-fact contract exists based upon the prior dealings of the two parties and the price should be the fair market price.

Indefiniteness

To form an agreement, the essential terms of the agreement must be present. An offer, acceptance, or an agreement with indefinite terms could not constitute a contract under the common law. The necessary terms to a contract are 1) identified parties, 2) subject matter, 3) time for performance, and 4) price. The lack of one of these necessary terms does not automatically make a contact void. For example, Aaron hires Levi to plant his field with corn seed. The price is to be $50 per acre. The time for performance is not identified but a court would more than likely hold a contract exists and that the deadline for performance should be the last day possible for planting that would give the plants adequate time to grow and be harvested. Courts often look at past transactions or dealings of the parties, common trade terms, and performance to date under the contract at hand to fill a missing term.

UCC § 2-204(3) provides an agreement that two parties intended to be a contract does not become void because of indefinite terms if there is a reasonable basis for determining remedies. UCC 2-306(1) even allows for output contracts and requirements contracts that were once thought to be unenforceable agreements since the terms were indefinite and consideration was lacking. An **outputs contract** is one in which the buyer agrees to purchase all of the output a seller produces. For example, Jerry agrees to buy all the wool Harry, a sheep farmer, can produce on his farm. A **requirements contract** is a contract in which the seller agrees to sell the buyer all the product a buyer would need. For example, Roadway Incorporated is building a new road for the state of Minnesota. Gravel Pit Incorporated agrees to sell Roadway all the sand and rock they will need to build the road.

Duty to Act in Good Faith

Parties to a contract must act in good faith with fair dealing. UCC §1-203 states "[e]very contract or duty within this Act imposes an obligation of good faith in its performance or enforcement." UCC § 1-201(19) states **good faith** means "means honesty in fact and the observance of reasonable commercial standards of fair dealing." For example, Josie hires Clint to paint her house red. Clint shows up to paint the house but Josie says she does not know whether or not she wants the house to be painted red. Unknown to Clint, Josie does not have

- Outputs contract
- Requirements contract
- Good faith

money to pay Clint so she makes up more excuses to prevent Clint from performing. Clint continues to show up seven days in a row but Josie keeps making up excuses. Josie is not acting in good faith because she is preventing Clint from providing performance under the contract. Good faith has been held to apply to cases other than those governed by the UCC.

Shelton v. Oscar Mayer Foods Corp.

459 S.E.2d 851 (1995)

The following are excerpts from the opinion of Judge Goolsby of the Court of Appeals for South Carolina.

This case arises out of an alleged wrongful termination of employment and, so far as is pertinent here, involves claims by Julian Harris Shelton against Louis Rich, a subsidiary of Oscar Mayer Foods Corporation, for breach of contract, breach of contract accompanied by a fraudulent act, fraudulent misrepresentation, and breach of covenant of good faith and fair dealing. Louis Rich discharged Shelton after a security guard reported he observed Shelton and another

Figure 7.7 This case involves a dispute involving Oscar Mayer

employee smoking marijuana in the Louis Rich parking lot. Judge James W. Johnson, Jr., granted Louis Rich's motion for a directed verdict on the breach of contract claim. All other claims were previously disposed of on motions to dismiss or for summary judgment by either Judge Johnson or Judge T.L. Hughston, Jr. Shelton appeals. We affirm in part, reverse in part, and remand.

Shelton worked at the Louis Rich processing plant in Newberry. When he was hired, he received the 1979 employee handbook. The handbook contained employee conduct rules and company policies. In 1983, Louis Rich distributed another handbook that included a change in company policies, but Louis Rich did not otherwise notify the employees of the change. In 1987, William Brown, a security guard, told Louis Rich management that he had observed Shelton and a co-worker smoking marijuana in the Louis Rich parking lot in the co-worker's van. There is conflicting testimony concerning whether Louis Rich investigated the allegation before it discharged Shelton. Shelton claims Louis Rich failed to "[e]nsure," as its *854 handbook provided, that its rules governing employee conduct "[would] be enforced fairly and equally with regard to all employees."***

Under South Carolina law, there exists in every contract an implied covenant of good faith and fair dealing. *Parker v. Byrd*, 309 S.C. 189, 420 S.E.2d 850 (1992). Further, we find no authoritative case law holding the implied covenant of good faith and fair dealing is not applicable to employment contracts that alter the employee's at-will status. If, therefore, the jury finds the handbook issued to Shelton created an employment contract that altered his at-will status, then the question of whether Louis Rich breached an implied covenant of good faith and fair dealing based on an employment contract is for the jury to decide.

Questions

1. How might an employee handbook form an agreement with employees?
2. What types of contracts does the UCC govern? Why was an implied duty of good faith incorporated by this court?
3. What actions taken by the company Oscar Mayer may have proven they were not acting in good faith?

Nonconforming Acceptance

As discussed, additional terms that are added by the offeree may or may not become part of the agreement, depending upon whether or not the parties are merchants or if the additional terms were material or prohibited by the original offer. Under UCC 2-206, acceptance may be made by any method that is reasonable. It also states an offer for the purchase of goods may be accepted by shipment of goods or the promise of prompt shipment of goods. In the event a seller promptly ships nonconforming goods, the seller is deemed to have accepted the offer while simultaneously breaching the contract unless the seller sends the goods as an accommodation and notifies the buyer that the goods are an accommodation. For example, Rita orders 100 couches to be sold at her furniture store. She specifies the size and type of material she wants for each couch. The factory does not have 100 of the type of couches Rita wants. Instead they send her 100 different couches. Unless they notify Rita the shipment was an accommodation, the factory has accepted her offer and simultaneously breached their contract with Rita. Rita may recover damages caused by the breach.

Discussion Questions

1. What is the Freedom to Contract and how is it different from the Freedom from Contract?
2. Which sources of law apply to contractual relationships?
3. Who is a merchant under the UCC?
4. What are the elements of a legally enforceable contract?
5. Who is an offeror and what is their relationship to the offeree?
6. What is consideration?
7. How is an-implied-in fact contract different from an express contract?
8. How is an executory contract different from an executed contract?
9. How is a voidable contract different from a void contract?
10. How is a formal contract different from an informal contract?
11. What does it mean for a contract to be unenforceable?
12. What is a bilateral contract and what is an example of bilateral contract?
13. What is a unilateral contract and what is an example of a unilateral contract?
14. What are the three requirements for a legally enforceable offer?
15. What is the significance of UCC § 2-204(3)?
16. What are two examples of statements that are not legally binding offers?
17. Is an advertisement an offer and when?

18. How is an auction with reserve different from an auction without reserve?
19. What is an options contract?
20. If an offer does not state a specific time, when will it terminate?
21. What is a counteroffer and how is it legally different from an inquiry?
22. What happens to additional terms made by an offeree under the common law and the UCC?
23. How can an offer be revoked under UCC § 1-202(e)?
24. What is the mailbox rule and when does it apply?
25. Can silence ever constitute acceptance?
26. How is an outputs contract different from a requirements contract?
27. What does UCC § 1-201(19) require of contracting parties?

Critical-Thinking Questions

28. What challenges do cyber transactions create in regards to contracting?
29. Is a promise by itself a legally enforceable contract and if not, why is it important that it not be considered a legally enforceable contract?
30. A merchant is often held to a higher standard than a nonmerchant is under the UCC—why is this?
31. Why is it important that an additional term proposed by an offeror not become part of a contract?
32. Why would a seller ship nonconforming goods if such shipment was considered an acceptance and a breach?

Essay Questions

1. Gwen is considering hiring a painter to paint her house. She runs an advertisement in a local newspaper seeking a painter. Rico answers the advertisement and visits Gwen's house. Rico says he might be able to paint the house this weekend. Gwen promises to pay him $1,000 if he does so. Rico arrives that weekend and begins painting. What type of contract do Gwen and Rico have and can Gwen tell Rico she has changed her mind once he has started to paint?
2. Tamara wants a tree removed from her yard. She posts an advertisement on the Internet offering $600 to anyone who removes the tree by Saturday of the following week. Alex contacts Tamara by email and says he will remove the tree the following Thursday for $600. What is the legal significance of Alex's statement?
3. Seneca is interested in buying a home listed for sale by Slow Moving Realty Company. Seneca calls the agent listing the house. The listing agent states the homeowner would like to offer the house for a sales price of $185,000. Seneca says, "One hundred eighty-five thousand dollars seems too high; would you consider $180,000?" What is the legal significance of this question?

4. Amos is considering selling his car. Britney offers Amos $4,000. Amos says, "I will sell you the car for $4,000, but I get to keep the stereo from the car." Has Amos accepted Britney's offer? If not, can the two parties still contract?

5. David would like to buy a business being offered for sale by Adam. David offers Adam one million dollars as a purchase price. Adam says he needs to think about the offer. Three weeks later, Adam calls David and leaves him a message stating that he accepts. Was a contract formed? If not why not? If a contract was formed, at what moment is it formed?

6. Tabitha is interested in buying a tractor for her farm. She sees Ralph has a tractor for sale. She stops at his farm and offers him $80,000. Ralph says $80,000 is not enough, but says he would consider $95,000 as a purchase price. One week later, Tabitha drives past Ralph's farm and notices the tractor is no longer sitting by the road with a "for sale" sign. Tabitha drives to the post office that Wednesday afternoon and sends Ralph a letter accepting his offer of $95,000 along with a promise to pay $95,000 the next Monday. Ralph receives the acceptance on Thursday. Was a contract formed? Assuming a contract was formed, when was it formed?

7. Dexter works for Internet Seller Incorporated. He sends a purchase order form to Laptop Manufacturing Company. The purchase order states Internet Seller will buy 200 laptop computers at the price of $500 per computer. The computers are to have a nineteen-inch screen and be delivered on January 19. Laptop Manufacturing sends back a confirmation order stating the computers will be delivered on January 20 and that Internet Seller must pay for shipping. Internet Seller receives the purchase order. Do the additional terms regarding shipping automatically become part of the contract?

8. Cylinder Company offers to sell 5,000 cylinders to Tractor Builder Company for $100 per cylinder. Tractor Builder Company agrees and sends an acceptance letter to Cylinder Company, stating Cylinder Company should send the cylinders in shipments of 1,000 on the first of each month beginning in March. The acceptance also states Cylinder Company is to pay for shipping. After the third shipment, Tractor Builder Company refuses to take delivery, stating it does not want to take any additional cylinders. Does Tractor Builder Company have to take delivery under contract law principles?

9. Dee has been selling his corn crop to a local ethanol plant each fall. The ethanol plant and Dee do not have a written agreement. The ethanol plant always pays the current market price for the corn. Do Dee and the ethanol plant have a contract and what type of contract is it: express or implied? Is it formal or informal? If the ethanol plant is taking all the corn Dee produces, is the contract a requirements contract? When will the contract come to an end?

10. Megan has been selling eggs to Barbara's bakery for three years. Barbara and Megan originally had a contract under which Megan and Barbara agreed Barbara would buy all her eggs from Megan at the price of $2 per dozen. The original contract ended two years ago. Megan has been selling Barbara all the eggs Barbara needs and Barbara pays the current market price for the eggs. Do Barbara and Megan have a contract and what type of contract is it: express or implied? Is it formal or informal? If Megan is selling all the eggs Barbara needs, is the contract a requirements contract? When will the contract come to an end?

CHAPTER EIGHT

CONTRACTS, PART II: CONSIDERATION, CAPACITY, AND LEGALITY

By Michael Bootsma

Alex has just inherited 100 acres of farmland from an uncle. Alex does not know it, but the farmland has a fair market value of $10,000 per acre. Alex sells the farmland to Donald for only $500 per acre. Alex then finds out his error. Alex now wants to get out of his contract.

Quan is 16 years old. He buys a brand-new sports car from a local dealership. He drives the car home in a reckless manner and damages the car in an accident. Quan takes the car back to the dealership and says he does not want anymore. The dealership says the sales contract Quan signed will not allow him to return it. Quan wants to know if he really has to keep the damaged car and pay for it.

Learning Objectives

1. Identify legally sufficient consideration
2. Understand legal principles that justify a lack of consideration
3. Understand the legal consequences of contracting with a minor
4. Identify situations involving diminished capacity by contracting parties
5. Understand the necessity of legality in the context of contracts

A contract requires 1) an agreement, 2) consideration, 3) capacity by both parties, and 4) legal subject matter. This chapter focuses on the elements of consideration, capacity, and legal subject matter. As a general rule, a promise alone is not a legally enforceable contract. For example, Stephanie promises her favorite student Eduardo $50 as a gift on his birthday. If Stephanie does not provide the gift, Eduardo cannot sue her. However, if a promise is given in exchange for something of value, the promise is legally enforceable. For example, Diane promises $50 to Cliff if Cliff will clean her apartment. If Cliff cleans the apartment, a unilateral contract is formed and Diane is legally bound to pay Cliff $50.

Consideration is something of legal value offered in bargain for a promise. As a general rule, courts are not interested in the sufficiency or amount of consideration. For example, Stewart pays twice the fair market value of a used car. Stewart cannot ask a court to order the seller to give him half of the money back. As an administrative matter, courts cannot get involved in hearing cases where one party believes they have not gotten enough consideration or where one party believes they have provided too much consideration. The number of trials would never end if someone could claim they entered into a bad deal or bargain.

One exception to the general rule that a court will not consider the value of consideration is when the amount of consideration is extremely small. Historically, it was said a court would not be interested in the adequacy or sufficiency of consideration unless it was but a peppercorn. A peppercorn is a very small berry that grows on a vine. The existence of a peppercorn as consideration leads the court to believe there may be a legal issue with the contract or its formation. For example, Mike is about to file bankruptcy so he sells his prized Corvette to his brother Steve for $10 when it is really worth $50,000. Mike may be doing this so he can later get the car back from his brother without losing the car as part of his bankruptcy.

Two common types of consideration are 1) something of value and 2) a return promise. For example, Martina offers George $100 for his basketball autographed by LeBron James. Martina has promised $100 in exchange for George's basketball. The basketball is the consideration. However, George could also promise Martina the basketball to be delivered next Tuesday and his return promise would also constitute consideration. The fact that a return promise can be consideration is an important legal concept because it allows the contract to be formed as of the moment a return promise is formed, which creates legal liability. Consideration can include refraining from doing something that a person has a legal right to do, as well.

Hamer v. Sidway

124 NY 538, (1891)

The following are excerpts from the opinion of Judge Parker for the New York Court of Appeals. The words in italics are not the words of the court but instead a summary of events leading to the controversy at issue.

The question which provoked the most discussion by counsel on this appeal, and which lies at the foundation of plaintiff's asserted right of recovery, is whether by virtue of a con-

Figure 8.1 A nephew agreed not to pay billiards in *Harner v. Sidway*

tract defendant's testator William E. Story became indebted to his nephew William E. Story, 2d, on his twenty-first birthday in the sum of five thousand dollars. The trial court found as a fact that "on the 20th day of March, 1869, William E. Story agreed to and with William E. Story, 2d, that if he would refrain from drinking liquor, using tobacco, swearing, and playing cards or billiards for money until he should become 21 years of age then he, the said William E. Story, would at that time pay him, the said

William E. Story, 2d, the sum of $5,000 for such refraining, to which the said William E. Story, 2d, agreed," and that he "in all things fully performed his part of said agreement."***

The court went on to find the uncle promised to keep the $5,000 on interest until such time as the nephew requested it. Unfortunately, the uncle passed away before the nephew ever requested the money. The nephew William E. Story, II, assigned the right to collect the money to Ms. Louisa Hamer. When she tried to collect payment, the executor of the estate of William Story, Mr. Franklin Sidway, refused to pay the money to Louisa Hamer.

The defendant contends that the contract was without consideration to support it, and, therefore, invalid. He asserts that the promisee, by refraining from the use of liquor and tobacco, was not harmed but benefited; that that which he did was best for him to do independently of his uncle's promise, and insists that it follows that unless the promisor was benefited, the contract was without consideration. A contention, which if well founded, would seem to leave open for controversy in many cases whether that which the promisee did or omitted to do was, in fact, of such benefit to him as to leave no consideration to support the enforcement of the promisor's agreement. Such a rule could not be tolerated, and is without foundation in the law. The Exchequer Chamber, in 1875, defined consideration as follows: "A valuable consideration in the sense of the law may consist either in some right, interest, profit or benefit accruing to the one party, or some forbearance, detriment, loss or responsibility given, suffered or undertaken by the other." Courts "will not ask whether the thing which forms the consideration does in fact benefit the promisee or a third party, or is of any substantial value to anyone. It is enough that something is promised, done, forborne or suffered by the party to whom the promise is made as consideration for the promise made to him." (Anson's Prin. of Con. 63.)

Now, applying this rule to the facts before us, the promisee used tobacco, occasionally drank liquor, and he had a legal right to do so. That right he abandoned for a period of years upon the strength of the promise of the testator that for such forbearance he would give him $5,000. We need not speculate on the effort which may have been required to give up the use of those stimulants. It is sufficient that he restricted his lawful freedom of action within certain prescribed limits upon the faith of his uncle's agreement, and now having fully performed the conditions imposed, it is of no moment whether such performance actually proved a benefit to the promisor, and the court will not inquire into it, but were it a proper subject of inquiry, we see nothing in this record that would permit a determination that the uncle was not benefited in a legal sense.

1. Who was Hamer and who was Sidway?
2. What did the nephew have to do to earn $5,000 from his uncle?
3. What legal argument did the executor Sidway raise against having to pay the money?
4. What did the court hold?
5. If the uncle had promised $5,000 in exchange to his nephew for the sole act of abstaining from drinking until age 14, would we have the same result?

Examples Where Consideration Is Lacking

The lack of consideration results in the lack of a legally enforceable contract. The first type of agreement that might be lacking consideration is the conditional gift. A **conditional gift** is a gift that can be accepted or demanded only after a certain condition has been met. For example, Nurulu offers $5 to the first student to come down to the front of his classroom. Nurulu is not bargaining for a student to come to the front of the classroom. Nurulu is offering a gift conditioned upon the fact a person must be the first to come down to accept. The promisor must receive some benefit in exchange for their promise for a contract to exist. The bargained-for benefit is what constitutes consideration. For example, Nurulu offers $5 to the first person who volunteers to help him carry a stack of exams to his office. Madeline accepts his offer and promises to help him carry the exams. Her return promise to carry the exams is consideration, as he will receive a benefit.

Past consideration is consideration that would be legally sufficient to form a contract but the consideration was given before the offer was made. For example, Jeff says to Shannon, "Remember when I helped you move into your new apartment; well, I need help moving this week." Shannon agrees to help Jeff move the following weekend but does not actually do so. Jeff cannot sue Shannon for not helping him move. The consideration he offered Shannon was a legal detriment he had suffered before she offered to help him move.

Assume Alfredo and Luigi work at a factory that makes pasta. One day Alfredo sees that Luigi is about to be run over by a tractor. Alfredo pushes Luigi out of the way, but Alfredo is badly hurt in the process. Luigi is overcome with gratitude and says, "Don't worry Alfredo—I will pay for your medical bills." Alfredo incurs $250,000 in medical bills. Luigi does not have enough money to pay the bills. His promise to pay the medical bills of Alfredo is a nonbinding promise for the purpose of contract law because it was not supported by consideration. The consideration provided by Alfredo was provided before Luigi gave his offer.

A **preexisting duty** is a duty that one already legally owes. The duty already owed cannot constitute legally binding consideration. For example, Andrew contracts with Amy. Andrew promises to build a garage for Amy for the price of $20,000. He promises to have the project completed by July 1. On June 15, Andrew says to Amy, "If you would like the garage completed by July 1, you will need to pay me another $5,000." Amy agrees. Upon completion of the project, Amy gives Andrew a check for $20,000. Andrew demands the additional $5,000. Amy's promise for the extra payment of $5,000 is not a legally binding promise because Andrew already had the duty to finish the job by July 1. He provided no consideration in exchange for her promise to make the additional payment.

An **illusory promise** is a promise that appears to be consideration but is not, as the promise itself does not legally obligate the promisor to a specific detriment. For example, assume Mary promises to deliver perfume to Aleisha in exchange for Aleisha's promise to pay if Aleisha wants to pay for it. Aleisha's promise to pay is an illusory promise and Mary is not obligated to deliver the perfume.

Agreements Enforceable Without Additional Consideration

The doctrine of unforeseen circumstances is an exception to the preexisting duty rule. The **doctrine of unforeseen circumstances** allows a contract to be modified from its original

Figure 8.2 Unforeseen circumstance may be a defense against contract enforcement

terms without requiring additional consideration, as long as the unforeseen circumstance was not foreseeable. Assume Carie hires Nolan to build her a swimming pool. Nolan agrees to build the swimming pool for the price of $30,000. After Nolan begins to dig the hole for the swimming pool, he finds a huge rock. It will cost $10,000 to have the rock removed. The Doctrine of Unforeseen Circumstances would allow Nolan to renegotiate the price of his original contract with Amy, as long as the rock was not foreseeable on his part. As an additional example, if Nolan should have known a rock may be present in the ground upon normal investigation, he cannot rely upon the Doctrine of Unforeseen Circumstances.

The UCC also removes the requirement of additional consideration in the event a contract is modified. UCC § 2-209(1) states, "An agreement modifying a contract within this Article needs no consideration to be binding." This means two parties of a contract governed by the UCC may modify the terms of the contract without providing new consideration. For example, assume Rexon Inc. agrees to sell Moffit Inc. ten thousand machine parts for the price of $15,000. Moffit is supposed to pick up the machine parts at Rexon's place of business. However, Moffit requests delivery by Rexon at no additional charge. Rexon agrees. Rexon must deliver the additional parts even though Moffit provided no additional consideration.

Promissory estoppel is another example of an agreement that is enforceable even though it lacks consideration. **Promissory estoppel** requires four elements: 1) a person makes a promise, 2) the person receiving the promise justifiably relies upon the promise, 3) the person relying on the promise suffers a detriment, and 4) Justice is served by the enforcement of the promise that was not supported by consideration.

For example, Nadia visits the university where she earned a business degree. She is taken on a tour of the building by the dean of the college of business whose name is Angelica. Nadia sees how out of date the computers in the computer lab are. She promises Angelica a gift of $20,000 to buy new computers. One week later, Angelica calls Nadia and asks about the gift. Angelica explains she is about to purchase the computers but cannot pay for them without Nadia's gift. Nadia tells her not to worry, as the money will arrive in one week. Two weeks later the money has still not arrived and Angelica calls Nadia again. Nadia informs her that she has decided to take a European vacation instead and needs the money for the trip. A promise was made by Nadia. Angelica was justified in relying on Nadia's promise because she informed her of her plans to buy the computers and received reassurance about the delivery of the gift. The reliance of Angelica was to her detriment, as the school now owes money for the computers. Therefore, a court will have to decide if this is an instance where Justice will be better served by enforcing the legal rule that a promise is legally binding only if it is supported by consideration, or whether Justice requires Nadia to make good on her promise because the dean relied on her promise.

- Promissory estoppel

A promise to pay for a past debt is often enforceable even if no consideration is present. **A promise to pay for a debt** that is not legally required to be paid is often enforceable by courts. An example is when Mike files bankruptcy and the bankruptcy court discharges Mike's debt to Jason. After the bankruptcy proceedings, Mike tells Jason he will repay him even though the bankruptcy court discharged Mike's debt. The bankruptcy court had eliminated Mike's obligation to pay Jason. Jason has not provided new consideration to Mike in exchange for his promise to *reaffirm* his debt to Jason. However, many courts would allow Jason to sue Mike for breach of contract if Mike does not make payment after reaffirming his debt to Jason.

Consideration Provided by Additional Agreements

Parties may have a preexisting duty to perform under a contract. However, an additional agreement, if supported by consideration, may form the basis of relieving a party from a preexisting duty.

Parties may agree to a mutual rescission. A **mutual rescission** occurs when both parties agree to return to their pre-contracting positions and suspend performance under their previous contract through a new contract. Agreements to mutually rescind a contract are enforceable by a court if both still have duties to perform (executory) and are supported by consideration. The promise to no longer perform and hold the other accountable under the original contract may constitute consideration in the eyes of the court for a new contract. For example, Bill and Chad have a contract under which Chad is to buy Bill's prized cow. The cow becomes sick and both Bill and Chad agree to rescind the contract. A court may view their mutual promises not to pursue the exchange and sale of the cow to be "new" consideration for a new contract to rescind their previous contract. If Chad had advanced any money to Bill, the money must be returned.

A **novation** occurs when a party agrees to discharge their duties under a previous contract by substituting a new contract that creates new obligations on the behalf of the parties. It is different from a rescission, as the parties are assigned additional duties under the new contract other than suspending performance under the old contract. For example, Bill and Chad have a contract under which Chad is to buy Bill's prized cow. The cow becomes sick and both Bill and Chad agree Chad will instead buy Bill's prized dog instead of the cow but for a lesser price than the cow.

A novation in which a new obligation replaces a preexisting obligation is often referred to as a **modification** or a **release**. A release generally requires 1) a writing to evince the new agreement, 2) new consideration, and 3) the parties to negotiate in good faith. For example, Matthew is concerned he might not be able to make his car loan payments. He approaches a bank manager and says, "I will give you the car I purchased with your loan proceeds if you promise not to sue me for the remaining payments." If the bank agrees and the agreement is put in writing, and Matthew was negotiating in good faith and not lying, the act of giving the car to the bank can constitute new consideration and a legally enforceable release has been created.

A novation can also occur when a new contract is formed by substituting a third party as part of a new contract if the new contract discharges the duties of the parties to the original contract. For example, Burt contracts to sell his fruit farm to Allison for $300,000. Allison becomes ill and her sister Amie agrees to buy the farm from Burt. A new contract is formed under which Amie, and not Allison, will be the purchaser of the farm for $300,000.

An **accord and satisfaction** is an agreement (also known as an accord) where the parties agree to satisfy a preexisting duty by imposing a new contractual duty. An accord and satisfaction is different from a modification because the original duty under the original contract is not discharged until the satisfaction (new duty) has been performed. In addition, an accord and satisfaction occurs only when an amount of performance required by a party is disputed by the parties to the contract. For example, Mike hires Rita to mow his lawn while he is on vacation in Europe for six weeks. Mike tells Rita he will pay her $50 each time she mows the lawn, but she should only mow the lawn if the grass needs it. A drought occurs while Mike is on vacation. Mike assumes Rita mowed his lawn maybe once while he was in Europe. Rita claims she mowed his lawn ten times. Mike claims her work was unnecessary because of the drought. He offers $100 instead of the $500 she believes she is owed, but states this payment settles any debt he owes her. If Rita accepts the payment of $100, she has accepted an accord by Mike and his debt to her is satisfied. She can no longer sue Mike for the $500 she believes she is owed.

Capacity

In order to assent (agree) to a contract, a party must have contractual capacity. Society would be disadvantaged if contractual capacity was not a key legal element required for a contract. For example, Robert could visit his neighbor Linda in the hospital, and after he finds out she is under the influence of heavy medication and unable to comprehend what is happening, he could get her to agree to contract for the sale of half of her property. Assuming Linda would not normally agree to such a contract, Robert has taken advantage of the situation. In order to prevent unjust consequences, the law requires a contracting party to have contractual capacity. The law of contracts gener-

Figure 8.3 Contracts entered into by those with limited capacity are often voidable

ally focuses on those who do not have contractual capacity or those with limited contractual capacity, including those it labels as infants, intoxicated, and mentally incompetent.

Infants

The common law referred to those who were not of the age of majority as "infants." Today, contract law generally refers to these individuals as "minors." A **minor** (or infant) is someone who has not reached the age of majority, which is the age of 18 in most states, but is age 19 in a few states such as Nebraska and Alabama, and even 21 in Mississippi. The common law as adopted by US states held a contract entered into by a minor was voidable at the minor's option. The common law allowed a contract to be voidable at the option of the minor in an attempt to protect minors from unscrupulous adults who might prey on innocent minors.

- Accord and satisfaction
- Minor

- Disaffirm
- Ratification
- Restitution

Under the common law and present-day state law, the minor can disaffirm the contract until the age of majority or a reasonable amount of time after reaching the age of majority. To **disaffirm** a contract means to declare the voidable contract will not be honored or abided by. The minor must disaffirm an entire contract and not just select provisions of the contract. If a minor does not disaffirm a contract upon reaching the age of majority, or during a reasonable amount of time afterwards, the contract is said to be ratified. **Ratification** in the context of a minor's contract means the minor chooses not to disaffirm the contract. Ratification can be express, meaning the minor states either orally or in written form their intent to ratify a contract entered into while they were a minor. Ratification can also be implied, meaning the minor, by their actions or conduct, chooses not to disaffirm a contract.

Assume Molly buys a used car from a local car dealership at the age of 15. Assuming the age of majority is 18 in Molly's state, Molly can disaffirm the purchase contract any time before reaching age 18 or a reasonable amount of time afterwards. The common law required Molly to simply return the car without making restitution for a decrease in the value of the car.

Restitution means restoring the other party to their original position. As a general rule, a minor is not required to make restitution for a product that he or she no longer possesses or services that have been consumed. In addition, only a minority of states would require Molly to make restitution equal to the fair value of the car on the day she originally received it. Therefore, in a majority of states, Molly could return the car, if she still had it, in whatever its existing condition might be.

State law also differs on the effect of misrepresentation. A majority of states allow a minor to disaffirm a contract even if the minor misrepresented their age. However, these states differ on whether or not the minor must make full restitution or merely return what they still possess. Further complicating matters is the fact that some states hold the minor can be liable for the tort of misrepresentation and others do not. Therefore, Molly, a minor, could buy a car after lying to a salesperson by telling the salesperson she is of the age of majority. Depending upon which state she lived in, she may or may not be able to disaffirm the contract, and if she can disaffirm the contract, she may nor may not be required to make restitution of the full value of the car on the day she received it. Also, Molly may or may not be liable for a separate tort of misrepresentation.

The general rule allowing minors to disaffirm a contract until the age of majority or a reasonable amount of time afterwards is subject to several important exceptions. State law may dictate certain contracts are not voidable at the option of the minor.

Shields v. Gross

448 N.E.2d 108 (1983)

The following are excerpts from Judge Simons of the New York Court of Appeals.

The issue on this appeal is whether an infant model may disaffirm a prior unrestricted consent executed on her behalf by her parent and maintain an action pursuant to section 51 of the Civil Rights Law against her photographer for republication of photographs of her. We hold that she may not.

Plaintiff is now a well-known actress. For many years prior to these events she had been a child model and in 1975, when she was 10 years of age, she obtained several modeling jobs with defendant through her agent, the Ford Model Agency. One of the jobs, a series of photographs to be financed by Playboy Press, required plaintiff to pose nude in a bathtub. It was intended that these photos would be used in a publication entitled "Portfolio 8" (later renamed "Sugar and Spice"). Before the photographic sessions, plaintiff's mother and legal guardian, Teri Shields, executed two consents in favor of defendant.[*] After the pictures were taken, they were used not only in "Sugar and Spice" but also, to the knowledge of plaintiff and her mother, in other publications and in a display of larger-than-life photo enlargements in the windows of a store on Fifth Avenue in New York City. Indeed, plaintiff subsequently used the photos in a book that she published about herself and to do so her mother obtained an authorization from defendant to use them. Over the years defendant has also photographed plaintiff for *Penthouse Magazine, New York Magazine* and for advertising by the Courtauldts and Avon companies.

In 1980 plaintiff learned that several of the 1975 photographs had appeared in a French magazine called "Photo" and, disturbed by that publication and by information that defendant intended others, she attempted to buy the negatives. In 1981, she commenced this action in tort and contract seeking compensatory and punitive damages and an injunction permanently enjoining defendant from any further use of the photographs.***

Historically, New York common law did not recognize a cause of action for invasion of privacy. In 1909, however, responding to the *Roberson* decision, the Legislature enacted sections 50 and 51 of the Civil Rights Law. Section 50 is penal and makes it a misdemeanor to use a living person's name, portrait, or picture for advertising purposes without prior "written consent." Section 51 of the statute states that the prior "written consent" that will bar the civil action is to be as "above provided," referring to section 50, and section 50, in turn, provides that: "A person, firm or corporation that uses for advertising purposes, or for the purposes of trade, the name, portrait or picture of any living person *without having first obtained the written consent of such person, or if a minor of his or her parent or guardian, is guilty of a misdemeanor*" (emphasis added).***

Concededly, at common law an infant could disaffirm his written consent.*** Notwithstanding these rules, it is clear that the legislature may abrogate an infant's common-law right to disaffirm or, conversely, it may confer upon infants the right to make binding contracts. Where a statute expressly permits a certain class of agreements to be made by infants, that settles the question and makes the agreement valid and enforceable. That is precisely what happened here. The Legislature, by adopting section 51, created a new cause of action and it provided in the statute itself the method for obtaining an infant's consent to avoid liability. Construing the statute strictly, as we must since it is in derogation of the common law, the parent's consent is binding on the infant and no words prohibiting disaffirmance are necessary to effectuate the legislative intent.***

It should be noted that plaintiff did not contend that the photographs were obscene or pornographic. Her only complaint was that she was embarrassed because, "They [the photographs] are not me now."***

A parent who wishes to limit the publicity and exposure of her child need only limit the use authorized in the consent, for a defendant's immunity from a claim for invasion of privacy is no broader than the consent executed to him.

Questions

1. What was the common law right of the plaintiff in regards to the contract entered into on her behalf by her parent?
2. Which code section allowed the mother to consent on behalf of her daughter?
3. What did the court think a parent should do to limit the consent given to a third party on behalf of a minor child?

Necessaries

Another important exception to the general contractual rule allowing disaffirmance by a minor is in the context of necessaries. A minor can disaffirm a contract for necessaries but remains liable for the value received. A necessary in the context of a contract is an item necessary to sustain a minor's existence. Examples include food, clothing, and housing. It is important to note a necessary cannot be provided by the minor's parents. For example, Michelle moves out of her parents' house at age 15. They are willing to provide her with housing. Therefore, if she leases an apartment, it is not considered a necessary and she can void the contract without being required to make any payments to the landlord (depending on the state in which she resides). The policy behind holding a minor liable for the value of a necessary received is to provide the adult an incentive to contract with a minor who needs the necessary to maintain their existence.

Figure 8.4 Groceries are a necessity for existence

Emancipation

Minors lose their ability to avoid a contract upon emancipation. **Emancipation** is the legal process by which a minor becomes independent of their parents under the law, thereby losing their status as a minor. A minor may become emancipated from their parents by a formal legal proceeding. In addition, a minor may also be emancipated by engaging in certain acts such as marriage.

Incompetency

An individual who is incompetent lacks contractual capacity. In *Dexter v. US*, 83 US (15 Wall) 9 (1872), the US Supreme Court stated the ability to enter into a contract is consensual, and therefore, a person suffering from mental illness cannot enter into a contract because he lacks the ability to consent. In regards to those who suffer from a mental illness or who are intoxicated because of ingesting drugs or alcohol, the general legal rule is the contract is voidable at the option of the mentally ill or intoxicated person if they are unable to understand the consequences of their actions at the time of contract formation.

For example, Mark is extremely intoxicated and sells his golf clubs to Lloyd for $200. The next day Lloyd delivers payment of $200 If Mark was intoxicated to the extent he did not understand the consequences of his actions at the moment he sold the golf clubs to Lloyd, the contract is voidable at Mark's option. Mark might believe $200 is a good price, in which case he would accept payment for the golf clubs and deliver them to Lloyd.

If a party to a contract who is suffering from a mental illness, or who is intoxicated, enters into a contract but is lucid, then the contract is fully enforceable and not voidable. To be **lucid** in the context of a contract negotiation means to understand the consequences of one's actions. For example, if Mark is intoxicated but understands that he is contracting to sell his car to his brother James for $6,000, Mark cannot void the contract at his option since he understands the consequences of his actions.

Finally, if a party has been adjudicated mentally incompetent by a court and a court has appointed a guardian to make financial decisions for the party, the party lacks contractual capacity because it has been legally removed by the court. In this situation, any contract entered into by the mentally incompetent individual is void. For example, Sid is adjudicated mentally incompetent by a court. Two months later he agrees to sell his house to Mary for $200,000 Two hundred thousand dollars is actually twice the fair market value and Sid has entered into an advantageous contract. However, it does not matter; the contract is void because Sid lacked contractual capacity. The contract is not enforceable by either party.

First State Bank of Sinai vs. Hyland

399 N.W.2d 894 (1987)

The following are excerpts from the opinion of Judge Henderson of the South Dakota Supreme Court.

Plaintiff-appellant First State Bank of Sinai (Bank) sued defendant-appellee Mervin Hyland (Mervin) seeking to hold him responsible for payment on a promissory note which he cosigned.*** On March 10, 1981, Randy Hyland (Randy) and William Buck (Buck), acting for Bank, executed two promissory notes. The notes remained unpaid on their due date and Bank sent notice to Randy informing him of the delinquencies. On October 20, 1981, Randy came to the Bank and met with Buck. Buck explained to Randy that the notes were past due. Randy requested an extension. Buck agreed, but on the condition that Randy's father, Mervin, act as cosigner. According to Randy, Mervin signed the note on October 20 or 21, 1981.

Mervin had transacted business with Bank since 1974. Previously, he executed approximately 60 promissory notes with Bank. Mervin was apparently a good customer and paid all of his notes on time. Buck testified that he knew Mervin drank, but that he was unaware of any alcohol-related problems.***

On April 20, 1982, the note was unpaid.*** On July 14, 1982, Buck sent a letter to Randy and Mervin informing them of Bank's intention to look to Mervin for the note's payment. On December 19, 1982, Bank filed suit against Mervin, requesting $9,800 principal and interest at the rate of 17% until judgment was entered. Mervin answered on January 14, 1983. His defense hinged upon the assertion that he was incapacitated through the use of liquor when he signed the note. He claimed he had no recollection of the note; did not remember seeing it, discussing it with his son, or signing it.

Randy testified that when he brought the note home to his father, the latter was drunk and in bed. Mervin then rose from his bed, walked into the kitchen, and signed the note. Later, Randy returned to the Bank with the signed note.

The record reveals that Mervin was drinking heavily from late summer through early winter of 1981. During this period, Mervin's wife and son accepted responsibility for managing the farm. Mervin's family testified that his bouts with liquor left him weak, unconcerned with regard to family and business matters, uncooperative, and uncommunicative. When Mervin was drinking, he spent most of his time at home, in bed.

Mervin's problems with alcohol have five times resulted in his involuntary commitment to hospitals. Two of those commitments occurred near the period of the October 1981 note.***

Incapacitated intoxicated persons have been treated similarly to mental incompetents in that their contracts will either be void or voidable depending upon the extent of their mental unfitness at the time they contracted.*** A void contract is without legal effect in that the law neither gives remedy for its breach nor recognizes any duty of performance by a promisor.*** Therefore, the term "void contract" is a misnomer because if an agreement is void, at its genesis, no contract (void or otherwise) was ever created.***

Mervin had numerous and prolonged problems stemming from his inability to handle alcohol. However, he was not judicially declared incompetent during the note's signing. Therefore, a void contract could only exist if Mervin was "entirely without understanding" (incompetent) when he signed the note.

The phrase "entirely without understanding" has been a subject of this Court's scrutiny from at least 1902.*** It has evolved in the law to apply in those situations where the person contracting did not possess the mental dexterity required to comprehend the nature and ultimate effect of the transaction in which he was involved.*** A party attempting to avoid his contract must carry the burden of proving that he was entirely without understanding when he contracted.*** Lapse of memory, carelessness of person and property, and unreasonableness are not determinative of one's ability to presently enter into an agreement.*** Neither should a contract be found void because of previous or subsequent incompetence.***

To show that he was entirely without understanding when he signed the note, Mervin points to his family's testimony that he was unconcerned with family and business, [**9] uncooperative, antisocial, and unkempt. He also notes his involuntary commitments in the Fall of 1981.

Yet, Mervin engaged in farm operations, drove his truck, executed a promissory note (on October 3, 1981, for cattle he bought, which note was paid approximately two months thereafter), and paid for personal items by check drawn on his bank circa the period that he signed the note. Obviously, Mervin had an understanding to transact business; the corollary is that he was not entirely without understanding.***

Contractual obligations incurred by intoxicated persons may [also] be voidable. Voidable contracts (contracts other than those entered into following a judicial determination of incapacity, or entirely without understanding) may be rescinded by the previously disabled party.*** However, disaffirmance must be prompt, upon the recovery of the intoxicated party's mental abilities, and upon his notice of the agreement, if he had forgotten it.***

Mervin received both verbal notice from Randy and written notice from Bank on or about April 27, 1982, that the note was overdue. On May 5, 1982, Mervin paid the interest owing with a check which Randy delivered to Bank. This by itself could amount to ratification through conduct. If Mervin wished to avoid the contract, he should have then exercised his right of rescission.***

We conclude that Mervin's obligation to Bank as not void because he did not show that he was entirely without understanding when he signed the note. Mervin's obligation on the note was voidable and his subsequent failure to disaffirm (lack of rescission) and his payment of interest (ratification) then transformed the voidable contract into one that is fully binding upon him.

Questions

1. Who was the original party to the promissory note in dispute? What role did Mervin play?
2. According to the court, what makes a contract void in the context of intoxication?
3. According to the court, what makes a contract voidable in the context of intoxication?
4. Was Mervin allowed to void the contract he entered into with the bank? What was the court's rationale for its holding?

Illegality

Besides requiring an agreement, consideration, and contractual capacity, a contract must be formed for a legal purpose. The discussion of legality starts with some general rules.

If an offeror makes an offer that later becomes illegal to perform, the offer terminates as an operation of law because a contract must have legal subject matter. In addition, a contract can be considered illegal because its subject matter violates a state or local statute or because it is found to violate public policy.

If the subject matter of the contract is illegal, a court is likely to find the contract to be void, meaning no contract at all. As an example, Ricky hires Bobby to deliver illegal drugs in exchange for $5,000. Bobby delivers the drugs but Ricky refuses to pay. A court will find this contract to be void and will not provide either party relief. Therefore, the general rule is a contract that provides for illegal subject matter will not provide any party with a remedy in the event of a breach. However, there are exceptions.

In the event a party made an innocent mistake of fact, or if the contract provides for additional subject matter that is not illegal, the court may provide relief in the form of restitution or reformation. For example, Melvin hires Olena to build him a swimming pool in his backyard and to build a fence around his backyard. Olena requires Melvin to provide a deposit of $5,000 for the building of the swimming pool. After paying Olena, Melvin finds out it is against the law of his city to have a swimming pool. A court might allow Melvin to recover his $5,000 deposit under the theory of restitution. A court might also reform the contract by stating the swimming pool is no longer part of the contract but allow Olena to build the fence as originally agreed.

If the actions of only one of the parties are illegal, then the court may find the contract to be voidable at the option of the innocent party. An example is a contract where one party was induced into the contract by duress or threat of physical harm. The innocent party who was threatened may find the contract to be beneficial and might elect to enforce the contract.

Contracts Violating Public Policy

Contracts that violate public policy are sometimes referred to as unconscionable contracts. **Unconscionable contracts** are contracts that "shock" the conscience of the court. Unconscionable contracts can be segregated into two categories: 1) substantive unconscionability and 2) procedural unconscionability.

Substantive unconscionability includes contracts whose terms a court finds to be egregious or extremely unfair. For example, assume Mitchel is extremely desperate for employment. Molly offers Mitchel employment but Mitchel must work in her salt mine for fifteen years and will receive only $9.50 per hour for his labor. Mitchel agrees because he needs the money to feed his family. If Mitchel quits his job with Molly and seeks other employment before the end of fifteen years, Molly may sue him for breach of contract. A court, however, could hold the terms of the contract to be so unfair that the contract must be considered unconscionable and unenforceable against Mitchel.

Procedural unconscionability includes contracts that are created as part of a process that a court finds to be unconscionable. For example, assume Louis needs a mortgage loan to buy a home. Big Bank Inc. promises to advance him funds to buy a home as part of a mortgage loan. Louis purchases a home and on the day he is supposed to pay the seller, Big Bank Inc. says, "We will give you the money you need but you have to sign this document first." Big Bank then produces a 10,000-page document that Louis must sign. He does not have time to read it. Unbeknownst to Louis, in the fine print on page 9,556, the bank has inserted that he must use their insurance company to buy insurance for his home as well as any cars he owns. The bank later sends Louis a letter informing him he needs to switch his insurance policies to their bank. Louis might claim the process by which was forced to sign the contract with Big Bank was procedurally unconscionable and that he should not have to buy insurance from their bank.

Covenants in the Restraint of Trade

Contracts in the restraint of trade are another example of a contract which violates public policy. Parties often include a covenant not to compete in a contract for the purchase of a business or in employment contracts. Assume Craig wants to buy a barbecue restaurant from Sophia. Sophia's business is named NC's Best BBQ. Craig purchases the business for the sum of $100,000. Sophia then starts Salem's Best BBQ restaurant and buys a building on the opposite side of the street from Craig. Everyone in their town knows Sophia has started a new restaurant and so they frequent her new restaurant instead of Craig's because of Sophia's reputation. Craig should have included a covenant in the purchase contract that would prohibit Sophia from starting a new competing restaurant in the area.

Courts will allow contracting parties to include *a non-compete clause, also known as a covenant not-to-compete* in the contract as long as it is 1) reasonable in length, 2) reasonable in geography, and 3) reasonable in scope. The question of what is reasonable in length, reasonable in geography, and reasonable in scope is a question of fact for a court.

Generally, the geography must not be larger than the area in which the business serves customers. For example, if Craig buys a restaurant in Salem, North Carolina, the geographic area in the non-compete clause of the contract should be no larger than the city of Salem and the surrounding areas from which a customer might travel to the restaurant.

The length of the non-compete clause should be no longer than necessary to prevent competition from the selling party. For example, after 20 years, very few customers are likely to remember Sophia was once the owner of NC's Best BBQ.

The scope of the non-compete clause should be no wider than necessary. If Craig prevents Sophia from working the restaurant industry as part of the purchase contract, a court is likely to say the scope of this prohibition in the contract is too broad. Sophia cannot even work as a waitress or bartender.

Now, consider Lee who is a great computer programmer. He is hired by High Tek Industries to help develop a new type of software. After helping the company develop the new software, Lee quits and starts a competing business where he creates the same type of software and even tries to sell it to existing High Tek customers. High Tek would have been wise to include a non-compete clause in the employment contract of Lee. A non-compete clause as part of an employment contract will be met with stricter scrutiny from a court than in the context of a sale of business. Generally courts are more likely to allow a non-compete clause if it prevents an employee from using trade secrets or taking customers from the employer.

- Exculpatory clause
- Adhesion contract

Exculpatory Clauses

Figure 8.5 Exculpatory clauses seek to eliminate risk of a contracting party

An **exculpatory clause** relieves a party from liability in the event an injury results from performance of the contract. For example, assume Rod rents a large machine to grind a stump left from a large tree he cut down. The rental contract Rod signs will most likely have a clause stating the owner of the machine will not be responsible for injuries arising from Rod's use of the grinder.

A court hearing a contract case involving an exculpatory clause will have to determine whether public policy is furthered by enforcement of the clause. Courts are interested in whether the activity that took place is one for amusement or pleasure as opposed to a necessity. For example, Celeste signs up to run a ten-kilometer race and signs a release form that eliminates the race sponsors from liability. Celeste suffers heat stroke and sues the race sponsors for negligence because they did not provide enough water stations. A court is more likely to enforce the exculpatory clause or waiver because Celeste was engaging in a race for pleasure or personal benefit as opposed to necessity.

State law as well as common law may prevent the use of exculpatory clauses in a variety of contexts. For example, at most, an exculpatory clause can eliminate liability from ordinary negligence. Therefore, damages from gross negligence or intentional torts cannot be eliminated by an exculpatory clause.

Courts are also interested in whether the party seeking to enforce the exculpatory clause had superior bargaining power. An **adhesion contract** is a contract in which one party has a superior amount of bargaining power that eliminates the other party from bargaining for better terms in a contract. For example, someone in the need of emergency care at a hospital is unlikely to be in a position to negotiate better terms from the hospital. A court might find an adhesion contract, or certain terms in an adhesion contract, to be in violation of public policy. However, a student must remember, only certain adhesion contracts that violate public policy will be held as unenforceable. A contract with a local cable television company is likely an adhesion contract, but a court is likely to enforce the provisions of such contract against the consumer unless the provision is found to violate public policy.

Tunkl v. Regents of University of California

60 Cal. 2d 92 (1963)

The following are excerpts from the opinion of Judge Tobriner of the California Supreme Court.

Hugo Tunkl brought this action to recover damages for personal injuries alleged to have resulted from the negligence of two physicians in the employ of the University of California Los Angeles Medical Center, a hospital operated and maintained by the Regents of the

University of California as a nonprofit charitable institution. Mr. Tunkl died after suit was brought, and his surviving wife, as executrix, was substituted as plaintiff.

The University of California at Los Angeles Medical Center admitted Tunkl as a patient on June 11, 1956. Upon his entry to the hospital, Tunkl signed a document setting forth certain "Conditions of Admission." The crucial condition number six reads as follows: "Release: The hospital is a nonprofit, charitable institution. In consideration of the hospital and allied services to be rendered and the rates charged therefor, the patient or his legal representative agrees to and hereby releases The Regents of the University of California, and the hospital from any and all liability for the negligent or wrongful acts or omissions of its employees, if the hospital has used due care in selecting its employees."***

We begin with the dictate of the relevant Civil Code section 1668. The section states: "All contracts which have for their object, directly or indirectly, to exempt anyone from responsibility for his own fraud, or willful injury to the person or property of another, or violation of law, whether willful or negligent, are against the policy of the law."***

In *Stephens v. Southern Pac. Co.* (1895) 109 Cal. 86, a railroad company had leased land, which adjoined its depot, to a lessee who had constructed a warehouse upon it. The lessee covenanted that the railroad company would not be responsible for damage from fire "caused from any … means." (P. 87.) This exemption, under the court ruling, applied to the lessee's damage resulting from the railroad company's carelessly burning dry grass and rubbish. Declaring the contract not "violative of sound public policy" (p. 89), the court pointed out "… As far as this transaction was concerned, the parties when contracting stood upon common ground, and dealt with each other as A and B might deal with each other with reference to any private business undertaking. …" (P. 88.) The court concluded "that the interests of the public in the contract are more sentimental than real" (p. 95; italics added) and that the exculpatory provision was therefore enforceable.

In applying this approach and in manifesting their reaction as to the effect of the exemptive clause upon the public interest, some later courts enforced, and others invalidated such provisions under section 1668.***

If, then, the exculpatory clause which affects the public interest cannot stand, we must ascertain those factors or characteristics which constitute the public interest. The social forces that have led to such characterization are volatile and dynamic. No definition of the concept of public interest can be contained within the four corners of a formula. The concept, always the subject of great debate, has ranged over the whole course of the common law; rather than attempt to prescribe its nature, we can only designate the situations in which it has been applied. We can determine whether the instant contract does or does not manifest the characteristics which have been held to stamp a contract as one affected with a public interest.

In placing particular contracts within or without the category of those affected with a public interest, the courts have revealed a rough outline of that type of transaction in which exculpatory provisions will be held invalid. Thus the attempted but invalid exemption involves a transaction which exhibits some or all of the following characteristics. It concerns a business of a type generally thought suitable for public regulation. The party seeking exculpation is engaged in performing a service of great importance to the public, which is often a matter of practical necessity for some members of the public. The party holds himself out as willing to perform this service for any member of the public who seeks it, or at least for any member coming within certain established standards. As a result of the essential nature of the service, in the economic setting of the transaction, the party invoking exculpation possesses a decisive advantage of bargaining strength against any member of the public who seeks his services. In exercising a superior bargaining power, the party confronts the public with a standardized adhesion contract of exculpation, and makes no provision whereby a purchaser may pay additional reasonable fees and obtain protection against negligence. Finally, as a result of the transaction, the person or property of the purchaser is placed under the control of the seller, subject to the risk of carelessness by the seller or his agents.

While obviously no public policy opposes private, voluntary transactions in which one party, for a consideration, agrees to shoulder a risk which the law would otherwise have placed upon the other party, the above circumstances pose a different situation. In this situation the releasing party does not really acquiesce voluntarily in the contractual shifting of the risk, nor can we be reasonably certain that he receives an adequate consideration for the transfer. Since the service is one which each member of the public, presently or potentially, may find essential to him, he faces, despite his economic inability to do so, the prospect of a compulsory assumption of the risk of another's negligence. The public policy of this state has been, in substance, to posit the risk of negligence upon the actor; in instances in which this policy has been abandoned, it has generally been to allow or require that the risk shift to another party better or equally able to bear it, not to shift the risk to the weak bargainer.

In the light of the decisions, we think that the hospital-patient contract clearly falls within the category of agreements affecting the public interest. [W]e have concluded that an agreement between a hospital and an entering patient affects the public interest and that, in consequence, the exculpatory provision included within it must be invalid under Civil Code section 1668.

Questions

1. What does Civil Code Section 1668 prohibit?
2. Was the contract entered into by the patient an adhesion contract?
3. What factors did the court consider when determining whether public policy was violated by the enforcement of the exculpatory clause?
4. What effect will the court's decision have on hospitals and patients?
5. Do you think the outcome would have been different if Tunkl was having a cosmetic surgery that was purely elective?

Licensing Statutes

A licensing statute requires individuals who practice a certain trade to be licensed under state or local law. Common examples are doctors, lawyers, accountants, real estate brokers, electricians, plumbers, and cab drivers. Assume Samir wants to start a taxi cab business. He buys a van and starts picking up passengers at the local airport. If he is not properly licensed as a taxi cab driver, then any contract he enters into for taxi cab services is illegal and is void as a matter of law. If the purpose of a licensing statute is primarily regulatory, the contract is void and the unlicensed professional cannot sue for breach of contract. However, if the purpose of the statute was primarily to raise money for the government, the unlicensed professional may be able to sue for breach of contract. For example, assume Misty flags down Samir, an unlicensed cab driver, at the local airport. She convinces Samir to drive 240 miles because she missed her flight. The cab fare is $500. Misty refuses to pay. If the purpose of the licensing statute that applies to Samir is primarily to raise revenue, then Samir may be able to sue Misty for breach of contract and collect his fare.

Discussion Questions

1. Why does a contract require the existence of consideration as a general rule?
2. Can a promise to do something be consideration and what about a promise not to do something?
3. What is a peppercorn and how does this term relate to the requirements of a contract?
4. What is a conditional gift and how is it different from a contract?
5. What is a preexisting duty and how is it different from past consideration?
6. What is an illusory promise and can it be consideration for purposes of forming a contract?
7. What is the doctrine of unforeseen circumstances and when will it allow a promise to be enforceable without consideration?
8. If an individual promises to pay for a debt that has been discharged in bankruptcy, can such a promise be enforced without additional consideration being offered by the offeree?
9. What is mutual rescission?
10. What is a novation and can it allow a new party to a contract?
11. What is a release and what are the requirements for an enforceable release?
12. What is an accord and satisfaction and can it exist when a debt is liquidated?
13. When would a release be an appropriate action as opposed to an accord and satisfaction?
14. Can a minor enter into a contract and what rights do they have?
15. What is ratification and how might it occur in a contract by a minor?
16. What is the effect of misrepresentation of age by a minor when contracting?
17. What is restitution and is it required if a minor disaffirms a contract that is not for a necessity?
18. What is a contract for a necessity and how is treated differently from other contracts entered into by a minor?
19. What is emancipation and how might it change the ability of a minor to disaffirm a contract?
20. Can a contract be entered into by an individual who is intoxicated and what is the legal effect of such contract?
21. When would a contract entered into by someone with a mental incompetency be considered void? Voidable? Fully enforceable?
22. What relief is available to a party who contracts for a service that the party knows is illegal, such as prostitution?

23. What is a licensing statute and can a party ever enforce a contract that is in violation of a licensing statute?
24. What is a covenant-not-to-compete and what factors does a court decide in regards to whether it should enforce such an agreement?
25. What is an exculpatory clause and in which situations is a court more likely to enforce an exculpatory clause?
26. What is an adhesion contract and will a court automatically void an adhesion contract?
27. What is substantive unconscionability and how is it different from procedural unconscionability?

Critical-Thinking Questions

28. How is the requirement of consideration closely related to the concepts of Freedom to Contract and Freedom from Contract?
29. Why would the law allow a minor to purchase, wreck, and then return a car without having to make restitution?
30. Why does the law require a minor to make restitution for necessities when it does not require restitution for contracts for frivolous items such as fancy stereos?
31. Why would a contract be voidable by an intoxicated person but only if they are extremely intoxicated?
32. Does the concept of unconscionability relate more to the concept of Freedom to Contract or the Freedom from Contract?

Essay Questions

1. Maurice takes his car to a local automotive repair business. Maurice agrees to pay $2,500 to have his antique Ford Pinto painted. The auto repair business starts to prepare the car for painting but discovers the car actually has been painted several times before. The owner of the auto repair business calls and asks Maurice if he will pay $3,000 instead of $2,500 to have the car painted. Maurice agrees. The car is painted. Does Maurice have to pay $2,500 or $3,000? Why?
2. Hillary is hoping to attend law school. She needs an updated transcript of her grades. Her professor Mazimoto offers to post her grades if she will pay him $500. She agrees to pay him $500 if he posts the grades by the next day. He does so but Hillary refuses to pay him the $500. Does she have to legally pay her professor? Why or why not?
3. Melvin recently hired a painter to paint the hallways and offices of his business property. He agreed to pay the painter $10 per hour. Melvin assumed it would take about 100 hours. The painter now claims it took him 200 hours. Melvin believes the painter has exaggerated the number of hours he has worked. How might Melvin be able to settle this dispute and also eliminate the possibility of a future lawsuit by the painter?
4. Adrian is a bank manager. A customer Neo has come into the bank. Neo has a mortgage loan with the bank. Neo claims he has lost his job and will not be able to pay the loan

back. His monthly payment is $1,000. Neo offers Adrian $7,500 as an accord and satisfaction. Can Neo enter into an accord and satisfaction with the bank? If not, how can he extinguish his liability to the bank?

5. John is a sixteen-year-old high school student. He lives with his mom Mary and dad Roger in North Dakota; John attends a school forty miles from his house. The temperatures in North Dakota often dip below –20° F. Roger and Mary cannot provide a car for John to drive to school. John is on the basketball team so his schedule precludes him from riding the bus provided by the high school. John buys a brand-new Mustang from a local car dealership for $42,000. He wrecks the car. Can John disaffirm the contract and does he need to make restitution if he does disaffirm the contract?

6. Rebecca is angry at her parents. She decides at age 15 to move out of their house. She rents an apartment. Her parents are extremely poor so Rebecca decides to rent an apartment with a pool, heated garage, and fitness facility. Rebecca lies when she fills out the rental application. She claims to be 19 years of age. After two months Rebecca decides she does not want the apartment and that she wants to move back in with her parents. What is the result if her lease contract has ten months remaining? Can she disaffirm the contract and will she need to make restitution?

7. Bud becomes intoxicated after his girlfriend breaks up with him. Miller approaches Bud and asks Bud if Bud would sell his car to Miller for $800. Bud agrees and the two sign a written agreement on paper provided by the bartender. The next day Miller arrives at Bud's house with $800. Bud remembers talking to Miller about the sale of the car the night before, but he does not remember any specifics. If Bud does not deliver title to the car to Miller, what will be the result if Miller sues Bud?

8. Gilbert suffers from a mental incompetency. One day his son Robert stops at his home to visit him. Robert says, "Dad what is the deal with the huge boat you have parked in your front yard? You have never been boating before, have you?" Gilbert claims to know nothing about the boat. Does Gilbert have to keep the boat or can he void the contract for the purchase of the boat?

9. Lucy applies for a job at a local restaurant. She is hired but the restaurant requires Lucy to pass a drug test at a local healthcare clinic as part of her contract or she will be fired. Lucy visits the clinic and the clinic accidentally hurts Lucy while performing the drug test. The drug test results are not conclusive. Lucy is fired. Can Lucy sue her employer for breach of contract? Can Lucy sue the health care clinic even if she signed a release of liability contract before having the drug test?

10. Enrico attends a major sporting event. Before entering the stadium he sees a sign that reads, "By providing your ticket to the ticket-taker, you are agreeing not to hold us responsible for any injuries resulting from negligence or gross negligence." Enrico enters the stadium and falls on the steps after a stadium employee spilled beer on the steps. The employee made no attempt to clean up the beer. Can Enrico sue the stadium and will he be successful?

11. Anthony visits a local appliance store and purchases a big-screen television. The cost of the television is $2,000. Anthony does not have enough money to buy the television but agrees to make monthly payments of $300 for two years. If he defaults, the contract states the appliance store can take back the television without returning any of

his payments. Anthony defaults on the agreement after eighteen months. What analysis would a court provide in a lawsuit for Anthony to recover his television?

12. Nancy is purchasing her first home. The date of the sale is August 1. Nancy arrives at the bank on August 1 so she can sign her mortgage documents and receive the keys to the house from the seller. Nancy is handed a 1,500-page mortgage document by the bank. Nancy asks how she is supposed to know what it says and the bank representative says Nancy can take it home if she wants to review it, but the closing will be delayed. Nancy signs the document. Later she finds out the mortgage has terms she does not want to abide by. Can Nancy ask a court to reform the contract and exclude those terms? What legal theory would she advance and will she be successful advancing this argument?

CHAPTER NINE

CONTRACTS, PART III: STATUTE OF FRAUDS, MISTAKE, FRAUD, AND CONSENT

By Michael Bootsma

Melissa has entered into a contract for the purchase of a home from Brad. Melissa arrived at the place specified by Brad with her money. However, Brad is now claiming the purchase price of the home to be $300,000. Melissa has an email from Brad stating the purchase price was to be $250,000. Does Melissa have to buy the house? Do the two parties have a contract? Does she have to pay $300,000?

Rick recently saw an advertisement for an old sewing machine. He called and spoke with the owner Marla. Marla said she thought the sewing machine was at least 100 years old. Rick said he would pay her $40 for the sewing machine. Marla agreed and delivered the sewing machine. After taking delivery of the sewing machine, Rick quickly realized the sewing machine was less than ten years old. Does Rick have to keep the sewing machine? Can he demand his money back?

Learning Objectives

1. Identify contracts that must satisfy the Statute of Frauds
2. Understand the legal significance of mutual and unilateral mistakes
3. Describe the elements necessary to prove misrepresentation
4. Understand affirmative defenses that may be used in contract cases
5. Define the basic objective of the Parole Evidence Rule

Statute of Frauds

The Statute of Frauds was a common law concept requiring certain contracts to be in writing before the contract would be enforceable in a court of law. For example, the contract for a sale of real estate must be in writing to be enforceable. If Samantha agrees to sell her home and the land on which it sits to Deb, the contract must be in writing for a court to enforce the contract. If the contract is not reduced to writing but is instead an oral contract, then a court would not enforce the oral contract unless an exception to the Statutes of Frauds applied. There are a few important things to remember in regards to the Statute of Frauds.

First, the Statute of Frauds was meant to help prevent fraud by requiring certain contracts to be in writing. The contracts required to be in writing are generally contracts that involved an important economic interest or a contract in which parties are likely to disagree to the terms at a later point.

Second, the Statute of Frauds does result in a contract being considered fraudulent. Parties may orally agree to contract for subject matter that is subject to the Statute of Frauds, and as long as neither party objects to the performance of the other, the contract will be performed as agreed. Whether the contract is contained in a sufficient writing is an issue only if one party to the contract seeks assistance from a court.

Figure 9.1 Some contracts must be in writing before a court will enforce such agreemen

Third, the written contract only needs to be signed by the party against whom the contract is being enforced. For example, assume Rick agrees to sell his farmland to Jan for $340,000. If Rick intends to enforce his contract with Jan in court, the written contract he provides as evidence must be signed by Jan. The court will generally not care if Rick has not signed the contract, as he is attempting to enforce it. Digital signatures are required to be respected under the federal ESIGN Act as well as the Uniform Electronic Transactions Act (UETA) that has been adopted by numerous states.

UCC § 2-201(2) allows an exception where the defendant need not have signed the contract if the transaction is between merchants and the party against whom the contract is being enforced received a written confirmation and did not object within ten days.

Fourth, under the common law, partial performance and promissory estoppel were exceptions to the Statute of Frauds. For example, assume Charlie sells Erica farmland. Erica pays for the land, takes possession of the land, and builds a fence around it. Charlie then claims no contract exists and refuses to transfer ownership. Erica may request a court require Charlie to transfer legal ownership to her since she relied upon his oral promise to transfer ownership. If she can prove payment for the land, she may be able to claim partial performance.

Finally, the Statute of Frauds requires only certain essential terms to be included in the writing. In addition, the writing may be a written document that was formed after the contractual agreement was made. The writing can also consist of multiple documents as long as the documents show the essential terms such as the defendant, the required signature, and the duties of the defendant as part of the contract.

Contracts Subject to the Statute of Frauds

- Prenuptial agreement
- Palimony
- Alimony

Contracts in Consideration of Marriage

A contract that was made in consideration of marriage must satisfy the contract of frauds. Mutual promises to marry may be considered a bilateral contract, but this agreement is not subject to the Statute of Frauds. One of the parties must promise something in consideration of marriage, such as money or an interest in land such as a home for the Statute of Frauds to apply.

Prenuptial agreements are agreements that are made in contemplation of marriage. The purpose of the **prenuptial agreement** is to determine what will happen to each party's assets in the event of a divorce or death after the two parties are married. A prenuptial agreement is subject to the Statute of Frauds. A promise made to support another in a marital-type relationship may be subject to the Statute of Frauds even if a legally binding marriage never results but the two parties live as if though they are married. New Jersey has a statute that requires promises for "palimony" to be in writing. **Palimony** is the promise to pay alimony to a pal who is not a spouse. **Alimony** is a court-ordered requirement of payment to be made by a divorced spouse.

Wright v. Wright
87 N.W. 709 (1901)

Excerpts from the opinion of Judge Given of the Supreme Court of Iowa are as follows:

Figure 9.2 A contract in consideration of marriage must be in writing to be enforceable under the S/F

PLAINTIFF states as her cause of action, in substance, as follows: That on and prior to October 17, 1895, she was unmarried; that on April 18, 1894, she gave birth to a son, of whom Ed Wright, son of the defendant, was the father. That about October 17, 1895, the plaintiff and said Ed Wright entered into a written contract to marry, by which said Wright acknowledged said child as his son. That at the same time, and as a part of the same transaction, the defendant executed a contract in writing as follows: "I, E. H. Wright, father of Edward Wright, the party of the first part to the foregoing contract, hereby agree by and with Amy Leretta Thomas, the party of the second part, that if she shall marry said Edward Wright on this day, and perform the duties of a wife to said Edward Wright to the best of her ability, and said Edward Wright should forsake her or her child, Edward Wayne Wright, referred to in the foregoing contract, within five years from this date, or during said period should refuse or wilfully neglect to properly provide for her and said child, then I will furnish a home for her and said child, and properly provide for her and said child, until five years from this date. E. H. Wright."

Plaintiff alleged that, in consideration of and in compliance with said contract, she married Ed Wright, and has ever since performed all the duties of a wife to him; that, notwithstanding, the said Ed Wright about January 1, 1897, forsook and abandoned her and said child, and ever since has refused and wilfully neglected to provide for the plaintiff and said child and to live with plaintiff, though frequently requested to do so; that plaintiff notified the defendant that Ed Wright had forsaken her and said child and refused and wilfully neglected to provide for them, and demanded that the defendant furnish them a proper and suitable home and support, which he refuses to do; that, because of the failure of said Ed Wright and of the defendant to provide for her and said child, the plaintiff has done so from January 1, 1897, to September 5, 1898, which was of the value of $7 per week, amounting to $652, for which she asks judgment. The defendant answered denying generally, and, upon trial had, verdict and judgment were rendered in favor of the plaintiff for $280 and costs.

Appellant's first contention is that the contract sued upon is "void for want of consideration, and as being contrary to public policy." It is said that the defendant derives no benefit, and that there was no consideration moving from the plaintiff to him. Plaintiff's promise was to marry, and to perform the duties of a wife to him, and mother to the defendant's son. In 14 Am. & Eng. Enc. Law (1st Ed.) 544, under title "Marriage Settlement," it is said: "The consideration of such a contract may be any valuable consideration, reciprocal stipulations, or the marriage itself. Marriage is a consideration of the highest value, and any contract or promise which brings about or helps to bring about a marriage is binding when the marriage has taken place," etc. In *Michael v. Morey*, it was held that "the consideration of marriage is a valuable consideration, and not only sustains covenants in favor of the wife and the issue of the marriage, but also covenants for settlements in favor of children of a former marriage as a moral consideration."*** As we have said, it was wise and timely, under the circumstances, that the plaintiff should exact this guaranty of a support in case of desertion and neglect by her husband. The contract is not against public policy. The court also hinted the easiest way the husband could have relieved his duties under this contract was to perform his duties as a father and husband.

Questions

1. Who was the defendant? Father Wright or son Edward Wright?
2. What consideration was provided in exchange for the promise of the young lady to marry?
3. What legal arguments did the defendant make against contract enforcement?
4. Was the Statute of Frauds met in this case?

Guarantees

The promise to pay for the debt of another is required to be in writing to be enforceable if the promise is made by a third party to the creditor. For example, Eleanor promises First Bank of Atlantic that she will pay the debt due by her daughter Crystal, if Crystal does not pay the bank. The only exception to this rule is when the party who promises to pay for (guarantee) the debt of another obtains an economic benefit from the guarantee. For example, Hao needs a car loan. He goes to First Star Bank. His best friend Paul (the third party) guarantees First Star Bank (the creditor) the loan payments will be made. Paul promises to make the loan payments if Hao does not. Paul's promise must be in writing to be enforceable in a court of law unless Paul is gaining an economic benefit from guaranteeing the debt of Hao.

A promise made to guarantee performance of another would also fit within the Statute of Frauds. For example, Derreck has a painting business. Carl is considering hiring Derreck. Derreck's friend Christine guarantees to Carl that Derreck will finish the job or she will provide performance. Her promise must be in writing to be enforceable by Carl.

Interests in Land

For most individuals, their home will be one of the most valuable assets they own. Therefore, the Statute of Frauds requires a contract involving the transfer of an interest in land to be in writing.

Interests in land include a sales contract to buy land, leases of land, mortgages secured by land, and easements. It should be noted many states have created an exception for leases of property that last one year or less. For example, Mike agrees to rent an apartment from Ted for the months of June, July, and August. If Mike lives in Iowa, the writing requirement of the Statute of Frauds does not apply under Iowa law because it is a lease for less than one year and the state legislature of Iowa has created an exception for this type of contract.

Contracts Longer Than One Year

A contract that cannot be performed within one year by the terms of its agreement must be in writing to be enforceable under the Statute of Frauds. The one-year period starts on the day the contract is formed. For example, Mitch hires Kerry to babysit his kids from September 1, 2014 until May 31, 2015. The agreement is signed on May 15, 2014. The one-year period begins on May 15, 2014, and therefore, the contract cannot be fully performed within one year of formation.

This provision of the Statute of Frauds is not applicable if the contract can possibly be performed within one year. For example, Michael Robinson, a famous basketball player, is hired to be the national spokesperson for the National Retired Basketball Players' Society. The contract is for life-time employment. Michael could die within one year of formation, and therefore, the contract could be performed within one year of formation and does not have to be in writing.

Most courts recognize an important exception exists for contracts that cannot be performed within one year when the contract has been fully performed by one of the parties. For example, Kayla hires Jon as her assistant for a period of two years and agrees to pay him a bonus if he remains in her employment at the end of two years. Their agreement is oral and no written evidence exists of their agreement. Jon works for Kayla for two years. Kayla refuses to pay Jon the bonus she promised him. She raises the Statute of Frauds as a defense. However, the fact Jon has worked for her for two years is full performance of Jon's duties and he can raise this as an exception to the Statute of Frauds.

• Parole Evidence
Rule

Contracts for the Sale of Goods for $500 or More

UCC §2-201(1) requires written evidence of a contract for the sale of goods priced $500 or more. The UCC does not have the same requirements for the writing or writings that the common law has. Remember, the under the UCC the writing does not need to have been signed if both parties are merchants and the party against whom the contract is being enforced had a chance to object to the terms of the written correspondence being used to satisfy the Statute of Frauds.

Figure 9.3 Contracts for goods costing more than $500 must be evinced by a writing under the S/F

The UCC contains several other important exceptions. First, if a plaintiff alleges an oral contract existed for one of the contracts covered by the Statute of Frauds, a defendant's admission of the existence of the oral contract may be enough for a court to allow evidence of an oral agreement. For example, Julie files a complaint against Bob stating Bob's Organic Market agreed to buy $1,000 worth of garden seed. Bob answers Julie's complaint by stating that their agreement was never reduced to writing and the court should dismiss this action. A court may accept this as proof a contract existed.

Second, if a party manufactures custom-made goods that cannot be sold to another party, the contract for those custom-made goods does not need to be in writing to be enforceable. For example, Chase Automotive orders a custom-made engine costing $3,000 from Varoom Engines. Varoom has started to make the engine when Chase informs Varoom it no longer wants the engine. If the engine cannot be sold to another party because it was specially manufactured for Chase, the sales contract need not be proven with written evidence.

Finally, if a party accepts part or all of a shipment of goods costing $500 or more, the party must pay for the goods accepted. For example, Bottling Company takes delivery of a thousand glass bottles costing $650. Even if this was an oral agreement, a court will look at the acceptance as proof a contract must have existed and Bottling Company will be required to pay for the bottles received and accepted.

Parole Evidence

The Parole Evidence Rule is another evidentiary rule meant to aid the judge in the administration of Justice in the area of contract law. The **Parole Evidence Rule** disallows evidence of prior oral negotiations prior to the integration of their agreement into a written contract if the purpose of the evidence of prior oral negotiations is to contradict the terms of the written contract. For example, Sydney is interested in having an architect draw her plans for a new house. Sydney and the architect talk about including a garage and swimming pool. However, Sydney does want to pay extra for the plans to include the garage and swimming pool. Sydney signs a written contract under which she promises to pay $4,000 and the architect promises to draw plans for a house. If this contract was meant to be their final integrated agreement, Sydney cannot introduce evidence of the prior negotiations if she later sues the architect and claims the garage or swimming pool should be included in the final plans.

In the event the parties intended a written document to embody their complete agreement, the Parole Evidence Rule prevents evidence of any prior negotiations if the purpose of the negotiations is to show the clauses of the written contract are missing some terms or if the purpose of the evidence is to change the terms of the contract. In the event the parties intended a written contract to document only part of their agreement, the Parole Evidence Rule disallows only evidence meant to contradict the terms of the written agreement. It does not prevent evidence being offered to prove agreements or terms not included in the written document. For example, Samantha hires Tom to put a new engine in her car for $4,000. Tom says Samantha's brakes also need to be replaced and the brakes will cost $500. Since the engine will be very expensive, Tom and Samantha write down their agreement, stating Samantha will pay $4,000 for a new engine. The document also states when the work must be completed and what type of engine is to be installed. Both parties sign the document. The brake replacement work is part of an oral agreement. If a dispute later arises about the work Tom is supposed to do, evidence can be introduced in court to prove the terms of their oral agreement for the brakes because the writing did not embody their entire agreement. It should be noted Samantha cannot provide evidence about prior negotiations of how much the engine should cost to replace under the Parole Evidence Rule, as the written document specified how much it should cost.

The Parole Evidence Rule has a few important points to remember other than the issue of whether the written document contained the entire agreement or part of the parties' agreement. The first point is when an agreement is made at the same time as the document is signed. Most courts will treat oral agreements as being inadmissible in court. UCC § 2-202 also prohibits the use of contemporaneous agreements as evidence in court. However, the UCC allows additional written agreements. The additional written agreements will be considered as part of the originally signed document. For example, assume Huston Enterprises contracts with Aviation Co for the sale of airplane parts. Aviation Co then decides it would like to defer the delivery date from June 1 to July 1. It would also like to add several component parts to the contract. Aviation Co and Huston Enterprises can sign an additional agreement and such written agreement can be offered as evidence under the Parole Evidence Rule.

The second point to remember regarding exceptions to the Parole Evidence Rule is the possibility of subsequent modifications. A **subsequent modification** to a written agreement is a modification that occurs after the written agreement is signed. It is allowed as evidence whether it is written or oral. For example, Stewart buys a new car for the price of $24,000. He signs a purchase contract with Kar Dealership Inc. with delivery to occur in six weeks. Later in the week that Stewart ordered the car, Stewarts calls Kar and states, "I would like to have different tires put on the car." The dealership agrees but states the tire exchange will cost an additional $200. Stewart agrees. This verbal agreement for exchanging tires would be allowed in court because it is a subsequent modification of the original written agreement.

A final point to consider is that the Parole Evidence Rule does not preclude the admission of prior negotiations if the purpose of such evidence is to prove the meaning of ambiguous terms. UCC § 2-202 specifically states evidence regarding course of performance, course of dealing, and usage of trade is allowed to explain or supplement terms of the agreement. **Course of performance** means how the parties have interpreted terms in a contract as

• Subsequent modification

evinced by performance under the contract. For example, Rita has a contract with Phil to provide housecleaning services. The contract states Rita shall clean the dwelling rooms. What is meant by "dwelling rooms" might be explained by what rooms Rita has been cleaning in Phil's house during the course of performance of the contract. **Course of dealing** means how the parties have acted in previous dealings with one another. For example, Charlie hires Layne to do repair work on Charlie's office. The contract, which Layne and Charlie sign, requires Layne to furnish Charlie with receipts for materials purchases. If Charlie previously allowed Layne to type up a summary of expenditures as opposed to providing individual receipts, Layne should be allowed to do so as part of this contract, as the court would construe the term "receipts" as meaning a summary of expenditures as the parties have done in previous dealings. The term **usage of trade** means a court will look to see how those engaged in the type of business involved in the contract dispute define similar terms. For example, Alex orders two truckloads of dirt for a landscaping project. If a dispute arises in regards to the term "truckload" and how much a truckload really is, a court may look to the industry of transportation of materials such as dirt for a common definition of "truckload."

Consent

It is important that parties to a contract enter into the contract of their own free will. The law strives to prevent parties from being tricked or forced into a contract that the party would not normally agree to but has because of deception or threats of another. A contract requires 1) an agreement, 2) consideration, 3) capacity, and 4) legal subject matter. A lack of consent results in a lack of an agreement. **Consent**, for purposes of contract law, means to agree to the terms of the contractual agreement. An individual cannot freely consent to the terms of an agreement if they are mistaken, have been lied to, or have been influenced. However, one must remember, not all instances of mistake, duress, and undue influence will prevent the formation of a contract.

Mistakes

A mistake by one or both parties could potentially prevent an agreement from existing. For example, Roger owns two laptop computers and offers one for sale. Mariah contacts Roger and they strike a deal. Roger thinks he is selling Mariah his old laptop computer and Mariah thinks she is buying his new laptop computer. Both parties are mistaken about what they are agreeing to. Therefore, no contract exists. Even if they agreed on a sales price and delivery date, they are agreeing to the sale of different items.

The area of mistakes in contract law is difficult to navigate. Some mistakes do not prevent the formation of a contract. For example, a mistake of law is rarely an acceptable defense against contract enforcement. In addition, mistakes as to the value of consideration are also rarely accepted as a defense against contract enforcement by courts. Parties often pay more than they should for goods and parties often sell goods for less than what they have agreed to, so courts cannot begin to hear cases involving "bad deals." The following discussion will focus on the distinction between two different types of mistakes: 1) unilateral and 2) bilateral.

Unilateral Mistakes

A **unilateral mistake** occurs when only one party to a contract is mistaken. Courts generally do not provide relief when one party to a contract is mistaken. For example, Gary buys land that he believes to have oil reserves. He does not tell the seller about his beliefs because he does not want the seller to increase the price of the land. Gary receives ownership of the land but then finds out he was mistaken about the oil reserves. Gary cannot sue the seller for damages claiming he, Gary, would not have paid as much for the land if he had known the truth. Gary was the only party mistaken.

Figure 9.4 A mistake might prevent contract enforcement

There are two important exceptions to the general rule regarding unilateral mistakes. First, a court may provide relief in the event the non-mistaken party knew or had reason to know of the mistake. For example, Scott is selling a bicycle. Todd asks Scott how much he wants for the bike. Scott replies $40. Todd says, "I have always wanted a bike with ten speeds." Scott knows the bike has only five speeds, but does not say anything. Instead Scott states, "This is a great bike, I used it yesterday." A court would likely grant Todd damages in a contract lawsuit regarding the fact the bike has only five speeds because Scott knew of Todd's mistake and did not correct his belief.

The second exception includes situations involving bookkeeping or mathematical errors in construction bids if the result is unconscionable. For example, the city of Primghar wants to build a new recreation center. It notifies the public it will be taking bids from June 1 to July 15. The city receives three bids from three different construction contractors. Two of the bids are almost $3,000,000 each. The other bid submitted by Fly-By-Night Construction is only $1,000,000. The city notifies Fly-By-Night that it has been awarded the contract. Fly-By-Night then realizes it made a multiplication error and really would have bid $3,120,000. A court may be inclined to allow rescission of the contract based upon the arithmetic error since Fly-By-Night may be bankrupted by such an error.

Aydin Corp. v. US

229 Ct. Cl. 309 (1982)

The following are excerpts from the opinion of Judge Nichols of the Court of Claims.

On January 28, 1975, the Naval Electronic Systems Command (NAVELEX) solicited offers for 18 AN/TRC-97A radio sets (hereinafter called radio sets). Because urgency was assigned to this acquisition, formal advertising was suspended in favor of the expedited procedures of direct negotiations with two prior qualified producers of the radio sets. Plaintiff,

Aydin, and its competitor, Radio Corporation of America (RCA), submitted bids. No other bids were submitted.

Plaintiff responded to NAVELEX's solicitations offering to furnish the 18 radio sets for a total price of $2,866,808 or approximately $158,800 per unit. RCA's bid was for a total of $3,989,790 or approximately $221,655 per unit, revealing an almost 40 percent disparity between the two.

In March of 1975 defendant conducted an evaluation of the two proposals and their respective prices. Defendant thereafter cleared the award of the contract to plaintiff. Included with the "business clearance" memorandum was a statement in longhand that "[t]he price offered will be verified by the contractor's signature on the bilateral award sheet." The price was never verified with the contractor. At some time around the end of March in 1975 plaintiff was awarded the instant contract for the production of the 18 radio sets.

In July 1975 plaintiff, through a Freedom of Information Act request, learned of the bid price submitted by its competitor, RCA. On December 5, 1975, plaintiff advised defendant by letter that plaintiff had made a substantial error in the material estimate which was included in plaintiff's bid calculations. Plaintiff contends that on several occasions between July and December of 1975, it orally advised the government that plaintiff had discovered a mistake in bid. The government disagrees that such oral representations were in fact made. The government further contends that even if such oral notice was promptly provided, plaintiff apparently notified persons without contractual authority.

More than 2 years later, on December 19, 1977, plaintiff submitted a claim to the contracting officer under the provisions of 50 USC. §§ 1431-1435, alleging the existence of a mistake in its offer. This mistake, plaintiff claimed, was due to "clerical oversights" which consisted of a failure to estimate quantities and costs of required items, and an omission from its estimate of a standard allowance factor for shrinkage, breakage, and loss of low priced items; "estimating judgment errors," and, finally, "errors in the compilation of the computerized material list." Plaintiff contended that the mistake was so obvious, given the 40 percent discrepancy between its bid and that of RCA, that it should have been apparent to the contracting officer. The contracting officer was then under a duty to verify the bid with Aydin which she failed to do.***

[P]laintiff's case seems constructed on the thesis that a bidder's mistake of judgment will invalidate an agreed contract price. Plaintiff's "substantial mistake in the material estimate" appears to be nothing more than that plaintiff simply underestimated the cost of materials, hence its bid. Plaintiff's moving papers do not attempt to show that the material estimate mistake was a "clear cut clerical or arithmetical error," nor is there any claim of misreading specifications. At oral argument, plaintiff's counsel was unable to add to its moving papers.***

In a letter to NAVELEX dated December 19, 1977, of the $494,768 in excess material cost, plaintiff attributed $107,212 to "clerical oversights." The remainder (thus the greater part) was attributed to "estimating judgment errors, and errors in the compilation of the computerized material list." (Deft's Exhibit 10, p. 2) To the extent that such errors were *judgment* errors, relief is precluded by our *Ruggiero* decision, *supra*. Very likely plaintiff simply assumed its material vendors would adhere to previous prices in face of the then current inflation; at least that it happened this way is nowhere ruled out.

Plaintiff's "clerical oversights" are described in the above letter as consisting of "(1) failing to estimate quantities and costs for several hundred items listed 'as required' on the computerized mailing list, and (2) omitting the standard nonproductive allowance (NPA) factor (3%) for shrinkage, breakage and loss of low priced items***." Some of these arguably could be shown to be clear cut mathematical or clerical errors. Defendant relies on *Eriez Magnetics Corp. v. United States,* 209 Ct.Cl. 673 (1976). We are unwilling to follow that oversimplified treatment of the case. First, *Eriez,* was a congressional reference case and though well reasoned, is not a binding precedent on this court. Second, following a low bid due to the omission of required materials in the estimate and numerous other irresponsible errors on the part of the bidder, defendant requested confirmation of bid price or verification, saying it did so because of the variance between plaintiff's low bid and other bids, which suggested the possibility of error. The verification was negligently and inefficiently performed. The casual treatment of it was rightly held to be a mistake in judgment.***

The "clerical oversights" and compilation errors, without more specific facts, do not fall into the "clear cut clerical or arithmetical error" camp. Neither do they clearly constitute errors of judgment. Giving them the most favorable reading for plaintiff, they are but a minor part of the adjustment claimed, and of the entire procurement. Defendant contests the nature of the error claiming it was due to bad or inefficient judgment. [P]laintiff should have been far more specific as to the nature of the mistakes it says occurred, and the money allocable to each mistake. Summary judgment is therefore unavailable to plaintiff and its motion must be denied. Whether defendant could have summary judgment on this issue by itself we need not decide.

Questions

1. What mistake was made and when was it discovered?
2. What differences existed that allowed the court to distinguish the Eriez case?
3. What is the difference between a judgment in error and a clerical error?
4. What types of unilateral mistakes does this court recognize as a basis for rescinding a contract?

Bilateral Mistakes

A bilateral mistake is often referred to as a mutual mistake. A **bilateral mistake** occurs when both parties to a contract are mistaken. To serve as a defense against contract enforcement, a mutual mistake must be material and not trivial. Assume Cynthia is interested in buying a rare set of coins. The seller has the coins in a display box. Cynthia believes the box will be included as part of the sale. The seller does not normally provide a display box as part of the sale. Assuming the box is of relatively small value, and Cynthia would have bought the coins without the box, the mistake is probably not a material mistake so neither party can use the mistake as grounds for rescission of the contract or as a defense against contract enforcement.

Besides refusing to grant relief when both parties to a contract are mistaken because the mistake is not material, courts will also generally refuse to provide relief when parties have

• Bilateral mistake

made mistakes about the fair value of property being exchanged. For example, Matthew sells a rare baseball card to Sally for half its fair value. Even if both parties were truly mistaken as to the value of the card, courts would generally not intervene.

A famous case involving a mutual mistake is *Sherwood v. Walker*, 33 N.W. 919 (1887). Mr. Sherwood was a banker who contracted to buy a cow from the Walker family. Both parties thought the cow was barren, which means it could not give birth. It turned out the cow was not barren. The Walker family refused to tender, which means offer to make available for delivery, the cow to Mr. Sherwood. The court found both parties were mistaken as to a material aspect of the contract. The court stated the two parties could not have reached an agreement if they were both mistaken as to the ability of the cow to produce a calf. Therefore, the court held no contract had existed because the parties had agreed to the sale of a barren cow and not a cow that could produce a calf. Therefore, a material bilateral mistake prevented the parties from forming a contractual agreement.

Misrepresentation

Related to the concept mistake is that of misrepresentation. A **misrepresentation** occurs when a party to a contract makes a misstatement of a material fact upon which the other party relies and suffers damages because of their reliance. For example, Hosea purchases a trumpet from Gideon. While negotiating the purchase price of the trumpet, Hosea asked Gideon the brand of the trumpet. Gideon lied about the brand of the trumpet. This lie caused Hosea to pay more than he would have if he had known the truth. Gideon may be able to sue for rescission or possibly for money damages.

Courts generally do not allow claims of misrepresentation if a salesperson has puffed up a product. **Puffing** is the process by which a seller overstates or exaggerates the value or performance of a good. For example, Samantha visits a car dealership where the salesman tells Samantha the car she is interested in buying is the most reliable car on the market. This is an exaggerated statement that the salesman cannot necessarily prove to be true. Under the common law, judges adhered to the concept of caveat emptor, which means "buyer beware." Therefore, contracting parties should beware of less than genuine efforts

Related to the concept of caveat emptor and puffery is the duty of disclosure. Under the common law, there was not a duty to disclose facts the other party to a contract would like to know. This area of contract law is changing and parties are required to disclose certain facts under state law. For example, in the state of Iowa, a seller of an automobile must mark on the title whether or not the car has ever been severely damaged in an auto accident.

Besides intentional misrepresentation, innocent misrepresentation and negligent misrepresentation may prevent the formation of a contract. An **innocent misrepresentation** occurs when a party makes a representation that turns out to be false but does not do so intentionally. For example, assume Malaki wants to buy a new truck from a local car dealership. He asks a sales agent what color the truck is. The salesman states the truck is emerald green but it is actually forest green. Assuming the salesman honestly believed the truck was emerald green, the statement was an innocent misrepresentation. Unfortunately for Malaki, unless the misrepresentation was of a material fact, the misrepresentation will not serve as a defense against contract enforcement or as grounds for rescission or monetary damages.

A **negligent misrepresentation** occurs when a party breaches their duty of care toward another by stating something that is untrue. For example, assume Steve wants to buy an engagement ring for his girlfriend Cherie. Steve asks the jeweler whether the diamond ring he is viewing is ten carats or fourteen carats. The jeweler says it is fourteen carats even though the jeweler is not entirely sure the statement is true. The jeweler has not intentionally lied but has breached his duty of care toward his customer Steve. Assuming this is a material mistake, Steve may refuse to take delivery of the diamond ring. He might also be able to sue for damages or ask a court to rescind the contract if Steve later discovers the misrepresentation but has already taken delivery.

Undue Influence

Undue influence means a party to a contract is unfairly influenced (persuaded) and agrees to contractual terms that the party would not normally consent to absent the undue amount of influence. Courts may be willing to allow a claim of undue influence as a defense against contract enforcement. Undue influence is recognized by courts in one of two scenarios. First, an individual enjoys a special fiduciary relationship with the contracting party, such as being the party's doctor or lawyer. Second, a party has a weak mind or infirmity that makes them susceptible to influence by another party.

As an example, Melissa visits her doctor Mary. Mary tells Melissa that Mary does not have long to live. Melissa says she would like to travel the world with the time she has left. Mary then tells Melissa that Mary will buy her home for half its fair market value. Melissa would not normally agree to such a contract but does so because she trusts Mary. If Melissa wants a court to grant her relief, she will have to prove she would not have entered into the contract but did so because she and Mary had a special relationship that influenced her decision to agree to enter into the contract.

Kase v. French and French
325 N.W. 2d 678 (1982)

The following are excerpts from the opinion of Judge Wollman of the Supreme Court of South Dakota.

This is an appeal from a judgment in an action brought by the administrator of the estate of Olivia M. McWilliams, deceased, (appellant) against Kenneth and Betty French to vacate a contract for deed and to recover various cash transfers allegedly obtained through undue influence. The trial court upheld the validity of the contract for deed and the cash transfers, holding that no confidential relationship existed at the time of the sale and that no undue influence resulted from the confidential relationship that subsequently did develop. We affirm.

A widow in her eighties, Mrs. McWilliams lived in a large, somewhat rundown two-story house in Rapid City. As she had a fourth-grade education and no business experience, her nephew, Charles Bruggeman, had been assisting her in the conduct of her business affairs. There was no dispute, however, that Mrs. McWilliams was mentally competent.***

Mr. and Mrs. French moved to Rapid City in 1971, where they purchased a small neighborhood grocery store. They delivered groceries as part of their service. In 1972 Mr. French delivered an order of groceries to Mrs. McWilliams. As he made her acquaintance he was struck by her resemblance to his grandmother. He commented upon this to Mrs. French and suggested to her that she also make Mrs. McWilliams' acquaintance. Once the two women met, a friendship quickly developed between them. Soon after their meeting, Mrs. French stopped by to see Mrs. McWilliams and found that she had injured herself in a fall. From that time on Mrs. French called on Mrs. McWilliams daily and started to help her with household work and other chores. About a month after meeting, Mrs. French told Mrs. McWilliams that she need never be lonely again because they, the Frenches, would take care of her for the rest of her life.

During the latter part of 1972 or early in 1973, the Frenches suggested to Mrs. McWilliams that she move to a dwelling that was less dilapidated. They testified that Mrs. McWilliams countered with the suggestion that they buy her home and fix an apartment in it for her. Within a few months, and after the Frenches had the property appraised (at $35,000), it was agreed that Mrs. McWilliams would sell her property, consisting of two lots, the home, a separate dwelling called the annex, and the personal property and fixtures in the home and the annex, to the Frenches for $40,000. There was to be no down payment, and the purchase price was to be paid, with interest at the rate of one percent per year, in monthly payments over a period of twenty years ($184 per month) beginning two years after the date of sale. Mrs. McWilliams was to continue to occupy an apartment in the house, rent free, for two years.

Either Mrs. French or Mrs. McWilliams asked Mr. Eugene Christol, Mrs. McWilliams' attorney, to go to the McWilliams home to discuss the impending transaction. Both the Frenches and Mrs. McWilliams participated in this conversation and related the terms of the sale already agreed to. Mr. Christol attempted to dissuade Mrs. McWilliams from selling her property under terms so inadequate to provide for her support and expenses for the rest of her life. He explained to her that one of the shortcomings of the proposed transaction was that the interest rate was not proper.***

Mr. Bruggeman (a relative) was also unable to convince Mrs. McWilliams to take a second look at the terms and was informed by Mrs. McWilliams that she no longer needed him to take care of her business because the Frenches would do that for her. Eventually, Mr. Christol prepared a contract for deed according to the terms specified by Mrs. McWilliams and the Frenches. Very shortly thereafter Mrs. McWilliams removed Mr. Bruggeman's name from all her bank, savings and loan accounts, and certificates of deposit, and opened a joint account with the Frenches. Mr. Bruggeman continued to visit his aunt but no longer counseled her on her business affairs.***

A confidential relationship 'exists whenever trust and confidence is reposed by the testator in the integrity and fidelity of another.'***

In the light of the contracts Mr. and Mrs. French had with Mrs. McWilliams and of the fact that the promise to take care of Mrs. McWilliams was made prior to the sale of her home, we conclude that a confidential relationship existed between Mrs. McWilliams and the Frenches at the time of the sale of the property. The existence of a confidential relation requires the dominant party "to exercise the utmost good faith and to refrain from obtaining any advantage at the expense of the confiding party."***

The Frenches were therefore under a duty to go forward with the evidence and show that the transaction was free from undue influence.***We cannot say that the contract for deed clearly shows the effect of undue influence.

The trial court found that the Frenches had neither taken unfair advantage of Mrs. McWilliams nor exerted undue influence upon her in any of their dealings. Given the trial court's opportunity to judge the credibility of the Frenches on the basis of their courtroom demeanor and testimony, we cannot say that this finding is clearly erroneous.

Questions

1. Who was Mrs. McWilliams and who were the Frenches?
2. How did the Frenches become friends with Mrs. McWilliams?
3. Did the Frenches influence Mrs. McWilliams with their actions and how?
4. Did the court find a confidential relationship between Mrs. McWilliams and the Frenches that would cause the case to be set aside?

Duress

The threat of physical force would eliminate or diminish the ability of an individual to determine whether or not they wanted to consent to a contract. The courts use a subjective standard as opposed to an objective standard in determining whether or not the person's ability to enter into a contract was influenced or diminished. Over time the law has come to recognize three primary threats that constitute duress. First, the threat of physical harm or imprisonment. Second, the threat of wrongfully taking a person's property. Third, the threat of economic hardship, referred to as economic duress.

The first two concepts are easy enough to understand. Phil wants to buy Elissa's farm. Phil tells Elissa to sell him the farm by signing a sales contract, or he, Phil, will shoot Elissa with a gun. Elissa's ability to determine whether not she wanted to contract has been affected. She did not have freedom of mind. A contract entered into because of duress may be avoided by the party subject to duress.

Figure 9.5 duress might be a defense against contract enforcement

The area of economic duress is less clear in contract law. Generally, the party claiming economic duress must prove the other party to the contract engaged in 1) wrongful behavior 2) that caused financial hardship and 3) the damaged party had no other alternatives.

As an example, assume Molly hires Dan to install plumbing in a house Molly is building for her parents. At the last minute, Dan threatens to breach the contract unless Molly agrees to double his pay as part of a new contract. Molly has no option but to agree. Dan has engaged in 1) wrongful conduct 2) that caused Molly damages and 3) left her with no other options. Therefore, Molly may be successful raising the defense of economic duress.

Generally wrongful behavior consists of illegal behavior. However, predatory behavior may be considered wrongful as well. For example, assume Randy is two months behind on his mortgage with Big Bank. Randy had pledged his car as collateral for the mortgage loan. Big Bank threatens to take Randy's car from him and Big Bank has the legal right to do this. Big Bank then then promises not to take the car if Randy will agree to sign a new mortgage contract with an interest rate more than double what he is paying now. A court may allow Randy to argue economic duress because of the actions of Big Bank.

Questions

1. What is the purpose of the Statute of Frauds?
2. Who must sign a written contract subject to the Statute of Frauds?
3. If Alex enters into an oral contract with Melanie for the purchase of real estate, has Alex engaged in fraudulent behavior?
4. What does UCC § 2-201(2) provide and what is an example of the application of this provision?
5. Does a writing need to be present at the time a contract is formed that is subject to the Statute of Frauds?
6. What is a prenuptial agreement and is it subject to the Statute of Frauds?
7. How is alimony different from palimony?
8. Is a promise to pay the debt of another legally enforceable if it is not evinced in a writing?
9. Would a contract for a lease for an apartment need to be in writing?
10. Would the sale of a home be subject to the Statute of Frauds as a normal rule? Why?
11. Must all personal-services contracts be evinced by a contract; if not, which personal-service contracts would need to be in writing?
12. What does UUC § 2-201(1) require in regards to the Statute of Frauds?
13. What exceptions to the requirement of a writing under the Statute of Frauds does the UCC provide?
14. What is the Parole Evidence Rule and when does it apply?
15. What is a subsequent modification and is a subsequent oral modification enforceable?
16. Can an oral agreement ever be introduced as evidence used to contradict a written contract under the Parole Evidence Rule?
17. What is the definition of course of performance, course of dealing, and usage of trade, and how do they differ?
18. What are the requirements of a legally enforceable contract and how does the term "consent" relate to these requirements?
19. Which types of mistakes can be used as a defense against contract enforcement and which cannot?
20. What is a unilateral mistake and which unilateral mistakes may suffice as a defense against contract enforcement?

21. What is a bilateral mistake and which bilateral mistakes may serve as a defense against contract enforcement?
22. What are the requirements for proving intentional fraudulent misrepresentation has occurred?
23. How does puffery differ from intentional misrepresentation?
24. What is innocent misrepresentation and how is it different from negligent misrepresentation?
25. What is undue influence and what type of relationship might give rise to undue influence?
26. What is physical duress and what effect does it have on a contract?
27. When might economic duress work as a defense against contract enforcement?

Critical-Thinking Questions

28. How can a retail store satisfy the Statute of Frauds as part of the check-out process?
29. Why would the drafters of the UCC require $500 as the threshold amount for a sale of goods under the Statute of Frauds and will this amount need to be increased over time?
30. What purpose does the Parole Evidence Rule serve?
31. Why do courts require a misrepresentation of a material fact and not just any fact?
32. How might a party protect against the defense of undue influence when entering into a contract where a fiduciary relationship exists between the two contracting parties?

Essay Questions

1. Jennifer works for a large furniture store retailer as a purchasing agent. She orders a thousand leather sofas from Sofa Manufacturing Company using a purchase order form provided by Sofa Manufacturing Company. Sofa Manufacturing Company accepts the order by prompt shipment. Each sofa costs $650. The sofas are specially made to fit the specifications provided by Jennifer. Jennifer receives the sofas but contests the price of $650. What arguments can Sofa Manufacturing make that the Statute of Frauds is satisfied? If a court found it was not satisfied, what exceptions to the Statute of Frauds may apply?
2. Bricks Manufacturing Company needs a commercial loan from Westing Bank. The loan officer at Westing Bank wants someone to act as guarantor of payment. The CEO of Quick Supply Company, which is the principal supplier of Bricks Manufacturing Company, sends the loan officer at Westing Bank an email saying it guarantees payment of the loan by Bricks. Two months later Quick Supply Company makes a payment on behalf of Bricks to Westing Bank. Was the Statute of Frauds satisfied in regards to the guarantee of Quick Supply Company? If not, what exceptions might apply?
3. Forest signs a contract for the lease of a commercial space in which he hopes to operate a business. After he starts to renovate the property, he notices the property has no drain system. Forest contacts the owner of the building and the owner says the cost of

installing plumbing will be a responsibility of Forest. Forest agrees to pay half of the cost of the plumbing and the owner agrees to pay for the remaining half of the cost. When Forest tries to obtain payment for half of the cost as a reimbursement from the owner, the owner says the lease contract states all repair costs are to be borne by Forest. How would the Parole Evidence Rule apply in this situation?

4. Connie needs to build a new greenhouse for her business. She hires Fast Construction Company. Connie signs a contract with Fast Construction for the construction of a new greenhouse. Upon completion of the project, Connie notices the greenhouse does not have a sprinkler system. She reviews her contract and notices the sprinkler systems were not included. In a lawsuit against Fast Construction, how might the Parole Evidence Rule prevent Connie from providing oral testimony about negotiations prior to the signing of the contract? What argument could Connie advance against the application of the Parole Evidence Rule?

5. Farmer Brown orders a thousand gallons of fertilizer from a local hardware store. Before making the purchase, Farmer Brown asked whether or not the fertilizer was safe for use on a potato crop. The salesman said it was. Upon receipt of the fertilizer, Farmer Brown reads the instructions on the back of a container and realizes it is not safe for his potato crop. Farmer Brown believes the hardware store salesman did not intentionally lie to him. What defenses might Farmer Brown raise in regards to contract enforcement?

6. Laptop Manufacturing Company orders four thousand component parts for use in its laptops. A supplier named Circuit Boards Producer Company offers Laptop Manufacturing Company one thousand new circuits that are made out of plastic instead of copper. Circuit Boards Producer Company ensures Laptop Manufacturing Company the plastic circuits will have the same dimensions as the circuits normally ordered by Laptop Manufacturing Company. It turns out the new circuits do not. Laptop Manufacturing Company believes the Circuit Boards had to know the circuits were a different size. What defenses can Laptop Manufacturing raise in regards to contract enforcement?

7. Richard is considering the sale of his farmland. He asks his accountant John about the tax consequences. John says the sale will be subject to a high amount of income tax. John suggests Richard sell the land to John as party of an exchange that would defer taxes for ten years. Richard agrees and the day before he is to transfer title, he learns the price offered by John is actually 20% less than the market price. What defenses might Richard raise against contract enforcement and will he be successful?

8. Rex visits his attorney Melody. Rex needs to create a will. Melody informs Rex he might be better off selling his family business as opposed to leaving it to his children. Melody informs Rex that Melody's brother Anthony would be interested in buying the business. Rex signs a contract for the sale of the business to Anthony. On the day before the sale is to occur, Rex realizes he has agreed to a price that is less than 50% of the true value of his business. What defenses might Rex raise and will he be successful?

9. Georgia has a rare car worth $150,000. She also owns a contracting business. Her business has a loan agreement with High Rate Bank. The terms of the loan are such that High Rate can demand full payment of the loan at any time. Georgia has made the same monthly payment for six years. During year 7, the CEO of High Rate Bank finds

out about the rare car owned by Georgia. The CEO demands full payment of the loan. When Georgia says she cannot pay the full balance, the CEO says he will accept her car as partial payment. He also agrees to continue to allow Georgia to make the same monthly payment. Georgia agrees but then changes her mind. What defenses might she raise?

10. Phillip is an intellectual property lawyer. A new client Seth comes to his firm. Seth needs a patent for a new invention he has. Phillip thinks the patent is a good idea and says he will do the work for free if he can be a 25% owner. Seth agrees after Roger, who is Phillip's law partner, says he believes it is a fair deal because often patents become worthless after the invention proves unpopular in the market. Two years later, the patented invention becomes a huge success. Seth would like to get out of the contract with Phillip. Can Seth raise undue influence as a defense? How about economic duress?

CHAPTER TEN

CONTRACTS, PART IV: THIRD PARTY RIGHTS, PERFORMANCE, DISCHARGE, AND BREACH

By Michael Bootsma

Donna hires Stewart to replace her air conditioner. Donna asks Stewart to use a special type of air conditioner. Stewart does not have a good opinion of the brand of air conditioner Donna has requested. If Stewart uses a brand of air conditioner he believes to be a better value and more reliable, can Donna sue Stewart for damages? How much in damages will Donna be awarded?

Ali has a contract to landscape Amy's backyard. Ali is worried because Amy wants a special type of deck behind her house that he has not built before. Ali would like to hire Mitch to build the deck. Ali would do the remaining work. Can Ali hire Mitch to work on Amy's house as a subcontractor?

Chapter Objectives

1. Identify the situations in which a party's duty is discharged under a contract.
2. Identify the liability created by different types of performance.
3. Understand the different types of damages a court may award a plaintiff in a breach of contract case.
4. Distinguish between a condition precedent and a condition subsequent.
5. Understand the rights and duties of third parties.

Breach of Contract

Damages are appropriate when a party has breached their duty or duties under a contract. For example, Kerry hires Mike to build her a tent for daughter's graduation party. Mike never builds the tent. Mike has breached his duty toward Kerry. Mike is liable to Kerry until he provides complete performance.

Complete performance means a party has performed the duties under the terms of the contract. Complete performance relieves a party of further contractual liability. For example, Dave contracts with Kris to refinish his deck. If Kris completes the job as required by the contract, then Kris no longer has any duties or liability toward Dave under their contract.

- Complete performance
- Substantial performance
- Material breach

If a party to a contract provides complete performance, the party is discharged of their performance and liability under the contract. Complete performance also allows a party to demand performance from the other party to the contract. For example, Carol hires Mark to build an addition to her house in exchange for $50,000. Once Mark has provided complete performance, he can require Carol to pay him $50,000. Carol cannot sue Mark for breach of contract because he has provided complete performance.

Substantial performance means a party has not provided complete performance but has not committed a material breach. A **material breach** occurs when a party does not perform a significant duty under their contract. Courts often look to what they call "the heart of the contract" to determine whether a material breach has occurred. For example, Stephanie hires Scott to fix her car by replacing the alternator; Scott does not replace the alternator. Scott has materially breached the contract.

If a party provides substantial performance, their duty to perform has not been discharged and they remain liable to the other party. For example, Irving hires Byron to paint Irving's entire car, including its bumpers, bright red in exchange for $10,000. Byron paints the body of the car but does not paint the bumpers. Irving may sue Byron because he has not provided complete performance. Assuming a court would find Byron has substantially performed his duties, Byron will be liable to Irving for damages. However, Irving will not be able to refuse to pay Byron. A court may reduce the payment of $10,000 required by Irving because of the substantial performance of Byron. For example, Irving might only have to pay $9,000.

A material breach of contract relieves the non-breaching party of its duties under a contract. For example, assume MSI Paper Company contracts to sell 500 reams of paper to Office Supplies Incorporated for $2,500. If MSI paper does not deliver any of the 500 reams, it has materially breached its contract and Office Supplies Incorporated is relieved of its duty to pay for the paper. In addition, Office Supplies Incorporated may sue MSI Paper for breach of contract.

Jacobs & Young v. Kent
230 NY 239 (1921)

Excerpts from the opinion by Justice Cardozo for the New York Court of Appeals.

The plaintiff built a country residence for the defendant at a cost of upwards of $77,000, and now sues to recover a balance of $3,483.46, remaining unpaid. The work of construction ceased in June, 1914, and the defendant then began to occupy the dwelling. There was no complaint of defective performance until March, 1915. One of the specifications for the

Figure 10.1 Pipe used in the construction of a home was at issue in *Jacobs & Young v. Kent*

plumbing work provides that "all wrought iron pipe must be well galvanized, lap welded pipe of the grade known as 'standard pipe' of Reading manufacture." The defendant learned in March, 1915, that some of the pipe, instead of being made in Reading, was the product of other factories. The plaintiff was accordingly directed by the architect to do the work anew.

The plaintiff left the work untouched, and asked for a certificate that the final payment was due. Refusal of the certificate was followed by this suit.

The evidence sustains a finding that the omission of the prescribed brand of pipe was neither fraudulent nor willful. It was the result of the oversight and inattention of the plaintiff's subcontractor. Reading pipe is distinguished from Cohoes pipe and other brands only by the name of the manufacturer stamped upon it at intervals of between six and seven feet. Even the defendant's architect, though he inspected the pipe upon arrival, failed to notice the discrepancy. The plaintiff tried to show that the brands installed, though made by other manufacturers, were the same in quality, in appearance, in market value and in cost as the brand stated in the contract—that they were, indeed, the same thing, though manufactured in another place.

We think the evidence, if admitted, would have supplied some basis for the inference that the defect was insignificant in its relation to the project. The courts never say that one who makes a contract fills the measure of his duty by less than full performance. They do say, however, that an omission, both trivial and innocent, will sometimes be atoned for by allowance of the resulting damage, and will not always be the breach of a condition to be followed by a forfeiture.*** Those who think more of symmetry and logic in the development of legal rules than of practical adaptation to the attainment of a just result will be troubled by a classification where the lines of division are so wavering and blurred. Something, doubtless, may be said on the score of consistency and certainty in favor of a stricter standard. The courts have balanced such considerations against those of equity and fairness, and found the latter to be the weightier.*** Nowhere will change be tolerated, however, if it is so dominant or pervasive as in any real or substantial measure to frustrate the purpose of the contract***. There is no general license to install whatever, in the builder's judgment, may be regarded as "just as good". The question is one of degree, to be answered, if there is doubt, by the triers of the facts, and, if the inferences are certain, by the Judges of the law***. We must weigh the purpose to be served, the desire to be gratified, the excuse for deviation from the letter, the cruelty of enforced adherence.***

In the circumstances of this case, we think the measure of the allowance is not the cost of replacement, which would be great, but the difference in value, which would be either nominal or nothing. Some of the exposed sections might perhaps have been replaced at moderate expense. The defendant did not limit his demand to them, but treated the plumbing as a unit to be corrected from cellar to roof. In point of fact, the plaintiff never reached the stage at which evidence of the extent of the allowance became necessary.***

The owner is entitled to the money which will permit him to complete, unless the cost of completion is grossly and unfairly out of proportion to the good to be attained. When that is true, the measure is the difference in value. Specifications call, let us say, for a foundation built of granite quarried in Vermont. On the completion of the building, the owner learns that through the blunder of a subcontractor part of the foundation has been built of granite of the same quality quarried in New Hampshire. The measure of allowance is not the cost of reconstruction. The rule that gives a remedy in cases of substantial performance with compensation for defects of trivial or inappreciable importance, has been developed by the courts as an instrument of Justice. The measure of the allowance must be shaped to the same end.

Questions

1. What did the construction contractor do to make the homeowner bring this lawsuit?
2. What amount of damages did the court think appropriate?
3. Did the court find the contractor had breached its duty of performance?
4. Was the breach in this case material or was substantial performance present?

Conditions

Contracts often contain conditions. A **condition precedent** is a condition that must be satisfied before performance is required by another party under a contract. For example, Stan contracts with Samantha to paint his house and the job must be complete within two weeks. Samantha is worried about the time period so she inserts a clause in the contract that states she is not required to perform the painting services within two weeks if it rains more than three days each week. Samantha has protected herself against liability by inserting a condition precedent into the contract.

A **condition subsequent** is a condition that requires performance until a condition is no longer satisfied. For example, Cindy hires Cory to work as an accountant for her business. She stipulates Cory will be paid a certain sum of money each Friday if he works forty hours that week. The requirement he works forty hours is a condition precedent. However, she also states in the contract that he must maintain a valid CPA license or his employment will automatically terminate. The requirement to maintain a valid CPA license is a condition subsequent. This example also illustrates the fact a contract may have multiple conditions as part of its terms. If both parties are subject to conditions, the existence of mutual conditions is referred to as **concurrent conditions**.

Conditions can also be classified as either express or implied conditions. An **express condition** is a written or verbal condition to a contract. An **implied condition** is a condition which is neither written nor oral but nonetheless exists as a part of the contract and can be inferred from the facts surrounding the contract. Assume Nellie hires Amanda to help her plant a vegetable garden on June 1 of the current year. Nellie tells Amanda that she must first receive approval from the local city officials before they plant the garden. The requirement of city approval is an express condition. The fact that it must not be raining on June 1 is an implied condition that Nellie might not necessarily state as part of their contract but could be inferred as being an implied condition.

Conditions may be objective or subjective in nature. An **objective condition** contains a reasonableness standard in regards to determining or judging when the condition has been met. A **subjective condition** is determined to be satisfied by the subjective opinion of a party to a contract. Hal hires Sal to paint his house. The two sign a written contract that requires Hal to pay Sal once the painting is complete. Under the terms of the contract, Hal has the authority to determine when the house painting has been finished. This condition would be a subjective condition precedent because Hal is not required to pay unless he is satisfied the house has been painted. If Hal is very hard to please, Sal might be unhappy with the outcome of this contract, as Hal might keep requiring Sal to touch up his painting work.

Types of Damages

There are two main categories of remedies for breach of contract: remedies at law and equitable remedies. Remedies at law generally require the defendant to pay monetary damages to the plaintiff. For example, Melissa damages Doug's property in the amount of $1,500. A court may require Melissa to compensate Doug by paying him $1,500. Equitable remedies are generally nonmonetary in nature. The four main forms of equitable relief are 1) specific performance, 2) injunction, 3) rescission and 4) reformation. Courts have different methods for determining the amount of monetary damages a plaintiff is entitled to in the event of a breach.

- Compensatory damages
- Expectation damages
- Reliance damages

Measures of Damages

Compensatory damages are meant to compensate or reimburse the plaintiff for what they have lost. Compensatory damages can be calculated based on three different interests.

First, a court may award damages to fulfill a party's expectations. This form of damages is referred to as the plaintiff's expectation interest. **Expectation damages** are the difference between the position where the plaintiff expected to be and where the plaintiff was left after the breach. The formula for expectation damages = what plaintiff was promised – what plaintiff received from defendant – cost savings to plaintiff of breach. For example, assume Pipe Fitter incorporated agrees to sell one thousand pipe fittings to Fast Manufacturing for the price of $2.20 per pipe fitting. Pipe Fitter breaches the contract and Fast Manufacturing is forced to buy the pipe fittings from another supplier for $2.50 per pipe fitting. Fast Manufacturing's expectation damages are $.30 per pipe fitting. If the breach allowed Fast Manufacturing to save $.05 in shipping expense per pipe fitting, Fast Manufacturing's expectation damages would be reduced to $.25 per unit because of the savings.

Sometimes the difference between what the plaintiff received is slightly different from what the plaintiff was promised but the cost to remedy is substantially more than the difference in value. For example, Madison hires Nicholas to paint the hallways in Madison's office building for $600. Madison stipulates Nicholas is to use German Boy brand paint. Nicholas uses a different brand of paint that is actually cheaper and a better quality than German Boy. Nicholas has provided substantial performance but not complete performance. Assume the cost to repaint the hallway is $600. Therefore, Madison can argue she should be awarded $600 in damages. However, the difference in economic value between what Madison was promised and what Madison may only be $50. Most courts would award $50 instead of the cost of $600, which is the cost to complete the project (repaint the hallways). Courts are likely to use this approach of awarding the difference in value as opposed to the cost to complete where the contract is not a contract for construction services or where economic waste would result.

If expectation damages cannot be proved in a matter the court finds to be reliable, a court may award a plaintiff damages based upon their reliance interest. **Reliance damages** compensate the plaintiff for expenses they have incurred by relying on the contract that was breached by the defendant. Reliance damages attempt to put the plaintiff back in their pre-contracting position. For example, Eddie hires Natasha to put a new sign on his building. He rents special equipment to keep his customers safe. Natasha does not complete the contract. Reliance damages are meant to put the plaintiff in the same position as they would have been if the contract had never been formed. Therefore, Eddie's reliance interest is the cost of the special equipment he rented for his store. If he receives this money in damages from Natasha, he will be in the same position he was if he had not formed a contract with Natasha. Eddie might feel he is entitled to lost profits he might have realized because of better advertising with a new sign. However, courts are reluctant to award lost profits to Eddie if the damages are hard to quantify with a reasonable amount of certainty.

The plaintiff's restitution interest is the amount of benefit the plaintiff has conferred upon the defendant who has now breached the contract. **Restitution damages** are equal to the amount of value the defendant has received. Restitution damages are often awarded in cases where expectation damages cannot be adequately calculated and where reliance damages do not adequately compensate the plaintiff. Assume Mick hires Joseph to build a horse barn on Mick's property. After Joseph has built a fence, but before he has started to build the barn, the county in which Mick lives outlaws agricultural buildings. Mick refuses to pay Joseph any money, as the contract is now void as a matter of law. Joseph sues Mick and the court awards him the value of the fence as restitution damages.

Restitution damages are also appropriate in the event a court imposes a quasi-contract on parties. For example, assume Joann helps her neighbor Tonya remove a tree limb from her property. In the event that no contract existed because of a lack of an agreement, a court may impose a quasi-contract. A court may award Joann restitution damages for helping her neighbor.

Regardless of the interest of the plaintiff used to calculate damages, the compensatory damages must come in one of two forms. First, the damages must be reasonably foreseeable. The defendant must not have actual notice of the possibility of damages if the damages are general in nature. These damages are often referred to as **general damages**. Second, if the damages are not reasonably foreseeable, the plaintiff must have put the defendant on actual notice that such damages may result. Damages which require notice to be received by the defendant are sometimes referred to as **special or consequential damages**.

For example, assume Taylor has a successful grocery business where customers can come and buy produce he grows on his thousand-acre farm. The roof to Taylor's grocery store starts to leak. Taylor hires Ace Company to repair the roof. Ace company agrees to fix the roof by Friday of the same week in exchange for $10,000. Ace Company does not complete the repairs on the roof until the end of the day on Saturday. Taylor sustains $5,000 in lost profits because he had to have his store closed on Saturday. A city inspector had given Taylor until Friday to get the roof fixed and required it to be closed on Saturday because it was not fixed. Whether or not Ace Company owes Taylor $5,000 for lost profits depends on whether Ace Company was put on notice that the store would need to be closed if the work was not complete by Friday, as the lost profit from Saturday would be considered *consequential* damages.

Hawkins v. McGee
84 N.H. 114 (1929)

The following are excerpts from the opinion of Judge Branch of the New Hampshire Supreme Court.

The operation in question consisted in the removal of a considerable quantity of scar tissue from the palm of the plaintiff's right hand and the grafting of skin taken from the plaintiff's chest in place thereof. The scar tissue was the result of a severe burn caused by contact with an electric wire, which the plaintiff received about nine years before the time of the transactions here involved. There was evidence to the effect that before the operation was performed the plaintiff and his father went to the defendant's

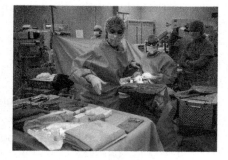

Figure 10.2 Damages arising out of a surgery was an issue in the *Hawkins v. McGee* case

office and that the defendant in answer to the question, "How long will the boy be in the hospital?", replied, "Three or four days, … not over four; then the boy can go home, and it will be just a few days when he will be able to go back to work with a perfect hand." Clearly this and other testimony to the same effect would not justify a finding that the doctor contracted to complete the hospital treatment in three or four days or that the plaintiff would be able to go back to work within a few days thereafter. The above statements could only be construed as expressions of opinion or predictions as to the probable duration of the treatment and plaintiff's resulting disability, and the fact that these estimates were exceeded would impose no contractual liability upon the defendant. The only substantial basis for the plaintiff's claim is the testimony that the defendant also said before the operation was decided upon, "I will guarantee to make the hand a hundred percent perfect hand" or "a hundred percent good hand." The plaintiff was present when these words were alleged to have been spoken, and if they are to be taken at their face value, it seems obvious that proof of their utterance would establish the giving of a warranty in accordance with his contention.

The present case is closely analogous to one in which a machine is built for a certain purpose and warranted to do certain work. In such cases, the usual rule of damages for breach of warranty in the sale of chattels is applied and it is held that the measure of damages is the difference between the value of the machine if it had corresponded with the warranty and its actual value, together with such incidental losses as the parties knew or ought to have known would probably result from a failure to comply with its terms.*** We, therefore, conclude that the true measure of the plaintiff's damage in the present case is the difference between the value to him of a perfect hand or a good hand, such as the jury found the defendant promised him, and the value of his hand in its present condition, including any incidental consequences fairly within the contemplation of the parties when they made their contract.*** Damages not thus limited, although naturally resulting, are not to be given.

The extent of the plaintiff's suffering does not measure this difference in value. The pain necessarily incident to a serious surgical operation was a part of the contribution which the plaintiff was willing to make to his joint undertaking with the defendant to produce a good hand. It was a legal detriment suffered by him which constituted a part of the consideration given by him for the contract. It represented a part of the price which he was willing to pay for a good hand, but it furnished no test of the value of a good hand or the difference between the value of the hand which the defendant promised and the one which resulted from the operation.

Questions

1. What type of damages interest did the court feel was appropriate to apply here?
2. Did the court believe the pain and suffering of surgery should be considered?
3. Why was it important the doctor had promised a one hundred percent good hand?

Equitable Remedies

Specific performance means to do specifically as promised. Specific performance is appropriate as a remedy when breach of the contract by one party cannot be compensated by monetary damages. For example, assume Roger contracts to buy a house once owned by his grandparents; they had since lost the home due to foreclosure by a bank. If the seller breaches their duty to deliver ownership of the house to Roger, Roger will not be satisfied by monetary damages. Rogers wants this specific house.

In the United States, courts are often slow to award specific performance as a remedy when personal services are involved, as this would be a means of involuntary servitude (slavery). However, courts might be willing to impose an injunction in a breach of employment contract involving personal services. An **injunction** is a court order that demands a defendant stop performing an action. For example, assume Brett is hired by a movie producer to be the lead actor in a movie. The contract prohibits Brett from acting in any other movies during that year. Brett breaches his contractual duties and takes a job acting in a similar type of movie. A court may award an injunction to prevent Brett from starring in the second movie.

The third type of equitable relief is rescission. **Rescission** is the act by which a court cancels or undoes a contract. For example, assume Hunter and Sierra have a contract for the sale of a car. Hunter gives Sierra $500 as a deposit or down payment on the car. Sierra informs Hunter two days later that the car has been damaged as part of an accident. Sierra does not want to fix the car and Hunter does not want to buy a car that was badly damaged. A court might award Hunter his $500 deposit back and then relieve Sierra of her duty to deliver the car.

Reformation is an equitable remedy that a court uses to change or modify the terms to a contract. Reformation is most often applied by courts in cases involving mistake or fraud. In addition, it may be appropriate when parties memorialize their agreement in the form of a written contract, mistakes may occur. A **scrivener's error** is a typographical error. For example, assume Mitchel and Jerry have a contract for the sale of a computer. Mitchel and Jerry put their contract in writing but accidentally write down the wrong price. A court may reform the contract price to preserve the original intent of the parties. Reformation can also be used in cases when a contract contains unconscionable terms. For example, a covenant not to compete that has an unconscionably wide area of coverage. The court may revise the covenant to a narrower area of coverage.

- Punitive
- Liquidated damages
- Nominal damages

Liquidated Damages and Punitive Damages

Courts generally do not award punitive damages in a breach of contract case unless an intentional tort such as fraud has also occurred. A **punitive** damage is a damage that is not meant to compensate a party for a loss suffered from the breach of contract but is instead designed to punish the breaching party for improper behavior. For example, Natalie rents an apartment with her boyfriend Alex for $1,000 per month for a period of twelve months. As part of the lease contract they signed, the contract has a clause that requires Natalie and Alex to pay damages of $15,000 in the event they breach their contractual duties. A court would most likely find this to be a penalty (punitive damages clause) that is unenforceable. The landlord is trying to deter Alex and Natalie from breaching their contract with the threat of a penalty.

Liquidated damages are damages provided in a contract that are meant to compensate the non-breaching party in the event of a breach of contract. For example, assume Natalie and Alex's lease contract requires liquidated damages equal to one month's rent in the event of a breach of contract; a court is likely to allow this amount as liquidated damages. It is reasonable for a landlord to believe they would lose one month's rent in the event a tenant breached their lease contract and moved out early.

In trying to determine whether a contract is providing for an unenforceable penalty or enforceable liquidated damages clause, a court will look to see 1) whether the damages of a breach of contract would be hard to calculate and 2) whether the amount of damages is reasonable. For example, a court would find one month's rent to be appropriate in the event of a breach of a lease contract because the landlord might lose one month's worth of rent trying to find another tenant. However, a court would object to a landlord receiving a damages amount greater than the entire amount of payments required by the lease. For example, Natalie and Alex rent an apartment at the rate of $1,000 per month for twelve months. Their lease contains a provision that is labeled "liquidated damages." The provision requires Natalie and Alex to pay $14,000 in liquidated damages if they breach their lease contract. A court would likely find the $14,000 amount to be an unenforceable penalty disguised as a liquidated damage.

Nominal Damages

Nominal damages are a small amount of damages awarded in a contract breach case that are intended to establish liability on the part of the breaching party but not necessarily compensate the party for damages realized. For example, in 1986 the United States Football League was awarded $3 in damages in an antitrust case against the National Football League. The award proved the National Football League had violated antitrust laws and provided $3 in nominal damages. The court case marked the end of the United States Football League, which was unable to maintain its operations.

Mitigation

In certain circumstances, a plaintiff is required to attempt to mitigate (reduce) his or her damages by taking actions to reduce the loss suffered from a breach of contract. For example, Sarah rents an apartment from Abe in College Town where she attends the state university. After one month, Sarah decides to transfer to another university; she moves out of her apartment and leaves a note for Abe saying she will not be returning. Depending on the law of Abe's jurisdiction, Abe may be required to try to immediately find another person to rent Sarah's apartment in an attempt to mitigate his damages. If Abe is required to mitigate his damages, but does not make reasonable efforts to lease the apartment again, the damages he tries to seek from Sarah might be reduced by a court.

Courts generally look to see whether the plaintiff made a reasonable effort to mitigate damages. What constitutes reasonable efforts depends upon the situation. For example, Abe would be wise to advertise the apartment in a local newspaper and on the Internet through a popular listing website. In addition, the courts will not require Abe to simply accept any tenant who applies to rent the apartment. The tenant must be a good tenant of the type to whom Abe would normally rent an apartment. Likewise in the context of employment contracts, if the employer breaches the employment contract, the employee is not required to take just any job the newly unemployed individual can find. The job must be comparable to that job that was lost through breach of contract.

UCC Provisions on Damages

The UCC has several key provisions related to breach of contract and related damages. First, UCC § 1-305 states damages shall be liberally awarded to put the plaintiff in as good a position as he or she would have been had the defendant performed as promised. Therefore, the UCC generally incorporates the expectancy interest of the plaintiff when awarding damages. Before discussing the provisions awarding monetary damages, it should be noted UCC § 2-716 allows for nonmonetary damages in the form of specific performance in the event the buyer cannot be compensated by monetary relief.

UCC § 2-712 allows a buyer to recover damages who never receives goods from the seller or a buyer who lawfully rejects goods delivered by the seller. The buyer can then buy conforming goods from another supplier and demand the difference in price from the seller under UCC § 2-712. The buyer can also seek damages without buying the goods, in which case the amount of damages would be the difference in market price and contract price at the time of breach under UCC 2-713.

Regardless of the action taken by the buyer, the buyer can seek incidental damages and consequential damages as well under UCC § 2-715. **Incidental damages** are damages arising because of the breach of the seller and include costs such as shipping the goods back to the seller or having the goods inspected by a third party. **Consequential damages** are damages that compensate the injured party for costs or lost profits caused because of the breach or damages and that the seller knew would result or had reason to know would result. Consequential damages can also be awarded in the event of a breach of warranty by the seller. For example, buyer informs seller that buyer needs a lot of fifty goods so it can fulfill an order to a customer of buyer. Seller breaches. Buyer is entitled to the lost profits on the sale to their customer because the seller was informed of the consequences of a breach when contracting.

Under the UCC, a buyer who accepts goods, but then determines the goods to be defective, may sue for damages. Under UCC § 2-607, the buyer must notify the seller of any defect within a reasonable amount of time. The UCC also allows a buyer to sue a seller for damages if the seller breaches the contract by failing to perform other required duties such as supplying missing or defective parts. The courts may award compensatory damages as well as consequential damages in the event of a breach of a sales contract.

Under UCC § 2-601, a seller of goods must make perfect tender to constitute complete performance. The courts have relaxed this rule to only require the goods must be free from a material defect. If a material defect is present, the buyer may reject the entire shipment of goods, accept part of the shipment and send back the rest, or accept the entire shipment. The buyer is given a reasonable amount of time to inspect the goods before accepting or rejecting. In addition, even if the buyer has accepted the goods, the buyer may be allowed to revoke their acceptance if a later inspection reveals a defect. UCC § 2-508 provides the seller with an important safeguard, as it allows the seller the right to cure (or fix defective goods) if the time for delivery has not yet expired.

Under UCC § 2-709, a seller may seek damages from the buyer when the buyer has accepted the goods but not yet paid for them as required by the contract. The amount of damages would be the contract price. Under UCC § 2-710 the seller is entitled to incidental damages. UCC § 2-718(1) allows for liquidated damages clauses. However, in similar fashion to the common law, the UCC requires the amount to be reasonable based upon the circumstances surrounding the contract. In addition, the UCC states unreasonable amounts of damages are to be considered unenforceable penalties.

In regards to mitigation of damages, UCC § 2-712 allows a buyer to recover consequential damages if the buyer attempts to cover (buy replacement goods) in the event of a seller breaching by not delivering the contracted goods to the buyer. If the buyer breaches, the seller is allowed to attempt to sell the goods and recover the difference in price between the original contract and the subsequent sales contract under UCC § 2-706. If the seller decides not to try to find another buyer and mitigate his damages, the seller is limited to the difference between the contract price and the fair market value under UCC § 2-708. If fair market value declines, UCC § 2-708 would limit the seller's recovery because of the seller's failure to mitigate.

Construction Contracts

If a construction contractor, who is the party in charge of building something, breaches a contract, the other party to the contract is generally awarded damages based upon their expectation interest. For example, Monica hires Kyle, a construction contractor, to build her a home. Kyle starts the project but fails to finish. Monica will be awarded as damages the cost to complete the building of her house.

If the party who contracted with the construction contractor breaches their duties under the contract, the construction contractor will be awarded damages based upon the extent the construction project has progressed. First, if the construction project has not yet started, the

- Anticipatory
  repudiation

Figure 10.3 Construction projects often involve a breach of contract because complete performance is hard to obtain

construction contractor is entitled to the profit they would have earned under the contract. If the construction project has already begun, then the construction contractor is entitled to the lost profit under the contract as well as any costs incurred to date. If the constructions project is complete, then the construction contractor is entitled to the full contract price.

Assume Theodore hires Fast Build Incorporated to build a new house for the contract price of $320,000. The expected costs to complete the project are $280,000. The expected profit is $40,000. If Theodore loses his job and informs Fast Build he cannot perform under the contract, Fast Build would be entitled to $40,000, assuming they had not made any expenditures. If Fast Build has expended $100,000 toward the completion of the house, and Theodore informs Fast Build he cannot perform and they should not continue building the house, Fast Build would be entitled to recover the costs they have expended along with the $40,000 of profit.

Anticipatory Repudiation

If a party to a contract anticipatorily repudiates its duties, the party has committed a material breach. An **anticipatory repudiation** occurs when a party to a contract informs the other party to a contract that it will be unable to perform under the terms of the contract. The legal significance of an anticipatory repudiation by a party to a contract is it allows the other party to immediately bring a lawsuit for breach of contract. For example, Ronald hires Brad to plant a corn crop in Ronald's field by May 1. The contract is signed on February 1. On March 1, Brad calls Ronald and informs Ronald that Brad's mom is dying from cancer and Brad will not be able to plant the crop. Ronald may immediately sue Brad for breach of contract because Brad has anticipatorily repudiated his contract. The outcome may seem harsh, as Brad's mother is suffering from a life-threatening condition. However, by allowing Ronald to look for another person to fulfill his needs, a court may limit the amount of damages Brad may owe Ronald. Furthermore, the common law allowed Brad to change his mind and required Ronald to accept his performance if Ronald has not already changed his position in regards to the contract. For example, if Brad anticipatorily repudiates his contract with Ronald, Ronald is not required to allow Brad to tender performance if Ronald has already hired Alan to plant his field.

- Objective impossibility
- Commercial impracticability

Discharge by Operation of Law

At certain times, a court will intervene and discharge a party from their contractual duties even though the party has not provided complete performance. For example a party to debt contract may be discharged from their duty to pay their debt by a *bankruptcy proceeding*. In addition, a *statute of limitations* may bar a party from bringing a breach of contract lawsuit if the lawsuit is not initiated within a certain time period. For example, under UCC § 2-725, a party has four years to bring a breach of contract claim for the sale of goods. The parties may agree under UCC § 2-725 to shorten the statute of limitations for a contract of the sale of goods to one year.

Objective impossibility is a legal doctrine that discharges a party from their contractual duties if it is impossible to perform such duties and the difficulty was not foreseeable at the time of contracting. For example, Mariah is about to be married to her college sweetheart Ashton. Mariah rents a reception hall where the wedding dance will be held. The reception hall is owned by Good Times Inc. One week before the wedding, the reception hall is burned to the ground. Good Times Inc. will be discharged from their duty to provide a reception hall under the theory of objective impossibility.

Some of the most common factual scenarios where a court will find objective impossibility are

1. Death or incapacity of a party to a personal services contract.
2. Death or incapacity of a third party who was key to the contract.
3. Destruction of subject matter important to the execution of the contract.

In a situation where impossibility is claimed on behalf of one of the parties, a court will consider many important factors. For example, did the parties consider the possibility that subject matter could be destroyed when they negotiated their contract? In a contract for the sale of goods, was the means for creating the goods destroyed or were the goods themselves destroyed?

Commercial Impracticability

Commercial impracticability is a legal doctrine where a court discharges a party from their contractual duty because it is commercially impractical but not objectively impossible. Under the common law and UCC § 2-615, only extreme circumstances will warrant commercial impracticability. As with objective impossibility, the impracticability must not have been reasonably foreseeable. For example, assume Midwest Tires agrees to sell 10,000 tires to Auto Warehouse at the price of $55 per tire. A shortage of petroleum products occurs because of an outbreak of war. This shortage of petroleum products causes the cost of producing tires to quadruple from $50 to $200. Midwest Tires fears this contract will bankrupt its business. The possibility of increasing petroleum prices must not have been foreseeable to Midwest Tires. In addition, the court must be convinced the enforcement of the contract will create such devastation that Justice requires the duty of performance to be discharged. Therefore, sellers sometimes face resistance from courts when claiming the price of inputs requires their performance be discharged. Courts are not sympathetic because of increased costs toward those who routinely sell goods that they produce.

In regards to both objective impossibility and commercial impracticability, parties may contract away their right to claim impossibility or impracticability as a means of satisfying the discharge of their duties. For example, assume Pier agrees to sell his corn crop to Northern Ethanol for the price of $7.50 per bushel. Pier and Northern Ethanol may state in their contract that neither commercial impracticability nor impossibility is to be used as a defense against contract enforcement. If this clause is included in their contract, it is assumed Pier will negotiate for a higher price. In addition, Pier may hedge or protect against certain risks, such as a bad storm, by purchasing crop insurance.

Frustration of purpose is a legal doctrine that discharges the duty of parties to perform where the original purpose of their contract can no longer be achieved. It is not necessary for both parties to have their purposes frustrated. For example, Bobby wants to learn martial arts from Scott who is an expert in martial arts. Bobby has contracted with Scott for ten individual lessons for the price of $250 per lesson. One week before the lessons are to begin, Bobby is involved in an auto accident. The accident leaves him in a full body cast. He is unable to move any of his body parts. As agreed, Scotts arrives at Bobby's home to teach him martial arts. Bobby and Scott would both be discharged from their duty to perform because the purpose of their contract cannot be achieved. Even if Scott is willing to teach Bobby, the purpose of their contract is frustrated and Bobby is relieved from his duty to accept the lessons and pay Scott.

Third Party Rights

Contracts often include more than two parties. For example, assume the city of Sheldon wants to build a new city office building. The city of Sheldon accepts an offer from Sturdy Incorporated. Sturdy Inc. will act as a general contractor. It will be responsible for ensuring the completion of the project. Sturdy Inc. will subcontract various parts of the construction project to third-party contractors, referred to as "sub-contractors" in the construction industry. For example, Sturdy Inc. might subcontract with High Voltage Electrical Company. High Voltage will be responsible for the electrical components of the construction project.

A third-party intended beneficiary enjoys the right to hold a party to a contract liable for breach of contract. A third-party **intended beneficiary** is a party whom the original parties to a contract intend to benefit. A common example of an intended beneficiary is the beneficiary to a life insurance contract. For example, Amanda purchases an insurance policy with Benefit Life Insurance Company that will pay her beneficiary Matt a lump sum of $500,000 if she dies in the next ten years. Matt is a third-party beneficiary to the contract between Amanda and Benefit Life Insurance Company. An **incidental beneficiary** is a party whom the original parties did not intend to benefit with their contract. An incidental beneficiary does not have standing to sue for breach of contract. For example, Benefit Life Insurance

Company may use Efficient Print Company to copy and print all their insurance applications. The life insurance contract between Benefit Life Insurance Company and Amanda did not intend to benefit Efficient Print Company.

The distinction between an intended beneficiary and incidental beneficiary is hard to define. Courts will consider the intent of the parties when forming their contract. If this is not clear, courts will look to see whether performance required as part of the contract was directed to be made to the beneficiary. Finally, the courts will look at the contract from the beneficiary's point of view to determine whether it would be reasonable for the party to believe they were an intended beneficiary.

For example, Dallas hires Nathan to fix his mom Linda's car. Dallas promises $500 to Nathan in exchange for his services. Linda is an intended beneficiary. Nathan formed the contract with the intention of benefiting his mother Linda. In addition, the subject matter of the contract was directed toward her.

Now assume Martin hires Joan to knit a sweater for his girlfriend Nadia. Martin states in his contract with Joan that Joan must buy all the necessary supplies from Max Fabrics. Joan is an intended beneficiary. A court would most likely find Max Fabrics to be an incidental beneficiary, assuming Martin was merely worried about the quality of fabric used and was not intending to benefit Max Fabrics with additional profit. The purpose of the contract was to benefit Joan, not Max Fabrics.

Historically, courts have categorized intended beneficiaries as being one of two types. **Creditor beneficiaries** are owed performance by one of the parties because of a preexisting obligation owed to the intended beneficiary. In the famous case of *Lawrence v. Fox*, 20 N.Y. 268 (1859), a debt was owed by Fox to Holly. Instead of making payment to Holly, Holly asked Fox to pay Lawrence. Lawrence was owed a debt by Holly and this debt made Lawrence a creditor beneficiary. The position of creditor beneficiary is advantageous because it allows the beneficiary to sue the promisor of the contract if they breach their duty but also the other party because that party originally owed a debt to the creditor beneficiary. **Donee beneficiaries** are not owed a performance because of an existing duty but because a party to the contract has decided to provide them a benefit. The beneficiary to a life insurance contract is generally a donee beneficiary.

- Creditor beneficiaries
- Donee beneficiaries

Bain v. Gillispie
357 N.W.2d 47 (1984)

The following are excerpts from the opinion of Judge Snell of the Iowa Court of Appeals.

James C. Bain serves as a referee for college basketball games. During a game which took place on March 6, 1982, Bain called a foul on a University of Iowa player which permitted free throws to a Purdue University player. That player scored the point that gave Purdue a last-minute victory. Some fans of the University of Iowa team blamed Bain for their team's loss, asserting that the foul call was clearly in error.

Figure 10.4 Hawkeye basketball was at the center of *Bain v. Gillespie*

John and Karen Gillispie operate a novelty store in Iowa City, specializing in University of Iowa sports memorabilia. The store is known as Hawkeye John's Trading Post. Gillispie's business is a private enterprise for profit having no association with the University of Iowa or its sports program.

A few days after the controversial game, Gillispies began marketing T-shirts bearing a reference to Bain. It showed a man with a rope around his neck and was captioned "Jim Bain Fan Club." On learning of it, Bain sued Gillispies for injunctive relief, actual and punitive damages. Gillispies counterclaimed, alleging that Bain's conduct in officiating the game was below the standard of competence required of a professional referee. As such, it constituted malpractice which entitles Gillispies to $175,000 plus exemplary damages. They claim these sums because Iowa's loss of the game to Purdue eliminated Iowa from the championship of the Big Ten Basketball Conference. This in turn destroyed a potential market for Gillispies' memorabilia touting Iowa as a Big Ten champion. Their claim for actual damages is for loss of earnings and business advantage, emotional distress and anxiety, loss of good will, and expectancy of profits. Exemplary damages are asked because Bain's calls as a referee were baneful, outrageous, and done with a heedless disregard for the rights of the Gillispies.

The trial court found the Gillispies had no rights and sustained a motion for summary judgment dismissing Gillispies' counterclaim. They appeal, contending the trial court erred in finding no genuine issue of material fact.

As the trial court properly reasoned "This is a case where the undisputed facts are of such a nature that a rational fact finder could only reach one conclusion—no foreseeability, no duty, no liability. Heaven knows what uncharted morass a court would find itself in if it were to hold that an athletic official subjects himself to liability every time he might make a questionable call. The possibilities are mindboggling. If there is a liability to a merchandiser like the Gillispies, why not to the thousands upon thousands of Iowa fans who bleed Hawkeye black and gold every time the whistle blows? It is bad enough when Iowa loses without transforming a loss into a litigation field day for 'Monday Morning Quarterbacks.' There is no tortious doctrine of athletic official's malpractice that would give credence to Gillispies counterclaim."

The trial court also found that there was no issue of material fact on the Gillispies' claim that they were beneficiaries under Bain's contract with the Big 10. Gillispies argue that until the contract is produced, there exists a question of whether they are beneficiaries. There is some question of whether there is a contract between Bain and the Big 10. In his response to interrogatories, Bain stated that he had no written contract with the Big 10, but that there was a letter which defined "working relationship." Although this letter was never produced and ordinarily we would not decide an issue without the benefit of examining the letter's contents, we nevertheless find the issue presently capable of determination. By deposition Gillispies answered that there was no contract between them and Bain, the Big 10 Athletic Conference, the University of Iowa, the players, coaches, or with anybody regarding this issue. Thus, even if the letter were considered a contract, Gillispies would be considered third-party beneficiaries. Because Gillispies would not be privy to the contract, they must be direct beneficiaries to maintain a cause of action, and not merely incidental beneficiaries.***

Gillispies make no claim that they are creditor beneficiaries of Bain, the Big 10 Athletic Conference, or the University of Iowa. "The real test is said to be whether the contracting parties intended that a third person should receive a benefit which might be enforced in the courts."*** It is clear that the purpose of any promise which Bain might have made was not to confer a gift on Gillispies. Likewise, the Big 10 did not owe any duty to the Gillispies such that they would have been creditor beneficiaries. If a contract did exist between Bain and the Big 10, the Gillispies can be considered nothing more than incidental beneficiaries and as such are unable to maintain a cause of action.*** Consequently, there was no genuine issue for trial that could result in the Gillispies' obtaining a judgment under a contract theory of recovery. The ruling of the trial court sustaining the summary judgment motion and dismissing the counterclaim is affirmed.

- Assignment
- Assignor
- Assignee
- Obligor

Questions

1. Who were the Gillispies? Who is James C. Bain?
2. Who was party to a contract with Mr. Bain?
3. Why did the court feel it inappropriate to hold a referee liable for making a bad call?
4. What type of beneficiary did the Gillispies claim to be? Did the court agree?

Assignment and Delegation

Third parties may be added to the contract by the means of an assignment or delegation after the contract is formed. An **assignment** occurs when a party transfers its rights under a contract to a third party. The third party does not have to provide consideration to the assignor. The **assignor** is the party who transfers a right. The **assignee** is the party receiving the right. An **obligor** is a party who owes a performance under a contract. As a general rule, the assignor extinguishes their interest in a right upon assignment of such right.

For example, assume Jonathan owes David $400 as part of a debt contract. David might later decide the money should be paid to his mother Donna. David assigns his right to collect the money to his mother Donna. David is the assignor and Donna is the assignee. It should be noted that an assignment is different from a novation. A novation substitutes an initial party to a contract for a new third party. The novation effectively removes a party from the contract. In an assignment, the assignor remains a party to the contract.

As a general rule, all rights provided by a contract can be assigned. Exceptions include 1) contracts that prohibit assignment by their own terms, 2) contracts for which a state statute prohibits assignment, and 3) the assignment or rights will substantially change the duties of the obligor.

For example, assume Rebecca hires Lee to shovel snow from her home's driveway in northern Michigan. Rebecca pays Lee in advance but finds out two weeks later that she will be moving to Florida. Rebecca attempts to assign her right to receive snow removal services to her dad Andrew. Andrew lives on a farm in northern Michigan and his driveway is two miles long. This assignment would be unenforceable by Andrew because the driveway to his farm is substantially longer than Rebecca's driveway. Therefore, the assignment increased Lee's duties as the obligor.

Even though parties can prohibit assignment, a court of law may override such a provision to a contract. Similarly, UCC § 9-406 prohibits parties from disallowing an assignment of the right to collect payment under a contract. In addition, state law might disallow the prohibition of the assignment of certain rights in a contract, such as the right to transfer an interest in real property.

Finally, the assignee steps into the shoes of the assignor. The assignee can sue the obligor for nonperformance but is subject to the same defenses the obligor held against the assignor. The assignee may also be able to sue the assignor if the assignee gave consideration in exchange for the assignment of rights. For example, Big Bank Inc. assigns its right to collect mortgage payments from Dennis. Big Bank makes the assignment to Trust Corp in exchange for valuable consideration. If Dennis does not make the required payment to Trust Corp, Trust Corp can sue Dennis as well as Big Bank.

Delegation

A party can delegate duties or obligations under a contract in a similar fashion to assigning rights under a contract. A **delegator** is the party who delegates a duty. The **delegatee** is the party to whom a delegation of duty has been made. The **obligee** is the person to whom a duty is owed. For example, United Delivery Service is to deliver a package to Smithson Corporation. United Delivery hires Fast Transit Company to make the delivery since it cannot do so on time. Smithson Corporation is the obligee. United Delivery is the delegator and Fast Transit Company is the delegatee.

As with assignments, delegations are not always given legal effect. Delegations are not legally enforceable if 1) the delegation is prohibited by the terms of the contract, 2) the delegation violates public policy or state law, or 3) the obligee has a substantial interest in having the delegator perform the duty. An example of when the obligee would have a substantial interest in having the original obligor perform is in the context of a personal services contract. Assume Danielle hires Michelangelo, a famous artist, to paint a picture of her daughter Rose. Michelangelo delegates his duties to Craig, a business law professor, who has limited painting abilities. Danielle, the obligee, has a substantial interest in having Michelangelo complete the painting as opposed to Craig.

A delegator remains liable to the obligee for performance. The delegatee becomes liable to the obligee once she assumes the obligation to perform. A delegator who wishes to relinquish liability should effect a novation instead of a delegation.

Questions

1. What is complete performance and what is its legal effect on a contract?
2. What is substantial performance and what is its legal effect on a contract?
3. What is a material breach and what is its legal effect on a contract?
4. What are a condition precedent and a condition subsequent and how are they different?
5. What are concurrent conditions?
6. What are an objective condition and a subjective condition and how are they different?
7. What is the definition of compensatory damages?
8. What is the definition of expectation damages and how are these damages calculated?
9. What is the definition of reliance damages and how are these damages calculated?
10. What is the definition of restitution damages and how are these damages calculated?
11. How are general damages different from special damages?
12. What are the three forms of equitable remedies and when are they appropriate for a court to award?
13. What are liquidated damages and how are they different from punitive damages?
14. What are nominal damages and when are they appropriate to award?
15. What is mitigation and when is mitigation always required?
16. What do UCC Provisions 2-712 and 2-713 provide?
17. What are incidental damages and how are they different from consequential damages?
18. What does UCC § 2-607 provide?
19. What do UCC Provisions 2-601 and 2-508 provide?
20. What does UCC § 2-709 provide?
21. What remedies are provided to a contractor in a construction contract that is breached by the person for whom the item is being built?
22. What is anticipatory repudiation and what is the legal effect of an anticipatory repudiation?
23. What is objective impossibility and how is it different from commercial impracticability?
24. What is an intended beneficiary and how is an intended beneficiary different from an incidental beneficiary?
25. What is a creditor beneficiary and how is a creditor beneficiary different from an incidental beneficiary?
26. What is an assignment and what contractual rights cannot be assigned?
27. What is a delegation and what contractual duties cannot be delegated?

Critical-Thinking Questions

28. Why is a party who received substantial performance still able to sue the breaching party?
29. How might damages based upon an expectation interest lead to economic waste?
30. Why do courts prohibit the enforcement of penalties as a general rule in regards to contractual breach?
31. Why is it important that actual notice be given to a breaching party when the plaintiff desires to receive special damages from the breaching party?
32. Why should courts be reluctant to allow a defense of commercial impracticability?

Essay Questions

1. Veronica owns a retail business. During the past year she purchased the building that she had been leasing. She contracts with a landscaper to install a sprinkler system as well as some shrubs. The total cost of the contract to Veronica will be $14,000. The landscaper quits three fourths of the way through the job and says he will not finish the job. The only thing he had left to do was connect the sprinkler systems to Veronica's building. The value of what he had done is approximately $9,000. Veronica has received a quote for $7,500 from another landscaper to finish the job. She has made payment of $4,000 to the first landscaper. What amount of damages should Veronica be rewarded based upon her expectation interest? Her reliance interest? A restitution interest? Assume this is not considered a construction contract.

2. Bethany owns an organic farm. She needs to build a new barn to house a milking cow and some free-range chickens. Bethany contracts with Harvey to build the barn for the contract price of $24,000. Bethany has purchased the materials at the cost of $16,000 and contracted Harvey to provide the labor. One week before he is to perform, Harvey calls Bethany and tells her he has broken his leg and cannot perform. Bethany obtains another quote for $30,000 to build the barn. What would be the appropriate amount of damages for Bethany based upon her expectation interest? Her reliance interest? A restitution interest? What if a court applies the rules above, especially applicable to a construction contract?

3. Mickey hires Donald to perform accounting services for Mickey's business. Donald and Mickey sign a contract under which Donald will perform certain accounting functions in exchange for the payment of $50 per hour to be paid biweekly. The contract also contains a clause that states Mickey will owe Donald $600 in damages if Mickey is ever more than ten days late with payment for Donald's services. During October of the current year, Donald performed twenty hours of accounting work for Mickey. Donald invoiced Mickey for the services and Mickey did not pay within ten days. Donald now wishes to seek the $600 in damages he is owed under the contract on top of the money he is owed for twenty hours of work. Will a court enforce the clause requiring payment of $600? Why or why not?

4. Gerald enters into a contract with a local television company. The contract specifies Gerald will receive cable and Internet services for two years at the price of $120 per month. The cable company will provide Gerald with equipment valued at $650. The equipment is necessary for Gerald to access the Internet and cable programming. In the contract it specifies Gerald will owe the company $2,500 in damages if Gerald ever breaches his contract, plus $120 per month for the remaining period of the contract. After eight months of bad service and limited Internet connection, Gerald quits paying his bill. Assuming a court finds Gerald has breached the contract, will the court require Gerald to pay the $2,500 amount? Why or why not?

5. Office Work Company orders 200 staplers from Office Supply Store at the price of $3 per stapler. Office Supply Store accepts the offer by promising prompt shipment. Office Supply does not make a prompt shipment and no staplers are ever delivered. Office Work Company proceeds to buy 200 staplers from another supply company. What are

Office Work Company's damages under the UCC, assuming it paid A) $3.20 for the replacement staplers; B) $3.50 plus $.10 in shipping expense for the replacement staplers, C) $2.80 for the replacement staplers?

6. Fresh Fruit Distributors buys fresh fruit from local farmers and then resells it. Fresh Fruit has a large order from a local grocery store for lettuce. Farmer Joe contracts with Fresh Fruit for the delivery of one hundred heads of lettuce at the price of $1 per head of lettuce. Farmer Joe calls Fresh Fruit the day before delivery is to take place and says he cannot perform. Fresh Fruit buys similar heads of lettuce from another farmer. What are the appropriate amounts of damages under the UCC, assuming Fresh Fruit paid A) $1.20 per head of lettuce, B) $1.05 per head of lettuce plus $.06 per head for shipping expense, C) $.90 per head of lettuce? What if Fresh Fruit lost the sale to the grocery store and the profit it was to make was $250? Can Fresh Fruit recover this amount under the UCC?

7. Ben Driven Motor Company owes the Farola Bank $200,000. Ben Driven Motors enters into a contract with Speedy Delivery for the sale of eight delivery vans costing $180,000 in total. Ben Driven Motors requires Speedy Delivery to make the payment of $180,000 directly to Farola Bank. Speedy Delivery takes possession of the vans but never makes payment. Who can sue Speedy Delivery and on what theory? Can Farola Bank sue Ben Driven and under what theory?

8. Smart Build Construction contracts with Yummie Foods for the construction of a new food processing plant for the price of $2,000,000. Smart Build will realize $300,000 in profit. Smart Build names Subfloor Company as a subcontractor in the contract with Yummie Foods. Subfloor estimates its profit will be $100,000. One week before construction is to begin, Yummie informs Smart Build that they will not need the plant and that they will breach the contract. Who can sue Yummie and for what amount and under which theory?

CHAPTER ELEVEN

REAL AND PERSONAL PROPERTY LAW

By Michael Bootsma

Alex and his business partner Melissa are interested in buying houses that are being offered for sale at discount prices. They want to buy the houses, renovate the houses, and then rent the houses to local college students. Alex and Melissa are interested in the legal concepts pertaining to a purchase of real property as well as the basics of tenant and landlord law.

Juan and his brother Philippe have started a restaurant and they are concerned about students from the local college parking in their parking lot. Customers of their restaurant are complaining that they do not have enough spaces from which to use for parking.

Objectives

1. Understand the process by which one becomes the owner of property
2. Distinguish between the different types of property ownership
3. Identify important concepts in transferring ownership
4. Understand basic legal principles associated with bailments
5. Understand major principles of tenant–landlord law
6. Identify different restraints on the use of property

Capture, Creation, Purchase, or Possession

A person can become the owner of property in one of several ways. An old saying is "possession is nine tenths of the law." This saying has a lot of merit. However, in most civilized societies valuable pieces of property will be subject to title ownership rules. Regardless, in some cases a person might still become an owner by capture, creation, or possession, so possession might still be nine tenths of the law.

Real property is defined as land and everything permanently attached to the land. For example, a house and the lot of land on which it sits are considered real property. **Personal property** is defined as all property that is not real property. Personal property is generally movable objects such as a car or laptop computer. Unless noted otherwise in this chapter, the discussion of law will apply to both real property and personal property. Personal property is often referred to as chattel. A **fixture** is a piece of personal property that has been attached to real property in such a manner that the personal property becomes a part of the real property. Since a fixture is considered real property once it is attached, the fixture transfers with the real property when such real property is sold unless the purchaser and buyer agree otherwise. A **trade fixture** is an item of personal property attached by a tenant who wishes to carry out a trade or business in a leased area. For example, Cindy rents an office in which she intends to do accounting work for customers. The office does not have carpet, so Cindy has carpet installed. The carpet is considered a trade fixture.

Rule of Capture

The **rule of capture** awards ownership to the first person who captures property and is most commonly applied to natural resources in the United States. Under the common law, the person who ultimately captured a wild animal was considered to be the owner as long as the animal was wild and had not been domesticated already by another person. It is important to note the owner was not the person who pursued the wild animal but the person who ultimately captured the animal. For example, Craig is pursuing a wild deer. Charlie comes along toward the end of the chase and captures the wild deer. It does not matter if Craig had been pursuing the deer for three days, and Charlie only for two hours; Charlie becomes the owner, as he is the first to capture.

Figure 11.1 Wild horses are an example of animal which used to be captured and possession was obtained by the captor

In the United States, through their lawmaking abilities, the states and the federal government restrict the capture of wild animals. For example, states create a system for obtaining licenses for hunting and fishing. In addition, the licenses allow for the capture of only certain animals during certain periods of time during the year. For example, hunters might only be able to shoot and kill a rooster pheasant during the month of October. Finally, the states and the federal government often pass laws to protect certain species. The Endangered Species Act of 1973 creates a federal system for protecting endangered species. An **endangered species** is a species that may face extinction (complete elimination) if not protected.

The rule of capture is also applied to oil and gas deposits. A landowner who properly drills an oil well under their land becomes the owner of the oil that they capture. Due to the fact that oil may run from underneath a neighbor's land into a well created by another neighbor, many states have created legislation limiting the number of wells a landowner may have per acre as well as the size and type of well. This prevents one neighbor from creating such a large well that it would drain the oil and gas deposits of neighbors.

Water Rights

Water rights are becoming an important issue for many locations throughout the United States, including the areas of the southwest United States where water is scarce. Courts often apply the rule of capture to water rights. However, the application of the rule will depend upon which type of water is being captured.

Percolating Water

In many states, the owner of land has the right to drill a well in order to obtain water. The water that exists underneath the surface of land is referred to as **percolating water**. In some states the English rule of absolute ownership is followed. Under the rule of absolute ownership, a landowner can use as much percolating water as she wants and for whatever use.

In other states, the use of percolating water is subject to a **reasonable use standard**, where the water can be used only to benefit the property where the water source is located and the use must be reasonable. For example, Farmer Brown creates a well underneath his land. If Farmer Brown uses the water from his well for his family and the animals he has on his land, he will be considered to have engaged in reasonable use even if it causes his neighbor's well to go dry. However, if he attempts to transport the water and irrigate a field far from his house, the use might not be considered reasonable.

Closely related to the concept of a reasonable use standard is the correlative rights theory. Under the **correlative rights doctrine**, the owner of land overlaying percolating water is considered to be a joint owner with other property owners whose property overlays the percolating water. Each owner is subject to a reasonable use standard. California is often accredited with the correlative rights doctrine.

Some states follow a prior appropriations rights doctrine. Under the **prior appropriation rights doctrine**, the first person to use a water source has a greater priority than a subsequent user. For example, Misty digs a well on her farm and finds an underground water source. She has a legal priority in using the found water as compared to subsequent individuals who find the same water source.

Surface Water

As a general rule, the person who captures surface water is the only owner of it. Also, a person can capture an unlimited amount of surface water on their own property. **Surface water** is water that has no natural stream or way of passage. An example of surface water is the water that flows across a parking lot after a large rain.

Landowners are allowed to divert surface water from their property. However, whether or not they are liable to neighbors for such diversion will depend in part on which legal doctrine their state recognizes. The first legal doctrine is called the common enemy doctrine. Under the **common enemy doctrine** at the common law, a landowner could use any means possible to divert surface water from their property. The landowner could use various drainage methods and even build a dam. However, most states now have changed the common enemy doctrine as applied to surface water and now limit the types of drainage permitted.

- Percolating water
- Reasonable use standard
- Correlative rights doctrine
- Prior appropriation rights doctrine
- Surface water
- Common enemy doctrine

Under the **natural servitude doctrine**, the landowner is considered to be a servant of surface water and cannot change the natural flow of the water by building a dam to push water backwards or by building a drainage mechanism that would hasten the flow of the water to other property owners. Some states have carved out exceptions for areas in which development of housing requires builders to be able to divert the land water. Approximately half the states follow the common enemy doctrine and half follow the natural servitude doctrine.

Stream Water and Lake Water

A stream or lake is a body of water that is treated differently from percolating or surface water. A stream is considered to be water that flows following a certain path. A lake is different. A lake is generally a resting body of water. Some states follow the prior appropriation rights doctrine where the first person to use a stream or lake has a superior right in regards to those who use the stream or lake later.

A person with **riparian rights** is a person who owns land that adjoins or butts up against the stream or lake. The right to use lake water or stream water is enjoyed by those with riparian rights in many states. These states often apply a reasonable use standard to those who own adjoining land. Those owners cannot materially interfere with another adjacent owner's use of the land.

As a general rule, domestic use receives greater protection than commercial use under a riparian system. Commercial use is the use of the water supply for a business purpose such as irrigating farmland. Landowners cannot use the water source for commercial use if such use will diminish the ability of a domestic user. For example, Daniel owns a farm. He can use the water from a river that runs between his land and Terry's land if such use is commercial, such as watering his crops (not a small garden), unless his use will reduce the water level to a point where his neighbor Terry cannot obtain enough water for domestic purposes such as drinking, washing clothes, or irrigating a small garden of vegetables.

Figure 11.2 The right to use water is an increasingly important property right

In most states, the public will generally have the right to use large streams and lakes for recreational purposes such as boating and swimming. The federal government enjoys the right to regulate public waters under the US Constitution. The states enjoy the right to regulate public waters as well under the 10th amendment Police Power. Whether a lake or stream is private or public will depend partially on federal law and partially on state law. There are different factors that may make a lake or stream a public body of water such as whether the land underneath the body of water is privately owned, whether the land around the stream or lake is privately owned, and whether the stream or lake can be used for navigation purposes.

- Abandoned property

Property Ownership by Creation

The concept of ownership in regards to creating property seems easy enough: One who creates property owns property. However, problems quickly arise with this rule. For example, one individual creates property using property that was already owned by another or two individuals both contribute labor and materials to the creation of property.

Here are some general rules in regards to creation of property:

1. If Y adds labor to X's materials, X is considered the owner unless Y substantially increased the value of X's materials. For example, David fixes Amy's car by adjusting the engine settings. Amy is still the owner of the car. However, Amy may be liable to David for compensation for services.

2. If Y adds labor and materials to the property of X, Y becomes the owner as long as the amount of labor and materials added by Y were substantial and Y was acting in good faith. For example, Marissa finds what she believes to be an abandoned wheel from a car. The wheel is worth about $10 and the true owner is Daniel. If Marissa adds a significant amount of materials and labor making the wheel a home decoration worth $1,000, Marissa is awarded ownership although she may be liable to Daniel for the amount of $10.

Figure 11.3 The person finding lost property might become to the owner!

3. If X and Y commingle their goods, then both become owners of a proportionate share. For example, Farmer Brown and Farmer McDonald store their soybeans in the same storage bin. Each maintains a proportionate interest but loses the ownership interest in the actual soybeans they placed in the storage bin.

Property Ownership by Possession

As a general rule an owner of personal property will lose their ownership right only to someone who finds their property if the property was abandoned. **Abandoned property** is property that an owner intentionally leaves or discards. For example, Misty throws her

- Lost property
- Mislaid property

engagement ring into a lake after learning her fiancé Jeremy once dated her sister Angie. Scott, an avid swimmer, finds the ring and becomes the owner since Misty threw her ring into the lake and abandoned it.

Lost property is property that was unintentionally lost, which means the owner accidentally lost possession of the object and did not misplace the property. The finder of lost property becomes the owner of the property subject to the prior owner's property interest. For example, Renetta's diamond ring slipped from her finger at a movie theatre. Cory finds the ring while sitting in the same seat a week later. Under the common law, Cory became the owner of the ring but would be subject to a superior property right interest by Renetta. The general rule regarding lost property is subject to several important exceptions under the common law as well as present-day statutory law:

1. An employee who finds property in some states must turn the property over to their employer,
2. A guest at a private home must generally turn the property over to the homeowner,
3. State law may impose duties on the finder of lost property, which requires the finder to advertise the found property in an attempt to locate the true owner.

Mislaid property is property that was intentionally placed but subsequently forgotten by the person who placed the property. Mislaid property does not become the property of the person finding it. The person finding the property is considered to be a caretaker for the property and must give the property to the owner of the property on which it was found so the true owner may regain possession. For example, assume Renetta places her ring on the bathroom sink of a movie theatre and forgets to put it back on her finger. Marissa finds the ring while using the same bathroom; she must turn the ring over to the owner of the property on which the ring was found.

Adverse Possession

Under the theory of adverse possession, if a party does not sue another for possessing their property within a required period of time, the original owner loses their ability to protect their property interest. If a party adversely possesses property and meets the requirement of state law, the party gets legal title (legal ownership) and the previous owner loses their title. If a party obtains property by adverse possession, the party must then bring a lawsuit to quiet title so the party can have the local courthouse record their ownership. The following rules apply to adverse possession in regards to *real* property.

The requirements for proving adverse possession include:

1. **Actual entry and exclusive possession**. A party must actually enter onto the land and then must not share possession with the true owner or the public generally. For example, Rob owns a building where he works on cars. His buddy Jeff routinely uses the building to work on his own personal car. Jeff has actually entered the property but he is not exclusively using the property.

Figure 11.4 Adverse possession means the person entered onto the land without the owner's consent

2. **Open and Notorious Possession**. The person adversely possessing the land must do so in a way that gives notice to the true owner. The adverse possessor cannot possess the land in secret. For example, Gale enters on the farmland of Harry. Gale builds a small home and puts a sign up on the property that reads, "Gale's All-Natural Farm." Gale is engaging in open and notorious possession of the land.

3. **Adverse or Hostile Possession**. A party does not have to be at war with the true owner but the adverse possessor has to occupy the land without consent of the owner. For example, Katie asks Carol if Katie can park her old car on Carol's land. Carol says Katie may until Carol decides it is no longer appropriate. Katie is not adversely possessing the land because Carol has given Katie permission.

4. **Continuous Possession**. Continuous possession means uninterrupted possession of the land. Each state will determine the required period of time that a person must adversely possess the property to obtain ownership. For example, in the state of Iowa, a party must adversely possess property for a period of ten years. The continuous requirement means if Jake, an Iowa resident, moves off the land he is adversely possessing in Iowa, his period of adverse possession has ended and the ten-year period would start over again when he moves back onto the real property.

Stewart v. Judy

No. 8-251/07-1510 (Iowa Ct. App. Apr. 30, 2008)

Donald Stewart and his wife had farmed a 3.1 acre tract of land since 1987. However, it turned out they were not the owners of a 3.1 acre tract of land which happened to be adjacent to the land they were rightfully farming. The Stewarts believed they were the owners of the 3.1 acres of land and farmed it without the permission of the true owners. The Stewarts put a fence up around the land they actually owned as well as the 3.1 acre tract of land they did not own.

In 2006, Clarence Judy and his wife purchased a tract of land by the Stewarts. Mr. Judy had the land surveyed and took out the fence of the Stewarts encompassing the 3.1 acre tract of land. At trial evidence was produced which showed Mr. Stewart had been warned by the previous owner of the disputed property that Mr. Stewart should quit farming the 3.1 acre tract of land. Mr. Stewart replied he would not quit farming it and farmed it until Mr. Judy purchased the 3.1 acre tract and the lawsuit began. An Iowa District Court held the possession of the 3.1 acre tract of farmland did not constitute adverse possession because the Stewarts did nothing more than put up a fence and farm the land. An Iowa Court of Appeals reversed the decision finding the 3.1 acre tract of land had been adversely possessed in a hostile, actual, exclusive, open, continuous manner under the color of title for at least 10 years. The Appellate Court stated it is not necessary in Iowa for the adverse possessor to pay the property taxes associated with the property.

Questions

1. Why were the Stewarts rewarded for using what they knew was not theirs?
2. Assume the facts were different and the Stewarts had purchased the land in 1996 and had been told in 2002 that they should not be farming the land so they quit for one year but started farming the land again in 2003. When is the soonest they could bring a claim for adverse possession?
3. What if the 3.1-acre tract of land had not been good for farming and no fence had been built around it? Assuming the children of the Stewarts used the land to ride horses, could the Stewarts bring a claim for adverse possession?

Ownership and Possessory Interests in Property

The common law has several different types of ownership in regards to real property. The most comprehensive form of ownership is referred to as a fee simple. A **fee simple** ownership interest is an estate of land that may last perpetually. The owner of land can pass ownership to his or her heirs (descendants). A **life estate** is an ownership interest that will lapse at the time the owner dies. For example, Sherri grants Mary the right to possess and occupy her land during Mary's life. Mary has a life estate. A **leasehold estate** gives a tenant the right to possess an estate for a period of time, such as one year, or until the tenant and landlord desire it to end. The common law was not as concerned with personal property because real property was, for the most part, the only property that had any substantial value.

Absolute ownership means the ownership of personal property and the ownership interest will last perpetually. Finally, a **trust** is a form of ownership, applicable to both real and personal property, where the trustee holds legal title to the property for the benefit of beneficiaries who enjoy equitable rights. For example, Robin retires from his carpet cleaning business. He transfers ownership of the business to a trust and names Craig as the trustee. He names his nephew Brady as the sole beneficiary.

Legal title means the ownership of property that is granted by the government and respected by a court. **Equitable title** is the ownership of property that provides benefits to the owner such as use of the property. For example, assume Matt buys a new car using money he borrowed from Midwest Bank. Matt is the equitable owner. The bank will most likely keep the title to the car, which means the bank has legal title.

The common law **Rule Against Perpetuities** prevents an owner from devising a property ownership interest that may or may not vest within 21 years after the owner's death. For example, Brad conveys ownership to his house to the first descendant of his who graduates from college. If none of Brad's children go to college, then it may very well be more than 21 years after Brad's death before any of his descendants attend college. Therefore, the conveyance by Brad is void under the rule against perpetuities. Some states such as South Dakota, Rhode Island, and Pennsylvania have abolished the Rule Against Perpetuities as a way of attracting investments to their state.

An **easement** is an interest in a land that allows the holder of the easement to use the land even though they are not the owner. For example, Mindy has a gas station that is located behind a retail shoe store. The only way to get to Mindy's gas station is by driving over the retail store's parking lot. The owners of the shoe store might agree to grant an easement to Mindy. The easement might specify Mindy may use a portion of the shoe store's land to form a driveway.

A **license** is the right to go *onto* another's land. For example, the driver of a delivery truck has the implied license to drive their truck onto the recipient's property. As a general rule, a license is revocable. For example, Scott attends a party at Emily's house. Scott becomes intoxicated and Emily asks him to leave. When Emily asks Scott to leave, she is revoking his license to be on her property.

Types of Tenancy

The previous discussion concerned the length of ownership by a party and his heirs. However, ownership might also be granted to more than one party at the same time. The most common types of joint tenancy are 1) tenancy in common, 2) joint tenancy with right of survivorship, and 3) and tenancy by the entirety.

A **tenancy in common** exists when multiple owners own a distinct share of an undivided interest in property. For example, Molly dies and conveys her interest in her Blackacre estate to her daughter Alexandra and her son Joey as tenants in common, with a 50% ownership interest granted to each. Alexandra and Joey each own a half interest in the undivided Blackacre. A co-tenant such as Alexandra can devise or convey her ownership interest in Blackacre to her children. To **devise** property means to transfer ownership by use of a will. To **convey** property means a grantor transfers legal title to a grantee. A common example of a conveyance is a sale of property.

A conveyance to tenants who are not husband and wife is presumed to be made in the form of a tenancy in common. Tenants in common also do not have to have equal ownership interests. For example, Alexandra can be granted a 75% ownership interest and Joey can be granted a 25% ownership interest.

- Legal title
- Equitable title
- Rule Against Perpetuities
- Easement
- License
- Tenancy in common
- Devise
- Convey

A **joint tenancy with right of survivorship** is an ownership interest where two or more persons own an undivided interest in property. A joint tenancy is similar to a tenancy in common except for the fact the joint owners cannot convey their ownership interests to another without ending the joint tenancy. Upon the death of a joint tenant, their ownership interest reverts to the remaining tenants. For example, Steve and Cherie own property as joint tenants. Steve dies. Steve's interest in the property transfers to Cherie upon his death. A joint tenancy can be severed (ended) by a sale of an ownership interest by a joint tenant. It can also be severed by agreement of the parties or by court order.

A **tenancy by the entirety** is an ownership interest held by a husband and wife as one person. The common law rule was the tenancy by entirety could not be severed by either the husband or wife individually. The tenancy by the entirety can terminate upon the agreement of the husband and wife or when a divorce of the husband and wife occurs. For example, Keith and April buy a house after they are legally married in their state. If Keith and April's state recognizes tenancy by the entirety, they will be presumed to own the house as part of a tenancy by the entirety. If Keith owes money to a creditor and the creditor tries to take possession of Keith's interest in the house, the creditor could not do so under the common law.

Tenant/Landlord Law

A common form of a periodic tenancy is the relationship between a tenant and a landlord. A tenancy is different from a license or an easement because the tenant enjoys possession of the land he or she rents. A **tenancy for years** is tenancy that ends after a certain date. A tenancy for years does not require notice the tenancy will be ending. For example, Nathan rents a home from Rebecca for a period of one year. Nathan's rental lease is a tenancy for years and Rebecca does not have to give him notice that his lease will end. Often a tenancy for years will convert into a periodic tenancy if the tenancy for years is not reviewed.

A **periodic tenancy** is for a fixed period of time but it automatically renews until either the landlord or tenant gives notice of their intent to quit the lease. For example, Daniel rents a home from Kevin as part of a month-to-month lease.

Figure 11.5 Landlords allow tenants to rent their real property

The lease will automatically renew each month. As a general rule, either Kevin or Daniel can quit the lease, but they must give at least 30 days' notice. The periodic tenancy requires notice be given at the beginning of a period unless it is a tenancy for one year or more in which the tenant may have to give notice only six months before the end of the lease. Some states may reduce the period for notice to an even shorter period of time.

Common duties of the landlord in residential lease situations include the implied warrant of habitability. The **implied warranty of habitability** requires the landlord to keep the premises fit for habitation both before and after a tenant takes possession. Some courts have implied this requirement even if the lease does not expressly contain this warranty.

The implied warranty of habitability applies primarily to residential leases (example: person rents a place to live) but has been extended to commercial leases (example: business rents office space) in some cases. Many jurisdictions also allow a tenant to withhold payment of rent if the landlord has refused to make repairs that are necessary to maintain the habitability of the apartment. However, the tenant should take note that the landlord has a reasonable amount of time to make repairs.

The landlord also must keep common areas in good working order. For example, a stairway in an apartment building must be maintained by the landlord so it is safe to use by tenants. The common law imposes an ordinary duty of care by the landlord in common areas.

The landlord has a duty not to interfere with the tenant's possession of the leased property. In most states a landlord must give at least 24 hours' notice before entering onto the leased property. In some states the tenant can object to the landlord's entry. As a general rule, the landlord may enter the premises in the event of an emergency. For example, if a water pipe bursts, a landlord could enter the apartment dwelling of a tenant. A landlord may be liable for damages if the landlord enters a leased property without proper notice.

The tenant has the duty to make rental payments on time. Many states have legislation that states a rental payment made within a certain number of days, such as three, will be counted as timely. In the event of nonpayment, most states require a variety of judicial steps be taken before a tenant can be forced to vacate a leased property. For example, in Iowa, a three-day notice must be filed with a court; if rent is not paid within seven days, another judicial filing must be made with the court in order to obtain possession of the property. Other common duties of the tenant: to make certain repairs, not to damage the property, and not to interfere with the use of another tenant's property.

Landlords are not allowed to discriminate against protected classes when deciding to whom they will rent. The Fair Housing Act of 1968, as amended, makes it illegal for a landlord to base rental decisions based upon mental or physical disability, race, color, sex, national origin, familial status, or religion. State and municipalities (example cities) often create additional protected classes such as sexual orientation and gender identity. The city of Madison, Wisconsin, has twenty-three protected classes that include, physical appearance, arrest record, conviction record, status as a student, political belief, and source of income.

Methods for Transferring Ownership of Property

Gifts

A **donor** is the person giving a gift to a recipient who is the **donee**. A gift is different from a sales contract since a gift requires no consideration. A **gift inter vivos** is a gift made during the lifetime of the donor. A gift inter vivos is irrevocable, which means the donor cannot revoke the gift once it is made. A **gift causa mortis** is given by a donor who believes death is imminent. The gift is automatically revoked if the donor recovers from the illness or survives the event that led the donor to believe death was imminent. For example, assume Rick believes is going to die in the next week from cancer so he gives his favorite car to his

- Donor
- Donee
- Gift inter vivos
- Gift causa mortis

- Testamentary gift
- Will
- Testator

son Luke. Rick miraculously recovers. The gift of the car to Luke is automatically revoked because it was a gift causa mortis. However, Rick can then make a gift inter vivos to Luke if he so wishes.

The three requirements for a valid gift are, 1) intent to make a gift by the donor, 2) delivery to the donee, and 3) and acceptance by the donee. These requirements are the same for a gift inter vivos and a gift causa mortis.

A **testamentary gift** is a gift of property made through a will. A **will** is a legal document which governs the distribution of property of a person upon their death. The person who creates a will is often referred to as a **testator**.

Intent seems to be a simple concept. The donor must intend to give ownership of the property to a donee. However, gifts must be distinguished from sales and bailments. A bailment assumes the bailee will return the property and that the donor does not relinquish ownership. Therefore, intent may not be easy to prove.

Delivery is often proof of the intent to give a gift. Delivery may be accomplished through actual delivery or constructive delivery. Constructive delivery is when the donor gives something to the donee that signifies ownership but is something other than actual object. For example, Monica gives her daughter the keys to a new car. The keys to the car are a means of delivery possession to her daughter. Finally, the law assumes acceptance on the part of the donee.

Marriage of Heinzman

579 P.2d 638 (1977)

Colorado Court of Appeals, Div. II

STERNBERG, Judge

Beth Lovato and William Heinzman lived together from 1969 to 1973 with some brief periods of separation. William was married at the time he began living with Beth but obtained a divorce in 1970. In the fall of 1970, William purchased the home in Boulder which Beth had been leasing. The court found, on supporting evidence, that Beth and William had become "engaged" and had agreed to marry. Thereafter, William deeded the home to "William Heinzman and Beth Lovato as joint tenants." The parties lived there until June 1973, when Beth left the state.

In October 1973, Beth petitioned the Boulder District Court to dissolve what she claimed was her common law marriage to William and requested a property settlement. The parties presented testimony on the common law marriage issue and on the issue of property division. The court ruled there was no common law marriage, and that judgment is not appealed. The court ordered the parties to submit briefs on the property division question. They did so, and neither party questioned the power of the court to proceed. Therefore, the property division matter was tried by consent. See C.R.C.P. 15(b) and 54(c). After considering the briefs, the court ordered the reconveyance of the Boulder residence to William. Beth appeals this order and we affirm.

Beth alleges that insufficient evidence was presented to the court to support its findings that the gift of real property was made during the parties' engagement period and that she was at fault in breaking the engagement. Although the facts were in dispute, testimony was presented that supported the court's conclusion that, before the conveyance of the house, Beth had agreed to marry William ceremonially, that he had bought her an engagement ring, and that Beth had later changed her mind. These factual determinations may not be disturbed on review, because there was sufficient evidence to support them.***

The trial court found, in effect, that William would not have given the joint interest in the home to Beth if he had not expected her to marry him formally at some future date and that Beth had broken the engagement. These circumstances warrant the imposition of an equitable trust. In *Beatty v. Guggenheim Exploration Co.*, 225 N.Y. 380, 122 N.E. 378 (1919), after characterizing trusts of this type as "the formula through which the conscience of equity finds expression," Judge Cardozo explained the doctrine as follows:

"When property has been acquired in such circumstances that the holder of the legal title may not in good conscience retain the beneficial interest, equity converts him into a trustee."

In *Semenza v. Alfano*, 443 Pa. 201, 279 A.2d 29 (1971), a case involving facts similar to those here, after quoting this passage from Beatty, the court said, "[t]he receipt of an ante-nuptial gift in contemplation of a marriage which never takes place is just such a circumstance." Consequently, to avoid unjust enrichment here, based upon the factual findings of the trial court, Beth, an equitable trustee, must reconvey her interest in the home to William.

Questions

1. Did William make a gift to Beth?
2. Whom did the court find to be a trustee of the property?
3. Which of the three requirements for a gift was missing: intent, delivery, or acceptance?

State law primarily governs the sale of property. Often state law will require a certain type of title or deed be used to transfer ownership. In addition, certain transfers of property may require specific disclosure. For example, in the state of Iowa, a person selling an automobile must transfer the title to the automobile and disclose whether the car has ever been in an accident severe enough that the damage was more than the value of the car (the automobile is often referred to as "totaled" in this situation.) Legal title means the proof of legal ownership that would be respected by the legal system. Legal title can also be referred to as "certificate of title." In the United States, titles for automobiles and recreational vehicles generally have to be filed with the local government where the citizen lives, such as the city or county of residence. A bill of sale generally accompanies the title in a sales transaction of an automobile. **A bill of sale** is a written statement from a seller that proves the seller has transferred ownership to the buyer.

A **deed** is a legal instrument that allows the **grantor**, person transferring an interest in real property, to a **grantee**, the person to whom the ownership interest in real property is being transferred. The sale of land is subject to the Statute of Frauds, which means the contract for the sale of land must be reduced to a writing and signed by the party against whom

- Bill of sale
- Deed
- Grantor
- Grantee

• Title opinion

the contract is being enforced. The sales contract for real property is commonly referred to as a purchase agreement. The buyer and seller are often represented by real estate agents.

The real estate agent is generally paid by commission. The commission is generally a percentage of the purchase price of the real property. An offer drafted by a real estate agent on behalf of the buyer or seller will generally contain the date of the closing, which is the date on which the seller delivers the deed to the property and the buyer provides payment. Of great importance is the time and date on which the offer expires. A typical offer will expire approximately 24 hours after it is made. This allows the buyer to pursue other properties and the seller to entertain other offers with neither having to worry about an existing offer.

An offer drafted by a real estate agent will also generally contain a clause stating the buyer will have a certain number of days to inspect the property. The buyer also generally has the right to inspect the property on the day of the closing to make sure no new issues have arisen. In addition, the buyer generally makes their offer contingent on the ability to obtain favorable financing.

In some cases the buyer will also make their offer contingent on the ability to sell an existing piece of property, such as the home in which the offeror is living. Another common condition is the requirement the seller pay all property taxes due for periods ending on the date of the closing. For example, Gary

Figure 11.6 The sold sign gives notice offers cannot be made any longer

buys a home from Louise and the closing date is July 1. The state where they live requires property taxes be paid one year after they are initially due. The state's fiscal year ends on July 1. Louise will have to provide payment for the year's worth of property taxes that are accrued as of the date of closing.

In many states, the seller is required to provide a disclosure statement, which reveals known defects related to the real property being sold. In addition, a buyer will generally hire an attorney to prepare a title opinion. A **title opinion** traces the record of ownership as far back in time as possible. Often the title opinion will trace the record of ownership to the date on which the United States Federal Government granted ownership for the first time. The purpose of a title opinion is to reveal any defects in the ownership interest of the grantor. For example, another party might be a tenant in common with the seller. The seller cannot convey title on part of the co-tenant. A common discovery by a title opinion is a lien or other judgment being levied against the property. As an example, Dorthy is interested in buying a piece of property from Larry. Larry refused to pay a plumber's bill four years before. The plumber filed a lawsuit against Larry and placed a lien on the property. Often a bank will not finance Dorthy's purchase unless Larry pays off the lien.

Title insurance is available in all fifty states. **Title insurance** is a form of an insurance policy that provides insurance protection in regards to whether the buyer is taking good title. The title insurance policy is based upon public records only. The insurance policy protects against mistakes in public records. The policy does not protect against liens or other ownership interests that are not part of a public record.

Types of Deeds

There are several common types of deeds for real property. Each deed makes different covenants, or promises, in regards to the seller's liability if the title to the property ends up having a defect. A **quitclaim deed** promises and warrants nothing besides the fact the seller is giving their interest in said property to the buyer. For example, Kenny creates a quitclaim deed for the university president's house. The deed would convey Kenny's ownership interest in said house even though Kenny presumably has no ownership interest!

A **warranty deed** makes the promise the seller has good title free from lien or ownership claims by another party. The seller must defend the title against any claims arising before or after the seller obtained ownership up until the date the buyer takes ownership. A **special warranty** deed makes the same covenants as a general warranty deed but limits the covenants to the time period during which the seller owned the property. As an example, Kristen provides a deed to Katie that states she has title and is conveying her ownership interest to Katie. Kristen warrants no claims have arisen while she has owned the property. However, she does not make any covenants or warranties in regards to time periods before she owned the property. This would be an example of a special warranty deed and not a general warranty deed.

Bailments

A **bailment** occurs when a piece of property is possessed lawfully by someone other than the owner. For example, Tricia takes her automobile to a mechanic to be repaired. Tricia has effected a bailment. The mechanic is the bailee and Tricia is the bailor. The **bailor** is the true owner of the property and the **bailee** is the person who rightfully possesses the property. The three major requirements for a bailment are 1) intent, 2) possession, and 3) physical control by the bailee. The intent to create a bailment without actual delivery and possession of the property will not create a bailment. In addition, possession without control of the property will not constitute a bailment. For example, assume Tricia pays $25 to park her car in an empty lot so she can visit the Iowa State Fair. If she keeps her keys, a bailment has not been created, as she is in control of the vehicle. She has leased a parking space.

The law recognizes three types of bailments: 1) A bailment for the sole benefit of the bailee, 2) A bailment for the sole benefit of the bailor, and 3) A bailment for the benefit of both the bailor and the bailee. If the bailment is for the sole benefit of the bailor, the bailee owes a lower standard of care and must not commit gross negligence in regards to the bailed property. If the bailment is for the sole benefit of the bailee, the bailee owes a higher duty of care, which requires extraordinary care. If the bailment is for the mutual benefit of both parties, the bailee is held to an ordinary standard of care.

Assume Lori gives her car to Dilini so Dilini can drive the car to get groceries. This is an example of a bailment for the sole benefit of the bailee Dilini. If Lori gives Dilini possession of her car so Dilini can wash the car, then assuming Dilini does not use the car for his own benefit, the bailment is one for the sole benefit of the bailor and Dilini owes a lower duty of care than when the bailment was solely for his benefit. If Dilini uses the car to get groceries but also promises to wash it in return for using it, the bailment is for the mutual benefit of both Lori and Dilini and Dilini must exercise a reasonable amount of care.

Besides the duty to take care of the bailed property, bailees must deliver the bailed property at the bailor's direction. The bailee might also have to compensate or pay the bailee for use of their property. For example, assume Ivan uses Harry's tractor to plant his field. Ivan the bailee may have to pay Harry for the use of his property unless the parties had agreed it would be a gratuitous bailment.

A bailor has the duty to warn the bailee of known risks associated with the bailed property. If the bailment is for mutual benefit of both the bailor and bailee, the bailor must also make an inspection of the bailed property. In addition, the bailor may also have a duty to compensate the bailee in the event the bailment was for the sole benefit of the bailor or the mutual benefit of both the bailor and bailee.

Types of Carriers

A **common carrier** is a carrier who agrees to carry property or persons for anyone who requests. A common carrier cannot refuse to carry a person or property without reasonable grounds for denying such request. A common carrier is licensed by the government. Examples of common carriers are trucking companies, taxicab companies, and airlines. A common carrier is a bailee.

A common carrier is held to a higher duty of care than a private carrier is. A common carrier is responsible for any damages to bailed goods unless the goods were damaged by 1) an act of God, 2) an enemy of the government, 3) the bailor's actions, or 4) the goods themselves. As an example, assume Big Dairy Incorporated ships a thousand gallons of milk by common carrier. If the common carrier has a properly cooled truck but the milk spoils because of its age, the common carrier is not liable because the milk caused its own deterioration.

A **private carrier** is a carrier who selects its customers and often does not have any customers at all. For example, Balli Furniture Incorporated has ten trucks that it uses to deliver furniture it has sold to customers. Balli Furniture is a private carrier. A **contract carrier** is a carrier who routinely transports property or persons for a select group of customers. A trucking service that delivers used cars for three local car dealerships only would be considered a

Figure 11.7 Trucking companies are often a prime example of a common carrier

contract carrier. The private and contract carrier owe an ordinary duty of care and not the heightened duty of care imposed on a common carrier.

Innkeepers

The innkeeper is much like the common carrier because the innkeeper is held to higher duty of care. The innkeeper is responsible for any damages to property of guests unless the goods were damaged by 1) an act of God, 2) an enemy of the government, 3) the bailor's actions, or 4) the goods themselves. However, an innkeeper is not technically a bailee. The innkeeper does not generally have exclusive possession or total control over a guest or their property. Some states have passed legislation limiting the liability of innkeepers.

In addition to the property of guests, innkeepers must also warn guests of any hidden risks such as a wet floor in a bathroom. The innkeeper must make routine inspections of property to identify potentially dangerous situations. The innkeeper must also protect guests against negligence and intentional torts of its own employees.

Ellish v. Airport Parking Co.

42 A.D.2d 174 (1973)

The following are excerpts from the opinion of Judge Hopkins of the New York Court of Appeals for the 2nd district.

About to leave on a flight from John F. Kennedy International Airport on September 1, 1966, the plaintiff parked her automobile in a lot operated by the defendant under an agreement with the Port of New York Authority. When she returned on September 5, 1966, her automobile had disappeared. Claiming that the defendant was responsible for the loss, she brought this suit.*** Under the circumstances of this case we do not find the defendant liable for the plaintiff's loss.

Briefly stated, the parties stipulated that the plaintiff drove into the parking lot at the airport, receiving from an automatic vending machine a ticket stamped with the date and time of entry. On one side the ticket was labeled "License to Park" and stated that the lot provided self-service parking; it warned the holder that the lot was not attended and that the car should be locked. On the other side the ticket contained the words in smaller print: "This contract licenses the holder to park one automobile in this area at holder's risk." Further, it provided that the defendant was not responsible for the theft of the automobile. Upon the plaintiff's receipt of the ticket, a gate opened, permitting the entry of the automobile into the lot. The plaintiff drove the automobile into a parking space, locked it and took the keys with her.

Under the practice of the defendant, on leaving the lot, the holder of the ticket would drive to the point of exit, present the ticket to a cashier and pay the amount due based on the time elapsed. If the driver did not have a ticket, the cashier would demand proof of ownership of the automobile. The defendant employed personnel to maintain the lot and to check automobiles left overnight in order to make certain that the cashiers collected proper fees. The lot was patrolled by Port of New York Authority police, in the same manner as the airport.*** At common law when a chattel was placed by the owner in the possession of another under an agreement by the latter to deliver it on demand, a convenient short hand expression of a duty cast on the bailee was found by establishing a presumption of negligence if the bailee did not come forward with a satisfactory explanation to rebut the presumption.***

[I]n formulating a rule to determine the extent of the liability of the defendant, we must concern ourselves with the realities of the transaction in which the parties engaged. The nature of the circumstances themselves leads to the determination whether the transaction should be considered a bailment, in which event the defendant is liable to the plaintiff, or whether the transaction should be considered a license to occupy space, in which event the defendant is not liable to the plaintiff.

Against this general background we think these considerations are paramount:

1. The service provided by the defendant to the plaintiff was clearly a space for her automobile to stand while she was away on her trip. That space was located in a lot where many other automobiles were similarly standing and to which the operators of the automobiles and others were given access. The plaintiff was not treated differently from the other automobile operators; nor was she led to believe that the lot would not be open to others.
2. The service provided by the defendant was impersonal. The plaintiff was aware that the defendant had no employees either to deliver the ticket for the automobile or to park the automobile. She accepted the ticket from an automatic dispensing device and she parked the car herself, choosing her own space, not at the direction of the defendant.
3. The plaintiff retained as much control as possible over the automobile. She locked the car and kept the keys. She did not expect or desire the defendant to move the automobile in her absence.
4. The plaintiff followed the directions contained in the ticket she received. In her favor, we think that the plaintiff should not be closely bound by the terms of the ticket, for plainly it was a contract of adhesion. The plaintiff was hardly in a position to bargain over the conditions of the ticket and, indeed, the condition of nonliability for theft sought to be imposed by the defendant is unenforceable under the public policy of our statute (General Obligations Law, § 5-325). Nevertheless, it is still the fact that the plaintiff heeded the warning of the ticket to lock her automobile.***

In the absence of any proof of neglect by the defendant, then, we do not think that the defendant should be held responsible for the loss of the automobile.***We do not find *Dunham v. City of New York* (264 App. Div. 732), in which we allowed recovery for the loss of an automobile parked in a lot at the World's Fair held in 1939, a precedent requiring us to hold for the plaintiff here. In *Dunham*, though the motorist locked his car after parking it and retained the keys, an attendant gave a ticket to the motorist before parking and directed him to the space to be occupied, thereby giving the appearance of the acceptance of custody for the car. Here, instead, the defendant by its procedures of impersonal parking disclaimed any appearance of custody.

Questions

1. Why wasn't the parking lot operator liable for the lost car?
2. What did the court state about the ticket's wording that warned the driver that the parking lot was not responsible for any damages?
3. Why did the court discuss the case of Dunham v. City of New York?
4. Would the driver have prevailed in her lawsuit if the parking lot operator had a hole in its fence that it knew about? Why or why not?

- Covenant
- Real covenants
- Zoning
- Variance
- Eminent domain

Restrictions on Ownership

A **covenant** is a promise to do something or refrain from doing something with one's property. For example, Melanie buys a house from Christa. In the deed of sale it states the owner of such land may not build a fence that is taller than six feet. Covenants that apply to real property are called **real covenants**. Real covenants often pass from one owner to the next. Real covenants are common in housing developments. The housing developer will often buy a large plot of land and subdivide it into smaller plots. The housing developer will place covenants in the deed of each subdivided plot. Common examples of covenants are prohibitions against parking recreational vehicles or boats on driveways of a personal residence.

Zoning is the process by which municipalities divide their geographic locations and limit the permissible uses by landowners for their property. For example, assume the city of Sanborn creates four zones. Zone 1 allows landowners to build only commercial properties such as businesses. Zone 2 allows landowners to build only single-family houses. Zone 3 restricts landowners so they can build only multiple-family housing. Zone 4 allows for only recreational use such as city parks. Zoning laws might also limit the size and height of buildings within a zone.

A **variance** is an exception granted to a landowner by the municipality. A variance will allow the landowner to do something with their real property that would normally not be allowed under the zoning law of the municipality. For example, assume zoning law prohibits building any structure within fifteen feet of the edge of a piece of real property. Arlene wants to build a garage but the garage will be only fourteen feet from the edge of her property. The municipality might allow her a variance that allows her to build the garage even though it would normally violate the local zoning laws.

Government Takings of Property

Eminent domain is the process by which the government confiscates the real property of a landowner for a public purpose and provides just compensation in return. The fifth amendment to the Constitution allows for such taking as long as the taking serves a public benefit. The right has been extended to states and cities by the Due Process clause of the 14th amendment. What qualifies as a public benefit is very broad. For example, the Supreme Court has allowed a city to take land that it considered blighted so the city can sell the land to a private developer.[1] The Supreme Court also held the state of Hawaii could take land from what the state felt was an oligarchy in an attempt to create a free market for land ownership.[2] The court looks for the taking of property to be *rationally related to a conceivable* public purpose. Therefore, what qualifies as a constitutional taking is very broad.

A government taking may include the government taking title to land, taking possession of land, or regulating the land in such a manner the land is considered to be taken by the government. However, a court might view a regulation as a valid exercise of police power meant to prevent public harm as opposed to an instance of eminent domain. For example, in *Hadacheck v. Sebastian*, 239 US 394 (1915) the US Supreme Court found a local zoning ordinance was a valid exercise of police power because the brickyard that it affected was a nuisance. The line between a nuisance, which can be regulated without just compensation, and a public good, which requires just compensation, is a blurred line at best.

The government does not have to take all of an owner's land for the owner to receive compensation. A partial taking, such as a small amount of land for a roadway, also qualifies as a taking that must be compensated. Additionally, the government does not have to actually do the taking. For example, in *Loretto v. Teleprompter Manhattan CATV Corp.*, 458 US 164 (1979), the Supreme Court required apartment building owners be given compensation after a statute allowed cable operators to install cable lines in the apartment buildings.

The government engaging in the taking, or allowing the taking by another party, must provide just compensation. In the event of a partial taking, the government must pay the landowner the difference between the fair market value before the taking and the fair market value after the taking. For example, the city of Sibley takes a portion of Ted's land to build a bike path. The city will owe Ted the difference in value calculated as the fair market value of his property before the taking as compared to after the taking. In the event of a non-partial taking, the government must pay the fair market value of the property.

Questions

1. How is real property different from personal property?
2. What is a fixture and what makes a fixture a trade fixture?
3. Who could claim to be the owner of a wild animal that is captured?
4. What is percolating water and what doctrines exist in regards to determining the ownership of percolating water?
5. What is surface water and what doctrines exist in regards to diverting surface water from an owner's land?
6. What is stream water and what doctrines exist in regards to determining the ownership of stream water?
7. What are the definitions of abandoned, misplaced, and lost property, and what is the legal distinction between these classifications?

---

1   See example *Berman v. Parker*, 348 US 26 (1954)
2   *Hawaiian Housing Authority v. Midkiff*, 467 US 229 (1984) & *Kelo v. City of New London*, 545 US 469 (2005)

8. What is adverse possession and what requirements must be proven to assert adverse possession as a claim against property?
9. Who is a donor and who is donee?
10. What are the three elements needed to prove a gift has occurred?
11. How is a gift causa mortis legally different from a gift inter vivos?
12. What is the legal distinction between a fee simple, a leasehold estate, and a life estate?
13. How is legal title different from equitable title?
14. What is the Rule Against Perpetuities and what might be an example of a device that violates the Rule Against Perpetuities?
15. How is a license different from an easement?
16. What is a tenancy by the common and how is it different from a joint tenancy with right of survivorship and a tenancy by the entirety?
17. What is a tenancy for years and how is it different from a periodic tenancy?
18. What is the implied warranty of habitability?
19. What are common duties and rights of both landlords and tenants?
20. What are common provisions included in a purchase contract for real estate?
21. What is a title opinion?
22. How is a warranty deed different from a special warranty deed and a quitclaim deed?
23. What is a bailment and who is a bailor and who is a bailee?
24. What is the duty of a bailee in regards to 1) a bailment for the sole benefit of the bailee, 2) a bailment for the sole benefit of the bailor, and 3) a bailment for mutual benefit?
25. What is the legal distinction between a common carrier, a private carrier, and a contract carrier?
26. What duties does an innkeeper owe toward guests of the inn?
27. What does the term "eminent domain" mean?

Critical-Thinking Questions

28. Why does the law have so many specific rules in regards to water rights and how might this area of law become an issue in the future?
29. Why would the law provide ownership to someone who has adversely possessed land they did not own?
30. Why would the law treat a gift made causa mortis differently from a gift made inter vivos?
31. How might nonpayment of rent by one tenant cause negative effects for other tenants?
32. What economic purpose is severed by prohibiting common carriers from discriminating against which customers they will serve?

Essay Questions

1. Miguel recently purchased his first home. He is very excited about making improvements to the home. He decides it would be cheaper if he had his own water source so

he digs a well in his backyard. Next he decides to construct a large building right next to the edge of his property. The following winter provides almost no precipitation in the form of snow or rain. Miguel gets a letter from his neighbor Stephen claiming Miguel has stolen Stephen's water source by digging a well. Miguel decides to see what happens with his neighbor. Much to Miguel's relief, summer rains are heavy and the rainwater bounces off his shed and creates a lake in Stephen's backyard. Miguel has received another letter from Stephen again claiming wrongdoing on the part of Miguel. What is Miguel's liability in regards to the well and the rainwater that is deflecting off his shed?

2. Jim has just purchased a marina where he sells and rents boats to be used on the lake that is located right next to his marina. Jim notices many members of the public are using his boat ramp for personal boats that are not rented from the marina Jim owns. In addition, he is also concerned because a construction company is building a restaurant uphill from the marina. Jim is worried rainwater will run downhill from the restaurant and flood his building where he keeps his new boats. Jim has asked you who is considered to be the owner of the water in the lake. He also wants to know what his rights are in regards to the potential for water run-off from the restaurant.

3. Eric grew up on a farm outside of town. His family has owned the farm for eighty years. The boundaries of the family farm are marked by a fence. Eric is interested in obtaining a mortgage to build a new barn. As part of the application process, the bank has a surveyor mark the boundaries of the farm. Much to the surprise of Eric, the fence his grandfather built is actually on a neighbor's farmland. Adverse possession in Eric's state requires ten years of continuous adverse possession. Eric moved back to the farm eight years ago. Eric is interested whether or not he can claim adverse possession as a way of claiming title to the land he thought his family owned. He believes he has a good case because the county has been assessing taxes on the portion of land that does not actually belong to him and his family has paid those taxes since they purchased the farm 80 years ago.

4. Philip has an auto body shop. Right next door to Philip's business is a group of storage sheds. To access the storage shed, a person must drive on Philip's driveway. Philip knows the owner of the storage sheds and does not want to offend them but he is concerned about whether or not he might lose his driveway through adverse possession. Should Philip be concerned about adverse possession if his driveway has been used continuously to access the storage sheds for a period of sixteen years?

5. Harlan owns a piece of beachfront property. He is about to be married to his long-time girlfriend Rhonda. Harlan wants Rhonda to be an owner of the property if he predeceases her, but he wants her to own the property with his children, with each having an equal ownership interest. He wants the property to remain in his family for many generations. What ownership form might best serve Harlan's objectives without violating the Rule Against Perpetuities?

6. Natalie owns a successful beachfront hotel and restaurant. Natalie would like her son Alex to own the property someday but is concerned he might mortgage the property. She decides to leave the property in her will to both her son Alex and the children of her son Alex as joint tenants with the right of survivorship. Alex does not have any children at the present time. What legal issues might arise because of this device if Alex does

not have children? Assuming he does have children before his mother dies, what will happen to Alex's interest when he dies?

7. Herb inherited a house from a great uncle. Herb believes the house will eventually double in value because of new construction that is happening nearby. Herb is considering renting the house to his nephew Mitch. Herb would like to be able to remove Mitch with as little notice as possible. However, he would like Mitch to at least stay through the winter before moving out. What type of lease should Herb enter into with Mitch? If Herb does sign a lease with Mitch, what are his duties regarding the house, as its bathroom is not currently in working order?

8. Sophia has inherited a large commercial building that has suites that are rented out to different businesses. The largest suite is currently being rented by a company that is often late with its payments. The lease Sophia currently has with the tenant was for ten years. However, the lease expires in three months. Sophia would like to keep the tenant but does not want to sign a lease for more than twelve months, as she is hoping she can find a better tenant. What type of lease should Sophia enter into with the current tenant? Also, what are her duties in regards to common areas such as the parking lot and sidewalks?

9. Susan just received bad news. A business developer in her town is going to build a new shopping mall. The mall will be located near her house. She received a letter in the mail today stating the city would be buying her house for the assessed value of the land. The assessed value is a value created by a local board for property tax purposes. Susan wants to know if the city can take her land and then sell it to a private business and whether or not she can claim she is owed more money than the assessed value of her home.

10. Jacklyn has owned a salvage yard for 26 years. She routinely buys old trucks and then removes parts from the trucks and then sells the parts to repair shops across the state. Jacklyn has been constrained in regards to growing her business because she does not have enough land. Her business is located in the area of a city that is populated with abandoned stockyards that are decaying. How might Jacklyn use the process of eminent domain to benefit her business and what factors will determine whether or not she is successful?

CHAPTER TWELVE

CONSUMER LAW

By Michael Bootsma

B ethany is interested in offering handmade jewelry online. She is interested in advertising the goods as "American Made" but she is unsure where the inputs for her product are made. She plans on selling the products online through a commercial website. She is also interested in knowing whether or not she must collect sales tax.

Taylor is interested in starting a debt-collection business. He will collect outstanding balances owed to credit card companies. He is interested in knowing what limitations exist in regards to contacting debtors at home. He is also interested in the possibility of recording the unpaid debt on the credit report of those who do not pay.

Objectives

1. Distinguish the government agencies involved in consumer law standard setting
2. Identify limitations placed on the sales process
3. Understand common product labeling requirements
4. Identify the warranties associated with the sale of a product
5. Understand principles associated with sales, use, and value-added taxes
6. Identify restrictions placed on debt collection

Government Agencies Involved in Regulating Marketing

Before discussing the limitations placed upon the sales process, several important government agencies must be discussed. The Federal Trade Commission (hereinafter FTC) is an independent federal government agency that was created in 1914 under the Federal Trade Commission Act. Its primary purpose is to further fair trade practices. One of its earliest missions was to "bust the trusts," as many wealthy families were using trusts to operate their family businesses from one generation to the next. It was feared these trusts would continue to add additional assets and the trusts would create anticompetitive

- Fraud
- Misrepresentation
- Puffery

dynasties. At the present time, the FTC is heavily involved in promoting fair trade practices through its rulemaking and enforcement capabilities. The FTC enforces federal law in several areas, including antitrust law and consumer protection laws such as the Telemarketing and Consumer Fraud and Abuse Protection Act. The FTC has five commissioners who head the agency and three bureaus: 1) the Bureau of Consumer Protection, 2) the Bureau of Economics, and 3) the Bureau of Competition.

The Federal Communication Commission (hereinafter FCC) is also an independent federal government agency. As with the FTC, the FCC is governed by five commissioners who are appointed by the President and affirmed by the Senate. The FCC governs communications made through the television, radio, and telephone industries when such communications begin or end in the United States. The FCC has rulemaking authority and enforcement capabilities. However, it also has the unique role of granting licenses to those who wish to operate communication companies, such as a cell phone carrier or a radio station.

The US Food and Drug Agency (hereinafter FDA) is a division of the Department of the US Health and Human Services. It is responsible for regulating food products, cosmetics, drugs such as vaccines, and medical devices. Unlike the FTC and FCC, it is considered to be part of the Executive Branch and is not considered an independent agency.

Prohibited Disclosures: Fraud

A salesperson is engaged in the profession of selling a good or service. The common law prohibits fraud in the context of a sale. **Fraud**, also known as **misrepresentation**, requires a plaintiff to prove 1) the defendant intentionally misrepresented a 2) material fact that 3) would have made a difference in the decision-making process of the plaintiff and 4) the plaintiff was justified in relying on the misrepresentation. The common law allows for a plaintiff to recover damages if the misrepresentation was intentional or if the misrepresentation was made negligently.

For example, Samuel is selling a house. Marissa is interested in buying a house. Marissa asks Samuel whether or not his house has ever had problems with flooding in its basement. Samuel knows it has but tells Marissa that the house has never had water problems. Marissa buys the home and later has issues with water damaging her basement. She asks a neighbor about the house and the neighbor tells her that she told Samuel the house had water problems when he bought it. Marissa has a good case of fraud against Samuel if she can prove that he knew the house had water problems. In the context of fraud, knowledge or negligence in regards to the truth can be difficult to prove in court. For example, if the previous owner of the house, Samuel, had lied to Marissa and told her the house never had water problems, it would be hard to prove Samuel lied to Marissa without additional evidence such as a neighbor's testimony. In addition, Marissa might also have trouble proving Samuel lied if his statement was verbal. She might claim in court that he made the misrepresentation but he might lie and say he did not. Therefore, Marissa would be wise to keep all writings such as emails and text messages from Samuel.

The common law recognized puffery as a defense against a claim of fraud. **Puffery** is an exaggerated, puffed, or outlandish claim about a product that a normal person would believe not to be an accurate factual representation or difficult to prove as true. For example, Erika works at a car dealership where she sells cars. She tells a customer a particular car for sale is, "The best-driving car I have driven in the past ten years." Erika's statement is puffery and her statement cannot be considered a misrepresentation giving rise to a claim of fraud by the buyer of the car.

Vulcan Metals Co., Inc. v. Simmons Mfg. Co.
248 F. 853 (2d Cir. 1918)

The Simmons Manufacturing Company contracted for the sale of its vacuum cleaner manufacturing business to Vulcan Metals Company. Vulcan Metals Company sued Simmons, alleging Simmons had misrepresented the capabilities of the vacuum cleaners that Vulcan Metals believed to be ineffective. In addition, Vulcan claimed Simmons misrepresented the fact the vacuum cleaners had been placed on the market by Simmons.

The following are excerpts from the opinion written by Judge Hand for the Second Circuit Court of Appeals.

The conceded exception in such cases has generally rested upon the distinction between "opinion" and "fact"; but that distinction has not escaped the criticism it deserves. An opinion is a fact, and it may be a very relevant fact; the expression of an opinion is the assertion of a belief, and any rule which condones the expression of a consciously false opinion condones a consciously false statement of fact. When the parties are so situated that the buyer may reasonably rely upon the expression of the seller's opinion, it is no excuse to give a false one.*** And so it makes much difference whether the parties stand "on an equality." For example, we should treat very differently the expressed opinion of a chemist to a layman about the properties of a composition from the same opinion between chemist and chemist, when the buyer had full opportunity to examine. The reason of the rule lies, we think, in this: There are some kinds of talk which no sensible man takes seriously, and if he does he suffers from his credulity. If we were all scrupulously honest, it would not be so; but, as it is, neither party usually believes what the seller says about his own opinions, and each knows it. Such statements, like the claims of campaign managers before election, are rather designed to allay the suspicion which would attend their absence than to be understood as having any relation to objective truth. It is quite true that they induce a compliant temper in the buyer, but it is by a much more subtle process than through the acceptance of his claims for his wares.***

In the case at bar, since the buyer was allowed full opportunity to examine the cleaner and to test it out, we put the parties upon an equality. It seems to us that general statements as to what the cleaner would do, even though consciously false, were not of a kind to be taken literally by the buyer. As between manufacturer and customer, it may not be so; but this was the case of taking over a business, after ample chance to investigate. Such a buyer, who the seller rightly expects will undertake an independent and adequate inquiry into the actual merits of what he gets, has no right to treat as material in his determination statements like these.***

As respects the representation that the cleaners had never been put upon the market or offered for sale, the rule does not apply; nor can we agree that such representations could

- Deceptive advertising
- Unfair advertising
- Obscene
- Indecent material

not have been material to Freeman's decision to accept the contract. The actual test of experience in their sale might well be of critical consequence in his decision to buy the business, and the jury would certainly have the right to accept his statement that his reliance upon these representations was determinative of his final decision. We believe that the facts as disclosed by the depositions of the Western witnesses were sufficient to carry to the jury the question whether those statements were false. It is quite true, as the District Judge said, that the number of sales was small, perhaps not 60 in all; but they were scattered in various parts of the Mountain and Pacific States, and the jury might conclude that they were enough to contradict the detailed statements of Simmons that the machines had been kept off the market altogether.

Questions

1. What were the facts of this case?
2. What misrepresentations were alleged by Vulcan?
3. What is the difference between a fact and an opinion?
4. Does a different standard apply in a business-to-business transaction as compared to a business-to-personal consumer transaction?

Federal Marketing Law

Under the Federal Trade Commission Act of 1914, advertising must be truthful and cannot be deceptive or unfair. In addition, advertising claims must be supported by evidence. For example, if an advertisement claims nine out of ten doctors prescribe a certain medicine, the company must have a study proving nine out of ten doctors prescribe such medicine.

The FTC has enforcement authority in regards to deceptive and unfair advertising. The FTC defines **deceptive advertising** as advertising that states or omits a fact that makes the advertising misleading about a material fact to the reasonable consumer. **Unfair advertising** is advertising that causes or is likely to cause substantial consumer injury that cannot be avoided and is not outweighed by the benefits it produces. As part of its enforcement authority, the FTC can issue cease and desist orders regarding deceptive advertising and it can also require counter advertising. The Lanham act allows a company to sue a competitor if the competitor is engaging in deceptive advertising. For example, Large Pharma Company could sue Ineffective Drug Corporation if Ineffective Drug Corporation is engaging in deceptive advertising.

Programming and advertising on television or radio may not be **obscene**. Whether or not advertising is to be considered "obscene" depends upon the test found in the Supreme Court case *Miller v. California*, 413 US 15 (1973). Under the *Miller* test, obscenity is determined by deciding whether the communication 1) appeals to a prurient interest based upon community standards, 2) depicts a patently offensive sexual act or conduct, and 3) lacks serious literary, or artistic, political, or scientific value. Obscene material is prohibited by the FCC at all times. **Indecent material** is less offensive than obscene material and is not allowed to be aired on television or radio broadcasts during times when a child might regularly be exposed to such programming. The FCC has designated 6:00 AM to 10:00 PM as times when a child might be exposed to such programming. An example of indecent material is a picture of a nude man. **Profane language** is language that is grossly offensive and constitutes a nuisance to the general public. It is prohibited on radio and television between 6:00 AM and 10:00 PM. Satellite radio, Internet, and cable television are generally not subject to the limitations placed on television and radio operators because cable television and satellite radio services are generally subscription based so the consumer controls the content delivered.

• Profane language

Specific industries such as the insurance industry, the pharmaceutical industry, the tobacco industry, and the alcohol industry face restrictions on the content of advertising both as part of the products' packages and as part of a marketing campaign. For example, the Family Smoking Prevention and Tobacco Control Act of 2009 prohibits advertising of tobacco products to minors. In addition, it prohibits the use of the words "mild," "light," and "low tar" on tobacco packages.

Figure 12.1 Profane speech is not protected speech

Limitations on advertising can also be found at the state level as well as the federal level. For example, in many states, lawyers are prohibited from advertising the number of cases they have won. Therefore, it is important for a company to understand the limitations applicable to their specific product or services at the federal, state, and local level. Furthermore, if the product is to be sold internationally, the company will want to understand the applicable laws of the foreign countries in which its product will be marketed and eventually delivered.

Discount Tobacco City & Lottery v. USA, formerly Commonwealth Brands v. FDA

674 F.3d 509 (2012)

The following are excerpts from the opinion written by Judge Clay for the 6th Circuit Court of Appeals.

On June 22, 2009, President Obama signed into law the Family Smoking Prevention and Tobacco Control Act. The stated purpose of the Act is to provide authority to the FDA to regulate tobacco products, in order to "address issues of particular concern to public health officials, including the use of tobacco by young people and dependence on tobacco."

Now challenged are the Act's requirements (1) that tobacco manufacturers reserve a significant portion of tobacco packaging for the display of health warnings, including graphic images intended to illustrate the hazards of smoking; (2) restrictions on the commercial marketing of so-called "modified risk tobacco products"; (3) ban of statements that implicitly or explicitly convey the impression that tobacco products are approved by, or safer by virtue of being regulated by, the FDA; (4) restriction on the advertising of tobacco products to black text on a white background in most media; and (5) ban on the distribution of free samples of tobacco products in most locations, brand-name tobacco sponsorship of any athletic or social event, branded merchandising of any non-tobacco product, and distribution of free items in consideration of a tobacco purchase (i.e., "continuity programs").***

[In regards to the ban of the use of colors in advertising tobacco products the court offered the following opinion]. Misleading advertising may be prohibited entirely." *In re R.M.J.*, 455 US at 203. This includes speech that "is inherently likely to deceive or where the record indicates that a particular form or method of advertising has in fact been deceptive." *Id. at 202.* But, "[t]ruthful advertising related to lawful activities is entitled to the protections of the First Amendment." *Id.* at 203.

Though the government may have an interest in decreasing the use of a product, "the State may not seek to remove a popular but disfavored product from the marketplace by prohibiting truthful, non-misleading advertisements that contain impressive endorsements or catchy jingles. That the State finds expression too persuasive does not permit it to quiet the speech or to burden its messengers." *Sorrell*, 131 S. Ct. at 2671.***

All use of color and imagery in tobacco advertising, of course, is not deceptive or manipulative. As Plaintiffs underscore, some advertising, like that for the "Camel Crush" product, is largely informational.*** Other tobacco advertising is used to reinforce consumer preference "by simply showing the package" of the customer's preferred brand. (Finally, some uses of color imagery are simply attention grabbing in a crowded marketplace, letting consumers know that their preferred brand or product is available at a particular retailer.*** Furthermore, there are surely certain color graphic tobacco ads that have nominal to zero appeal to the youth market. Each of these forms of advertising has great expressive value for the tobacco industry, and its suppression would be an undue burden on Plaintiffs' free speech.***

Although the government can show a substantial interest in alleviating the effects of tobacco advertising on juvenile consumers, the provision of the Act banning the use of color and graphics in tobacco advertising is vastly overbroad, and therefore the government cannot meet its burden of demonstrating that the Act is properly tailored under *Central Hudson*.

Questions

1. What public good was Congress trying to serve with the Family Smoking and Prevention Act?
2. Is misleading speech protected under the first amendment?
3. Why would Congress want to prohibit tobacco firms and distributors from using color?
4. The *Central Hudson* case requires a government restriction on speech: 1) advance an important government interest, 2) directly advance the interest by the means employed, and 3) not be overly broad. Which of these requirements was not met in this case?

Required Disclosures

The common law contains a concept known as caveat emptor. **Caveat emptor** is a Latin phrase that means "buyer beware." Caveat emptor means a seller does not have to disclose known facts about a product or a service that might deter a buyer. A buyer is responsible for inquiring as to the details or condition of the product or service they are purchasing.

Both federal law and state law require certain disclosures to be made depending upon the type of product or service being sold. For example, in the state of Iowa, a person selling a car must state the odometer reading on the back of the title of ownership. In addition, if a car has been significantly damaged, a disclosure of such damage is required. States also require certain disclosures be made in the context of the sale of a home. As an example, the state of Illinois requires a seller to disclose the answers to twenty-three specific questions about the knowledge of the seller in regards to various items of concern, such as whether or not the house has had termites, water problems in a basement, sewer issues, or methamphetamines manufactured inside the dwelling. The disclosure statement, if answered untruthfully by the seller, may provide evidence of a misrepresentation. The burden of proof will remain with the plaintiff to prove knowledge on the part of the seller. For example, a plumber might be able to verify whether or not a house has had sewer problems in the past.

In regards to disclosure statements:

1. The salesperson and marketing department must know what disclosure statements are required
2. The disclosure statement may provide proof of a misrepresentation on the part of a seller
3. The buyer should beware of undisclosed defects and inspect a product carefully before purchasing

The purchase of a home is often the largest single financial transaction a person will conduct in their lifetime. A buyer should beware of dishonest sellers. It may be advisable for a buyer to have the property inspected for sewer problems, termite or bug infestations, and structural problems, to name a few areas where repairs may be expensive. The buyer should also ask questions of the seller and the seller's agent as to what defects the house currently has. For example, "Has this house had any problems with water leaking into its basement?"

Certain products such as automobiles, textiles, and furs must contain certain disclosures such as whether the product was made in the USA. Other products cannot use "Made in the USA" on their packaging unless the product was "all or virtually all" made in the USA, which is the fifty states, District of Columbia, and US territories and possessions.

Clemens v. Lesnek

505 N.W.2d 283 (1993)

The following are excerpts from the opinion of the Michigan Court of Appeals.

This case arises from the plaintiffs' purchase of the defendants' house in June of 1987. The purchase agreement stated that the buyers were purchasing the house in an "as is" condition. The plaintiffs took possession of the house in December of 1987. In March of 1989, the plaintiffs filed a complaint against the defendants for fraudulent concealment of latent defects in the property. The complaint alleged that the defendants had a duty to disclose numerous defects of the property, including a leaky roof and a faulty septic system. During a jury trial in the Oakland Circuit Court, the trial court granted a partial directed verdict in favor of defendant Helene Lesnek. The court did not inform the jury about the directed verdict, and the jury returned a verdict against both defendants for $96,500 in damages.***

Figure 12.2 The roof of the house was at issue in the *Clemens v. Lesnek* case

In *Christy v. Prestige Builders, Inc.*, 415 Mich 684; 329 NW2d 748 (1982), the principal issue was whether a vendor landowner owes subvendees of his vendee a common law duty whose breach would be actionable as negligence. In discussing this issue, our Supreme Court stated:

> Under the common law, a land vendor who surrenders title, possession, and control of property shifts all responsibility for the land's condition to the purchaser. Caveat emptor prevails in land sales, and the vendor, with two exceptions, is not liable for any harm due to defects existing at the time of sale.
>
> The first exception is the vendor's duty to disclose to the purchaser any concealed condition known to him which involves an unreasonable danger. Failure to make such a disclosure or efforts to actively conceal a dangerous condition render the vendor liable for resulting injuries. The second exception is that a vendor is liable to those outside the land for a dangerous condition on the land after the sale until the purchaser discovers or should have discovered it. Once the purchaser discovers the defect and has had a reasonable opportunity to take precautions, third parties such as subvendees have no further recourse against the vendor. Under both exceptions, then, knowledge of the defect on the part of the purchaser relieves the vendor of any duty or liability. [*Christy, supra*, pp 694–695.]

Citing this language from *Christy*, this Court in *Farm Bureau Mutual Ins Co v. Wood*, 165 Mich App 9, 16; 418 NW2d 408 (1987), held that the plaintiffs in that case were required to prove the following in order to prevail on their claims: (1) at the time of the sale, there was on the property a concealed condition that involved an unreasonable danger; (2) the condition was known to the sellers; and (3) the buyers had no knowledge of the defect. Accordingly, the trial court in the present case required the plaintiff to prove these elements, including unreasonable danger.

We agree with the plaintiffs that they were not required to prove that undisclosed hidden defects were unreasonably dangerous in order for them to recover damages for fraud despite the fact that the purchase agreement contained an "as is" clause.

In *Christy*, the cause of action was premised upon negligence because there was no contractual relationship between the defendant and the plaintiffs. Consequently, there was no reason for the Court in *Christy* to decide whether the provision of an "as is" clause in the purchase agreement would have relieved the seller of liability. See *Niecko v. Emro Marketing Co*, 769 F Supp 973, 978 (ED Mich, 1991). This Court in *Wood, supra*, stated that the plaintiffs' causes of action were based on the principle announced in *Christy*. However, the principal issue in *Wood* was not whether the defendants, as property owners, owed a duty to disclose the defective artesian well and the flood damage, but concerned whether the defendants fraudulently concealed the latent defects. Although an "as is" clause in the purchase agreement indicates that the parties in the present case considered that between them the risk of the present condition of the property should lie with the purchasers, the clause did not preclude the plaintiffs from alleging fraud. *{our Supreme Court has }* held that if a seller makes fraudulent representations before a purchaser signs a binding agreement, then an "as is" clause may be ineffective. Thus, the plaintiffs could recover damages for fraudulent concealment even if the defects did not involve unreasonable danger.***

We find that the plaintiffs provided sufficient evidence of damages with respect to the property's value to create an issue for the jury, and reasonable minds could differ with regard to the issue. The trial court accordingly denied the defendants' motion for judgment notwithstanding the verdict with respect to this issue.***

Questions

1. What damages did the plaintiffs allege they were owed?
2. What is the law in Michigan regarding caveat emptor?
3. What is an "as is" clause and why did it not shift the risk of defect to the buyer?
4. What should a homeowner disclose to potential buyers based upon this case?

Food Package Labeling

The FDA requires food packages to contain the product name and net quantity of the food product on its front label or on the right side of the product. These are just two of potentially numerous disclosures a food product must bear. Food manufacturers are also required to list all the ingredients of a food product on its label. The ingredients are to be listed in the order of greatest input to the least input. FDA-certified color additives must be listed as well.

The Nutrition Labeling and Education Act of 1990 requires certain disclosures be made on a food package in an attempt to inform consumers of the nutritional attributes of the product. The act requires certain disclosures be made in a vertical box with no less than eight-point font. The minimum requirements are 1) serving size or other common household unit, 2) number of servings per container, 3) number of calories per serving and derived from total fat and saturated fat, 4) amount of total fat, saturated fat, cholesterol, sodium, total carbohydrates, complex carbohydrates, sugars, total protein, and dietary fiber per serving or other unit, and 5) amount of vitamins, minerals, or other nutrients. The act

• Nutrition content claim

also requires the percentage of daily value each item represents based upon a 2,000-calorie diet. For example, a product label might state, "25% of daily calories are from saturated fat."

Some firms are granted an exemption from these disclosures. Examples are firms that meet the definition of a small business because of their gross sales revenue are exempted, and firms that are considered small businesses because they have a low volume of product relative to their number of full-time equivalent employees.

A **nutrition content claim** is a claim that directly or indirectly states a food product has a certain characteristic. For example: "Low Fat." According to the FTC, a food package label can claim it is a "good source" of a particular food element if it contains between 10 and 19% of the required daily intake. For example, a product might state it is a "good source of vitamin C." A product can claim it is a "high" source if it contains at least 20% of the daily recommended value. In addition, only foods that would normally have a high amount of a daily value of a certain nutrient can use the terms "low" or "free." For example, a processed product such as soup may make the claim it is "sodium free" if such claim is true. However, a packaged fruit such as an apple is not expected to contain sodium and cannot use the term "sodium free" on its label.

Figure 12.3 Nutrition labels are required on most food products in the US

The FDA often places additional requirements on certain phrases such as "sugar free" and "gluten free." Celiac disease causes inflammation of the lower intestine. The protein gluten, a natural component of wheat, rye, and barley, causes the inflammation associated with celiac disease. To use the phrase "gluten free" on a package, a product must not contain any ingredients from a gluten-producing grain, or if processed to remove gluten from a gluten-producing grain, it must have fewer than 20 parts per million.

State Licensing Laws

Food processing plants, caterers, and restaurants are generally required by the states in which they operate to obtain licenses before selling food and/or drinks to the general public. The business is then subject to inspection by state or local health officials on a periodic basis. Rules vary by state, but exceptions might apply to those not selling their product to the general public. For example, a church generally does not have to be licensed to prepare food for a religious gathering.

Certain trades also require a license before an individual can hold herself out as providing such service. For example, lawyers are generally required to obtain a law license before providing legal services. An accountant cannot call himself a Certified Public Accountant until he has passed a uniform exam and met the requirements of his state. Some states even require cosmetologists and plumbers to be licensed. Those who provide services or advertise their services without proper licensure can be fined by the state in which they operate.

Direct Marketing

Direct marketing is the process by which marketing is made directly to a consumer. **Telemarketing** is the use of phone or similar electronic device to make a sale of a product or service. In 1991, Congress enacted the Telephone Consumer Protection Act (TCPA). The TCPA provides numerous protections to the recipient of a telemarketing phone call, such as prohibiting marketing calls from occurring before 8:00 AM or after 9:00 PM if placed to a personal residence. The Act as enforced by the FTC and FCC prohibits companies from calling a person who has asked to be put on their company do-not-call list. In addition to a company-specific do-not-call list, a federal do-not-call list exists. Several states have created a similar registry.

Under the TCPA, prerecorded messages are not allowed to be made as part of an automatically placed call unless a consumer has agreed to receive these prerecorded messages. The process of playing recorded messages by a machine is referred to as *robodialing* and the phone number is often dialed by a machine, which is referred to as *autodialing*. The FCC requires written consent be obtained before a marketer can engage in robodialing or autodialing.

Mobile marketing is the process by which sellers market to a consumer through a mobile device such as a cell phone. Mobile marketing can occur through a phone message, text message, or an email. Consumers who receive unwanted marketing calls in violation of federal law can file a complaint with the FCC. The FCC does not generally award individual damages but may assess penalties against the company making the illegal calls. Consumers who receive emails in violation of federal law can file a complaint with the FTC.

Figure 12.4 Cell phones are subject to direct marketing calls

The federal Telemarketing Consumer Protection Act of 1991 prohibits autodialing of cell phone numbers. The act even applies to foreign calls. Direct sales agencies and marketing agencies can circumvent this prohibition by simply manually dialing cell phone numbers.

The CAN-SPAM act places limitations on the transmission of commercial emails. To be considered commercial, a message must be promoting a commercial good or commercial service. Political advertisements are not considered commercial messages for purposes of the CAN-SPAM act.

A commercial email sent to advertise a product or service must, among other requirements, identify the sender, contain a physical postal address, and provide the recipient a method for opting out. The Act also prohibits the harvesting of email addresses. For example, Ricky has a new bike repair service he would like to advertise. Ricky cannot harvest email addresses from a local college online directory.

As part of the Telemarketing Sales Rule of 1995, a telemarketer must identify the name of the company being represented, the product or service being provided, and any material facts such as whether the product comes with a warranty. Total cost of the product or service and the quantity of the product or service being purchased are also considered material facts by the FTC in accordance with this rule.

Warranties

As a general rule, a manufacturer of a product as well as businesses which distribute the product will be strictly liable for a defect in a product that causes an injury to the purchaser of such product. For example, Todd buys a car from Mass Car Production Company, and the car has defective brakes. Todd is hurt in an auto accident because the brakes do not work properly. It does not matter if Todd was speeding and partly to blame, as the manufacturer is strictly liable because of the product defect.

Those businesses that do not manufacture products but instead sell the products manufactured by another business may also be liable if a warranty is breached. Warranties are generally categorized as either implied or express. **Express warranties** are written or oral assertions (promises) about a product or a service made by a seller. Express warranties are often made by sellers of products in order to provide the buyer with peace of mind. For example, automobile dealerships often sell new automobiles with an express warranty that the car will not need repairs for the first few years of its life, and if it does, the dealership will pay for such repairs.

The Magnuson-Moss Warranty Act is a federal law that provides detailed rules regarding express warranties in the context of the sale of consumer goods. The Magnuson-Moss Warranty Act also prohibits merchants from disclaiming implied warranties if an express warranty has been provided.

Implied warranties are nonverbal or non-written assertions about a product or a service at the time they are sold. Implied warranties do not cover a specific period of time, as an implied warranty makes an implied promise at the time the product or service is sold. However, in most states, a consumer has several years to discover defects that existed at the time of sale and seek damages.

The **implied warranty of merchantability** is the assertion by the selling merchant that a consumer product is fit for its general purpose and contains no defect. For example, Katie buys a new computer from Big Box Store Inc. The implied warranty of merchantability provides the computer should start and work for normal computing purposes.

The **implied warranty of fitness for a particular use** is the implied promise a consumer good will achieve a particular purpose or perform a specific function. For example, Amanda told a truck salesman she needed a large truck to routinely carry 10,000 pounds of rock. The salesman remained silent as to the capabilities of the truck to carry such a weight. Amanda purchased the truck. The truck's rear axle then broke while carrying 10,000 pounds of rock. The implied warrant of fitness for a particular use has been breached. The salesman implied the truck could carry 10,000 pounds of rock.

The implied warranty of merchantability applies to new goods and used goods as long as a merchant is selling the goods. A **merchant** is defined in most states as someone who routinely sells goods of this nature or holds himself out as having specific knowledge or skill related to the product. The implied warranty of merchantability does not apply to non-merchants. The implied warranty of fitness for a particular use may apply to a non-merchant who knew or should have known the buyer was going to use a product for a particular use and did not tell the buyer the product would not work for such purpose.

Under state law, implied warranties can generally be disclaimed by expressly stating in writing the product is being sold "as is" or without warranties of "merchantability." However, some states do not allow a merchant to sell a good as is. Finally, it should be noted that consumers cannot abuse a product, or use the product in a way that it was not intended, and then claim a breach of the warranty of merchantability.

Sales Tax

- Sales tax
- Nexus
- Optional sales tax
- Use tax

Many states, counties, and municipalities levy (impose) a sales tax on goods and services sold within their jurisdiction. A **sales tax** is a tax levied on the gross price of a sale of a good or service. The sales tax rate might differ depending upon the item sold. A company must collect sales tax for sales made in each state for which it has a nexus. A **nexus** is a substantial presence in a state. Building a retail store in a state would generally create a nexus in that state. What constitutes a nexus or substantial presence varies by state.

States determine which items and services will be subject to sales tax. Some items such as groceries and food that has not been prepared to eat, as it would be in a restaurant, are exempt from sales tax in most states or are subject to a lower rate of sales tax. The rules regarding sales tax vary from geographic location to location. For example, in the state of Iowa, new home construction services are not subject to sales tax but repairs of an existing home are generally subject to a sales tax.

Some counties and cities may levy an **optional sales tax**, which is an additional amount of sales tax imposed in conjunction with a state sales tax. For example, assume a state imposes a 6% sales tax but a city within the state has been affected by a flood. The city decides to impose an optional sales tax of 2%. Rudy operates an appliance store in this city. Rudy will have to collect 8% sales tax from his customers at the time of sale.

Some states require an individual or business to remit the proper sales tax when they make purchases of products or services that have not been subject to sales tax. A tax on goods purchased that is required to be remitted is referred to as a **use tax**. For example, some Internet businesses do not collect sales tax when making an online sale of a good or service. If Rhonda were to purchase a new television from an Internet retailer, she would be responsible for paying a use tax if the Internet retailer did not collect the appropriate sales tax from her.

If Rhonda had bought the item in a different state and that state had a lower rate of sales tax, Rhonda might be required to pay the difference to her state. For example, Rhonda lives in State A, which has a sales tax of 7%. She buys a television in State B where the rate of sales tax is 6%; State A may require her to remit the difference of 1%.

When starting a business or offering a new product, a company must consider whether or not they need to collect a sales tax. The sales tax is collected by the selling company and remitted to a state or local government. Some states require a business to apply for a sales tax permit before they start to sell goods subject to a sales tax. The state will issue the business a tax identification number, which it uses when remitting sales tax to the state or local government.

Internationally, many countries impose a value-added tax (hereinafter VAT). A **VAT** is a tax assessed against the value added by a manufacturer or a distributor. For example, assume Tool Manufacturing Inc. purchases steel that it uses to create handheld tools used by automobile mechanics. It is located in a country with a VAT rate of 6% on its products. The steel used by the company has a cost of $1 per pound. The finished tool has a value of $12 per pound. Tool Manufacturing Inc. must pay the 6% VAT on $11 ($12 − $1). The value of a VAT system is that it does not directly tax the end user as a sales tax does. It does require extra burdensome accounting by all parties involved in the supply chain, but may prevent individuals from engaging in activities such as buying products online to avoid a sales tax.

Collection of Payment

Businesses often allow customers to purchase goods or services "on credit" or "on account," which means the customer does not have to immediately pay for such good or service. Before allowing a customer to purchase a good or service without paying first, a business should enter into a written contract with the customer. The contract should address key issues such as long the customer has to pay, what interest rate will be applied to outstanding balances, and what actions will be taken to collect outstanding accounts. If a customer does not pay in a timely fashion, a company may 1) sue the customer for nonpayment, 2) contract with a collection agency to recover the debt, and 3) report the outstanding debt to a credit-reporting agency.

Suing a customer for nonpayment incorporates the principles learned in other chapters regarding contract law, torts, and the process of a filing a lawsuit. Businesses must be especially careful not to run afoul of state law or common law when collecting debt. For example, Rod's Repair Service is angry about a customer who has not paid his overdue bill. Samantha, the company's accountant, posts the overdue bill in their front store window. The company may be liable to the customer for invasion of privacy or another civil wrong under state law. Finally, if a business prevails in a court against a debtor, the business will have to enforce its judgment. The process of garnishment is a legal process by which a creditor can order a third party to withhold payment. For example, XYZ Corporation wins a lawsuit against Bob. XYZ Corporation is awarded $5,000 in damages. XYZ Corporation may be able to require Bob's employer to garnish or withhold payment from Bob's paycheck.

Congress passed the Fair Debt Collections Practices Act of 1998 (hereinafter FDCPA) in an effort to stop abusive practices by debt-collection agencies. The act covers debt incurred by consumers but generally not businesses. For example, a personal home loan, a credit card balance, or an amount due to a hospital would be covered by the provisions of this law.

A **debt collector** is anyone who routinely collects debts that are owed to another party. A debt collector cannot:

1. Call debtors at inconvenient times such as before 8:00 AM and after 9:00 PM unless a debtor agrees.
2. Call the debtor at any time if the debtor is being represented by an attorney.
3. Call the debtor at work if the debtor's employer objects.
4. Engage in harassment such as using abusive language.
5. Contact the debtor if the debtor asks for verification of the debt or if the debtor states he or she does not owe any or all of the debt.

Under the FDCPA, debt collectors are not allowed to garnish an employee's social security benefits or civil service benefits. Debtors who believe they have been subject to unfair practices under the FDCPA can file a complaint with their state attorney general, the FTC, or the Consumer Financial Protection Bureau. Consumers who are being harassed by debt collectors should consider sending the debt collection agency a cease and desist order by certified mail. A **cease and desist** letter informs a party they are engaging in unlawful behavior and must immediately stop such actions.

Consumer Credit Protection Laws

The purpose of the Truth in Lending Act of 1968 (hereinafter TILA) was to provide consumers with certain minimum disclosures so consumers could compare one credit opportunity (for example, a loan or credit card account) against another. The Federal Reserve implemented TILA largely through a regulation known as Regulation Z. TILA and Regulation Z apply primarily to consumer credit and not to business-to-business credit arrangements. Under the TILA and Regulation Z, a business must disclose the following to consumers:

1. The Annual Percentage Rate (periodic statements must show effective annual rates)
2. Finance charges (includes interest, transactions fees, and origination fees)
3. The length of time required to pay a credit card balance if only the minimum balance is made
4. Amount financed

TILA and Regulation Z provide many other important protections, such as the prohibition of issuing credit cards unless a consumer has requested a credit card. In addition, a consumer cannot be held liable for more than $50 for the unauthorized use of a card, such as when a credit card is stolen.

Under the Fair Credit Billing Act of 1974, an individual can dispute a charge to their credit card, or other credit account such as a department store credit account, which they believe was made in error. For example, Jeannie believes her credit card was charged for a good she did not purchase. She must notify her credit card company within sixty days of

- Debt collector
- Cease and desist

issuance of the first statement showing the charge (state law or a credit card company may extend the 60-day period). The company must then notify her of their findings in regards to the disputed amount. The credit card company may not require payment on the disputed amount and it cannot assess finance charges on the disputed amount until a resolution is reached. If reported after sixty days of the purchase, liability of the consumer is unlimited under the Fair Credit Billing Act of 1974. Therefore, the consumer should immediately report any suspicious or unauthorized transactions.

Under the Federal Electronic Funds Transfer Act of 1978, a consumer is not liable for unauthorized electronic funds transfers if they notify their bank immediately of a lost access device such as a debit card or an ATM pin. The consumer may be liable for up to $50 in charges if they notify their bank within two business days after the loss of their access device. Finally, a consumer's liability may be limited to $500 if they notify the bank after two business days but before sixty days after the unauthorized charges appear on a periodic statement. After sixty days, a consumer's liability will be unlimited under federal law.

In 2009, Congress passed the Credit Card Accountability, Responsibility and Disclosure Act (hereinafter CARD). CARD was passed in response to alleged abuses by financial institutions, such as credit card companies. CARD provided several important safeguards for consumers. The following is a list of some general rules applicable to credit card companies under CARD.

1. Credit card companies cannot generally increase interest rates on existing balances unless a consumer has missed two consecutive payments.
2. Credit card companies cannot charge a late fee of more than $25 for the first late payment and $35 for a second late payment in a six-month period.
3. Credit card companies must mail or deliver a consumer's credit card statement 21 days before payment is due.
4. Credit card companies must disclose how long it will take to pay off an existing balance if making only the minimum payment as well as the amount needed to be paid monthly to pay off the balance in three years.
5. Credit card companies must allocate payments to higher-interest-rate debt balances first.

Credit Reporting and Identity Protection

There are three credit-reporting agencies (companies): TransUnion, Equifax, and Experian. The most common score is referred to as the "FICO" score. Scores range from 300 to 850, with higher scores signifying a better chance of repayment of debt by a debtor. A consumer's FICO score is an average of the scores reported by the three credit-reporting companies. The exact formula for determining a consumer's credit score is difficult to state but is based upon the following factors:

1. Amount of Outstanding Debt
2. History of Making Timely Payments

3. History of Maintaining Credit Accounts (example: number of years you maintained a credit card with a specific bank)
4. How Many Inquiries a Consumer Has Had (example: how many creditors have done credit checks)
5. Types of Outstanding Debt (Home mortgages and student loan debt generally have less of a negative effect as opposed to credit card debt)

Private businesses can report to the credit-reporting agencies past due balances owed by consumers. The private business is generally required to establish an account with these institutions. The reporting agencies also utilize public records such as those containing judgments from lawsuits.

Under the Fair Credit Reporting Act of 1970, consumers have the following rights:

1. To request information maintained in their personal file by a credit-reporting agency
2. To be notified if a creditor has used a credit score against the consumer
3. To contest inaccurate information contained in a credit score report
4. To request a copy of a their personal credit report
5. To have negative credit actions removed after seven years (or ten years if a bankruptcy was involved)

Consumers who believe incorrect information is being used by a credit-rating agency should notify the credit-rating agency in writing of the error and provide as much proof of the error as possible. For example, Jack Johnson has a very common name. A past-due credit card balance is showing up on his credit report. He should contact the credit-rating agencies in writing and provide as much information has he can to prove that a different Jack Johnson is responsible for the past-due balance.

Under the Equal Credit Opportunity Act of (1974), a person cannot be denied credit based upon their race, religion, national origin, color, gender, marital status, age or dependence on public assistance. Often financial institutions will have access to information such as a consumer's age or marital status because of their application process. However, these factors cannot be used to deny an applicant credit and the factors cannot influence the terms of a credit agreement if the person is granted credit. Items such as the amount of income, expense, current debt are common factors used to determine whether or not a person should be granted credit and what the terms of a credit agreement should be.

Identity Theft

Under the Fair and Accurate Credit Transactions Act of 2003, consumers are allowed to alert the credit-rating agencies when they believe they have become the victim of identity theft. The credit-rating agencies will then alert creditors who make inquiries about the consumer's credit score. In addition, consumers are allowed to request a free copy of their credit report once a year. Consumers should visit annualcreditreport.com or ftc.gov.

If a consumer becomes a victim of identity theft, the FTC provides the following guidance: 1) the consumer should contact the reporting agencies and alert the agencies of the potential theft of identity, 2) the consumer should then file a report with the FTC, and 3) the consumer should file a police report. Finally, the FTC suggests consumers obtain a copy of their credit report to monitor activity in their name. Additional steps such as contacting the IRS to receive a special pin for filing taxes might be needed as well.

Questions

1. What are the three US government agencies involved in consumer protection? Describe and distinguish these agencies.
2. What is the test used to determine whether fraud (also known as misrepresentation) has occurred?
3. What is puffery and it can be the basis of a fraud claim?
4. What is deceptive advertising and how is it different from unfair advertising?
5. What are the definitions of obscene speech, indecent speech, and profane language, and how is each type of speech treated differently under the law?
6. What does the term "caveat emptor" mean and does it prevent sellers from having to disclose material facts under the law today?
7. Which food ingredients are required to be listed on a food package label and in what order?
8. What does the Nutritional and Education Act of 1990 provide?
9. What is a nutrition content claim and what rules apply to a nutrition content claim?
10. What types of businesses have to apply for a license before they can begin providing products or services to the general public?
11. What do the terms "direct marketing," "telemarketing," and "mobile marketing" mean?
12. What restrictions are placed on telemarketers in using a phone to contact potential customers?
13. What protections does the CAN-SPAM provide to consumers?
14. What negligence standard is applied to a manufacturer who creates a defective product that is sold to a customer?
15. What is the definition of an express warranty and what is an example of an express warranty?
16. What is the implied warranty of merchantability and does it apply to non-merchants?
17. What is the implied warranty of fitness for a particular use and can it be disclaimed?
18. What is a sales tax and how is it different from a use tax?
19. What is a VAT tax and how does it differ from a sales tax?
20. What steps can a business take to recover an outstanding debt?
21. What actions are prohibited under the Fair Debt Collections Act of 1998?
22. What disclosures must be made to consumers under the Truth in Lending Act of 1968 as well as Regulation Z?
23. What protections are provided against unauthorized charges to a credit card under the Fair Credit Billing Act of 1974?
24. What protections are provided against unauthorized electronic transfers under the Federal Electronic Funds Transfer Act of 1978?

25. What is CARD and what protections does it provide consumers?
26. What factors do the credit-reporting agencies use when calculating a FICO score for a consumer?
27. What rights are afforded consumers under the Fair Credit Reporting Act of 1970?

Critical-Thinking Questions

28. Does the concept of caveat emptor further the right of Freedom to Contract or the right of Freedom from Contract?
29. The Nutrition Labeling and Education Act was controversial, especially among businesses producing food products. Why do you suppose this law was controversial?
30. With the rise of acceptance of marijuana in the US, what disclosures might federal agencies require on the package of a marijuana product?
31. Why is a manufacturer of a product held strictly liable for manufacturing a product and not subject instead to a reasonable manufacturer standard like negligence?
32. Why did Congress pass laws like the Fair Debt Collection Act—won't the law encourage individuals not to pay outstanding debt?

Essay Questions

1. Olga sells electronics at a department store. Olga often tells customers a certain big-screen television is "the best on the market." Alex purchases the television on the advice of Olga. He then reads several online reviews that state the television he bought is possibly one of the most unreliable televisions on the market. Will Olga be liable to Alex? Why or why not?
2. Stacy works a real estate agent. She tells Nancy a certain house is in the "best neighborhood in town." The house is actually not in a good neighborhood. Nancy buys the house and immediately realizes that the neighborhood is not safe for her children. Can Nancy sue Stacy for fraud? Why or why not?
3. Gone Bananas Incorporated grows and sells bananas to grocery stores across the US. Gone Bananas would like to run a commercial advertisement that shows a person dancing and doing dance moves with a banana that might be considered obscene by some. What is the test for obscenity? What is the effect of the commercial being considered obscene or being considered indecent?
4. Rodrick is hired by a local radio station to provide the morning news. Rodrick has a history of saying shocking things on the radio. The radio station is trying to learn what obscene language is as opposed to indecent behavior. What is the test for determining whether or not language is obscene? What limitations are placed on obscene language? What about indecent behavior?
5. Karen is excited about a new website she has created. The website provides networking opportunities for college students. Karen would like to market this product to college

students. Can Karen harvest emails of students from college directories? Can Karen place sales marketing calls to mobile phones using a prerecorded message?

6. Brad is considering expanding his construction business and having his sister work as a marketing agent. Brad and his sister Angelina are considering calling homeowners in the surrounding twenty-mile area to see if they need any construction services. What limitations are placed on the ability of Brad and Angelina to call consumers on their home telephones? What information must Angelina provide over the phone in the event she speaks with a potential customer?

7. Nathan buys a blender at a local appliance store. Before buying the product, Nathan asks the salesperson whether or not he can use the blender to blend whole pieces of fruit such as an apple. The salesperson says the blender can handle anything except for cement. Nathan takes the blender home and puts in three apples. He starts the blender and is hurt by a piece of flying plastic that came from the blender. Under what theories, other than fraud, may Nathan use to recover damages incurred because of the blender accident?

8. Troy goes to AutoParts Store Incorporated and buys a new clutch for his 1970 Shelby Cobra Mustang. He takes the clutch home and tries to install it. The clutch does not seem to fit well but does eventually fit into place. Troy drives the car for twelve weeks before the clutch malfunctions. Troy removes the clutch and notices the holes in the bottom of the clutch were improperly drilled by the manufacturer. Troy takes the clutch back to AutoParts Store Incorporated. The store refuses to refund Troy his money because he has passed their store sixty-day return policy. Can Troy recover damages? Under what legal theory?

9. Dallas Johnson is contacted by a debt collector. The debt collector claims Dallas owes $8,000 on a credit card account. Dallas believes he might have been mistaken for another Dallas Johnson. What actions should Dallas take if the debt collection continues to contact him at home and at work? What steps should he take if he thinks he has become a victim of identity theft?

10. Libby is applying for a home loan. The bank informs Libby that they cannot give her a loan because she has an outstanding balance with a credit card company. Libby has never had a credit card. What steps should Libby take to have this information removed from her credit report? What should Libby do if she has been the victim of identity theft?

CHAPTER THIRTEEN

EMPLOYMENT LAW AND DISCRIMINATION

By Michael Bootsma

Allison has an employee Stan who has been showing up late to work. Allison is considering firing Stan. However, she is concerned because Stan has accused Allison and the company of discriminatory practices in the past. She is worried he might raise discrimination as an issue if she tries to fire him. She is concerned about what to do.

Rhonda was recently propositioned by her manager. He told Rhonda she should come to his vacation home this weekend. He said he was considering promoting her. Rhonda felt uncomfortable and said she had a birthday party for a relative that weekend. Her manager has now propositioned her again this week. He said he would like to take her on his sailboat overnight. Rhonda is concerned about what to do.

Objectives

1. Identify the legal issues arising from an at-will employment agreement
2. Understand the liability created by sexual harassment in the workplace
3. Identify protected classes under federal and state employment law
4. Identify basic employment rights afforded to employees under federal law
5. Identify an employer's obligations regarding employment benefits

Types of Employment Arrangements

Many employment arrangements in the United States provide for an at-will employment relationship. An **at-will employment** agreement allows an employer to terminate an employment relationship without providing a cause (reason) to the employee and without legal liability (as a general rule). The most recognizable benefits of the at-will arrangement are the right of the employee to quit at any time and the right of the employer to discharge, meaning fire or let go, the employee at any time. An at-will employment agreement can still be considered a contract; however, the contract is not for a fixed term.

- At-will
  employment

For example, assume Karen gets a job at Fast Food Incorporated. Karen is hired to be a manager and will receive pay of $1,000 per week. Karen can be discharged from her job at any time, without cause, and she can also quit her job at any time. Karen has an at-will employment contract. Her employer can terminate her contract without telling her why or providing her a good reason for her termination.

Not all employment arrangements are at-will. An employee can negotiate an employment contract that requires the employer provide good cause for termination such as a reduction in sales or noncompliance with company rules. Some employment contracts provide for a fixed term such as six months, one year, or ten years. For example, in 2013 the New York Yankees baseball organization signed Derek Jeter to a 12 million dollar contract for the 2014 baseball season. The fixed term of this contract was one year.

It is possible an employer in some states could draft an employment contract that is both at-will and for a fixed term. However, the presumption is that a fixed term contract is not an at-will contract which means the employer would have to provide cause for termination of the employment agreement. The key to identifying the at-will employment contract is the specific language used in the contract governing the employment relationship.

The benefits of a fixed-term employment agreement include the certainty the employee will not quit within a given period of time without certain repercussions, such as the loss of pay and the application of a non-compete clause. Companies spend very large sums of money in regards to recruiting and maintaining employees and they often protect their investment in the employee with a contract for a fixed term. The employee gains assurance they will not be terminated or discharged before a certain date unless a previously agreed-upon circumstance arises. This knowledge may allow employees to make difficult decisions that may be unpopular or unprofitable in the short run but economically beneficial in the long run. However, in a fixed-term employment arrangement, the rules of contract law apply and the employer may be liable for damages if the employer does not perform as promised under the fixed-term contract. In addition, the terms of the contract will provide the terms and conditions that allow an employee to be terminated.

Even though the common law doctrine of at-will employment provides flexibility to both the employer and the employee, as either can terminate the relationship without providing a justification, there are legal issues that may arise in the discharge of an employee in an at-will employment relationship. The first issue is whether or not an implied-in-fact contract was formed. The existence of an implied-in-fact-contract may prevent the employer from discharging an employee without cause. The second issue is whether the employer has violated federal or state law regarding employment contracts, which often protects employees from being terminated or discharged from employment based upon a protected class. For example, an employer who fires someone based upon their race has violated Title VII of The Civil Rights Act of 1964, even if the employee was hired under an at-will employment contract. In addition, the state of Montana requires employers to provide good cause for terminating employees who have passed a probationary period even if they were originally hired as an at-will employee. Finally, the courts in many states have created public policy exceptions that create liability for an employer discharging an employee under an at-will employment arrangement. For example, assume Lacorsha is terminated from her job after she misses work because of jury duty. Most courts would

EMPLOYMENT AGREEMENT

By and between Accountants R US. (Company) referred to as "Company", and Michael J. Bootsma (Employee) referred to as "the Employee".

The Company, located at Making Money Street, Suite 101, New Jack City, Iowa 55555, shall employ Employee, and Employee hereby agrees to be employed on the following terms and conditions:

1. DURATION: Employment shall commence on March 1, 2015, with time being of the essence. The employment agreement shall stay in force for five calendar months from the date the agreement is assigned at which time the agreement will renew for a one year period unless either (1) Employee gives written notice that Employee agrees to terminate the employment relationship or (2) the Company and the Employee decide to renegotiate this contract.

2. DUTIES: Employee agrees to perform the duties set out herein: (Describe general duties)

- Update Quickbooks with month-end financial information.
- Prepare year-end tax returns.
- Make phone calls as needed to collect past due accounts.
- Verify payroll and health insurance payments are made each month.
- Provide monthly financial reports.
- Cross train so that Employee understands job duties of all employees.
- Investigate new business opportunities.
- Contact potential clients.
- Organize and maintain all financial records necessary for the operation of the Company.

3. COMPENSATION: In consideration of the foregoing, Company shall pay Employee a salary of $4,000.00 per month, for Employee's services, payable biweekly. Employee will also be eligible for a matching contribution to his qualified IRA for purposes of the SEP rules of 26 U.S.C. Section 408(k).

4. TITLE: The title of the Employee shall be Chief Financial Officer and Treasurer.

5. TERMINATION: This agreement may be terminated earlier upon (1) death of Employee or illness or incapacity that prevents Employee from performing his/her duties for a period of more than 6 weeks in any calendar year and (2) breach of the agreement by Employee. Such option shall be exercised by Company giving a notice to Employee by certified mail, addressed to him in care of employer. With such notice, this agreement shall cease and come to an end 14 days after in which the notice is mailed.

6. MISCELLANEOUS: (1) Employee agrees not to disclose any of Company's nonpublic information during or after the employment. (2) In the event of any dispute over this agreement, it shall be resolved through binding arbitration under the rules of the American Arbitration Association.

7. NON-COMPETE. Employee agrees to the following "Non-Compete" clause. Employee will not start a competing business within 8 years after the termination of employment. In addition, Employee agrees that Employee will not ever start a similar business which serves any clients who were at one time clients of the Company. If the Employee were to serve any clients of the Company, Employee agrees to forfeit the revenue of the clients to the Company payable each year on 12/31.

In witness whereof, both parties have executed this agreement at _____ (place of execution), on _____ (date).

_____
Company

_____
Employee

Figure 13.1 Sample employment contract

• Whistle-blower

find Lacorsha's termination to violate public policy if she properly notified her employer of her jury duty. Another situation in which public policy would be violated is if an employee notifies local authorities that a law has been violated by the company. The person who notifies proper authorities of a violation of law by a company or its employees is referred to as a **whistle-blower**.

Torosyan v. Boehringer Ingelheim Pharmaceuticals, Inc.
662 A.2d 89 (1995)

Anushavan Torosyan filed suit against his former employer Boehringer Ingelheim Pharmaceuticals alleging breach of an implied contract as well as several other causes of action including defamation. The trial court held for Mr. Torosyan regarding breach of implied contract and defamation. Boehringer appealed the trial court's decision. Relevant excerpts from the opinion of the Supreme Court of Connecticut's opinion written by Judge Peters are reproduced below.

The plaintiff was employed as a chemist by the defendant beginning in November, 1982. Because of representations made to the plaintiff in his preemployment interviews and in an employee manual given to the plaintiff on his first day of work, there was an implied contract between the parties that the plaintiff's employment could be terminated only for cause. On May 17, 1985, the plaintiff's supervisors falsely accused the plaintiff of having falsified an expense request form. The defendant then terminated the plaintiff's employment without cause. The plaintiff made extensive efforts to seek other employment, but he was unable to earn an equivalent salary at another job. Because of the defendant's acts, the plaintiff experienced humiliation, embarrassment and damage to his reputation.***

At several of the interviews, the plaintiff informed the defendant's employees that he was seeking "long-term" employment, and that he did not want to move his family from California unless the defendant could guarantee him job security. In response, one interviewer told the plaintiff that if the plaintiff did a good job, the defendant would "take care" of him. Another interviewer told the plaintiff that he hoped that the plaintiff would stay forever and that the plaintiff would have the opportunity to examine the company's employee manual to determine whether it provided the guarantees that he sought.

The plaintiff, whose native language was not English, testified as follows:

***

"Q. And what went on during [the next] interview [with Stuart Rapp, personnel manager]?
"A. He was very nice, sensitive person. ... I questioned Mr. Rapp how long you expect to stay in this company. He says, I hope you will stay forever.
"Q. You questioned Mr. Rapp?
"A. I questioned Mr. Rapp.
"Q. As to how long?
"A. How long I should stay in this company.
"Q. How long you should stay. And Mr. Rapp said?

"A. I hope you will stay forever. ... And also Stuart promised me more details of the terms of our employment, we can provide your company's book and you can see and read and study that book to see if it is your favor or not. And he promised that book also.

"Q. What book was that?

"A. That is the company's policies and procedures."

On August 31, 1982, the defendant wrote to the plaintiff, stating that "this letter confirms our offer to you for employment as Biochemist III at an initial salary of $30,000 per year." Although the letter from the defendant further represented that the defendant would provide the plaintiff with various fringe benefits, it did not state that the plaintiff's employment would be terminable only for cause.***

The defendant moved to Connecticut in late October, 1982, and began work for the defendant on November 1. On that day, he was provided a copy of the defendant's employee manual, which he immediately proceeded to read. In a section titled, "The Right to Manage," the manual provided that "the company recognizes its right and obligation to operate and manage its facilities. This includes the right to hire, discharge for cause, promote, demote, reclassify and assign work to employees." (Emphasis added.)***

Sometime in 1984, the plaintiff was provided with an updated copy of the defendant's employee manual.*** In a section titled "The Right to Manage," the new manual provided that "the company recognizes its right and obligation to operate and manage its facilities. This includes the right to hire, discharge, promote, demote, reclassify and assign work to employees." As the trial court found, "conspicuous by its absence was the theretofore requirement 'for cause.'" The new manual contained the same provisions relating to the "Management's 'Open Door'" policy as did the old manual. The plaintiff did not believe that the new manual applied to him. (Emphasis Added.) On the basis of the foregoing facts, the trial court rejected the plaintiff's claim that there had been an express contract between the parties that the plaintiff's employment could be terminated only for cause. Nevertheless, the trial court found that there had been an implied contract between the parties containing such an agreement. "The defendant, in its brief, argues that the words 'just do a good job and Boehringer will take care of you' and 'hope you will stay forever,' even if uttered to the plaintiff, do not amount to words or action or conduct which could, arguably, constitute some form of contract commitment. This court finds that when used as part of an employment interview involving a gainfully employed chemist who was seeking reassurance that a trans-continental relocation would be a worthwhile career move, such words could and did amount to a contractual commitment to the plaintiff that if he took the job he would not be terminated without just cause.

Questions

1. Why was Mr. Torosyan discharged from his job?
2. Did the court believe the common law principle of an at-will doctrine applied?
3. What facts led the court to find an implied contract existed?
4. What was the significance of the employee manual Mr. Torosyan was provided?

Federal Law Protecting Employees

EEOC

The Equal Employment Opportunity Commission (EEOC) is a federal agency that enforces federal law governing discrimination based upon a person's race, religion, sex, pregnancy, age, national origin, color, disability, or genetic information. The EEOC has local offices across the United States that help it implement federal law preventing workplace discrimination of employees and job applicants. The EEOC has the power to investigate claims of discrimination. Employees are often required to first submit a claim of discrimination under federal law to the EEOC before the employee is allowed to proceed with a legal claim in court. For example, Donald believes he is passed over for promotion because he is male and the company owner is a female who prefers to work with females on a daily basis. If Donald wants to enforce federal law against his employer, he will need to first register his complaint with the EEOC. If the EEOC decides not to pursue legal recourse against the employer, the employee can then commence a legal proceeding against the employer.

Title VII of the Civil Rights Act of 1964

Title VII of the Civil Rights Act of 1964 makes it unlawful for an employer to discriminate against an existing employee or job applicant based upon their race, color, national origin, sex, or religion. Title VII applies to businesses with fifteen or more employees and federal, state, and local governments, no matter how many employees they have. **Discrimination** means treating an applicant differently from others in regards to work-related matters because the employee or job applicant belongs to a protected class.

The term **race** is not defined by Title VII but has been interpreted as encompassing ancestry, cultural identification, cultural association, or a perceived belief that a person is associated with a certain ancestry or culture. For example, Samuel is not hired for a position because the hiring company believed he was Hispanic and the company did not want to hire Hispanic workers. **National origin** is interpreted as encompassing those who are born in a certain nation or descendants of someone who was born in a certain nation. There is often overlap between the definition of race and national origin. **Color** has been interpreted as encompassing a person's skin pigmentation or the general shade of their complexion. For example, Maria is denied employment because she is brown skinned. Acts that may result in liability to an employer include, but are not limited to, decisions regarding hiring, promotion, tenure, compensation, and termination if the decisions are made based upon a protected class such as national origin, race, or color.

There are two forms of discrimination recognized by US Courts. **Disparate treatment** is intentional discrimination. For example, Ali is told he will not be hired because of his religious affiliation to Islam. Ali has suffered disparate treatment. **Disparate impact** arises when an employer's job requirements or hiring qualifications discriminate against those of a protected class even if the employer did not intend to discriminate against a protected class. In *Griggs v. Duke Power Co.*, 401 US 424 (1971), the Supreme Court first recognized disparate impact discrimination. Duke Power Company had been intentionally discriminating against African Americans in their hiring practice before the Civil Rights Act of 1964 had been passed. After the passage of the Civil Rights Act, Duke Power instituted certain policies such as requiring a high school diploma, which indirectly kept African Americans from obtaining employment. The Supreme Court found Duke Power Company was discriminating by using company policies which on their face were not per se discriminatory.

The EEOC and courts require some proof that employment criteria are discriminating against a protected class to prove disparate-impact discrimination. The EEOC, and ultimately a court, may look at the rates of hiring to determine if a job application requirement or another employment qualification is discriminatory in effect. When investigating potential occurrences of discrimination based upon hiring criteria, the EEOC looks to see if at least 80% of the protected class was represented in the final hiring statistics as compared to those of another class. For example, assume XYZ Corporation requires all employees have a college degree by the start date of their employment. Veronica believes this is discriminating against individuals of her nationality because most are recent immigrants who have not had the chance to yet obtain a college degree. Veronica is from the (fictitious) country of Zanashkia. Of the 100 employees hired by XYZ Corporation in the past year, 80 were born in the United States. Only one applicant was from Zanashkia. Since one employee is less than 80% of 80 or 64 employees, the EEOC may view this as evidence of disparate impact in the rates of hiring.

Sex Discrimination

Gender discrimination is also referred to as sex discrimination and may occur in a variety of ways. An employer cannot engage in disparate treatment by refusing to hire members of one gender or by providing different job opportunities and benefits for employees of one gender as opposed to another. In addition, the Equal Pay Act of 1963 also prohibits a company from providing unequal pay between men and women performing substantially the same job functions.

Gender discrimination can also be found in employment decisions related to pregnancy or childbirth. For example, in *UAW v. Johnson Controls Inc.*, 499 US 187 (1991), the Supreme Court held it was impermissible gender discrimination for a company to discriminate against female workers by prohibiting them to work in the battery division unless the female workers proved they could not bear children. Johnson Controls Inc. was concerned with potential harmful effects on the fetus of a pregnant woman. The Supreme Court justified its holding based upon the Pregnancy Discrimination Act of 1978, which states sex discrimination includes employment decisions based upon pregnancy, childbirth, or other related conditions.

Federal law as it stands at the date of the publication of this text does create a protected class for those who are lesbian, gay, bisexual, or transgender. The EEOC has held that employment decisions based upon transgender could be a form of sex discrimination but Title VII has not been interpreted by a court as protecting against discrimination of those who are lesbian, gay, bisexual, or transgender. The laws of many states and cities, however, make it illegal for an employer to discriminate against an employee of this class. For example, Iowa

• Anti-nepotism

code section 216.6 prohibits employment decisions based upon gender identity or sexual orientation.

Finally, in numerous states, and the District of Columbia prevent employers from basing employment decisions on marital status. This does not mean a company in these jurisdictions cannot refuse employment based upon who a person is married to but it does mean companies in these jurisdictions cannot base employment decisions upon whether or not a person is married. For example, assume Smith works for Delton Manufacturing. Smith is married to Natalie. Delton Manufacturing can refuse to hire Natalie because she is married to Smith and he works for the company. The refusal to hire family members or spouses is referred to as an **anti-nepotism** policy. However, the company cannot refuse to hire Natalie simply because she is married.

Age Discrimination

Under the Age Discrimination in Employment Act of 1967, employers are prohibited from discriminating against employees because of their age if the employee is 40 years old or older. State law or municipal law may protect a larger class of workers beyond age 40. A unique feature of the Age Discrimination in Employment Act is an employee can waive his or her rights. The Older Workers Benefit Protection Act of 1990 prevents employers from providing a difference in benefits such as severance because of the age of the affected employees. The Older Workers Benefit Protection Act also creates minimum standards for a waiver of rights under the Age Discrimination in Employment Act.

As an example, Gilbert is 67 years old and applies for a job at Quick Decision Corp. Quick denies his employment application and hires Patricia who is only 43 years old. Gilbert has faced an adverse employment decision based upon his age and he has a claim under the Age Discrimination in Employment Act.

Disability Discrimination

Under the Americans with Disabilities Act of 1990 (hereinafter ADA") and the ADA Amendments Act of 2008, employers are prohibited from discriminating in employment-based decisions against someone with a disability. A disability is defined as 1) a physical or mental impairment that substantially limits one or more major activities of an individual, where 2) the impairment has been documented, and 3) the impairment is ongoing.

What constitutes a disability is sometimes an issue that a court must decide. As a general rule, physical characteristics such as being left-handed or having red hair are not considered disabilities. Under the ADA Amendments Act, Congress rejected the Supreme Court's prior rulings that stated a disability could not be correctable by medication if it were to count as a disability. However, specifically excluded from the definition of a disability are sexual behavior disorders such as a pedophilia and other specifically defined conditions such as compulsive gambling, kleptomania, pyromania, or the use of illegal drugs.

Under the ADA, a disability must substantially impair a major life function such as seeing, walking, hearing, or sitting. The limitation must impair major life activities and not just a single activity required to be performed at work. The ADA Amendments Act broadened the definition of major life activity to include bladder, bowel, and respiratory functions. Under the ADA it is also illegal to discriminate against someone who has had a disability previously or who is perceived by others as having a disability.

In the event an employee has a disability, the employer cannot make adverse employment decisions against the employee if the employee could be reasonably accommodated without an undue hardship. For example, Kendall is disabled and uses a wheelchair. He applies to work as an accountant at Fast Figure Accounting PLC. If Fast Figures could easily accommodate Kendall by installing a ramp to their office, Fast Figure cannot deny Kendall employment based upon his disability. Courts have ruled an economic hardship does not have to be incurred to provide reasonable accommodations. For example, if Kendall were instead without sight and needed someone to read all documents out loud to him, the cost of the designated reader may be an undue economic hardship to the firm if the firm is relatively small with limited economic resources.

Vande Zande v. Wisconsin
44 F.3d 538 (7thCir. 1995)

Lori Vande Zande brought this case against her employer the state of Wisconsin. She alleged discrimination under the ADA. The following are excerpts from the opinion written by Judge Posner.

Even if an employer is so large or wealthy—or, like the principal defendant in this case, is a state, which can raise taxes in order to finance any accommodations that it must make to disabled employees—that it may not be able to plead "undue hardship," it would not be required to expend enormous sums in order to bring about a trivial improvement in the life of a disabled employee. If the nation's employers have potentially unlimited financial obligations to 43 million disabled persons, the Americans with Disabilities Act will have imposed an indirect tax potentially greater than the national debt. We do not find an intention to bring about such a radical result in either the language of the Act or its history. The preamble actually "markets" the Act as a cost saver, pointing to "billions of dollars in unnecessary expenses resulting from dependency and nonproductivity." § 12101(a)(9). The savings will be illusory if employers are required to expend many more billions in accommodation than will be saved by enabling disabled people to work. The concept of reasonable accommodation is at the heart of this case. The plaintiff sought a number of accommodations to her paraplegia that were turned down. The principal defendant as we have said is a state, which does not argue that the plaintiff's proposals were rejected because accepting them would have imposed undue hardship on the state or because they would not have done her any good.***

Lori Vande Zande, aged 35, is paralyzed from the waist down as a result of a tumor of the spinal cord. Her paralysis makes her prone to develop pressure ulcers, treatment of which often requires that she stay at home for several weeks. The defendants and the amici curiae argue that there is no duty of reasonable accommodation of pressure ulcers because they do not fit the statutory definition of a disability. Intermittent, episodic impairments are not disabilities, the standard example being a broken leg.*** But an intermittent impairment that is a characteristic manifestation of an admitted disability is, we believe, a part of the underlying disability and hence a condition that the employer must reasonably accommodate. Often the disabling aspect of a disability is, precisely, an intermittent manifestation of the disability, rather than the underlying impairment. The AIDS virus progressively destroys the infected person's immune system. The consequence is a series of opportunistic diseases which (so far as relevant to the disabilities law) often prevent the individual from working. If they are not part of the disability, then people with AIDS do not have a disability, which seems to us a very odd interpretation of the law, and one expressly rejected in the regulations. We hold that Vande Zande's pressure ulcers are a part of her disability, and therefore a part of what the State of Wisconsin had a duty to accommodate—reasonably.

[The defendant complains her employer did not go far enough in accommodating her. One of her] complaints concerns a period of eight weeks when a bout of pressure ulcers forced her to stay home. She wanted to work full time at home and believed that she would be able to do so if the division would provide her with a desktop computer at home (though she already had a laptop). Her supervisor refused, and told her that he probably would have only 15 to 20 hours of work for her to do at home per week and that she would have to make up the difference between that and a full work week out of her sick leave or vacation leave. In the event, she was able to work all but 16.5 hours in the eight-week period. She took 16.5 hours of sick leave to make up the difference.***

She argues that a jury might have found that a reasonable accommodation required the housing division either to give her the desktop computer or to excuse her from having to dig into her sick leave to get paid for the hours in which, in the absence of the computer, she was unable to do her work at home. No jury, however, could in our view be permitted to stretch the concept of "reasonable accommodation" so far. Most jobs in organizations public or private involve team work under supervision rather than solitary unsupervised work, and team work under supervision generally cannot be performed at home without a substantial reduction in the quality of the employee's performance. This will no doubt change as communications technology advances, but is the situation today. Generally, therefore, an employer is not required to accommodate a disability by allowing the disabled worker to work, by himself, without supervision, at home.

Questions

1. What were the facts of this case?
2. Did the court believe the plaintiff to have a disability for purposes of the ADA? What was her disability?
3. Did the court believe a state government could face an undue hardship in the context of providing reasonable accommodations?
4. Did the court believe the plaintiff should be allowed to work from home as a reasonable accommodation? Could their holding change in a future case if the facts were different?

Genetic Information Nondiscrimination Act of 2008

The Genetic Information Nondiscrimination Act of 2008 makes it unlawful for an employer to discriminate in employment-related decisions if the discrimination is based upon a person's genetic information or a family member's genetic information. Employers are not only prohibited from asking about genetic information, but employers are also prohibited from requesting or purchasing such records. Insurance carriers are also prohibited from requesting genetic information in relation to the employer's group health program.

For example, in 2013 Fabricut Corporation settled with the EEOC for $50,000 after it had asked a job applicant for her medical history as part of a physical she underwent after being offered a job. The applicant had told Fabricut she had carpal tunnel syndrome.

Employers often request employees to undergo a physical. Employers must instruct the doctor's office not to request family medical information as is often required when a new patient enters a medical office. If the doctor has done so, the employer should avoid viewing such information.

Harassment

Harassing an employee because of their age, disability, genetic information, race, color, sex, religion, or national origin may result in liability for an employer under federal law. Harassment is categorized as either quid pro quo or hostile work environment. **Quid pro quo** harassment means an employment decision is based upon a protected class being subject to offensive behavior as a condition of employment. For example, Jerry is told by his supervisor (the person whom he reports to) that in order for him to be promoted, he must have a sexual affair with his supervisor. Jerry has been subject to sexual harassment in the form of quid pro quo, which means "this for that."

Hostile work environment harassment occurs when a workplace becomes hostile because of an employee's membership in a protected class and the reasonable person would find the workplace intimidating. For example, Monica is a practicing Mormon. Monica's coworkers continually make jokes about the Mormon religion in Monica's presence. They also continually ask her questions about her faith and then laugh at her answers. If a reasonable person would be intimidated by the behavior Monica is facing, Monica's workplace has become a hostile work environment. It should also be noted, any coworkers who are affected by the harassment of Monica might be able to bring a claim of a hostile work environment.

Constructive discharge occurs when an employee quits their job because their workplace was a hostile work environment. If an employee quits there job because a hostile work environment existed, the employer will be subject to liability in the same manner as if the employee continued to work for the employer.

Employers are automatically liable for harassment by a supervisor if the harassment results in a change in employment status such as being fired or demoted or if the harassment results in a denial of benefits such as a raise. For example, Mariah's boss tells her if she would have a sexual affair with him, she would get promoted. As a supervisor, her boss has created liability on the part of the employer.

- Prima facie
- Business necessity

Employers are also liable for a hostile work environment created by a supervisor unless the 1) the employer tried to prevent the harassment and 2) the employee did not attempt to use the company's resources in relation to the harassment. For example, Mark harasses Michelle. Michelle informs her supervisor Janet. Janet tells Mark his behavior is not appropriate and sends him home for the day without pay. The next day Mark returns and smiles at Michelle. Michelle feels uncomfortable. Michelle decides to do nothing about the situation and quits. Michelle might not have a claim against her employer on the grounds of a hostile work environment because she did not inform her employer of her belief the harassment was going to continue and the employer had tried to prevent the behavior by reprimanding Mark.

A company may be legally responsible for harassment committed by employees who are not supervisors, as well as independent contractors and customers, if the employer knew or should have known about the harassment and the employer did not take measures to prevent or correct the behavior. For example, Anita is a bank teller. Rod comes in and makes an inappropriate remark about Anita's body. The bank supervisor hears the statement but does not say anything to Rod. The bank now has notice of Rod's behavior and may be liable for harassment on the part of Rod if Rod acts in this manner again.

Defenses to Discrimination

Once a prima facie case has been proven by the plaintiff in regards to discrimination, the employer has to prove the employment criteria in question have a business necessity. **Prima facie** means the plaintiff has proven their case unless contradictory evidence can be provided to convince the court otherwise. There are several different defenses an employer may raise.

Business Necessity

Business necessity is a defense allowed by courts in regards to a claim of disparate-impact discrimination. When proving business necessity as a defense against discrimination, the employer must prove the criteria that may be causing discrimination are a business necessity. The exact definition of a **business necessity** is a subject of debate, but for purposes of this chapter, the reader should think of a business necessity as an employment requirement that is uniformly applied and consistent with a necessary part of business operations. For example, assume National American Bank Corporation prohibits the hiring of employees who have been convicted of a theft-related felony. Mark was convicted of grand theft auto, which is a felony in his state. Mark proves in court that National's employment criteria related to theft convictions have a disparate impact on a protected class, of which he is a member. National may prove the job requirement is a business necessity by showing those with theft-related convictions are statistically more likely to repeat their offense. Since National is in the banking business, a court may find that employment criterion to be a business necessity.

Bona Fide Occupational Qualification

A **bona fide occupational qualification** is a defense that employers can raise by proving their discriminatory policy is necessary to the normal operation of a business. This defense is allowed in cases of disparate treatment. The bona fide occupational qualification defense allows discrimination in the context of employment for all classifications except race and color. For example, a police department may require mandatory retirement at age 55 because of safety and performance concerns, which would normally be considered age discrimination. Another common example is the requirement by a church or religious institution that certain employees such as a priest have the same religious beliefs as those held by the religious institution.

• Bona fide occupational qualification

Bona Fide Seniority Systems

An employer may use a bona fide seniority system even if it causes disparate-impact discrimination. The bona fide seniority system must 1) have a legitimate goal other than discrimination and 2) be based upon length of service. For example, Old School Solutions has a seniority system in regards to assigning office space. The company provides offices to those who have worked for the company for more than ten years. If the purpose of this seniority system was to reward those who maintain employment with the company, the company can continue with this policy even if in application, only Caucasian males receive offices, while female employees and non-Caucasians do not receive offices.

Reasonable Accommodations

Reasonable accommodations are required to accommodate those who have a disability and those who may have a religious objection to a job duty or requirement. In the context of a disability, the accommodation cannot cause a hardship on the employer. A hardship may be a substantial economic burden, a disruptive work environment, an extensive change, or a fundamental change in business operations.

In the context of religion, an employer must make accommodations to allow an employee to observe their religious practices unless such accommodation would cause more than a minimal burden on the operation of the business. For example, an employer may allow an employee to arrive later than usual on the day of their worship service to allow the employee time to attend their worship service.

Technical Defenses

There are several technical defenses that an employer may raise in regards to a lawsuit regarding discrimination. First, a plaintiff basing a claim of discrimination on federal law must first file a charge with the EEOC unless the basis for the lawsuit is the Equal Pay Act. The plaintiff must then receive a Notice of the Right to Sue from the EEOC before they may bring their lawsuit. A plaintiff in an age-discrimination case does not need a Notice of the Right to Sue from the EEOC. Once a Notice of the Right to Sue has been received, an aggrieved employee has a certain time limit in which they can file a claim. A defendant employer can raise the lack of a Notice of the Right to Sue as a technical defense.

The second defense that is technical in nature has to do with the number of employees an employer has for purposes of claims of discrimination under federal law. If the basis of discrimination is religion, sex, race, color, national origin, disability, or genetic information, the employer must have more than fifteen employees to be subject to federal law. If the basis of discrimination is age, the employer needs to have more than twenty employees. Finally, there is no required number of employees under the Equal Pay Act. It should be noted in *Arbaugh v. Y & H Corp*, 546 US 500 (2006), the Supreme Court rejected the lack of the requisite number of employees as a defense in a case where the employer did not raise the lack of requisite employees as a defense until later in a trial. Furthermore, state laws prohibiting discrimination may have a lower threshold number of employees than corresponding federal law. Therefore, employers may face liability under state law even if they do not have the requisite number of employees for purposes of federal law.

Federal Law Providing Employee Benefits and Rights

Under the Fair Labor Standards Act of 1938 (hereinafter FLSA) a covered employee is required to be paid the federal minimum wage per hour. A youth worker (under the age of 20) can be paid a lesser amount (currently $4.25) for the first 90 consecutive days of employment.

If an employee works more than 40 hours in a work week, the employee must be paid time and one-half for each hour worked in excess of 40 hours. Workers exempt from overtime pay and minimum wage requirements include teachers, executives, and administrative and professional employees. Some companies offer time and one-half pay or even double pay on holidays or weekends, but this is not required by law. Only hours worked in excess of 40 hours during a consecutive seven-day period are eligible for time and one-half pay under the FLSA.

There are multiple limitations for those under age 18 who enter the workforce.

- Those under age 14 may hold only certain jobs, such as agricultural related, newspaper delivery, acting, babysitting, or in a business owned by their parents unless it is a manufacturing, mining, or a labeled hazardous job. (It is expected these children will work a small number of hours.)
- Children ages 14 and 15 may work in most jobs as long as the jobs are not considered manufacturing or labeled as hazardous by the US Department of Labor. They may work up to 3 hours on a school day, 8 hours on a non-school day, up to 18 hours a week while school is in session and 40 hours when school is not in session.
- Children ages 16 and 17 may work an unlimited number of hours in any job that is not labeled as hazardous by the Department of Labor.

Under the Federal Insurance Contributions Act of 1935 (hereinafter FICA), employees and employers alike contribute toward federal retirement health care and wage assistance programs available once a worker reaches retirement age. The law requires two taxes. First, a Social Security tax of 6.2% is levied against the wages of an employee. For example, assume Rick is paid $100. He would owe Social Security tax of $6.20. His employer would have to pay a matching amount $6.20. Second, a Medicare tax of 1.45% is levied against wages of workers. If Rick earns $100 of wages, he will also owe $1.45 of Medicare tax in addition to his $6.20 of Social Security tax. His employer will have to pay a matching amount of Medicare tax. Rick's net paycheck after taxes are withheld would be $100 − 6.20 − 1.45 = $92.35. Rick's employer would also have to pay a matching amount of $6.20 and $1.45 of Social Security and Medicare tax.

Medicare tax is levied against an unlimited amount of wages. Social Security tax is required on only the first $117,000 ($117,000 is the 2014 wage limit). As of January 1, 2013, the Affordable Care Act required employers to withhold an additional .9% Medicare tax on individuals who earned more than $200,000. The tax due is calculated at the rate of .9% for taxpayers filing as single who have wage income of more than $200,000. If a person is married and files as Married Filing Jointly, the .9% tax is assessed against wages of more than $250,000. For example, Rick and Veronica have combined wage income of $225,000 and file their US tax return as Married Filing Jointly. They will not owe the additional .9% Medicare tax because their combined wages are less than $250,000.

Under the Federal Unemployment Tax Act of 1935 (hereinafter FUTA), the federal government provides unemployment compensation through state-run programs. Employers pay a federal tax of 6.2% on the first $7,000 of wages per employee and are granted a credit for the amount of unemployment tax assessed at the state level of up to 5.4%. Therefore, in some cases, the employer may only be subject to a .06% federal unemployment tax (6.2% − 5.4%). The unemployment tax assessed at the state level is based largely upon the employer's claim history of causing employees to become unemployed. For example, a seasonal business like a lawn-mowing business will have a higher "experience rating" and owe a larger amount of state unemployment tax as a percentage of wages. It is important to note only the employer is responsible for paying this tax. To be eligible for unemployment compensation, employees cannot be unemployed through any fault of their own and must meet additional state law eligibility requirements. The benefit period for unemployment compensation lasts for a set period of time, such as 26 weeks in some states, but may end earlier if the employee finds new employment.

All fifty states and the District of Columbia have a system of providing for workers' compensation. Eligible employees who are hurt or injured on the job, through no fault of their own, benefit from a state-run workers' compensation program. Employees must be performing job duties when they are injured. Commuting to and from work is generally not covered. If an employee accepts workers' compensation benefits, the employee is barred from bringing a lawsuit against the employer for negligence. The sources of funds for benefits paid by a workers' compensation program are privately held insurance policies paid for by employers; self-insurance, which means the employee covers the costs themselves; or a state insurance program.

Under the Consolidated Omnibus Reconciliation Act of 1985 (hereinafter COBRA), employees of federal, state, or local government agencies or businesses with twenty or more employees are eligible to receive benefits from an employer-sponsored health insurance plan after a qualifying change in employment event. It is important to note the company must have a group health insurance plan and the employee, if eligible, must pay the full amount of premiums and not simply the share of the premium they paid before the qualified change in employment took place. A qualifying change in employment covers an employee quitting their job or even being terminated for reasons other than gross misconduct. Former employees, spouses, and their dependent children are eligible for coverage under COBRA. The benefit period is *generally* up to either 18 or 36 months, depending upon the qualifying change in employment event.

Under the Patient Protection and Affordable Care Act of 2010 (hereinafter ACA), employers of 50 or more full-time equivalent employees must offer a health insurance plan that meets minimum requirements. The minimum requirements include the individual covered pays a maximum of 40% of the cost of medical services. The law also requires the employee pay less than 9.5% of their household income toward their insurance plan. The amount the individual contributes toward their health insurance plan is generally withheld from the employee's paycheck. The IRS has provided several safe harbor tests to help employers determine whether or not they are covering enough of the employee's health insurance, since the employer will not know the household income of an employee.

The purpose of the ACA was to expand health insurance coverage in the United States by 1) requiring certain employers to provide health insurance programs, 2) incentivizing individuals who are not covered by an employer-sponsored plan to enroll in a health insurance plan operated by a state or federal exchange, and 3) expanding state-run Medicaid programs. Medicaid is a federally subsidized state-run program, which provides insurance to low-income individuals. The ACA provided several statutory prohibitions regarding insurance plans.

1. Insurance companies cannot impose lifetime limits on benefits.
2. Insurance plans must provide certain preventive procedures cost-free to the insured.
3. Insurance companies cannot exclude benefits for preexisting conditions for those under age 19.
4. Insurance companies must cover beneficiaries until age 26.
5. Insurance companies are limited to approximately a 20% profit margin on most plans.

The ACA has been subject to much debate. In *National Federation of Independent Business v. Kathleen Sebelius*, 132 S. Ct. 2566 (2012), the Supreme Court held the individual mandate that required individuals to purchase health insurance as constitutional. However, the Supreme Court held the requirement that states expand their Medicaid programs or lose all Medicaid funding as unconstitutional. In *Hobby Lobby Inc. v. Kathleen Sebelius*, the Supreme Court held a private for-profit corporation did not have to provide certain contraceptives under their corporate health insurance plan. The owners of the corporation believed the contraceptives in question terminated the life of a fetus and violated their religious principles.

Under the Employee Retirement Income Security Act of 1974 (hereinafter ERISA), employers may provide additional retirement savings opportunities to employees in addition to the contributions made through Social Security and Medicare taxes. Common examples of programs offered by employers are defined contribution plans such 401(k)'s or Simple IRA's or defined benefit plans such as a private company–run pension plan. Compliance with ERISA often results in tax-exempt contributions from employees' wages and tax-deferred growth in earnings of investment accounts. The employee may contribute a portion of their wages toward an ERISA plan. The money contributed by the employee is often then withheld from the employee's check. Some employers will match contributions of employees to their retirement plan. For example, Michelle has a 401(k) plan. She contributes 3% of her wages toward the plan. Her employer matches her 3% contribution, resulting in an immediate 100% return for Michelle. Michelle's employer will impose restrictions on how long Michelle must work for the employer before the employer's contribution vests and legally becomes her property.

Under the Family Medical Leave Act of 1933 (hereinafter FMLA), businesses employing fifty or more employees in a seventy-five-mile radius must offer up to twelve weeks of unpaid leave during a calendar year for certain absences. Federal, state, or local government agencies are subject to FMLA provisions no matter how many individuals are within their employ. When calculating the number of employees a business has, both part-time and full-time employees count toward the fifty employee minimum requirement. To be eligible for benefits under the FMLA, an employee must have worked 1,250 hours during the previous twelve-month period. The FMLA covers absences related to pregnancy, adoption, sickness of the employee that leaves the employee unable to perform their job duties, or sickness of a family member such as a spouse, child, or parent. Under FMLA, employers are required to continue making contributions toward the health insurance plan of the employee and are required to provide an "equivalent" job on the return of the employee. State law requirements may differ and employers may choose to provide even greater benefits than those required under FMLA.

EEOC NOTICE

Number 915.002

Date 5/2/97

The Supreme Court has held that the "ultimate touchstone" in determining whether an employer has a sufficient number of employees to satisfy the jurisdictional prerequisite for coverage under Title VII of the Civil Rights Act of 1964, as amended, 42 USC. § 2000e(b), is "whether an employer has employment relationships with 15 or more individuals for each working day in 20 or more weeks during the year in question." Equal Employment Opportunity Commission and Walters v. Metropolitan Educational Enterprises, Inc., 117 S.Ct. 660, 666 (1997). The Court adopted the EEOC's position that employees should be counted whether or not they are actually performing work for or being paid by the employer on any particular day.

• Worker's union

In Metropolitan, the Court interpreted § 701(b) of Title VII, which defines a covered employer as one who "has fifteen or more employees for each working daily in each of twenty or more calendar weeks in the current or preceding calendar year. The Commission has interpreted this provision to include employers who have an employment relationship with 15 or more employees for the relevant days, regardless of the daily work schedules of the individual employees. See EEOC Policy Guidance No: N-915-052, "Whether Part-time Employees Are Employees Within the Meaning of § 701(b) of Title VII and § 11(b) of the ADEA," April 20, 1990, 8 FEP Manual (BNA) 405:6857, EEOC Compliance Manual (CCH) & 2167 ("part-time employees are counted whether they work part of each day or part of each week").

The method the Court adopted is often called the "payroll method" because "the employment relationship is most readily demonstrated by the individual's appearance on the employer's payroll." Id. at 663-64. However, the Court stressed that "what is ultimately critical is the existence of an employment relationship, not appearance on the payroll." 2 Id. at 666. The Court upheld the EEOC's interpretation, reasoning that "an employer 'has' an employee if he maintains an employment relationship with that individual" on the day in question. Id. at 664 (emphasis added). The Court rejected Metropolitan's interpretation that an employer "has" an employee for a particular working day only when it is actually compensating the employee for that day. Id. at 664.***

Questions

1. Does a part-time employee count as an employee for purposes of federal employment law?
2. What is the payroll method of determining whether a person counts as an employee?
3. What is "ultimately crucial" in the counting of employees for federal law purposes?

Unions

Employees have a right to organize and form a union under the Norris-LaGuardia Act of 1932. The Norris-LaGuardia Act specifically prohibited the use of so-called yellow-dog employment contracts, which specifically provided an employee would face adverse employment consequences if they joined a union. A **worker's union** is a group of workers who have organized for the purpose of representing their interests in workplace matters such as pay rates, benefits, and working conditions. The process of **collective bargaining** is when the worker's union, on the behalf of its individual members, negotiates workplace matters with the owners or managers of a company. The Norris-LaGuardia Act also prohibited federal courts from imposing anti-labor injunctions. The injunctions often prevented workers from striking, picketing, or becoming part of a union.

The National Labor Relations Act of 1935 created additional rights in regards to unions and is often referred to as the "Wagner Act" because its sponsor was Robert Wagner. The National Labor Relations Act's major purpose is to prevent employers from discriminating against employees who join or wish to join a union. Specifically, the law prohibits employers from 1) interfering with the formation of a union, 2) discriminating against an employee because of their affiliation with a union, and 3) refusing to collectively bargain with a union. The National Labor Relations Board is heavily involved with the enforcement of National Labor Relations Act. The National Labor Relations Board is an independent agency governed by five board members who are appointed by the president after confirmation by the Senate.

The Taft-Hartley Act of 1947 created rights for non-union employees and employers in regards to unions and union activities. In particular the Act prohibits 1) employers from discriminating against non-union employees, 2) employers from requiring union membership as a prerequisite for employment, 3) employees from engaging in a secondary boycott. A **secondary boycott** is a practice by union employees who threaten adverse actions such as a strike or a refusal to work with a second company that does not have a dispute with the union. For example, the auto workers at the Green Car Company threaten to strike because it gets its supplies from Parts Manufacturing Company with whom workers have a labor dispute. Under the Taft-Hartley Act, closed shops are prohibited. A **closed shop** is an employer's requirement that an employee be a member of a union before being hired. A union shop is not prohibited. A **union shop** does not require union membership before an employee can be hired but it does require the employee eventually join the union. Many states have passed right-to-work laws. A right-to-work law will prohibit the adoption of a union shop by an employer.

- Collective bargaining
- Secondary boycott
- Closed shop
- Union shop

Employee Privacy Rights

Employees enjoy limited rights to privacy in regards to their employment. The following is a brief list of privacy rights.

- The Employee Polygraph Act of 1988 protects employees from being required to take a polygraph test, also known as a lie detector test. The act generally applies to private employers but not government agencies.
- The Consumer Credit Protection Act of 1968 protects employees from being discharged because their wages have been garnished. It also limits the amount of wages that can be garnished.
- Under tort law as well as federal and often state law, most employees enjoy a right to privacy. Therefore, as a general rule, employers must notify employees when they are being monitored or their correspondence is being monitored.

- The Fourth Amendment protects government employees from unreasonable searches and seizures. This right might protect an employee's workspace as well as prohibit certain types of drug testing. The Fourth Amendment, however, applies only to government employers and not private employers. In addition, email correspondence of government employees is often available for inspection by the public.

Discussion Questions

1. What advantages do both the employer and employee receive under an at-will employment agreement?
2. Can an employee be fired for any reason under an at-will employment agreement? Which exceptions exist?
3. What is the EEOC? What does the EEOC do?
4. What classes of individuals are protected from employment discrimination under Title VII of the Civil Rights Act of 1964?
5. What distinguishes "race" from "national origin" and "color"?
6. How is disparate treatment different from disparate-impact discrimination?
7. What behavior of an employer does the Equal Pay Act of 1963 prohibit?
8. What is an anti-nepotism policy?
9. Are workers of any age protected under the Age Discrimination in Employment Act of 1967?
10. What is the definition of a disability under the Americans with Disabilities Act of 1990?
11. What behavior does the Genetic Information Nondiscrimination Act of 2008 prohibit?
12. How is quid pro quo sexual harassment different from harassment arising from a hostile work environment?
13. Is a company liable for harassment created by a 1) supervisor, 2) employee, or 3) a customer?
14. What is the business necessity defense and when can the business necessity be used?
15. What is the bone fide occupational qualification defense and when can it be used as a defense?
16. What is a bona fide seniority system and when can it be used as a defense?
17. What are reasonable accommodations and what are not reasonable accommodations in the context of employment?
18. What does the FLSA provide in regards to rights of workers and prohibitions for employers?
19. What two taxes constitute FICA and who pays FICA tax?
20. What is workers' compensation and how is it different from unemployment insurance?
21. What is COBRA and what rights does it provide an employee or former employee?
22. What is the Affordable Care Act and does it provide free health insurance for workers of large companies?
23. What is ERISA and what is an example of a plan provided under ERISA to employees?
24. What is the FMLA and does it provide for paid leave?
25. What is collective bargaining?

26. How is a closed shop different from a union shop and are either legal in the US?
27. What privacy rights do employees enjoy?

Critical-Thinking Questions

28. Why does the US place restrictions on the number of hours a 15-year-old can work instead of the child's parents deciding how much a child should work?
29. Why does US law prevent a worker from suing their employer for an injury incurred on the job if the employee has accepted payments from a workers' compensation fund?
30. How might expanding health insurance under the Affordable Care Act reduce health insurance costs?
31. What benefits does a worker's union provide its members and what disadvantages might it provide its members?
32. What arguments can an employer make in support of monitoring an employee's email and Internet usage?

Essay Questions

1. Malcom is employed by Big Industry Company. Malcom was hired after a short interview and background check. A Human Resources manager then provided Malcom with an employee handbook that stated he could be fired at any time for any reason except for being a member of a protected class under federal law. Malcom was not required to sign the employee handbook. Malcom then asked the manager how long he would be employed. The manager said if you don't get fired before the end of the year, then at least one year because we have employee evaluations yearly. What type of employment agreement does Malcom have and why?

2. Josie is a graduating senior in Management Information Systems. She is at the top of her class and has several employment opportunities from which to choose. Josie decides to take a job with Database Incorporated. During her interview she is told she can work for Database as long as she wants. She is also told about how female employees routinely work from home after starting a family. Josie signs a contract to work for the company for two years with a salary of $65,000 per year. The contract states Josie will only be let go upon good cause. What will Josie's employment status be after the two-year period expires? Stated another way, will Josie be an at-will employee at the end of two years?

3. John is interviewing at Good Times Incorporated. John is asked about his country of birth during his interview. John says he was born in the US but also adds his parents emigrated from Nepal. His interviewer says, "Nepal is one place I have never been and never intend to go." John says, "You wouldn't know how beautiful my country is until you have visited it." The interviewer then says, "Now it is your country. You just said you were born here—are you telling me the truth?" John says, "I was born here but think of Nepal as my country of heritage." John is not hired for the job. Has John faced discrimination? If so, what type and what facts support your conclusion?

4. Peter is interviewing at No Rules Incorporated, which operates its store seven days a week. New employees are required to work Thursday through Monday from 8:00 AM to 4:00 PM. The manger interviewing Peter asks if Peter has any issues working on weekends. Peter says not as long as he can attend church. The manager then responds, "Great, another right-wing nut, just what we need here." Peter does not know what to say so he responds, "I only need to be absent at most two hours." The manager says, "I will write down you need to be absent two hours each Sunday morning, is that ok?" Peter says, "Yes, thanks." Peter is not hired for the job. He feels he has been subject to discrimination. What types of discrimination might have Peter been subject to and what facts support your conclusions?

5. Martha is employed by Notoriously Wild Enterprises. Martha has recently been promoted to the position of manager. She asks her manager if she will be given an office. The manager says he will check. Martha is not given an office. Martha asks her manager why and he says they have a seniority system for offices, and all the other managers have longer tenure. Martha then asks why another employee, Geraldo, was given an office, as he was promoted at the same time as she was. The manager says it has to do with the fact he has to routinely hold sensitive meetings with company customers. Has Martha been subject to discrimination and what facts support your conclusion? As part of your answer, please incorporate any defenses the company might raise.

6. Cal Dar Enterprises is trying to reach new markets of consumers. One group of consumers it would like to attract is the Hispanic community. Cal Dar starts a new division called Emerging Markets. Karl applies to be the head of the new division. Sandra is hired instead of Karl. Sandra is of Hispanic descent and her parents currently live in the northern part of Mexico. Karl believes he has been discriminated against because of his ethnicity. Assuming Sandra is fluent in Spanish and Karl has had only two years of Spanish as a second language in high school, do you believe Karl has a good case under Title VII? Why or why not?

7. Terri uses a wheelchair as a result of an accident she suffered while riding a motorcycle with her boyfriend in college. Terri applied for a job as a sales representative at Big Sales Incorporated. Big Sales specializes in the sale of software systems to health care organizations such as hospitals. Terri is not hired. She believes she has been discriminated against because of her disability. The hiring manager had asked Terri about her ability to travel to a customer's business to demonstrate the software. Will a court hold Big Sales liable for discrimination under the Americans with Disabilities Act? Why or why not?

8. Michael has type 1 diabetes and often has low blood sugar episodes that require him to drink a high-content sugar drink. Michael applies for a job as an emergency dispatch operator at a local police station. Michael is not given the job. Michael believes he has been discriminated against unlawfully. Will a court hold the local police station liable for discrimination under the Americans with Disabilities Act? Why or why not?

9. Allison has been hired to work for an auto repair business. She is 24 years old. The auto repair business employs 50 employees. Allison is paid a salary and is not eligible for overtime pay under federal law. Besides the right of not being discriminated against, what government-required benefits will Allison be eligible for and who will pay for these benefits?

10. Ricky was just terminated from his job as a store manager at large clothing store. The clothing store has 20,000 employees nationwide. Ricky was let go from his job because of an accident that occurred at the store. The accident was the fault of the store. Ricky is wondering what rights he has against his employer under federal law now that he has been terminated from his job.

CHAPTER FOURTEEN

SECURED TRANSACTIONS AND BANKRUPTCY

By Sophia Harvey

A rty was recently let go from his job and is having trouble making his credit card, student loan, and house payments. He is considering filing bankruptcy. He does not know what chapter of the bankruptcy code he should file under. Arty is also curious as to whether all of his debts will be discharged in bankruptcy or if some cannot be discharged.

Barbara incorporated her business almost ten years ago. She had a successful business until she hired a bookkeeper who embezzled almost 1 million dollars. Now Barbara's business is struggling to make its loan payments. She is wondering what the effect of filing bankruptcy will be on her business. She is concerned that she might lose her business.

Chapter Objectives

1. Understand the economic rationale behind bankruptcy.
2. Distinguish between the major chapters of the bankruptcy code.
3. Identify the key components in a bankruptcy proceeding.
4. Understand the significance of secured transactions.
5. Identify debts that cannot be discharged as well personal assets that are exempt from liquidation in a bankruptcy proceeding.

Bankruptcy Theory

Individuals and companies can file for bankruptcy protection under federal law. Bankruptcy protects the individual or business filing for protection by stopping immediate collection actions by creditors. It establishes an orderly process for creditors to be paid in a predetermined order of priority. The creditors are paid by proceeds from a liquidation of the individual's or business' assets. The economic theory behind the Bankruptcy Code is to enable individuals and corporate entities to get a "fresh start" in their financial affairs while providing creditors a universal set of rules for resolving outstanding debts. This ensures that individuals who encounter financial trouble are not crushed by their debt load and payment obligations. Without the relief provided by the bankruptcy code, an individual might pursue only jobs that pay cash wages that cannot be tracked by creditors, or the individual might not work at all. With regard to businesses, the bankruptcy code ensures that financially troubled companies have an opportunity to reorganize their debts in order to allow the company to continue operating in a way that treats all creditors equitably, including employees, taxing authorities, suppliers, and lenders. The economic theory behind allowing a business to reorganize their debts is that businesses struggling to pay their debts might be forced to shut down if not allowed to file for reorganization, resulting in job loss in the community and a complete financial loss to creditors.

Bankruptcy does not come without a price. It is not a "get out of jail free card" that lets an individual get rid of all their debt without any consequences. Bankrupt individuals and companies may have great difficulty finding loans in the future, and if they do, the interest rates on those loans are likely to be very high. Some argue that bankruptcy makes it possible for people to avoid responsibility for their debts and encourages reckless lending and borrowing. In addition, creditors might not recover the full amount of money they are owed. However, the American legal system upholds the belief that the benefits of bankruptcy outweigh the burdens and that businesses and individuals need an orderly mechanism to resolve their financial difficulties. Therefore, the burdens and benefits must be carefully considered, and much thought must be given to legislation regarding the parameters of bankruptcy protection. If the law is too lenient, individuals and business will take advantage of bankruptcy filings and there is a great potential for abuse. On the other hand, if bankruptcy is not a rational economical choice, individuals and businesses may defraud creditors or cease contributing to the economy altogether.

Bankruptcy Law and Courts

Bankruptcy legislation is promulgated by the United States Congress. Article 1, Section 8 of the United States Constitution authorizes Congress to establish the Federal Bankruptcy Courts. All bankruptcy cases are then heard by judges in federal bankruptcy courts. Cases arising in the bankruptcy courts are appealed to federal District Courts or bankruptcy appellate panels. As with other federal cases, the decision of a federal District Court in a bankruptcy case can be appealed to a federal Court of Appeals and ultimately the United States Supreme Court. Thus, the sources of bankruptcy law are the United States Code as passed by Congress and decisions from the bankruptcy courts and courts with appellate jurisdiction over the bankruptcy courts, including Federal District Courts, Bankruptcy Appellate Panels (BAPs), the eleven Federal Courts of Appeal, and the United States Supreme Court.

Bankruptcy courts also apply state laws in determining certain matters, such as which assets are exempt from liquidation as part of bankruptcy proceedings. While many state laws are different, the federal bankruptcy code creates a nationwide set of rules on which creditors and debtors may rely. For example, state law governing judgments, secured transactions, and certain exemptions are applied by the bankruptcy court in its interpretation and enforcement of the federal bankruptcy law. As a result, it is appropriate to think of bankruptcy law as a set of federal laws that create a universal set of rules that may be applied slightly differently based on the state where the bankruptcy is taking place.

- Debtor
- Creditor
- Automatic stay
- Adequate protection doctrine

Types of Bankruptcies

The laws that make up the bankruptcy code are found in Title 11 of the United States Code. There are different types of bankruptcy proceedings available to address various financial situations. The most common types of proceedings are chapter 7, chapter 11, and chapter 13 bankruptcies. The types of bankruptcy are referred to by chapter because of the chapter of the bankruptcy code in which the governing statutes are found.

A chapter 7 bankruptcy is a complete liquidation of a debtor's assets. A **debtor** is a party who owes money to another. A **creditor** is a party to whom money is owed. The proceeds of the liquidation of the debtor's assets are paid to the debtor's creditors under a set priority scheme, depending on the type of debt owed to each. A chapter 11 bankruptcy is a reorganization of the debtor's business with the goal of enabling it to pay its existing debts while it continues to operate as a business. This is commonly used by corporations that have difficulty meeting their obligations to creditors. Recent well-known examples of chapter 11 bankruptcies are the General Motors and Chrysler car company bankruptcies. Finally, under a chapter 13 bankruptcy, individual debtors are able to adjust the amount of their debt. Chapter 13 debtors make monthly payments according to a plan that is agreed to by all the creditors. Chapter 13 is available only to individuals. It is not available to partnerships, LLCs, or corporations. It is considered one of the simplest chapters of the bankruptcy code an one of the cheapest ways to seek bankruptcy protection.

In addition, there are chapter 9, chapter 12, and chapter 15 bankruptcies. A chapter 9 bankruptcy is specifically designed for adjustment of a municipality or other state-created organization's debt. A chapter 12 bankruptcy is designed to address debt issues of family farmers and family fishermen. Chapter 15 is recognition and management of insolvency proceedings of other countries, the so-called international bankruptcy.

Bankruptcy Basics

The procedure for chapters 7, 11, and 13 are largely the same. The following discussion will address the principles and concepts consistent between bankruptcy proceedings under chapters 7, 11, and 13 of the bankruptcy code. Upon the filing of a bankruptcy petition, an automatic stay is instituted. An **automatic stay** prevents creditors from taking any collection action such as repossessions of cars and foreclosures on houses. For example, Brenda files chapter 7 bankruptcy. She is four months behind on her mortgage payments. The moment she files her chapter 7 bankruptcy petition, the automatic stay comes into place and the bank that holds her mortgage cannot foreclose on her house.

The automatic stay does not leave the creditor without any protection. Under the **adequate protection doctrine**, the court may require the debtor to make certain payments to its secured creditors in an attempt to protect the creditor's interest while the creditor is subject to the automatic stay. For example, a car lender may receive payments in order to protect it from loss in value due to depreciation of the car between the time a bankruptcy is filed and the time a plan that provides for payment to the car lender is confirmed. These payments are called **adequate protection payments**.

The debtor's property is referred to by the court as the bankruptcy **estate**. The bankruptcy estate generally includes all of the property that the debtor has obtained before the petition was filed. The bankruptcy estate also includes certain property received within 180 days after the filing of the petition, including gifts, inheritances, and profits from property owned by the estate. The court will appoint a **trustee** to administer the bankruptcy estate. The responsibility of the trustee varies depending on the type of bankruptcy that is filed.

Between twenty and forty days after the date the debtor's petition is filed, a meeting of all the debtor's creditors is held. All the creditors have the ability to pose questions to the debtor at this meeting. The meeting of creditors is generally attended by the debtor, creditors, and a bankruptcy trustee. Bankruptcy judges are not normally present at the meeting of creditors. The creditors need to substantiate the claims that they file in the case by stating the amount they claim as being owed. The document submitted by the creditors to verify their claim is called a **proof of claim**.

In re Jha
461 B.R. 611 (Bankr. N.D. Ca. 2011)

The following is a summary of the court's opinion. Byron Jha was a single father with two minor children who filed for Chapter 13 bankruptcy on June 23, 2008 in Northern California. Mr. Jha worked as an operations manager. He owed the Internal Revenue Service approximately $126,000 in unpaid federal income taxes for previous tax years. The day after he filed his bankruptcy petition, his bankruptcy attorney sent notice of his bankruptcy proceeding to the IRS. The debtor's attorney also had telephone conversations with IRS employees about Mr. Jha's bankruptcy case. In addition, his attorney sent the IRS a notice of the meeting of creditors in his case.

On July 16, 2008, the debtor received nine letters from the IRS in the mail. The letters were all Notices of Intent to Levy his assets issued by the IRS to pay for the taxes he owed for tax years 1999 through 2007. Mr. Jha brought an action against the IRS in his bankruptcy case seeking damages for the IRS's violation of the automatic stay. The Debtor claimed that the Notices of Intent to Levy caused him increased stress and forced him to cancel a vacation he had planned with his children in order to deal with the situation. In addition, the IRS letters required him to stay home from work, resulting in lost earnings. He also claimed that as a result of receiving the IRS's letters, he was forced to incur $20 in additional medication charges to calm his stomach distress.

In order to receive an award of damages for a violation of the automatic stay, the debtor must prove by a preponderance of the evidence that (1) a bankruptcy petition was filed; (2) the debtor is an individual; (3) the creditor received notice of the petition; (4) the creditor's actions were in willful violation of the automatic stay; and (5) the debtor suffered damages.

The bankruptcy court found that the parties did not dispute that a bankruptcy petition was filed, that the debtor was an individual, that the IRS received notice of the debtor's petition, and that the IRS willfully violated the automatic stay when it sent the nine Notices of Intent to Levy to the debtor. The IRS did challenge, however, whether the debtor suffered any damages.

The bankruptcy court acknowledged that the debtor may have suffered distress as a result of the Notices of Intent to Levy sent by the IRS, but concluded that the debtor had planned to take the days off as vacation before he received the notices from the IRS and did not provide any evidence of lost or canceled vacation plans with his children. The bankruptcy court concluded that the debtor appeared to have taken the same number of days off as he had originally planned but spent those days at home instead of on vacation with his children and declined to award lost wages as damages. The court did, however, award the debtor $20 in actual damages for the additional medication he was prescribed by his doctor for the stomach distress caused by the IRS's actions in sending the Notices of Intent to Levy.

• Exempt property

Questions

1. How does the automatic stay affect creditors?
2. How did the IRS violate the automatic stay?
3. What must a debtor prove to recover damages for a violation of the automatic stay?
4. What damages did the bankruptcy court award to the debtor in this case?
5. Why was the debtor's request for lost wages denied?

Exempted Property

Certain property of the debtor is exempt from being used to pay creditors and is referred to as **exempt property**. Exempt property under federal law includes a certain amount of home equity, equity in a motor vehicle, a certain value of household goods, and tools of the trade up to a certain value. To the extent the homestead exemption is not exhausted, certain interest in other property will be exempt. For example, Chris files for chapter 7 bankruptcy. He owns a $10,000 car against which no creditors have a claim, so he has $10,000 of equity in his car. This is above the federal exemption amount for equity in his car, which was $3,675 in the year 2014. He would have to pay the bankruptcy trustee the value of equity he has in the car that is above the federal motor vehicle exemption, $6,325, or the bankruptcy trustee would take his car and sell it, pay him the exemption amount of $3,675, and then distribute the rest to creditors. As another example, Chris' house is worth approximately $80,000 and he owes $60,000 on his mortgage debt contract for the house. This means he has $20,000 in equity in his house. The amount of equity Chris has in his house is below the federal exemption amount of $22,975 as of 2014; therefore, he will not be forced to sell his house to pay his creditors.

In addition to the exemptions provided by federal law, the bankruptcy code also allows states to adopt their own set of exemptions. If a debtor does not want to use the state law exemptions, he or she may always select the federal exemptions. However, the debtor

• Preferential
transfers

generally can choose the state law exemptions only of the state in which he or she is a resident. For example, Iowa allows a unique list of exempted assets, including clothing, a shotgun and a rifle or musket, a wedding or engagement ring, farming equipment, and the family Bible.

Nevertheless, even though a debtor may have a choice between federal and state exemptions, in certain instances federal law may limit the amount of an exemption under state law. The debtor may choose to use either the federal or the state exemptions, depending on their situation and the laws of specific states.

US Trustee Program

The federal government participates in the bankruptcy process by providing neutral, third party oversight of the parties and the proceedings. The Department of Justice has a United States Trustee Program through which it participates in the bankruptcy process. The goal of the United States Trustee is to "promote the efficiency and protect the integrity of the Federal bankruptcy system."[1] The US Trustee does not work for the bankruptcy court or the debtor, but is an independent third party that provides a safeguard for the parties in the bankruptcy courts. US Trustees exist in all bankruptcy jurisdictions except for the six bankruptcy districts located in Alabama and North Carolina.[2] In those two states, the Bankruptcy Administrator serves in a similar oversight function as the US Trustee. The US Trustee or the Bankruptcy Administrator appoints private bankruptcy trustees to oversee and administer consumer bankruptcy cases under chapters 7, 12 and 13 of the bankruptcy code. Case trustees in chapter 11 cases are appointed by the bankruptcy court upon motion by an interested party, the US Trustee, or the Bankruptcy Administrator.

Powers of the Trustee

Most bankruptcy cases involve the appointment of a case trustee, as distinguished from the US Trustee or Bankruptcy Administrator. The role and responsibilities of the trustee depends on the type of bankruptcy. In Chapter 7 proceedings the bankruptcy trustee's job is to liquidate the debtor's assets. In chapters 11 and 13, the trustee might also be required to liquidate assets as well as be tasked with helping operate the business of a debtor. The trustee has the power to require other individuals who possess the debtor's assets to deliver them to the trustee. The trustee also has the power to set aside sales by the debtor of his property as well as preferential and fraudulent transfers.

Preferential transfers are payments of cash or a transfer of assets in payment of a pre-existing debt that favors one creditor over another by providing the creditor more than they would have received under the bankruptcy code. Routine payments for goods and services are not considered preferential transfers. Such transfers must generally have occurred within 90 days before the filing of the petition. If the creditor falls within the definition of

1   http://www.Justice.gov/ust/eo/ust_org/index.htm
2   http://www.uscourts.gov/FederalCourts/Bankruptcy/BankruptcyAdministrators.aspx

an "insider," there is a one-year look-back period for preferential transfers rather than a 90-day look-back period. For example, Daniel is considering filing chapter 7 bankruptcy. He decides to pay a supplier the full amount he owes the supplier. Daniel hopes this will keep the supplier happy and that the supplier will continue to do business with him after his bankruptcy proceedings are complete. Daniel's actions may be considered a preferential transfer if the supplier received more than it would have as part of the bankruptcy proceedings and he paid the supplier during the look-back period.

A **fraudulent transfer** is a payment of cash or transfers of assets that were made within two years of the filing of the petition when such transfers are made for less than adequate consideration. In certain cases, the look-back period may be even longer. Transfers that left the debtor insolvent or close to insolvent may also be considered fraudulent transfers. For example, assume Perry is considering filing for bankruptcy. He has a rare Babe Ruth baseball card worth $50,000. He sells the card to his best friend for $500 two months before filing a chapter 7 bankruptcy petition. The sale of the baseball card by Perry to his best friend would be considered a fraudulent transfer.

Commodity Futures Trading Commission v. Weintraub et al.
471 US 343 (1985)

On October 27, 1980, the Commodity Futures Trading Commission (the "Commission") filed a complaint against Chicago Discount Commodity Brokers (the "CDCB") in the United States District Court for the Northern District of Illinois for violations of the Commodity Exchange Act. On the same date, Frank McGee, the sole director and officer of CDCB, agreed to allow the Commission to appoint a receiver who would then file CDCB into a chapter 7 bankruptcy. John Notz, Jr. was appointed as the receiver and, ultimately, the trustee in bankruptcy after he filed a voluntary petition on behalf of CDCB.

As part of the Commission's investigation, a Mr. Gary Weintraub, former legal counsel for CDCB, was questioned. Mr. Weintraub refused to answer some of the Commission's questions on the basis that the communication was protected by the attorney-client privilege. The Commission asked Mr. Notz, Jr. to waive CDCB's right to the attorney-client privilege, to which Mr. Notz Jr. agreed. The court directed Mr. Weintraub to answer the Commission's questions based on Mr. Notz Jr.'s waiver of the attorney-client privilege on behalf of the CDCB. Mr. Weintraub objected to Mr. Notz Jr.'s waiver of the privilege and appealed, arguing the trustee could not validly waive the privilege over his objection.

The Supreme Court acknowledged the existence of the attorney-client privilege for corporations. It went on to state, "[a]s an inanimate entity, a corporation must act through agents. A corporation cannot speak directly to its lawyers. Similarly, it cannot directly waive the privilege when disclosure is in its best interest. Each of these actions must necessarily be undertaken by individuals empowered to act on behalf of the corporation. The parties in this case agree that, for solvent corporations, the power to waive the corporate attorney-client privilege rests with the corporation's management and is normally exercised by its officers and directors. The managers, of course, must exercise the privilege in a manner consistent with their fiduciary duty to act in the best interests of the corporation and not of themselves as individuals."

• Fraudulent transfer

- Unsecured debt
- Secured debt
- Collateral

The Supreme Court went on to hold that a trustee in bankruptcy could waive the attorney-client privilege because the trustee was expected to act as a manager. The Supreme Court also noted that the actual managers of the corporation could be stripped of their power by a bankruptcy court, and the corporation's powers could be allocated back to the trustee. Therefore, in his or her role as a manager, the trustee was authorized to waive the attorney-client privilege with respect to pre-bankruptcy communications.

Questions

1. What are the facts of this case?
2. What was the issue for the court to resolve?
3. What did the court hold and what was its rationale?
4. How might this case make it harder for trustees to do their job?

Debt and Secured Transactions Law

In order to understand the treatment of debt in bankruptcy proceedings, it is important to know the difference between different classifications of debt. Debts can be classified broadly in two categories: secured and unsecured. An **unsecured debt** is a debt for which the creditor did not obtain a security interest. The typical example of an unsecured debt is a credit card loan. The credit card company agrees to loan the borrower money in exchange for the borrower's promise to repay the loan. If the borrower defaults on the loan or files bankruptcy, the credit card company does not have the ability to go after any of the borrower's assets to satisfy repayment of the loan because it does not have a security interest. Besides credit card debt, student loan debt is also a common type of unsecured debt.

A **secured debt** is one, where in addition to the borrower's promise to pay, in the event of default the lender also can also take possession of specified collateral because the creditor has a security interest. The assets that a creditor holds a security interest in are called **collateral**. The lender's security interest arises from a security agreement between the lender and the borrower. The security agreement is a contract. Security agreements concerning personal property are governed by Article 9 of the Uniform Commercial Code.

For example, if a restaurant owner borrows money to buy a pizza oven, the lender can require that the pizza oven serve as collateral for the loan. The lender holds a security interest in the collateral, here the pizza oven. If the borrower defaults on the payments to the lender or files bankruptcy, the lender has the right to recover lost payments on the loan by taking possession of the collateral, the pizza oven.

Another common example of a secured creditor is a car financing company. In exchange for lending the borrower money to buy a car on credit, the lender obtains a security interest in the car. If the borrower defaults on his or her car payments, the lender can repossess the car, sell the car, and take the money it obtains from the sale to reduce the amount of the car loan owed by the borrower.

The secured creditor's claim is generally secured only to the extent of the value of the collateral that constitutes a security interest. For example, if Mike buys a $2,000 flat screen television from Appliance Retail Company and grants Appliance Retail Company a security interest in the television, when he files bankruptcy, Appliance Retail Company's secured claim is limited to $2,000, the value of the television, which is the collateral.

In re Johnson

269 B.R. 246 (Bankr. M.D. Ala. 2001)

The debtors took out a mortgage for the purchase of land. Regions Bank held the mortgage loan and secured it to the debtors' real property. The debtors owned and lived in a mobile home that sat on their land, but that was not permanently affixed to the land. Regions Bank claimed that its security interest covered both the land and the mobile home that was sitting on the land, as both were real property. Therefore, the bank's claim for payment on the loan it had made was secured up to the value of the real property, which it argued included both the land and the mobile home. The debtors argued that Regions' claim was secured only by the land, not their mobile home, because the mobile home was personal property and not real property.

The Bankruptcy Court agreed with the debtors, holding that Regions' security interest did not extend to the debtors' mobile home because the mobile home was considered personal property. Under Alabama law, a mobile home does not become real properly until it is permanently affixed to the land by means such as removing the wheels and axles, enclosing it with concrete blocks, or building a porch around the mobile home. As a result, the court concluded Regions' claim was secured only to the land on which the mobile home sat and did not extend to the debtors' mobile home.

Questions

1. What are the facts of this case?
2. Was Regions Bank's claim secured or unsecured?
3. Why did Regions Bank want a greater amount of its claim secured?
4. Why do you think there's a difference between a mobile home that sits on land and one that is more permanently affixed to the land?

Under the bankruptcy code, unsecured and secured creditors are treated differently. Generally, a secured creditor's right to be repaid will have a higher priority than the unsecured creditor's claim. This is mainly because a secured creditor has a contract with the borrower that entitles the secured creditor to repossess the collateral in the event of default. The unsecured creditor does not have a legal right to any of the debtor's assets. The unsecured creditor must wait for the bankruptcy court to determine whether there is any money left over after repaying creditors with a higher priority, such as the secured creditors, to determine whether the unsecured creditor will recover any payments.

Chapter 7 Liquidation

- Voluntary petition
- Involuntary petition

Individuals, partnerships, and corporations can all make use of the provisions in chapter 7 of the bankruptcy code. A chapter 7 bankruptcy involves the complete liquidation of all the debtor's nonexempt assets. The parties involved are the debtor, creditors, and the trustee. The debtor is the person or business owing money to creditors. The creditor is the party to whom money is owed. The trustee oversees the orderly liquidation of the debtor's assets.

The process for a chapter 7 bankruptcy begins with the filing of a petition. A petition can be filed either voluntarily or, in rare circumstances, involuntarily. The court institutes an automatic stay, stopping all collection actions. The debtor then negotiates the turnover of his or her nonexempt assets to the trustee. The trustee then liquidates the debtors' nonexempt assets and distributes the proceeds to creditors in accordance with the priority set forth in the bankruptcy code. The debts that are unsatisfied are discharged, unless the debt is within a class of debts that is non-dischargeable.

A chapter 7 debtor is allowed to maintain ownership of certain exempt assets. For example, the family Bible, a certain amount of equity in a motor vehicle, a certain amount of equity in a home, and a certain amount of tools used in a trade. Nonexempt assets will be liquidated by the trustee and the proceeds will be used to pay secured creditors first, followed by unsecured creditors. A chapter 7 bankruptcy will discharge certain debts. Once a debt is discharged in a completed bankruptcy process, the debt ceases to exist and the creditors who were owed those debts before the bankruptcy filing cannot take any further collection action. However, it should be noted that not all debts will be discharged. Debts that are not discharged in bankruptcy include child support payments and alimony, certain taxes, and most student loans.

In the case of an individual filing a chapter 7 petition for bankruptcy, the debtor is required to complete credit counseling before filing a petition. After completing the credit counseling, the individual must complete a chapter 7 petition, listing certain items including income and expenses, secured and unsecured creditors, and property owned by the debtor. It must also be accompanied by documentation such as a copy of the debtor's most recent tax return and copies of paystubs from the last 60 days.

There are two types of chapter 7 bankruptcy petitions. A **voluntary petition** is a bankruptcy petition filed by an individual or business at their own option. An **involuntary petition** is filed by creditors who are concerned the debtor may incur more debt and lose more assets if legal action is not taken to protect the debtor's assets.

A voluntary petition may be dismissed if there is a determination that substantial abuse exists. Any interested party may allege substantial abuse. Substantial abuse is assumed if the debtor's family income is greater than the median family income for the state in which the debtor resides. The family income is calculated using an average of the last six months' income after subtracting allowable expenses. The debtor may be able to avoid a finding of substantial abuse by claiming certain special circumstances such as medical costs or anticipated future job loss.

Abuse is not presumed if the debtor's income is less than the state's median income. Even if abuse is not presumed, it can still be established by showing bad faith or abuse of the bankruptcy laws. For example, cause would exist for substantial abuse if a court were to make a finding that a debtor spent $10,000 on lottery tickets in bad faith in the month preceding his filing for bankruptcy. The court may dismiss the petition for reasons other than substantial abuse as well. Those additional grounds for dismissal include the failure to provide all necessary documentation, past conviction for certain felonies, and the failure to pay child support.

In re Miller

302 B.R. 495 (Bankr. M.D. Pa. 2003)

The Miller coupled filed for bankruptcy jointly. The female debtor did not work but the male debtor was a civilian employee at the United States Navy depot with a yearly income of $67,735 at the time of filing his chapter 7 bankruptcy petition. The US Trustee brought an action in bankruptcy court to have the debtor's case dismissed based on substantial abuse of the chapter 7 bankruptcy process.

The determination of substantial abuse is largely within the discretion of the court. The policies that guide the analysis are, on one end, the statutory presumption that a chapter 7 debtor's voluntary petition for relief should be granted and, on the other end, the policy that "it was not the design of the bankruptcy laws to allow the debtor to lead the life of Riley while his creditors suffer on his behalf." *In re Bryant*, 47 B.R. 21 (Bankr. W.D.N.C. 1984). The standard applicable to substantial abuse varies from jurisdiction to jurisdiction.

In determining the existence of substantial abuse, the Judge in this case focused her analysis on the ability of the debtor to pay his debts out of future income and compared the payments unsecured creditors would receive under a chapter 7 plan against what such unsecured creditors would receive in a hypothetical chapter 13 plan by the debtors.

The US Trustee argued that the debtor's case should be dismissed because after paying all of their reasonable and necessary expenses, the debtors had significant disposable income with which they could pay off a substantial portion of their debt. Specifically, the US Trustee argued that the husband debtor's voluntary contribution to a retirement account, excessive withholding for tax payments, his voluntary contribution to an account for car insurance, and payments made on a second mortgage for his mother's house were not necessary and reasonable expenses. When all of those expenses are added back to his income, the debtor's monthly disposable income is over $1,000. The US Trustee further presented evidence that under a hypothetical chapter 13 repayment plan, the debtors would be able to repay 35% of their unsecured debt.

The bankruptcy court dismissed the debtors' case for substantial abuse despite the fact that there was no evidence the debtors had filed their chapter 7 petition in bad faith. Among the factors the court considered was the amount of unsecured debt that the debtors had taken out far exceeded their ability to repay and the fact that their proposed family budget was unreasonable due to the inclusion of voluntary contributions to a retirement plan and payment of a mortgage on the male debtor's mother's house.

- Discharged

Questions

1. What are the facts of this case?
2. Who asked the court to dismiss the debtors' petition?
3. What expenses did the court find to be unreasonable and unnecessary?
4. What was the purpose of comparing the payout to unsecured creditors in a chapter 7 case to the payout they would receive in a chapter 13 case?
5. Did the court find any bad faith by the debtors?

The chapter 7 bankruptcy proceedings may be involuntary if creditors file a petition to force an individual, and usually only an individual, into bankruptcy. In order to do so, a creditor has to meet certain minimum requirements, including a minimum amount owed. There are also a minimum number of creditors who must file the involuntary petition. The requisite number of creditors and amount of debt depend upon the circumstances of the debtor. The debtor is able to object to an involuntary bankruptcy petition. However, the court may still provide relief to creditors requesting an involuntary bankruptcy if either the debtor is not paying debts as they come due, or a receiver, assignee, or a custodian took possession of the debtor's assets within the last 120 days. Frivolous petitions filed by creditors for involuntary bankruptcy may result in severe penalties being assessed against the creditors filing the frivolous petition.

Once a petition has been accepted by a court, a chapter 7 trustee is appointed to oversee the case of each chapter 7 debtor. The trustee's job is to liquidate the debtor's assets. The trustee has the power to require other individuals who possess the debtor's assets to deliver them to the trustee. The trustee also has the power to set aside sales by the debtor of his property as well as preferential and fraudulent transfers.

Distributions of the debtor's liquidated assets are made using a priority scheme set forth in the bankruptcy code. The secured creditors are paid before the unsecured creditors are. With respect to property on which there is secured debt such as a house or a car, the debtor may pay for the property, reaffirm the debt, or surrender the property to the creditor. Unsecured creditors are paid under a distribution order by the bankruptcy court in accordance with bankruptcy law, with some unsecured creditors being paid before others. For example, unpaid child support obligations are paid first, then administrative expenses associated with the bankruptcy proceedings, then wages to employees, then amounts due for certain employee benefit programs, and the list goes on.

At the end of a chapter 7 case, debtors are **discharged** of unpaid liabilities that are allowed to be discharged under the bankruptcy code. The discharge prevents creditors from bringing collection proceedings for the discharged debt. For example, Andrew took out a $100,000 unsecured personal loan from Fast Lane Bank. He repaid about $20,000 of the personal loan before filing for chapter 7 bankruptcy. He is granted a discharge under chapter 7 of the $80,000 he owed on his personal loan to Fast Lane Bank before he filed chapter 7 bankruptcy. Due to the discharge of his debt to Fast Lane Bank, he no longer owes Fast Lane Bank any money. Thus, Fast Lane cannot pursue Andrew for the $80,000 he owed on the personal loan before the chapter 7 bankruptcy and discharge.

Although there is a general presumption that all debts are discharged, there are a number of exceptions to dischargeability. This means that after a bankruptcy proceeding is over, the individual continues to owe those debts and the creditors can still collect. Debts that are not discharged are those that arise from fraud, willful misconduct, or an intentional tort. Most taxes, fines, and penalties owed to local, state, and federal governments are not dischargeable in bankruptcy either. In addition debts that arise from purchasing luxury items are not dischargeable in bankruptcy. Finally, an exception that causes much chagrin to students is that student loan obligations are not subject to discharge, as a general rule.

When filing for protection under the bankruptcy code, a debtor must follow all the requirements of the code or risk losing its protection. For example, a debtor must declare all assets truthfully in filings to the court. If the debtor is found to have concealed assets, then the court may take away the protection of the bankruptcy code.

Rembert v. Citibank South Dakota
219 B.R. 763 (E.D. Mi. 1996)

Benethel Rembert worked for Chrysler Motor Company for almost 29 years. As of 1996, she was making between $36,000 and $45,000 per year as an hourly factory inspector. Ms. Rembert routinely gambled at the Windsor Casino in Ontario, Canada. In the years leading up to the bankruptcy proceedings, Ms. Rembert began to suffer large losses from her gambling. To obtain more cash for the purposes of gambling, she opened credit card accounts with two credit card companies. She would take out cash advances on those credit cards at the Windsor Casino. To pay for her gambling habit, she also took out a second mortgage on her home. The Judge presiding over her bankruptcy proceedings found some of her credit card debts to be non-dischargeable debts because at the time she took out the cash advances she possessed fraudulent intent. The bankruptcy court Judge found, based on Ms. Rembert's testimony in court, that when she took out the cash advances, she never intended to repay the credit card companies and knew that she would not reasonably be able to repay the cash advances from gambling winnings.

Ms. Rembert appealed this decision to the Federal District Court for the Eastern District of Michigan. The District Court considered whether the advances Ms. Rembert took were fraudulent under 11 USC. § 523(a)(2)(A), which provides that, "A discharge … does not discharge an individual debtor from any debt … obtained by false pretenses, a false representation, or actual fraud, other than a statement respecting the debtor's or an insider's financial condition." The creditor bears the burden of showing a debt is non-dischargeable by a preponderance of the evidence. The District Court disagreed with the finding of the Bankruptcy Court Judge. The District Court Judge stated there was no actual fraud toward the credit card companies on Ms. Rembert's part. The District Court Judge also did not believe there was enough evidence to prove that Ms. Rembert did not intend to repay her debt when she took out the cash advances or that she made misrepresentations when borrowing the money she used to gamble. The District Court stated, "Gambling is a risky investment. But so too is trying to start a successful small business, or investing in derivatives, or investing in heating oil futures or penny stocks. These are all risky endeavors that most of the time do not pan out. Unfortunately, bankruptcy is the route taken by many individuals whose risky investments do not pan out. If the risky investment succeeds, the lenders, be they credit card companies or banks are made whole. If the investment fails, then their risk does

- Reaffirmation
- Debtor-in-possession

not pay off. That the credit card company's risk in advancing money does not pan out does not turn the debtor into an individual guilty of defrauding the creditor."

Questions

1. What are the facts of this case?
2. On what basis did the credit card company argue the debt was non-dischargeable?
3. What did Ms. Rembert hope to gain by appealing the ruling in her bankruptcy proceeding?
4. Why did the District Court Judge disagree with the bankruptcy Judge?
5. Why did the Judge draw a parallel between starting a business and gambling?
6. Do you agree or disagree with the court's decision and rationale?

Although outstanding debts are generally discharged in a chapter 7 proceeding, the debtor is allowed to agree to the non-discharge of debts that would normally be dischargeable. This is called **reaffirmation**. A reaffirmation is often required if the debtor wants to keep property that secures a debt. However, reaffirmation is not generally required for car loans and home mortgages, which are treated differently under the bankruptcy code. To reaffirm a debt, the debtor must file a notice with the court before obtaining a discharge. The court may object to a debtor's reaffirmation if they feel it is not in the best interest of the proceedings. For example, assume Tom has a ski boat that he loves to use for water sports. He lives right next to a lake and enjoys taking his kids out on the boat. He reaffirms the debt he owes to the bank that advanced money for him to buy the boat. The bankruptcy court hearing his case would have to approve of his reaffirmation. If the court does, Tom can keep but the boat but will have to make payments to satisfy the outstanding debt.

Chapter 11 Reorganizations

Chapter 11 of the bankruptcy code is designed to allow debtors the opportunity to reorganize their debts instead of liquidating their assets. Although the provisions of this chapter are generally used by corporations, they are also available to certain individuals. Many of the same principles underlying chapter 7 bankruptcies also apply to chapter 11 proceedings. For example, a chapter 11 bankruptcy can be either voluntary or involuntary.

In a chapter 11 proceeding, the debtor's business continues to operate as it was previously. A debtor who is operating under a chapter 11 plan is called a **debtor-in-possession** and continues to operate the business. In some situations, a trustee is appointed to run the debtor's business. In a chapter 11 proceeding, a plan for repaying creditors is created for the debtor. Under the plan of reorganization, some but not all debts are dischargeable. For example, past due taxes for which no tax returns were ever filed are generally not dischargeable.

For the first 120 days from the initiation of a chapter 11 proceeding, only the debtor has the right to file a reorganization plan. If the 120-day mark passes without the debtor proposing a plan, then the debtor's creditors are allowed to file a reorganization plan. The debtor must obtain the consent of creditors to a plan within 180 days of the beginning of its chapter 11 case or the creditors have the right to propose a plan of their own. Creditors are divided into different classes based on the type of claim they hold, but all classes of creditors must consent to a reorganization plan. If only one class consents to the plan, the court can force acceptance of the plan by other creditors by using the "cram-down" provisions of the bankruptcy code. If the court feels the plan is not in the best interests of the parties, it may refuse to enforce a proposed plan.

At the end of a chapter 11 proceeding, the court grants a chapter 11 individual debtor a discharge only if he or she has abided by and fulfilled all the terms of the reorganization plan. Technically, a discharge for organizations can be granted at any time after the court has confirmed a reorganization plan, but there is no time limit on how long a reorganization plan can last in a chapter 11 bankruptcy proceeding. For example, a debtor might be forced to make payments for four years before the reorganization plan is met and the remaining debts that are eligible to be discharged are discharged.

Due to the fact that the debtor's business continues to operate in a chapter 11 bankruptcy, the bankruptcy code requires that the plan be in the best interests of the creditors. Some creditors may prefer to settle their claims for payment through a private negotiation with the debtor through a process generally referred to as a **workout** or **debt workout**.

- Workout
- Debt workout

Ohio v. Kovacs
469 US 274 (1985)

The state of Ohio had obtained an injunction against William Kovacs who was doing business as B&W Enterprises. The state of Ohio wanted to force Mr. Kovacs to clean up a hazardous waste site that he had been operating. Shortly after the state of Ohio obtained an injunction forcing him to clean up the site, Mr. Kovacs filed for protection under chapter 11 of the bankruptcy code. He then converted his chapter 11 filing into a chapter 7 liquidation proceeding.

In Mr. Kovac's bankruptcy proceeding, the state of Ohio asserted that its claim against Mr. Kovacs was not a "debt" or a "liability on a claim" that could be discharged under the bankruptcy proceeding. The bankruptcy court disagreed, as did the District Court and the Appellate Court.

The Supreme Court granted certiorari review to the case. It was tasked with deciding whether the claim under the injunction was to be considered a "debt" or a "liability on a claim" that would have been dischargeable under the bankruptcy code. The Supreme Court looked at the legislative history of the bankruptcy code to see if the drafters offered guidance on the definitions of a "debt" or a "liability on a claim." The Supreme Court found the legislative history did not necessarily define the terms, but it did not eliminate an equitable remedy such as an injunction as a debt or a liability on a claim.

The Supreme Court did note that a claim arising from embezzlement or larceny would fit the definition of a liability, which is not dischargeable in bankruptcy. However, this was an environmental issue and not larceny or embezzlement.

The Supreme Court agreed with the bankruptcy court Judge's opinion that the state of Ohio would be owed a payment by Mr. Kovacs because he did not clean up the hazardous waste site. Since the state of Ohio was owed money damages for nonperformance by Mr. Kovac, the state was owed a "debt" for purposes of the bankruptcy code and that debt was properly discharged under chapter 7 of the bankruptcy code.

Questions

1. What were the facts of this case?
2. Why did the state of Ohio try to claim Kovacs did not owe them a "debt"?
3. What was the court's holding and rationale?
4. How could Congress change the outcome of a case like this?

Chapter 13 Bankruptcy

A chapter 13 bankruptcy proceeding is one in which an individual debtor is allowed to pay back creditors through a repayment plan. It is the least expensive method of seeking the protection of the bankruptcy code and is also the least complicated. Unlike chapter 7 and chapter 11 proceedings, a chapter 13 petition can only be made voluntarily by the debtor. However, a chapter 13 petition can be converted to a chapter 7 or 11 petition and vice versa.

In order to qualify for a chapter 13 bankruptcy, an individual must have unsecured debt of less than $360,475 and secured debts of less than $1,081,400. The individual must also have regular income. Regular income might include wages, profits from a small business, or social security income.

The chapter 13 debtor is the only party that can file a repayment plan. Although unsecured creditors and the trustees have the right to object to the debtor's chapter 13 plan, the court can overrule the objections of unsecured creditors. The court will overrule their objections to a repayment plan if the plan will distribute property and payments in an amount equal in value of the claims and all of the debtor's disposable income is being applied toward payments under the plan.

The plan must provide for the transfer of all future income realized by the debtor to pay debts pursuant to the terms of the plan. Claims are given priorities in accordance with the bankruptcy code. Creditors are organized into classes for purposes of repayment under the chapter 13 plan and creditors within the same class are treated equally. The chapter 13 payment plan is between 36 and 60 months, depending on the income of the debtor. A trustee is appointed to collect payments from the debtor and distribute the payments to the creditors in accordance with the terms of the repayment plan.

Upon fulfillment of the terms of the chapter 13 repayment plan, the debtor's remaining debts are discharged. Certain debts remain non-dischargeable include, as discussed before, some taxes, intentional torts, student loans, and domestic support obligations.

Discussion Questions

1. What economic arguments can be made to support the availability of bankruptcy under the law as a means of discharging excess debt?

2. What economic arguments can be made against the availability of bankruptcy under the law as a means of discharging excess debt?

3. What kind of law governs bankruptcy proceedings?

4. What court has jurisdiction to hear cases involving bankruptcy law?

5. What chapters of the bankruptcy code were discussed in this chapter and how do they differ?

6. John D. Tractor owns a farm on which he plants corn and soy beans. In the past few years, he borrowed a lot of money to upgrade his farm machinery. Although the farm is making money, it is not making enough to cover the amounts owed on a monthly basis. What chapter of bankruptcy should he explore?

7. Of chapter 7, 11, and 13 bankruptcies, which one(s) allows a creditor(s) to force a debtor into bankruptcy proceedings?

8. What is an automatic stay and what is its legal effect?

9. What is the adequate protection doctrine?

10. What are the definitions of 1) a creditor, 2) a debtor, and 3) a trustee?

11. What property is included in the estate of the debtor?

12. What property is exempt from discharge in a bankruptcy proceeding?

13. What powers does the trustee have?

14. What is a secured debt and how is it different from an unsecured debt?

15. What is a voluntary petition and how is it different from an involuntary petition in a chapter 7 bankruptcy proceeding?

16. How does the trustee determine in which order to distribute assets to creditors?

17. What types of debt are not discharged in a bankruptcy proceeding?

18. What is reaffirmation and must a court approve of reaffirmed debt?

19. How is a chapter 11 proceeding different from a chapter 7 proceeding?

20. Who is a debtor in possession?

21. What is a workout and when does it occur?

22. When is a debtor discharged of debts in a chapter 11 bankruptcy?

23. How is a chapter 13 bankruptcy proceeding different from a chapter 11 bankruptcy, and how is it different from a chapter 7 bankruptcy?

24. When is a debtor discharged from their dischargeable debt obligations in a chapter 13 proceeding?

25. Sally Spender owes $1,500 on a Visa credit card, $25,000 in student loans, and $18,000 on her convertible. She cannot make her monthly payments.
    a. What kind of bankruptcy should she file?
    b. If she files bankruptcy, what debts will be discharged?

26. Bob Burgundy files a petition for chapter 7 bankruptcy. Two weeks before he filed for bankruptcy, Mr. Burgundy transferred title to his vintage 1972 Corvette to his mother. His mother paid him $5 for the car. How would this transfer be viewed by the bankruptcy court?

27. Billy Lopez recently filed for chapter 13 bankruptcy and has made all of his monthly plan payments. He woke up one morning to go to work to find that his car, which he reaffirmed under the chapter 13 bankruptcy plan, had been repossessed. He is current on payments to the auto financing company. Is the repossession legal?

Critical-Thinking Questions

28. In the priority of payments to creditors in bankruptcy, secured creditors are paid before unsecured creditors. Is this is fair to the unsecured creditors? How are unsecured creditors compensated for this risk?
29. Credit card debt is usually dischargeable in bankruptcy. What behavior do you think this encourages in consumers? What could Congress do to remedy this situation?
30. Congress has ruled that student loan debt cannot be discharged in bankruptcy. Often student loans are obtained from an agency backed by the federal government. Is it fair for Congress to exempt student loans from discharge, and what would it take to change the law regarding student loans?
31. If asked of the average citizen, who would they say should not be able utilize federal bankruptcy proceedings?
32. If you could add items to the list of exempt property in a chapter 7 liquidation, what would they be?

Essay Questions

1. Martin had a successful small business before a recession hit his community. Martin believes the economy will improve in the next year and he may be able to regain a significant portion of the revenue he lost during the past few years. Martin's business owes a substantial amount of money on a commercial loan to Quick Repo Bank. He also is three months behind on his home mortgage. Finally, he has been paying for most of his groceries and other personal expenses by using a credit card. Martin knows he will have to file bankruptcy in the next two months. What type of bankruptcy proceeding should Martin file and why? Include a discussion of advantages and disadvantages of chapter 7, chapter 11, and chapter 13 bankruptcies.
2. Allison was married to Tom until last year when she found out Tom had been taking out credit card loans as well as other personal loans in Allison's name. Tom even bought a beach property in her name. The beach property is now in foreclosure. Allison has a fairly successful contracting business. However, she does not believe she can keep up with the minimum payments on the loans her husband has taken out in her name. What type of bankruptcy proceeding should Allison file and why? Include a discussion of advantages and disadvantages of chapter 7, chapter 11, and chapter 13 bankruptcies.
3. Fast Eddy has just filed a petition for a chapter 7 bankruptcy proceeding. Fast Eddy is unemployed but receives $60,000 a year from a settlement resulting from an auto

accident four years ago. The payments will continue for three more years. Fast Eddy owes $85,000 in credit card debt and he is three months behind on his mortgage. Fast Eddy is also behind on child support payments to his ex-wife in the amount of $24,000. Fast Eddy did own a rare 1963 Corvette worth $140,000 but he recently sold the Corvette to his brother Slick Willy for $100. On what grounds might the trustee move to have Fast Eddy's bankruptcy proceeding dismissed?

4. Roselyn Motor Corporation has filed a chapter 11 bankruptcy. The day before it filed their bankruptcy petition, Roselyn made the following payments: a) $134,000 in employee salaries, b) $40,000 to Roselyn's main supplier Auto Parts Supplier, and c) $1,200 for a utility bill. Roselyn also transferred ownership of a plant to its main customer for a fraction of the plant's fair market value. In addition, Roselyn returned merchandise to its second most important supplier because Roselyn had not yet paid for said merchandise. Which payments and transfers may a trustee set aside in the chapter 11 proceeding?

5. Meredith Doctor recently divorced her husband who does not work outside the home. She is required to pay child support of $2,500 a month under the divorce decree. Ms. Doctor owns a house that is worth approximately $500,000 on which there is a mortgage of $450,000. She also owns a car on which she owes $45,000 and has student loans outstanding in the amount of $100,000. Finally, she owes $12,000 on an American Express card.

    a. What are her secured debts?
    b. What are her unsecured debts?
    c. How much equity does she have in her house?
    d. If she files chapter 7 bankruptcy, what debts are discharged?
    e. If she files chapter 13 bankruptcy, what debts are discharged?
    f. What debts can she reaffirm in bankruptcy?
    g. What debts cannot be discharged in bankruptcy?
    h. What type of bankruptcy would you advise her to file?

6. The Hawkeye Brewing Company was founded by Rikki and Bobbi. Hawkeye Brewing Company is in the business of making and selling specialty micro-brews. To start the company, the Hawkeye Brewing Company borrowed $300,000 from Wells Fargo. It also bought a Ford F-250 truck for $35,000 to transport the beer. The Ford truck was bought on credit from Ford Auto Financing. Hawkeye Brewing Company operated profitably for three years until Rikki and Bobbi started to spend more time in Myrtle Beach than running the company. The Hawkeye Brewing Company has not made a payment to Wells Fargo or Ford Auto Financing in six months. In addition, the Hawkeye Brewing Company has not paid its bottle supplier and owes Cyclone Bottles $15,000. Wells Fargo has sent letters demanding payment and Ford Financing is threatening to repossess the truck.

Hawkeye Brewing Company could operate profitably if it could hold off creditors until after the bowl games so it could sell beer during the college football season.

a. Who are Hawkeye Brewing Company's creditors?
b. Who are Hawkeye Brewing Company's secured creditors and unsecured creditors?
c. What type of bankruptcy should Hawkeye Brewing Company file?
d. What document does the Hawkeye Brewing Company have to file with the court within 120 days of filing?

CHAPTER FIFTEEN

AGENCY, CORPORATE, AND PARTNERSHIP LAW

By Michael Bootsma

Jeff is considering investing in rental real estate. He hopes to buy a house in a college town and rent it to students. He is curious as to whether he should start a corporation and have the corporation own the house or whether he should just own it personally.

Emily has always wanted to own her own coffee shop. Her best friend Alex is great at customer service and would like to be a partner in Emily's coffee shop business. Emily and Alex are trying to decide whether they should form their business as a partnership or as a corporation or maybe an LLC.

Objectives

1. Understand the differences between various business entity forms
2. Identify the liability exposure associated with different business entity forms
3. Identify the tax consequences of various types of business entity forms
4. Identify key organizational documents
5. Distinguish between an employee and an independent contractor
6. Understand tenets of agency law

Business Entities

Sole Proprietorships

According to the US Small Business Administration (hereinafter SBA) over 70% of the businesses in the United States are organized as a sole proprietorship. A **sole proprietorship** is a business that has no separate legal existence from its single owner. There are several limitations to having a sole proprietorship. A sole proprietorship cannot have more than one owner. The sole proprietorship cannot raise funds beyond that which its owner can obtain from personal sources or from sources of credit, such as a bank loan. However, there are advantages.

To start a sole proprietorship, an individual must simply start engaging in business activities. For example, Norman routinely fixes automobiles for his friends and family. He charges $60 per hour. Norman has a sole proprietorship unless he organizes his business as a formal business entity other than a sole proprietorship or shares his profits and losses with a co-owner. The sole proprietorship is popular, as it requires no official filing with the state to actually form the business. Norman, the mechanic, simply needs to offer to fix someone's car in exchange for money. In some states, state law will require the sole proprietor to obtain licenses and permits, depending upon the nature of the business. For example, restaurants often need licenses before they can serve food to the general public. Many states require a sales tax permit before a business can sell products and collect sales tax.

The sole proprietorship creates no additional level of taxation for the owner. The sole proprietorship's income is reported by the sole proprietor on their federal individual income tax form as well as their state income tax return if the state has an income tax. The income from the sole proprietor will be subject to 1) federal income tax, 2) Social Security tax, 3) Medicare tax, and, if applicable, 4) state income tax. A sole proprietor would also be responsible for employment taxes if the sole proprietorship has employees. Examples of employment taxes are Social Security tax, Medicare tax, federal unemployment tax, and state unemployment tax. Losses from a sole proprietorship may offset taxable income from other sources, such as wages from a job. The ability to use losses from the business to offset other sources of income is another advantage of the sole proprietorship.

Many business owners will decide against forming their business, or continuing to operate their business as a sole proprietorship because a sole proprietorship creates unlimited liability for its owner. The law views the business and its owner, the sole proprietor, as a single economic entity. If a sole proprietorship owns a delivery truck and the delivery truck's brakes malfunction, the sole proprietor will be legally responsible for any damages arising from an accident. The sole proprietor is also liable for any debt issued by the sole proprietorship. For example, Melanie starts a home remodeling business and borrows $60,000 from a local bank to pay for advertising and other start-up costs; Melanie is personally responsible for the repayment of the $60,000 loan. The exposure to liabilities, including lawsuits, often prompts business owners to form their business as another entity such as an LLC or a corporation. Some individuals still choose the sole proprietorship but try to minimize the risk of exposure to a lawsuit by obtaining liability insurance.

Partnerships

A **partnership** is a business entity formed by two or more persons who engage in a profit-seeking activity and share the profit and loss of such activity. A partnership that does not provide limited liability to any of its members is often referred to as a "**general partnership.**" Partners in a partnership can decide to share profits and losses equally or in unequal percentages as long as the IRS approves of such allocation. For example, Kerry and Kristin form K&K Partnership. Kristen is allocated 60% of all profit and loss. Kerry is allocated the other 40% of all profit and loss. Partnerships are often popular because partners believe the duties of operating a business will be shared equally. In addition, the partnership can presumably raise more funds than an individual can on his or her own operating as a sole proprietorship.

The definition of a partnership makes reference to "persons" and a person can be a human being or another business entity such as an LLC, a corporation, or a partnership. For example, Ryan could form a partnership with Orange Computer Corporation in which Ryan receives 75% of all profits and Orange Corporation receives 25%. A partnership can be formed through a formal process of drafting a partnership agreement or it can be formed informally by two persons merely engaging in business and sharing profits. For example, Lindsay and Erin decide to offer painting services to local property management companies. Lindsay and Erin charge $50 per hour for painting and they split all the profits equally. Lindsay and Erin never intended to form a partnership but did so inadvertently by sharing profits from a business activity.

The federal taxation of partnerships is governed by Subchapter K of the Internal Revenue Code. For states who impose an income tax, state law in regards to income tax generally follows the Internal Revenue Code. The partnership is viewed as a flow-through entity. A partnership does not pay income tax at the business-entity level. Each partner is allocated their share of profit and loss and reports it on their individual income tax return. Income from a partnership, in which a partner actively participates in the activities of the partnership, is subject to federal income tax as well as Social Security and Medicare taxes at the individual level. Losses from a partnership, in which a partner actively participates in the activities of the partnership, are allowed to offset income from other sources, such as wage income. Income and loss from a partnership in which a partner does not actively participate is subject to passive income and loss limitations.

Partners of a general partnership are jointly liable for the debts of the partnership. **Joint liability** means all partners share liability but any one partner can be required to pay the full amount of the debt. As a general rule, partners in a general partnership are also jointly liable for the torts committed by other partners in the ordinary course of business. Partnership assets are generally liquidated to satisfy a debt or liability claim by a third party before a partner is required to contribute personal assets to satisfy a liability. However, the fact that partners in a general partnership may be liable for the actions of another partner and may have to contribute personal assets to satisfy a debt or liability arising from a tort claim makes general partnerships somewhat risky.

Limited Partnerships

Limited partnerships are partnerships with one or more general partners and one or more limited partners. A **general partner** has unlimited liability for the liabilities of the partnership, including debts incurred by the partnership or torts committed by the partnership's activities. General partners usually are involved in the day-to-day affairs of the partnership and are actively involved in its business activities. A **limited partner** has liability that is limited to its investment in the partnership. Limited partners generally do not actively participate in the partnership. For example, assume Delilah and Sampson form the Stronghold Partnership. Sampson is a general partner and Delilah is a limited partner. Sampson and

- Joint liability
- Limited partnerships
- General partner
- Limited partner

- Limited
  liability limited
  partnership
- Corporation

Delilah both contribute $10,000 in cash to start the partnership and its business activities. Sampson can be liable in excess of his $10,000 investment but Delilah will not be liable in excess of her $10,000 investment. Assume the partnership secures an additional $80,000 loan from a bank in the name of the partnership. Stronghold partnership then defaults on its $80,000 loan. At most, Delilah can lose her $10,000 investment since she is a limited partner. Sampson may lose his $10,000 but could also be required to use personal assets to satisfy the rest of the liability since he is a general partner.

Limited Liability Limited Partnerships

Since a limited partnership provides for limited liability, a partnership must file the appropriate paperwork with its state of formation to achieve the status of "limited" in regards to the liabilities of limited partners. The same is true for a limited liability partnership. In states that recognize a **limited liability limited partnership**, all partners in the limited liability partnership receive limited liability protection. Creditors, such as banks as well as suppliers, will often refuse to contract with a limited liability partnership, as the credit they extend might exceed the assets of the partnership in which case, no general partner will exist to satisfy the balance of the obligation owed to the creditor or supplier.

Corporations

A corporation is a creature of state law. A **corporation** is a separate legal entity that provides limited liability to its owners who are called stockholders. Owners of a corporation are referred to as stockholders, as their ownership interest is evinced by ownership of stock in the company. A corporation's taxable income is assessed an income tax by the federal government as well as the state government if the state in which it derives taxable income has an income tax. Subchapter C of the Internal Revenue Code provides the rules regarding taxation of corporations so many in the business world refer to a corporation that faces double taxation as a "C Corporation." Stockholders share in profits by receiving dividends that are a return of profit by the company. Stockholders also realize a return on their investment if their stock holdings increase in value. A financial expert would say the primary goal of a corporation is maximizing shareholder wealth. Varying rates of federal income tax may apply to shareholders who receive a dividend or realize a gain by selling stock. The fact stockholders face a tax on distributed profits that were already taxed at the corporate level means the profit of a corporation is subject to double taxation, which is a disadvantage of the corporation as compared to a partnership or sole proprietorship.

A corporation is formed by filing articles of incorporation with a state agency. The corporation's founders will then also need to draft bylaws that govern the operation of the corporation. One of the major advantages of a corporation is its ability to issue stock certificates to investors in exchange for money. The shareholder can contribute services or other assets in exchange for an ownership interest. Corporations are the primary legal entity allowed to have their ownership interests traded on a public stock exchange such as the New York Stock Exchange (NYSE).

Stockholders generally elect a Board of Directors. The Board of Directors is often composed of outside individuals who help make top-level decisions such as when to pay a dividend to stockholders. The Board of Directors might also have the power to vote in favor of a merger with another corporation. The Board of Directors hires executives to manage the company. Sometimes executives may also sit on the Board of Directors, as their knowledge of the business and its affairs is beneficial to the Board. Executives often hire additional managers who will hire and supervise staff. The staff provide the labor that creates a good or service for customers.

Perpetual Real Estate Services, Inc. v. Michaelson Properties, Inc.
974 F.2d 545 (4th Cir. 1992)

The following are excerpts from the opinion of Judge Wilkinson of the United States Court of Appeals for the Fourth Circuit. (The case involved an appeal based upon a jury instruction in a lower court.)

In this case plaintiff has sought to pierce the corporate veil of its former business partner, Michaelson Properties, Inc. (MPI), and to hold MPI's sole shareholder, Aaron Michaelson, personally responsible for MPI's contractual liability.***

In August 1981, defendant Aaron Michaelson formed Michaelson Properties, Inc., for the purpose of entering into joint real estate ventures. MPI was incorporated under the laws of the state of Illinois with initial paid-in capital of $ 1,000. Michaelson was the president and sole shareholder. MPI subsequently entered into two joint ventures with Perpetual Real Estate Services, Inc. (PRES), the plaintiff in this case, involving the conversion of apartment buildings into condominiums. (One of these joint ventures was a partnership named the Arlington Apartment Associates, or AAA partnership.)***

During 1985 and 1986, the AAA partnership made various distributions of the profits from the condominium units. Prior to each distribution, the partners made the determination, as required by the partnership agreement, that they were leaving sufficient assets to permit the partnership to meet its anticipated expenses. Three distributions were made to PRES and MPI, totalling approximately $ 456,000 to each partner. MPI then authorized distributions of its profits to its sole shareholder, Aaron Michaelson.

In 1987, more than a year after the last of these distributions, several condominium purchasers filed suit against AAA, asserting breach of warranty claims in the amount of $ 5.5 million. Shortly before the case went to trial, counsel for AAA entered into settlement negotiations. The case was ultimately settled for $ 950,000. PRES paid the full amount on behalf of the partnership; MPI made no contribution toward the settlement since its profits had been distributed years earlier.

PRES then filed this diversity action against Michaelson and MPI. The complaint sought indemnity from MPI pursuant to the AAA partnership agreement and asserted that Michaelson had received unlawful distributions from MPI. PRES also asserted two theories for holding Michaelson personally responsible for MPI's debt.***

Virginia courts have long recognized the basic proposition that a corporation is a legal entity separate and distinct from its shareholders.*** A fundamental purpose of incorporation is to "enable a group of persons to limit their liability in a joint venture to the extent of their contributions to the capital stock."*** This concept of limited liability "supports a vital economic policy***, a policy on which "large undertakings are rested, vast enterprises are launched, and huge sums of capital attracted."***

• S corporation

Virginia courts have assiduously defended this "vital economic policy," lifting the veil of immunity only in "extraordinary" cases.*** Under Virginia law, plaintiff bears the burden of convincing the court to disregard the corporate form, and must first establish that "the corporate entity was the *alter ego,* alias, stooge, or dummy of the individuals sought to be charged personally."*** This element may be established by evidence that the defendant exercised "undue domination and control" over the corporation.***

The Supreme Court of Virginia has specifically held, however, that proof that some person "may dominate or control" the corporation, or "may treat it as a mere department, instrumentality, agency, etc." is not enough to pierce the veil.*** Hence, plaintiff must also establish "that the corporation was a device or sham used to disguise wrongs, obscure fraud, or conceal crime."***

The jury instruction in this case simply failed to communicate the essence of Virginia law in this area. Virginia adheres to a rigorous standard requiring proof that the defendant used the corporation to "disguise" some legal "wrong." This strict standard contrasts starkly with the rather soggy state in which the law was submitted to the jury, which was permitted to impose personal liability on Michaelson if it found that Michaelson dominated MPI and used MPI to perpetrate "an inJustice or fundamental unfairness." The fact that limited liability might yield results that seem "unfair" to jurors unfamiliar with the function of the corporate form cannot provide a basis for piercing the veil

Questions

1. What wrong was supposedly committed by Mr. Michaelson?
2. What does it mean to "pierce the corporate veil"?
3. Did the court believe piercing the corporate veil was appropriate in this case?

An **S corporation** is a corporation that was formed under state law like a C corporation but that makes an election under subchapter S of the Internal Revenue Code. The S corporation provides the same limited liability protection as a C corporation but is allowed flow-through tax treatment like a partnership. The shareholders are allocated profit and loss in proportion to their ownership of stock in the company, like partners in a partnership. The shareholders are responsible for recording their share of profit or loss on their individual tax return. As with partnerships, an S corporation's shareholders might face passive activity gain and loss limitations for income tax purposes if they do not actively participate in the day-to-day activities of the corporation. Unlike partnerships and LLC's, an S corporation's shareholders can be paid a salary, which allows the shareholders to reduce the amount of income that is subject to Social Security and Medicare taxes. For example, assume Melanie and Todd form a business named Fast Clean. If they have $100,000 of taxable income and form a general partnership sharing profits and losses at 50%, then they will both be subject to individual income tax as well as Social Security and Medicare tax on their $50,000 share of taxable income. If they form as an S corporation, they could each be paid a $20,000 salary, which would be subject to individual income tax as well as Social Security and Medicare tax. However, it will reduce the S corporation's taxable income to $60,000: $100,000 – $20,000 salary for Melanie – $20,000 salary for Todd. The remaining taxable income of $60,000 would be subject to only individual income tax and not Social Security and Medicare Tax. For this reason, S corporations are more popular for profitable business entities that have only a few shareholders.

Business Entity	Advantages	Disadvantages
Sole Proprietorship	1) Easy to form 2) Owner has total control 3) No double income taxation	1) Unlimited liability 2) Limited ability to raise capital
General Partnership	1) Easy to form 2) Partners can pool capital and share responsibility 3) No double income taxation 4) Ability to use partnership debt to increase the use of losses at the individual level subject to certain income tax limitations	1) Unlimited liability 2) Partners may face Social Security and Medicare taxes on all profits
Limited Partnership	1) Partners can pool capital and share responsibility 2) No double income taxation 3) Limited partners will enjoy limited liability 4) Ability to use partnership debt to increase the use of losses for tax purposes at the individual level subject to certain limitations	1) General partner still has unlimited liability 2) Partners may face Social Security and Medicare taxes on all profits 3) More complicated and expensive to form than other types of business entity forms, such as sole proprietorship or general partnership
Limited Liability Limited Partnership	1) Partners can pool capital and share responsibility 2) No double income taxation 3) Partners will enjoy limited liability 4) Ability to use partnership debt to increase the use of losses at the individual level subject to certain limitations	1) Third parties might refuse to extend credit to entity because of limited liability shield 2) More complicated and expensive to form than other types of business entity forms, such as sole proprietorship or general partnership
Limited Liability Company	1) Members can pool capital and share responsibility 2) No double income taxation 3) Members will enjoy limited liability 4) Ability to use LLC's debt to increase the use of losses at the individual level subject to at risk limitations	1) Third parties might refuse to extend credit to entity because of limited liability shield 2) Members may face Social Security and Medicare taxes on all profits 3) More complicated and expensive to form than other types of business entity forms, such as sole proprietorship or general partnership 4) State LLC law might not be as developed as corporate or partnership law

• Limited liability
company

Business Entity	Advantages	Disadvantages
C Corporation	1) Ability to raise capital by issuing stock certificates to investors 2) Stockholders will enjoy limited liability 3) Can be traded on a public exchange	1) Double taxation on profits in most cases 2) Corporate losses will not flow through to the stockholders' individual tax returns 3) More complicated and expensive to form than other types of business entity forms
S Corporation	1) Ability to raise capital by issuing stock certificates to investors 2) Stockholders will enjoy limited liability 3) Can convert to a C corporation 4) No double taxation and losses flow through to shareholders 5) Shareholders can reduce Social Security and Medicare Taxes by paying themselves a salary	1) Restrictions on ownership of shares 2) Restrictions on distributing company profits 3) More complicated and expensive to form than other business entities

As a general rule, an S corporation's shareholders cannot count the debt of the business entity for which they are personally liable as basis for allowing losses to be utilized on their individual income tax returns. For example, assume Melanie and Todd's Fast Clean business has $100,000 in taxable losses during year 1. Todd and Melanie each contributed $10,000 in cash to start the business. They also borrowed $80,000 from a local bank. They are both personally responsible for the $80,000 debt. They are equal owners. If Fast Clean is a general partnership, the $50,000 loss allocated to each partner could be shown as a deduction on their personal tax return because they both had a basis of $50,000 ($10,000 investment of cash + $40,000 half share of debt). If Fast Clean was an S corporation, each shareholder could deduct only $10,000 of the $50,000 allocated loss because their share of debt cannot be considered as basis in their ownership interest.

The S corporation faces several limiting requirements, which if not met under the Internal Revenue Code, would cause the S corporation to lose its flow-through taxation treatment. An S corporation cannot have different classes of common stock that provide different participation rates for distributions. In addition, the S corporation cannot have more than 100 shareholders. Partnerships, corporations, and non-resident aliens cannot be shareholders in an S corporation.

Limited Liability Companies

A **limited liability company** (hereinafter "LLC") is a separate legal entity that provides limited liability protection to its owners like a corporation while preserving pass-through taxation similar to that of a partnership. For this reason, real estate investments that create large losses are generally owned in an LLC, which follows the tax treatment of a partnership. The LLC provides flow-through tax treatment and allows the owners to increase their basis by their share of debt.

Owners of an LLC are referred to as "members" instead of stockholders or partners. As with a partnership, profits and losses may be allocated to the members in any proportion to which the members agree as long as such allocation is respected for tax purposes. As with partnerships, an LLC's members might face passive activity gain and loss limitations for income tax purposes if they do not actively participate in the day-to-day activities of the LLC. Fortunately, members of an LLC are usually able to participate in the day-to-day affairs of the company with more flexibility in regards to such participation as compared to partners in limited liability limited partnership. LLC's also provide favorable flow-through taxation; however, as with a partnership, the member's allocation of profit is generally subject to Social Security and Medicare taxes.

A **non-profit** or **not-for-profit** business entity is a business entity that does not intend to make a profit, as it spends its revenues and other sources of income on its designated programs. Special state law provisions and Internal Revenue Code provisions apply to a non-profit. An LLC, a corporation or a partnership can elect to be taxed as a non-profit by the IRS. For the most part a non-profit will not be subject to income tax.

A **professional service corporation** is a corporation form required by state law for individuals such as doctors, lawyers, and accountants. The states require the use of a professional service corporation as opposed to a regular C corporation so the owners of the corporation cannot totally shield themselves from torts claims such as negligence. Professional limited liability companies and professional limited liability partnerships are offered as alternatives to professional corporations in many states.

Franchise is a term used to describe a contract that allows one business entity to enjoy benefits such as advertising, access to products, and use of trademarks and trade names. A business entity might be referred to as a "franchise," but the label merely describes the contractual benefits it enjoys and not the type of business entity that was actually formed. Due to the fact franchise agreements can sometimes be economically burdensome on the franchisee, some states have developed specific laws pertaining to franchise contracts.

As an example of a franchise arrangement, assume Tubby's is a famous fast food restaurant. Tubby's Corporation is a publicly traded corporation (its common stock is traded on the NYSE). Marco wants to start a Tubby's restaurant in his hometown. Marco forms an LLC called Marco's Fast Food LLC. His LLC then enters into a franchise contract with Tubby's. His LLC Marco's Fast Food will be considered a *franchisee* and Tubby's Corporation will be considered a *franchisor*. Marco is allowed to use the Tubby's name for his restaurant. He can also use the product names developed and trademarked by Tubby's. However, Marco has to pay 10% of all his profits to the Tubby's Corporation. In addition, he must buy his food from Tubby's Corporation. Finally, he must decorate his store and run his restaurant in compliance with standards set by Tubby's Corporation.

Independent Contractor vs. Employee

An **employee** is defined as one who provides services for another, generally on a continuing basis, under the direction of the hiring person, and subject to the control of the hiring person. An independent contractor is not an employee because an **independent contractor** does not work under the direct control or supervision of the hiring person but is instead hired to perform a task or complete a project which the independent contractor completes independently.

- Non-profit or Not-for-profit
- Professional service corporation
- Franchise
- Employee
- Independent contractor

- Vicarious liability
- Respondeat superior

Whether an individual is an employee or an independent contractor creates different legal responsibilities for the person contracting with the individual. An employee is provided numerous benefits under federal law such as the right to join a company's health insurance program, the right to be compensated equally with members of the opposite sex, and the ability to participate in retirement programs. The employee also creates employment taxes that the employer must pay such as Social Security, Medicare, federal unemployment, and state unemployment. Equal amounts of Social Security and Medicare taxes are due from an employee and the employer is responsible for deducting this amount from the employee's paycheck along with federal income tax, state income tax, and other elective deductions such as union dues. In contrast, an independent contractor is generally responsible for their own health insurance, retirement, Social Security, Medicare, and income tax payments. The business that employs and independent contractor generally pays them a lump sum from which they are generally not required to withhold any payments. Therefore, many businesses view independent contractors as less expensive labor providers.

The courts have distinguished between employees and independent contractors by considering several factors, none of which by itself determines the classification of a worker as an employee or independent contractor. The following is the list of the most common factors used by the courts and the Internal Revenue Service.

1. The amount of control the contracting company exercises over the individual worker,
2. The classification given the individual worker by contracts or other business agreements
3. The length of the relationship,
4. Whether the individual worker supplies their own tools or uses the tools of the contracting company,
5. Whether the individual worker is paid by the hour or by completed job,
6. Whether the individual worker is engaged in a distinct trade separate from the contracting company,
7. Whether the individual worker incurs unreimbursed expenses, and
8. Whether the individual worker serves other clients.

Liability for Employee's Actions

Under the concept of vicarious liability, an employer is liable for the actions of an employee while the employee is acting within the scope of their employment. **Vicarious liability** means a court may impose liability on an individual who did not commit the act that caused injury but who has a special relationship with the person who did commit the act that caused injury. For example, some states impose liability on the owner of a car that is involved in an accident even if the owner was not the person driving the car. Employers are subject to vicarious liability on the part of their employees because of the employment relationship that exists between employees and employers. The common law doctrine of **respondeat superior** held masters strictly liable for the actions of their servants. Respondeat superior is applied to hold employers vicariously liable for the actions of their employees when the employees are acting within the scope of their employment. Therefore, the first question is whether an individual worker is an employee or an independent contractor. The second question is whether or not the act resulting in damages was within the scope of employment.

Since the analysis for determining whether an individual worker is an employee or an independent contractor was discussed previously, the analysis of the scope of employment is considered next. First, an employer becomes liable for an employee's actions if they authorize an employee to do an action. For example, Kenny works for Fast Construction Inc. Kenny's boss tells him to remove a section of sidewalk using a jackhammer. Kenny does this but in the process damages a passing car with flying debris. Fast Construction Inc. is liable for Kenny's actions, as he was acting within the scope of his employment. Second, an employer may also be liable for actions committed by an employee even if the employee was not expressly ordered to do so. Courts will often ask

1. Whether the action was one the employee was hired to do,
2. Whether the action took place at the place of employment and during work hours,
3. Whether the action benefited the employer,
4. Whether the employer furnished an instrumentality used to commit the act (for example, an employer-owned car), and
5. Whether the employer had reason to know the employee might commit the act if an intentional act occurred.

State law varies on the subject of what constitutes an act within the scope of employment. However, the above items are common factors evaluated by courts and will be used for the purposes of this chapter.

As an example, assume Mark is an employee at a grocery store. He is having a bad day and a customer asks him for help finding a can of soup. Mark tells the customer, "Any jerk with half a brain could find a can of soup in this store." The customer becomes angry and threatens to report Mark to the store supervisor. Mark then proceeds to punch the customer, breaking the customer's nose. If the customer sues the grocery store under the theory of respondeat superior, the grocery store may claim Mark was not ordered to do this action. Mark was in the store during normal business hours. However, hitting customers is not part of the job duties he was hired to perform, the action did not promote the interest of the grocery store, and the store had no reason to know Mark could act in this way. Therefore, the store would more than likely not be responsible for the actions of Mark.

Courts tend to draw a line between minor deviations from normal employment activities and serious deviations from normal employment activities when deciding whether or not an employer is to be liable for the actions of an employee based upon whether the act was in the normal course of employment. For example, assume Jordan drives a company car to make sales calls. Jordan has been expressly told not to use her personal car for company purposes. Jordan stops at a gas station to buy a soft drink. While leaving the store, she accidentally damages the car of another customer. Jordan's action would probably be considered a minor deviation from her normal job duties and her employer would be liable for the accident. If Jordan had instead decided to take the company car on a summer vacation and was involved in an accident while in another state, her employer would not be liable because this would be considered a major deviation from her normal job duties.

To summarize, an employer is liable for the actions of an employee when such action occurs within the scope of their employment. A minor deviation from normal employment activities is not considered substantial enough to prohibit the employer from being held liable for its employee's actions. A substantial deviation from normal employment activities that was not ordered by an employer would negate (eliminate) liability on the part of the employer.

Under the common law, employees could be held liable for negligence even if the act was committed within the scope of their employment. This means an employee creates liability for themselves as well as their employee through the concept of vicarious liability. However, some states have passed statutes declaring certain employees not be held personally liable for actions that were negligent or reckless as long as the action was within the scope of their employment. However, even in states that protect employees from claims of negligence when acting within the scope of their employment, intentional torts committed by an employee will almost always subject the employee to liability unless the action was ordered to be committed by the employer. A common example of an employee protected by state law from personal liability would be a government employee.

Liability for an Independent Contractor's Actions

As a general rule an organization or individual hiring an independent contractor is not liable for torts committed by the independent contractor because the independent contractor is not subject to the control of the hiring individual or business. There are exceptions to this rule. First, if the activity to be performed by the independent contractor is inherently dangerous, the hiring individual or business will be responsible. For example, Fast Dig Mining Company hires an independent contractor to use dynamite to blast a large rock from a mine shaft. This activity is inherently dangerous and a court would likely hold Fast Dig Mining Company responsible for any damages resulting from the blasting because the activity is dangerous and the company should be responsible for any damages.

Second, an individual or business hiring an independent contractor can be liable for the actions of an independent contractor when the independent contractor is performing a non-delegable duty of the hiring individual. For example, Malachi is an attorney hired by Beth to sue her former employer. Malachi knows the statute of limitations has almost run so he decides to hire a delivery agency to deliver the necessary documents to the courthouse. The delivery agency misplaces the documents and upon finding them delivers the documents after the statute of limitations has run. The delivery of the documents may be viewed as a non-delegable duty by a court and Beth may be allowed to sue Malachi for missing the deadline even though Malachi hired an independent contractor.

Third, an individual or business can be liable for the actions of an independent contractor if the individual or business was negligent in hiring, supervising, or instructing the independent contractor. For example, Harlan hires Hunter to cut down some trees on his property. Hunter is an independent contractor. Harlan mistakenly believes trees owned by Jerry are actually on Harlan's property. At Harlan's instruction, Hunter cuts down the trees belonging to Jerry. Harlan is liable to Jerry because he was at fault for giving instructions to Hunter on which trees to cut down.

Liability for an Agent's Actions

Agency Law

Principals are liable for certain actions undertaken by agents. An employee is generally considered an agent under state law. However, state law may differ in regards to actions taken by an agent who is an employee. An independent contractor is generally not considered an agent under the common law because they are not subject to the control of the hiring individual or business. Agents who are not typically labeled as either independent contractors or employees but are still agents include partners in a partnership, insurance agents, real estate agents, and purchasing agents.

To have an agency relationship a principal and an agent must have a relationship in which the principal authorizes the agent to act on behalf of the principal and the agent must consent to act on behalf of the principal and subject to the control of the principal. A **principal** is the one on whose behalf an agent acts. An **agent** is the one who agrees to act on behalf of a principal and subject to the control of the principal. There are several important aspects of the agency relationship.

1. The principal must create the power for the agent to act on his behalf. This power can be created expressly or in another manner such as by an operation of law.
2. The agent must consent to the agency relationship and agree to act on the behalf of the principal and under the control of the principal. For example, Cree is a famous football player. He requests that Jerry Mac represent him as his agent in contract negotiations with a professional football team. Cree is the principal and Jerry is his agent if Jerry agrees. Since Cree's contract will determine his compensation and benefits, Cree may limit the power Jerry has in negotiating with the football team. For example, Cree might inform Jerry that Jerry cannot sign a contract on his behalf but instead can only negotiate on his behalf. Jerry must act within Cree's control.

An agency relationship is often coupled with a contractual relationship but an agency relationship does not have to create a contractual relationship. A **gratuitous agency relationship** is one in which the agent is not compensated by the principal. Under contract law, a contract would not normally exist in the case of a gratuitous agency relationship because no consideration was received by the agent in exchange for their promise to work as an agent. For example, Peter wants to win the affection of Kalli. He offers to move her furniture from her old apartment to her new apartment. He is a gratuitous agent if he acts within her control and on her behalf.

There are different types of agents under the law. For example, a **general agent** is an agent who has the authority to provide all the business services a principal would need for a given purpose or at a given location. A **special agent** is an agent who is authorized by the

- Principal
- Agent
- Gratuitous agency relationship
- General agent
- Special agent

principal to perform a specific undertaking. For example, Mitchell is the managing employee of Data Corporation. Martha is the owner. She has authorized Mitchell to manage the affairs of the business, including all meetings with both suppliers and customers. Mitchell also manages the finances of the company. Mitchell is a general agent. Now consider Cassie. She is hired by Danielle to help sell Danielle's farmland. Since there is only one transaction, she is considered a special agent.

A **subagent** is an agent of an agent authorized by the principal to perform acts as part of the agency agreement. For example, Phillip is hired by Cynthia to collect outstanding balances owed to her by customers. Phillip is not an attorney and cannot file a lawsuit against customers who do not pay. Therefore, he requests that Heather be allowed to work as his subagent, as she is licensed to practice law. Cynthia agrees and authorizes Phillip to employ Heather as a subagent.

Types of Agencies

An **express agency** is an agency that is formed either through a written agreement or an oral agreement. As an example, Harrison hires Melody to negotiate the purchase of a piece of real estate. Melody and Harrison sign a written contract that details the duties of each party.

An **implied agency** arises from facts and circumstances that result in the parties believing an agency has been formed. For example, Stephanie is chasing her dog, which runs onto Mark's lawn. Mark immediately begins to help Stephanie chase her dog. Mark has implied his consent to act on Stephanie's behalf. Stephanie, by her actions, has authorized Mark to act on her behalf and take control of her dog.

An **agency by ratification** is formed when an agent acts without authority from a principal but the principal ratifies the action afterwards. For example, Rodney returns home from college to find his mom Ellen has sold his prized baseball card collection. Rodney is very angry and tells his mother she had no right to act as his agent. Ellen then informs Rodney as to the price the buyer has agreed to pay and Rodney is impressed. He ratifies her as his agent agrees to allow her to deliver the baseball card collection to the seller as his agent.

An **agency by estoppel** occurs when a principal acts in a manner that leads a third party to reasonably believe an agency relationship exists. The law will estop a principal from denying an agency relationship exists when the principal has acted in a manner as to create the appearance of an agency. For example, Horace is a successful businessman. He volunteers to participate in a mentorship program. He is paired with Silva. Silva is a very bright and promising young professional. Horace takes Silva to meet each one of his customers. While meeting with his customers, Horace makes statements such as, "Silva is the brightest young professional I know. I hope she will take over my business someday." He makes other statements of praise and his customers start to believe Silva is in his employ and has authority to act as his agent. An agency by estoppel may have been created by Horace.

Types of Agency Authority

If an agent is acting within the scope of their authority, they will create liability for the principal. **Express authority** is authority that was given in written or verbal form. For example, Suzie asks Stan to drive her car. Stan agrees. Stan has the express authority to drive Suzie's car. The **equal dignity rule** holds that if an agent will be entering into contracts on behalf of the principal, which must be in writing under the Statute of Frauds, the agent's authority as granted by the principal must be in writing.

Implied authority arises from 1) express authority or 2) custom. For example, Suzie asks Stan to wash her car at the local carwash and return it to her by 5 PM. Stan has express authority to wash Suzie's car but has implied authority to drive her car to the carwash and back. As another example, Terri is hired by Martin to help Martin purchase a home. Terri has the express authority, under a written contract with Martin, to call prospective sellers and arrange showings. She also has the express authority to submit offers that Martin wishes to make. Upon acceptance of an offer, it may be customary for an agent such as Terri to schedule inspections even though her contract with Martin is silent on the issue of arranging inspections. The arrangement of such inspections might have arisen from implied authority. Implied authority and express authority are often referred to as **actual authority** since the principal actually gives authority to the agent before the agent acts on his behalf.

Authority by ratification occurs when a principal grants authority after the agent has acted on her behalf without authority. The principal must have all the material facts in order to grant authority by ratification. For example, Tommy is Mandy's purchasing agent. He buys goods that Mandy sells in her grocery business. One day Tommy is picking up meat from a supplier when the supplier notices Tommy has a fifty-pound bag of salt in his truck. The supplier asks Tommy if he can buy it. Tommy says its Mandy's bag of salt but he does not see why it would hurt. The supplier hands Tommy a check for the salt. Tommy delivers the check to Mandy. Mandy tells Tommy he does not have authority to sell her goods but she will ratify his action this one time and accept the check.

Emergency agency powers arise when an emergency situation arises and an agent must act without actual authority. For example, Marissa works at a hotel. She had been expressly told her job duties do not involve contacting public officials on the behalf of the hotel. Her contract even specifically forbids the contacting of public officials. One night a guest becomes ill and Marissa calls 911. An ambulance is dispatched to the hotel. The guest refuses assistance. The county hospital now wishes to bill the hotel for the ambulance service. The hotel refuses to pay the bill based upon the fact Marissa did not have the authority to contact public officials. A judge may declare Marissa had an emergency power in the situation. The court may feel public policy will be well served by not discouraging employees from calling for an ambulance. If that is the case, then the hotel might be required to pay for the ambulance services.

Apparent authority exists when a principal leads a third party to reasonably believe an agent possesses authority to perform an action or actions on behalf of the principal. As an example, Toyin works for Mad Max Construction Company. One day a supplier delivers a large shipment of lumber to the job site where Toyin is working. Toyin's boss yells to the truck driver, "Toyin can sign, he is second in command on this job." Later that day

- Equal dignity rule
- Implied authority
- Actual authority
- Authority by ratification
- Emergency agency powers
- Apparent authority

Toyin stops at the supplier's main office and orders 10,000 pounds of bricks. The supplier believes Toyin has this authority based on the representations of his boss at the job site. If the construction company later claims they do not want the bricks, a court could say the supplier held a reasonable belief Toyin had the authority to make this order.

Liability for the Acts of Agents

If a court finds 1) an agency relationship existed and 2) the agent was exercising some form of authority as discussed above, the agent will create liability for the principal in regards to a third party. Whether or not an agent is liable to a third party depends upon the type of action taken by the agent.

Liability for Contracts

As a general rule, a principal is bound by a contract entered into by an agent if the agent is exercising authority granted to her by the principal. The principal will then be liable to a third party if the contract is breached. The agent too may be liable to a third party if the contract is breached if the agent is acting on behalf of an undisclosed principal. An **undisclosed principal** is one whom the agent does not make known to a third party that results in the third party believing they are contracting with the agent. The agent is subject to liability for breach of contract if they are representing an undisclosed principal and the principal breaches the contract. A **partially disclosed principal** is one whom the agent does not disclose the identity of to a third party but does inform the third party the agent is acting on behalf of a principal. If an agent represents a partially disclosed principal, state law differs from state to state on whether or not the agent may be held liable for breach of contract on the part of the principal. A **fully disclosed principal** is one whom an agent discloses the existence and identity of to a third party. A fully disclosed principal alleviates the agent from liability from third parties in regards to contractual breach.

As an example, assume Hailey is interested in buying a piece of property next to her business.

1. Assume the owner of the land dislikes Hailey because her customers almost always park on his land. Hailey hires her friend Mark to approach the seller as her agent. She tells Mark not to disclose the fact he is working on behalf of a principal. Mark follows her instructions and signs a purchase contract with the seller. Hailey is an undisclosed principal in this situation and Mark would be liable to the seller for contractual breach if Hailey changes her mind and decides not to purchase the land.
2. Now assume the same facts except the seller asks Mark if he will use the land or whether he is actually acting on behalf of a principal. Mark cannot lie and says, "I am acting on behalf of a principal but I can't disclose their name." The seller agrees to sign the purchase contract. Hailey is now a partially disclosed principal and may be liable for breach of contract if Hailey refuses to buy the property. Mark's liability will depend on the applicable state law.

3. Now assume the same facts but when the seller asks Mark if he is acting on behalf of a principal, Mark says he is acting on behalf of a principal. The seller refuses to sell the land unless he discloses the name of the principal. Mark does and the seller raises the price but the purchase price is still within the price range Hailey agreed to pay, so Mark signs the contract. Hailey is now a disclosed principal and, as a general rule, Mark will not be subject to liability for breach of contract by Hailey if she refuses to purchase the land.

Liability for Negligence

A principal is liable for negligence resulting from their own acts. For example, Dan hires an agent to deliver products for his business on Saturdays. Dan provides the agent a truck to use. The truck has faulty brakes because of negligence by Dan. Dan would be liable to third parties for any damages caused by his negligence in maintaining the truck. An agent is subject to liability for their own negligence. For example, Dan's delivery agent would be responsible for damages resulting from causing an accident while speeding in the delivery truck.

Liability for Intentional Torts

A principal is liable for intentional torts he commits himself or orders an agent to commit. The agent will also be liable for intentional torts that they commit. For example, Jimmy hires Buff to be a bouncer at his bar. Jimmy orders Buff to strike an unruly customer in the jaw. Buff does so. Since Buff was acting for Jimmy as his agent, Jimmy may be held liable for battery. Buff will also likely be liable to the customer for his intentional act.

A principal might also be subject to liability if the principal knew or should have known the agent may commit an intentional tort even if the principal did not order such action. For example, assume Jimmy hired Buff knowing Buff has a history of violence. One day Buff pushes a customer who falls and breaks an arm. Jimmy may be liable to the customer, as Jimmy had been aware of the potential for Buff to act in this manner. Finally, it is important to note the principal is not liable for intentional torts that an agent commits if the intentional tort was not ordered by the principal, was not foreseeable, and did not arise out of the context of the normal course of the agency.

Liability for Crimes

A principal is responsible for crimes that they commit. A principal may also be liable for crimes of an agent if the principal ordered the agent to commit the crime, had knowledge the agent was likely to commit the crime, or if state law imposes criminal liability on the principal. For example, assume state law requires annual reports for corporations be filed with the Secretary of State. State law might impose criminal liability on a company for false annual reports filed by an executive of such company. Finally, agents are criminally liable for any acts that they commit unless the agent has a defense against criminal liability.

Termination of Agency Relationship

An agency may terminate in a variety of ways. The following is a list of ways in which an agency may terminate.

1. <u>By agreement</u>. The principal and agent mutually decide to terminate their agency relationship.
2. <u>By agent's resignation</u>. An agent may terminate an agency relationship by informing the principal of their resignation or taking action that notifies the principal the agency relationship has been terminated.
3. <u>By principal's action</u>. A principal may terminate the agency relationship by notifying the agent of their desire to terminate the relationship or by conduct that notifies the agent of the termination.
4. <u>Completion of purpose</u>. An agency may have been created to achieve a specific purpose such as the purchase of a rare coin collection. Once the purpose has been achieved, the agency terminates.
5. <u>Predefined event occurs</u>. An agency may terminate once an agreed-upon event takes place. For example, an agency agreement may state the agency is to last one year. Once one year has lapsed the agency terminates. In addition, the agency agreement may state an agent's ability to solicit purchases for a home will terminate if the seller experiences a change in employment.
6. <u>Death or incapacitation of party</u>. If either the principal or agent dies or becomes incapacitated, then the agency terminates. For example, an owner of a business hires an agent to sell his business. Before any offers are accepted, the seller of the business becomes mentally incapacitated. The agency is terminated upon the occurrence of this event.
7. <u>Impossibility or frustration of purpose</u>. An agency may terminate once it becomes impossible for the purpose of the agency relationship to be achieved or if a change in events frustrates the purpose of the relationship. For example, assume Dexter hires Melissa to purchase an industrial-sized oven for Dexter's new restaurant business. Melissa is then informed Dexter did not receive a license from his city to operate a restaurant. Depending upon their agreement, most courts would state the agency relationship was terminated when Melissa had notice Dexter would not be opening a restaurant.
8. <u>Bankruptcy</u>. Bankruptcy of a principal will terminate the agency relationship. The bankruptcy of an agent may terminate an agency relationship as well in certain circumstances if the agent's financial situation is of importance to the agency. For example, Sally hires Nathaniel to collect rent from tenants who occupy her building. Nathaniel's ability to pay his creditors may become an issue, as he is in control of Sally's money.

Whether or not an agency is terminated is of great importance to both the principal and the agent. Once the agency relationship is terminated, neither party will normally owe any further duties toward the other. However, the termination of an agency relationship also ends the principal's liability for actions of the agent. One major exception to this general rule is where an agent continues to act on behalf of the principal, exercising apparent authority. For example, Charlie hires Erika to help him sells copies of the computer software he developed. After Erika demands more compensation, Charlie becomes angry and terminates their agency relationship. In an effort to win back Charlie's approval, Erika contacts customers who have purchased the software in the past and offers them additional copies at a reduced price. Erika may be exercising apparent authority and Charlie may be bound by her actions. If he is going to terminate the relationship, he would do well to inform his customers of the termination.

• Fiduciary duty

Rights and Duties

Duties of Agents

The agency relationship imposes a fiduciary duty upon the agent. A **fiduciary duty** is a duty that requires one party act in the best interest of another party. The agent must act in the best interest of the principal and put the principal's interest before their own. The following duties arise from this fiduciary relationship. They can be categorized into duties of loyalty and duties of performance.

1. Duty of Loyalty. The agent must be loyal to his principal. The agent cannot represent two principals if the principals are engaged in competition. The agent cannot engage in self-dealing with the principal. For example, Monica knows her employer needs large quantities of soy to make their products. Monica cannot start her own corporation and buy the needed soy from herself as an agent of her employer.
2. Duty of Notification. The agent must notify the principal of matters important to the principal. For example, Harry manages a dairy cow farm for Eleanor. One day Harry notices a rising river is about to start flooding the pasture where the cows graze. Harry must notify Eleanor of the potential for the flood.
3. Duty of Care. An agent must exercise reasonable care when representing the principal. For example, an agent operating a forklift at the factory of a principal must not drive the machinery in a negligent fashion.
4. Duty to Abide by Orders. An agent has the duty of abiding by a principal's instructions. Even if an agent thinks she knows a better way of accomplishing a task, she must follow the directions of the principal.

Diamond v. Oreamuno, et al.
248 N.E.2d 910 (1969)

The following are excerpts from a New York Court of Appeals opinion by Judge Fuld.

Upon this appeal from an order denying a motion to dismiss the complaint as insufficient on its face, the question presented—one of first impression in this court—is whether officers and directors may be held accountable to their corporation for gains realized by them from transactions in the company's stock as a result of their use of material inside information.

The complaint was filed by a shareholder of Management Assistance, Inc. (MAI) asserting a derivative action against a number of its officers and directors to compel an accounting for profits allegedly acquired as a result of a breach of fiduciary duty. It charges that two of the defendants—Oreamuno, chairman of the board of directors, and Gonzalez, its president—had used inside information, acquired by them solely by virtue of their positions, in order to reap large personal profits from the sale of MAI shares and that these profits rightfully belong to the corporation. Other officers and directors were joined as defendants on the ground that they acquiesced in or ratified the assertedly wrongful transactions.***

This information, although earlier known to the defendants, was not made public until October of 1966. Prior to the release of the information, however, Oreamuno and Gonzalez sold off a total of 56,500 shares of their MAI stock at the then current market price of $28 a share. After the information concerning the drop in earnings was made available to the public, the value of a share of MAI stock immediately fell from the $28 realized by the defendants to $11. Thus, the plaintiff alleges, by taking advantage of their privileged position and their access to confidential information, Oreamuno and Gonzalez were able to realize $800,000 more for their securities than they would have had this inside information not been available to them.***

Just as a trustee has no right to retain for himself the profits yielded by property placed in his possession but must account to his beneficiaries, a corporate fiduciary, who is entrusted with potentially valuable information, may not appropriate that asset for his own use even though, in so doing, he causes no injury to the corporation. The primary concern, in a case such as this, is not to determine whether the corporation has been damaged but to decide, as between the corporation and the defendants, who has a higher claim to the proceeds derived from the exploitation of the information. In our opinion, there can be no justification for permitting officers and directors, such as the defendants, to retain for themselves profits which, it is alleged, they derived solely from exploiting information gained by virtue of their inside position as corporate officials.***

The sale of shares by the defendants for the reasons charged was not merely a wise investment decision which any prudent investor might have made. Rather, they were assertedly able in this case to profit solely because they had information which was not available to anyone else—including the other shareholders whose interests they, as corporate fiduciaries, were bound to protect.*** Restatement, 2d, Agency § 388, comment C:

> "An agent who acquires confidential information in the course of his employment or in violation of his duties has a duty*** to account for any profits made by the use of such information, although this does not harm the principal.*** So, if [a corporate officer] has 'inside' information that the corporation is about to purchase or sell securities, or to declare or to pass a dividend, profits made by him in stock transactions undertaken because of his knowledge are held in constructive trust for the principal."***

In the present case, the defendants may be able to avoid liability to the corporation under section 16(b) of the Federal law since they had held the MAI shares for more than six months prior to the sales. Nevertheless, the alleged use of the inside information to dispose of their stock at a price considerably higher than its known value constituted the same sort of "abuse of a fiduciary relationship" as is condemned by the Federal law. Sitting as we are in this case as a court of equity, we should not hesitate to permit an action to prevent any unjust enrichment realized by the defendants from their allegedly wrongful act.

• Indemnification

Questions

1. What actions had the employees taken that were alleged to be illegal?
2. Who was the plaintiff in this lawsuit and what gave the person the standing to sue?
3. What duty was breached by the agents in this case?
4. What harm might have been done to the company by the actions of these employees?
5. Is it ever permissible for an agent to put their own interests before the interests of a principal?

Duties of Principals

The duties of principals toward agents include:

- Cooperation. The principal cannot interfere with the agent's completion of required duties. For example, Clint hires Jessica to be his agent in negotiations between Clint's company and its employees. On at least five occasions, Jessica has reached an agreement with the employees that Clint said he would accept and each time Clint has refused to consider the agreement. Clint is not cooperating with Jessica.
- Reimbursement. The principal must provide reimbursement for expenses incurred by the agent on behalf of the principal. In addition, the agent may seek reimbursement for liabilities incurred because of tortious or unlawful acts by the principal. For example, if a principal breaches a contract when the principal was undisclosed, the agent may be liable to the third party. The agent may sue the principal for reimbursement. The act of seeking reimbursement arising from a legal liability is referred to as **indemnification**.

Questions

1. What is the definition of a sole proprietorship and is the owner of a sole proprietorship subject to unlimited liability and double taxation?
2. What is the definition of a partnership and is the partner in a partnership subject to unlimited liability and double taxation?
3. What is the definition of a limited partnership and is the limited partner in a partnership subject to unlimited liability and double taxation? What about a general partner?
4. What is the definition of a corporation and is the shareholder in a corporation subject to unlimited liability and double taxation?
5. What is the definition of an S corporation and is the shareholder in an S corporation subject to unlimited liability and double taxation?
6. What is the definition of an LLC and is a member of an LLC subject to unlimited liability and double taxation?
7. Can a not-for-profit be formed as an LLC?
8. What is a franchise agreement and what are its advantages and disadvantages?
9. How does a court determine whether a person is an employee or an independent contractor?
10. What is the definition of vicarious liability and respondeat superior?
11. When is an employer not responsible for torts committed by an employee?
12. Is a company responsible for torts committed by an independent contractor?
13. What are the required elements to form an agency relationship?
14. How is a general agent different from a special agent?
15. How is an express agency different from an implied agency?
16. How is an agency by ratification different from an agency by estoppel?
17. Can express authority give rise to implied authority?
18. How is authority by ratification different from apparent authority?
19. In regards to disclosed principals, partially disclosed principals, and undisclosed principals, when does a principal have contractual liability and when does an agent have contractual liability?
20. When is a principal liable for the intentional torts committed by an agent?
21. When is a principal liable for the negligence committed by an agent?
22. When is a principal liable for crimes committed by an agent?
23. In what ways might an agency terminate other than when the parties agree to terminate the agency relationship?
24. How might an agent still create liability for a principal even after the agency has been terminated?
25. What is a fiduciary duty and does an agent owe a fiduciary duty toward the principal?
26. What duties of performance does an agent owe a principal?
27. What duties does a principal owe toward an agent?

Critical-Thinking Questions

28. It is it ethical for business owners to use the corporate shield to limit the amount of damages they might owe a plaintiff for damages caused by the corporation's tortious activities?

29. Once the state of Wyoming offered the LLC as a form of business entity, most states quickly followed suit. Why would they do this if it meant losing state income tax revenue?

30. Why would the law hold an employer liable for the negligence of an employee who was acting within the scope of their employment?

31. Why is a principal held liable for the actions of an agent acting with apparent authority if the agent knows the agency relationship has terminated?

32. Why can't an agent work for competing principals? What if the principals agree in writing to allow the agent to represent them even though they are competitors?

Essay Questions

1. Loretta has started a veterinary business. She has numerous clients. She also has two employees. Loretta is considering partnering with Dan who also is a veterinarian. What type of business entity should Loretta and Dan form?

2. Kyle and Penelope want to borrow money to purchase commercial rental real estate. The business will have a positive cash flow but will create a taxable loss. What business entity should Kyle and Penelope utilize?

3. Rachelle was hired by Quick Loan Corporation to process mortgage applications. Rachelle is paid a certain amount for each application processed. Rachelle has been working for the company for two years. She has quarterly reviews provided by the same supervisor. Rachelle brings her own computer to use. Is Rachelle an employee or an independent contractor?

4. Kevin has his own plumbing business. He has been working for Large Manufacturing Company for two years. Kevin spends about three hours each day working on the plumbing of Large Manufacturing Company. Kevin spends the rest of the day working for other clients. Kevin bills Large Manufacturing by the hour for work performed. Kevin has his own tools. Is Kevin an employee or an independent contractor?

5. Lawrence is hired by Big Construction Company to lay a cement floor for a new building for Office Square Company. Big Construction Company directs Lawrence to lay the cement at the thickness of three inches. It turns out that thickness is not thick enough. Office Square Company suffers high economic damage from the floor being only three inches thick. Who is liable to Office Square? Big Construction Company? Lawrence? Both?

6. Marissa hires Ashley to be her real estate agent. Marissa is selling her house. Ashley asks Marissa whether or not the house has ever had issues with flooding. Marissa says once but it was because the gutters were plugged with leaves. Ashley says, "We should just say the house has had no issues with flooding because that problem was fixed when you cleaned the gutters." Tom is interested in buying the house. He asks Ashley

whether the house has had water problems. Ashley claims it has not. Tom buys the house from Marissa and has issues with flooding. He finds out from a neighbor that the house had flooding issues when Marissa lived in it. Whom can Tom sue for the tort of misrepresentation?

7. Dale is an employee of Fast Sales Incorporated. Dale sells knives as a door-to-door salesman. Dale has had a history of making inappropriate comments to female customers. Dale has been warned not to make such comments again. One day Dale makes a very inappropriate comment to Morgan at her home while trying to sell her a set of knives. Is Fast Sales Incorporated liable to Morgan for Dale's actions?

8. Richard has a history of drinking too much alcohol. Richard is employed by Fast Build Construction Company. One day the project supervisor brings a case of beer to a job site where Richard is working. Richard drinks too much beer and becomes intoxicated. He decides to drive a piece of construction equipment across the job site. While doing so, he runs into a parked car owned by Aimee. Who is liable to Aimee for the damages to her car?

9. Melvin works as a traveling salesman for Insurance Corporation. One day while driving a company car he stops to see an old friend. While backing out of the friend's driveway, he damages a parked car owned by Ellen. Is Melvin liable to Ellen? Is Insurance Corporation liable to Ellen?

10. Hannah works for Emily's All-Natural Products as a sales representative. Hannah drives a car owned by Emily's. One day Hannah decides to visit her grandma in another town. She takes the company car to visit her grandma even though she is not supposed to use the car for personal purposes. Hannah is involved in an accident with Alan. The accident is Hannah's fault. Can Alan hold Hannah liable for his damages? How about Emily's All-Natural Products?

11. Janelle recently hired Fast Debt Recovery Service to help her collect debts owed by customers. She signed a written contract with Fast Debt Recovery Service in which they promised to take all actions necessary to recover debts owed to Janelle. For each $1 recovered of debt, the firm would be paid $.50. Janelle is surprised to find out Fast Debt Recovery Service has been collecting payments from customers and requiring the payment of interest charges. Janelle is interested in whether or not an agency relationship has been created. Has an agency relationship been created? If so, what type and does the agent have the power to collect interest from customers?

12. Tiffany is a successful business tycoon who would like to find the car her dad owned when he graduated from college. Tiffany hires a private investigator to help her track down and purchase the car for her dad's birthday on July 10. Tiffany signs a contract with the private investigator and authorizes the private investigator to purchase the car if found, but not for more than $20,000. The private investigator finds the car on July 12, two days after the birthday of Tiffany's father. The private investigator signs a purchase agreement for the car and now wishes to seek payment from Tiffany for the car. Did Tiffany have an agency relationship with the private investigator on July 12? If so, what type of agency is it? Also, can a third party hold Tiffany liable for breach of contract if she does not provide payment for the car?

CHAPTER SIXTEEN

SUSTAINABILITY AND ENVIRONMENTAL LAW

By Joel Boon

Introduction: Elk River Spill

On January 9, 2014, up to 7,500 gallons of crude 4-methylcyclohexanementhol (MCHM), a chemical foam used to clean coal in coal preparation plants, leaked into the ground by the Elk River near Charleston, West Virginia. The leak was from a storage tank at a facility operated by a chemical-producing company called Freedom Industries.[1] The spill took place less than two miles upstream from a drinking water intake, treatment, and distribution center operated by West Virginia American Water.

The consequences were drastic. The leak affected up to 300,000 residents within a nine-county region. They were advised not to use tap water from the West Virginia American Water facility for drinking, cooking, bathing, or washing. Very little was known about the health effects of exposure to the toxic MCHM. However, within days of the spill, scores of people sought hospital treatment for symptoms from chemical exposure, including nausea and vomiting, and more than a dozen were hospitalized.

West Virginia's governor declared a state of emergency in response to the spill. The official do-not-use advisory on drinking water was gradually lifted from five to ten days after the leak. However, as of the date this chapter was written and several months

Figure 16.1 Elk River in West Virginia

after the incident, many people still will not use the water. Many can still smell the chemical in their water. The legal consequences may be both criminal and civil. Freedom Industries filed a chapter 11 bankruptcy petition in response to the lawsuits it faced after the spill. Many lawsuits have been filed

---

1   The actual manufacturer of the leaked MCHM was a company called Eastman Chemical Co.

by businesses affected by the spill, including those forced to close during the immediate hazard, such as restaurants and bars.

The Nature of the Problem

When an accident occurs like the one at Elk River, there is no mistaking the disaster that occurred or its source. However, perhaps the greatest environmental threats come in the form of resource depletion and resource degradation (i.e., pollution). Individuals may not readily connect the cumulative impact of their personal energy consumption, which overwhelmingly comes from fossil fuels, to health effects or the consequences of climate change, but those impacts exist just the same.

Risk Analysis

Several historic events that greatly affected the environment are the Love Canal, Three Mile Island, Bhopal, Chernobyl, *Exxon Valdez*, and Deepwater Horizon. Some environmental incidents can be attributed to criminal actions or to negligence, but many are regarded as accidents. While it is true that incidents are largely unintentional, thinking of these events as accidents may result in thinking of them as unforeseeable or unpreventable.

Two key contributing factors toward organizational linked environmental incidents may be inadequate risk analysis and risk management. **Risk analysis** entails identifying risks, their probabilities of occurring, and the options for addressing those risks. **Risk management** involves the actions taken to prevent risks from occurring and minimizing the consequences when they do occur. Risks can include all environmental harms, and the process for analyzing and managing risks can be undertaken by policymakers, academia, public interest groups, and, most importantly, businesses.

Ultimately, hazardous emergencies are risks that are known or should have been known. This is not to say that an incident is a result of improperly cutting corners to save on costs, although that it is possible. Although some believe improper risk taking and cost reductions had a primary role in the Deepwater Horizon oil spill in 2010. There are system design improvements that can be made to reduce uncertainty and the risk of unpredictability. One might compare risk analysis for any business that may deal with an environmental disaster with an airplane that experiences a serious mechanical issue or even the tragedies that occurred with the *Challenger* and *Columbia* space shuttles.

Both technical issues and human error may play a role. An organization involved in such an incident may ask itself several questions. Was there a system design flaw? Was there a design flaw involving the specific parts at issue? Was there an issue with inadequate training of personnel? Was there inadequate safety inspection processes and procedures? Was there an issue with employees not performing inspections or completing checklists? Aviation safety has improved significantly over time, not because there have been fewer "accidents" but because of improvements in engineering, systems, and processes. Businesses that can cause major environmental hazards, like the Elk River spill, are presented with the same opportunities. The business can identify what factual situations caused the problem.

- Sink
- Economic efficiency
- Market failure
- Externality

The Tragedy of the Commons

The concept of the tragedy of the commons was developed by biologist Garrett Hardin in a 1968 essay of the same name. Hardin challenged the belief, implicit in Adam Smith's concept of the "invisible hand," that individuals acting in their own rational self-interest will necessarily benefit society as a whole. He adopts the illustration of a pasture open to all for the use of their cattle to show the limits of the invisible hand. If a herdsman were to add one animal to the pasture, he receives all of the benefit of the sale of that animal, a positive utility of +1. But the corresponding negative aspect of adding one more animal is that its contribution to overgrazing the pasture is shared among all the herdsmen. Therefore, the negative utility of adding an animal is much less than –1 for each individual herdsman. Each herdsman therefore has the incentive to keep adding more cattle to the pasture, to the ultimate ruin of all the herdsmen. The cumulative effect of everyone using common resources is that no one gets to benefit from them, and therein is the tragedy of the commons.

Ocean fisheries and national parks are also examples of common natural resources subject to the tragedy of the commons. Hardin also cites pollution as an inverse application of the tragedy of the commons. He believes pollution is added to the common resource and its burden is shared by all. Each enterprising person or entity lacks a disincentive to pollute the environment because that individual experiences an economic benefit, but the harm of that pollution, such as health impacts to the public and effects upon flora, which is plant life associated with a certain region, and fauna, which is animal life associated with a certain region, are shared by many more than the polluter. In this way, air and water resources can also be exploited to the overall detriment of society if measures are not implemented to curb the harm.

Individuals often think of the direct benefit of resources only. For example, the ability to drink clean water. However, one should also think of natural resources for their ability to act as *sinks*. A **sink** is an environmental service that provides an indirect benefit. Examples of sinks are vegetation, which take in carbon dioxide, and wetlands, which limit the impacts of flooding. Actions that reduce the ability of the environment to act as a sink is an additional side effect associated with the consumption of natural resources.

Market Failure

Both environmental disasters and pollution are examples of market failure. **Economic efficiency** is the use of resources in a way that maximizes the production and distribution of goods and services. In an efficient market, everyone is better off in relative terms than they are in an inefficient market. **Market failure** describes an inefficient distribution of goods and services in a free market. One specific type of market failure is called an externality. An **externality** is a cost or benefit not included in the price of a market good. Pollution is a classic example of an externality. An industrial plant may produce widgets with air pollution being created as a byproduct of the manufacturing process. That pollution is not built into the price of the widget but is instead is a cost borne by the public in the form of poorer health. The market price of the widget therefore does not represent all of the costs associated with the widget. Therefore, a market failure has occurred. A **free market** is a market economy where the government does not intervene. Since market failures often occur, governments such as the federal government in the United States, often exercise some regulation of the free market for goods and services. The approaches taken by governments when confronting market failures associated with natural resources include taxes, economic bargaining between parties, government regulation through lawmaking, and allowing private lawsuits.

Pigovian Tax

One response to externalities is the **Pigovian tax**, an idea developed by economist Arthur C. Pigou. These taxes are added to environmentally harmful products with the goal of *internalizing* the external costs so that the price of widgets represents their full costs. Without the taxes, under this view, the price is artificially low, and the market will operate inefficiently by selling the widgets for less than their true cost to the market. With the price bearing the full costs of the product, market behavior will reward those goods and services that are environmentally friendly.

Pigovian taxes have been proposed in the environmental arena in the form of a carbon tax to address climate change. From an economist's standpoint, a carbon tax would be an effective response to climate change. Politically, however, a carbon tax appears to be unpopular in the United States. Instead, the standard means of dealing with externalities in the United States is to limit them or prevent them from occurring in the first place through a *command and control* approach. Under a **command and control approach** the government enforces regulations that prescribe which activities are illegal and which are not. The government imposes penalties for noncompliance. Because there are costs associated with regulations, this approach does have the effect of at least partially internalizing the external costs of pollution similar to what a Pigovian tax would do.

Coase Theorem

Ronald Coase took a different view on dealing with externalities. His theorem states that there are reciprocal harms done upon both parties, the polluter and the public, and if transaction costs are low enough, the parties can bargain for the most efficient outcome. The public is harmed when they have negative health effects because of air pollution. However, forcing the cost of pollution on a business also creates a negative economic effect.

The Coase Theorem requires the parties negotiate for an efficient outcome. The polluter may agree to pay an affected party for having to deal with the pollution. Likewise, the affected parties might pay the business not to pollute. The cost to the business of not creating pollution is referred to as the **abatement cost**. The dollar value placed on the ability to avoid pollution is referred to as **abatement benefits**. The optimal point of pollution, under the

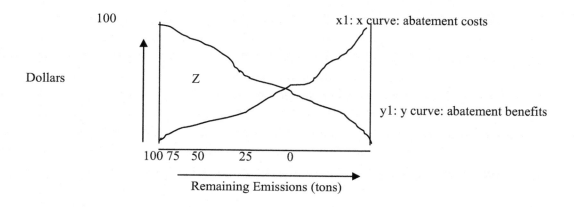

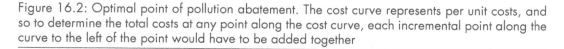

Figure 16.2: Optimal point of pollution abatement. The cost curve represents per unit costs, and so to determine the total costs at any point along the cost curve, each incremental point along the curve to the left of the point would have to be added together

Coase Theorem, is where the abatement costs curve, when plotted on a graph, meets the abatement benefits curve (Figure 16.2, point Z). Under the Coase view, rights to the polluter and to the public should be assigned so that this negotiation can take place and the optimal point is reached.

It is likely to be much easier, and therefore, cheaper for a business to abate the first X tons of a pollutant. However, it is incredibly difficult, and costly, to abate the last few tons of the pollutant, especially when the final tons do not contribute to any detrimental health effects. The harm upon the business in that situation is much greater than the societal costs of the pollution.

One problem with developing the Coase Theorem into a real-world model for allocating rights efficiently between polluters and the public is the high information costs involved. It is difficult to say that a particular chemical caused a particular health outcome because individuals are constantly subject to a myriad of environmental exposures and it is hard to pinpoint that one causes a given harm. There are also high transaction costs. It is difficult for parties to bargain in the manner needed to control pollution. Imagine a business that is creating a harmful substance and putting it into the air. The members of the local community will be affected differently depending on how close they live to the business. In addition, some members of the community might invest in the company, while others may work for the company. It may be difficult for the community and the company to negotiate with so many different parties involved. Therefore, the economic positions of the parties, the information available to the parties, and a range of other factors make the implementation of the Coase Theorem very difficult.

Many (but not all) environmental regulations deal with economic uncertainty and impracticality by incorporating the *precautionary principle*. The precautionary principle means acting in anticipation of potential harm to prevent it from occurring. This approach therefore errs on the side of protecting public health and safety over economic interests, and for sound reasons. First, because those harms can be quite severe. Second, because it is much easier to prevent a harm than to deal with the consequences once they occur.

The burden of proof under the precautionary principle is upon those whose position is that an action or policy is not harmful. By incorporating this concept into laws, policymakers are in essence acknowledging the high information and transaction costs associated with pollution and deciding to favor the public in the allocations of rights between the public and polluters. Under the Coase Theorem, an optimal point of pollution can be determined regardless of the initial allocation of rights, but in practicality, there is a great deal of political struggle over that initial allocation. Notwithstanding the precautionary principle, a certain level of pollution and waste will always be tolerated, simply as a byproduct of economic activity. For political and other reasons, some forms of economic activity receive more favorable treatment than others, with agriculture being a prime example of a favored economic activity when allocating property rights in this context.

What specific methods can be used to limit externalities? Garrett Hardin suggested several options with respect to common resources and the tragedy of the commons. One is to sell the public resources as private property, as with grazing land. Another is to keep property public but allocate accessibility, by auction, by merit (using agreed-upon standards), by lottery, or on a first-come, first-served basis. For example, publicly owned parks and lakes generally require permits for visitors to camp, fish, or boat.

What about the inverse tragedy of the commons issue of pollution, where resources such as air and flowing water cannot be so readily divided up and allocated? We've already considered two economists' views. Here Hardin says that coercive laws and taxing devices are necessary to make compliance with the law more cost effective than the economic gain that would otherwise be had by noncompliance. The phrase Hardin coins is *mutual coercion mutually agreed upon*—an acceptance of legal restrictions upon our behavior and activities for the good of society, no different from the acceptance of taxes as a price of living in a functioning society with various public goods.

Case Study: "The Wager"

Biologist Paul Ehrlich wrote one of the seminal texts of the early environmental movement with his 1968 book *The Population Bomb*. Ehrlich's book warned of Malthusian mass starvation and major social upheaval as a result of unchecked population growth. A premise of Ehrlich's concern was that the earth consists of finite natural resources and that the growing number of people would overwhelm those resources and cause severe shortages.

Natural resources can be thought of as *renewable*—those resources that are inexhaustible, such as solar energy, or that can renew themselves on a human timescale, such as biomass and fertile soil—or *nonrenewable*—those resources that exist in a fixed quantity and that can be depleted much faster than the geologic processes used to form them, such as fossil fuels and minerals. The fear voiced by Ehrlich was that many renewable resources could be depleted faster than the ability to regenerate them and that renewable resources could be depleted entirely.

In 1980, economist Julian Simon challenged Ehrlich's assertions. Simon's position was that markets would respond to growing demands for resources in ways that would not be disruptive, making those resources, in a sense, unlimited. Price adjustments would permit the extraction of resources that currently were not economically feasible to develop, the resources would be used more efficiently, or there would be incentives to develop alternatives to meet the resource needs. To Simon, population growth was a good thing, as it would supply the human ingenuity that would help to make these market adjustments. Simon wagered with Ehrlich over how the price of five metals, essential for a variety of products, would change over ten years. Simon allowed Ehrlich to select the metals; they were copper, chromium, nickel, tin, and tungsten.

If Simon's position was correct, the prices of the metals would stay stable or go down, even as the world population grew. If Ehrlich was correct, the prices would increase. Simon won the wager decisively. All five metals dropped in price from 1980 to 1990 in inflation-adjusted terms (and three in nominal terms), with the total supply of three of the metals actually increasing. The global population increased by 800 million people in that time span, even as prices for the metals were, on average, half of what they were in 1980. For each metal, Simon's predictions held true—substitute resources were developed, or improved technologies made better use of the resources. Ehrlich sent Simon a check for $576.07, the difference in price between the metals from 1980 to 1990.

Free-market proponents have pointed to the Simon-Ehrlich bet as an argument against the politics of scarcity. However, economists have since shown that Ehrlich would have won the bet in the majority of ten-year periods from 1900 to 2008. This debate is likely to continue, while the world's population continues to increase.

Ehrlich developed a model for measuring the environmental impact of population as the multiplied numbers of (1) the number of people in the population, (2) the number of resource units used per person, and (3) the environmental impact per unit of resource used. Thus, the environmental impact of a developed country, with a low population but high amount of resources used per person and high amount of impact per resource (e.g., a heavily meat-based diet, a heavy reliance on cars), might be the same as a developing country that has a high population but low resource use per person and low impact per resource (e.g., a heavily plant-based diet, primary reliance on walking and bicycling for transportation).

Questions

1. Consider each element of this equation. How desirable and feasible is it to promote policies that manage population growth (a position advocated by Ehrlich)?

2. How desirable and feasible is it to promote policies that limit the amount of resources that a population uses (e.g., the consumption of water, electricity, and gasoline)?

3.   How desirable and feasible is it to promote policies that manage the impact of resource use (e.g., forcing the utilities that produce electricity to do it in a more environmentally friendly manner)?

The Legal Response to Environmental Problems

Environmental Statutes

In the United States, environmental externalities are addressed through statutes and regulations, whose goals are both preventative and remedial. An exhaustive review of all federal environmental statutes is beyond the scope of this chapter, but a very brief overview of some of the most significant environmental laws follows. These statutes are accompanied by an expansive amount of administrative regulation and other policy guidance issued by the agencies tasked with implementing and enforcing the statutes, primarily the Environmental Protection Agency (EPA). Much case law interpreting the statutes also exists, as these laws have been heavily litigated.

The interplay between federal and state law results in a staggering degree of complexity of environmental law. The Clean Air Act alone is comparable to the tax code in intricacy and complication. Any business activity that may cause environmental impact is likely to be subject to regulation, with environmental permits playing an essential role in conducting that activity. These regulations and permits establish requirements for recordkeeping, design standards, corrective action requirements, planning requirements, closure standards, pollution-generation limits, pollution-release limits, ambient standards, training requirements, pollution-treatment requirements, monitoring requirements, and reporting requirements, among others.

The **National Environmental Policy Act** (NEPA) of 1969 requires that all major actions by federal agencies affecting the quality of the human environment undergo analysis to review any environmental impacts that agency action may have. The reach of NEPA is substantial, since it includes any permits issued by federal agencies or any projects that include funding from a federal agency. NEPA also created the Council on Environmental Quality, which advises the president on environmental matters.

At the first level of analysis of agency action, the proposed action can be categorically excluded from an extensive analysis by meeting certain criteria. At the next level of analysis, an agency can prepare an environmental assessment to determine if the agency action would significantly impact the environment. If no, then the agency can issue a "finding of no significant impact." If yes, then the third level of analysis is to prepare an environmental impact statement (EIS), which sets forth in more detail the need for the proposed action, the impact of the proposed action, and any alternative actions available to the agency. A public comment period takes place after a draft EIS is prepared, and the input obtained in that period is considered before the issuance of a final EIS. One example of when an EIS is needed is for a proposed passenger rail project, which would involve the Federal Transit Administration.

All federal agencies take part in the preparation of NEPA documents, and the EPA plays a particular role in reviewing and publicly commenting on EIS documents. NEPA also provides for a private right of action to compel judicial review of agency actions that fail to adhere to the NEPA process. Damages are not awarded, but injunctive relief is available to prevent agency action until the agency has complied with the statute.

NEPA plaintiffs have experienced broad success in cases where agencies have outright failed to prepare an EIS and it was clear they should have prepared one and in cases where an EIS was prepared but inadequately so. Where NEPA plaintiffs will not prevail is if an agency has prepared an adequate EIS, but made a decision the plaintiffs disagree with. As long as the statute is adhered to and environmental consequences are considered, courts will not review the underlying merits of agencies' actions, a position established by the Supreme Court case of *Strycker's Bay Neighborhood Council v. Karlen*, 444 US 223 (1980). The result of *Strycker's Bay* and other cases is that a significant environmental statute, and the model for similar legislation worldwide, today elevates process over substance.

The **Clean Air Act** (CAA) of 1970 focuses primarily on stationary sources. A key aspect of the CAA was for the EPA to develop *national ambient air quality standards* (NAAQS) for common air pollutants, called criteria pollutants. That list of criteria pollutants has been modified slightly over time and today includes sulfur oxides, particulate matter (soot), carbon monoxide, ozone (smog), nitrous oxides, and lead. The NAAQS set permissible concentration limits of the criteria pollutants within the ambient air, with a margin for safety to protect public health. Costs are not a consideration when developing the NAAQS.[2] States are tasked with developing a way to achieve compliance with the NAAQS targets by developing state implementation plans, or SIPs.

States develop SIPs in a complicated process by determining present ambient (or surrounding on all sides) air concentrations, determining present emissions, calculating the necessary emission reductions to achieve compliance, and rationing allowable emissions to regulated sources. A portion of SIPs include transportation control plans to address mobile sources of air pollution, as well as provisions for limiting emissions that affect downwind states. All SIPs are reviewed by the EPA and are formally accepted or rejected. If the EPA rejects a state's SIP, the EPA is obligated to issue a federal implementation plan (FIP) within two years of rejecting the SIP, although the state can correct its deficient SIP prior to the FIP being issued.[3]

States are allowed to set standards for stationary sources in their SIPs that are stricter than the NAAQS, but the standards cannot be less restrictive at the state level. The CAA also provides that states determine whether each criterion pollutant is in attainment of NAAQS or nonattainment. Because the goal of clean air would be impaired if states with already clean air allowed for emissions that resulted in concentrations approaching the NAAQS as a ceiling, the EPA requires that states issue *prevention of significant deterioration* (PSD) permits for sources in attainment regions and *nonattainment* permits for sources in nonattainment regions. The permitting process is called *new source review*

- Clean Air Act (CAA)

---

2   *Whitman v. American Trucking Associations, Inc.*, 531 US 457 (2001).

3   *EPA v. EME Homer City Generation, L.P.*, 12-1182, slip op. (US April 29, 2014, http://www.supremecourt.gov/opinions/13pdf/12-1182_bqm1.pdf.

- Major sources
- Area sources

(NSR), and these permits apply for each criterion pollutant. Because of the costs and regulatory burdens associated with obtaining PSD permits, regulated sources want to avoid actions that trigger PSD permit requirements, which limit the incremental emissions that a source can add to a region's baseline emissions level. Nonattainment permits prevent the construction of new major emission sources unless those emissions are offset, a condition that can be obtained by retiring emissions from other sources.

SIPs are directed at existing sources of criteria pollutants. For stationary sources in designated industries that are new or significantly modified, the EPA provides direct oversight of criteria pollutants and limited other pollutants through what is called *new source performance standards* (NSPS). NSPS differ from NAAQS in that the NAAQS is a health-based standard focusing on the pollution levels, whereas NSPS are technology based.

A 2007 Supreme Court decision opened the door for carbon dioxide and other greenhouse gases (GHGs) to be included within NSPS oversight. The EPA previously determined that it did not have the authority to regulate GHGs for their role in causing climate change, and even if it did have the authority, it declined to issue rules setting vehicle emission standards for GHGs. In *Massachusetts v. Environmental Protection Agency*, 549 US 497 (2007), the Supreme Court held that the EPA did have the statutory authority to regulate GHGs, as they fit within the Clean Air Act's definition of "air pollutant."

The CAA also provides for *national emission standards for hazardous air pollutants* (NESHAPs). NESHAPs, like NSPS, are technology based. Those technology standards are derived from the industry leaders among those industries generating HAPs. The Act applies differing technology standards based on the source of the pollution.

Major sources are those that emit ten tons per year or more of any HAP or 25 tons per year or more of any combination of HAPs. Major sources are subject to more stringent requirements than all other sources, called **area sources**. All major sources and a limited number of area sources must obtain permits in order to operate. These operating permits, called Title V permits, are administered by the states and are intended to address all CAA technology and emissions requirements for a regulated source. Title V permits contain requirements for emissions limits and monitoring, recordkeeping, and reporting. These permits are issued for terms of up to five years and so they must be renewed regularly.

The CAA has been successful in reducing air pollution. Some scientists believe it has prevented millions of premature deaths and illnesses. An EPA report of the first twenty years of the CAA measured compliance costs in the hundreds of billions dollars. However, the economic benefit of the Act was measured in the trillions of dollars.

Case Study: Buying the Right to Pollute

• Cap and trade
system

Acid deposition results when sulfur dioxide (SO_2) and nitrogen oxides (NO_x) are emitted into the air and form secondary, acidic substances that then descend back to the earth's surface in dry form as acidic gases or particles, or in wet form as rain, snow, fog, or mist. Most commonly thought of in the form of acid rain, this pollution causes respiratory diseases in humans, stresses trees, depletes soil, harms wildlife, and damages buildings, cars, and other stone and metal objects. The most common sources of sulfur dioxide and nitrogen oxides are from coal-burning power plants and other industrial facilities.

An innovative market-based approach for dealing with the acid rain problem was introduced in the Clean Air Act Amendments of 1990. The law created what is called a *cap and trade* system. A **cap and trade system** involves setting a cap on the total number of allowable SO_2 emissions, and establishing a system of tradable allowances where regulated sources can buy and sell (trade) SO_2 allowances in a market administered by the EPA. In this system, an allowance is equal to one ton of SO_2, and power plants cannot produce more emissions than they have allowances. The limitation is included in their Title V permit. These plants can achieve compliance by reducing their emissions, by emitting unused allowances from prior years that they banked, by purchasing allowances from other sources, or by using some combination of these approaches.

Under a cap and trade system, regulated sources have an economic incentive to reduce their emissions, thereby reducing the need to purchase allowances and also providing the potential possibility to sell allowances to other entities. As with any business activity, some sources will be able to reduce emissions more cost-effectively than others. That is, the cost to reduce each incremental ton of SO_2 emissions, referred to as marginal control costs, is lower for some sources than for others.

It makes more sense, both from an economic and an environmental standpoint, that sources that can reduce emissions cost-effectively do so, and for the less cost-effective sources to purchase allowances from the cost-effective one. When the goal is reduction of emissions, from an environmental perspective, it makes no difference how those reductions are achieved, as the desired outcome is the same.

From an economic perspective, it is in the interests of the covered entities, as well as society, for reductions of emissions to be achieved as efficiently as possible. By contrast, examples of non-market-based strategies are a government mandate for each entity to reduce its emissions by a certain percentage or for each entity to install prescribed pollution-control technologies. The environmental outcome may be the same as under a cap and trade approach, but how cost-effectively those emission reductions are achieved may vary widely among entities. A cap and trade system instead provides the regulated entities with the flexibility to achieve emission reductions in the most productive manner available.

Any party has the ability to buy SO_2 allowances at the EPA's annual auction. In many years environmental student groups or classes will buy one or more allowances, for the simple fact that they can retire that allowance and not ever emit the SO_2. The actual impact these purchases has is negligible, given the total number of allowances auctioned off, but it does make a social statement.

Questions

1. What is a cap and trade system?
2. What are the benefits of a cap and trade system?
3. What might be some disadvantages of a cap and trade system?

The **Clean Water Act** (CWA) of 1972 is administered by the EPA, the Army Corps of Engineers, and state and tribal governments. The CWA focuses primarily upon **point sources** that are a single identifiable cause of pollution. An example is a discharge of waste from a facility. Point source pollution can be contrasted with nonpoint source (NPS) pollution, which has no confined and discrete conveyance, such as pesticide runoff from agricultural land.

The CWA requires that all point sources obtain a National Pollution Discharge Elimination System (NPDES) permit before they may add any pollutant to navigable waters. **Navigable waters** are a broadly defined term that includes channels of waters that can be used for the transport of people or goods. Obtaining a permit requires that applicants engage in treatment of the effluent—or wastewater discharged into surface waters—to limit the impact of the discharge, with both technology-based and water-quality-based standards built into the permit. "Pollutant" is a broadly defined term and can include dredged and fill material, i.e., excavated material incidental to any activity, including mechanized land clearing, ditching, channelization, or other excavation. Enforcement actions can be brought for discharging without a permit, violating a permit, and failing to provide information required under the Act. The Act also allows citizen suits against persons who violate the Act and against the EPA itself (and their state counterparts) to force them to comply with the statute.

The CWA also makes states responsible for addressing nonpoint source pollution. States must first identify waters that fail to meet applicable water quality standards (called Water Quality Limited Segments (WQLS)). States must then determine the **total maximum daily load** (TMDL), which is the maximum amount of pollutant in water that meets water quality standards. It accounts for point sources and nonpoint sources, plus a margin for safety to address uncertainty, with waste load levels rationed out to the various dischargers of the polluted water. The EPA approves or disapproves of the TMDLs established by states, and where the EPA disapproves a TMDL, it establishes its own for the state.

The **Federal Insecticide, Fungicide, and Rodenticide Act** of 1972 (FIFRA) regulates the use of pesticides and is administered by the EPA and by state environmental agencies. FIFRA requires that all pesticide products be registered with the EPA. Pesticides generally consist of a chemical which is meant to attract and destroy pests such as a plant known as a weed.

The registration process requires that manufacturers of a pesticide review a pesticide for its potential environmental, health, and safety impacts. The EPA then reviews those data prior to approving the pesticide for sale, use, and distribution. Registered pesticides are then monitored for any new information about the pesticide, and based on that information, a product's registration can later be amended or canceled. The EPA and state agencies also carry out enforcement actions for the use of banned or unregistered pesticides.

The **Endangered Species Act** of 1973 (ESA) was enacted to prevent the extinction of plants and animals. It is administered for ocean species by the National Marine Fisheries Service (NMFS), a division of the National Oceanic and Atmospheric Administration, an agency within the Department of Commerce. The ESA is administered for all other species by the US Fish and Wildlife Service (FWS), an agency within the Department of Interior.

Figure 16.3 The National Wildlife Federation believes polar bears are endangered for extinction

The ESA focuses on listed species. A species may be either **endangered**, meaning it is at risk of extinction throughout all or a significant portion of its geographic habitat, or **threatened**, meaning likely to become endangered within the foreseeable future. Once listed, a number of protections are provided to the species. Whether or not a species is to be listed must be based on scientific data; economic factors may not be considered.

Economic concerns may be considered after a species is listed, when formulating a species recovery plan, which the NMFS and FWS develop after a species has been listed. A key component of recovery plans is the designation of critical habitat for species, which can include both public and private property. A critical habitat is a geographic area that contains the necessary habitation and environment for an endangered species to survive. Federal agencies may not take actions that adversely impact the critical habitat of listed species. This can include the issuance of federal permits for actions taken on private land. If a species has sufficiently recovered, it can then be reclassified from "endangered" to "threatened," or it can be delisted altogether.

The **Toxic Substances Control Act** of 1976 (TSCA, pronounced "TOSS-ca") provides the EPA with regulatory authority over the manufacture, importation, and sale of chemicals. The EPA maintains an inventory of every chemical processed or manufactured in the United States. Controls available to the EPA for those chemicals that post unreasonable environmental, health, and safety risks are bans, usage limitations, label requirements, and other restrictions.

The **Resource Conservation and Recovery Act** of 1976 (RCRA, pronounced "RICK-ra"), is a significant amendment to the Solid Waste Disposal Act of 1965. RCRA regulates the generation, transportation, treatment, storage, and disposal of hazardous waste, and is again administered by the EPA. The statute's goals include reducing the amount of waste generated and managing wastes in an environmentally sound manner to help protect human health and the environment. Complex rules exist throughout the cradle-to-grave lifecycle of the hazardous wastes, with extensive recordkeeping and reporting requirements.

RCRA further contains provisions aimed at helping state and local governments manage nonhazardous solid waste, including household garbage. RCRA regulates primarily solid wastes, which is part of the definition of hazardous wastes, but it also regulates underground storage tanks used to store petroleum and other chemical products.

While RCRA is directed at materials destined for disposal, the **Comprehensive Environmental Response, Compensation, and Liability Act** of 1980 (CERCLA), or Superfund, deals with the remediation of abandoned sites containing hazardous substances. CERCLA is an example of the **polluter pays principle**, where the party responsible for generating pollution is made financially liable for the harm, including the remediation of the harm. The EPA can sue a party responsible for contributing waste to a hazardous waste site. Also liable would be the owner of the site, the owner or operator of the site at the time of disposal of the contaminant, and those responsible for transporting the pollutant to the site.

CERCLA imposes joint and several liability for indivisible harms. **Joint and several liability** means any party who is responsible for helping create the harm is jointly liable for the damages and could be called upon to pay all the damages. In the context of the CERLCLA, any one polluter to a site can be made responsible for the entire cleanup costs of the site, no matter the contributions by other parties. This aspect of the statute shifts the legal burden of assessing liability to all of the polluters of a site to the polluters themselves, who can sue each other to recover remediation costs that the polluters believe are in excess of their own contributions to the waste site. Strict joint and several liability also acts as a powerful incentive for parties to avoid future instances of improper waste disposal. For those hazardous waste sites where the EPA is not able to identify a responsible party, it can do the cleanup itself and draw upon money from the Superfund. The **Superfund** is a trust fund initially created primarily by a tax on the petroleum and chemical industries.

CERCLA authorizes two kinds of response actions by the EPA: short-term removal actions addressed at releases or threatened releases that require a prompt response (less than twelve months), and long-term remedial actions aimed at reducing the risks associated with hazardous substances that are not immediately life threatening. Remediation actions take place at sites designated on a National Priorities List (NPL, www.epa.gov/superfund/sites/npl/). Because many Superfund sites predate RCRA and other environmental laws that, if adhered to, would have prevented the site from becoming a contaminated site in the first place, the number of Superfund sites should, ideally, go down over time as the sites are cleaned up and removed from the NPL.

The **Emergency Planning and Community Right-to-Know Act** (EPCRA) of 1986 is an emergency preparedness law that places reporting requirements on facilities that manufacture or store specified chemicals. Regulated facilities must report annually to state emergency response commissions (SERCs) and local emergency planning committees (LEPCs) the presence of certain chemicals at the facilities in excess of threshold limits. Regulated facilities must also report to SERCs and LEPCs any environmental releases of hazardous substances exceeding threshold quantities. This reported information is maintained in a publicly available database called the Toxic Release Inventory (TRI). TRI data have contributed to the enactment of new legislation and regulation, to a variety of academic research, to advocacy efforts by public interest groups, and to industry action to preemptively avoid a public response. One example is the use of TRIA data by the Sierra Club of Illinois to block the permitting of a hazardous waste landfill in Peoria, Illinois.

Enforcement

Most environmental statutes provide for both civil and criminal penalties for noncompliance (a notable exception is NEPA, which directs federal agency actions rather than regulates actions by the public). While the costs to comply with the law can be substantial, the costs for failing to comply can be even higher. That being said, the public resources available for enforcement are limited, and the practical matter is that the number of actors and activities subject to regulation under these and other statutes is so broad that many violations go undetected. To account for this, the EPA has an audit policy designed to encourage self-policing by regulated entities that voluntarily discover violations of statutes and promptly disclose them. If various conditions are met, entities make disclosures under this policy face significantly reduced civil penalties and recommendations for no criminal prosecution.

Case Study: The Ozone Layer

This chapter references several US laws addressing environmental concerns. But a variety of environmental issues go beyond what any one country can handle and require international solutions. Pollutants do not respect boundaries drawn on maps, and some issues are truly global in that the harm generated in one country is felt the world over, and perhaps most acutely in nations far away from the source of the harm.

One such global issue is the thinning of the ozone layer. The ozone layer is part of the earth's stratosphere (located roughly 10–16 miles above the earth's surface, or 17–26 kilometers). It provides important protection against harmful ultraviolet (UV) radiation from the sun. Ozone (O_3) in ambient air is a pollutant caused by smog and is believed to diminish the ozone layer. Several halogenated hydrocarbon compounds, when released into the air, can eventually reach the ozone layer and break down the ozone, thereby thinning the ozone layer and allowing more UV radiation to reach the earth's surface. This problem is most pronounced at the earth's poles, with holes in the ozone layer over the Arctic and Antarctic. Most prominent among these compounds are chlorofluorocarbons (CFCs), chemicals used as a coolant in refrigerators and air conditioners, as a propellant in aerosol spray cans, and in the bubbles of plastic foam used for packaging and insulation.

• Nuisance
• Trespass

The CFC industry initially opposed efforts to phase out CFCs by attacking the science behind the ozone layer issue. Eventually, however, scientific consensus on the effects of ozone-depleting substances (ODS) such as CFCs resulted in the Montreal Protocol on Substances that Deplete the Ozone Layer. The Montreal Protocol is a treaty ratified by all United Nations members, making it one of the most successful international agreements ever.[4] It phases out the use of ODS, with a goal of restoring the ozone layer by 2050. Recent scientific analysis points to the success of the Montreal Protocol—commercial substitutes for CFCs were developed, the concentrations of CFCs and other harmful compounds in the atmosphere are decreasing, and the ozone layer is showing evidence that it is recovering.

Questions

1. What is the ozone layer?
2. Could the ozone layer be considered a tragedy of the commons?
3. What factors may affect the ability of the United States to reduce effects on the ozone layer?

Tort Claims

Although negative environmental externalities are resolved primarily through public laws, there are other means of addressing market failure with respect to environmental issues. One example is a common law tort claim in court. One legal theory for a cause of action under the common law is **nuisance**, where the plaintiff must show causation of significant interference with the plaintiff's private use and enjoyment of the plaintiff's land. In a case such as the Elk River spill, causation may be easy to establish, but in many instances, establishing the causal link between the harm and the source of the harm is very difficult. For example, proving water has entered a house because of a local building project may be very difficult.

Another potential cause of action under the common law is **trespass**, which is the intentional entering above or below another's real property without permission. This cause of action has the benefit of not requiring a demonstration of harm in order to prevail. All that is necessary is to prove the trespass was intentional. However, here, too, there are limitations. For instance, at what point does pollution become a "thing" that can trespass? Can a particle of air pollution trespass? Different courts have answered this question differently, with many saying that air pollution can constitute a trespass, but others saying that it cannot.

Both nuisance and trespass claims must also address the defendant's rights. Even if it can be established that Factory A's emissions of a pollutant caused a specific harm, courts must

---

4   United States legislation providing for the phase-out of ozone-depleting chemicals came in the 1990 Amendments to the Clean Air Act.

weigh the consequences of holding Factory A liable. Factory A may have been in existence before the housing development, which is now affected, was built. Closing Factory A will also mean a loss of jobs. These and other difficult questions limit the effectiveness of torts as a way of successfully resolving many environmental issues.

• Greenwashing

Voluntary Initiative

Another response to negative environmental externalities and other environmental problems is for business interests to act on their own. In one sense, this idea seems paradoxical in that we have claimed externalities result from market failure. However, there are reasons that companies can take an environmentally conscious approach.

One reason is that it does actually help the business from a financial standpoint. For example, Swiss Re, one of the world's largest reinsurance companies, has taken a proactive stance to climate change, pointing to severe weather events that are said to be greater in frequency and in intensity as a result of climate change. These natural disasters cost the global insurance industry tens of billions of dollars annually, to say nothing of the thousands of lost lives attributed to these events. Examples of actions by Swiss Re are founding and supporting the nonprofit group Swiss Climate Foundation that helps businesses make climate-conscious actions; contributing to a report in partnership with the European Commission and others to be used by various decision-makers in developing climate mitigation and adaptation strategies; and developing programs to help the company and its employees reduce their own carbon footprint, meaning their contribution to climate change.

There are also public relations benefits associated with being green (environmentally conscious). While some self-promotion can be an attempt to be recognized for the responsible measures a company has taken, these actions are sometimes criticized as *greenwashing*. **Greenwashing** is the spin that oversells how environmentally friendly a produce, policy, or company is. For example, banks often prompt customers to select the use of electronic bank statements. It is true that use of electronic statements reduces the use of paper, but it also saves a tremendous amount of expense for banks, as they do not have to pay for printing and postage.

Yet another reason for voluntary measures is to preempt government action. If an industry can sufficiently engage in self-policing, it reduces the impetus for laws to address the area of concern. The concern is that such laws would engage in overreach, be too inefficient, and be too costly.

Finally, a business may take a green approach because its principals consider sustainable development to be the right thing to do. An increasing number of shareholders care as much about the social and environmental responsibility of the companies they have a financial interest in as they have in the return on their investments. There are even socially responsible investment funds with portfolios comprising companies that meet the funds' standards for good corporate citizenship on the environment or other issues. For example, iShares MSCI USA ESG Select Index is an index fund which tracks the value of companies who follow high environmental and social standards (ticker symbol KLD).

IV. The Future

- Greenhouse
  effect

The review of the major environmental statutes in this chapter shows they were passed in and around the 1970s. The laws that came out of this period addressed environmental issues being reported in the major media such as serious problems with air, water, and land. The major medium not addressed by any national laws is the climate. The response to climate change is *the* dominant environmental topic today and will be for years to come. It's a massively complicated issue that is global in nature. It draws upon complex scientific models and analysis in a variety of fields. It has far-reaching economic implications for businesses, governments, and the public.

The basic concept behind climate change is this: a layer of gases around the globe form the basis of what is called the **greenhouse effect** on our planet. Energy from the sun penetrates the atmosphere and warms the earth, and some of that heat radiates back to the atmosphere and escapes into space. But greenhouse gases (GHGs) trap some of that heat, making life as we know it possible. By burning fossil fuels, more GHGs are released into the atmosphere. More heat gets trapped and less escapes into space, resulting in a warming climate. The main GHGs are carbon dioxide, chlorofluorocarbons, methane, nitrous oxide, ozone, and water vapor. Of these, carbon dioxide (CO_2) receives the most attention because of its sheer volume relative to the other GHGs.

One early effort to address this issue was the Kyoto Protocol to the United Nations Framework Convention on Climate Change. The Kyoto Protocol, adopted in 1997, has as its goal the reduction of GHG emissions using 1990 emission levels as a baseline for most parties. The treaty sets binding emission-reduction targets for industrialized countries to be achieved in two commitment periods. Developing countries commit to reducing their GHGs but have no binding targets. One of the mechanisms the Kyoto Protocol allows for reducing emissions is the use of international emissions trading, not unlike the trading of SO_2 discussed previously. Reaction to the protocol has been mixed, with industrialized countries achieving emission reductions but with global emissions having increased.

Conclusion

Some of this chapter has been economic in its focus. On a certain level this is fitting. After all, economics is the study of the production and distribution of scarce resources, and the environment consists of the very physical resources we depend upon for the food we eat, for the air we breathe, for everything we consume. We are not always aware of just how acutely our lives are interconnected with the environment until something we take for granted is impacted.

But to start and end our study of the environment with an exclusively economic focus is to ignore, at our peril, the immense noneconomic value that the environment provides and the moral considerations that should inform our thinking on these issues. The purpose in offering these final thoughts is to remind ourselves, even if briefly, that the value of the environment extends well beyond the bottom line.

Discussion Questions

1. What were the facts of the Elk River incident and who was affected?
2. What is risk analysis and how is it related to the concept of risk management?
3. What is the theory of the tragedy of the commons?
4. What is a sink and how is it beneficial to a community?
5. How are the concepts of economic efficiency and market failure related to the concept of environmental regulation?
6. What is an externality? In what way can environmental problems be externalities?
7. What is a Pigovian tax and how is it related to environmental regulation?
8. What is the Coase Theorem and how can it be used to help further the goal of sustainability?
9. What are abatement costs? What are abatement benefits?
10. What is the precautionary principle?
11. What is the EPA and what is its purpose?
12. What is the basic requirement of NEPA?
13. What is the Clean Air Act and what does it provide?
14. What are state implementation plans (SIPs)?
15. What are major sources, and how are they different from area sources?
16. What are Title V permits, and who must obtain them?
17. What is a cap and trade system?
18. What is the Clean Water Act and what does it provide?
19. What is the Federal Insecticide, Fungicide and Rodenticide Act and what does it provide?
20. In what way can the Endangered Species Act affect private property?
21. What is the Toxic Substances Control Act and what does it provide?
22. What does RCRA regulate?
23. What is the purpose of CERCLA, also known as the Superfund?
24. What is the polluter pays principle?
25. How might the tort claims of nuisance and trespass be used to control pollution?
26. What is greenwashing?
27. What is the greenhouse effect?

Critical-Thinking Questions

28. Why is pollution considered a market externality?
29. What are three reasons a business may voluntarily seek to reduce its impact on the environment?
30. What makes the Coase Theorem difficult to apply in the business world?
31. How might "The Wager" be used by both a proponent and an opponent of a new environmental regulation?

376 | BUSINESS LAW

32. How might banks and other companies that provide monthly statements use sustainability as a rationale for decreasing the number of statements they send via postal mail and how might this green initiative save them money?

Essay Questions

1. Assume the US Congress is worried about carbon emissions being produced by private jets used by wealthy individuals. How might the US use a Pigovian tax to reduce the carbon emissions from these jets? How might Congress use a command and control approach?
2. Assume the town of Lakeview is located next to a factory that creates a large amount of heavy smoke that settles as a black residue on the town. Assume the town places a value of $100,000 on preventing the residue and the factory values the ability to create the residue at $80,000. How might the town and the factory use the Coase Theorem to settle their dispute? What might be the difficulties in incorporating the Coase theorem?
3. A large flood has affected the state of Iowa. Jerry owns an automobile repair shop. He has ten drums of recycled oil. He normally pays $250 per drum to dispose of the oil. He decides to instead dump the oil in the flooded river. What environmental law might he have violated?
4. Assume Rexcon is a large oil production company and that it has an oil well that malfunctions and lets large amounts of oil into a local lake. What laws might apply to Rexcon's situation?
5. Assume the federal government would like to build a new highway across the nation. Assume one area of the highway would disrupt the habitat of an endangered species. What federal legislation might apply to this situation?
6. Marissa's neighbor Edward likes to burn his trash in a large bin behind his house. Marissa is angry because particles from the fire continually land in her swimming pool. Assuming it is not against the law to burn one's trash, what civil torts might Marissa bring against her neighbor Edward?

APPENDIX A

THE CONSTITUTION OF THE UNITED STATES: A TRANSCRIPTION

W e the People of the United States, in Order to form a more perfect Union, establish Justice, insure domestic Tranquility, provide for the common defence, promote the general Welfare, and secure the Blessings of Liberty to ourselves and our Posterity, do ordain and establish this Constitution for the United States of America.

Article. I.

Section. 1.

All legislative Powers herein granted shall be vested in a Congress of the United States, which shall consist of a Senate and House of Representatives.

Section. 2.

The House of Representatives shall be composed of Members chosen every second Year by the People of the several States, and the Electors in each State shall have the Qualifications requisite for Electors of the most numerous Branch of the State Legislature.

No Person shall be a Representative who shall not have attained to the Age of twenty five Years, and been seven Years a Citizen of the United States, and who shall not, when elected, be an Inhabitant of that State in which he shall be chosen.

Representatives and direct Taxes shall be apportioned among the several States which may be included within this Union, according to their respective Numbers, which shall be determined by adding to the whole Number of free Persons, including those bound to Service for a Term of Years, and excluding Indians not taxed, three fifths of all other Persons. The actual Enumeration shall be made within three Years after the first Meeting of the Congress of the United States, and within every subsequent Term of ten Years, in such Manner as they shall by Law direct. The Number of Representatives shall not exceed one for every thirty Thousand, but each State shall have at Least one Representative; and until such enumeration shall be made, the State of New Hampshire shall be entitled to chuse three, Massachusetts eight, Rhode-Island and Providence Plantations one, Connecticut five, New-York six, New Jersey four, Pennsylvania eight, Delaware one, Maryland six, Virginia ten, North Carolina five, South Carolina five, and Georgia three.

When vacancies happen in the Representation from any State, the Executive Authority thereof shall issue Writs of Election to fill such Vacancies.

The House of Representatives shall chuse their Speaker and other Officers; and shall have the sole Power of Impeachment.

Section. 3.

The Senate of the United States shall be composed of two Senators from each State, chosen by the Legislature thereof, for six Years; and each Senator shall have one Vote.

Immediately after they shall be assembled in Consequence of the first Election, they shall be divided as equally as may be into three Classes. The Seats of the Senators of the first Class shall be vacated at the Expiration of the second Year, of the second Class at the Expiration of the fourth Year, and of the third Class at the Expiration of the sixth Year, so that one third may be chosen every second Year; and if Vacancies happen by Resignation, or otherwise, during the Recess of the Legislature of any State, the Executive thereof may make temporary Appointments until the next Meeting of the Legislature, which shall then fill such Vacancies.

No Person shall be a Senator who shall not have attained to the Age of thirty Years, and been nine Years a Citizen of the United States, and who shall not, when elected, be an Inhabitant of that State for which he shall be chosen.

The Vice President of the United States shall be President of the Senate, but shall have no Vote, unless they be equally divided.

The Senate shall chuse their other Officers, and also a President pro tempore, in the Absence of the Vice President, or when he shall exercise the Office of President of the United States.

The Senate shall have the sole Power to try all Impeachments. When sitting for that Purpose, they shall be on Oath or Affirmation. When the President of the United States is tried, the Chief Justice shall preside: And no Person shall be convicted without the Concurrence of two thirds of the Members present.

Judgment in Cases of Impeachment shall not extend further than to removal from Office, and disqualification to hold and enjoy any Office of honor, Trust or Profit under the United States: but the Party convicted shall nevertheless be liable and subject to Indictment, Trial, Judgment and Punishment, according to Law.

Section. 4.

The Times, Places and Manner of holding Elections for Senators and Representatives, shall be prescribed in each State by the Legislature thereof; but the Congress may at any time by Law make or alter such Regulations, except as to the Places of chusing Senators.

The Congress shall assemble at least once in every Year, and such Meeting shall be on the first Monday in December, unless they shall by Law appoint a different Day.

Section. 5.

Each House shall be the judge of the Elections, Returns and Qualifications of its own Members, and a Majority of each shall constitute a Quorum to do Business; but a smaller Number may adjourn from day to day, and may be authorized to compel the Attendance of absent Members, in such Manner, and under such Penalties as each House may provide.

Each House may determine the Rules of its Proceedings, punish its Members for disorderly Behaviour, and, with the Concurrence of two thirds, expel a Member.

Each House shall keep a Journal of its Proceedings, and from time to time publish the same, excepting such Parts as may in their Judgment require Secrecy; and the Yeas and Nays of the Members of either House on any question shall, at the Desire of one fifth of those Present, be entered on the Journal.

Neither House, during the Session of Congress, shall, without the Consent of the other, adjourn for more than three days, nor to any other Place than that in which the two Houses shall be sitting.

Section. 6.

The Senators and Representatives shall receive a Compensation for their Services, to be ascertained by Law, and paid out of the Treasury of the United States. They shall in all Cases, except Treason, Felony and Breach of the Peace, be privileged from Arrest during their Attendance at the Session of their respective Houses, and in going to and returning from the same; and for any Speech or Debate in either House, they shall not be questioned in any other Place.

No Senator or Representative shall, during the Time for which he was elected, be appointed to any civil Office under the Authority of the United States, which shall have been created, or the Emoluments whereof shall have been encreased during such time; and no Person holding any Office under the United States, shall be a Member of either House during his Continuance in Office.

Section. 7.

All Bills for raising Revenue shall originate in the House of Representatives; but the Senate may propose or concur with Amendments as on other Bills.

Every Bill which shall have passed the House of Representatives and the Senate, shall, before it become a Law, be presented to the President of the United States; If he approve he shall sign it, but if not he shall return it, with his Objections to that House in which it shall have originated, who shall enter the Objections at large on their Journal, and proceed to reconsider it. If after such Reconsideration two thirds of that House shall agree to pass the Bill, it shall be sent, together with the Objections, to the other House, by which it shall likewise be reconsidered, and if approved by two thirds of that House, it shall become a Law.

But in all such Cases the Votes of both Houses shall be determined by yeas and Nays, and the Names of the Persons voting for and against the Bill shall be entered on the Journal of each House respectively. If any Bill shall not be returned by the President within ten Days (Sundays excepted) after it shall have been presented to him, the Same shall be a Law, in like Manner as if he had signed it, unless the Congress by their Adjournment prevent its Return, in which Case it shall not be a Law.

Every Order, Resolution, or Vote to which the Concurrence of the Senate and House of Representatives may be necessary (except on a question of Adjournment) shall be presented to the President of the United States; and before the Same shall take Effect, shall be approved by him, or being disapproved by him, shall be repassed by two thirds of the Senate and House of Representatives, according to the Rules and Limitations prescribed in the Case of a Bill.

Section. 8.

The Congress shall have Power To lay and collect Taxes, Duties, Imposts and Excises, to pay the Debts and provide for the common Defence and general Welfare of the United States; but all Duties, Imposts and Excises shall be uniform throughout the United States;

To borrow Money on the credit of the United States;

To regulate Commerce with foreign Nations, and among the several States, and with the Indian Tribes;

To establish an uniform Rule of Naturalization, and uniform Laws on the subject of Bankruptcies throughout the United States;

To coin Money, regulate the Value thereof, and of foreign Coin, and fix the Standard of Weights and Measures;

To provide for the Punishment of counterfeiting the Securities and current Coin of the United States;

To establish Post Offices and post Roads;

To promote the Progress of Science and useful Arts, by securing for limited Times to Authors and Inventors the exclusive Right to their respective Writings and Discoveries;

To constitute Tribunals inferior to the supreme Court;

To define and punish Piracies and Felonies committed on the high Seas, and Offences against the Law of Nations;

To declare War, grant Letters of Marque and Reprisal, and make Rules concerning Captures on Land and Water;

To raise and support Armies, but no Appropriation of Money to that Use shall be for a longer Term than two Years;

To provide and maintain a Navy;

To make Rules for the Government and Regulation of the land and naval Forces;

To provide for calling forth the Militia to execute the Laws of the Union, suppress Insurrections and repel Invasions;

To provide for organizing, arming, and disciplining, the Militia, and for governing such Part of them as may be employed in the Service of the United States, reserving to the States respectively, the Appointment of the Officers, and the Authority of training the Militia according to the discipline prescribed by Congress;

To exercise exclusive Legislation in all Cases whatsoever, over such District (not exceeding ten Miles square) as may, by Cession of particular States, and the Acceptance of Congress, become the Seat of the Government of the United States, and to exercise like Authority over all Places purchased by the Consent of the Legislature of the State in which the Same shall be, for the Erection of Forts, Magazines, Arsenals, dock-Yards, and other needful Buildings;—And

To make all Laws which shall be necessary and proper for carrying into Execution the foregoing Powers, and all other Powers vested by this Constitution in the Government of the United States, or in any Department or Officer thereof.

Section. 9.

The Migration or Importation of such Persons as any of the States now existing shall think proper to admit, shall not be prohibited by the Congress prior to the Year one thousand eight hundred and eight, but a Tax or duty may be imposed on such Importation, not exceeding ten dollars for each Person.

The Privilege of the Writ of Habeas Corpus shall not be suspended, unless when in Cases of Rebellion or Invasion the public Safety may require it.

No Bill of Attainder or ex post facto Law shall be passed.

No Capitation, or other direct, Tax shall be laid, unless in Proportion to the Census or enumeration herein before directed to be taken.

No Tax or Duty shall be laid on Articles exported from any State.

No Preference shall be given by any Regulation of Commerce or Revenue to the Ports of one State over those of another: nor shall Vessels bound to, or from, one State, be obliged to enter, clear, or pay Duties in another.

No Money shall be drawn from the Treasury, but in Consequence of Appropriations made by Law; and a regular Statement and Account of the Receipts and Expenditures of all public Money shall be published from time to time.

No Title of Nobility shall be granted by the United States: And no Person holding any Office of Profit or Trust under them, shall, without the Consent of the Congress, accept of any present, Emolument, Office, or Title, of any kind whatever, from any King, Prince, or foreign State.

Section. 10.

No State shall enter into any Treaty, Alliance, or Confederation; grant Letters of Marque and Reprisal; coin Money; emit Bills of Credit; make any Thing but gold and silver Coin a Tender in Payment of Debts; pass any Bill of Attainder, ex post facto Law, or Law impairing the Obligation of Contracts, or grant any Title of Nobility.

No State shall, without the Consent of the Congress, lay any Imposts or Duties on Imports or Exports, except what may be absolutely necessary for executing it's inspection Laws: and the net Produce of all Duties and Imposts, laid by any State on Imports or Exports, shall be for the Use of the Treasury of the United States; and all such Laws shall be subject to the Revision and Controul of the Congress.

No State shall, without the Consent of Congress, lay any Duty of Tonnage, keep Troops, or Ships of War in time of Peace, enter into any Agreement or Compact with another State, or with a foreign Power, or engage in War, unless actually invaded, or in such imminent Danger as will not admit of delay.

Article. II.

Section. 1.

The executive Power shall be vested in a President of the United States of America. He shall hold his Office during the Term of four Years, and, together with the Vice President, chosen for the same Term, be elected, as follows

Each State shall appoint, in such Manner as the Legislature thereof may direct, a Number of Electors, equal to the whole Number of Senators and Representatives to which the State may be entitled in the Congress: but no Senator or Representative, or Person holding an Office of Trust or Profit under the United States, shall be appointed an Elector.

The Electors shall meet in their respective States, and vote by Ballot for two Persons, of whom one at least shall not be an Inhabitant of the same State with themselves. And they shall make a List of all the Persons voted for, and of the Number of Votes for each; which List they shall sign and certify, and transmit sealed to the Seat of the Government of the United States, directed to the President of the Senate. The President of the Senate shall, in the Presence of the Senate and House of Representatives, open all the Certificates, and the Votes shall then be counted. The Person having the greatest Number of Votes shall be the President, if such Number be a Majority of the whole Number of Electors appointed; and if there be more than one who have such Majority, and have an equal Number of Votes, then the House of Representatives shall immediately chuse by Ballot one of them for President; and if no Person have a Majority, then from the five highest on the List the said House shall in like Manner chuse the President. But in chusing the President, the Votes shall be taken by States, the Representation from each State having one Vote; A quorum for this Purpose shall consist of a Member or Members from two thirds of the States, and a Majority of all the States shall be necessary to a Choice. In every Case, after the Choice of the President, the Person having the greatest Number of Votes of the Electors shall be the Vice President. But if there should remain two or more who have equal Votes, the Senate shall chuse from them by Ballot the Vice President.

The Congress may determine the Time of chusing the Electors, and the Day on which they shall give their Votes; which Day shall be the same throughout the United States.

No Person except a natural born Citizen, or a Citizen of the United States, at the time of the Adoption of this Constitution, shall be eligible to the Office of President; neither shall any Person be eligible to that Office who shall not have attained to the Age of thirty five Years, and been fourteen Years a Resident within the United States.

In Case of the Removal of the President from Office, or of his Death, Resignation, or Inability to discharge the Powers and Duties of the said Office, the Same shall devolve on the Vice President, and the Congress may by Law provide for the Case of Removal, Death, Resignation or Inability, both of the President and Vice President, declaring what Officer shall then act as President, and such Officer shall act accordingly, until the Disability be removed, or a President shall be elected.

The President shall, at stated Times, receive for his Services, a Compensation, which shall neither be encreased nor diminished during the Period for which he shall have been elected, and he shall not receive within that Period any other Emolument from the United States, or any of them.

Before he enter on the Execution of his Office, he shall take the following Oath or Affirmation:—"I do solemnly swear (or affirm) that I will faithfully execute the Office of President of the United States, and will to the best of my Ability, preserve, protect and defend the Constitution of the United States."

Section. 2.

The President shall be Commander in Chief of the Army and Navy of the United States, and of the Militia of the several States, when called into the actual Service of the United States; he may require the Opinion, in writing, of the principal Officer in each of the executive Departments, upon any Subject relating to the Duties of their respective Offices, and he shall have Power to grant Reprieves and Pardons for Offences against the United States, except in Cases of Impeachment.

He shall have Power, by and with the Advice and Consent of the Senate, to make Treaties, provided two thirds of the Senators present concur; and he shall nominate, and by and with the Advice and Consent of the Senate, shall appoint Ambassadors, other public Ministers and Consuls, Judges of the supreme Court, and all other Officers of the United States, whose Appointments are not herein otherwise provided for, and which shall be established by Law: but the Congress may by Law vest the Appointment of such inferior Officers, as they think proper, in the President alone, in the Courts of Law, or in the Heads of Departments.

The President shall have Power to fill up all Vacancies that may happen during the Recess of the Senate, by granting Commissions which shall expire at the End of their next Session.

Section. 3.

He shall from time to time give to the Congress Information of the State of the Union, and recommend to their Consideration such Measures as he shall judge necessary and expedient; he may, on extraordinary Occasions, convene both Houses, or either of them, and in Case of Disagreement between them, with Respect to the Time of Adjournment, he may adjourn them to such Time as he shall think proper; he shall receive Ambassadors and other public Ministers; he shall take Care that the Laws be faithfully executed, and shall Commission all the Officers of the United States.

Section. 4.

The President, Vice President and all civil Officers of the United States, shall be removed from Office on Impeachment for, and Conviction of, Treason, Bribery, or other high Crimes and Misdemeanors.

Article III.

Section. 1.

The judicial Power of the United States, shall be vested in one supreme Court, and in such inferior Courts as the Congress may from time to time ordain and establish. The judges, both of the supreme and inferior Courts, shall hold their Offices during good Behaviour, and shall, at stated Times, receive for their Services, a Compensation, which shall not be diminished during their Continuance in Office.

Section. 2.

The judicial Power shall extend to all Cases, in Law and Equity, arising under this Constitution, the Laws of the United States, and Treaties made, or which shall be made, under their Authority;—to all Cases affecting Ambassadors, other public Ministers and Consuls;—to all Cases of admiralty and maritime Jurisdiction;—to Controversies to which the United States shall be a Party;—to Controversies between two or more States;—between a State and Citizens of another State,—between Citizens of different States,—between Citizens of the same State claiming Lands under Grants of different States, and between a State, or the Citizens thereof, and foreign States, Citizens or Subjects.

In all Cases affecting Ambassadors, other public Ministers and Consuls, and those in which a State shall be Party, the supreme Court shall have original Jurisdiction. In all the other Cases before mentioned, the supreme Court shall have appellate Jurisdiction, both as to Law and Fact, with such Exceptions, and under such Regulations as the Congress shall make.

The Trial of all Crimes, except in Cases of Impeachment, shall be by Jury; and such Trial shall be held in the State where the said Crimes shall have been committed; but when not committed within any State, the Trial shall be at such Place or Places as the Congress may by Law have directed.

Section. 3.

Treason against the United States, shall consist only in levying War against them, or in adhering to their Enemies, giving them Aid and Comfort. No Person shall be convicted of Treason unless on the Testimony of two Witnesses to the same overt Act, or on Confession in open Court.

The Congress shall have Power to declare the Punishment of Treason, but no Attainder of Treason shall work Corruption of Blood, or Forfeiture except during the Life of the Person attainted.

Article. IV.

Section. 1.

Full Faith and Credit shall be given in each State to the public Acts, Records, and judicial Proceedings of every other State. And the Congress may by general Laws prescribe the Manner in which such Acts, Records and Proceedings shall be proved, and the Effect thereof.

Section. 2.

The Citizens of each State shall be entitled to all Privileges and Immunities of Citizens in the several States.

A Person charged in any State with Treason, Felony, or other Crime, who shall flee from Justice, and be found in another State, shall on Demand of the executive Authority of the State from which he fled, be delivered up, to be removed to the State having Jurisdiction of the Crime.

No Person held to Service or Labour in one State, under the Laws thereof, escaping into another, shall, in Consequence of any Law or Regulation therein, be discharged from such Service or Labour, but shall be delivered up on Claim of the Party to whom such Service or Labour may be due.

Section. 3.

New States may be admitted by the Congress into this Union; but no new State shall be formed or erected within the Jurisdiction of any other State; nor any State be formed by the Junction of two or more States, or Parts of States, without the Consent of the Legislatures of the States concerned as well as of the Congress.

The Congress shall have Power to dispose of and make all needful Rules and Regulations respecting the Territory or other Property belonging to the United States; and nothing in this Constitution shall be so construed as to Prejudice any Claims of the United States, or of any particular State.

Section. 4.

The United States shall guarantee to every State in this Union a Republican Form of Government, and shall protect each of them against Invasion; and on Application of the Legislature, or of the Executive (when the Legislature cannot be convened), against domestic Violence.

Article. V.

The Congress, whenever two thirds of both Houses shall deem it necessary, shall propose Amendments to this Constitution, or, on the Application of the Legislatures of two thirds of the several States, shall call a Convention for proposing Amendments, which, in either Case, shall be valid to all Intents and Purposes, as Part of this Constitution, when ratified by the Legislatures of three fourths of the several States, or by Conventions in three fourths thereof, as the one or the other Mode of Ratification may be proposed by the Congress; Provided that no Amendment which may be made prior to the Year One thousand eight hundred and eight shall in any Manner affect the first and fourth Clauses in the Ninth Section of the first Article; and that no State, without its Consent, shall be deprived of its equal Suffrage in the Senate.

Article. VI.

All Debts contracted and Engagements entered into, before the Adoption of this Constitution, shall be as valid against the United States under this Constitution, as under the Confederation.

This Constitution, and the Laws of the United States which shall be made in Pursuance thereof; and all Treaties made, or which shall be made, under the Authority of the United States, shall be the supreme Law of the Land; and the judges in every State shall be bound thereby, any Thing in the Constitution or Laws of any State to the Contrary notwithstanding.

The Senators and Representatives before mentioned, and the Members of the several State Legislatures, and all executive and judicial Officers, both of the United States and of the several States, shall be bound by Oath or Affirmation, to support this Constitution; but no religious Test shall ever be required as a Qualification to any Office or public Trust under the United States.

Article. VII.

The Ratification of the Conventions of nine States, shall be sufficient for the Establishment of this Constitution between the States so ratifying the Same.

The Word, "the," being interlined between the seventh and eighth Lines of the first Page, The Word "Thirty" being partly written on an Erazure in the fifteenth Line of the first Page, The Words "is tried" being interlined between the thirty second and thirty third Lines of the first Page and the Word "the" being interlined between the forty third and forty fourth Lines of the second Page.

Attest William Jackson Secretary

done in Convention by the Unanimous Consent of the States present the Seventeenth Day of September in the Year of our Lord one thousand seven hundred and Eighty seven and of the Independance of the United States of America the Twelfth In witness whereof We have hereunto subscribed our Names,

G°. Washington
Presidt and deputy from Virginia

Delaware
Geo: Read
Gunning Bedford jun
John Dickinson
Richard Bassett
Jaco: Broom

Maryland
James McHenry
Dan of St Thos. Jenifer
Danl. Carroll

Virginia
John Blair
James Madison Jr.

North Carolina
Wm. Blount
Richd. Dobbs Spaight
Hu Williamson

South Carolina
J. Rutledge
Charles Cotesworth Pinckney
Charles Pinckney
Pierce Butler
Georgia

William Few
Abr Baldwin

New Hampshire
John Langdon
Nicholas Gilman

Massachusetts
Nathaniel Gorham
Rufus King

Connecticut
Wm. Saml. Johnson
Roger Sherman

New York
Alexander Hamilton

New Jersey
Wil: Livingston
David Brearley
Wm. Paterson
Jona: Dayton

Pensylvania
B Franklin
Thomas Mifflin
Robt. Morris
Geo. Clymer
Thos. FitzSimons
Jared Ingersoll
James Wilson
Gouv Morris

APPENDIX B

THE UNITED STATES BILL OF RIGHTS

THE TEN ORIGINAL AMENDMENTS TO THE CONSTITUTION OF THE UNITED STATES

PASSED BY CONGRESS SEPTEMBER 25, 1789

RATIFIED DECEMBER 15, 1791

I

Congress shall make no law respecting an establishment of religion, or prohibiting the free exercise thereof; or abridging the freedom of speech, or of the press, or the right of the people peaceably to assemble, and to petition the Government for a redress of grievances.

II

A well-regulated militia, being necessary to the security of a free State, the right of the people to keep and bear arms, shall not be infringed.

III

No soldier shall, in time of peace be quartered in any house, without the consent of the owner, nor in time of war, but in a manner to be prescribed by law.

IV

The right of the people to be secure in their persons, houses, papers, and effects, against unreasonable searches and seizures, shall not be violated, and no Warrants shall issue, but upon probable cause, supported by oath or affirmation, and particularly describing the place to be searched, and the persons or things to be seized.

V

No person shall be held to answer for a capital, or otherwise infamous crime, unless on a presentment or indictment of a Grand Jury, except in cases arising in the land or naval forces, or in the Militia, when in actual service in time of War or public danger; nor shall any person be subject for the same offense to be twice put in jeopardy of life or limb; nor shall be compelled in any criminal case to be a witness against himself, nor be deprived of life, liberty, or property, without due process of law; nor shall private property be taken for public use without just compensation.

VI

In all criminal prosecutions, the accused shall enjoy the right to a speedy and public trial, by an impartial jury of the State and district wherein the crime shall have been committed, which district shall have been previously ascertained by law, and to be informed of the nature and cause of the accusation; to be confronted with the witnesses against him; to have compulsory process for obtaining witnesses in his favor, and to have the assistance of counsel for his defense.

VII

In suits at common law, where the value in controversy shall exceed twenty dollars, the right of trial by jury shall be preserved, and no fact tried by a jury shall be otherwise re-examined in any court of the United States, than according to the rules of the common law.

VIII

Excessive bail shall not be required nor excessive fines imposed, nor cruel and unusual punishments inflicted.

IX

The enumeration in the Constitution, of certain rights, shall not be construed to deny or disparage others retained by the people.

X

The powers not delegated to the United States by the Constitution, nor prohibited by it to the States, are reserved to the States respectively, or to the people.

APPENDIX C

AMENDMENTS XI - XXVII

XI

Passed by Congress March 4, 1794. Ratified February 7, 1795.
The Judicial power of the United States shall not be construed to extend to any suit in law or equity, commenced or prosecuted against one of the United States by Citizens of another State, or by Citizens or Subjects of any Foreign State.

XII

Passed by Congress December 9, 1803. Ratified June 15, 1804.
The Electors shall meet in their respective states and vote by ballot for President and Vice-President, one of whom, at least, shall not be an inhabitant of the same state with themselves; they shall name in their ballots the person voted for as President, and in distinct ballots the person voted for as Vice-President, and they shall make distinct lists of all persons voted for as President, and of all persons voted for as Vice-President, and of the number of votes for each, which lists they shall sign and certify, and transmit sealed to the seat of the government of the United States, directed to the President of the Senate; -- the President of the Senate shall, in the presence of the Senate and House of Representatives, open all the certificates and the votes shall then be counted; -- The person having the greatest number of votes for President, shall be the President, if such number be a majority of the whole number of Electors appointed; and if no person have such majority, then from the persons having the highest numbers not exceeding three on the list of those voted for as President, the House of Representatives shall choose immediately, by ballot, the President. But in choosing the President, the votes shall be taken by states, the representation from each state having one vote; a quorum for this purpose shall consist of a member or members from two-thirds of the states, and a majority of all the states shall be necessary to a choice. [And if the House of Representatives shall not choose a President whenever the right of choice shall devolve upon them, before the fourth day of March next following, then the Vice-President shall act as

President, as in case of the death or other constitutional disability of the President. The person having the greatest number of votes as Vice-President, shall be the Vice-President, if such number be a majority of the whole number of Electors appointed, and if no person have a majority, then from the two highest numbers on the list, the Senate shall choose the Vice-President; a quorum for the purpose shall consist of two-thirds of the whole number of Senators, and a majority of the whole number shall be necessary to a choice. But no person constitutionally ineligible to the office of President shall be eligible to that of Vice-President of the United States.

XIII

Passed by Congress January 31, 1865. Ratified December 6, 1865.
Section 1.
Neither slavery nor involuntary servitude, except as a punishment for crime whereof the party shall have been duly convicted, shall exist within the United States, or any place subject to their jurisdiction.

Section 2.
Congress shall have power to enforce this article by appropriate legislation.

XIV

Passed by Congress June 13, 1866. Ratified July 9, 1868.
Section 1.
All persons born or naturalized in the United States, and subject to the jurisdiction thereof, are citizens of the United States and of the State wherein they reside. No State shall make or enforce any law which shall abridge the privileges or immunities of citizens of the United States; nor shall any State deprive any person of life, liberty, or property, without due process of law; nor deny to any person within its jurisdiction the equal protection of the laws.

Section 2.
Representatives shall be apportioned among the several States according to their respective numbers, counting the whole number of persons in each State, excluding Indians not taxed. But when the right to vote at any election for the choice of electors for President and Vice-President of the United States, Representatives in Congress, the Executive and Judicial officers of a State, or the members of the Legislature thereof, is denied to any of the male inhabitants of such State, being twenty-one years of age,* and citizens of the United States, or in any way abridged, except for participation in rebellion, or other crime, the basis of representation therein shall be reduced in the proportion which the number of such male citizens shall bear to the whole number of male citizens twenty-one years of age in such State.

Section 3.
No person shall be a Senator or Representative in Congress, or elector of President and Vice-President, or hold any office, civil or military, under the United States, or under any State, who, having previously taken an oath, as a member of Congress, or as an officer of the United States, or as a member of any State legislature, or as an executive or judicial officer of any State, to support the Constitution of the United States, shall have engaged in insurrection

or rebellion against the same, or given aid or comfort to the enemies thereof. But Congress may by a vote of two-thirds of each House, remove such disability.

Section 4.

The validity of the public debt of the United States, authorized by law, including debts incurred for payment of pensions and bounties for services in suppressing insurrection or rebellion, shall not be questioned. But neither the United States nor any State shall assume or pay any debt or obligation incurred in aid of insurrection or rebellion against the United States, or any claim for the loss or emancipation of any slave; but all such debts, obligations and claims shall be held illegal and void.

Section 5.

The Congress shall have the power to enforce, by appropriate legislation, the provisions of this article.

XV

Passed by Congress February 26, 1869. Ratified February 3, 1870.

Section 1.

The right of citizens of the United States to vote shall not be denied or abridged by the United States or by any State on account of race, color, or previous condition of servitude--

Section 2.

The Congress shall have the power to enforce this article by appropriate legislation.

XVI

Passed by Congress July 2, 1909. Ratified February 3, 1913.

The Congress shall have power to lay and collect taxes on incomes, from whatever source derived, without apportionment among the several States, and without regard to any census or enumeration.

XVII

Passed by Congress May 13, 1912. Ratified April 8, 1913.

The Senate of the United States shall be composed of two Senators from each State, elected by the people thereof, for six years; and each Senator shall have one vote. The electors in each State shall have the qualifications requisite for electors of the most numerous branch of the State legislatures.

When vacancies happen in the representation of any State in the Senate, the executive authority of such State shall issue writs of election to fill such vacancies: Provided, That the legislature of any State may empower the executive thereof to make temporary appointments until the people fill the vacancies by election as the legislature may direct.

This amendment shall not be so construed as to affect the election or term of any Senator chosen before it becomes valid as part of the Constitution.

XVIII

Passed by Congress December 18, 1917. Ratified January 16, 1919. Repealed by amendment 21.
Section 1.
After one year from the ratification of this article the manufacture, sale, or transportation of intoxicating liquors within, the importation thereof into, or the exportation thereof from the United States and all territory subject to the jurisdiction thereof for beverage purposes is hereby prohibited.

Section 2.
The Congress and the several States shall have concurrent power to enforce this article by appropriate legislation.

Section 3.
This article shall be inoperative unless it shall have been ratified as an amendment to the Constitution by the legislatures of the several States, as provided in the Constitution, within seven years from the date of the submission hereof to the States by the Congress.

XIX

Passed by Congress June 4, 1919. Ratified August 18, 1920.
The right of citizens of the United States to vote shall not be denied or abridged by the United States or by any State on account of sex.

XX

Passed by Congress March 2, 1932. Ratified January 23, 1933.
Section 1.
The terms of the President and the Vice President shall end at noon on the 20th day of January, and the terms of Senators and Representatives at noon on the 3d day of January, of the years in which such terms would have ended if this article had not been ratified; and the terms of their successors shall then begin.

Section 2.
The Congress shall assemble at least once in every year, and such meeting shall begin at noon on the 3d day of January, unless they shall by law appoint a different day.

Section 3.
If, at the time fixed for the beginning of the term of the President, the President elect shall have died, the Vice President elect shall become President. If a President shall not have been chosen before the time fixed for the beginning of his term, or if the President elect shall have failed to qualify, then the Vice President elect shall act

as President until a President shall have qualified; and the Congress may by law provide for the case wherein neither a President elect nor a Vice President elect shall have qualified, declaring who shall then act as President, or the manner in which one who is to act shall be selected, and such person shall act accordingly until a President or Vice President shall have qualified.

Section 4.

The Congress may by law provide for the case of the death of any of the persons from whom the House of Representatives may choose a President whenever the right of choice shall have devolved upon them, and for the case of the death of any of the persons from whom the Senate may choose a Vice President whenever the right of choice shall have devolved upon them.

Section 5.

Sections 1 and 2 shall take effect on the 15th day of October following the ratification of this article.

Section 6.

This article shall be inoperative unless it shall have been ratified as an amendment to the Constitution by the legislatures of three-fourths of the several States within seven years from the date of its submission.

XXI

Passed by Congress February 20, 1933. Ratified December 5, 1933.
Section 1.
The eighteenth article of amendment to the Constitution of the United States is hereby repealed.

Section 2.

The transportation or importation into any State, Territory, or possession of the United States for delivery or use therein of intoxicating liquors, in violation of the laws thereof, is hereby prohibited.

Section 3.

This article shall be inoperative unless it shall have been ratified as an amendment to the Constitution by conventions in the several States, as provided in the Constitution, within seven years from the date of the submission hereof to the States by the Congress.

XXII

Passed by Congress March 21, 1947. Ratified February 27, 1951.
Section 1.
No person shall be elected to the office of the President more than twice, and no person who has held the office of President, or acted as President, for more than two years of a term to which some other person was elected President shall be elected to the office of the President more than once. But this Article shall not apply to any person holding the office of President when this Article was proposed by the Congress, and shall not prevent any person who may be holding the office of President, or acting

as President, during the term within which this Article becomes operative from holding the office of President or acting as President during the remainder of such term.

Section 2.
This article shall be inoperative unless it shall have been ratified as an amendment to the Constitution by the legislatures of three-fourths of the several States within seven years from the date of its submission to the States by the Congress.

XXIII

Passed by Congress June 16, 1960. Ratified March 29, 1961.
Section 1.
The District constituting the seat of Government of the United States shall appoint in such manner as the Congress may direct:

A number of electors of President and Vice President equal to the whole number of Senators and Representatives in Congress to which the District would be entitled if it were a State, but in no event more than the least populous State; they shall be in addition to those appointed by the States, but they shall be considered, for the purposes of the election of President and Vice President, to be electors appointed by a State; and they shall meet in the District and perform such duties as provided by the twelfth article of amendment.

Section 2.
The Congress shall have power to enforce this article by appropriate legislation.

XXIV

Passed by Congress August 27, 1962. Ratified January 23, 1964.
Section 1.
The right of citizens of the United States to vote in any primary or other election for President or Vice President, for electors for President or Vice President, or for Senator or Representative in Congress, shall not be denied or abridged by the United States or any State by reason of failure to pay any poll tax or other tax.

Section 2.
The Congress shall have power to enforce this article by appropriate legislation.

XXV

Passed by Congress July 6, 1965. Ratified February 10, 1967.
Section 1.
In case of the removal of the President from office or of his death or resignation, the Vice President shall become President.

Section 2.

Whenever there is a vacancy in the office of the Vice President, the President shall nominate a Vice President who shall take office upon confirmation by a majority vote of both Houses of Congress.

Section 3.

Whenever the President transmits to the President pro tempore of the Senate and the Speaker of the House of Representatives his written declaration that he is unable to discharge the powers and duties of his office, and until he transmits to them a written declaration to the contrary, such powers and duties shall be discharged by the Vice President as Acting President.

Section 4.

Whenever the Vice President and a majority of either the principal officers of the executive departments or of such other body as Congress may by law provide, transmit to the President pro tempore of the Senate and the Speaker of the House of Representatives their written declaration that the President is unable to discharge the powers and duties of his office, the Vice President shall immediately assume the powers and duties of the office as Acting President.

Thereafter, when the President transmits to the President pro tempore of the Senate and the Speaker of the House of Representatives his written declaration that no inability exists, he shall resume the powers and duties of his office unless the Vice President and a majority of either the principal officers of the executive department or of such other body as Congress may by law provide, transmit within four days to the President pro tempore of the Senate and the Speaker of the House of Representatives their written declaration that the President is unable to discharge the powers and duties of his office. Thereupon Congress shall decide the issue, assembling within forty-eight hours for that purpose if not in session. If the Congress, within twenty-one days after receipt of the latter written declaration, or, if Congress is not in session, within twenty-one days after Congress is required to assemble, determines by two-thirds vote of both Houses that the President is unable to discharge the powers and duties of his office, the Vice President shall continue to discharge the same as Acting President; otherwise, the President shall resume the powers and duties of his office.

XXVI

Passed by Congress March 23, 1971. Ratified July 1, 1971.

Section 1.

The right of citizens of the United States, who are eighteen years of age or older, to vote shall not be denied or abridged by the United States or by any State on account of age.

Section 2.

The Congress shall have power to enforce this article by appropriate legislation.

XXVII

Originally proposed Sept. 25, 1789. Ratified May 7, 1992.
No law, varying the compensation for the services of the Senators and Representatives, shall take effect, until an election of Representatives shall have intervened.

IMAGE CREDITS

Chapter One

1.3. Library of Congress Prints and Photographs Division / Copyright in the Public Domain.

1.4. Copyright in the Public Domain.

1.5. Joseph Abel / Copyright in the Public Domain.

1.6. US Department of Justice / Copyright in the Public Domain.

1.7. Copyright © 2012 by Biswarup Ganguly / (CC BY-SA 3.0) at http://commons.wikimedia.org/wiki/File:Crashed_Taxi_-_Multiple_Car_Accident_-_Rabindra_Sadan_Area_-_Kolkata_2012-06-13_01323.jpg.

Chapter Two

2.1. Copyright © 2007 by swatjester / Flickr / (CC BY-SA 2.0) at http://commons.wikimedia.org/wiki/File:Marbury_v_Madison_John_Marshall_by_Swatjester_crop.jpg.

2.2. Copyright © 2006 by Jarle Vines / (CC BY-SA 3.0) at http://commons.wikimedia.org/wiki/File:Burger_King_Paa_Karl_Johan.jpg.

2.3. Copyright © 2008 by Matt Dempsey / (CC BY-SA 2.0) at https://www.flickr.com/photos/matt44053/3245510424.

2.4. Copyright in the Public Domain.

2.5. Copyright in the Public Domain.

2.6. User:Ammodramus / Wikimedia Commons / Copyright in the Public Domain.

Chapter Three

3.1. Bureau of Engraving and Printing / Copyright in the Public Domain.

3.2. Warren K. Leffler / US News & World Report / Copyright in the Public Domain.

3.3. Copyright © 2010 by Jeffrey Pang / (CC BY 2.0) at https://www.flickr.com/photos/jeffpang/4784912702.

Chapter Four

Chapter Five

Chapter Six

Chapter Seven

Chapter Eight

Chapter Nine

Chapter Ten

Chapter Eleven

11.4. PublicDomainPictures / Pixabay / Copyright in the Public Domain.

11.5. geralt / Pixabay / Copyright in the Public Domain.

11.6. tkoch / Pixabay / Copyright in the Public Domain.

11.7. Nemo / Pixabay / Copyright in the Public Domain.

Chapter Twelve

12.1. Nemo / Pixabay / Copyright in the Public Domain.

12.2. PublicDomainPictures / Pixabay / Copyright in the Public Domain.

12.3. FDA / Copyright in the Public Domain.

12.4. Mcability / Pixabay / Copyright in the Public Domain.

Chapter Sixteen

16.1. Craig Stihler / FWS / Copyright in the Public Domain.

16.2. PublicDomainPictures / Pixabay / Copyright in the Public Domain.

ABOUT THE AUTHORS

Michael Bootsma is a licensed CPA and attorney in the state of Iowa. Mr. Bootsma holds a Juris Doctorate as well as an M.A. from the University of Iowa. He received a B.S. from Iowa State University in the areas of accounting and finance. He has held various professional positions in the areas of education, accounting, and law.

Charles Damschen is a Registered Patent Attorney and partner at Hamilton IP Law. Mr. Damschen is also an adjunct at the University of Iowa College of Law where he received his Juris Doctorate with high distinction. He received a bachelor of chemical engineering and a B.S. in chemistry from the University of Minnesota.

Sophia Harvey is an attorney in the state of North Carolina. Ms. Harvey holds a Juris Doctorate from the University of Iowa and a B.A. in Government from Harvard University. She studied tax law at the University of Florida and is currently pursuing an S.J.D. in tax law at the University of Florida. She has practiced law in the areas of bankruptcy, tax, civil litigation and criminal defense. Ms. Harvey was certified and testified as a tax expert in a Chapter 11 bankruptcy case.

L. Craig Nierman completed his undergraduate work at the University of California, Davis. Mr. Nierman then spent seven years working for a Fortune 100 insurance company after which he earned a Juris Doctorate with high distinction from the University of Iowa College of Law. He has held several adjunct teaching positions. He currently practices insurance law in Iowa and serves nationally as an expert witness and consultant in insurance litigation.

Michael Thieme received a Juris Doctorate from the University of Iowa. Mr. Thieme currently serves as an assistant professor for the Department of Law at the United States Air Force Academy. He was previously assigned to the Office of Military Commissions, Defense where he represented multiple detainees held in United States custody at Guantanamo Bay, Cuba. The views and opinions of the author expressed herein do not necessarily reflect those of the United States Air Force. No federal endorsement of this book is intended.

GLOSSARY

A

Abandoned property is property that an owner intentionally leaves or discards.

Abatement benefits the dollar value placed on the ability to avoid pollution.

Abatement cost is the cost to the business of not creating pollution.

Absolute ownership means the ownership of personal property and the ownership interest will last perpetually.

Absolute privilege applies to statements made in legal proceedings such as a trial or debate in the legislature.

Accord and satisfaction is an agreement (also known as an accord) where the parties agree to satisfy a preexisting duty by imposing a new contractual duty.

Active inducement under which theory one who distributes a device with the intent to induce infringement is liable.

Actual authority Implied authority and express authority are often referred to by this term since the principal actually gives authority to the agent before the agent acts on his behalf.

Actual duty is a duty one must perform in a given scenario.

Actus Reus is the criminal or guilty act, or in some cases omission, that society has deemed unlawful.

Adequate protection doctrine under which the court may require the debtor to make certain payments to its secured creditors in an attempt to protect the creditor's interest while the creditor is subject to the automatic stay.

Adequate protection payments are payments that a lender might receive in order to protect them from loss in value due to depreciation of a product between the time a bankruptcy is filed and the time a plan that provides for payment to lender is confirmed.

Adhesion contract is a contract in which one party has a superior amount of bargaining power that eliminates the other party from bargaining for better terms in a contract.

Administrative law creates the rules agencies must follow when making regulatory law and when enforcing regulatory law.

Advertisements are generally not legally binding offers unless they contain words of limitations such as limiting the quantity of the item being sold or the number of people who can accept.

After a reasonable amount of time when an offer terminates. Determining what a reasonable amount of time is depends on the facts and circumstances of each case.

Agency by estoppel occurs when a principal acts in a manner that leads a third party to reasonably believe an agency relationship exists.

Agency by ratification is formed when an agent acts without authority from a principal but the principal ratifies the action afterwards.

an Agent is the one who agrees to act on behalf of a principal and subject to the control of the principal.

an Agreement is generally evinced by an offer and an acceptance.

The Agreement on Trade Related Aspects of Intellectual Property Rights (TRIPS Agreement) highlights the fact that intellectual property (and the respect for the intellectual property rights of others) is not only of great importance to fully developed economies but also to economies in the developing world.

Alimony is a court-ordered requirement of payment to be made by a divorced spouse.

Alternative dispute resolution includes ways to resolve legal disputes without a trial.

Answer is the defendant's formal response to the complaint.

Anticipatory repudiation occurs when a party to a contract informs the other party to a contract that it will be unable to perform under the terms of the contract.

Anti-nepotism refers to the refusal to hire family members or spouses.

Apparent authority exists when a principal leads a third party to reasonably believe an agent possesses authority to perform an action or actions on behalf of the principal.

Appeal of Right means the entitlement to appeal to the Court of Appeals.

Appellant refers to the party who appeals.

Appellate Court parties usually have the right to have trial court decisions reviewed by a state Appellate Court.

Appellee refers to the other party from the one who appeals (the appeallant).

Appropriation is the wrongful use of another's name or likeness for the defendant's benefit.

A promise to pay for a debt is often enforceable by courts even if the debt is not legally required to be paid.

Arbitrary marks are those that have no relation to the goods or services associated with the mark other than identifying the source.

Arbitration is like a trial provided by an entity other than the government. It uses a third party but differs from negotiation and mediation in that it is more certain to produce a final, legally binding resolution.

Area sources are those other than major sources (see below), which are subject to more stringent requirements.

Arraignment is the initial step in a criminal prosecution, whereby the defendant is brought to court to hear the formal charges and enter a plea.

Arson in common law is the malicious burning of the dwelling of another person.

Assault claims will prevail only if the plaintiff can prove that the defendant intentionally put them in fear of imminent physical harm; that a reasonable person in the same situation would be fearful of imminent physical harm; and that the defendant had no permission or privilege to act.

Assignee refers to the party receiving the right.

Assignment occurs when a party transfers its rights under a contract to a third party.

Assignor is the party who transfers a right.

Assumption of risk results when the plaintiff increased the likelihood of injury by knowingly engaging in a risky activity.

Attorney work product is the attorney's own notes, strategies, and intra-office communication.

Attractive nuisance is a potentially dangerous object that might attract others onto a property owner's land.

At-will employment refers to an agreement that allows an employer to terminate an employment relationship without providing a cause (reason) to the employee and without legal liability (as a general rule).

Auction refers to a situation where the auctioneer places an item for sale and solicits bids from those in attendance. The bidders make an offer to purchase and the auctioneer decides which bid to accept.

Authority by ratification occurs when a principal grants authority after the agent has acted on their behalf without authority. The principal must have all the material facts in order to grant authority by ratification.

Award is the final decision of the arbitrator during an arbitration and is much like a judgment in a trial.

B

Bailee refers to the person who rightfully possesses the property in relation to bailments.

Bailment occurs when a piece of property is possessed lawfully by someone other than the owner.

Bailor is the true owner of the property in relation to bailments.

Bankruptcy Courts are one of several types of court that hear cases of a specific nature within the federal system; they hear only bankruptcy matters.

Bankruptcy fraud occurs when a person knowingly and fraudulently conceals assets or destroys, falsifies, or withholds documents in violation of the law governing a bankruptcy proceeding.

Battery involves intentional physical contact that is offensive or harmful and was not consented to. The requirements are that the defendant touched the plaintiff with an object or the defendant's body; that the touching was unwelcome or offensive; that a reasonable person in the same situation would find the touching harmful or offensive; and that the defendant had no permission or privilege to act.

Bench trial refers to a trial without a jury (since it is tried to the judge sitting at the bench).

Berne Convention is an international treaty for copyright which provides international protection for copyrights of citizens of any member country.

Beyond a reasonable doubt To prove a defendant is guilty *beyond a reasonable doubt* means the trier of fact, a judge or a jury, can have no reasonable doubt that the defendant is guilty.

Bilateral An offer in a *bilateral* contract is accepted by a return promise.

Bilateral mistake or mutual mistake occurs when both parties to a contract are mistaken.

Bill of sale is a written statement from a seller that proves the seller has transferred ownership to the buyer.

Bribery is offering, giving, receiving, or requesting something of value with the intent to unlawfully influence a person or entity in a position of trust.

Bribery of a public official is a federal crime designed to ensure that government officials act with the interest of the constituents in mind instead of their own financial interests.

Brief After the notice of appeal, each party files a *brief*, which is a lengthy written argument with citations to the law and evidence.

Burglary under the common law was the breaking and entering into the dwelling house of another at nighttime with the intent to commit a felony.

Business ethics is a term generally used to refer to the application of ethics in the business context.

Business necessity is an employment requirement that is uniformly applied and consistent with a necessary part of business operations.

C

Cap and trade system involves setting a cap on the total number of allowable SO_2 emissions, and establishing a system of tradable allowances where regulated sources can buy and sell (trade) SO_2 allowances in a market administered by the EPA.

Case of first impression refers to when a court hears a case for the first time.

Categorical Imperative Immanuel Kant's *Categorical Imperative* asks "what if everyone acted this way?" Kant believed human beings had a duty to act in such a way that the individual would find their action to be acceptable as a universal law.

Cause in fact is often referred to as the "but for" cause of the damages. The judge or jury asks "but for" the defendant's breach of duty, would the plaintiff have been injured?

Caveat emptor means "buyer beware"—a seller does not have to disclose known facts about a product or a service that might deter a buyer. A buyer is responsible for inquiring as to the details or condition of the product or service they are purchasing.

Cease and desist A *cease and desist* letter informs a party they are engaging in unlawful behavior and must immediately stop such actions.

Certification mark is a mark used to certify a good or service.

Challenge for cause If a potential juror indicates that he or she is biased against one of the parties or will not be able to conform to the judge's instructions, an attorney may issue a *challenge for cause*, which is a request that the judge remove the juror for a specific reason.

Civil law is a body of law that defines private rights and remedies of a citizen. It primarily governs the legal issues arising between citizens and between citizens and their government, and is often enforced by one citizen against another, but can be enforced by a government entity in the United States.

Civil procedure is the procedural law for civil, rather than criminal, cases.

Clean Air Act (CAA) of 1970 was intended for the EPA to develop *national ambient air quality standards* (NAAQS) for common air pollutants, called criteria pollutants.

Clean Water Act requires that all point sources obtain a National Pollution Discharge Elimination System (NPDES) permit before they may add any pollutant to navigable waters.

Clear and convincing evidence can be thought of as requiring the plaintiff to prove it is more substantially likely than not that the defendant is liable.

Click-on agreement is used to describe online transactions where the user must click on a box to certify their assent.

Closed shop is an employer's requirement that an employee be a member of a union before being hired.

Closing arguments After all of the evidence is presented, each side is allowed time to orally summarize the evidence presented and assist the factfinder in how to analyze the evidence through *closing arguments*.

Coase Theorem is an economic theorem which holds an efficient outcome will be obtained through bargaining as long as transaction costs are low.

Collateral refers to the assets in which a creditor holds a security interest.

Collective bargaining is a process whereby the worker's union, on behalf of its individual members, negotiates workplace matters with the owners or managers of a company.

Collective marks are marks used by a group of individuals such as a union or an association.

Color has been interpreted, in relation to civil rights, as encompassing a person's skin pigmentation or the general shade of their complexion.

Command and control approach under which the government enforces regulations that prescribe which activities are illegal and which are not.

Commercial impracticability is a legal doctrine where a court discharges a party from their contractual duty because it is commercially impractical but not objectively impossible.

Commercial speech includes speech that promotes a product or service, communicates information that benefits the economic interest of the speaker, or intends to create goodwill for the company.

Common carrier agrees to carry property or persons for anyone who requests; cannot refuse to carry a person or property without reasonable grounds for denying such request; and is licensed by the government.

Common enemy doctrine enables a landowner to use any means possible to divert surface water from their property.

Common law is a term used to refer to a set of general legal principles and definitions largely derived from the precedent of court cases as opposed to statutes.

Comparative negligence compares the contribution of the defendant toward the plaintiff's injury with the contribution of the plaintiff toward their own injury.

Compensatory damages refers to an award of money calculated to compensate a person for the harm caused by the tortfeasor.

Complaint or petition is the document that initiates an action (or lawsuit). It is a pleading setting forth the names of the parties, a description of the controversy, and the specific legal theories that justify the plaintiff's request for relief.

Comprehensive Environmental Response, Compensation, and Liability Act (CERCLA) of 1980, or Superfund, deals with the remediation of abandoned sites containing hazardous substances.

Concurrent conditions refer to when mutual conditions exist and both parties are subject to those conditions.

Concurrent jurisdiction means two or more courts have jurisdiction over the same matter.

Concurring opinion is the opinion of one or more judges who agree with the outcome of the majority opinion but for different legal reasons.

Conditional gift is a gift that can be accepted or demanded only after a certain condition has been met.

Conditional privilege exists when the defendant's communication was made in good faith with the proper motive.

Condition precedent is a condition that must be satisfied before performance is required by another party under a contract.

Condition subsequent is a condition that requires performance until a condition is no longer satisfied.

Confession of judgment refers to when the defendant offers to pay a certain amount of money to settle the case. If the plaintiff rejects the offer and the final judgment is for that amount or less, the plaintiff may be required to pay for the defendant's court costs and/or attorney fees.

Confidentiality clause is the portion of the settlement agreement that keeps the terms secret.

Consent in relation to contract law means to agree to the terms of the contractual agreement.

Consequential damages are those which require notice to be received by the defendant.

Consideration is the legal value provided in a bargained-for exchange of a promise.

Continuation application An inventor may allow a patent to issue with the narrow claims and then file another patent application called a *continuation application* that is related to the first application. The continuation application is virtually identical to the first except for the claims.

Continuation-in-part application is filed if new subject matter is to be included after the first application (as this cannot be included in a continuation application).

Contract carrier is a carrier which routinely transports property or persons for a select group of customers.

Contractual capacity is the capacity required by law to enter into contracts.

Contributory infringement is a type of indirect infringement that occurs when a party provides a component that has a specific use as part of another article that is covered by a patent, even though that component standing alone does not infringe any patents.

Contributory negligence means negligence on the part of the plaintiff contributed in some fashion to their injury.

Conversion is essentially a civil remedy for theft and is committed when the defendant takes or retains another's personal property.

Convey To *convey* property means a grantor transfers legal title to a grantee. A common example of a conveyance is a sale of property.

Copyright is an intellectual property right designed to protect artistic works, and broadly extends to "original works of authorship fixed in any tangible medium of expression."

Corporation is a separate legal entity that provides limited liability to its owners who are called stockholders.

Correlative rights doctrine Under this doctrine, the owner of land overlaying percolating water is considered to be a joint owner with other property owners whose property overlays the percolating water.

Counterclaim When a defendant is sued and the defendant responds with a lawsuit against the plaintiff, this is called a *counterclaim*.

Counteroffer An offeree may reject an offer by simply stating "no" or by making a counteroffer. A *counteroffer* rejects the original offer and makes a new offer.

Course of dealing means how the parties have acted in previous dealings with one another.

Course of performance means how the parties have interpreted terms in a contract as evinced by performance under the contract.

Courts of general jurisdiction State courts are *courts of general jurisdiction*, i.e., they have authority over every matter not specifically reserved for other courts.

Courts of limited jurisdiction Federal courts have the power to hear only cases arising out of the Constitution and laws passed by Congress so, instead of being courts of general jurisdiction, they are *courts of limited jurisdiction*.

Covenant refers to a promise to do something or refrain from doing something with one's property.

Credibility often focuses on bias, or past acts of the witness such as lying or cheating, but it can also relate to the witness's competence.

Credit card fraud is committed when, without authorization, a criminal uses a credit card holder's information to obtain a benefit with such information.

Creditor refers to a party to whom money is owed.

Creditor beneficiaries are owed performance by one of the parties because of a preexisting obligation owed to the intended beneficiary.

Criminal law defines what is a crime. It can generally be enforced only by a government representative such as the attorney for a city or state.

Cross examination During witness testimony, *cross examination* takes place after *direct examination* (where the side that called the witness asks questions) and involves the other side asking questions, but only on subjects related to the direct examination.

Cybercrime involves the use of a computer or computer-related technology.

Cyber hacking is the unauthorized access of another's computer with the intent to change its settings or to access information on that computer.

Cybersquatting refers to a party registering a domain name that was identical or very similar to a well-known mark and attempting to resell that domain name to the mark owner for a profit.

Cyber torts are torts based on computer-, Internet-, or technology-related activities.

D

Debt collector refers to anyone who routinely collects debts that are owed to another party.

Debt workout refers to a process that creditors can use to settle their claims for payment by negotiating privately with the debtor.

Debtor refers to a party who owes money to another.

Debtor-in-possession refers to a debtor who is operating under a chapter 11 plan and continues to operate the business.

Deceptive advertising is advertising that states or omits a fact that makes the advertising misleading about a material fact to the reasonable consumer.

Deed refers to a legal instrument that allows the grantor to transfer an interest in real property to the grantee.

Defamation There are two types of defamation: libel and slander. Libel applies to a defamatory written statement, while slander concerns defamatory oral communication.

Defamation by implication A defendant who uses the truth in a malicious manner and publishes their statement to a third party causing harm to a defendant's reputation might still be liable for defamation under the theory of defamation by implication.

Defamation per se means that the statements are inherently harmful. The statements can be either written (libel) or verbal (slander).

Default judgment means that the plaintiff obtains a judgment against the defendant because of the defendant's failure to defend the case.

Defendant or respondent, is the person against whom a lawsuit is being brought.

Defense of laches means that the defendant is asserting that the patent owner waited too long to bring the infringement claim.

Delegatee refers to the party to whom a delegation of duty has been made.

Delegator refers to the party who delegates a duty.

Depositions are an opportunity for each side to interview the other party, or other potential witnesses such as an employee, under oath prior to trial.

Design patents cover the nonfunctional ornamental aspects of the invention.

Devise means to transfer ownership of a property by use of a will.

Direct examination is the phase of witness testimony when the side that called the witness asks questions.

Direct marketing is the process by which marketing is made directly to a consumer.

Disaffirm To disaffirm a contract means to declare the voidable contract will not be honored or abided by.

Discharged At the end of a chapter 7 case, debtors are *discharged* of unpaid liabilities that are allowed to be discharged under the bankruptcy code. The discharge prevents creditors from bringing collection proceedings for the discharged debt.

Discovery rule as an exception to the statute of limitations, extends it by the amount of time that a reasonable person would not have had any idea that a claim existed.

Discretionary Appeals are appeals to the Supreme Court which mean that the Supreme Court will not necessarily agree to hear a case appealed to it.

Discrimination means treating an applicant differently from others in regards to work-related matters because the employee or job applicant belongs to a protected class.

Disparate impact arises when an employer's job requirements or hiring qualifications discriminate against those of a protected class even if the employer did not intend to discriminate against a protected class.

Disparate treatment is intentional discrimination.

Dissenting opinion sometimes referred to as a minority opinion, means a minority number of judges hearing a case have the same opinion as to the outcome of a case which is different from the majority opinion.

District Court Judges as well as judges of the Court of Appeals and Supreme Court Justices, are appointed by the president, subject to confirmation by the United States Senate. The judges serve a life term and can be removed from office only for certain egregious misconduct.

Diversity jurisdiction Article III of the Constitution gives Congress the power to give the federal courts overlapping jurisdiction over certain cases between citizens of different states on matters that would otherwise be heard in state court. Currently, the law allows this if the amount in dispute exceeds $75,000. The authority to hear these cases is called *diversity jurisdiction* because it involves people of diverse citizenship.

Doctrine of Unforeseen Circumstances allows a contract to be modified from its original terms without requiring additional consideration, as long as the unforeseen circumstance was not foreseeable.

Donee A donor is the person giving a gift to a recipient who is the *donee*.

Donee beneficiaries are not owed a performance because of an existing duty but because a party to the contract has decided to provide them a benefit.

Donor A *donor* is the person giving a gift to a recipient who is the donee.

Dormant Commerce Clause is a constitutional principle that states only Congress can regulate interstate commerce. It prohibits states from regulating an area of interstate commerce even if Congress has not.

Double Jeopardy prohibits the state from trying a defendant twice for the same crime. Double Jeopardy even prevents the state from appealing a not-guilty decision in a criminal case to a higher court.

Dram shop action is brought by a plaintiff against an establishment that served too much alcohol to a patron, who caused the plaintiff's injury.

Due process prevents the federal government from arbitrarily taking a citizen's life, liberty, or property. There are two types of due process; substantive and procedural.

Duty-based ethical theories determine ethical behavior by focusing on a prescribed set of duties one must follow.

E

Economic efficiency is the use of resources in a way that maximizes the production and distribution of goods and services.

Emancipation is the legal process by which a minor becomes independent of their parents under the law, thereby losing their status as a minor.

Embezzlement occurs when a fiduciary is lawfully entrusted with personal property of another and then fraudulently takes or uses that property for his own gain.

Emergency agency powers arise when an emergency situation arises and an agent must act without actual authority.

Emergency Planning and Community Right-to-Know Act of 1986 is an emergency preparedness law that places reporting requirements on facilities that manufacture or store specified chemicals.

Eminent domain The Fifth Amendment protects property owners from having their property confiscated by the state without just compensation. Just compensation has been held to mean the fair value of the property and does not include lawyer's fees or other costs incurred by the property owner in defending their ownership of the property. The process of a government taking property of a citizen in this manner is referred to *eminent domain*.

Endangered means a species is at risk of extinction throughout all or a significant portion of its geographic habitat.

Endangered species refers to a species that may face extinction (complete elimination) if not protected.

Endangered Species Act of 1973 (ESA) was enacted to prevent the extinction of plants and animals. It is administered for ocean species by the National Marine Fisheries Service (NMFS), a division of the National Oceanic and Atmospheric Administration, an agency within the Department of Commerce.

Equal dignity rule holds that if an agent will be entering into contracts on behalf of the principal, which must be in writing under the Statute of Frauds, the agent's authority as granted by the principal must be in writing.

Equal Protection is a concept that holds states cannot treat classes of citizens differently under the law unless they have a legitimate, important, or compelling reason for doing so.

Equitable damages are damages not consisting of money damages and include 1) rescission, 2) injunction, or 3) specific performance.

Equitable title is the ownership of property that provides benefits to the owner such as use of the property.

Erie Doctrine can be applied in diversity cases, and originates from the 1938 United States Supreme Court decision in *Erie Railroad Co. v. Tompkins*. This case establishes that when federal courts exercise jurisdiction over cases arising out of state law, they must apply state rather than federal law. Thus, theoretically, litigants should expect to get the same result regardless of whether their cases are heard in state or federal courthouses.

Errors and omissions When malpractice claims are made against professionals like insurance agents or brokers, real estate agents, or other agents who help individual fill out applications or sign purchase contracts, the malpractice claim is often called an *errors and omissions* claim.

Estate The debtor's property is referred to by the court as the bankruptcy *estate*.

Ethics refers to the principles of wrong and right held by an individual and derived from various sources such as custom, societal norms, and personal beliefs that guide an individual when deciding which behavior is morally acceptable.

Evidence, clear and convincing can be thought of as requiring the plaintiff to prove it is more substantially likely than not that the defendant is liable.

Exclusionary rule excludes any evidence which was obtained in violation of a defendant's fourth, fifth, or sixth amendment rights.

Exculpatory clause relieves a party from liability in the event an injury results from performance of the contract.

Executed contracts are contracts under which both parties have performed and no performance is still due.

Executive Branch refers to the offices of president and vice president in the US.

Executory contracts are contracts for which one party still owes performance.

Exempt property refers to certain property of the debtor which is exempt from being used to pay creditors

Exhibits refer to much of the information presented in court which was obtained in discovery.

Expectation damages are the difference between the position where the plaintiff expected to be and where the plaintiff was left after the breach. The formula for expectation damages = what plaintiff was promised – what plaintiff received from defendant – cost savings to plaintiff of breach.

Expert testimony Providing but-for causation in malpractice cases is generally established through *expert testimony*, which is evidence provided through the testimony of professionals with similar credentials to those of the defendant.

Expert witnesses While most witnesses testify merely as to what they actually saw or heard, *expert witnesses* provide opinions about the incident. During discovery, each side is required to disclose not only what experts they may call as witnesses, but also certain information about their experts' credentials and expected testimony.

Express contracts are contracts that are generally either verbal or written.

Express agency is an agency that is formed either through a written agreement or an oral agreement.

Express authority is authority that was given in written or verbal form.

Express warranties are written or oral assertions (promises) about a product or a service made by a seller.

Expression of opinion is generally not an offer and cannot be accepted by someone hearing this statement.

Externality is a cost or benefit not included in the price of a market good.

Extortion was the fraudulent use of one's public office to obtain assets from a victim. Today most states have a criminal statute outlawing blackmail, which is the obtaining of assets by threatening harm to a victim or their property.

F

Factfinder is the judge in a bench trial or the jury in a jury trial.

False imprisonment occurs when a defendant confines the plaintiff through the use of physical force or verbal threats without permission or privilege.

Fanciful marks are those that did not exist in the language prior to their use as a mark, such as "Exxon" or "Kodak."

Federal Circuit based in Washington, D.C., is the only division of the Court of Appeals to receive cases based on the subject matter of the case rather than the geography of the lower court.

Federal Insecticide, Fungicide, and Rodenticide Act (FIFRA) of 1972 regulates the use of pesticides and is administered by the EPA and by state environmental agencies. FIFRA requires that all pesticide products be registered with the EPA.

Federal law refers to laws created by an entity of the federal government or to the US Constitution.

Fee simple A *fee simple* ownership interest is an estate of land that may last perpetually. The owner of land can pass ownership to his or her heirs (descendants).

Felony refers to a serious crime, punishable by imprisonment for more than one year or by death.

Fiduciary duty requires one party act in the best interest of another party. The agent must act in the best interest of the principal and put the principal's interest before their own.

Firm offer Under UCC § 2-205, an offer can become a *firm offer* if 1) the offer was made by a merchant, 2) there is a signed writing, and 3) the writing clearly states the offer is to remain open. If a period of time has not been stated, the offer is to remain open to the offeree for a reasonable period of time not to exceed three months.

First-sale doctrine requires the patent owner to relinquish all rights in an individual article after an authorized sale so that the purchaser is free to use or resell that article without any restrictions.

Fixture refers to a piece of personal property that has been attached to real property in such a manner that the personal property becomes a part of the real property. Since a fixture is considered real property once it is attached, the fixture transfers with the real property when such real property is sold unless the purchaser and buyer agree otherwise.

Foreseeability is sometimes referred to as legal causation or proximate causation.

Forgery refers to the making or altering of a writing with the intent to defraud another.

Franchise is a term used to describe a contract that allows one business entity to enjoy benefits such as advertising, access to products, and use of trademarks and trade names.

Fraud The tort of *fraud* is designed to provide a remedy to those who are damaged through deceit.

Fraudulent transfer is a payment of cash or transfers of assets that were made within two years of the filing of the petition when such transfers are made for less than adequate consideration.

Free Market refers to a market economy where the government does not intervene.

Frustration of purpose is a legal doctrine that discharges the duty of parties to perform where the original purpose of their contract can no longer be achieved. It is not necessary for both parties to have their purposes frustrated.

Fully disclosed principal is one where an agent discloses the existence and identity of to a third party. A fully disclosed principal alleviates the agent from liability from third parties in regards to contractual breach.

G

General agent is an agent who has the authority to provide all the business services a principal would need for a given purpose or at a given location.

General damages compensate for losses resulting from the tort that do not have a precise economic value. They compensate the injured person generally, but are not calculated by using a specific mathematical model.

General deterrence When someone commits a crime, society has an interest in punishing the lawbreaker such that the rest of society sees the harsh consequences and is deterred from breaking the law themselves; this is referred to as *general deterrence*.

General partner has unlimited liability for the liabilities of the partnership, including debts incurred by the partnership or torts committed by the partnership's activities.

General partnership refers to a partnership that does not provide limited liability to any of its members.

Generic term refers to a mark that only names the product associated with the term.

Gift causa mortis is given by a donor who believes death is imminent. The gift is automatically revoked if the donor recovers from the illness or survives the event that led the donor to believe death was imminent.

Gift inter vivos is a gift made during the lifetime of the donor. A gift inter vivos is irrevocable, which means the donor cannot revoke the gift once it is made.

Good faith means honesty in fact and the observance of reasonable commercial standards of fair dealing.

Grand jury In federal courts, if the crime is a felony, the accused has a constitutional right to a *grand jury*. This means the prosecutor must present evidence to a panel of citizens and they decide if there is enough evidence to proceed.

Grantee and Grantor A deed is a legal instrument that allows the *grantor*, person transferring an interest in real property, to a *grantee*, the person to whom the ownership interest in real property is being transferred.

Gratuitous agency relationship refers to one in which the agent is not compensated by the principal. Under contract law, a contract would not normally exist in the case of a gratuitous agency relationship because no consideration was received by the agent in exchange for their promise to work as an agent.

Greenhouse effect The basic concept behind climate change is that a layer of gases around the globe form the basis of what is called the *greenhouse effect* on our planet.

Greenwashing is the spin that oversells how environmentally friendly a produce, policy, or company is.

H

Hearsay evidence is when a witness states what the witness heard someone else say.

Hostile work environment harassment occurs when a workplace becomes hostile because of an employee's membership in a protected class and the reasonable person would find the workplace intimidating.

I

Idea–expression dichotomy refers to the concept that states an idea is not separable from its expression.

Identity theft occurs under federal law when a person has been found to "knowingly transfer or use, without lawful authority, a means of identification of another person with the intent to commit, or to aid or abet, any unlawful activity that constitutes a violation of Federal law, or that constitutes a felony under any applicable State or local law.

Illusory promise refers to a promise that appears to be consideration but is not, as the promise itself does not legally obligate the promisor to a specific detriment.

Immunity is a promise from the government not to prosecute some or all of the crimes charged, in exchange for the accused's willingness and cooperation in catching and testifying against others engaged in even more serious crimes.

Implied agency arises from facts and circumstances that result in the parties believing an agency has been formed.

Implied authority arises from 1) express authority or 2) custom.

Implied contract also called an implied-in-fact contract, is different from an express contract because it is inferred from the actions of the parties and is not evinced by an oral or written agreement.

Implied warranties are nonverbal or non-written assertions about a product or a service at the time they are sold. Implied warranties do not cover a specific period of time, as an implied warranty makes an implied promise at the time the product or service is sold.

Implied warranty of fitness for a particular use is the implied promise a consumer good will achieve a particular purpose or perform a specific function.

Implied warranty of habitability requires the landlord to keep the premises fit for habitation both before and after a tenant takes possession.

Implied warranty of merchantability is the assertion by the selling merchant that a consumer product is fit for its general purpose and contains no defect.

Incidental beneficiary is a party whom the original parties did not intend to benefit with their contract. He or she does not have standing to sue for breach of contract.

Incidental damages arise because of the breach of the seller and include costs such as shipping the goods back to the seller or having the goods inspected by a third party.

Indecent material is less offensive than obscene material and is not allowed to be aired on television or radio broadcasts during times when a child might regularly be exposed to such programming.

Indemnification is the act of seeking reimbursement arising from a legal liability.

Independent contractor refers to a person who is not an employee because an *independent contractor* does not work under the direct control or supervision of the hiring person but is instead hired to perform a task or complete a project which he or she completes independently.

Indirect infringement requires that the infringer has knowledge of the patent and that the accused infringer intended that its product infringe the patent.

Informal contracts are contracts that are not subject to formal requirements under the law.

Information is a formal criminal charge made by a prosecutor without a grand-jury indictment.

Infringement is the unlawful use of another's right without their permission.

Injunction An *injunction* requires a party to quit and refrain from engaging in certain behavior.

Innocent infringement occurs when a defendant did not have notice of a copyright. It is allowed by courts as a defense to a claim of copyright infringement.

Innocent misrepresentation occurs when a party makes a representation that turns out to be false but does not do so intentionally.

Inquiry An *inquiry* is not a counteroffer but a tentative or indefinite request for a better offer or a comment upon the terms of the offer.

In rem jurisdiction gives a state court authority over a dispute when the property at issue is located within that state, even if its owner is not a resident of that state.

Insider trading can be legal—when corporate directors buy and sell stock in their own company, though such actions must be reported to the SEC and placed during certain times of the year specified by the SEC. *Insider trading* is illegal when someone buys or sells while possessing nonpublic information.

Integrity means a person has a strong character for being honest, fair and consistent in the application of their moral beliefs of right and wrong.

Intellectual property is the broad term that generally refers to products of the human creative spirit such as inventions, creative works, trade and service marks, trade secrets, and other know-how.

Intended beneficiary A third-party *intended beneficiary* is a party whom the original parties to a contract intend to benefit.

Intentional infliction of emotional distress When a defendant causes an injury to a plaintiff by engaging in intentionally outrageous behavior, the defendant may be liable for *intentional infliction of emotional distress*.

Interference with a prospective business advantage While bona fide competition is not actionable, a business that unreasonably targets a competitor's customers or engages them may be liable for *interference with a prospective business advantage.*

Interference with contractual relationship A person who induces another to breach a contract with a third party can be held liable for *interference with contractual relationship.*

Interlocutory appeal The vast majority of appeals are heard after judgment. However, the parties may seek an *interlocutory appeal,* which is an appeal prior to trial.

Intermediate Appellate Court is a court that hears appeals from state trial courts and is subject to the authority of a higher court usually called the Supreme Court.

International law is composed of the laws and judicial customs of all nations or countries.

Interrogatories Discovery often begins with written requests for information. Among the most common requests are questions, called *interrogatories,* which are written questions that the other side must answer.

Intervening cause also known as superseding cause, is a defense to a negligence action. When a defense is raised based upon an *intervening cause,* the defendant asserts that something beyond the defendant's control intervened to cause the plaintiff's injury.

Invasion of privacy The tort of *invasion of privacy* helps to protect the privacy and identity of ordinary citizens.

Involuntary petitions are filed by creditors who are concerned the debtor may incur more debt and lose more assets if legal action is not taken to protect the debtor's assets.

J

Joint and several liability means any party who is responsible for helping create the harm is jointly liable for the damages and could be called upon to pay all the damages.

Joint liability means all partners share liability but any one partner can be required to pay the full amount of the debt.

Joint tenancy with right of survivorship is an ownership interest where two or more persons own an undivided interest in property.

Judge is a court-appointed official who governs a court's proceedings.

Judgment is a final ruling on the result of the trial. The *judgment* may differ slightly from the verdict.

Judicial Branch interprets and applies federal law to cases and controversies.

Judicial review is a review by the Supreme Court "to say what the law is" and declare whether a statute passed by Congress violates constitutional principles.

Jurisdiction is the power of a court to decide a case regarding certain legal matters. In order to hear case, a court must have the appropriate jurisdiction.

Jury instructions The judge instructs the jury on what the law is in the form of *jury instructions.* Each side presents the judge with a list of instructions it would like the jury to hear. Then, immediately after the evidence has been presented, the judge decides which instructions to give.

Jury trial In civil cases, one of the parties must ask for a *jury trial* within a certain amount of time of filing the complaint or answer. The number of jurors varies by jurisdiction ranging from six to twelve.

Justices Judges who sit on the Supreme Court are often referred to as *Justices*.

L

Larceny is the taking and carrying away of another's tangible property with the intent to deprive them of such property.

Law The *law* defines what is legal and what is illegal and provides a minimum threshold for acceptable behavior in society.

Leasehold estate gives a tenant the right to possess an estate for a period of time, such as one year, or until the tenant and landlord desire it to end.

Legal injury refers to an injury that rises above a certain legal threshold. While hurt feelings do not constitute a legal injury, a physical injury or lost money does.

Legal subject matter is a requirement that a contract not accomplish an illegal goal or act.

Legal title means the ownership of property that is granted by the government and respected by a court.

Legislative Branch The US Congress is referred to as the *Legislative Branch* because it creates legislation.

Levy means to seize assets or funds. A *levy* can also be on other assets, including what other parties owe the defendant.

Libel is one of two types of defamation. The other is *slander*. *Libel* applies to a defamatory written statement.

License is the right to go *onto* another's land. For example, the driver of a delivery truck has the implied *license* to drive their truck onto the recipient's property. As a general rule, a *license* is revocable.

Life estate is an ownership interest that will lapse at the time the owner dies.

Limited liability company is a separate legal entity that provides limited liability protection to its owners like a corporation while preserving pass-through taxation similar to that of a partnership.

Limited liability limited partnership In states that recognize a *limited liability limited partnership*, all partners in the limited liability partnership receive limited liability protection.

Limited partner has liability that is limited to its investment in the partnership. *Limited partners* generally do not actively participate in the partnership.

Limited partnerships are partnerships with one or more general partners and one or more limited partners.

Liquidated damages are damages provided in a contract that are meant to compensate the non-breaching party in the event of a breach of contract.

Long-arm statute is a law passed by the legislature, giving courts power over people who have sufficient connections with the state. It is said the "long arm" of the law can reach beyond the state's borders.

Lost property is property that was unintentionally lost, which means the owner accidentally lost possession of the object and did not misplace the property. The finder of *lost property* becomes the owner of the property subject to the prior owner's property interest.

Lucid To be *lucid* in the context of a contract negotiation means to understand the consequences of one's actions.

M

Madrid Protocol provides mark owners with an international system for registering their marks in multiple countries.

Magistrate judges who handle cases, or portions of cases, assigned to them by a district judge—are appointed by the chief judge of the District Court. So, a magistrate judge might handle only the initial appearance in a criminal case or a discovery dispute in a civil case while the district judge would normally preside over the trials.

Majority opinion means a majority of the judges hearing a case have the same opinion as to the outcome of the case.

Major sources are those that emit ten tons per year or more of any HAP or 25 tons per year or more of any combination of HAPs. *Major sources* are subject to more stringent requirements than all other sources,.

Malpractice is a claim asserted against a professional, such as a physician, dentist, attorney, or accountant, for injuries a plaintiff sustains because the defendant failed to exercise the appropriate standard of care required in their profession.

Market failure describes an inefficient distribution of goods and services in a free market. One specific type of *market failure* is called an externality.

Material breach occurs when a party does not perform a significant duty under their contract. Courts often look to what they call "the heart of the contract" to determine whether a *material breach* has occurred.

Maximum profit is defined as the most profit a company can create even if it means acting unethically.

Mediation is when the parties rely on a neutral third party called a *mediator* to help them negotiate.

Mediator The *mediator* is often an attorney or sometimes a retired judge who does not represent either side. *Mediators* often have specific training on helping parties to resolve differences. The parties usually split the charge for the *mediator's* time.

Mens Rea is the legal term for a guilty mind.

Merchant in most states refers to someone who routinely sells goods of this nature or holds himself out as having specific knowledge or skill related to the product.

Merger doctrine holds a criminal defendant cannot be convicted of lesser included offenses and the greater offense.

Minor (or infant) is someone who has not reached the age of majority, which is the age of 18 in most states, but is age 19 in a few states such as Nebraska and Alabama, and even 21 in Mississippi.

Mirror-image rule prohibits the offeree from accepting an offer while adding additional terms.

Misdemeanor crimes are those crimes where the maximum punishment is a year in jail or less.

Mislaid property is property that was intentionally placed but subsequently forgotten by the person who placed the property. *Mislaid property* does not become the property of the person finding it.

Misrepresentation occurs when a party to a contract makes a misstatement of a material fact upon which the other party relies and suffers damages because of their reliance.

Missouri Plan is a judicial selection process that utilizes a commission to appoint judges. The commission is generally composed of a judge, attorneys selected by the state's lawyers, and citizens appointed by the governor.

Mobile marketing is the process by which sellers market to a consumer through a mobile device such as a cell phone.

Modification also known as a *release*, refers to a novation in which a new obligation replaces a preexisting obligation.

Money laundering is the act of transferring illegally obtained money through legitimate people or accounts so that its original source cannot be traced.

Motions for directed verdict are requests to dismiss the plaintiff's case because the plaintiff failed to assemble enough evidence to carry the plaintiff's burden of proof. These motions are rarely granted, but are often made for strategic reasons for appeal purposes.

Motions for summary judgment are often filed around the end of the discovery process to ask the judge to decide some or all matters in controversy before the trial. Summary judgment is granted only when there is so much evidence for one side that a reasonable judge or jury could only decide the issue in one party's favor.

Motions for the judgment on the pleadings request the judge rule based upon the pleadings only. They are appropriate when there are no factual discrepancies from the pleadings made by the parties and the judge can provide a ruling by applying the appropriate law.

Motions in limine meaning "at the start," are filed just before the trial to prevent juries from hearing about certain irrelevant information learned during discovery.

Motions to compel discovery are often filed around the end of the discovery process to ask the judge to decide some or all matters in controversy before the trial.

Motion to dismiss describes the specific grounds for its argument and asks the judge to dismiss the case before any other proceedings are held.

Mutual assent Acceptance of an offer creates an agreement and this agreement is sometimes referred to as *mutual assent* in the legal world.

Mutual rescission occurs when both parties agree to return to their pre-contracting positions and suspend performance under their previous contract through a new contract.

N

National Environmental Policy Act (NEPA) of 1969 requires that all major actions by federal agencies affecting the quality of the human environment undergo analysis to review any environmental impacts that agency action may have.

National origin is interpreted as encompassing those who are born in a certain nation or descendants of someone who was born in a certain nation. There is often overlap between the definition of race and national origin.

Natural servitude doctrine Under this doctrine, the landowner is considered to be a servant of surface water and cannot change the natural flow of the water by building a dam to push water backwards or by building a drainage mechanism that would hasten the flow of the water to other property owners.

Navigable waters are broadly defined as including channels of waters that can be used for the transport of people or goods.

Negative right refers to the right to exclude others from performing certain acts (infringing the owner's rights) using either a state or federal court system.

Negligence results when a defendant breaches a duty of care owed to the plaintiff by acting in a way that a reasonable person would not act. It frequently involves property damage and/or personal injury claims.

Negligence per se or "negligence in itself," occurs when a violation of the law establishes a breach of duty on the part of the defendant.

Negligent misrepresentation occurs when a party breaches their duty of care toward another by stating something that is untrue.

Negotiation occurs when the parties, with or without an attorney representing them, directly negotiate with each other, either through written or oral communication.

Nexus refers to a substantial presence in a state. Building a retail store in a state would generally create a nexus in that state.

Nominal damages are a small amount of damages awarded in a contract breach case that are intended to establish liability on the part of the breaching party but not necessarily compensate the party for damages realized.

Non-profit or not-for-profit business entities are those that do not intend to make a profit, as they spend their revenues and other sources of income on their designated programs.

Notice of appeal refers to a formal notice requesting an appeals court to review the case.

Novations occur when a party agrees to discharge their duties under a previous contract by substituting a new contract that creates new obligations on the behalf of the parties.

Nuisance A legal theory for a cause of action under the common law is *nuisance*, where the plaintiff must show causation of significant interference with the plaintiff's private use and enjoyment of the plaintiff's land.

Nutrition content claims are claims that directly or indirectly state a food product has a certain characteristic.

O

Objective conditions An *objective condition* contains a reasonableness standard in regards to determining or judging when the condition has been met.

Objective impossibility is a legal doctrine that discharges a party from their contractual duties if it is impossible to perform such duties and the difficulty was not foreseeable at the time of contracting.

Obligee is the person to whom a duty is owed.

Obligor is a party who owes a performance under a contract.

Obscene speech occurs when 1) the work or speech appeals to a prurient interest, 2) the work or speech is patently offensive, and 3) the work or speech lacks serious literary, artistic, political, or scientific merit.

Obtaining goods by false pretenses refers to the act of intentionally misrepresenting a material fact to a person in order to persuade the person to transfer property to the person making the misrepresentation.

Offeree In relation to an agreement, the offeree is the person to whom the offer is made.

Offeror The *offeror* makes an offer to the *offeree*.

Optimal profit is defined as the most profit a company can create without violating its ethical duties.

Optional sales tax Some counties and cities may levy an *optional sales tax*, which is an additional amount of sales tax imposed in conjunction with a state sales tax.

Options contract is a contract under which the offeror promises to keep his or her offer open to the offeree until a specified date.

Ordinances are a form of statutory law that generally applies to a small geographic area such a city or a county.

Organized crime is defined as widespread criminal activities that are coordinated and controlled through a central syndicate.

Outcome-based ethical theories focus on the potential outcomes of a particular situation as opposed to the duties of the actors involved.

Outputs contract is one in which the buyer agrees to purchase all of the output a seller produces.

P

Palimony is the promise to pay *alimony* to a pal who is not a spouse.

Parole Evidence Rule disallows evidence of prior oral negotiations prior to the integration of their agreement into a written contract if the purpose of the evidence of prior oral negotiations is to contradict the terms of the written contract.

Partially disclosed principal is one whom the agent does not disclose the identity of to a third party but does inform the third party the agent is acting on behalf of a principal.

Partnership refers to a business entity formed by two or more persons who engage in a profit-seeking activity and share the profit and loss of such activity.

Past consideration is consideration that would be legally sufficient to form a contract but the consideration was given before the offer was made.

Patent Cooperation Treaty There is a type of international patent application that is valid in nearly 190 countries. This international patent application is a result of the *Patent Cooperation Treaty* and is called a "PCT application."

Percolating water is the term used for water that exists underneath the surface of land.

Peremptory challenges are those in which potential jurors are excused without the attorneys having to disclose a certain reason.

Periodic tenancy is for a fixed period of time but it automatically renews until either the landlord or tenant gives notice of their intent to quit the lease.

Perjury is the intentional telling of an untruth while under oath to tell the truth.

Personal jurisdiction refers to the court's authority over a particular person or organization.

Personal property is defined as all property that is not real property and generally refers to movable objects such as a car or laptop computer.

Phishing is the act of accessing another's computer with the intent to use information from that computer to commit a fraud.

Pigovian tax This is added to environmentally harmful products with the goal of *internalizing* the external costs so that the price of widgets represents their full costs.

Plaintiff sometimes referred to as a petitioner, is the party who initiates a lawsuit.

Plant patents which cover newly invented strains of asexually reproducing plants.

Pleadings are documents filed with the court that state the legal position of the parties. It is important to note pleadings do not include discovery documents.

Point sources The Clean Water Act focuses primarily upon *point sources* that are a single identifiable cause of pollution.

Police Power allows a state to regulate the health, safety, and morals of its citizens.

Polluter pays principle refers to where the party responsible for generating pollution is made financially liable for the harm, including the remediation of the harm.

Ponzi scheme is an investment fraud that involves the payment of purported returns to existing investors from funds contributed by new investors.

Post-trial motions Either side may ask the judge to adjust the verdict or convene a new trial by arguing that the jury did not follow the right procedure or that the verdict was not supported by the evidence; these are examples of *post-trial motions*.

Precedent is the holding, or legal ruling, provided in a court's opinion.

Preemption is the process by which federal law overrules or preempts state law. Congress can expressly state its intention to preempt state law. Congress, however, can also be found to have implied preemption of state law by leaving no room for state regulation.

Preexisting duty is a duty that one already legally owes. The duty already owed cannot constitute legally binding consideration.

Preferential transfers are payments of cash or a transfer of assets in payment of a preexisting debt that favors one creditor over another by providing the creditor more than they would have received under the bankruptcy code.

Prenuptial agreement are agreements that are made in contemplation of marriage. The purpose of the *prenuptial agreement* is to determine what will happen to each party's assets in the event of a divorce or death after the two parties are married.

Preponderance of the evidence To prove a case by a *preponderance of the evidence* means the trier of fact finds it is more likely than not the defendant is liable for committing the wrongful act.

Pretrial conference A few weeks before trial, the judge may summon the parties to the courthouse for a *pretrial conference* to discuss the upcoming trial. At this conference, each party is required to disclose certain documents, such as instructions they would like the jury to receive, a description of the evidence each side plans to submit, and a brief containing legal arguments about the case.

Prima facie ethical duties are to be self-evident principles that one must strive to preserve or further.

Principal A *principal* is the one on whose behalf an *agent* acts.

Prior appropriation rights doctrine Under this doctrine, the first person to use a water source has a greater priority than a subsequent user.

Prior art means existing information and concepts that prove the components of a patent are not new or novel.

Private carrier is a carrier who selects its customers and often does not have any customers at all.

Privilege is a legally recognized justification entitling the defendant to make and communicate the statement. The courts recognize two types of privileges: conditional and absolute.

Privileged communication There are several classes of information that are exempt from discovery. For example, *privileged communication* involves communication between attorneys and their clients. The concept of privileged communication shields client and attorney discussions and other interactions from discovery, which allows clients to privately seek legal counsel without fear that those private communications will be exposed.

Probable cause To obtain a search warrant, the state must convince a judge *probable cause* exists. *Probable cause* is a reasonable belief that a crime has been committed.

Procedural due process means the federal government must follow certain procedures when taking away a citizen's life, liberty, or property. *Procedural due process* rights include the right to an attorney in certain cases, the right to be notified of a legal proceeding, and the right to cross-examine witnesses.

Procedural law defines the process by which an individual's rights can be taken away.

Procedural unconscionability includes contracts that are created as part of a process that a court finds to be unconscionable.

Process of service The law is very specific about the required *process of service*, which is the formal way the summons must be delivered to the defendant. In many cases it must be hand delivered to the defendant or the defendant's spouse.

Products liability claims are brought against manufacturers who allegedly produced the defective product that caused an injury to the defendant.

Profane language is language that is grossly offensive and constitutes a nuisance to the general public.

Professional service corporation is a corporation form required by state law for individuals such as doctors, lawyers, and accountants. The states require the use of a *professional service corporation* as opposed to a regular C corporation so the owners of the corporation cannot totally shield themselves from torts claims such as negligence.

Promissory estoppel is an example of an agreement that is enforceable even though it lacks consideration. *Promissory estoppel* requires four elements: 1) a person makes a promise, 2) the person receiving the promise justifiably relies upon the promise, 3) the person relying on the promise suffers a detriment, and 4) Justice is served by the enforcement of the promise that was not supported by consideration.

Proof of claim In relation to bankruptcy claims, the creditors need to substantiate the claims that they file in the case by stating the amount they claim as being owed. The document submitted by the creditors to verify their claim is called a *proof of claim*.

Property crimes include burglary, larceny, arson, or forgery, and include a crime being committed against the property of another.

Protective orders In terms of discovery disputes, *protective orders* are a direction from the court to limit discovery or to require the parties to treat certain produced information as confidential.

Provisional patent application allows an inventor to make the invention "patent pending" and preserve his or her patent rights around the world for less expense than that incurred with filing a non-provisional patent application.

Public-order crimes such as being intoxicated in public or prostitution, are generally focused on prohibiting behavior that reflects negatively on society even though there may not be a traditional "victim" of the crime.

Puffery is an exaggerated, puffed, or outlandish claim about a product that a normal person would believe not to be an accurate factual representation or difficult to prove as true.

Puffing is the process by which a seller overstates or exaggerates the value or performance of a good.

Punitive damages are money damages awarded primarily to punish the tortfeasor for outrageous behavior.

Q

Quid pro quo harassment means an employment decision is based upon a protected class being subject to offensive behavior as a condition of employment.

Quitclaim deed refers to a deed that promises and warrants nothing besides the fact the seller is giving their interest in said property to the buyer.

R

Race This term is not defined by Title VII but has been interpreted as encompassing ancestry, cultural identification, cultural association, or a perceived belief that a person is associated with a certain ancestry or culture.

Ratification in the context of a minor's contract means the minor chooses not to disaffirm the contract.

Reaffirmation Although outstanding debts are generally discharged in a chapter 7 proceeding, the debtor is allowed to agree to the non-discharge of debts that would normally be dischargeable. This is called *reaffirmation*.

Real covenants are covenants that apply to real property, and often pass from one owner to the next. *Real covenants* are common in housing developments.

Real property is defined as land and everything permanently attached to the land. For example, a house and the lot of land on which it sits are considered *real property*.

Reasonable person refers to the average person in society who exercises an average amount of care when conducting their affairs.

Reasonable suspicion is the belief a person may be engaged in a *criminal activity*. *Reasonable suspicion* is a lesser standard than probable cause is.

Reasonable use standard Using the example of the use of percolating water, the water is subject to a *reasonable use standard*, where it can be used only to benefit the property where the source is located and the use must be reasonable.

Receiving stolen goods is the act of receiving property that the defendant knew or should have known was stolen with the intent to deprive the true owner of such property.

Rescission The act by which a court cancels or undoes a contract.

Reckless A tortfeasor acts in a *reckless* manner when a tortfeasor is conscious of a risk but disregards it.

Redirect in relation to witness testimony, a *redirect* allows the party that originally called the witness to cover items covered during cross examination.

Reformation is an equitable remedy that a court uses to change or modify the terms to a contract. *Reformation* is most often applied by courts in cases involving mistake or fraud.

Registered agent If a defendant is a corporation or similar entity, the summons may be delivered to a *registered agent*, which is the person officially listed with the government in the state where the company is incorporated or organized.

Regulation is a law which has the same force as statutory law but is passed by an agency of the federal government whereas a statute is passed by Congress.

Regulatory law refers to regulations passed by an agency such as the Environmental Protection Agency or a state agency such as a state department of human services.

Rehabilitation is the process of seeking to improve the criminal's character and outlook so he or she can function in society without committing other crimes.

Rejection Offers can terminate by *rejection*, which is the offeree's statement or other conduct that states the offeree's desire to reject an offer and refuse acceptance.

Release (A) The contract between the parties that spells out the terms of the settlement is called a settlement agreement or *release* and that portion of the settlement agreement that keeps the terms secret is a confidentiality clause.

Release (B) A novation in which a new obligation replaces a preexisting obligation is often referred to as a modification or a *release*. A *release* generally requires 1) a writing to evince the new agreement, 2) new consideration, and 3) the parties to negotiate in good faith.

Reliance damages compensate the plaintiff for expenses they have incurred by relying on the contract that was breached by the defendant.

Removal When a resident of one state transfers a case to the federal court in another state, the transfer is called *removal*.

Reply In response to a counterclaim, the plaintiff is required to file a *reply*, just like the defendant is required to file an answer to the complaint.

Request for production is a demand for documents that are relevant to the issues being litigated.

Requests for admissions During the discovery process, either side can submit to the other *requests for admissions*, which ask the other side to admit that certain things are true.

Requirements contract is a contract in which the seller agrees to sell the buyer all the product a buyer would need.

Res ipsa loquitur is a Latin phrase for "the thing speaks for itself." It is another special negligence standard that helps prove breach of care by the defendant.

Rescission means to undo a contract and return both parties to their pre-contract positions.

Resource Conservation and Recovery Act (RCRA) of 1976 regulates the generation, transportation, treatment, storage, and disposal of hazardous waste, and is again administered by the EPA.

Respondeat superior is applied to hold employers vicariously liable for the actions of their employees when the employees are acting within the scope of their employment.

Restitution means restoring the other party to their original position. As a general rule, a minor is not required to make restitution for a product that he or she no longer possesses or services that have been consumed.

Restitution damages are equal to the amount of value the defendant has received. They are often awarded in cases where expectation damages cannot be adequately calculated and where reliance damages do not adequately compensate the plaintiff.

Riparian rights A person with *riparian rights* is a person who owns land that adjoins or butts up against the stream or lake.

Risk analysis entails identifying risks, their probabilities of occurring, and the options for addressing those risks.

Risk management involves the actions taken to prevent risks from occurring and minimizing the consequences when they do occur.

Robbery under the common law was the taking by force, intimidation, or threat of violence of a person's tangible personal property with the intent to deprive them of that tangible personal property.

Rossian Ethics focuses on *prima facie* ethical duties and actual ethical duties. *Prima facie* ethical duties are to be self-evident principles that one must strive to preserve or further.

Rule 10b-5 of the Securities Exchange Act of 1934 makes it illegal to engage in any act, practice, or course of business that would operate as a fraud or deceit upon a person when purchasing or selling securities.

Rule Against Perpetuities The common law *Rule Against Perpetuities* prevents an owner from devising a property ownership interest that may or may not vest within 21 years after the owner's death.

Rule of capture awards ownership to the first person who captures property and is most commonly applied to natural resources in the United States.

Rule of Four requires that at least four of nine Supreme Court Justices must vote to hear a discretionary appeal.

S

Satisfaction is the formal document indicating that the judgment has been paid.

S corporation refers to a corporation that was formed under state law like a C corporation but that makes an election under subchapter S of the Internal Revenue Code.

Scrivener's error refers to a typographical error.

Secondary boycott is a practice by union employees who threaten adverse actions such as a strike or a refusal to work with a second company that does not have a dispute with the union.

Secured debt refers to a type of debt where in addition to the borrower's promise to pay, in the event of default the lender also can also take possession of specified collateral because the creditor has a security interest.

Self-defense is a common example of a justification type of defense.

Service mark A *trademark* generally refers to a name, logo, tagline, symbol or other distinguishing characteristic of a product or associated with the product, and a *service mark* refers to the same subject matter when associated with a service provided.

Settlement agreement or release The contract between the parties that spells out the terms of the settlement is called a *settlement agreement* or *release*.

Shrink-wrap agreement exists when the terms and conditions of the contract are contained in a product's packaging but the terms cannot be accessed until the plastic wrap is removed from the box.

Sink refers to an environmental service that provides an indirect benefit.

Slander There are two types of defamation: libel and slander. *Libel* applies to a defamatory written statement, while *slander* concerns defamatory oral communication.

Slander of property is similar to defamation, but it requires untrue statements that diminish the value of property.

Slander of title is a specific form of slander of property, which is committed by knowingly casting doubt on the ownership interest of another in property.

Small Claims Court is a court that hears civil law cases where a small amount of money is in dispute.

Sole proprietorship is a business that has no separate legal existence from its single owner.

Solicitation of bids is a common example of a statement of future intention.

Sovereign means no one country is superior to another country

Special agent is an agent who is authorized by the principal to perform a specific undertaking.

Special damages are damages that arise "out of pocket" because of expenses incurred after the tortious act.

Special or consequential damages are damages which require notice to be received by the defendant.

Special warranty A *special warranty* deed makes the same covenants as a general warranty deed but limits the covenants to the time period during which the seller owned the property.

Specific deterrence is a goal of a specific conviction and sentence to dissuade the offender from committing crimes in the future.

Specific performance requires a party to perform a certain action. The key difference between an injunction and *specific performance* is an injunction requires a person to refrain from acting while *specific performance* requires a person to complete a certain action.

Stakeholder approach requires company officials to consider the consequences of their actions on all relevant stakeholders of the firm.

Standing Before a person or organization can bring a civil lawsuit, it must have *standing*, which is a sufficient interest in the controversy to bring the case.

Stare Decisis Under the doctrine of *Stare Decisis*, a court should not overturn its previous rulings except in rare situations where Justice requires a departure from precedent.

State law refers to laws created by an entity of a state government. Most states have a similar structure to the federal government.

Statement of future intention A *statement of future intention* is not considered a legally binding offer. A common example of a statement of future intention is a *solicitation of bids*.

Statute of limitations A Complaint must be filed before the *statute of limitations*—the maximum amount of time after the alleged incident occurs in which one must file suit—expires.

Statutory law refers to statutes passed by legislatures such as the United States Congress or a state legislature.

Strict liability imposes liability on the defendant regardless of whether the defendant acted with reasonable care. Strict liability is applied to situations where a defendant engages in activities that are inherently dangerous.

Subagent refers to an agent of an agent authorized by the principal to perform acts as part of the agency agreement.

Subjective condition is determined to be satisfied by the subjective opinion of a party to a contract.

Subject matter jurisdiction refers to whether the court has authority over the specific matter in controversy.

Subpoena Some information relevant to a controversy may be controlled by third parties not directly involved in the litigation. In order to obtain the relevant information, the court may issue an order to a third party, called a *subpoena*, requiring them to allow inspection of their property, turn over copies of documents, sit for a deposition, or appear for trial as a witness.

Subsequent modification to a written agreement is a modification that occurs after the written agreement is signed. It is allowed as evidence whether it is written or oral.

Substantial performance means a party has not provided complete performance but has not committed a material breach.

Substantive due process means citizens have certain rights that the government cannot take away by legislation; for example, the right to marry, raise children, or work at a job.

Substantive law refers to rights or obligations of an individual.

Substantive unconscionability includes contracts whose terms a court finds to be egregious or extremely unfair.

Suggestive marks provide some suggestion as to a quality or characteristic of the goods or services associated with the mark, but require some mental exercise to connect the mark with the product.

Summons also referred to as the *original notice*, is a document that formally advises the defendant that a complaint has been filed.

Superfund is a trust fund initially created primarily by a tax on the petroleum and chemical industries.

Surface water is water that has no natural stream or way of passage, e.g., water that flows across a parking lot after a large rain.

T

Tenancy by the entirety is an ownership interest held by a husband and wife as one person.

Tenancy for years is tenancy that ends after a certain date. A tenancy for years does not require notice the tenancy will be ending.

Tenancy in common exists when multiple owners own a distinct share of an undivided interest in property.

Testamentary gift is a gift of property made through a *will*.

Testator The person who creates a will is often referred to as a *testator*.

Theft crimes include larceny, burglary, and robbery.

Theft of trade secrets involves the intentional taking, copying, or using another's *trade secrets* with the knowledge the owner of the secret will be injured by such action.

Threatened In relation to species, *threatened* means likely to become *endangered* within the foreseeable future.

Title insurance is a form of an insurance policy that provides insurance protection in regards to whether the buyer is taking good title. This type of policy is based upon public records only.

Title opinion traces the record of ownership as far back in time as possible. Its purpose is to reveal any defects in the ownership interest of the grantor.

Tort The term *tort* is derived from a French word meaning "wrong" or "injury." In the US legal system, a tort is a civil claim other than a claim for breach of contract.

Tortfeasor The person who commits a *tort* is a *tortfeasor*, which finds its roots in a French word meaning "wrongdoer."

Total maximum daily load is the maximum amount of pollutant in water that meets water quality standards.

Toxic Substances Control Act (TSCA) of 1976 provides the EPA with regulatory authority over the manufacture, importation, and sale of chemicals.

Trade dress refers to the aesthetic of a product or its packaging.

Trade fixture This is an item of personal property attached by a tenant who wishes to carry out a trade or business in a leased area.

Trademark A *trademark* generally refers to a name, logo, tagline, symbol or other distinguishing characteristic of a product or associated with the product.

Trademark dilution allows the owner of the mark to prevent third parties from using the mark on completely unrelated products where there is no likelihood of confusion.

Trademark infringement exists when a party uses a mark associated with goods or services and that party's use of the mark is likely to cause customer confusion as to the source of those goods or services.

Trade name is the name a business uses when engaging in commerce but is not by itself a type of trademark. However, a trade name might become part of a trademark.

Transcript Depositions are often taken at an attorney's office in front of a court reporter, who develops a *transcript*, which is a written record of everything that is said. It can be used at trial to discredit or impeach the witness if the witness's trial testimony is different.

Treble damages If a jury finds that a party willfully infringed a patent, the infringer may be liable for *treble damages*, which is three times the actual monetary damages.

Trespass to real property occurs whenever the defendant enters on the plaintiff's land without permission. *Trespass* can occur through the defendant's presence on the land or something that is within the control of the defendant.

Trespass to personal property occurs when the defendant interferes with the plaintiff's use of plaintiff's personal property. The defendant can be liable even if the property was not actually removed from the defendant's possession.

Trust A *trust* is a form of ownership, applicable to both real and personal property, where the *trustee* holds legal title to the property for the benefit of beneficiaries who enjoy equitable rights.

Trustee The *trustee* holds legal title to the property for the benefit of beneficiaries who enjoy equitable rights. The court will appoint a *trustee* to administer a bankruptcy estate. The responsibility of the *trustee* varies depending on the type of bankruptcy that is filed.

U

Unconscionable contracts are contracts that "shock" the conscience of the court. They can be segregated into two categories: 1) substantive unconscionability and 2) procedural unconscionability.

Undisclosed principal An *undisclosed principal* is one whom the agent does not make known to a third party that results in the third party believing they are contracting with the agent.

Undue influence means a party to a contract is unfairly influenced (persuaded) and agrees to contractual terms that the party would not normally consent to absent the undue amount of influence.

Unenforceable contracts contain all the elements of a valid contract (agreement, consideration, capacity, and legality) but are unenforceable by a court.

Unfair advertising is advertising that causes or is likely to cause substantial consumer injury that cannot be avoided and is not outweighed by the benefits it produces.

Unilateral A *unilateral* contract contains an offer that can be accepted by providing complete performance only.

Unilateral mistake This occurs when only one party to a contract is mistaken. Courts generally do not provide relief when one party to a contract is mistaken.

Unintentional tort An *unintentional tort* involves a situation where the tortfeasor had no intention of creating a wrong, but, because of a lapse in judgment or a failure to be careful, harmed someone else.

Union shop A *union shop* does not require union membership before an employee can be hired but it does require the employee eventually join the union.

United States Court of Appeals also known as circuit courts, hear appeals from the District Courts.

United States District Court The main federal trial court is known as the *United States District Court* and federal lawsuits typically originate in them.

United States Supreme Court The *United States Supreme Court* is the final arbiter of federal law and all appeals from the United States Court of Appeals are appealed to the Supreme Court, which decides whether or not to hear the appeal.

Unprotected speech An individual cannot have his or her speech regulated by the government unless the person in engaging in *unprotected speech.*

Unsecured debt An *unsecured debt* is a debt for which the creditor did not obtain a security interest.

Usage of trade means a court will look to see how those engaged in the type of business involved in the contract dispute define similar terms.

Use tax A tax on goods purchased that is required to be remitted is referred to as a *use tax.*

Utilitarianism requires a cost-benefit analysis to determine the appropriate ethical action.

Utility patents cover the way something functions or the specific arrangement of parts.

V

Variance is an exception granted to a landowner by the municipality. A *variance* will allow the landowner to do something with their real property that would normally not be allowed under the *zoning* law of the municipality.

VAT is a tax assessed against the value added by a manufacturer or a distributor.

Venue is the proper court or forum to hear a case.

Verdict Jurors select a foreperson and then review and discuss the evidence to reach their conclusion or *verdict,* which is their rendering of liability, guilt, or the absence of it.

Vicarious infringement A defendant is liable for *vicarious infringement* when the defendant has the right and ability to control the infringer's conduct and receives a direct financial benefit from the infringement.

Vicarious liability means a court may impose liability on an individual who did not commit the act that caused injury but who has a special relationship with the person who did commit the act that caused injury.

Void A *void* contract is no contract at all and cannot be enforced by a court.

Voidable *Voidable* contracts are contracts for which one party has the option of nullifying the contract or enforcing it.

Voir dire In jury trials, immediately before trial, a group of potential jurors go through *voir dire,* which is a Latin phrase meaning "to speak truthfully."

Voluntary petition A *voluntary petition* is a bankruptcy petition filed by an individual or business at their own option.

W

Warranty deed makes the promise the seller has good title free from lien or ownership claims by another party. The seller must defend the title against any claims arising before or after the seller obtained ownership up until the date the buyer takes ownership.

Whistle-blower The person who notifies proper authorities of a violation of law by a company or its employees is referred to as a *whistle-blower*.

Will A *will* is a legal document which governs the distribution of property of a person upon their death.

With reserve At an auction *with reserve*, the seller or auctioneer may withdraw the item any time before the auctioneer accepts the highest bid and declares the item to be sold.

Without reserve In an auction *without reserve*, neither the auctioneer nor the seller can withdraw an item once bidding has started.

Witness testimony involves calling a witness to the stand and asking him or her questions.

Worker's union refers to a group of workers who have organized for the purpose of representing their interests in workplace matters such as pay rates, benefits, and working conditions.

Work for hire A work will be a *work for hire* under copyright law if the author was an employee and prepared the work within the scope of the author's employment, or if the author and a party with whom the author is contracted expressly agree in writing that the parties intend for the work to be a work for hire.

Workout Some creditors may prefer to settle their claims for payment through a private negotiation with the debtor through a process generally referred to as a *workout* or *debt workout*.

World Intellectual Property Organization (WIPO) is governed by the United Nations and oversees PCT applications.

Writ of Certiorari If at least four of the nine Supreme Court Justices decide to hear a case, the Supreme Court grants a *Writ of Certiorari*, sometimes referred to simply as a "Writ of Cert," that means the Court is exercising its discretionary power to hear an appeal.

Z

Zoning is the process by which municipalities divide their geographic locations and limit the permissible uses by landowners for their property.

INDEX

CPSIA information can be obtained
at www.ICGtesting.com
Printed in the USA
LVOW02s0310170117
521209LV00005B/20/P